CHRIST
IN THE
REVELATION

ROBERT SMITH

CHRIST IN THE REVELATION

Copyright © 2014 by Robert Smith
Published by 21st Century Press
Springfield, Missouri U.S.A.
Printed in U.S.A.

21st Century Press is a publisher dedicated to publishing books with high family values. We believe the vision for 21st Century Press is to provide families and individuals with user-friendly materials that will help them in their daily lives and experiences.

It is our hope that this book will help you discover truths for your own life and help you meet the needs of others. May you be richly blessed.

All rights reserved. No part of this book may be used or reproduced in any manner whatsoever or stored in any database or retrieval system without written permission except in the case of brief quotations used in critical articles and reviews. Requests for permissions should be addressed to:

21st Century Press
2131 W. Republic Rd. PMB 211
Springfield, MO 65807
800-658-0284
www.21stcenturypress.com

ISBN: 978-0-9911004-6-0
Cover Design: Keith Locke
Book Design: Lee Fredrickson

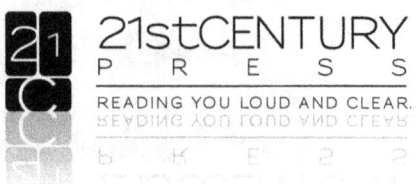

DEDICATION

I would like to give thanks to my lovely wife, Marvelle, love of my heart for 60 years; my "proof reader" who made me look good; for her dedication and support through these many years, and patience through 4 years of writing this book. Also to my dearest friend and companion in the ministry, the late Dr. Linfield Crowder, who shared with me many of the concepts in this writing; who encouraged me for years to write this book. He said, "When an old man dies, a library goes with him." Also a heartfelt thanks to our dear friend Debbie Bridgewater for many long and tiring days and hours critiquing the material and adding many suggestions; and to Phil Stewart and Robert Carter for their encouragement; and to Mindy, the computer lady who has walked us through the computer maze.

Thanks also to the late J.R. Church and also Gary Stearman, authors of Prophecy in the News. And to all of my acquaintances who have poured themselves into my life.

Also, so very much appreciation to Lee Fredrickson and the staff of 21st Century Press for their kindness, patience and support.

And of course, to our Wonderful Lord Jesus Christ, love of my life, since I met Him as my Lord and Savior in 1947, and whom, by the help of the Holy Spirit, we seek to Honor and glorify.

The Author

MY CLOSING PRAYER AS I WROTE THE LAST SENTENCES OF "THE CHRIST IN REVELATION."
January 4th 2014 at 4:30 P.M. through tears of Love and thankfulness:
To my dear Lord and Savior Jesus the Christ I dedicate this 4 year effort.

Please forgive me for all my lack of ability, fumbling for expression; my weakness through the fleshly mind and carnal soul. But somehow let it overlook my faults and express something of the longing and love that began in my youth, when you first spoke to me out on the mountain side. I have ached to know you, and to express your goodness and graciousness ever since I prayed the first prayer of my life at 17 years old: "God, if there is a God, I want to know you."

For nearly 60 years I have not known a day that that longing and love has not welled up in my soul. And when I sat out to try to express that love in the writing of "The Christ is Revelation" I have daily cried out in my soul for help to do the best my incapable mind and soul could express of your glory and greatness.

Now I present it to you, my Lord, and offer it to your blood bought Church as much as they will and can receive it. I leave It in your hands and the hands of my beloved brethren. Amen

Contents

INTRO: CHRIST IN THE REVELATION 7
PREFACE: OUTLINE 57
1. THE GLORIFIED CHRIST 77
2. DANIEL AND THE CHURCH AGE 107
3. THE CHURCH IN THE COURT ROOM 147
4. COURT IS SET 173
5. PREPARATION FOR JUDGMENT 199
6. HOLDING BACK TRIBULATION 225
7. EXECUTION OF JUDGMENT 241
8. THE HORDES OF HELL 261
9. THE LAST 3 1/2 YEARS OF JUDGMENT 285
10. CHRIST, THE TEMPLE AND THE WITNESSES 305
11. ISRAEL IN THE TRIBULATION 333
12. THE BEAST AND HIS WORLD ORDER 389
13. THE REAL REDEEMER COMES TO ZION 425
14. THE LAST PLAGUES AND JUSTICE EXECUTED ... 501
15. A QUICK CONCLUSION 529
16. THE WORLD CHURCH 569
17. FALL OF THE WORLD ECONOMY 603
18. OUTCOME OF CHRIST AND ARMAGEDDON 631
19. THE MILLENNIUM AND BEYOND 659
20. NEW HEAVEN AND NEW EARTH 683
21. THE HOME OF THE BRIDE 705
APPENDIX: CHRIST IN THE REVELATION 739

INTRODUCTION

CHRIST IN THE REVELATION

"The path of the just is like a shining sun, that shines ever brighter unto the perfect day" (Proverbs 4:18).

As we give ourselves to reading, hearing and keeping the Book of The Revelation of Jesus Christ, we will see that it is *not* pointing us toward total chaos and destruction as many believe, or toward the end of the world and demise of the human race; but is actually leading us to the fulfillment of God's complete plan which leads to the light of that *perfect day* promised to us and the world.

> *"The Revelation of Jesus Christ, which God gave Him to show his servants— things which must shortly take place. And He sent and signified it by His angel to His servant John" (Revelation 1:1).*

A lady with three little kids attended an evening testimonial service. All day had been a very frustrating and trying time with the children as she tried without success to bring them under control. During the service, she caught what she thought would be an opportune time for her to testify and in the midst of her confusion, she said to the congregation, "I've been sitting here on my thoughts with this bench running through my head." At that time, one of the children got up and headed down the pew; she grabbed him and said, "Sit down Jesus!"

My point is simply this: sometimes in our study of Revelation we may feel so frustrated it seems we are sitting on our thoughts with a bench running through our head. If we clear our head of all that the world has put into it and search for Christ and His purpose in the study, it need not be so.

Rather than to dwell on the scary parts of the book—the Beast, Antichrist, Dragon, 666, etc., we are going to look for and stay very close to, the Lord Jesus Christ in our comments in this writing. We will try to find Him in either His obvious and stated presence, or try to see Him behind the scene or in the person of His Angel, or in His cryptic appearance of symbols and metaphors. People often ask for the key to understanding Revelation. The above text is the key and Revelation provides its own key. The key is keeping Jesus in view and seeing Him either in the backdrop or in the scene of everything recorded in the Book. Proof of this is the fact that every phrase, thought, and symbol in Revelation, can be found in the Messianic texts of the Old Testament, and therefore represent the Revelation of Jesus Christ, the Messiah.

We believe that the greatest weakness made by so many of those who expound on the Book of The Revelation of Jesus Christ, is that they dwell on every other part of the book except Jesus Him. Consequently, most people think that it is a scary Book about odd-looking beasts with seven heads and ten horns, the terrible number 666, and an awful harlot. They miss the meaning of the Great Tribulation and Armageddon because they see it as the acts of an angry God out to destroy the world and all of the people in it with no consideration of Christ and His purpose for the Christian and the Jew.

SO MUCH MISUNDERSTANDING AND MISINFORMATION

In these last days, and especially as it pertains to prophesy, we have to be extremely careful what we believe and what we hear, even from some of our evangelical teachers. We should make careful note of the first warning that Christ gave us when He began to answer His Jewish disciples inquiry of, "*Tell us, when will these things be? And what will be the sign when all these things will be fulfilled?*" (Mark 13:4). Jesus then warned them about those who would come proclaiming that He is Christ, but would deceive many. Last-day deceptions will be so strong that well-meaning evangelical preachers, teachers, and even the very elect will be deceived if it was possible. (Mark 13:6, Matthew 24:24).

There is so much misunderstanding and false interpretation of Revelation among Christians who are not properly instructed in its meaning. Some Christians tend to understand it based on the delusions promoted in the world of media, by carnal-minded men who have no idea what Jesus is up to. Television documentaries, movies, and books by the scores are all giving their expert theory on what the Book really means. Consequently, because they have no concept of its real message, they keep people in fear about the end of the world, or the *Holocaust* of end-times. To the worldly fear-mongers, Armageddon will destroy everything. They say we are living in a dying universe. According to their interpretation of Revelation, we will soon destroy ourselves or uncontrollable forces will obliterate the whole human race and Earth will go off into a cold, silent, and lifeless forever.

A major misunderstanding involves the Battle of Armageddon. It is essentially not a battle between nations and neither is it a conventional warfare. It is a cosmic warfare between Christ and the beastly kingdoms. It involves only those who have taken the mark, name and number of the Beast; those who are responsive to the call of demons coming out of the mouth of the Dragon, Beast and False Prophet (Revelation 16:13), and have subscribed to His misuse of the *One World Order*. It does not see the demise of all people.

Remember, it is prophesied that another thousand years right here on old terra-firma, after which there is a new Heaven and new Earth. We will describe these things in greater detail when we expound on Revelation, Chapter 16.

NOT THE REVELATION OF BEAST, ANTICHRIST, 666 ETC., BUT JESUS CHRIST

Someone once said, "If we start out for nowhere, we will usually get there." Some go into the Book of Revelation for totally the wrong goals or reasons and usually end up getting nowhere. Those who start out by looking for the right answers usually always get there. The Key for our quest into Revelation is given in the very first verse. If you go into it looking for the Revelation, or revealing of Jesus Christ, you will discover Him revealed throughout the pages. If you go into it looking for beasts, dragons, and 666, that is all you will see. Or, if like so many of the world's experts who already believe that we are heading for total chaos, then that is where you will end up. If for political reasons or greed of money, you choose to keep people in a fear mode, then the Book of Revelation is an excellent tool. On the other hand, if you are a Christian and know that God's final plan is not destruction, but redemption; of the Church, Israel and the Gentile nations, then Jesus revealed in His glorious day becomes easy to see. This study will look for the hidden Christ in every part of its writings. Every statement, symbol, and thought in the Book of Revelation comes from the Old Testament Messianic Prophecies and is meant to reveal Jesus the Christ, as Messiah. Just as every cryptic symbol of the old Tabernacle—every board, piece of hide, color, and all other material spoke of Christ—so every symbol, thought, phrase and event in Revelation will reflect upon Jesus Christ. Most all of the Messianic texts are shrouded in shadow, symbolism, and mystery. Cryptic in nature for the analogous purpose of forcing us to search for understanding, so Christ in the Revelation is mostly hidden in cryptic symbols, shadows, and mystery, revealed only by intercalating Old Testament Messianic texts into Revelation. Only His beloved will be willing to seek and find Him.

This Book of the Bible is not the revelation of St. John the divine as it is sometimes captioned. It is however, written by John from exile on the Island of Patmos and comes to him while he was "in the Spirit on the Lord's day" (Revelation 1:10). It is dictated to him and therefore not in any way impressions of his own fantasy. In every part, it is revelations of scenes coming out of the unseen world of Heaven and narrated by Angels of the Lord's presence sent to John by none other than Jesus Christ our Lord, Himself.

The writing is first and foremost the "Revelation of Jesus Christ." It details what has been written of Him in the Old Testament of His Messiah ship, and which has been outlined by prophetic utterance in all of the Old and New Testaments. It reveals many details of what is known as the "Day of the Lord," "The Lord's Day" or "That Day." We will enlarge on the subjects later in this writing. (See more detail in Appendix: Christ in the Revelation)

It is not the Revelation of the beast, the false prophet, or the great whore. And it is not even intended to be a revelation of the great dragon, although it brings Satan out of obscurity and reveals his actions and nature more clearly than we have been able to ascertain in Scripture to this point. These entities are a part of the final drama, but not the stars of the story. There is only one star and that is Jesus Christ. The Antichrist is just the little horn; Jesus, the true Christ is the Big Horn.

INFLUENCE OF NEGATIVE NATURE

Our reading and contemplation of the Revelation is often influenced by our negative nature which tends to dwell on the bad at the expense of the good.

There are three reasons for this negative view of Revelation.

1. We seem to like tragedy, drama, the mysterious, the occult, the gruesome and the gory as shown by our choice of entertainment. Therefore, we often get hung up on these fascinating and intriguing images, and the negative tragedies of the Revelation and miss the real essence—Christ's victory over the world and the devil behind the world. The bazaar and scary images in Revelation tend to plague our imagination, causing the book to seem more like a Halloween spoof rather than any form of reality.

2. By nature, we are often more mindful of earthly things rather than heavenly. There is a tendency to sympathize with the world in prophesied tragedies of the ungodly world more than we rejoice in Christ's plan and purpose and in all of the glorious things done in defense of the Church and the avenging of its enemies; and what is done to restore the Jews. It is Christ's presence, power, and glory that permeate the Book of Revelation.

3. We do not see the esoterical beings spoken of in Revelation. And, we have a difficult time intercalating their influence on the church, Israel, and world into our natural wisdom and understanding.

We must encourage ourselves to read, hear, and keep the prophecies of this Book, both in and by the touch of the Holy Spirit who "will guide you into all truth" (John 16:13). As we contemplate the Book of Revelation under the leadership of the Holy Spirit, we can easily see that these seemingly scary symbols are not meant to form some sort of physical image in our thinking, but are to impress us with the spirit, character, and nature of evil. They are only pawns in the game where Christ is King and all else are but check-mates.

NO GLOOM AND DOOM!

Where is the gloom and doom here? We who love Him will not find it if we are looking for and finding Jesus, everywhere in the Book. As mentioned previously, this gloom and doom spirit is not helpful in understanding the Book of Christ's Revelation.

It may be helpful to observe another basic misunderstanding of The Revelation of Jesus Christ. We have already spoken of how many people see the Book as confusing and scary. It is shameful that even our Christian minds at times, seem inclined to be negative. We often think in a pessimistic mode; a gloom-laden attitude full of defeatist and critical spirits rather than a positive, affirmative, and optimistic outlook. To illustrate, let me submit that if I held up a clean white piece of paper with a small dot in the center and ask someone what they see, their answer would probably be, "I see a black dot." Isn't it strange that they did not see the larger and more obvious piece of white paper? We are so inclined to see the dark side instead of the light side. Another illustration: We call the traffic lights a *stop light*. Isn't that also strange? It is a *go light* as much as it is a *stop light*. So often our natural tendencies are to read the Bible seeing all of the black dots and stop lights rather than the bright side and the go side. We tend to read with a rather fearful view of God and Christ. Everything seems to have a sense of judgment with it.

However, to my delight, I have found that the Book of Revelation is more positive than negative. It is strange how our thoughts seem to move toward the Beast, the False

Prophet, the Number 666, the Seven Heads and Ten Horns, the Great Red Dragon, the Great Harlot, and the destruction of Babylon etc. While we are dwelling on these frightening and confusing parts of the Book, they seem to take center stage in the whole drama and be the main subject of our intense inquiry. I assure you that these elements and personages are only a small part of the message of the Book and are not the central theme.

NOT IMAGES BUT IMPRESSIONS

We should not attempt to formulate any kind of mental picture of these symbols. Instead, we should use the various parts of the description as a means to impress us about the nature and characteristics of evil that the symbol represents. Or on a positive note, of the nature and character of the good it represents. For instance, the Antichrist, or beast as we call him, is only a little horn with a big mouth (Daniel 7:8). We cannot visualize (nor is it meant to be visualized) an animal which looks like a leopard, a bear, and a lion with seven heads and ten horns. No wonder people have nightmares over the reading of Revelation. This visualization often distracts us from the real message meant by the symbol. However, when we put all those symbols into their proper impressions and characteristics of the Beasts of Daniel and the Empires of the past Mid-East history, they make perfect sense and represent the historical background of the One World Order shown to us in Revelation thirteen. This example may be used as a pattern for all the rest of the symbolic and allegorical images of Revelation.

BRIEF SYNOPSIS OF SOME OF THE SYMBOLS

The beast and false prophet reign only for a very short time of three and one-half years and then are delivered to Hell forthwith. The Great Dragon known also as the old serpent, devil, and Satan is thrown out of Heaven to Earth, then quickly eliminated from the earth's scenes (Revelation 12:9, 20:2). The great whore who has plagued the Church and Israel from the beginning, or at least as far back as Babylon, is completely destroyed and a rebellious population of Earth is defeated at Armageddon, leaving only the righteous nations to enter the Millennium (Matthew 25:33).

KEEP CHRIST IN VIEW AS HE CONQUERS ENEMIES

In all of the commentary and study on Revelation, we must contemplate every event, phrase, and development, but never stray far from Christ and His consistent presence in every part of every scene. We must see Christ in control of all events because every decree comes from Him; every angel as a messenger of His presence is sent, directed, and tutored by Him; every seal is opened by Him; every trumpet is ordered by Him; and every vial representing the wrath of God is poured out upon an ungodly world by His direct order from the temple in Heaven. This is all to accomplish Paul's prophecy to the Corinthians declaring:

> *"Then comes the end, when he delivers the kingdom to God the Father, when he puts an end to all rule and all authority and power. For he must reign till he has put all enemies under his feet"* (1 Corinthians 15:24-25).

And, again so clearly foreseen in other Scripture:

> *"And to give you who are troubled rest with us when the Lord Jesus is revealed from heaven with His mighty angels, in flaming fire, taking vengeance on those who do not know God, and on those who do not obey the gospel of our Lord Jesus Christ. These shall be punished with*

everlasting destruction from the presence of the Lord and from the glory of his power, when He comes, in that Day, to be glorified in His saints and to be admired among all those who believe...." (2 Thessalonians 1:7-10).

"And to wait for His son from heaven, whom He raised from the dead, even Jesus who delivers us from the wrath to come" (1 Thessalonians 1:10).

And again in Adam's pre-flood days, Enoch speaks of Revelation:

"Behold, the Lord comes with ten thousands of His saints, to execute judgment on all, to convict all who are ungodly among them of all their ungodly deeds which they have committed in an ungodly way, and of all the harsh things which ungodly sinners have spoken against Him"(Jude. 14, 15).

We must remember that:

"...the Father judges no one, but has committed all judgment to the Son" (John 5:22).

And also:
"He has appointed a day on which He will judge the world in righteousness by the Man whom He has ordained. He has given assurance of this to all by raising Him from the dead" (Acts 17:31).

These texts and many others speak directly of the Day of the Lord, and the day of judgment shown to us in the Revelation. Today, He is a Savior. In that day, He will be a righteous judge. Revelation 19:11 substantiates this by saying, "...in righteousness He judges and makes war."

FOLLOW THE LAMB

It will be easy to follow Christ in the events and scenes of the Revelation. Sometimes, He will name Himself and other times He will hide behind the curtain and be manifest in the person of angels or other enigmas such as signs, symbols, and cryptic shadows. One of the easiest trails to follow Christ through the Revelation will be to follow Him as the *Lamb*. Jesus calls Himself the *Lamb* twenty-seven times throughout the Book of Revelation.

It is Jesus the Lamb that opens the seven seals. In Chapter Six, the world cries to be hidden from the face of the Lamb in anticipation of the judgment. In Chapter seven, the Lamb is mentioned four times, all in protection and care for His own, namely the raptured Church and the righteous Jews, and in Chapter twelve, the blood of the Lamb that makes us overcomers. Chapter thirteen introduces the *Lamb's Book of Life* that keeps us from falling into Antichrist mesmerism. In Chapter fourteen, the Lamb is on Mt. Zion where He has led the 144,000 Jews. Chapter fifteen tells of the plagues called down on the Earth by the witnesses of Chapter eleven, while Christ is revealed as "a lamb that had been slain" to John and the Church is in Heaven at the throne, upon the sea of glass. (Revelation 5:6) They are again shouting praises to the Lamb. In Chapter seventeen, the Beast foolishly makes war with the Lamb. This war will be Armageddon.

Chapter nineteen describes the *marriage supper of the Lamb*. In the twenty first Chapter, the Lamb is mentioned five times, all associated with His Bride, the New Jerusalem, the twelve tribes of Israel, and the Temple. In the city, the Lamb is the Light, and the *Lamb's Book of Life* is mentioned again. Finally in Chapter twenty two, Christ is seen again on the throne as the Lamb of God. This trail is easy to follow. As we dig deeper into each of these passages we will see the superior role of Christ in the Revelation. By intercalating more cryptic references to Him, among the many references to the Lamb, it should not be difficult to trace Him. What an exciting walk to trail the Lamb through the last days.

JESUS IS THE ESSENCE OF ALL PROPHECY

Realizing Christ's pre-eminence in Revelation helps to better understand John's words in Chapter 19: *"The testimony of Jesus is the spirit of prophecy"* (Revelation 10:19).

Looking for Christ in the many texts in Revelation reveals that He is often esoteric to the natural mind, without observation in the normal sense, but seen through the Spirit of God. Insight is given into His personal presence throughout the whole Book if there is first an understanding of what Christ meant by this passage. The Living Bible reads this way: *"The Purpose of all prophecy is to tell you of Jesus."* And the Amplified Bible says: *"The substance and essence of all truth revealed by Jesus, is prophecy."*

Prophecy is all-encompassing. It can be said that the Old Testament is the New Testament concealed and the New Testament is the Old Testament revealed. The prophecies of the Old Testament are the New Testament foretold and concealed; and the New Testament is the place Old Testament Messianic Prophecies unfold and are revealed. Willis Beecher Stone, lecturer for Princeton Theological Seminary said of this text:

> "Messianic prophecy may be regarded as the New Testament in the Old. *The Messianic prophecies are the principle thing everywhere in the Bible, and underlie all biblical history and poetry, all preaching and teaching, all national worship, and all sayings of all wisdom.* The Old Testament is the record of God's promises and the New Testament is the record of their fulfillment."

In his commentary on Revelation 19:10, Tim LaHaye states:

> "Everything about Jesus is prophetic: His birth, life, passion, death, burial, resurrection; His church, His coming again for the saints, and His coming kingdom on the earth; and the wonderful future He has planned for those who love and serve Him, are also multiple" (Isaiah 64:4, I Corinthians 2:9).

The spirit of Christ is embedded in all of the Old Testament, given life in the New Testament, and revealed in a final and full disclosure in the Revelation. He is the one who *was* in the Old and New Testaments, who *is* today at the right hand of God making intercession for us, and who *is to come* in power and great glory (Revelation 1:8). The whole motif of the Old Testament and the entire message of the New Testament is the testimony of Jesus—the coming Messiah and the present Christ. He is the hope of all of the pre-flood and post-flood Patriarchs. Abraham "waited for the city whose builder and maker is God" (Hebrews 11:10). That city is revealed in the Revelation. Christ was the "Word of God" before He came in the flesh, and the image of God in the flesh. Such is His pre-eminence in all scriptures and more so in the Book of Revelation. The Word encourages all Christians to "search the Scriptures, for in them you think you have eternal life; and these are they which testify of Me" (John 5:39).

Later in Jesus' closing remarks to the disciples He says, "These are the words which I spoke to you while I was still with you, that all things must be fulfilled which were written in the Law of Moses and the Prophets and the Psalms concerning me" (Luke 24:44, 45). Certainly the testimony of Jesus is the spirit of prophecy, and that essence permeates the whole Bible, especially the Book of Revelation of Jesus Christ.

In the opinion of the author, the highest aspirations of

the Old Testament writers are their ascriptions of the God-like characteristics of a coming Prince, Messiah, the Son of David. These aspirations form the whole motif, or central theme and dominant idea, of the Scriptures, and are resident in one man. That man is Jesus Christ. Therefore, findings in a study of the Old Testament Messianic theme, points to Christ as the dominant idea behind everything in the texts and the personification of the whole distant design of the Old Testament.

Everything about Jesus is prophetic. Over seven hundred and seventy seven specific details of Him have already been fulfilled, and over one thousand are yet to be fulfilled. There are one hundred nine prophecies with over two-hundred seventy details of His birth alone; one-hundred twenty-five prophecies of His life and ministry, thirty prophecies of His last twenty four hours, fifty-nine prophecies of His resurrection, three hundred twenty nine prophecies of His second coming, and the list goes on.

With such enormous odds in the prophetic texts, many of which were written nearly fourteen hundred years before His birth, some seven hundred years earlier, and some over five hundred years before, it is absolutely impossible for Christ Jesus to be an impostor. The *Law of Compound Probabilities* establishes His authenticity. Jesus said *"search the scriptures [for] these are they which testify of Me"* (John 5:39).

In one of His last discourses with the disciples after His resurrection, Jesus made a direct appeal to them:

> *"O foolish ones, and slow of heart to believe in all that the prophets have spoken! Ought not the Christ to have suffered these things, and to enter into His glory? And beginning at Moses and all the Prophets, He expounded to them in all the Scriptures the things concerning Himself"* (Luke 24:27).

It would have been a privilege to sit there at that time and hear Jesus expose all of the Old Testament references to Himself. What great insight and experience of discovery to have been allowed that sacred privilege!

John, Chapter one, gives great insights into His immortal pre-existence from the beginning and the exposition that He is the very Word, Logos of God, proclaiming that "the Word became flesh and dwelt among us, and we beheld His glory, the glory as of the only begotten of the Father, full of grace and truth." (John 1:14) After John the Baptist recognized Jesus as the "*Lamb of God who takes away the sin of the world,*" Philip looked up to his brother and said:

"*We have found Him of whom Moses in the law, and also the prophets, wrote—Jesus of Nazareth*" (John 1:29, 45).

Paul spoke of His Old Testament supremacy by saying…

"[God] had promised before, through His prophets in the Holy Scriptures, concerning His Son Jesus Christ our Lord" (Romans 1:2-3).

And again in Hebrews, he found it important to declare His supremacy, by stating:

"God, who at various times and in different ways spoke in times past to the fathers by the prophets, has in these last days spoken to us by His Son, whom He has appointed heir of all things, through whom also He made the worlds" (Hebrews 1:1).

By the forgoing references and many others which could be sited, we seek to turn our attention to the supremacy of our Lord Jesus Christ. Before we ever expound upon the glory of His great day, it is our desire to show that all prophecy, and especially every part of the Book of Revelation, is meant to tell us about Jesus and His revelation. This very testimony is the spirit, or breath, of all prophecy.

We can also see that in order to reach a clear understanding of the Book of Revelation, it will be necessary to relate every part of the Book to its counterparts in the Old Testament, especially references to the Messiah. We will find that virtually every reference to the Messiah in the Old and New Testaments can find its counterpart, fulfillment, and meaning in the message of the Book of The Revelation of Jesus Christ, if we look for Him in every phase of the Book. Actually, the whole Book of Revelation is the fulfillment of all that is prophesied throughout the Old Testament as well as the New Testament under such phrases as *The Day of the Lord, The Great Day of the Lord,* and *That Day.*

KEEP REVELATION POSITIVE

The Book of The Revelation of Jesus Christ is far from scary. It has not occurred too many that over two-thirds of the book has nothing at all to do with what we normally think of when we think of Apocalypse. In fact, the word has taken on a symbolism of its own simply because of the negative view most people take of the Book of Revelation. In fact, the word Apocalypse does not even mean what we usually think it does. We see it as indicating a strange pseudonymic, symbolic imagery. It supposedly represents the expectation of cosmic cataclysm where God destroys the ruling powers of evil. In fact in the Middle Ages, it took on the meaning of Hell because of this fear-mongering.

The word simply means "Revelation or something viewed as a prophetic revelation; something that forecasts the ultimate destiny of the world." (Webster's Universal Dictionary) If convinced that Revelation is the revelation of the cosmic cataclysm of destruction of the earth and its peoples, then this meaning would be correct. But as we shall see in this study, the Book of Revelation has a far different theme—it is

The Revelation of Jesus Christ.

The Book of The Revelation of Jesus Christ very plainly forecasts some sad things to come. Remember that they are but a very short period, and whether they are catastrophic or not depends upon where your interests and alignments are. If one's devotion is to this present world and its purposes, then it may be Apocalyptic in the world's sense of the word. If your wealth is invested in this world and the things of this world, and your love is thus devoted to this present world with its satanic bent and materialistic goals, then you will think that Revelation is scary.

However, if your love and interest is aligned with God's purpose, and with Jesus Christ and His Kingdom, then there will be little or nothing at all scary about the Revelation. An illustration of what I am saying can be found in the first few verses of the nineteenth Chapter of Revelation. The entire eighteenth Chapter has been devoted to the destruction of the World Order's economic system, which Jesus plainly told us was evil and unrighteous. (Luke 16:9) While the world's people are mourning and tearing their clothes, Heaven is rejoicing. The only use of the word *Hallelujah* found in the New Testament is in these first four verses of Revelation nineteen. These verses show that among God's people who have long since given up their love for this world, are rejoicing that the Lord has destroyed the world's ungodly system of money. Now to the worldly, this is a great tragedy. But to those who have had enough of this world's crooked ways and have laid up their treasures in Heaven, this becomes not a sad and scary time, but a time for rejoicing. The *Apocalypse* or Revelation of that day is not seen as catastrophic to Heaven's crowd.

JUST HOW POSITIVE IS THE BOOK OF REVELATION?

We will show just how positive and supportive the

Revelation of Jesus Christ actually is. There are four hundred and four verses in the Book. A careful study of each one will show that of those verses, two-hundred and sixty-nine of them have absolutely nothing to do with wrath or judgment. That is exactly two-thirds of the whole Book. Only one hundred and thirty five verses have any part of wrath or judgment, and some are limited in the subject of judgment.

A further examination of the Book by Chapters, will show that at least ten of the twenty two Chapters have nothing to do with judgment, and several others are only partially about judgment. You have to read through five chapters before reaching any bad news at all. The first chapter is a revelation of the glorified Christ, where we find Him, and what His attitude is. Do we see Him standing on some mountain with a sword in His hands, calling out wicked curses upon the world He is about to destroy? Not so! We see Him in the midst of His church, with the leaders (or angels) of the churches in His hand. In the second and third chapters, do not find Him calling out condemnation on His church for their faults. Although there are some admonitions, all are supportive and encouraging. Nothing Apocalyptic or catastrophic can be in these three chapters.

We now come to the fourth and fifth chapters of Revelation. We see scenes of Heaven and the throne of God on the sea of glass. A rainbow can be seen over the throne, a symbol of peace and promise of protection. The church is in Heaven with the seven spirits of God, living creatures that protect the throne, the elders, and the angels. And what is heard in heaven? No wrath; no condemnation; not even a rebuke coming from the throne; and absolutely no hint of Judgment. We hear great adoration, praise, and triumph from all of those around the throne. We hear them giving honor and glory to Him who sits on the throne, and worship to Him who was and is and is to come, who lives forever and ever.

The only touch of sadness mentioned in these chapters is John weeping because there is not anyone able or willing to take the book of our inheritance, and pay the price to buy it back for us. But John is quickly told to weep no more. He looks up to see that what is coming out of the throne is not the expected and deserved wrath for sin, nor an angry God ready for vengeance. No! Coming into Johns view is an age-old symbol of God's love and forgiveness for our sin. It is an emblem and image which goes all the way back to Adam's and Abel's sacrifice of the lamb; to Calvary, and death of *"the Lamb of God who takes away the sin of the world "* (John 1:29), for there appears a *"Lamb who has been slain"* (Revelation 5:12). Hallelujah! No wonder all Heaven breaks out in a crescendo chorus of praise.

> *"Worthy is the Lamb who was slain to receive power and riches and wisdom and strength and honor and glory, and blessing! And every creature which is in Heaven and on the earth and under the earth, (even Hell is going to be forced to join in this praise service) and such as are in the sea, and all that are in them, I heard saying: blessing and honor and glory and power be to Him who sits on the throne and to the Lamb, forever and ever!"* (Revelation 5:12-13).

No saint of God or lover of Jesus can find anything scary or morbid about these scenes. In fact, we will be very comfortable in that kind of heaven and around that kind of throne. My point is this. We have covered five chapters of Revelation and found not one thing to be terrified about. In fact we have found every reason to rejoice at the reading, hearing, and keeping of this prophecy. But the end is not yet. When the sixth chapter is understood, it is worth rejoicing over if the heart is set on Jesus' promised inheritance. The opening of each seal simply reveals what Christ is going to do and the price He will have to pay to win our inheritance. The four horsemen are the four destructive spirits of Satan. Christ will have to overcome these sorrows upon the earth, not brought on by God, but by Satan.

Then we come to the seventh chapter and still find nothing to cry about unless you are against the Jews. Here we find more reminders of God's love and protection during the times of tribulation. The 144,000 Jews, who have suffered terribly during their lives, now have the testimony of Jesus. They are sealed and kept from any harm of the above mentioned four spirits of destruction during the short time of wrath to come. And then we see *"a great multitude which no one could number, of all nations, tribes, peoples, and tongues"* who are before the throne and the Lamb" (Revelation 7:9). They are crying with a loud voice saying *"Salvation belongs to our God who sits on the throne, and unto the Lamb!"* (Revelation 7:10). They are still singing the same songs of praise that we heard in the fifth Chapter. And where do we find Jesus? During this time, Jesus is still among His Church, just as He was in chapters two and three:

> *"For the Lamb who is in the midst of the throne will shepherd them and lead them to living fountains of water. And God will wipe away every tear from their eyes"* (Revelation 7:17).

There is little cause for fear or terror in at least six out of seven of these chapters. This brings us through the seventh chapter and except for a few scary things that only apply to the world, the Christian has nothing but exciting revelation to ponder. The eighth and ninth chapters have some scary elements, but we must realize they only account for approximately three and one-half years.

Chapter ten opens with an exciting insight into the esoteric world of Heaven, the same Heaven revealed in the fourth and fifth chapters. A mighty angel comes down from

Heaven. Thus, if he comes from Heaven, he must be on a mission from God and the Lamb, Jesus Christ. One of the first hints to his purpose is a rainbow on his head. This rainbow represents a mission of peace. The rest of verse one shows that this angel, or messenger is none other than the Lord, Himself. His proclamation is that Satan and sin have no more time. The jig is up!

All that God has said to the prophets is finished and the mystery of God is over. Heaven tells John to take a little book and eat it. This is probably not the same book found in chapter five. It is sweet to his taste, but sour to his stomach. Heaven's message to John is that the event in the next three and one-half years is going to be bitter-sweet. It will have its bitter side to the world of the Antichrist, but will be sweet to the redeemed. The only negative part of this whole chapter is simply the bitterness of the book.

Consider the fact now that seven out of ten chapters in Revelation have no judgment in them and the one other is simply a warning of coming judgment. So what is so scary about Revelation?

The eleventh chapter of the Book of Revelation starts at the Temple Mount in Jerusalem. The measuring of the Temple sight suggests plans to build. Then, we are introduced to two witnesses who are the fulfillment of Zechariah's prophecy in the fifth chapter. The world may be fearful when they hear these witnesses preaching about the coming kingdom of Christ. They have been sent from God to protect Israel's remnant from the Beast. Like with Elijah of old, (which one of them may be) plagues are called down on the Antichrist when he attempts to destroy the Jews. When their witness is over, they are killed. However, before paranoia sets in over the coming Christian or Jewish persecution, television news will broadcast what is about to happen. After a short three and one-half days, the two witnesses are raptured; caught up to meet the Lord in the air. All of this simply reflects Christ's love and work with the Jews during the tribulation. The only fear acknowledged here is this chapter is the fear that fell on the world as it witnessed right before their eyes over worldwide television, the rapture of God's Holy Spirit-filled saints.

Verses thirteen through eighteen show the beginning of the last three and one-half years of the wrath of God on that demonic, devilish beastly kingdom. Rather than being fearful to the saints of God, it is said to be a *"reward [to the] servants the prophets and the saints, and those who fear your name"* because God's purpose is to *"destroy them that destroy the earth"* (Revelation 11:18).

This chapter ends with the Temple in Heaven opened, and the ark of the testimony unveiled. This is a dramatic action as great signs accompany it in Heaven and on Earth, and should not be scary to the saint.

The twelfth chapter reveals the great red dragon that attempts for the seventh and last time, to destroy the Jews during the last half of the Tribulation after trying to destroy them through all of history. Very important information is given in this chapter that provides the backdrop of the whole scene in Revelation. Behind the *curtain*, a war is taking place in Heaven. The great angel, Michael casts the devil out of Heaven. Satan is sent to Earth, but Christians should not fear because the Church will not be here and the righteous Jews will be protected. This should be cause for great rejoicing to both Christians and Jews alike, as the angel Michael, *"who stands watch over the sons of [God's] people,"* casts the devil out of Heaven (Daniel 12:1). That is the message of this chapter—the great central theme found in verse eleven:

> *"And they overcame him by the blood of the Lamb and by the word of their testimony, and they loved not their lives to the death"* (Revelation 12:11).

To those who know their God, both Jews and Christians, there is nothing at all fearful about this entire chapter. It is mostly positive revelation and supportive encouragement to all Jews who will fall under Satan's wrath.

Chapters thirteen through eighteen can be frightening for those who do not know the Lord. The wrath of God is poured out on everyone whose names are not written in the Lamb's Book of Life (Revelation 13:8). This includes suffering for those who take the *Mark of the Beast* (Revelation 14:9-11). Out of eighteen chapters, only two hint of judgment and five that contain the last three and one-half years of God's wrath upon the Antichrist's kingdom. Thirteen of the eighteen are mostly or entirely positive and supportive.

The final four chapters in Revelation are totally positive with nothing scary for the saints and Jews to fear. They display the glorious coming of Christ with His saints following the *Marriage Supper of the Lamb*, and the millennial reign of Christ with the saints next to Him. This is followed by the new heaven and a new earth wherein dwells only righteousness and nothing unclean can enter there. The only negative showing through in these chapters is the defeat and judgment of the beast, the false prophet and the wicked, old dragon which has deceived the nations since the *Garden of Eden*.

Overall, what has been shown is that at least ten of the twenty-two chapters in Revelation contain absolutely no judgment whatsoever, and at least seven more are mostly positive. Therefore, over two-thirds of the book is completely void of fear, terror, cataclysm, or judgment. The only judgment in the other Chapters is upon the ungodly, rebellious, sinful world of the Antichrist's Kingdom, and upon the Beast himself with his cohorts—the false prophet, the great harlot, the wicked dragon, and those whose names are not written in the *Lamb's Book of Life*. We must drop our superstitions and get ready to enter into the *Great Day of God Almighty* and the *Revelation of Jesus Christ*.

THE TERRA FIRMA — A KINGDOM FOR GOD'S DEAR SON

It may be a bit difficult for some readers to understand why there must be a judgment. How can a loving God and His affectionate, caring Son be at such odds with the world they want to redeem? Why is the Creator at war with creation? How did the rift develop between God and His world? Who perpetrated the estrangement and why?

To adequately answer these questions we must have a basic under-standing of the whole scheme of scripture back to the beginning in Genesis. From a careful study of the texts relating to the pre-creation relationship between God and His Son, God established the earth to be the terra firma for the Throne and Kingdom of His Son. He placed man on earth to be the subjects to and objects of the love for the Son.

Lucifer, called light bearer, son of the morning, and the anointed cherub that covers, was made caretaker and steward of the Earth. However, rather than remain in the servitude position, he coveted Christ's place as being equal with God (Isaiah 14:12, Ezekiel 28:14). Satan rebelled against God, taking one-third of the angelic hosts with him. Note the revelation of the Antichrist's heart in Isaiah 14:12-14 where he declares his desire to be like the most-high God.

LUCIFER, THE USURPER, THE HIDDEN SIDE OF HISTORY AND OF REVELATION

Lucifer and the fallen angels set out to take over the earth and the Kingdom created for God's beloved Son (Isaiah 14, Ezekiel 28). In order to usurp complete authority over the earth and because man was the object of Christ's love, Satan saw it necessary to corrupt humanity, leading them in

CHRIST IN THE REVELATION 31

resistance against the divine Trinity. This began a cosmic war between Satan and his followers, and God's hosts. Satan has been allowed to run His course until he leads the whole unregenerate world to a stand-off against God and His Son. In the Book of Revelation 12:7-11, we see Satan cast out of Heaven where he resisted God and accused God's people day and night before the throne (Job 2:1-7). He is not in Hell yet, as many have thought, but rather moves back and forth from the throne room of Heaven to Earth. This can be seen in many texts including his earthly presence at the temptation of Jesus (Matthew 4:8-11).

Satan is cast to the earth and knowing His time is short, he becomes extremely violent. He cannot take his wrath out on God or any of His angels, nor the Church which is Raptured, so he turns to the vulnerable ones: the nations of the ungodly whom have already been ruling from space. Through his rogue and deranged, fallen angels (the principalities and powers which have been his viceroy's over nations. In Daniel, chapters ten and eleven, he wreaks havoc on a rebellious world and leads them to their final judgment by Christ and His armies at Armageddon. It is Satan's fall to Earth that perpetrates the tribulation.

The foregoing is the hidden side of Revelation. Satan is fully responsible for causing all of the wrath and destruction revealed and prophesied in its pages. Knowing the time of His judgment is near, he makes a heroic last stand. Cast out of Heaven, then from the air and coming to Earth, he takes up incarnate residence as a man (Daniel 7, 8, 11). The prophet Isaiah asked if "this [is] the man who made the earth tremble, who shook the kingdoms?" (Isaiah 14:16).

The Antichrist is a man who comes out of a deeply occult kingly line of European kings and has already been serving Satan. He no longer desires to control the earth and set up His kingdom in place of Christ. Now he only wishes to destroy the earth and all that is in it, leaving no possibility that Christ would finally reign on Earth. Much like Hitler's Parched Earth Policy at the end of World War II, he burned, looted, and destroyed everything on His way to retreat. Satan knows His end is near and hopes to leave nothing for man or God to possess.

It is interesting that the New Jerusalem will leave its construction site in Heaven to relocate in the atmosphere of Earth. In so doing, it will take ruler-ship and control over Earth. Thus, Christ and the Church will take permanent occupation of Satan's former domain which was His when he was prince of the power of the air (Ephesians 2:2).

God's plan concerning the Cosmic War is to make Earth—Terra Firma the location of the throne of His Son in Jerusalem. This is the reason that most of the warfare will be located in and around Jerusalem and the Holy Land. It was in this location that God chose to put His name and bring about the birth of His Son. And it is in this locale where He plans to set up the eternal throne and center of His Kingdom on Mount Zion and in Jerusalem on the Holy Mount.

SATAN'S WORK AMONG THE WORLD KINGDOMS

We must note in the Book of The Revelation of Jesus Christ, as well as in the prophecies of Daniel, Joel, Zephaniah, Isaiah, Micah, and Zechariah, that most of the final battles will take place in and around Jerusalem and Israel. This is where Christ lived, died, and rose again, and it is where He will also return. All of the Empires that are directly involved with the great dragon, depicted by the seven heads and ten horns of the beast, and representing the great Empires shown us in the Book of Daniel are the ones involved in an effort to destroy Israel.

The beasts of Daniel seven have morphed into a singular entity as we see in Revelation 13:1-2. The great battles of history have been fought around and concerning the Holy Land. The holy Roman empire tried to put a king of Jerusalem there and create the Millennium through its crusades. They will be revived by a European prince and ten kings (ten horns or powers) out of the old empire in a final effort to put an Antichrist in Jerusalem.

We observe from scripture that the world systems, even the culture and life-style of humanity, began their rebellion from the beginning with Adam and Eve leading the way. That rebellion became a seed sown in the hearts of the Adamic race of human beings and eventually has affected the whole charade of earthly governments beginning at Babel. The statement in Genesis 10:10, *"The beginning of his kingdom was Babel,"* may not only speak of Nimrod and his earthly kingdom, but may actually reach into the esoteric world and reflect the beginning of Satan's rule over the Gentile world kingdoms.

These worldly kingdoms and their rebellion against God are the subjects of Daniel's prophecy; their final end in the seven heads and ten horns of the Beast of Revelation. It is imperative that we understand that these cosmic, esoteric powers of darkness are the manipulators of the worldly nations. They are the principalities and powers under the control of the Prince of the power of the air, the God of this world. Understanding these underlying, unseen powers over the nations is a must if we are to comprehend events in our present world scene and how and why the nations end up in defiance and judgment toward God and therefore fall under the wrath of God in the last portion of Revelation.

Consequently, while many of the world's rebellious nations will be involved, the final battles will be fought at Jehoshaphat by Gog and Magog on the mountains of Israel, the West Bank, and in the Valley of Megiddo (Joel 3, Ezekiel 38-39). All of these are within a few miles of Jerusalem. Each terrorist nation to be destroyed by God will be those surrounding Israel that are in war against Jerusalem and Israel (Ezekiel 32:18-32). Thus, as we move into the final signs of the end, and hear the drums of Armageddon beat ever louder, let us keep our attention on Israel and the land of our Lord.

In His divine foreknowledge, God foresees the end of Satan's rebellion and the final outcome of man's resistance against God, led by these "rulers of the darkness of this age" and those who *committed "spiritual wickedness in heavenly places"* (Ephesians 6:12). We can see why the final scenes of this age will be centered in the Middle East and enacted around Israel, the land of our Lord Jesus Christ. Consequently, we have the whole scheme of prophecy, from the teleological Revelations starting with Genesis 3:15, to the eschatological insights of the prophets, and final apocalyptic texts of Daniel and Revelation. All-out war is the result.

A COSMIC WARFARE IN THE HEAVENLIES

It is difficult for those who are earthly minded to see into another dimension and comprehend its environs. Because this is our only perspective outside of the revealed scriptures, the personages, players, and theater of the cosmic conflict is most difficult to follow. It is only the insight that we receive through the revealed Word in the Bible that we can comprehend these activities and the reason behind them. Therefore the Book of Revelation becomes absolutely important and necessary in order to know the conclusion of all that is shown us in Scripture.

The cosmic war has as its main theater of conflict today in the heavenly realms of God and His angelic hosts, who are in conflict with the Devil and His angels. In Revelation, it is shifted to Earth (Revelation 12:9). It involves the whole universe inasmuch as the starry realms will suffer part of the judgment. We are told that the stars will fall and the Heavens will roll up like a scroll. (Revelation 6:14, Isaiah 34:4). What we term as the heavenlies is not only the Kingdom of God's heaven, but also the cosmic world of the unseen; the main battleground of a war of cosmic proportions occurring in outer space.

It is therefore, most difficult for us to understand this conflict in that it is mostly in the esoteric world, i.e. the world beyond our sight and hearing. Just because we cannot hear and see into that dimension does not mean that it is less real. In fact, it may be said to be more real than our physical world. Here again we should mention that this is why the Holy Scriptures are so important to us who have been given citizenship in that other world and are acutely interested in its reality. Without Scripture, we have no other insight into its activities and concerns.

Even though the main theater of conflict is in the heavenlies, it has also seriously affected our earthly realm because this earth is the part of God's creation where Satan was made steward. In his rebellion, he has become the god of this world and the prince of this world, as well as the prince of the power of the air (John 12:31, 14:30, II Corinthians 4:4, Ephesians 2:2, 6:12). This world is unwittingly involved in the cosmic war.

Satan's subtlety is effective by teaching the elite world that there is no cosmic or metaphysical realm of beings; no gods, angels, devils, etc. Of course, since he is the prince of this world, his influence is mostly upon the world's elite. His work on the underclass of the world is through his demonic hosts, but His personal persuasive manipulations are always upon the real movers and shakers of the world. This describes those whom David Rockefeller has identified as the Supranational Sovereigns, International Elite, and World Financiers of the world. This is one way Lucifer has worked his evil influence and kept them blind so He can pull strings behind the scenes. His subtle control of prestigious manipulators in the secret conclaves of international finance and international community planning who honestly believe they serve the real God who will bring about the Millennium and knows what is best for the world.

Satan has been given power over the darkness of this world (Ephesians 6:12). Therefore, he brings a part of the cosmic war to us hapless human beings. It was and is not our choice because we are given no choice, just as most civilians in war also have no choice.

Not only has humanity been diabolically affected by Satan's fall and his usurping of authority among "we the people," his fall has also caused chaos for the Earth itself. Paul helps us see how all creation has been subject to upset and upheaval, and must be delivered from this corruption (Romans 8:20). The physical earth will be delivered at the same time that the saints are delivered, and a "new heavens and a new earth" will ensue (Revelation 21:1). All of this will be congruent to the events of Revelation when Christ restores all things (Romans 8:19-23, Revelation 21:1, 2 Peter 3:13, Acts 3:21).

Because the bulk of humanity has chosen, or been deceived into joining Satan's rebellion, it follows with the world of nations in conflict with God and His plan for Christ.

REVELATION REVEALS THE COSMIC WORLD'S LAST WAR

The seals show the theater of Lucifer's last battle and what Christ must overcome to win our promised inheritance in the last battle of the cosmic world and its war against Christ. The trumpets show the first half of that war and the vials show the final three and one-half years of the final battle.

It is the book of Revelation following the lead of the book of Daniel, that finally alerts us to the cosmic side of the wars against evil that has set nations against each other and united them against God. It is only here that we see into the throne room of God as the Lamb prepares to open the seals—conditions necessary for Him to receive the purchased possession. The seals are the attestation and confirmation of ownership (or Warranty Deed) of God's book of inheritance of the earth. When they are opened and their demands met, transfer of ownership will be approved. They spell out the rules of conflict for the engagement of war between Christ the true and rightful owner, and Satan through his anti-Christ, the impostor throughout the ages. The earth and its environs is the theater of conflict (Ephesians 1:13-14). It is the Book of Revelation that represents the "*dispensation of the fullness of time*" that Paul spoke of, in which God will "*Gather together in one, all things in Christ, both which are in heaven and which are on earth, even in Him*" (Galatians 4:4, Ephesians 1:10).

Peter spoke of the same by declaring "*that He may send Jesus Christ, who was preached to you before whom heaven must receive until the times of restoration of all things, which God has spoken by the mouth of all his holy prophets since the world began*" (Acts 3:20-21)

This is what the Book of Revelation is all about. The return of Christ to put down all resistance to His Kingdom, both earthly and esoterically, seen and unseen, and redeem the purchased possession which is an earthly throne and kingdom, our promised inheritance.

It is in Revelation we see into the netherworld of Satan as the great dragon or serpent, and his hate and persecution of Israel from the beginning. Also, we see his diabolical hate toward all that are Godly and have the "*testimony of Jesus Christ*" (Revelation 12:17). It is in this Book that we see the real actor behind the Antichrist and his deception as he comes to mimic Christ and take away His Throne. Because the prophecies concerning Christ's return are so well-known among the nations, it will be necessary for Satan to mimic Christ's reappearance in order to convince the ungodly world of his assumed identity (John 5:43). Even the "*very elect*" will be deceived if at all possible (Matthew 24:24).

He must be convincing, because one third of the angels believed He could take the place of God's beloved Son.

The Book of Revelation gives us a sneak peek into the bottomless pit where demons abide under their king Abaddon, or Apollyon. The world does not acknowledge the reality of demons and will not understand the demonic plague that will torment the world for five months (Revelation 9). This opening of the pit of Hell will allow a deluge of demonic power on the earth in the last seven years. Only those who read and study the Book of Revelation will be able to see beyond natural understanding and into the involvement of demons in the final cosmic war where the forces of this world, influenced by demons, come out of the mouth of the beast and false prophet. They are spirits of devils drawing the worlds armies into a cosmic war with Christ and His armies at Armageddon (Revelation 16:13-17).

Revelation lets us see behind the scene of the world religions and understand their mysteries (Revelation 17:5). It is also here that we see satanic power behind the historical kingdoms represented by the seven heads of the beast. We also see the esoteric activities of Hell behind the world events that are driving the world toward a *One World Order* and the re-emergence of the holy Roman empire as the eighth head (Rev. 17:9-11). Here we become earthly observers of the cosmic theater of war occurring in space, involving both the seen and the unseen world, earthly powers and esoteric powers of angels, devils, demons and men. And, we can better understand the all-out insurgence of God to destroy the whole cosmic realm of Satan. His plan is to destroy the terra firma intended to be an eternal place for the throne and kingdom of God's beloved Son. Remember also, that Christ wants to share His inheritance with us.

Revelation, allows us to see through the veil of the flesh

and catch a glimpse into Heaven. There we see the Church and the Lamb before the Throne. We are able to see the multitude which no man can number, of the nations, kindred, tongues, and people participating in a great camp meeting in the presence of Christ. (Revelation 4-5, 7) And of course, we could not know about the promised New Jerusalem and the New Heaven and Earth if not for an outer space view into the next world.

The Book of Revelation records the final end of the war which we know as the Tribulation and Armageddon. It is the Revelation of Jesus Christ when in His glorious appearance at the Battle of Armageddon, Christ will set up His throne and kingdom (Revelation 1:1). It is His desire to share His glory with us since we have been adopted into His Kingdom.

MYSTERIES TO SOME

It is true that the Book of the Revelation of Jesus Christ is mysterious to many people. For example, to the worldly who may use it for personal advantage such as a political end or diplomatic tool, its true light never appears and it does not lead to a perfect day. When, as in the secret society's New Age movement of Alice Bailey and/or Madam Blavatsky's *New World Order*, it is used to dissuade Christians and gain world political dominance, or a pseudo-millennium peace and safety. It leads to confusion and *"sudden destruction"* (1 Thessalonians 5:3). Fear-mongers use it to speak of the end of the world; pseudoscience uses it as expert documentation to speculate about horrible natural disasters; the Media and Hollywood use it as a way to gain an audience by manipulating and sensationalizing a lie. Each one completely misses its real meaning. Revelation is far from being just a book about the end of the world. In fact, far from being a prediction of the end of the world and all humanity with it. It actually foresees a wonderful thousand years of perfect peace followed by a beautiful, eternal world. It becomes a provable fact that only those who hear, read, and keep the book in order to know and see the Revelation of Jesus Christ, will ever find the key.

Although many see Revelation as a mysterious book, it was not written as such. It is a revelation, not a mystery, and designed for only one thing: an unveiling of Jesus Christ in His latter-day coming.

The Book is *not* written for the worldly mind. For the ungodly that process everything through the natural mind, it is enigmatical. It speaks in riddles, symbols, obscure speech, and literary jumbles that are difficult to understand. It was *not* written for the casual critic, the scoffers and mockers, or the agnostics who are always try to fault God and His purpose. As they try to understand, its expression become entangled with their carnal criticalness and their observations end up going nowhere. Paul taught that the unsaved world is "*always learning and never able to come to the knowledge of truth*" (2 Timothy 3:7).

The Revelation of Jesus Christ is not written to those who think they know more than God and are more literate than His Word and those who would "add to" or "take away" from the Book. Conversely, it is written ...

> "*To everyone who hears the words of the prophecy of this book; and if anyone adds to these things, God will add to him the plagues that are written in this book; and if anyone takes away from the words of the book of this prophecy, God shall take away his part from the Book of Life, from the holy city, and from the things which are written in this book*" (Revelation 22:18-19).

This passage is not speaking of those who write commentaries, seek to analyze the book's content, or teach from the expanded concepts of the prophetic texts. It simply refers to those who add to or take away from its message showing no respect for the Lord Jesus Christ or God's Holy Word.

The message in Revelation is for those who are committed to keeping the truths of the Book. The word *keep* suggests a close look or giving careful attention to, preserving its contents. Only those who know the Lord can safely and successfully keep this book. To others it becomes an incentive to confusion. A study of church history shows that those who only read and hear but do not *keep* the book, soon wander off into heresy of one form or another. Heresy can be explained as truth carried to an extreme. One must be vigilant to divide it from truth that God gives. We find that the basic error of cultic doctrines often start with a misconception and wrong understanding of the Revelation. Another concept of heresy is a half-truth twisted and shaped into a lie. Or, in the words of the late A. N Trotter, we can call it *Technological Inexactitude*. Satan has no originality. He can only twist truth into a lie.

REVELATION NOT A MYSTERY, BUT ANALOGOUS

The word *analogous* means something written as an analogy and designed for study and contemplation. It is not written to be read like a story or novel, but is to be analyzed and scrutinized; meditated over and mused upon.

The Revelation is not mysterious then, but written in a mysterious, analogous manner. It is not a Book for the casual reader. That is to say its design is written for investigation, inquiry, evaluation and review. It is a diagnostic book to be analyzed and compared with all of the analogical texts of the Messianic message. It is true that the book's real meaning comes only to people who are biblically literate, able to analyze the book scripturally, and have at least a basic understanding of the Messianic prophecies of both the Old and New Testaments. They are committed to and serious about, Jesus Christ and His second coming. One thing seems critically clear: the book is often a dividing factor between the earnest spiritual seeker for God's truth, and those who have only *"a form of godliness but [deny] its power"* (2 Timothy 3:5).

I believe John was fully aware that this message from the Lord was not designed even for the casual critical Christian, let alone the agnostics of this world. Even for the majority of carnal Christians, it necessarily and purposefully remains an obscure writing. It was written just prior to, or near the beginning of the Roman persecution of both Jews and Christians which came in the early second century. Therefore, some say Revelation was written in an analogous way to keep the true message from being understood by the Roman leaders. At that time, some believed that its message was about Rome and brought condemnation on the empire. They believed that it was meant to deceive the Pagan rulers. Consequently, those who were using Christianity as a tool for state purposes would not be able to interpret its true meaning. Especially in the papal times, Christians tended to believe the Antichrist was the papal hierarchy. However, the real meaning of the book was designed to reach across the ages and far into the future. It has something to say about the future's seventh and eighth empires with their ten kings of Rome. Its real message was about the coming, or revealing, of Jesus Christ at the end of this age. The apparent reason for secret language was not to obscure it from Rome, but to obscure it from all of the ungodly, agnostic mockers and scoffers in the end time (2 Peter 3:3). It also gives incentive for real believers to do as the Bereans did as *"they received the word with all readiness, and searched the Scriptures daily to find out whether these things were so"* (Acts 17:11).

Keep in mind that any acceptable interpretation of the Revelation must be absolutely Christ centric, and also Biblically centric. In other words, every concept of it must be tied in and exegetically congruent with every other Messianic prophecy taken in their literal translation and interpretation.

One must be able to substantiate every phrase, thought, and expression in the Book of the Revelation of Jesus Christ in its comparison to all other Old and New Testament counterparts. I have nearly completed a diagnostic work in which I show that every praise, thought, symbol, and impression of the Book of Revelation can first be found in the thoughts, impressions, and motif of the Old Testament. Therefore, the Berean formula is a good one. We should receive the Word with an open mind, but search the Scriptures for the literal meaning.

We should not be surprised to find that God often withholds or makes obscure, certain portions of His Word. Jesus said to His disciples that there were some things they could not understand as of yet. He taught about things given to His followers that others cannot understand (Luke 8:10). And Peter said of Paul's teaching that there were *"some things hard to understand"* (2 Peter 3:16). We are taught that there are things understood only by the spiritual mind. If a person has not been born of the Spirit, he is still thinking with the natural mind and cannot discern spiritual things (I Corinthians 2:14-16).

Daniel said of the last-day prophecies that "none of the wicked shall understand, but the wise shall understand" (Daniel 12:10). Psalms teaches us that "the secret of the Lord is with those who fear Him" (Psalms 25:14). We are told not to depend on the experts and scholars, but depend on the Holy Spirit who *"will guide you into all truth...and He will tell you things to come"* (1 Corinthians 1:20, John 16:13). Also, in Deuteronomy 29: 29 we find that *"the secret things belong to the Lord our God, but those things which are revealed belong to us and to our children forever."*

As we search the secret things of God which are purposely left vague and obscure, let us be diligent to follow the Holy Spirit as He leads and guides us into truth. Do not be dismayed by the fact that many cannot understand. The simple plan of salvation is not difficult to understand, but it does have its mysteries. The deeper truths of His Kingdom are hidden so that we ourselves may dig them out.

THE BOOK OF REVELATION MUST REMAIN ANALOGOUS

We must never try to make the Revelation simple, only understandable to the regenerate mind. The book must remain analogously mysterious for the majority of carnal Christians and all others who seek to use it or understand it for any other purpose than the Revelation of Jesus Christ and His great day of glory, power, and dominion. To everyone else, it will remain an obscure book, not simply mysterious, but enigmatic. Its design is such that the half-hearted and insincere should not use it for self-serving purposes. Being so written, it necessarily distinguishes between the self-serving and the wholehearted and sincere seeker of Jesus Christ and His coming Kingdom.

Jesus kept Himself secret from those who sought Him for selfish purposes. He seems to follow His own instruction to us, teaching that we are not to "cast pearls [the very valuable truths of God] before swine [the ungodly and carnal minded]" (Matthew 7:6). Also, Paul gives us an interesting concept along this line when he said that heresies were necessary so that those who are approved may be manifest among us (1 Corinthians 11:19).

It is in the study of Revelation that the sincere believer in Christ can be distinguished from the visionary and fanatical interpreter whose effort can be easily seen as erroneous, making the true light of Christ even more manifest. Light always shines brighter against a dark backdrop. As it becomes offensive to some who love darkness rather than light, even so, to the church, Christ our light becomes the guiding light that directs our path into a fabulous future that awaits those who love Him (Isaiah 64:4, 1 Corinthians 2:9).

And to those who earnestly love and seek the Revelation of Jesus Christ, it is thrilling to share that the light which shines unto a perfect day, is shining brighter against the dark backdrop of today's corruption and confusion. Its hope for us is very attractive against the gloom of today's world. The Book of Revelation is far more relevant to the earth's events than it ever has been. However, as the signs of the times grow increasingly significant and we see the hope of a new world among so many different people, we find a new growth of the same old Chiliastic absurdities surging through the ambitions of the world planners. It is another major deception that began In the Middle Ages and is carried over to modern day delusion. It was known as the Chiliastic doctrine.

THE CHILIASTIC FALSE INTERPRETATION OF THE MILLENNIUM

It seems that there is no part of the book of Revelation that has inspired more incentive for the visionaries and also more encouragement for the true believer, than the concept of the Millennium as revealed to us in the Revelation. It was a misguided concept of the Millennium and also of the whole book of Revelation that inspired the crusades; for it was the idea that Rome was the one and only universal church that had many elite of the papal age. It was up to those in a heresy-ridden Holy Roman Empire to decide that it was time to take Jerusalem from the infidels and set up the millennial kingdom by putting a Roman prince on the throne in Jerusalem, known as the king of Jerusalem. Of course this was all without Christ. The Revelation of Jesus Christ clearly teaches that Christ will be the one who sits on the throne in Zion.

In the medieval ages, when the papal hierarchy began to see the Roman church as the one and only true, universal church, and the Pope as the vicar, or visual representation of

Christ on Earth, many of the elite of the papal dynasties in the heresy-ridden Holy Roman Empire began to see themselves in a Messianic role and see the Catholic Church as the Universal Church spoken of in Revelation. Increasingly, the millennial concept, inspired by their own private interpretation of Revelation caught the dreams of the papal hierarchy. By their own personally inspired and grandiose ideas of power and glory, and by their own strength and importance, they thought it was time to take the City of Jerusalem and the Holy Land back from the Muslims and develop the thousand years of peace in the Middle East. They thought in doing so, surely one of them would become the Christ.

Like a wild fire, that dream caught the imagination of the mysterious and superstitious Kings of the Holy Roman Empire, especially in France where the seat of the doctrine of the Blood of Christ was strong. Mary of Magdala had supposedly migrated into the area of Lorraine bringing with her a son of Jesus Christ. Many of the Kings, such as Fredrick the Great, supposedly were born of the son of Jesus Christ through Mary and therefore were literally of the bloodline of Christ.

It was these Kings and the promoters of this heresy that inspired and spawned the crusades. These so-called *Kings of the Blood* believed that they were worthy to sit upon a throne in Jerusalem in the stead of Jesus Christ and that out of them would also come the ten kings who would reign with the beast (2 Thessalonians 2:4, Revelation 17:12). Their purpose in the crusades was to overthrow the infidels in an apocalyptic-like seizure and take control of the Holy Land. They would set up one of their own Roman Kings in a palace on the Temple Mount in Jerusalem and secure a Millennium of peace and good will (Daniel 9:26). They did not completely annul Christ's part in the Millennium, but, since they saw themselves as Vicar, or earthy representation of Christ, assumed upon themselves to be the worthy creators of the Millennium.

After the conquest of Palestine, Godefroy de Bouillon set up a *Kingdom of God on Earth*, created a throne, and placed his brother, Baldwin on the throne as *King of Jerusalem*. He created what he expected to be a dynasty in Palestine to last one-thousand years. He inspired what became a deeply occult organization known as the "Priory de Zion" (the Priority is Zion) to be the *king-makers and keepers*. They built fortresses all around the Holy Land and guarded it as a kingdom. There is today among those kings of the blood, a king-in-waiting who holds the title *King of Jerusalem*. Juan Carlos was so named, and the son of the last reigning King of the Holy Roman Empire, Otto von Hapsburg. His son Karl carries that title today.

It was in their prideful and self-important minds to be the ones to set up the kingdom for Christ and to assume for one of their own, the kingship of Christ under the title *King of Jerusalem*. The title of that dream was a Chiliastic Empire, taken from the Greek *Chilliad* meaning the *Doctrine of the Millennium*. Such a grandiose idea was referred to and was a part of the basis of Augustine's "City of God."

Eventually, those with more level heads and solid minds prevailed against the Hierarchy and their false fantasies. The upset of this magic spell of the papacy was eventually broken by seeing through the Papacy and their anti-Christian ambitions. It was the seeing through of these grandiose dreams that actually exposed the Papacy for what it really was and had a part in opening a door for the Reformation. However, we believe it will be from the inspiration of that old Chiliastic dream that a new Pope will arise, and the hope of the present day Priory de Zion will again come to the forefront out of the chaos of a failed *One World Order* dream. The world will again choose a Roman prince of an occult nature and no doubt out of that same old bloodline who will again try to assume a throne on the Temple Mount and declare another messianic Kingdom. (See *Retrus Romanus* by Thomas Horn and Chris Putnam, Defender.)

Today, though an archaic word, Chiliast is still used in circles where the possession and title of the *King of Jerusalem* is yet held in expectation of one of their own being put on a throne in Jerusalem. The word actually depicts "one who believes that Christ will reign in person on an earthly throne for a thousand years" (*Oxford's Unabridged English Dictionary* 345).

In Lange's commentary, the author suggests that the analogous manner of writing of the Revelation is to lock out the understanding of the ungodly in their self-centered carnal pursuit (Schaff 62). This discourages carnal Christians from pursuing an understanding of Revelation out of curiosity or self-motivated reasons. It should, however, encourage born-again believers to seek the Holy Spirit's anointing and guidance in deciphering and understanding its message.

There is another rather negative side to the word *Chiliasm*. In this instance, it is a twisted dream coming out of the millennium concept in Revelation and becomes the base concept in the evil ambitions of the despot. It is being used by the deeply occultic, Luciferian-inspired plotters of a *One World Order*, who see this millennium concept as a promise of a coming ideal society created by a revolution. Many of their central offices can be located and in-housed in the basement of the UN headquarters in New York. It is picked up by the ungodly of political and social manipulators and used in humanists as a guide for world control. This idea was actually developed even before the Book of Revelation was ever written and used by the god-kings of the great empires.

The modern liberal dream of a perfect world, one without poverty, disease, social wrong, and war, injustice created by humanistic effort without the need of God or His Christ, has again created a false hope and false interpretation of Revelation. The Chiliastic visionaries are using the Book of Revelation to whip the world into their mold. Even in the evangelical churches, these Chiliastic ideas have found a root in the *Kingdom Now* theology.

The sad truth is, that when chaos of the Tribulation actually falls upon them, they will still totally miss the point and continue to be fascinated with their own form of the lie of Chiliasm. Be not dismayed, the hierarchy of this world, with their monarchial, dictatorial dreams like the emperors of old, will always use God and His Christ to promote their own ambitions. The book will always be "*a stone of stumbling and a rock of offense*" to many of the modern day Pharisees and Sadducees (1 Peter 2:8).

However, the Chiliastic hope is not in vain. It is still very real. After the demise of Satan and His Antichrist, the true Christ will set up the true Chiliastic age of a thousand year Millennium. To the godless mind of the unregenerate worldling, the Book of Revelation will always be obscure and confusing. To them it is only an intriguing mystery. The world loves a mystery. Therefore, they are fascinated by this book for the same reason and attracted to all types of occult, mystic, and metaphysical mysteries. Then, using the curiosities of the populous, they prey upon them with all kinds of devilish and demonic obscurities and only use the Book of Revelation to exploit the public.

OTHER MISGUIDED CONCEPTS OF REVELATION

A misguided concept of the Book of Revelation is spurning the radical branch of Shiite Islam. A false reading of Revelation teaches them to believe in the return of the twelfth Imam. He is their form of a returned savior as is alluded to in the Book of Revelation. To them, he is known as the twelfth Imam Mahdi. They believe that Revelation shows the return, not of Jesus Christ, but a powerful Islamic leader who will use Jesus as second in command and through Him, Islam must create the world chaos as shown in Revelation. It will be worldwide chaos that will supposedly overthrow all infidels in the United States and all western societies, including all of Christianity and Judaism, and set up a worldwide Islamic kingdom.

Furthermore, it is another misguided concept of the *New World Order* spoken of as the beastly kingdom as conceived in the Revelation, that has inspired Lucifer to bewitch the Secret Order Cults and the New Age crowd with their Aquarian age of peace—a type of the Millennium of Revelation. They join forces with the Humanists and their political cohorts, to decide they do not need Jesus and can set up their own Millennium of prosperity and world peace without Christ. Most of this is inspired by Lucifer himself, and they plainly say so. Satan reads the Book of Revelation, but does not have the light of understanding, and certainly does not want to promote Christ's victorious coming to defeat His kingdom, so He influences all of these groups to see it His way. He sees the coming one as he, himself, and struts around Heaven as if he was a great one (Isaiah 14:12).

There are the deeply misguided Gnostics who were such a hindrance to the early church and are again today a hindrance to the modern church. They are those mystical elite who believe they have some extra insight and knowledge through mystic wisdom. They cannot receive truth, although they seek it ardently, simply because their motives are wrong. But be sure that Jesus *"will appear a second time, apart sin for salvation"* (Hebrews 9:23). Paraphrased, this verse suggests that Jesus is not coming to deal with sin this time, but to bring salvation to those who wait for Him.

And lastly, even the socialist theology of Communism conceived by misguided Jews, has its twisted concept of Revelation and its perfect Millennium. Many heresies within the

Church world today have come about because of a lack of understanding of the Book of the Revelation of Jesus Christ. Many pastors steer away from the book because they believe its teaching is a cause of confusion. Many fundamental Bible colleges have limited curriculum that deals with Revelation for the same reason. It is also a fact that some pastors who do not choose to study and teach at least the fundamentals of prophecy, become reactionary and critical of those who do.

Over 180 years ago, Sir Isaac Newton had an insightful and almost prophetic thought proclaiming, "About the time of the end, a body of men will be raised up who will turn their attention to the prophecies, and insist on their literal translation and interpretation in the midst of much clamor and opposition."

A true story is told of a Pastor who taught the New Testament verse by verse, from beginning to end. He taught through the Book of Jude, and then turned around and started over. Someone asked him why he avoided the Book of Revelation. He answered, "Oh, it is a book that no one really understands; and besides, it has no practical teaching in it. It is full of quaint ideas, imaginations, and symbolic terms which are hard to understand. It only sows confusion in the church, so we will not bother to go into it."

The fact is however, by not bringing the Book of The Revelation of Jesus Christ and its message before God's people, it tends to cause its own confusion. Consider how *Kingdom Now* doctrine, the *Preterists* Diversion, the *Emerging Church* fallacy, *Replacement Theology*, and many more delusions are confusing the Church today. All of these diversions, if not deceptions, and many others are plaguing the Church. Because of a lack of understanding of the Book of Revelation, people are left to these many deceptions plaguing the Church today.

We are bound to mention those misguided in the Jewish

faith, even though they have limited contact with the Book of Revelation and its message. Except for a few today, they do not accept the book as credible. Still, in their concepts of the coming Messianic Kingdom, they tend to parallel much of nominal Christian mistakes. There was a tendency among the Pharisees and Sadducees crowd, along with the High Priests and elders, to contemplate the coming Kingdom of Messiah; to let their religiosity lead them into the lust for personal and national pride. They so misunderstood the Messianic promises that they completely missed His coming to Bethlehem's manger. Consequently, their complete misunderstanding of the Messianic Kingdom led to a disastrous effect upon most of the fanatically religious mass of Jewry.

At the same time the earthly representatives of Jewish culture and thoughts were led astray by worldly aims and ambitions, there was an elect few in each age who considered carefully the prophetic utterances, and seemed to clearly understand the true Messianic hope of Israel. With the aid of the prophetic text both in Judaism and Christianity, those few have been able to correctly interpret the true spiritual meanings of the symbolic and metaphysical language of Scripture. They are able to perceive the true purposes of God in them and from that proper understanding of prophetic scriptures, build their lives and hopes on a coming Messiah and His future Kingdom, leaving the rest of the world out.

Just as it has transpired in Jewry, so it is with the Christian church. Many in the church have, for power, pride, and denominational identity, strayed from the simple, literal truth of Christ's coming in power and great glory. Nevertheless, there was and is a remnant in every age; those fathers of the faith who were able to see through the hypocrisy and blindness of the Hierarchal elements of the church and keep focused on a true understanding of the Messianic hope.

We may seem to belabor the point, but before speaking

of Christ in the Revelation, we feel it is important to observe a world full of misunderstanding of the book's true message. These are all present-day delusions that come out of the millennium concept in Revelation. It is the same old misinterpretation that has plagued the Church since the early days.

NEED A SPIRITUAL BORN-AGAIN EXPERIENCE

This is why there is a strong recommendation by the author that a brother or sister in Christ simply read the Book for devotional reasons, but not try to comprehend the depth of Revelation before growing in the *"grace and knowledge of our Lord and Savior Jesus Christ."* (2 Peter 3:18) When a person is first saved, their attention turns to the life, death, and resurrection of the Lord, which is the true gospel by which we are saved (1 Corinthians 15:1-4). New converts may want to restrain their sense of curiosity, avoiding deeper study of the Book of Revelation. It could be confusing and scary, and probably would not suffice their need of growing closer to the Lord.

We also suggest that it is nearly impossible to understand the Book of Revelation of Jesus Christ unless you have received a born-again experience, where *"old things are passed away* [i.e. our old nature with its desires and lusts, and *all things have become new"* (2 Corinthians 5:17). Without a born-again experience, mankind is carnal in both sin and the natural minds, not having the mind of Christ. When Peter made his great profession to Jesus, proclaiming *"You are the Christ, the son of the living God,"* Jesus responded back to him, *"flesh and blood,* [that is men] *has not revealed this to you, but my father who is in heaven"* (Matthew 16:16-17).

Just as Jesus declared in the above text, it is a true fact that one must have a personal revelation of Jesus Christ before understanding the Christ in the Revelation. This is the only way we can be converted from a carnal mind to a spiritual mind.

Christ must be known personally in a born-again experience before comprehending Him in His great day of glory.

OUR APPEAL TO THE READER

Have you come out of this world and its love *of "the lust of the flesh, the lust of the eyes, and the pride of life"* by accepting your adoption as a child of God (1 John 2:16)? Have you accepted Christ and His saving grace? Or do you still love the world? If you love the world, the love of the Father is not in you, for the Word declares:

> *"Do not love the world, (not the Earth but the ungodly world systems) or the things in the world. If anyone loves the world, the love of the Father is not in him. For all that is in the world—the lust of the flesh, the lust of the eyes, and the pride of life—is not of the Father, but is of the world. And the world is passing away, and the lust of it; but he who does the will of God abides forever"* (I John 2:15-17).

If you still love this world and its lust of the flesh and pride of life; if you still count your wealth by earthly treasures, then the Book of Revelation of Jesus Christ will be a confusing and frightening book to you. It shows great loss of worldly gain. However, if you have given up your love of this world and its lusts and pride of life for a love for the Lord Jesus Christ and His coming Kingdom, the Book of the Revelation of Jesus Christ will be an exciting, thrilling and positive Book for you.

Let Christ and His Church extend to you that invitation:

> *"The Spirit and the Bride say, "come!" And let him who hears say, "come!" And let him who thirst come. And whoever desires, let him take the water of life freely"* (Revelation 22:17).

COME

Come, calls Christ, all who long to be free,
Weary, heavy-laden, and learn of me,
For rest of soul, light yoke, you'll see,
But you must come.
Come unto me all ye ends of the earth,
Come who thirst of sins parched dearth,
Come and receive a promised new birth,
But you must come.
Come unto me from the uttermost,
Come unto me in the innermost,
Come and be filled with the Holy Ghost,
But you must come.
Come, a final invitation call,
Spirit and Bride, on whom so e'er it fall,
For whosoever will, it reaches all,
But you must come.
(Robert J. Smith, 1988)

PREFACE

OUTLINE

MARVELOUS DESIGN SHOWS DIVINE INTELLIGENCE

(Please refer to outline at the end of this chapter.)

In the very first verse of the Bible, Genesis 1:1, there is scientific proof that intelligence far beyond our modern day genius, has designed and breathed inspiration into this text. Without considering the computer-generated marvels of Genesis 1:1, we can look at just the obvious script and see a scientific enigma. It becomes plain that the instant any thought was put into these texts, a divine mind beyond any human intelligence of the day, was involved.

To those who have had a touch of college level scientific background, an axiom of scientific truth is obvious in this verse. We have been told by professors and scientists that there are five absolutes of the physical universe. They are time, force, motion, space, and matter. Take another close look at this verse: *"In the beginning* (time), *God* (force), *created* (motion), *Heaven* (space), *and Earth* (matter). From the first verse of the Bible, we find the five absolutes of science, and therefore, proof of intelligence far beyond the supposedly barbaric minds of the age in which it was written. God's Holy Word contains not one "let us suppose" as is recorded over eight-hundred times in Darwin's *Origin of the Species*.

Our point is this: Before modern man could get involved, advanced science was already at work. Remember, Genesis was written at least as far back as Moses in the fifteenth century B.C. Evidence shows that parts of Genesis go even further back than that and draws from oral and written tradition back to the beginning. This puts the men who wrote it near the fringe of the *dark ages* of human intelligence. Now in the closing book of the Bible, we have continuing evidence of superior thinking. It is evidence that no man, even a sage or wizard of Intelligence, could have written this book. The writer was not John, but the Lord Jesus Christ Himself. It is written with a touch of mystery but, it is not mystic. A biblical mystery may be discovered and is part of God's marvelous design; but mysticism is part of the subtle deception of Satan and can never be discovered with logic. With all of the book's challenges, Christ the Revelator and John the writer, never moves outside of wisdom and logic, and always keeps the Logos as its central theme.

ESTABLISHING A LOGICAL OUTLINE

To establish a logical, reasonable, and plausible timeline, and to formulate an outline for the events in the Book of Revelation is one of those evident challenges. However, it is absolutely necessary in order to understand the book.

There is difficulty in outlining revelation, evidenced by the numerous outlines which have been suggested and presented for consideration. Serious study of the book began near the turn of the twentieth century. Following are some examples of the intrigue in the book's variety of designs:

REVELATION'S SEVENS.

Attempts have been made to use its marvelous series of "7's". There are at least twenty eight "7's" in Revelation.

Some have suggested as high as forty, but we present only these. There are 7 churches, 7 stars, 7 Spirits of God, 7 candle sticks, and 7 lamps in each; 7 angels, 7 seals, 7 trumpets, 7 vials, 7 plagues, 7 dooms or woes, 7 heads, 7 thunders, 7 eyes, 7 crowns, 7 I Am's, 7 thunders, 7 voices, 7 stones, 7 1000's, 7 mountains, 7 kings, 7 kingdoms, etc. There are forty verses in Revelation that speak of 7. In all of Scripture, there are over four-hundred, twenty "7's", and forty "70's." Several efforts have been made to align these 7's in a logical and chronological outline. If we try to outline the Book by its 7's as these efforts show, we find ourselves totally lost in finding a credible and rational timeline of events. The "7's" are evidence of design, but not evidence of order or time frame.

REVELATION: CHRONOLOGY

Many writings built various outlines by making an effort to place the events of Revelation in a consistent chronological order. Authors take it phrase by phrase as each event follows the other in a sequential and progressive order. Several honorable works have been written to establish a chronological outline and I do not propose to criticize them. There is evidence of a general sequence of events in a suggested chronological order, but not entirely. I see a different and more simple solution.

The problems that develop by using a chronological system of outline are many. Here are just a few of them:

A. The sixth seal includes all of the 7 trumpets, and the seventh trumpet includes all of the 7 vials, 7 plagues, 7 years of Tribulation, and 7 mentions of a Tribulation earthquake. It presents a type of telescoping effect where one lens slips down into the other. When one takes a reasonable, chronological concept alone as

B. In an outline based upon a sequential and consecutive order of events, one can arrive at so many duplications of what appears to be the same occurrence. For instance, there would be an earthquake in Revelation 6:12 and 8:5; then, more in 11:13 and 11:19. Still others in 12:16, 16:18-20, 18:21, and 20:11. Total, this adds up to eight earthquakes during a seven year period. That is possible, but when we consider that Babylon is mentioned as destroyed by earthquakes several times (Revelation 14:8, 16:19 18:21). There are other mentions of her destruction as well, but they strongly suggest the same earthquake (Revelation 18:2, 18:10). By trying to rationalize a consecutive outline, Babylon would be destroyed at least four times by earthquakes. Logic dictates that it is more reasonable to see at least some of these destructions of Babylon and the accompanying earthquakes to be the same phenomenon.

C. Trying to imagine how to telescope the 7th seal out into the 7th trumpet, and both of them projected into the 7th vial and 7 last plagues, becomes a nightmare for a progressive approach to an outline of events in the book.

NO ORDER SUGGESTED

This idea comes from agnostics, mockers, and scoffers who suggest that the events in Revelation are the rambling of a mystic and are on the order of the Secret Society's writings, with no meaning or logical sense. These unbelievers attempt to mystify.

There are many views that have developed their own

special terminology, and each has different ideas for an outline. For instance, there are those who believe in the a-millennial, the pre-millennial, and the post-millennial views. Each one of these suggests their own outline.

There is the pre-Tribulation view, meaning a persuasion that the Rapture of the Church takes place before the Tribulation. Then, there is the mid-Tribulation view which believes that the Rapture takes place in the middle of the Tribulation. And lastly, is the post-Tribulation view including those persuaded that the Rapture of the Church takes place at the end of the Tribulation period. Each of these will have their own outline.

REVELATION: NO ORDER, ONLY RANDOM REVELATION

Those who reject Revelation as authentic, suggest that it was never intended to be an orderly discourse of events in the real world, but randomly jotted down as individual inspirations from dreams, or hallucinations of mystics. This is certainly the case with Gnostic thinkers, but it would not hold true with John or the Lord who revealed these things. A mystic gets his inspiration from dreams, visions, and impressions on the mind, probably from hallucinating drugs. This could be reasonably so with the Gnostic thinkers of the day, but certainly not true with John or the Lord!

Each of these would have a completely different outline of events. The only one with no outline at all would be the a-Millennial view. They believe that no part of the Book of Revelation has any semblance to reality at all. To them the book is metaphorical and allegorical, and none of the stories are meant to relate to any real happenings in the real world at any time. They think that all of Revelation is symbolical and should only be used as allegorical and metaphorical illusions or illustrations. They compare it to events and attitudes at any given age and time. We will not bother to add any credibility to such nonsense or to insult the text by giving apologetics to these thoughts.

OUR PROPOSAL

To clarify my position in these writings, I take the Pre-Millennial view without question. This view adheres to the rapture taking place before the tribulation. We have given extensive study to each of the fore-suggested positions and find that none of them can begin to hold up to careful scrutiny in the basic motif of prophetic light. In my opinion, when taking into account the whole prophetic and Messianic texts—both Old and New Testaments, only the pre-Tribulation position can answer to a careful comparison to the whole.

Therefore, I propose a slightly different concept in a possible outline for the Book of the Revelation of Jesus Christ. This is an outline that will be more consistent with its design and one that helps keep Christ, and His people, the Jews, in view as the central motif of the entire book.

The outline will use some of the chronological order which has been suggested by others, but in following a very general sequence of events, we will find some parallels as well. By viewing the accompanying examples and illustrations of a suggested outline, and in keeping with Old Testament Messianic texts which parallel Revelation texts, the reader will be helped in following this particular concept of outline.

OUTLINE - A PAGEANT OF DIVINE JUSTICE

The following outline will be presented in the form of a play. Its subject, and the subject of Revelation as a whole, tells of the final judgment at the coming of the Lord in His *day*. Immediately following the Rapture of the Church, John is brought into the throne room of Heaven (Revelation 4:1). At this point it becomes the throne room of judgment and can be compared to the hall of justice. Court is set. The courtroom briefing, or indictment contained in the scroll will be opened. The book is a legal document of ownership. Its seals represent the conditions for redeeming the *promised possession* (Ephesians 1:14). An executor of the estate is found and chosen. He is the Lamb. He is also our *goel*, or the Kinsman redeemer; a near relative upon whom certain redemptive obligations fall to a nearest of kin. We will enlarge upon this *Right of Redemption* in our expose about the scroll.

Keeping our view of outline consistent with a general chronological order, we will interject another proposal which view the Book as written in the form of a theoretical play script that we have called *The Theatrical Scenes of Divine Justice*, or more simply *Scenes of Divine Justice*. Please note the use *justice* rather than *Judgment*. As a culture steep into the age of total theatrical drama and entertainment, this concept can be easily understood.

In keeping with a theatrical train of thought, it is interesting to consider the New Testament world of Greek, Hellenistic culture where theater played a prominent role in John's day. In efforts to Hellenize the culture of the empire from Macedonia to Persia and India, Alexander the Great, and later of his four Captains inherited power over the Greek Empire. Greek tragedy and drama was very popular and wide-spread, even in the Holy Land among the Jews.

In addition to the above, the author found that such a form would be consistent with the concepts, flow, and plan of the events in Revelation. Rather than try to reconcile the events in a strictly chronological order, or try to conceive some sequential or progressive flow of the happenings in the book, I set out to see what would happen to the logic of outline, if we put them in a playwright style. Consequently, we would have a curtain-up and curtain-down sequence with behind-the-scenes, showing the events in Heaven simultaneous with events taking place on stage in the human scene, and placing a few *mean-whiles* along the way. The only way old Greek theater, as well as the modern playwright, has been able to clarify actions and events in a story, is to show their simultaneous scenes by placing a *meanwhile* between them. We believe many of the events in the Book of the Revelation of Jesus Christ take place simultaneously and could be clarified with a *meanwhile*.

Several features of the outline should be mentioned and explained at the start. (1) We have taken the liberty to attempt to divide the book into *acts* and *scenes* as if you were reading the script of a stage production. (2) What many in the past have identified as *interludes,* or *parenthesis,* we see as events behind the scenes and between curtains, usually taking place in Heaven. (3) We must keep clearly in focus whether the described event we are considering at the time is it taking place on Earth or in Heaven, is behind the scenes as preparation for action, or a parenthesis. One of the beautiful features of the Book of Revelation is that it gives us the awesome privilege of penetrating the dimensional barrier between the unseen world of the esoteric dimension and the Earth's realm. (4) As in many story-line publications or productions, the time-line of events is usually divided into what we will call *meanwhile*.

For example, an old western novel might use the phrase: "meanwhile, back at the ranch…" several times in the script. It seems to be the easiest and most logical way to keep all of the events in order. We understand by *meanwhile*, that the events of one chapter and the events of the former chapter are taking place simultaneously. If we separate the series of events in Revelation into several *meanwhiles,* we see certain events taking place at the same time and overlapping in sequence as other happenings are taking place. (See *Chart of the Harmony in Revelation* at the end of this chapter.)

For instance, (see Act III, scene V of the outline) while the tragedies of chapters eight and nine are taking place on Earth, the 144,000 are sealed and hidden from the Antichrist (Revelation 12). The Church meanwhile, appears in Heaven above the calamities and afflictions on Earth, and found in the presence of the Lamb (Revelation 7). This design offers much clarity to the sequences of the events in Revelation.

GENERAL OUTLINE

The first three chapters of Revelation are not included in this outline, inasmuch as they show us *"things that are,"* they divide between the *"things that you have seen"* and the *"things which will take place after [the Church age"* (Revelation 1:19). These three chapters are designed to show the Lord's care of the Church and her rapturous transport before the actual time of Tribulation on the Earth. They represent the parenthesis between the sixty-ninth and the seventieth week of Daniel's seventy weeks, a Stop Gap which represent the Church age. They are the Church age. The Pageant of Divine Justice starts with the seventieth week of Daniel and is the seven years of Tribulation.

Beginning with chapters four and five, there are scenes displayed entirely in Heaven. According to our suggested form of outline, the scenes in chapters 6 and 7 have nothing to do with Earth and what is going on there. No indication is given as to what is happening on Earth, but we can assume that pre-Tribulation events (the beginning of sorrows talked about in Matthew 24:8) are happening. Here we see the throne room of the Divine Judge of all the Earth. Court comes into session revealing the book of judgment—the prosecutor's brief. At this time, the executor of the inheritance and administrator of the estate is chosen. He alone is worthy to take the scroll, or warrantee deed, and open the seals, each one displaying the demands that must be met before ownership can be transferred. These three scenes will be represented in Act 1.

In this Act Jesus is portrayed as the Executor and Prosecutor, God is the Judge, and the twenty-four elders are the jury. The guardians of the court are the living creatures. Confidence in the Executor of the Estate is shown in the accolades of praise offered. He is the Lamb wounded unto death. Here Jesus Christ is both Savior and Judge (John 5:22, 30).

PREPARATION AND PRELUDE OF COMING EVENTS

In Chapters five and six, we are led into the reading of the brief which, as the seals are opened, begin the whole sequence of events and presents us with the preparation for judgment and a prelude of what must come for the redemption to take place. I do not believe that the opening of the seals represent any action, or engagements in the actual Tribulation, but rather represent the signs of coming events. In fact, what is shown in chapter six closely matches the signs of His coming in Matthew twenty-four where Jesus said: *"All these are the beginning of sorrows"* (Matthew 24:8).

Each seal represents a condition leading up to the Tribulation, and a requirement to be met in order to buy back the inheritance. This will become clearer later when we go into the laws of redemption in the Old Testament. Each seal is a demand requiring Judgment; each, an indictment against Satan and his kingdom. They reveal the disaster Satan has caused and is still causing. I believe the actual Tribulation begins with chapter eight after the sealing of the 144,000, and after we see the church already transported into the presence of the Lord (Revelation 7). (Observe the seven scenes under Act II of the outline.)

Chapter six, Act II, is called *Fore view and Preparation for Coming Judgment*. It is the sentence handed down and a preview of coming events that will cause or trigger the Tribulation. These compare interestingly enough with signs of His coming in Matthew twenty-four. Jesus calls out:

"*...for all these things must come to pass, but the end is not yet*" (Matthew 24:6).

It is very important that we understand what is said here. These are what Gary Stearman's *Prophecy in the News* calls pre-pre-Tribulation sorrows, or sorrows that trigger the Tribulation, but the end—seven years of Tribulation is still a little ways off. These sorrows are evident in the seven seals, which represent the things that must be dealt with before the title deed to our inheritance can be opened.

As each seal is broken, a greater understanding is revealed of why Jesus must judge the earth. There appear to be no engagement or action in the Tribulation actually taking place here. These are fore-views of coming Judgment or signs of coming events. They are warnings, as shown in Matthew twenty-four. The seals represent conditions to be met and the demands which require justice to be administered to Satan's Earth. Each one shows Satan's destroying factors and are an indictment against the Devil.

To show that no actual acts of judgment have, or are taking place in chapter six, we find in chapter seven the destructive angels, depicted in the four horsemen, being held back from causing any destruction on the earth. He who has the seal of the living God cries out saying:

"*Do not harm the earth, the sea, or the trees, till we have sealed the servants of our God in their foreheads*" (Revelation 7:3).

Every hurt is enumerated and sequel to the trumpets in chapter eight. By this we see that no action toward and tribulation has taken place until the 144,000 Jews are sealed on Earth and an innumerable multitude of every nation, kindred, people, and tongues are safely above the Tribulation foray in Heaven and in the presence of the Lamb (Revelation 7:9). This is meant to be a comfort to the redeemed and Jews alike.

We will call Act III, *Demands for Judgment* as the prosecutor opens his brief *"to take peace from the earth"* (Revelation 6:4). Satan has been cast to Earth, taking out his vengeance upon the earth and later upon man (Revelation 12:9, 12). It is Satan's wrath not God's wrath, that is expressed in the four horses of Revelation chapter six, God's wrath is not expressed until the 11th chapter, after which the "wrath of God" is mentioned 11 times. These are the same evil spirits as seen in Zechariah chapter 6 and which were set to destroy The earth put held back by Christ until the servants of God, the 144,000 Jews were sealed in chapter 7, and were later released (chapter 9:14).

REAL TRIBULATION BEGINS

Chapters eight and nine appear to be in the first three and one-half years of the Tribulation. They depict the tragedies and human failures which will demand Christ's intervention, and are associated with a nuclear exchange between angry nations (Revelation 11:18). Prayers of intercession are offered in Heaven just before justice is administered (Revelation 8:1-4). These are scenes consistently shown to be the throne of mercy, the seat of intercession as a part of justice.

In both chapters eight and nine, justice, in the form of judgment falls upon the earth. These catastrophic events do not represent God's wrath, but are caused by exchange of nuclear war and wrath between the angry nations (Revelation

11:18, Psalm 2). They take place in the first half of the Tribulation but are also reflected in the plagues of chapter sixteen. Parallels will be listed in chapter sixteen's comments. God's wrath is mentioned eleven times, but they all come after the eleventh chapter and are involved with only the last three and one-half years of the Tribulation.

Chapter ten is an interlude behind the scene and generally takes place in Heaven. Chapter eleven is a *meanwhile*, showing events concerning the Jews and their temple and the witnesses during the last part of the first half of the Tribulation, moving us into the last three and one-half years.

Chapter twelve is another *meanwhile* that shows us the same period of time as relates to the Jews and Israel during the Tribulation. They reveal some of what we are calling the *triggers to Tribulation* which God will use to justify the last days of His wrath.

Act IV brings us to the last half of the Tribulation called *the wrath of God*. This is where justice is administered from on high. It correlates with the same period of time shown to us from the standpoint of several participators in this judgment. During the next few chapters we will suggest several *meanwhiles* in the events.

Chapters eleven through eighteen reveal the last half of a seven year Tribulation, showing the events from the view of two witnesses in Jerusalem, the Jews, the Beast with his economic, political and religious power, the plagues, Armageddon, the great harlot, and the One World Order economy called Babylon. Each of these is separated by a *meanwhile* and generally parallel to chapters thirteen through sixteen.

Chapters thirteen, seventeen, and eighteen are also *meanwhiles* that show us the Tribulation from the perspective of the Beast and His kingdom (Revelation 13), the Apostate Church (Revelation 17), and the World Economic situation during the Tribulation (Revelation 18).

The coming of the Lord is mentioned in chapter fourteen and detailed in chapter nineteen. It also brings us to the final reaping of the earth in two harvests (Revelation 19:15-18). Meanwhile, chapters fifteen and sixteen show us the same period of time, namely the last three and one-half years of Tribulation. They detail the plagues called down from Heaven by the two witnesses of Chapter eleven (Revelation 11:5-6). In chapter fourteen, a call is made to the Jews to serve God alone, and get out of the beastly system of Babylon. (Revelation 18:4) They were not to take the mark, name, or number of the beastly, one-world power of chapter thirteen.

In chapters seventeen and eighteen the beast, false prophet, his one world religious harlotry, and the world economic crash are all detailed. This shows Christ dealing with the three entities first revealed in chapter thirteen. Chapters eleven through eighteen contain many *meanwhiles* that cover the same general overlaps of time from these various perspectives. Each *meanwhile* leads to the end.

As described earlier, the real action begins with chapter eight. These events, represented in the outline by Act III, show the first half of the seven-year Tribulation. They are catastrophic events cause by the exchange of angry nations, not by God (Revelation 11:18, Psalm 2). God's wrath is mentioned eleven times in the Book of the Revelation of Jesus Christ, starting in chapter eleven and represented by the vials, plagues, and Armageddon. All eleven references of the *wrath of God* are associated with the last half of the Tribulation and the destruction of the Beast and His Kingdom.

Act IV of the outline shows events happening in the last part of the seven-year Tribulation. Chapters eleven through eighteen best illustrate the concepts of *meanwhiles*. Chapter eleven shows Jerusalem and the temple playing an important part in the cause of the angry nations while the plagues are called down from Jerusalem by the two witnesses (Daniel

9:27, 11:28-30; 2 Thessalonians 2:4). These plagues that are the antagonizing factors leading to Armageddon are detailed in chapters fifteen and sixteen. We can also follow the hate of the dragon and the beast toward Israel because of these plagues during the same time period (Revelation 12).

Meanwhile, we see the beast, his world government, and his world religion cohort exercising their political, religious, and economic control during the same time (Revelation 13). During the same time, the plagues drive the devil to entice the world by his demon spirits under the Beast, challenging the coming of the Lord at Armageddon.

Finally, after all the conditions of the seals are met, the angry nations are put down, and the beast, false prophet and dragon are bound, the Lord and His Church come to possess the promised inheritance. The earth and its people become the environment for Christ's throne and kingdom (Revelation 19). The Millennium and the new heavens and earth are revealed in chapters twenty and twenty-two. Keep in mind that the seven trumpets are included in the seventh seal, and the vials are included in the seventh trumpet. Therefore, the last seal includes the rest of the judgment, and all of the trumpets and vials, thus fulfilling the last seal of demand for judgment.

The outline will become clearer as the events of the book are covered in detail. I suggest you keep the outline and charts in hand as we proceed through the chapters of the book, making continual reference to them, as indicated on the outline. The great dragon, the Beast, and the false prophet are bound. The Lord and His Church come to possess the promised possession, inheriting the earth and its people who will become the kingdom under His throne—the throne of David. The demands for justice and judgment have been met.

The eternal life promised by our Lord Jesus Christ becomes a reality in these closing chapters of Revelation.

MANY OF THE DETAILS OF REVELATION ARE IN THE OLD TESTAMENT

As fore-mentioned, the Book of Revelation is actually an accumulation of all the Messianic prophecies and motifs of the Old Testament. Every thought, praise, symbol, and concept in the Book, are found in the Old Testament. Therefore, the Book of Revelation does not give us great detail about the Antichrist, the beast, the number 666, or the great harlot. Most of the information about these must be intercalated from the Old and New Testaments to get the complete story. At the same time, we are not given a lot of details about the Tribulation or Armageddon in the Old Testament Messianic prophecies, but most of the details about these events we will find in the prophets of Old and in the rest of the New Testament.

The Book of Revelation does not detail Christ's great triumph over Hell, the principalities and powers, rulers of the darkness of this age, nor His victory over the fallen angels, demons, or the dragon that administrates them (Ephesians 6:12). We are only told that there is a war in Heaven and we receive vague briefs of the event. Again, we are required to fill in the blanks from the Messianic Scripture. The separation of good and bad nations, and their destiny is given to us in Matthew twenty-five, but is not detailed in Revelation. So, as an analogue writing, I believe God designed us to search out Revelation's mysteries from all of the prophetic texts.

The Revelation of Jesus Christ moves quickly into the real aim and object to be accomplished in that short time of the Tribulation. It takes us directly into the millennial reign of Jesus Christ in His earthly kingdom and the New Jerusalem. Many of the details of the Millennium and life in the New Jerusalem must be intercalated into these Revelations from the Old Testament, namely Isaiah, where great details are given about the Millennium.

In Revelation twenty-one, we are carried into a deeply mysterious and cryptic understanding of this New Jerusalem which takes us deeper than the actual physical city described here. It is introduced as the *Bride, the Lamb's wife* (Revelation 21:9).

THEME IS CHRIST IN HIS GREAT DAY

The Book of the Revelation of Jesus Christ is totally, simply, and solely about Christ and His triumph over His enemies, which include the enemies of the Jews, Israel, and the Church. All other subjects are relative to Christ's Revelation and are not primary to the event. The only impression we are left to understand, is that these villains are the enemies of Christ Jesus the Lamb of God, and He will defeat them in His *Great Day* of Revelation. Therefore, we have to intercalate into Revelation all of the Messianic texts from the Old Testament which speak of *that day, that great day,* or *the day of the Lord*.

Act V reveals the consummation, and inheritance of the promised possession. In keeping with the main theme of our writing "Christ in the Revelation," and in harmony with this outline, we would like to suggest that Christ is seen in every part of this last-day *Pageant of Divine Justice* as in *the day of the Lord*. (See the Appendage for further discussion of the *Lord's Day* or *the Day of the Lord*.)

Now let us proceed with a study of Revelation, chapter by chapter.

PAGEANT OF DIVINE JUDGMENT

The Theatrical Scenes of Divine Justice
Act I   Hall of Justice – Court is set
        Scene I Throne of Judgment 4:1-11
        Scene II Book of Judgment and Inheritance 5:1-4
        Scene III Executor of the Inheritance Appointed   5:5-14

Act II	Preparation and Foreview of Judgment – Case presented
	Signs of coming Tribulation and Redemption
	Seven Seals broken to execute the Redemption
	These are the beginning of sorrows – conditions for Redemption

        Scene I   1-4 seals Prosecutor's Brief   6:1-8
        Scene 2   5th seal Demand for Judgment-Martyr's Blood
                  6:9-11
        Scene 3   6th seal World's terror of approaching judgment
                  6:12-17
                  Men's hearts failing them
        Scene 4   Interlude: Behind the scenes - righteous sealed
                  Redeemed Jews kept through judgment   7:1-8
        Scene 5   Godly, both Jew & Gentile, kept above judgment
                  7:9-17
        Scene 6   7th Seal Breathless expectation-Day of the Lord
                  The greatest moment in history has come

Act III   Prosecutor's Brief - Demand for Judgment
        Human failure under Satan's influence demands God's
        intervention
        FIRST 3 ½ YEARS OF TRIBULATION—Wrath of Nations
        11:18 & Psalm 2
        Scene 1   Preparation for Judgment- announcing the
                  Tribulation   8:1,2
                  Great High Priest of Heaven, Golden Censor- Voice
                  of Martyrs   8:3-5
        Scene 2   Trumpets 1-3   Judgment on Earth & Environment
                  8:7-11
        Scene 3   Trumpet 4   Judgment in the Heaven   8:12
        Scene 4   Trumpet 5   Hell is loosed   9:1-11
        Scene 5   Trumpet 6   Judgment upon world's systems
                  9:13-16
        Interlude: Behind the scenes in Heaven prior to last
                  3 ½ years in Tribulation
                  The Great Tribulation starts- God's wrath mentioned
                  11 times
        Scene 1   John, like Ezekiel 2:8 & 3:11 eats the Book   10
                  The Book of Sentence- both bitter and sweet

OUTLINE

Act IV: Simultaneous judgment on particular entities
    Scene 1 Two witnesses & the Temple in Tribulation 11
    Scene 2 Israel in Tribulation 12
    Scene 3 Beast & global government in Tribulation 13
    Scene 4 Christ captures Mt. Zion from Antichrist 14
    Scene 5 Harlot Church & Apostate economy in Tribulation 17 - 18

Act V: The Promised Possession
    The consummation and reception of the inheritance
    Scene 1 Coming of Christ at Armageddon   19
    Scene 2 The Millennial Reign of Christ & the Church 20:1-6
    Scene 3 The Great White Throne of Judgment- Death Toll 20:7-15

    Three enemies of the Lamb & Church, put down by Christ -
        1. Devil
        2. Beastly World Order
        3. Apostate Church
    Scene 4 The New Heavens & the New Earth   21 & 22

CHART OF THE HARMONY OF THE REVELATION

The Church in Heaven

- (Meet the Lord)
- Three events in the sky
- (Marriage Supper)
- (Court of Awards)
- Things that are to come

Second Coming of the Lord Chapter 19
With the saints - (Jude 14, Zechariah 14:9)

Chapter 20 - The Kingdom Age - The 1000 year Millennium
Hell Destroyed - Earth and Heaven cleansed
Chapter 21, 22 The New Heavens, Earth & New Jerusalem

God's wrath

- Chapter 7
- Chapter 9
- Chapter 11
- Chapter 12
- Chapter 14
- Chapter 16
- Chapter 18

3 1/2 yrs

Pause - Chapter 10 - Scene in Heaven

Man's wrath – Satan's wrath

- Chapter 6
- Chapter 8
- Chapter 11
- Chapter 12
- Chapter 13
- Chapter 15
- Chapter 17

3 1/2 yrs

Tribulation Time - 7 years

Chapter 4 & 5 — Preparation for Judgment in Heaven
Rapture of the Church

Chapters 2 & 3 The Church age - The things that are

CHAPTER 1

THE GLORIFIED CHRIST

We now come to the actual text of the Book of The Revelation of Jesus Christ starting with chapter one in the book. By way of introduction, allow me share a poem which came by me in a time of inspiration about the precious Word of God. It is entitled, *An Ode to the Word.*

AN ODE TO THE WORD

The Word of God must be <u>sought</u>
Like a treasure in a field,
And then withal, it must be <u>bought</u>
As a precious gem revealed.
Now let the Word of God be <u>taught</u>
To hungry souls that yearn,
And then finally it must be <u>caught,</u>
Kindled in the heart to burn.
And, oh how sweet as it is <u>wrought</u>
In the lives of those who heed,
So buy the Word and <u>sell it not,</u>
For we have no greater need.
(Copyright: 1991- Robert J. Smith)

Sought, bought, caught, wrought, and sell it not, tells the story of the Word.

To this point in our writing, much effort was spent sharing with the reader some basic information which provides a good background for an understanding of the Revelation of Jesus Christ, as well as our particular approach. There are hundreds of great books written on this wonderful and exciting finish to the inspired text. For every one I have read, I gained understanding. Some I agree with, while others reveal how far people can stray when they try to understand holy things with the carnal mind. As my dear friend and Pastor, Owen Carr use to say: "I am a composite of a multitude of wonderful people." So I say with Pastor Carr, I am a composite of all of those who have poured part of themselves into me throughout my lifetime.

ONLY AS THE SWEET HOLY SPIRIT LEADS INTO ALL TRUTH

As is true with all of God's Word, it is especially true with Revelation. No part of the Word can be understood and comprehended without a born-again mind touched by the Holy Spirit. Only the Holy Spirit can lead and guide into all truth (John 16:13). As the Apostle Paul so humbly expresses to the Corinthians:

> *"My speech and my preaching were not with enticing words of man's wisdom, but in demonstration of the Spirit and of power ... not the wisdom of men ... but we speak the wisdom of God in a mystery, the hidden wisdom, which God ordained before the ages for our glory ... for the Spirit searches all things, yes, the deep things of God ... now we have received, not the spirit of this world, but the spirit who is from God, that we might know the things that are freely given to us by God"* (1 Corinthians 2:4, 6-7, 10-12).

Especially when it comes to the Revelation of Jesus Christ,

we must pray and yield to the Holy Spirit's prompting. Most of the confusion over Revelation has been created by carnal minds (even with a PHD attached) that have not, and do not operate by the prompting of the sweet Holy Spirit of God.

All of our preaching and teaching, especially as pertaining to the understanding of Revelation, must always be under the direct anointing of the Holy Spirit, and in His demonstration and power. It must all come through the renewed mind of Christ. It must be preceded by the crucifixion of the old nature in a born-again experience and understood in the mysteries of a new birth from the hidden wisdom, which the Spirit of God gives.

As stated earlier, the Revelation of Jesus Christ cannot be fathomed without the insight of the Holy Spirit. We must pray until we sense the touch of the Holy Spirit before we ever begin a study of this Book or seek to explain it. So help us God! Let us seek Him in Prayer constantly as we study the Book.

GOD GAVE IT, JESUS REVEALED IT, CHRIST'S ANGEL TRANSMITTED IT, AND JOHN WROTE IT DOWN AS DICTATED. (V. 2)

We will call the first seven verses of chapter *The Prelude, Preface,* or *Forward,* to the book. Here, John introduces himself as the author of the book and tells what ought to be done with the writings. *The Revelation of Jesus Christ* actually begins with verse eight.

Many people have misunderstood the book simply because they do not read the first several lines? Revelation starts with the correct title and key to its understanding:

> *"The Revelation of Jesus Christ, which God gave Him to show unto His servants—things which must shortly take place. And He sent and signified it by His angel to His*

servant John" (Revelation 1:1).

Therefore, it is not called the *Revelation of Saint John* as some would suppose. John would have been horrified to know it had ever been called by his name.

JOHN, A VERY SPECIAL DISCIPLE; HUMBLE, SELFLESS, YET EXTRAORDINARY

John would never have wanted to be called by the exalted name of *Saint John* or *John the Divine*; or to receive any such glory to himself. And never would he want to be in competition with the Lord for the glory which solely and completely belonged unto Jesus Christ. He simply calls himself what any and all of us must be called *a servant of Jesus Christ,* or *the disciple whom Jesus loved.* Always, in the presence of Jesus our Lord we must be humbled, while He must be exalted.

No disciple selected by our Lord was more humble and less self-assuming. It is true, however, that the Apostle John knew the man well who was revealing these things to him. Of all the disciples chosen by our Lord to be the foundation stones of our faith, John was probably the most worthy to receive this very special and personal revelation from the Lord. No one knew Christ better, loved Him more, or demonstrated a closer relationship with than did John.

Christ is mentioned by name or by title fifty-nine times in the text of this book. He is called *The Lamb* twenty-seven times. By virtue of these titles alone, we are all encouraged to look for Christ throughout the Book of Revelation.

A special insight into the Lordship and Messiahship of Jesus was given to John. We only have to follow him during the final days before the crucifixion to see the close personal tie, both at the Lords table where it was John who lay on His breast, and at the crucifixion where the Lord committed

His own mother to John's care. We note the Lord's personal invitation to John who would join Him at the Transfiguration, and we also see John's very special respect and love for Christ at the tomb. John was known among the disciples as *the disciple "whom the Jesus loved"* (John 13:23).

All of this is so perfectly complimentary to what we read in the very special gospel written by John, which exposes the deity and eternal nature of the Lord. Only John had the insight to begin Christ's biography with the beginning when He was *"with God"* and *"was God"*; and to discern that He is the Logos, or Word of God made flesh and is dwelling among us (John 1:1, 14). A person must have that insight to say it, and John certainly did. He proved to be very stable, experienced, and reliable.

Christ would naturally choose one who deeply loved Him and was personally close to Him, to reveal the highly significant, consequential, and far-reaching revelation of Himself and the events of His great day of manifestation. Therefore, our Lord's personal selection of His beloved disciple, John had special insight into His divine nature, both by design and from His heart.

A PERSONAL RELATIONSHIP IMPERATIVE TO UNDERSTAND REVELATION

One can learn from this that Jesus only reveals Himself to those who love Him, respect Him, and care about Him personally. God's secrets are with those that fear Him (Psalms 25:14). If one expects to enjoy and *"see wondrous things from Your Law"* we must cultivate a close, personal relationship with the Lord Jesus Christ Himself (Psalms 119:18).

Extra time is spent on the personal aspect of John's relationship to Christ Jesus in order to emphasize John's personal position in the Lord. Only one that is close to another could ever be a reliable witness to the insight of another's character. Only someone close to Christ would be able to wisely interpret his actions. John's own personal witness and attestation will be observed a bit later.

Not only did it take a very personal relationship with Christ to be the one chosen to pen the dictation, but it likely takes a personal relationship to rightly understand the book. Only those who know Him will be able to properly understand the His Revelation. To those who know Him as "the way, the truth, and the life" (John 14: 6) also understand that knowing Him personally, is life eternal (John 14:6, 17:2-3).

IMPORTANT THAT THE AUTHOR KNOWS HIM IN A PERSONAL WAY

Please allow the author to establish his position with the Lord. I am not suggesting nor am I implicating that my relationship can be compared to John's special place with the Lord, but as it will be important to the most serious reader of this work, I want to say that I have come to love the Lord Jesus Christ as near as possible as a fallen human being can, with all my heart, soul, mind, and strength. This is the first and great commandment (Matthew 22:36-38).

For the first two decades of my life, I did not know Jesus. I did not even know of Him or know about Him. For reasons I, nor my friends and family will ever know until we see Him, Jesus called my name three times while I sat alone on a hillside during a spring cattle roundup. It was the first time that I had ever thought about eternity and whether or not there was even a God. For two years the only prayer I knew how to pray was a personal appeal. Each night I prayed, "God, if there is a God, I would like to know you." He so graciously saw fit to answer that prayer coming from a lost sinner boy, and He made Himself known to me.

At that time, I knew Him only out of fear and respect. It was two years later before I learned to love Him with Agape love. I was helping to pioneer a church when I met a young new convert whom I desired to disciple in Christ. One night, a guest speaker made a comment that he believed you could not make it to Heaven without a certain experience, an experience which I knew my new convert did not have. I found him weeping at the altar and was afraid he had been offended or discouraged by the speaker's comment.

I wanted to explain to him my disapproval of what the speaker said when he stopped me and made one of the most profound statements that I have ever heard from any of Christ's disciples. He said: "It doesn't matter to me whether I make Heaven or if the Lord ever blesses me again, nor if I ever amount to anything in Christ's Kingdom, but I would still serve Christ with all of my heart." I was astonished and asked him, "Why would you serve the Lord when you expect no returns?" I will never forget his answer. He looked at me with tears welling up in his eyes and said, "Because I love Him." Convicted and convinced, I knew immediately that I did not have, nor had I ever found that kind of love. I spent the whole night in the chapel weeping and asking the Lord to bless me with love like that. I did not leave the Lord's presence until I knew I could say that I loved Him. Since then, I have loved Him first and foremost. Others may not see or always know, but the Lord does. I speak the truth when I say simply and forthright, I love Him.

That young man's name was Norman Bachman. He later sold his lucrative business and went to the foreign-mission field at his own expense, blessing missionaries by providing his own boat to transport them up and down the rivers. He eventually became a support missionary.

BECAUSE I LOVE HIM

Since that time, with all that is within me and limited only by my fallen and human nature, I have sought to know

Him in a close and personal way, and want to obey all that He has so mercifully asked me to be and do. Since I came to know the Lord, I see His majesty and the wonder of it all about me. I have lost interest in the worldly society around me and only thrill to His presence and His plan. I desire Him more than any of these things, and even more than life itself. Even though I know I cannot force Him on anyone else, I travail in prayer until Christ is formed in my friends and family. John saw Him and gained a great heritage. I have never seen Him, yet I love Him with all of the heart I know how to give, and I know that someday I shall see Him.

Over the years, I have looked for Him in every verse I read in the passages of the Word. Like Balaam, I seem to sense a King in the camp of Israel. I hear his voice in the songs of David, feel His heartbeat in the breasts of the Patriarchs, and I long for His wisdom and feel His presence in the whisper of the Spirit of prophecy. When I study about the tabernacle, I see Jesus in every part. When I see Moses at the burning bush, I see Him standing before Jesus. I read the Song of Solomon and He is the sought-after beloved shepherd, and in Isaiah I find Him the Suffering Savior.

When I am in Jerusalem where I have visited thirty-four times, I weep at the sight of the Temple Mount, the Tomb, and dozens of other sights which speak softly, in mute, hushed tones of Him. I weep as we walk the Via Dolorosa, stand in the prison, or look awestruck at Calvary's Hill. I think you get my point—I only boast in the Lord and wish for the reader to know my heart as we approach the subject of "Christ in the Revelation."

In all of my unworthiness, I know Him, I love Him, I long for Him, and I weep in prayer and praise as I celebrate Him with all of my heart and soul. It is Him I long to see in every line and verse of The Revelation of Jesus Christ. This is the intrigue I have in Christ. He speaks to me from the pages of His Revelation and I long to know Him and see Him in all of His majesty and glory in His *Great Day*.

LET HIM REVEAL HIMSELF TO YOU PERSONALLY

Jesus, our wonderful Lord wants so much to reveal Himself to us today. He wants to step out of the shadows of mystery and obscurity, and meet us in our world and in our daily walk, as if it were face to face. As we look for and seek Him in the pages of Revelation, He will from time to time, peek out from behind the curtain or from around an impression or symbol, and reveal Himself to us in the now as the Lamb of God or an angel.

He may even wink at us understandingly as we ponder His mysteries. And, as we wait for Him to appear, He will move from impressions in our minds to a reality in our hearts.

Paul put it so clearly when he said:

"Now we see in a mirror dimly, but then face to face" (1 Corinthians 13:12).

An old song said it so well:

"Face to face shall I shall behold Him, far beyond the starry sky, Face to face in all His glory, I shall see Him by and by" (Carrie E. Beck, 1898).

How thrilling it is that this whole record of Revelation is centered in Jesus Christ. It contains the record of God's Word and the testimony of Jesus Christ, and the things which Christ personally showed to John. John continues to keep himself in the background as merely the scribe of the message.

LET'S OVER-EMPHASIZE HIM RATHER THAN UNDER-ESTIMATE HIM

As some would like us to do, we will not detail most of

the more intriguing and scary parts of the book, but will tend to keep Christ in our focus as the essence of this entire writing. It is the Revelation of Jesus Christ. We will name Him everywhere that He appears in the book; everywhere He is represented by His angel and responsible for an act or event; and everywhere we sense His spirit and presence.

Some may feel that God's presence is over-emphasized, but I do not want to miss any emphasis that should be on Him, or squander any opportunity to glorify Christ in the entire Revelation. I would rather over-emphasize the Lord, rather than under-estimate the attention He deserves. Just as in the Old Testament, if our spiritual senses are acute and keen to the Messianic overtones of the text, we can sense and feel the essence of the Christ in every facet of the Old Covenant.

Attention will be given to hundreds of Old Testament references which directly relate to *His Day of Revelation*. If the count is correct, there are approximately eight-hundred references to Old Testament passages in the Revelation. These have been traced and given adequate attention; and according to Chuck Missler, there are over two-hundred, eighty-five direct quotes from the Messianic Old Testament texts in Revelation.

Except for brief attestations from John, the entire first chapter of Revelation is a Revelation of Jesus Christ. Jesus sent this message through His angel. It is a clue to understanding that although many angels are evident in and throughout the book, most of them are direct representatives of Jesus Himself. Therefore we can know what they say, do, and accomplish is actually the acts of the Lord Jesus Christ.

REVELATION: THE UNVEILING

Another analogy can be found in the word *unveiling*. Imagine for a moment, a sculptor creating an artful statue.

He works on it daily, but keeps it under wraps from the public so they cannot see it until it is complete. When the day of its completion has come, the artist sets a time for the unveiling ceremony. The crowd gathers and waits expectantly to see the completed sculpture. With much fanfare, it is finally revealed. The veil is removed, and there it stands for all to see, study, and enjoy.

All throughout the Old Testament, Christ was veiled in cryptic and symbolic enigma. The Messiah was always in the shadows, seldom ever in the full light of Revelation. In the New Testament, He rarely spoke of Himself as the Messiah. Jesus said *"The works that I do in my Father's name, they bear witness of Me"* (John 10:25). He seldom even hinted that He was the Messiah or the Son of God, but instead, addressed himself as the *Son of Man* eighty-nine times in the gospels. The point is this: only here in Revelation does Jesus Christ finally come out from behind the curtain—off stage, where most of His activity has been enacted, and allowing Himself full disclosure. He even said that the Kingdom during His ministry on Earth was *without observation* and could not be readily seen (Luke 17:20).

So it is with the Book of Revelation. The *Day of the Lord* has been in process throughout the millennia of time. Each part has been detailed for us. And now we begin to see *"things which must shortly take place,"* starting with the unveiling of Jesus Christ and the Revelation of His glory, power, and majesty as revealed throughout the church age. In every sermon, teaching seminar, or act of worship, and in the building of every cathedral, mission compound, divinity school, or brush arbor in the world throughout the church age, He is revealed. It is also in every book, movie, or TV show designed for His glory. All of these have been part of the detail of His unveiling. All these things have been and are that *"which you have seen, and the things which are, and the things which will take place after that"* (Revelation 1:19).

MUST SHORTLY COME TO PASS (verse 1)

Some have questioned the statement in Revelation 1:1 which simply states *"things which must shortly take place"* as if it meant *"the time is at hand."* I believe this meant that the time to fully reveal Jesus Christ as Lord and Savior began here in the beginning of the age while Revelation was written. Since then, He has been revealed by the evangelism of the Church. God our Father never reveals anything before its time, and the time to reveal Christ as Lord and Savior, King of Kings, and Lord of Lords is now. It began at the start of the Church age which explains why Revelation chapter one begins with the Church age.

Soon we shall "see the King in His [full] beauty" (Isaiah 33:17). Yes, "I [shall] see Him ... I [shall] behold Him" (Numbers 24:17). *Behold* means to look upon with consideration and attentiveness and to see with wonder and awe. When we see Him in His entire splendor and wonder in that day, it will be with awe and amazement.

There is a sense in which the Kingdom of Christ is no longer hidden as it was throughout the Old Testament. Revelation moves it beyond existing only in us, but without earthly observation. Of course, it still exists in the hearts and lives of those who love and serve Him, but by bringing the Old Testament Messianic texts into the context of Revelation, we begin seeing the reality of His earthly millennial reign—His actual Kingdom on Earth. Revelation 11:15, 19:11, and 19:15 mirrors the rather obscure trappings of such Old Testament hints of the Earthly Kingdom of our Lord such as in Zechariah 14:9 and Daniel 2:44, 7:14, 22, and 27. In Revelation, the Abrahamic, Davidic, and Gentile church covenant all come together amalgamating their promises into one great Kingdom of Christ.

READ, HEAR AND KEEP (V. 3)

What are we instructed to do with this Revelation of Jesus Christ? As always, Jesus keeps it simple and direct. We are to read it, hear it taught, and then when we have received it, we are to *keep* it. As a comfort to many of us, our Lord did not say to understand it. If we were instructed to understand, most people would be in trouble. It has personally taken over half a century of study to dare venture any kind of understanding of revelation's message, and even then as we shared in the Preface, we approach its contents with fear, humility, and extreme caution. Even without completely understanding its contents and in spite of whether we study it in any depth, we are to read and hear it taught. Just reading or hearing it has a certain sanctifying effect upon the soul. Allowing its concepts to pass through our minds and sink into our souls, brings us closer to our

Lord and Savior, Jesus Christ and a revelation of Him. Those who refuse to hear it are in error.

KEEP IT IN ORIGINAL FORM

The exhortation to *keep* it has significance. The word in the Greek text is *tereo*. It carries the connotation of a vigil or watching over or caring for. In fact the same word is used nine times throughout Revelation. It is used four times in the exhortation to the Jews and churches where they are complimented for keeping the Word of God and the commandments of God. Its last use in Revelation 22:7 and 19 continues the above connotation. We are cautioned not to change it in any way. It is a dangerous practice to change any part of the Word of God except directly and carefully by a literal translation and interpretation into another language.

Revelation is the only book that carries this direct warning and a curse or a blessing dependent upon how we keep its context in the original form. We are told that this issue will come up in our record before the Judgment, where we will either receive the blessings in the book, or cursed with the plagues found there. It becomes a sacred trust to each one who reads it and gives ear to it. We are to keep it in its original form (Revelation 22:18, 19)

KEEP IT BY PRESERVING, GUARDING, AND WATCHING OVER IT

Along the command of not adding to or taking away from Revelation's text, we are also to guard and preserve it. For centuries during the medieval times, the book was seldom taught or considered, but thank God it was kept for us in these closing days of time. Only at the beginning of the nineteenth century and especially in the beginning of the twentieth century, did men begin seriously to consider it. Like the book of Daniel, it was closed until our modern time. It has been preserved by careful watch over the translations.

Isaac Newton, one of the greatest scientists the world has ever known; a devout believer in the inspiration of the Bible text and very knowledgeable in prophecy, made the following statement:

> "About the time of the end, a body of men will be raised up who will turn their attention to the prophecies and insist on their literal translation and interpretation in the midst of much clamor and opposition."

At the time Newton made this statement, there was virtually no attention given to prophecy as a whole, let alone any serious effort at understanding of teaching of Revelation.

KEEP BY CAREFUL CONSIDERATION

So many people today give very little consideration of

Revelation except to pick out allegorical or metaphorical examples to fit a sermon. Pastors and teachers often determine that it is too controversial and has no practical message for the church today, so they avoid it. That is not what Jesus taught us to do. According to Him, we are to give careful attention to the contents of the book. It deserves far more consideration than an occasional mention.

JOHN'S BRIEF ATTESTATION (V.4)

As is so true to John's nature, he only briefly refers to himself as might be necessary. Even then, he immediately concedes attention by giving deference back to Christ. Jesus states that the writing was to be given to the seven churches of Asia which are enumerated in chapters two and three (Revelation 1:11). These churches represent all of the church age; therefore it is given to the Church as a whole. The message is clearly *"from Jesus Christ, the faithful witness, the firstborn from the dead, and the ruler over the kings of the Earth"* (Revelation 1:5).

Christ gives witness of Himself and His position as overtaker of the princes of the Earth. His authority comes on the wings of the Resurrection from the dead by which he is "declared to be the Son of God with power according to the Spirit of holiness by the resurrection from the dead" (Romans 1:4).

It also comes through the seven spirits which are before the throne. Seven is the number of fullness and completeness and is therefore, the full manifestation of the Holy Spirit. Wherever Jesus is, we can be assured that the Holy Spirit is also manifest in His fullness. This is one of the reasons I do not ascribe to the idea that the Holy Spirit departs from the earth in the Rapture. He cannot be taken away from any place at any time (2 Thessalonians 2:7). The Holy Spirit fills the universe and is present everywhere. If He is not present in

Revelation, then Jesus cannot be there. Those that teach the above do not adequately understand God's Holy Spirit.

OUR POSITION IN HIM (vs. 5, 6)

All that we read of Christ in these texts is true to His character, and gives witness to Him as the beloved Jesus whom we know and serve. Even within this weighty testimony, we are quickly reminded of our personal worth to Him. We are the ones that He personally loves and washed from sin in His own blood sacrifice. He reminds us of that love and sacrifice twenty-seven times throughout the book by calling Himself the Lamb. This brings understanding that He is the same Old Testament Messiah who continues to the end of the age. Even in the glory of His place at the throne of God, He wants us to remember our special place in Him by appearing as *"a Lamb as though it had been slain"* (Revelation 5:6). John the Baptist was the first to reveal Him as the *"Lamb of God that takes away the sin of the world"* (John 1:29). Never before was the sacrificial lamb related to the Man, or Messiah—Jesus Christ, by the Jews.

We are encouraged and excited to think of Christ sharing His position with us in the coming Kingdom as "kings and priests to His God and Father" (Revelation 1:6). But immediately, attention is deferred back to Him. Although shared with us, the glory is never ours, because "to Him be glory and dominion forever and ever. Amen" (Revelation 1:6).

To keep us from getting side-tracked from the motif of the writing and help us center in on the single message of this communication, Revelation reveals to us a great promise:

> *"Behold, He is coming with clouds, and every eye will see Him, and they also who pierced Him; and all the tribes of the earth will mourn because of Him"* (Revelation 1:7, Zechariah 13:6).

THE SACRED *I AM* (V.8)

Verse eight begins the actual *Revelation of Jesus Christ*. Twice at this point, Jesus refers to Himself as *I AM* and is used a total of seven times in Revelation—four times in chapter one, verses 8, 11, 17, and 18, and also in verses 21:6, 22:13, and 22:16. Three more times in this chapter alone, Jesus refers to Himself as the Great *"I AM"* (Revelation 1:11, 17, 18).

No other term in all of scripture so exalts our Lord, than this revealing and yet mysterious designation of His name. Everywhere in both the Old and New Testaments, He is distinguished from all other deities, angels, and heavenly beings by this pure and simple term, *I AM*. From the time this name was given of Him to Moses at the burning bush in Exodus 3:14, it has permeated us with His essence.

The term simply means: I exist, I have always existed, and I will always exist of and by myself; I just am. One hundred, forty-seven times in the Old Testament and one hundred, sixty-two times in all of Scripture, we encounter this wonderful name. Seven times in the gospels, Jesus Himself uses the term as it relates to His ministry to us. The book of Isaiah refers to the name thirty-five times. There are twenty-one *I AM's* in Jeremiah, and eighty-five times Ezekiel says *"they shall know that I am the Lord"* (Ezekiel 12:15). Psalms records the name *I AM* seven times. A strange analogy is made of Jesus' death in Psalm twenty-two. The "I AM" is compared to a mother worm that dies, but in its death, secretes a scarlet fluid which protects the life of the young (Psalm 22:6). Also in Psalms 40:17, 69:8, 20, 29, 102:7 and 11, Jesus uses this name to identify Himself with the poor and common people. All of these references in Psalms relate to His suffering and rejection. In contrast each of the seven times it is used in Revelation, is a tribute to His victorious glory and exaltation.

We who are earthly beings of time, can never comprehend

the thought of a past eternity, present eternity, and a future eternity. We may be able to grasp in limited realization that God could live forever. However, I must place Christ the son, in the same mode. He not only lived in the present eternity, but He lived in the past eternity, and will live in the future eternity. John, the writer of this Revelation, only by insight given by the Holy Spirit, could begin his gospel with:

> *"In the beginning was the Word and the Word was with God, and the Word was God"* (John 1:1).

He was born into this dimension and He died. But, He quickly overcame death and can now say, *"I am alive forevermore"* (Revelation 1:18). And *"if we believe that Jesus died and rose again ... [then] we shall always be with the Lord"* (1 Thessalonians 4:14, 17).

THE BEGINNING AND THE END (V. 8)

It is true that Jesus seldom ascribed Himself as Deity. Only twice can I find Him even hinting that He was the Son of God. The term, *Son of God* was used by others, but not by Him. Most often He referred to Himself as the *Son of Man;* twenty-seven times in Matthew, fourteen times in Mark, twenty-four times in Luke, and nine times in John. This makes a total of seventy-four times that Jesus refers to Himself as the *Son of Man.* The text hints in fifteen other places at His self-designation as the *Son of Man,* making a total of eighty-nine times. Every reference where Jesus spoke of His Second Coming and His Revelation, He called Himself the *Son of Man.* In his vision of Christ in His glory, John proclaims that He appeared as *"one like the Son of Man"* and four more times in Revelation He is so called (Revelation 1: 13). Obviously, He desires to identify with us on His human side, especially in the day of His coming.

By the term Alpha and Omega, the Beginning and

the End, Jesus ascribes deity to Himself. This term is well recognized as a Messianic quality from antiquity. It is the first and the last of the Greek alphabet, comparable to the first and last Hebrew letters; a term used in various form in the Hebrew culture to designate the timelessness of the Almighty. Jesus also uses it in verse eight. The prophet Isaiah 44:6 uses this idiom to designate the eternal Almighty God:

"I am the First and I am the Last; besides Me there is no God" (Isaiah 44:6).

With the use of *Almighty*, which has the same connotation in the original language, the Alpha and Omega is used seven times in the Book of Revelation. It is significant to note in this passage that there a coming *face-to-face* with the Eternal—the one who was, and is, and is to come, the Almighty (Revelation 1:8). Death did not end His life and death will not end our lives. He gave us eternal life.

This term is part of the enigma of the Book of Revelation of Jesus Christ, as well as the whole prophetic tapestry of Bible prophecy. When one studies related texts, a puzzle is found. It appears in the texts that the end actually comes before the beginning. At least we know that the end had already been settled at the beginning. A cryptic shadow seems to follow all events as they develop in the plan of God, because each part fits into a tapestry of design that had already been determined at the very beginning. Christ was crucified before the foundations of the world, and the *Book of Life* was written at the same time. Those that come to Him have already been predestined to be conformed to His Son. It would be like the man who throws a ball and is already down at the other end to catch it. What an awesome thought that someone could throw a ball and be there to catch it, yet that is exactly what kind of God we serve. The end was already determined before the beginning.

Again, the prophet Isaiah enlightens us with an eternal perspective by asking:

> *"Who has declared from the beginning that we may know? And former times that we may say, 'He is righteous'"* (Isaiah 41:26)? Later, God asks, *"Who has declared this from ancient time? Have not I, the Lord"* (Isaiah 45:21)? *God admonishes us to "ask [Him] of things to come concerning [His] sons; and concerning the work of [His] hands, you command [Him]"* (Isaiah 45:11).

Following, Isaiah declares:

> *"I am God, and there is no other ... declaring the end from the beginning, and from ancient times things that are not yet done, saying My counsel shall stand, and I will do all My pleasure"* (Isaiah 46:9-10).

Isaiah 48:3-7: The Living Bible makes this text easily understood:

> *"Time and again I told you what was going to happen in the future. My words were scarcely spoken when suddenly I did just what I said. I knew how hard and obstinate you are....that is why I told you ahead of time what I was going to do ... You have heard my predictions and seen them fulfilled, now I will tell you new things I haven't mentioned before, secrets you haven't heard. Then you can't say, 'We knew that all the time!'"*

Romans 10:4 says, *"Christ is the end ..."* And thus we find Him in Revelation.

These texts make it possible for us to see that the end was before the beginning. Again, it is like throwing a ball and already being down at the end to catch it. Christ, the *Word of God* set things in motion toward the end, and then is down at the end to complete it. That is what we read in The Revelation of Jesus Christ.

In Revelation 1:9 John calls himself our "companion in Tribulation, and in the kingdom and patience of Jesus Christ." Again we see him humbly proclaiming that he is nobody in the presence of Jesus Christ. A dear friend of mine, the late Reed Gipson is one of the humblest companions in tribulation I have ever had the privilege of knowing. He penned a little saying which I use quite often to introduce myself. As eloquently as he can possibly be, he declares that "I'm a nobody, trying to tell everybody, that there is a somebody, who can save anybody."

In the presence of the great I AM, the Alpha and Omega, the Beginning and the End, and the Almighty, what more could John or anyone else say except "I'm a nobody." Even his banishment from Patmos for the Word of God merited just a mention, and then only as it was associated with the testimony of Jesus Christ.

THE LORD'S DAY (v. 10)

A tribute to Jesus Christ is suggested by John's mention of the Lord's Day. We should not believe that worship on the first day of the week began with the Catholic Church. Long before the Papacy, Christians were meeting on the Lord's Day—the first day of the week. After His resurrection, Jesus met with His disciples on Sunday morning and evening, and appeared to the disciples on the way to Emmaus and had fellowship on Sunday evening. Acts 20:7 mentions the church at Troas meeting on the *"first day of the week."* Paul admonished the Corinthian believers to bring their tithe and offerings *"on the first day of the week"* (I Corinthians 16:2). This pattern was well established in the early church. The term appears eight times in the Bible, the first six are in the Gospels. All of them refer to the Resurrection having occurred on the first day of the week, or the day after the Jewish Sabbath. In the old texts, it was well known that the eighth day represented the day of creation and renewal, and now it spoke of a new beginning. Twenty-five years after the resurrection, the Jewish believers were still taking the Sabbath, or seventh day, as a day of rest, and the eighth day as the day to celebrate the Lord by *breaking bread* with believers. It is plain to see that a new day has been ordained in honor of our Lord.

A VOICE AS A TRUMPET (v. 10)

All great events and important announcements in Israel, especially the calls to gather, were made with the Shofar, or Rams Horn. One long blast was to get attention and call to a gathering. Jesus also meant to get our attention and I think we ought to pay attention! The next verse directs John to get this message to the churches.

JESUS IN THE MIDST OF THE CHURCHES (v.12)

In Revelation twelve, John turns to see who was speaking and significantly, he saw the Lord Jesus Christ in His chosen place where He desires most to be—in the midst of the churches. If you look for Him today, you will always find Him in the midst of a Christ-honoring, Christ-glorifying church where He dwells in the midst of the praises of His people.

I still worship with wonder having some of my old country-kid love of the great outdoors. Much of my worship happens in the wonder of His creation. However, I had to discover that He does not yet redeem rocks and streams and trees and mountains. I can find the great Creator in these places, but not the Redeemer. Instead, I have to come among the redeemed if I am to celebrate the Redeemer, for His redemptive work is among people. His creative genius is always out there, but as redeemer you will always find Him among His precious called-out ones who are chosen and faithful, whether they are on Earth or in Heaven (Revelation 17:14). Throughout Revelation, you will find Christ among the Churches (Revelation 5:8, 7:9, 17, 17:14, chapters 19, 20, 21). That is where John always saw Him and that is where we will always find Him if we are looking for Him. He *"loved the church and gave Himself for it ... that He might present it to Himself a glorious church, not having spot or wrinkle, or any such thing, but that it should be holy and without blemish"* (Ephesians 5:25,27; Revelation 19:7).

It is of significance that the churches, chosen by the Lord, were purely Gentile churches consisting of Gentile congregations, but with Jewish converts. It is remarkable that the Jewish churches in Jerusalem or churches in Judaea or Samaria were not among those chosen to receive the message from Patmos. I believe, at least partially, it is because Jesus needed to emphasize the fact that now, during the Church Age which will be represented by the next two Chapters, He will be working among the Gentiles with all Jewish converts included. Of course, every born-again and Christ-honoring Jew is included in the Gentile church.

JOHN FOUND CHRIST AS THE LIGHT AMONG THE CHURCHES

John found Christ among the candlesticks, or *menorah*— an Old Testament symbol that naturally illustrates the light of the churches, for Jesus *is* the very essence of light. Everywhere He is manifest, He is the Light. From the very beginning, John saw the Lord's life as the Light of Men (John 1:4). He is the True Light (ibid v.9). Even then, John was sent to bear witness of the light so that all men might believe; the light that lights every man who comes into the world. (ibid v. 9) In the next two chapters, the voice of the Lord Jesus Christ is coming from the midst of the Menorah, the light of the Old Testament Tabernacle. It shows that His light is the light of the Church, and the voice of the Church should be the voice of Christ.

Christ dwells in a light that we cannot even approach in our natural state (1 Timothy 6:16). Jesus is so bright and brilliant that when He faces the beast or Antichrist at Armageddon, He *"will consume [them] with the breath of His mouth, and destroy with the brightness of His coming"* (2 Thessalonians 2:8). The sword of His mouth is the Word of God according to Ephesians 6:17. This is a very important tie to the Old Testament analogy. The menorah, located across from the showbread in the first sanctuary of the Tabernacle, was a symbol of the light of our testimony, both to the Church itself and to the world around us. If we are not carrying the light of Christ in the church and in the world, we have likely slipped off into the lukewarm Laodicean church (Revelation 3:14-22).

CHRIST'S ILLUMINOUS APPEARANCE IN HIS GLORIFIED FORM

It is this glorious and brilliant light, the very essence of His presence that John begins to behold as He sees Christ in the candlesticks. The description given by Paul in his first letter to Timothy speaks of the light we will see Him in at His coming:

> *"...until our Lord Jesus Christ's appearing, which He will manifest in His own time, He who is blessed and only Potentate, the King of kings, and Lord of lords, who alone has immortality, dwelling in unapproachable light, whom no man has seen or can see, to whom be honor and everlasting power. Amen"* (1 Timothy 6:14-16).

LIKE THE "SON OF MAN" (v. 13)

Out of respect to Jesus Christ, John always identifies Christ with the term, *Son of Man*. It is a very cryptic and symbolic term out of the Old Testament, and out of an even older antiquity. Here again in humility, as in the days of earthly sojourn, Jesus chooses to be identified as a man.

The term, Son of Man was and is a rather vague and cryptic expression used one-hundred, eleven times in the Old Testament and over ninety times in the New Testament. It was cultivated of the Holy Spirit in the hearts for the purpose of inclination for a deeper worship relationship and insight toward God and His expected Messiah and Son. It related to His Jewish name—Son of Man over and against His divine name—Son of God.

The prophet Daniel gives insight into the cryptic meaning of the term, Son of Man. In a vision, Daniel sees *"One like the Son of Man, Coming with the clouds of heaven! He came to the Ancient of days…"* (Daniel 7:13). This reveals a direct association with the coming of the one called the *Son of Man* into the presence of the *Ancient of Days* to receive a restored dominion over the earth. The first Adam was given dominion over the earth but lost it due to *the Fall* (Genesis 1:26). One of his sons, a son of Abraham, and a son of David after him was to come and restore that dominion over earth. The known *Christmas text* in Micah, chapters four and five follow this connection through to explaining that the One who receives the highest dominion over Earth would be born in Bethlehem.

The term exegetically seems to come to fruition in the Second Adam—Jesus Christ (1 Corinthians 15:45-49). The term originates with Adam—the first man, but finds its fulfillment in Jesus—the last man who is born of the natural as a Son of Man (ibid v. 45). He is the quickening one who will lead us into the reclamation, restoration, and restitution of the heritage that the first Adam lost (Genesis 1:26).

This term also seems to have an enigmatic connection to Genesis 3:15 where the son of a woman would ultimately defeat the serpent and take back the heritage. Therefore, the term relates to a man who would receive dominion over the earth. If the scribes and priests had been aware and well-studied in the deeper mysteries of the Messianic prophecies and promises, they would have quickly caught the subtle suggestion when Jesus continued to call Himself the *Son of Man* over eighty-nine times. If the Church is well-studied in the Messianic texts, it will be quickly discerned why He continues to call Himself the Son of Man in the record of His coming Revelation; the whole book is centered in His return to take possession of Earth.

Ezekiel alone uses the term Son of Man over one-hundred times. He was so enhanced by the Spirit of God, and in tune with the prophecies of the last days and coming of Christ that he easily associated with the strange, prophetic term of Son of Man. As a careful study is made of the term, it becomes clear there is an enigma attached to it that only the knowledgeable understood. This mystery is unveiled as one follows it through the Old Testament as far back as Adam, Seth, and Enoch (Genesis 3:15). With a definitive article attached, it signifies not the son of the first Adam, but the second Adam who overcame the sin of the first Adam, and now goes on to assume the title of the second Adam who takes dominion over the earth after the first Adam lost it to Satan's rule (Genesis 1:26, Psalm 8:4-8).

It now becomes obvious why Jesus uses this term throughout His earthly life and in the Revelation. His victory over Satan and redemption of the earth, promised back to the sons of Adam, is definitively known as the Son of Man in prophetic enigma. Because of the well-known promise of a redeemer who would take full dominion of the earth, every king and ruler imagined himself to be that chosen Son of Man who would rule—including Nebuchadnezzar of Babylon, Alexander the Great of the Greeks, and many others. Godefroy de Bouillon and his brother, Baudouin set themselves up as King of Jerusalem after the first Crusade, both imagining the same thing. Eve believed her son Seth, whose name means *man, or son of the promise,* might be that chosen one. Every woman after Eve hoped her womb would bring the Son of Man to birth. In all of this background information, the significance in finding the cryptic key to Jesus' name, Son of Man is discovered.

John is impressed that Jesus appears like the Son of Man, choosing to identify with His human nature to better relate to mankind. It was also necessary by the laws of sacrifice, that He be not only God, but also a Redeemer man-God, or a kinsman Redeemer. He wants us to know that even in His glorified state, He still honors His possession as one of us.

THE LORD INDESCRIBABLE BY HUMAN LANGUAGE (v. 14-16)

As we set out in the writing of this book, we must understand that there is no human language on earth which is adequate enough to describe the glorified Christ in all of His beauty. We can only express his glorified state as best we can, realizing our limited mode of expression.

THE THEOPHANY OF JESUS

Here we enter into a great study: the theophany of Jesus—one of His many appearances in various forms. John struggled to describe what he saw, finding that words in our earthly language cannot begin to express the full brilliance of His glorified person. All of these terms are symbolic. We will not imagine in earthly terms what John saw, but through the insight of the Spirit, catch the impressions intended.

Note that these descriptions are comparable to several other references to the glorified Lord in Revelation. Brief accounts of His beauty can be found in Revelation 10:1 and 14:14. His transfiguration had an illusion to His glorified form (Matthew 17:2). We will refer to just a few Old Testament texts which can be compared to this theophany of Jesus.

Ezekiel and Nebuchadnezzar saw Him in dreams (Ezekiel 1:28, Daniel 2:31). Daniel saw Him in the presence of *"the Ancient of Days,"* describing Him similar to what John saw—the same garment and same golden girdle (Daniel 7:13, 10:5-6). His face glowed brightly and His eyes were a flame of fire, just like John's description and impression of Him. His feet were as brass while it is burning in the furnace, and His voice was the voice of a multitude like the sound of many waters. The white hair does not speak of age, for there is no age with God. It represents to us wisdom, honor, and dignity in our language. Daniel 10:16 describes Him in terms that match both Revelation and Ezekiel's vision of Him: *"... and His countenance was like the sun shining in its strength"* (Revelation 1:16). This term is always used in relationship to His Day of Judgment upon the world. Every description matches what John saw of Him in Revelation 1:12-16, and represents the theophany of Jesus the Christ in both the Old and New Testaments.

JOHN FELL AS ONE DEAD (v. 17)

Like John in Revelation 1:17 who fell on his face as dead, Daniel also was overwhelmed at the great vision and presence of the glorified Lord; his face was distorted, strength left Him, and he lay on his face as dead. The men that were with him did not see the vision, but a great fear and quaking fell upon them and they fled the scene. Paul had a very similar experience when Christ appeared to him on the road to

Damascus (Acts 9).

Ezekiel was loved of God the same as Daniel. While in the far away land of the Medes on the anniversary of the day of the destruction of his beloved Jerusalem fourteen years before, Ezekiel said, "The hand of the Lord was upon me" (Ezekiel 40:1). He was brought to the land of Israel, and in vision, he saw, *"a man whose appearance was like the appearance of bronze"* (Ezekiel 40:3). This is the same Theophany as John saw in Revelation 1:15. By this same glorified Lord, Ezekiel had a hand laid on his shoulder and was shown the New Jerusalem of Revelation.

Daniel had a glorious experience in the presence of the glorified Lord when he said, "Suddenly, a hand touched me" (Daniel 10:10). Imagine the day when all believers come into His presence, and in turn, God reaches out and lays His hand on our shoulders! He said to Daniel what every faithful and loving follower desires to hear, "O Daniel, a man greatly beloved, understand the words that I speak unto you" (Daniel 10:11). What a day, when after all the toils of a life lived for Him, we come into His presence and He reaches out and lays the mantel on our shoulder and says "Well done, good and faithful servant ... enter into the joy of your Lord" (Matthew 25:23). All of these things again show the close tie between the Jehovah God of the Old Testament and Jesus the Christ of the New Testament.

AFFIRMATION A SECOND TIME (v. 18-19)

Christ is showing John and sending to His Church such far reaching revelations, that He chooses again to assure John and the Church that they are true and faithful, and can be relied upon because they come from the Man who was raised from the dead by His own power. He declares that He is the I Am, the first and the last; He who lived, died, and yet is alive evermore, and who has the key to hell and death. He wants us to know from Heaven's perspective, the things that have already been, the things that are in the church age, and the things to come after the church age.

THE STARS IN HIS RIGHT HAND (v. 20)

The Lord's great love for His Church kept the *stars* of the churches close to Him in His right hand (Revelation 1:16) The *stars* of the Church are the angels, or messengers/pastors. However, I do not believe this refers so much to those pastors who have drifted into the Laodicean mode of only a professional ministry where their interest is in building an earthly denomination, not God's Kingdom; those with desires toward earthly rewards and/or in seeking the glory and approval of man more than the approval and love of the Lord. They are nothing but hirelings, in it for themselves. Only the Lord can distinguish between the true shepherd and the hireling.

Therefore, these stars refer to the true shepherds of God's flock, whose hearts are set on bringing the people into a relationship with Christ and the glory of Christ to the people, disciplining the true believers and followers of our Lord Jesus Christ. This is a comforting thought that the humble, Christ-loving, people-serving stars are held securely in His right hand. This is reassuring. All of this mystery is revealed in the last verse twenty of chapter one. What a thought—our pastors are angels. Don't argue with me; I may be right! Besides, Revelation says it, so it must be true!

We will continue our expose' of Jesus Christ as we briefly follow Him among the Churches in chapters two and three. The next chapter of our writing will be called *Daniel and the Church Age*. The Church age as represented in chapters two and three has its introduction in Daniel. It is the untimed break between the sixty-ninth and seventieth week of Daniel's *seventy weeks of seven years* (490 years) of prophecy (Daniel 9).

CHAPTERS 2, 3

DANIEL AND THE CHURCH AGE

THE CHURCH AGE

People generate great excitement in anticipation of attending a play. One can also experience high exhilaration and enthusiasm when approaching the time to read a will from a rich relative. Both of these are comparable to a reading and a walk through the Book of Revelation; for as we enjoy the extravaganza of divine reconciliation of all things in the Book of Revelation, we will be led through scene after scene of the complete final stages of the defeat of Satan, the world, and the flesh. We will also see a return of the promised inheritance to the Church and to the Jews, as well as the righteous *sheep* nations. God has a covenant with each of the above, as we will see.

The final fulfillment of the three great and distinct Covenants which God made with man will be shown. He promised to return the Jews to their land after a long Diaspora, or scattering; to rapture the Church before the Tribulation period; and to redeem the nations from the power of Satan. This causes great excitement as we anticipate the opening of the pageant of divine justice which reveals the final fulfillment of these three covenants. As we proceed, the Revelation as it was written for the dictates given to John by our Lord Jesus Christ, will take on the form of a Greek style tragedy performance with all of the plot, pathos, theatrics, and curtain-up curtain-down, well known drama productions in the Hellenized Middle East of the day.

THE WATCHERS

In *Prophecy in the News*, the late J. R. Church, Henry Morris, and Gary Stearman, often spoke of the *watchers*. They put these *angel beings* in the context of watching the human drama on earth as if on stage acting out the saga of human affairs. They suggest that 1 Corinthians 4:9, using the term *spectacle*, is actually speaking of the theater used in the same way as Acts 19:29 and 3. This shows the Church on a make-shift stage, acting out our drama in the world with the angels watching us as if we were performing on stage. The same thought is suggested in Hebrews 12:1 where a spectacle on stage is watched by a *"great cloud of witnesses"* observing our actions and cheering us on to the finish. These thoughts indicate that thinking of Revelation as a theatrics production is not foreign to other contexts of Scripture. Thus, putting thoughts about Revelation in theater-production style is fitting and lines up with the Word according to 1 Corinthians 15:24-26. However, it may take some imagination to see it in this form. We will see Christ in His great day of glory and conquest while presenting the drama of the final years of this age as spelled out in 1 Corinthians 15:24-26.

First, let's take a short walk through the Book of Daniel before we enter the Hall of Justice. This will help us to see how we connect the Book of Daniel to Revelation, especially Chapters 2 and 3 as well as all the Chapters to follow.

DANIEL - AN OLD TESTAMENT INTRODUCTION TO REVELATION

Our first introduction to any theater is typically the vestibule. As one enters the imaginary entrance of the great hall of God's courtroom, there is a fascination with the emblems on the walls and the displays throughout the entrance hall to the court. The exhibits, shown for our consideration before we consider the Book of Revelation and enter into the courtroom of justice, are immediately recognized. We have become acquainted with the symbols from our study of the Book of Daniel.

For instance, the great image of Nebuchadnezzar's dream as we know it, represents the first of those powerful empires in the Middle East whose rule over Jerusalem and the Holy Land for twenty-five hundred years began what Jesus called *"the times of the Gentiles"* (Luke 21:24).

As this study progresses, the *times of the Gentiles* and final days of these Empires will be the primary subject of Revelation. These four mentioned empires are symbolized in the heads and horns of the beast.

Also from Daniel, we recognize the great beast known as the Little Horn which made war with the saints in Daniel chapters seven and eight, and symbols of the ten kings as mentioned in Revelation seventeen. They are the same ten kings first found in the ten toes of the great image of Daniel two and the ten horns of the fourth beast in Daniel seven and eight that now in Revelation, appears on the head of the beast in chapters thirteen and seventeen. There are various other scenes which relate to the Book of Daniel and are clearly representative of the symbols of Revelation.

There is a strong connection between these prophecies and many others from the Old Testament, and those found in Revelation. It is necessary to contemplate these scenes before we enter into the throne room of God and watch the pageant of God's justice unrolling of the scroll of our inheritance. While moving through the various chapters of Daniel, we will thoroughly answer the question: "Why should we imagine Daniel to be the introduction to Revelation?" Most of the thoughts and symbols in Daniel give preparatory information to understanding Revelation.

It is necessary to understand Daniel's disclosures as an introduction and prelude to Revelation. Before we begin to understand the Revelation of Jesus Christ, we are told to consider Daniel; for nearly all of the images, symbols, and impressions in the Book of Revelation are foreshadowed there. The Book of the Revelation of Jesus Christ is the completion and final end of the times of the Gentiles that was first introduced to us as the major theme of Daniel's writings. It is his exposure of the Gentile nations, their occupation of the land of Israel, and their control over the Jewish people from the time of Babylon's invasion of Jerusalem in 586 BC and their eventual try at another world order that we see defeated in the Revelation. Jesus called their occupation the *"times of the Gentiles"* (Luke 21:24) saying *"Jerusalem will be trampled by Gentiles until the times of the Gentiles are fulfilled"* (Luke 21:24). This was the situation from Babylon's invasion in 586 BC until now because Jerusalem is still very much in control of Gentile forces.

END OF THE TIMES OF THE GENTILES

Jesus gave us exact details concerning the signs and events that would surround the end of the times for the Gentiles (Luke 21:20-26). It is very interesting to see that what Jesus said in His Olivet discourse is so relative to Revelation. All of these signs and events in Daniel are exposed in the Book of the Revelation of Jesus Christ.

Revelation brings a conclusion to the times of the Gentiles which began when Jerusalem was given over to the Gentile world powers with Babylon's siege in 586 BC. Control was given to Satan, who also became the god of this world and the prince of the power of the air. In Daniel, Satan remains esoteric, but we finally see Him plainly exposed in

Revelation as the old dragon who gives power to the beast (Revelation 13).

For reasons not made clear, Satan was allowed a time-slot by God to rule the earth through the Gentile world powers in order to fulfill his transgression against God and make good on His boast recorded in Isaiah fourteen & Ezekiel twenty-eight. It was his desire to take over the throne of God and be like the God, the Most High. God has allowed Him to make good on his bragging, but will bring his time to a close in Revelation (Isaiah 14:12-14). It was Satan's desire to justify his criticism toward God in order to take over the throne of God. Calling upon the law of justice of Heaven, Satan demands of God before the holy angels of Heaven, to prove His right to give the earth to Christ and His bride as the terra ferma upon which to set the throne of His Son. Satan's appeal was somewhat successful, for He took one-third of the angels with Him.

Satan's control will be taken away from him and his angels at Christ's Revelation. According to Daniel 2:34 and 35, His control would end when the Rock cut out of the mountain without hands, who is Christ, attacks the whole structure of the Gentile nations in the final end (or feet of the image) bringing it crashing to the ground (Daniel 2). The crumbling of the great nations as seen in Daniel is the essence of Armageddon and the theme of Revelation. (Revelation 16-19). At that time, as shown in both the books of Daniel and Revelation, Christ sets up His Kingdom at the day of His coming (Daniel 2, 7, 8, 11; Revelation 11:15, 19, 20). He redeems the earth, including the Holy Land, Jerusalem, and the Temple, and returns all of Earth to its rightful owners—Christ, the elect nation of Israel, and His Church. Daniel's interpretation of the great image of the dream of Nebuchadnezzar, and his visions of the Gentile world power, the beast, and little horn of chapters 8-9, 11, and 12 are all essentially the essence of the whole book Christ's Revelation.

This is why we say that the Book of Revelation shows the end of the times of the Gentiles. God through Christ will finish the cosmic war with Satan as Satan tries to usurp the throne of God and lay claim to the earth and its Gentile power through final efforts of the Antichrist. Revelation is the exposure of the *Great Day of God Almighty*, the *Day of the Lord*, and *That Day*, that is often spoken of throughout the Old Testament. It is the time in which God, through Christ, will redeem the whole creation back to Himself and His Son, and give the earth to Christ and His bride, for which it was originally intended. That conquest will come at the Revelation of Jesus Christ. There are over eight-hundred references to, and two-hundred, eighty-five direct quotes from the Old Testament in Revelation, many of them from Daniel. A careful study of these will add great dimension to the understanding of the Revelation of Jesus Christ.

As we continue our walk through Daniel we view the great empires that have paraded themselves throughout the history of the Middle East, it becomes plain how each one sought to destroy the Jews in their time and thwart God's plan under the bidding of Satan (Daniel 2:28-33). The great beasts of Daniel seven and eight have for centuries, been striving with each other upon or in the area of the Great Sea—the Mediterranean. Frustrated in their failure to establish total rule, they gradually morph into a mutant form as the one great beast of Revelation thirteen. Note in Revelation 13:1-2 how each of the four beasts of Daniel chapter seven are mutations, morphed into one beast and becoming part of the character of the beast of Revelation and the last great Gentile power. This beast is the *little horn* and his ten Kings out of the fourth beast—Rome, which will come to the head of a world empire, or new world order (Daniel 7:20-22, 8:9-12). Finally, as we see the *Rock* slam into the feet of the great Gentile

New World Order, bringing it to total destruction, and accomplished by Christ at Armageddon (Daniel :34). Then we see the establishment of His Eternal Kingdom and the Saints inheriting the Kingdom (Daniel 2:44, 7:21, 22, 26, 27).

THE 70TH WEEK STOP-GAP AND THE PURPOSE OF THE GREAT TRIBULATION

One other insight from the Book of Daniel comes in the seventieth and final seven-year week of Daniel chapter nine. It is the prototype of the last seven years of this age—the motif of the Book of Revelation and its Tribulation period. From this chapter, we can best understand the last time of trouble to be seven years in duration (Daniel 12:1).

THE 70TH WEEK OF DANIEL

The Book of Revelation is the final seven years of the 70x7, or 490 years of the vision that Daniel received from the angel Gabriel (Daniel 9). One is totally lost in the Revelation without understanding this fantastic revelation of the history of the Jewish nation from the time of Daniel and Babylon, to the final seven years of Tribulation.

When Daniel sees the great destruction of world Kingdoms, he becomes deeply concerned about his nation Israel and his people, the Jews. After Daniel's earnest inquiry, Gabriel is sent to show him how Israel and the Jews would fare during these times of the Gentiles which would have control to the end over the Holy Land, the Jews, and world affairs. The angel, Gabriel's explanation of the future of Israel is found in Daniel chapter nine, eleven, and twelve. Chapter ten gives insight into the cosmic wars and the great esoterical "principalities and powers" (Ephesians 6:12) under Satan, who are given control over this world and who causes all of this grief (Ephesians 6:12). These esoteric and cryptic powers are carefully and subtly hidden in the Old Testament, yet plainly revealed in the Book of Revelation of Jesus Christ.

Daniel sees in his vision, seventy weeks of years, or four-hundred, ninety years of history coming to the Jews until the time of the end. He is shown four-hundred, eighty-three years of their history up to the crucifixion of Christ. It is fascinating to see how perfectly these years are fulfilled. Daniel then sees a suspended time, or a *stop-gap* in God's time clock for the Jewish nation when it will be dispersed (diaspora) into the whole world and their city, Jerusalem sacked (Luke 21:24). Desolation and wars were also prophesied upon Israel and the world for an undetermined amount of time. We have seen this since the Jewish disbursement in AD 70.

At the end of the sixty-nine weeks, Daniel saw an undetermined amount of time down to the final seven years at the end of this age. The last seven years are about the redemption of the Jews and Israel as Christ breaks the Gentile's reign over them. That is the essence of the entire book of Revelation. It is that last seven years called the Great Tribulation. While the believer tends to despair at the thought of those seven years of trouble, the book of Daniel gives hope and comfort to understand the Great Tribulation just as God planned it to be. It is *not* the end of the world, nor the total annihilation of the nations; or is it the demise of the Jews as the Arab world sees it, but the birth pangs of a whole New Age of one-thousand years of peace, health and hegemony ending with a new Heaven and new Earth. It is not only Israel's final redemption, but also the redemption of the nations of the world. Hope and comfort is found when we see that the tribulation is meant to accomplish these six wonderful things (Daniel 9:24).

SIX POSITIVE REASONS FOR THE TRIBULATION

Without comparing Revelation to Daniel's 70-week

vision, we would not be able to plainly see Christ's plan and the positive purpose for the Tribulation period. Daniel says that this great time of trouble is meant to accomplish six very positive and exciting things. All of these apply to the Jews:

1. To finish the transgression

2. To make an end of sin

3. To make reconciliation for iniquity

4. To bring in everlasting righteousness

5. To seal up the vision and prophecy

6. To anoint the Most Holy

Note that these accomplishments of the Great Tribulation are for both the Church and Israel's benefit. It is also the hope of the nation that survives the Battle of Armageddon. They represent our total and complete redemption, restoration, and restitution of all things. Daniel said this time of trouble in the redemption of mankind would be three and one-half years, *"time, times, and half a time"*, or one thousand, two hundred and ninety days; those who waited until the *"one-thousand three hundred and thirty-five days"* would be greatly blessed (Daniel 12:7, 11-12). This is when we will see the fulfillment of the above six accomplishments of Tribulation in the Book of Revelation and the setting up of the earthly Kingdom of Christ as foreseen by Daniel is revealed.

Therefore the Tribulation is designed to finish Satan's transgression, and to end the times of the Gentiles, ushering in a new world without rebellion against Christ, the Jews, and the Church. When we can lift our eyes heavenward and look above the tragedy of Earth under the devastation that Hell and God's wrath has left upon it, we may shout with joy at the accomplishments of the Tribulation, just as Heaven rejoices at the final destruction of Satan's Babylon. After it is all over, we may say with the redeemed:

> *"Alleluia! Salvation and glory and honor and power to the Lord our God! For true and righteous are His judgments ..."* (Revelation 19:1-2).

Although it is difficulty seeing this from an earthly perspective, we shall see that God's justice is right and His judgments are true and righteous. He is right to bring on the Tribulation.

To this end we shall point each step we take, as we are led through the proceedings of His court of justice in The Revelation of Jesus Christ. There is another tie which plainly illustrates how the Book of Daniel is the opening to the Book of Revelation.

THE 70 WEEKS STOP-GAP AND THE CHURCH AGE

The Revelation of Jesus Christ opens with the Church and church age because one of the obscure enigmas, yet realized purpose of the *stop gap* in the seventy weeks of Daniel, is that during this stop-gap of undetermined time while the Gentiles are in control of Jerusalem and the Holy Land, the Gentile Church was to be born and matured. In order to see this fact, keys must be found to another cryptic mystery in Scripture. Paul spoke of the Church as a mystery so we must look for it among the cryptic symbols of Scripture. In Ephesians 3:3, 4, and 9, he mentions that the mystery of the Church had been hidden from the beginning of the world. And in Ephesians 5:32, he calls it a *"great mystery."*

Remember, the stop-gap started with the death of the Messiah. The rest of verse twenty-six and twenty-seven shows the stop-gap and skips a period of time between the cutting of the Messiah and the end and beginning of the Tribulation by the confirming of a covenant. Fifty days later, the Church was born and Christ's full ministry and personality has been revealed through its preaching and teaching. Therefore, the Church is the introduction to Revelation and the *bridge leading* to the Great Tribulation. It becomes the bridge that ties Daniel and Revelation together. The book of Daniel is the *stop-gap* in the seventy-week prophecy that makes the direct connection.

After the Messiah was crucified, the undetermined amount of time represents the Church Age which began with Christ's Resurrection and ends just prior to the beginning of the last seven years. Hence the Lord began His Revelation with the Church age, starting His manifestation in the Church. The Church's position just before the beginning of the last seven years of the Tribulation places it in exact keeping with the stop-gap in Daniel's seventy weeks. When the Church is gone from the earth, Christ's final redeeming work ushers in the seven-year Tribulation (Revelation 4:1). In essence, this is the remaining part of the Book of Revelation.

DANIEL USHERS US INTO THE DISPENSATION OF THE CHURCH

At this point, the church age picks up at the stop-gap in Daniel's seventy weeks. This gap represents two important factors in our time. 1) It is *the times of the Gentiles* which will end with the Lord's return as shown in Revelation. 2) It is the time when the Lord suspends His work with the Jews and they are scattered among the nations. He turns to the Gentile nations to *"take out of them a people for His name"* (Acts 15:14). Immediately following the Church's Rapture, Christ will turn back to the Jews and begin completing their redemption by restoring the "tabernacle of David which has fallen down" (ibid v. 16).

According to Paul in Romans chapters nine, ten, and

eleven, it was necessary for Christ to cut off Israel for a time and turn His work to the Gentiles in order to fulfill His promise to Abraham and the nation of Israel. His purpose in establishing Israel was not to build an arrogant religious aristocracy, but to bring the world to Himself. Although Israel still honored the Messianic hope, they failed to recognize Christ as Messiah, let-alone His purpose through them to bring the world to Christ. Therefore, the Church was necessary. Christ's ultimate Revelation comes through the Gentile Church for the last two millenniums.

Paul shares the clear sequence found in Revelation by proclaiming, *"[when] the fullness of the Gentiles has come in ... all Israel will be saved"* (Romans 11:25-26). This places the salvation of the Jews squarely in the Book of Revelation. After the Church age and at the end of the *time of the Gentiles*, He will regather the Jews and bring them into their promised inheritance as prophesied in Revelation. This is why the seven-year Tribulation is called *"the time of Jacob's trouble"* (Jeremiah 30:7). All of this is clearly shown in Revelation.

Therefore, The Revelation of Jesus Christ completes the book of Daniel and brings us into the complete fulfillment of all of the covenants that God made with man: the Rapture and return of the Church, the restoration of Israel to her full promise, and the redemption of the Gentile nations from the power of Satan.

CHRIST IN THE MIDST OF THE CHURCH

The Revelation begins with Christ in the midst of His Church in the second and third chapters. Jesus Christ is, and always will be the head of the Church. In spite of the Church's faults and shortcomings, He refuses to step away, even in the day of His Revelation. He is never on the outside of the Church, but always in the middle of it, for He said *"I will never leave you nor forsake you"* (Hebrews 13:5). Jesus *"loved the church and gave Himself for it"* (Ephesians 5:25). He said *"this gospel of the Kingdom will be preached in all the world as a witness to all the nations, and then the end will come"* (Matthew 24:14). Then He said: *"I will build My Church and the gates of Hades shall not prevail against it"* (Matthew 16:18). Christ *is* working and leading in the Church. He holds the pastors of the true Church in His right hand and walks among the candlesticks, or light of the Church (Revelation 1).

SEVEN GENTILE CHURCHES ARE NAMED

Seven churches are named and each is a Gentile church. Not one of them named is a Jewish church in Israel. This is also a connection back to the book of Daniel and the stop-gap. Israel was to be cut out and the Gentile Church grafted in (Romans 9-11).

As the messages to the churches are explored, three stages of fulfillment are found and depicted here. As with all prophecy, it has an unfolding and progressive fulfillment.

1. Each church represents the churches in the day John wrote the Revelation at the end of the first century, about AD 96—approximately sixty years after the Lord's death and Resurrection.
2. They also represent a period in history of the Church from John's day to the present and beyond, until Jesus comes again.
3. They are each and altogether a perfect prototype, or analogy equivalent to an average church at any given time.
4. And lastly, they represent the entire end-time Church prior to the Rapture and Second Coming of Jesus Christ.

Only an omniscient and omnipotent God could have

inspired the writing in Revelation that typifies the Church Age so perfectly in so many capacities.

God's Word, knowledge, and foreknowledge of us can be declared as always up-to-date. He sees the past, how it reflects upon our situation today, and what it will look like in the future. Christ has a way of looking into the affairs of the Church today and seeing the seed, or DNA of the future Church.

HE STILL WALKS IN THE TRUE CHURCH TODAY

Jesus can be found everywhere in the Book of Revelation, overseeing and directing each event and scene. Like the director or playwright of a production, He is seldom in the scene itself, yet He is always in the background overseeing and controlling everything by His command.

He is the great *I Am* seven times; He is the *Lamb* twenty-seven times; He is often a great angel such as the one in chapter eight who throws the coals of the God's sensor to the earth to initiate the Tribulation. Or, He may be the thundering voice and bearer of the seal of God. Unmistakably, He is there in every part of the drama, behind the scenes pulling all of the strings. Consistently, we find Christ in the presence of the Church on Earth, in Heaven, and at the Marriage Supper. He is at the head of the Church—the great army of His return. He is not always obvious to the carnal man, but can be seen in the Spirit by the redeemed.

Christ is still walking in the Church today; in every sermon and lesson, every altar call, and in every appeal. He walks aisles of the churches, searching out His own for *"The Lord knows those who are His, and, let everyone who names the name of Christ depart from iniquity"* (2 Tim. 2:19). He even walks the altars of the heart (Revelation 3:20). Jesus whispers His will in times of prayer. He manifests His presence in signs and wonders. He moves mountains and works miracles. Yes, He is still in the midst of the Church today. He is *"with [us] always, even to the end of the age, Amen"* (Matthew 28:20).

THE SEVEN CHURCHES OF ASIA AND THE CHURCH AGE

(Refer to the chart at the end of this chapter. It shows how each promise to the Church is fulfilled in chapters 20-22.)

The following is a brief look at each church from a practical standpoint. For the historical and prophetic implications, we will depend largely upon the provided charts. We will also rely on the charts to show us the exact fulfillment of Christ's promise to each of the churches at the end of Revelation.

Nearly every church is given a complement, a comment, a warning, a promise and/or an exhortation. However, Philadelphia has no warning, Laodicea has no complement or promise, and Smyrna is not asked to repent. Each are exhorted to hear what the Spirit of God is saying to the Church.

Reflecting the image or symbol of the Jewish Menorah, there are seven lights of the raptured Church. Each one is a close reflection in the church of Jewish custom, for we must remember that the whole root system of the Church is from Jewish and Israelite practice and observance. Every one of our basic concepts comes from God's Revelation to and through the Jewish law and prophets. Each of the churches shows the connection and association with Christ including:

1. Where Christ stands in relationship to the Church.

2. What Christ sees and likes about the Church.

3. What Christ will not condone in His Church.

4. What instructions Christ gives to the Church.

5. What Christ promises to the faithful in His Church.

Each one eventually fails and has their lights removed and there are no churches at these locations today.

EPHESUS (Revelation 2:1-7) the Cooling Church (from AD 30 to AD 100)

Jesus leaves no question in each of the churches as to whom they are dealing with—who has the power to bless and curse, and to whom they are accountable.

Jesus reminds the church in Ephesus of His presence; that it is He who holds the seven stars in His right hand (Revelation 2:1). In most of our churches, Christians get so busy being religious that Christ is left sitting somewhere in the shadows, unobserved. From time to time we allow Him to come out of the shadows and make Himself known. He reminds each Church that He is not just a sentimental piece to sit on the mantel, a picture to hang on the wall, or a tattoo on the arm, but a vital, living part of our Church life.

Revelation 2:1 reveals the introduction, verses two, three, and four the commendation and comment, verses four and five the warning, and verse seven the Promise. This church would be of particular interest to John personally inasmuch as he was pastor of the Church of Ephesus when he was taken by Rome and left on the Isle of Patmos. John knew quite well the status of the Church and would not be pleased to learn it had lost its first love. It had not lost its love for Christ, but had grown cold and no longer had the freshness of that first love. They were told to repent and do their first works anew or lose their light. Evidently they did not repent and fire up their first love, because not many years after, the Church was gone.

Jesus saw their works and how they could not tolerate those who were evil—a task that befell each of the churches. Nevertheless, a group of heretics had influenced them.

NICOLAITANS

Nicolas, a conqueror of the people, was a proselyte of the Church at Antioch and a deacon of the Church at Jerusalem (Acts 6:5-6). His followers were infiltrated by a spirit that offered a diversion or delusion of which God hated. It caused division in the Church by launching a spirit of the Papacy, thereby introducing idolatrous practices. Leaders were elevated among the people and called *clergy*, while the rest of the people were called laity. The laity was then subject to the clergy. Neither of these words were used in the New Testament Church and were foreign to the Church that Christ inspired.

The Clergy claimed special privileges from God, and the people were hard set to obey them, even at penalty of excommunication. These Nicolaitans began introducing forms of idolatrous practices. Gradually, old heathen practices coming out of Babylon were adopted. They were not only the beginning of the Papal authority and idolatry, but they also laid much of the ground work, fitting in well with the spirit of the Gnostics.

Jesus hates any division or spirit of superiority in the Church. Clergy and laity are not pleasing terms. There is no respect of persons with God. The rich, poor, learned, and the unlearned are the same to Him. We do show honor, respect, and appreciation for those who assume responsibility and those with special calling and ability, but only as they live humble lives submitted to Christ. We should never elevate them in the position of lording over the Church (1 Peter 5:1-4). There is only one level of position in the Church and that is a servant of Jesus Christ and fellow laborer in His service (Philemon 1:1).

SMYRNA (Revelation 2:8-11) the Persecuted Church (AD 100 to AD 312)

Jesus—the first and the last, speaks to the Church today. He that was dead and is still alive must be the voice of the angel, or pastor of the Church. During this era, we have the Masada massacre and persecution of both Jews and Christians up to AD 135 and the Bar Kochba revolt. Tribulation and poverty were rampant among both Jews and Christians. Much of this Church lived and worshipped in the catacombs and became an underground Church.

Jesus said the church in Smyrna claim to be Jews, but is not. This was most likely an element of the Jewish and Gentile converts who, though they confessed Christ, still held to certain forms of Judeo-gnosticism. They embraced some of the legalistic Judaism, relied on a mystic enlightenment, proclaiming that Jesus came in spirit, but not in body. Some of this element may have become the thirteenth tribe known as Khazaria, becoming a part of Russian Jewry and Europe's Ashkenazi Jews. They probably were not true Jews, but claimed to be. We do not know for certain who these men were; we can only speculate.

There is no request for this Church to repent, and there is a reason. The Lord has great love and admiration for them. He knew their works, their tribulation, and their poverty. This is the ending age of the New Testament, and it was under great duress from Rome and from the Jews. However, the Lord said they were rich which is in stark contrast to the Laodicean Church.

Among the Jewish proselytes, there was a group making trouble regarding the old law. God said this group was being used of Satan. The devil was going to try them, but they were to be faithful till death, in martyrdom. There is no warning and no call to repentance for the Church in Smyrna.

PERGAMOS (Revelation 2:12-17) The Compromising Church (AD 312 to about AD 500)

The Church must pay attention to Him who is speaking from Heaven. He is not only loving and sweet, but He also bears a sharp, double-edge sword. This sword is the words of His mouth (Ephesians 6:17). Scripture declares that the *"Word of God is living and powerful, and sharper than any two-edged sword, piercing even to the division of soul and spirit, and of joints and marrow, and is a discerner of the thoughts and intents of the heart"* (Hebrews 4:12). That is Jesus' message to the Church today.

This period started with Constantine's conversion and his Edict of Toleration, ending persecution and unifying the Church with the State. This period of Church history saw the first Pontiff, Bishop Boniface.

The main body of the Church had developed the practice of the Nicolaitans which were getting a start in the days of the Ephesus Church. The Papacy began to take solid root among the main body of believers. They were turning away from Christ's concept of the Church and giving over to a worldly-minded Church which sought power and control in the world rather than a Kingdom of faith in Christ and God. The Church tied itself to worldly prestige, but felt the full pressure of the Papacy and its idolatrous ways.

It was during this period, the Church began to realize that Christ's return might still be some time away. The Roman Church began seeing itself as the all-encompassing body of Christianity. Replacement theology which said that the Jews no longer had a part in God's promise was running rampant. They were hated by Christ and the Church, so the Roman Church took the promises of Israel upon themselves. They began interpreting Revelation in a way that made them to believe it was their responsibility to develop the Millennium and get it ready for Christ's return. The Chiliastic interpretation of Revelation developed, which inspired the Crusades. (See introduction for more information about this doctrine.)

The sin of Balaam is mentioned in Jude eleven and Revelation 2:14. Keep in mind that Balaam was hired from Aram to curse Israel. God stood in his way and forced him to prophesy truth about the coming Messiah. Eventually, he did cast a stumbling block before Israel and brought in idolatrous practices, causing them to commit fornication. Evidently, there was in the Church of Pergamos a serious stumbling block. One can only assume it to be the conversion of Constantine who, although He brought acceptance to Christianity, also incorporated a lot of heathen practice into the Church of Pergamum, some of which we still wrestle with today.

The city of Pergamum was founded in the fourth century BC by King Atlas. From its beginning, it was a prototype of pagan idolatry and the god/king priestly order, fashioned after old Babylon's Paganism and emperor worship. It followed the Tzar system of Babylon's khans and bells. An excellent book by Alexander Hislop entitled *Two Babylon's*, gives adequate documentation of this relationship of Pergamum to Old Babylon. A famous *Seat of Satan* was moved from near the Ishtar Gate in Old Babylon and set in Pergamos in the second century before Christ. It was remodeled and called the *Great Altar of Satan* and the *Sanctuary of Zeus*. In John's day (first century AD) it was well known as *the Place where Satan dwells* and *Satan's Seat*. It was closely related to the synagogue of Satan in Smyrna.

In the later eighteenth and early nineteenth Centuries, the Wilhelm's were deeply into the occult and sought to revive the old god/king idea of ancient Paganism. They conceived to revive the Roman Empire from teachings in the book of Daniel and Revelation, wanting to build a revived Roman Empire out of the Holy Roman Empire. This can easily be seen in that Hitler's Nazi party which claimed to be the *Third*

Reich, or the *Third Empire*. It indicated the third try at re-establishing the Roman Empire, the first one being the work of the dreams of Charlemagne; the second was the Wilhelms, who created the First World War with Germany; and the third was the Nazis in the Second World War. A strong satanic spirit began to grip the Aryans of Germany, and was the inspiration behind moving of the *Seat of Satan* to Berlin. The occult was rampant among the kings and nobility of the Old Germanic Holy Roman Empire.

Near the beginning of the twentieth century (1902), the *Altar of Zeus*, or the *Seat of Satan* was moved to Berlin from Pergamum. Its spirit and influence lay heavy on the German people, and I believe it became the satanic drive that inspired the first and second world wars. Also out of Germany came the higher criticism of the Word of God, modern liberal theology, evolution, and most all of the heresies we have dealt with in the past two hundred years. Names such as Nietzsche, Darwin, and Freud came from this era. These are what Germany's *Seat of Satan* gave to them, and have permeated our whole society. I am not saying that there are necessarily mystic powers in the physical altar itself, but there was and still is a satanic spirit in the people who felt comfortable having it in their country and moved it there. Interestingly, it was at the great *Altar of Zeus*, or *Satan's Seat* where Obama made his speech after he was elected in 2008. Afterwards, he ordered a model of it built in the stadium at Denver where he made his inauguration speech. At that time, there was a strong Messianic mood that gripped Obama and his supporters. Our world and its political systems can never track or discern Satan's power behind wayward nations, but Jesus can see right through to the esoteric world and He knows where the power and inspiration is coming from. Through the Word of God, we can discern and counter it as did many people in Pergamum.

THYATIRA (Revelation 2:18-29) the Adulterated Church (AD 500 to AD 1500)

This period of History is best known as the *Dark Ages* or the *1000 years of darkness*. False doctrine ran rampant and many false heresies were born. Jesus again manifests Himself to the Church as the Son of God with eyes of fire and feet of fine brass (Revelation 1:14-15). In just two more chapters, He will be preparing to fulfill Justice and judgment upon a wayward world (See also Jude 14-15). The wayward worldly Church will suffer right alongside the wayward world.

This church represents a time in history during the Roman Empire when the strength of the political empire was gradually leaning more to the Papacy than to the Emperors. The Emperors and Papacy were ordaining each other, so it became a rulership made up of church and state. The Church scratched the back of the Emperors, and the Emperors scratched the back of the Popes. The Lord seems to recognize the charity, faith, and service of the Catholic Church, and we acknowledge it to be commendable as well. But their works had taken precedence over their commitment to Christ and to the true gospel. Salvation by works instead of by grace through faith had taken pre-eminence; therefore, it was all works and very little grace.

JEZEBEL AND MYSTERY BABYLON, MOTHER OF HARLOTS AND ABOMINATIONS OF ALL THE EARTH: The seductive spirit of false prophecy like that of Jezebel had infiltrated all of their good works and was leading the Church into fornication with the world. It was at this time that the old Babylonian, pagan spirit of worldliness began to invade the Church. Under influence of the Holy Roman Empire and its occult kings, the Roman church began preferring the Babylonian mystic religion rather than the simple gospel of Jesus Christ. No wonder it is called the adulterated church.

The Church is warned by God about Jezebel—the self-proclaimed prophetess, and given space to repent, but she repented not. The implication is that this adulterated church was given space and a warning to repent, but spiritual arrogance had gripped the greedy hearts of both the political and the religious leadership.

There was a small group of faithful New Testament, born-again believers, who were pure and unadulterated, and not moved by the politics of the day. They were warning the Church of its adultery. These were the early days of the first sparks of the Reformation, which became a Renaissance. Hess, Luther, and others were there and are commended by Christ. However, the main body of the Church remained in its adulterous mode and was part of the Church that became associated with the great Worldwide Harlot Church which would be destroyed in Revelation seventeen and eighteen, for it has not yet repented.

SARDIS (REVELATION 3:1-6) THE REFORMATION CHURCH (AD 1500 to 1700)

Sardis is the incomplete church—restored and reformed. Jesus comes to this church as the complete fullness of the seven Spirits of God; and by the power of the Spirit of God, He holds the pastors of the church in His right hand. Whether a pastor is right or wrong, we the people must put him in the hands of God who will deal with him in a way so as not to destroy the Church. To rise up against a God-called pastor is not wise, and compares to rising up against Jesus Himself.

Sardis is the Church that has endured all of the injustice of a church/state monopoly. It has dominated the church world of the time. The middle age Church was almost dead to Jesus and little remained, but thank God there were a few names even during this period that had not defiled themselves. Jesus said that they, and all who keep themselves pure in time of persecution, will *"walk with [Him] in white, for they are worthy"* (Revelation 3:4). They were pure, but imperfect (v.5).They that overcome will walk in white and not be blotted out of the Book of Life; Jesus will confess him before the Father (3:5).

Around this time, William Tyndale translated the scriptures from Latin into English. His life was threatened; nevertheless, he opened the Scriptures to individual Bible study, something that had been prohibited by the Roman Church for one thousand years. In 1517 Martin Luther began the Reformation at Wittenberg. All of this opened the way for the Evangelical Church as we know it today.

With this part of the Church Age happening just before the Reformation begins, the message is to watch for the coming of the Lord and strengthen that which you have because Jesus will come as a thief in the night (Revelation 3:2; 1 Thessalonians 5:2). This is the beginning of Christ's message of His Second Coming. The people were admonished to watch for the Lord's return.

The Reformation had only a limited amount of teaching about the Second Coming of Christ. The books of Daniel and Revelation were only considered in passing. Some of the classical churches of Germany and England began missionary work and spoke of the Second Coming of Christ. However, it was not until the Evangelical Church began in the early 1900s that the message of the Rapture and the Second Coming of Christ really began to take hold. Many of the great hymns of the church were written during these early years of revival; over one hundred of them spoke about Christ's Coming.

PHILADELPHIA (REVELATION 3:7-13) THE BELOVED MISSIONARY AND EVANGELICAL CHURCH (from 1700 to the present)

It was God's time for the final Rapture Church. Isaac Newton was born, and not only became the greatest scientist of our time, but he was also a student of prophecy, speaking and teaching about the Return of Christ. Ben Franklin caused the printed page to explode on the world. The Revolution in America, the U.S. Declaration of Independence, and the Constitution gave political clout to the Evangelical Church; the prophesied Philadelphia Church was born.

I believe the very name of the Church in Philadelphia is prophetically indicative of its character. The name means *brotherly love,* and that is certainly a reality. It reflects its missionary and evangelical endeavors today. The wonderful fellowship with believers of all denominations is enjoyed around the world. Having personally ministered in seventeen countries around the world, it is pure joy to find missionaries working with many groups and ministries in their respective countries. We live great days of the worldwide interchurch like Billy Graham Crusades, television, and other media evangelism.

Jesus identifies Himself immediately in Philadelphia as still being Lord of the Church and One who is holy. He proclaims to the church that "These things says He who is holy, He who is true, He who has the key of David ..."(Revelation 3:7) He begins to speak to the Church about Israel's restoration and the coming Kingdom of David that is soon to be established. At this time, the Church Age is about to end and God will return to build the House of David once again (Acts 15:15-16). This is just one indication that the current Church Age is living on the brink of His coming, and the coming of the Kingdom Age.

It began in 1906 with the outpouring of the Holy Spirit

across the country and around the world. C.M. Ward's great radio broadcast opened every day with a resounding, "It's Revival Time, across the nation and around the world." Jesus encourages us to do missionary work, saying He will *"... open door[s] that no one can shut"* (Revelation 3:8). We have seen that time in the history of the Church when the wind of the Holy Spirit blew across America. Then it began to blow across China who tried to shut the door to Christianity, but now houses the largest collective church body of Christians in the world. It began to blow across Russia, who also tried to build a wall to shut out Christians, but that wall came down and today Russia is said to have more open doors to the gospel than America. Today, the Church at large is preaching the gospel in over two hundred, eight countries of the world. The day after 911, Linda Stouffer speaking on CNN, made the statement that "we now have a universal religion. Christianity is now in every country of the world." Matthew's Gospel proclaims that *"This gospel of the kingdom will be preached in all the world as a witness to all the nations, and then the end will come"* (Matthew 24:14). This includes the Muslim nations as well.

This world is soon going to see that the Church is heaven bound to be with Jesus. It will be revealed and made manifested in glory, and kept from the Tribulation. Jesus said of the Church today that He would make them that are in the Church, but *"of the synagogue of Satan ... [to] come and worship before your feet"* (Revelation 3:9). This is why Jesus exhorts the Philadelphia Church to *"... hold fast what you have, that no one may take your crown"* (3:11) Many may make light of the weaknesses of the Church today, but Jesus gave His own opinion: "Because you have kept My command to persevere, I also will keep you from the hour of trial which shall come upon the whole world, to test those who dwell on the earth. Behold, I come quickly!" (3:10-11).

Jesus said those who endure to the end as overcomers, will enjoy the New Jerusalem that is soon to come (3:12).

LAODICEA (REVELATION 3:14-22) THE BACKSLIDDEN AND APOSTATE CHURCH (TODAY)

No compliments are paid to the church in Laodicea. There is only rebuke and instruction. Christ is seen outside the Church, knocking to get in. Christ Himself is not even welcome in this church. Only a socialistic and humanistic membership is welcome in this final day Church. Christ seems to be only an exultant prop to add sentimental religiosity to their program.

In like agreement with many other expositors of the Revelation, it too is my personal belief that the Church of Laodicea probably exists parallel to the Church of Philadelphia as the two contrasting forms of the Church of the end time. It seems we can easily identify both of these church types running side by side in our world today. While many churches today remain Christ centered and continue to preach the gospel as it has been delivered to us by writers of the New Testament, there are also many churches representing a cross-section of all denominations today, both Evangelical and nominal, who are drifting into *post-Christian* thinking. They feel a need to add modern liberal thinking to their church in order to relate to the present generation.

The sixties brought a great revival among the hippies and a new excitement to traditional religion. However, instead of holding to New Testament gospel, many churches allowed the worldly mind-set and loose living of the hippy generation detract them. These liberal churches have thrown out sound traditional doctrine for a modern, palatable gospel and lame lyrics with little or no scriptural basis. Paul warned believers in Romans chapter twelve to not allow the world to entice us into conformity with a worldly way of thinking (Romans 12:2).

Although edging along the lines of gospel, this post-Christian preaching seeks to add the modern liberal thinking of Behavioral and Psychological sciences rather than solid Biblical thinking. For instance, while seldom preaching the self-altering born-again message—the dying out to self and the crucifixion of the flesh through the empowering of the Holy Spirit, people drift into modern simulations to the simple message of Christ and the Apostles. Too often we are left to believe that improving our old nature by behavioral modification, psychological therapy, self-improvement, or reform and repair the old nature by works of righteousness, are equivalent to the born again experience. They believe that what makes us worthy of God's attention and blessing is our human goodness.

In this style of preaching and singing, sin and repentance is seldom mentioned and the need of total brokenness, humility, and complete consecration is rarely encouraged. The crucified self—dying out to the old nature and putting on the new nature in Christ, the indwelling Christ and the infilling of the Holy Spirit—are seldom mentioned in context of a dead self-life. A change in lifestyle by putting off offensive things and developing a hate for worldly things is virtually never suggested. It is replaced by self-fulfillment and self-empowerment. We are left to assume that the world's systems are okay with Christ, and that Christ likes us just the way we are in our old sinful nature; He wants to come in and live side by side with us, in harmony with the old self-nature.

Let us take seriously the Lord's rebuke to the Laodiceans. They are among us. These are the substitutes for the real thing as taught by the Word of God. The word *flesh* can generally be translated *self-life*. Galatians five teaches us what to do with the self-nature. According to our Lord, The first thing the Holy Ghost will do in us and our congregation when He is allowed to come in and move among us, is to "*convict the world of sin, and of righteous, and of Judgment [to come]*" (John 16:8). That coming judgment is shown to us in Revelation as the work and ministry of Christ among us.

Along with these errors in biblical concept, there are other qualities of the Laodicean Church evident in many of our modern churches: the lust of the flesh (desires of the self-life), the lust of eye (desiring everything pertaining to what we see in this life), and the pride of life, (self-esteem and pride of self) (1 John 2:16). One can find much of this rampant in many churches today. People entangle themselves with the affairs of the present social life rather than the affairs of eternal life. All of these issues were found in the Laodicean Church of Revelation.

There is another side of the Laodicean Church which can be seen in today's modern, liberal church. The meaning of *Laodicean* is the *People's Church*. The will of carnal people in the congregation is sought, rather than the true will of God. They tend to do what the people want—preach what the people want to hear, sing what the people want to sing, and act like the people want them to act. This behavior is justified through dependence upon the unconditional love of a good and merciful God. People seek out Bible versions or interpret scripture according to what they want it to say rather than what God is actually saying. Paul exhorts us to reach the Word because the time will come when people will not put up with sound doctrine. Instead, *"they will listen to a great number of teachers who say what they want to hear in order to suit their own desires. They will turn their ears away from the truth and instead, embrace myths"* (2 Timothy 4:2-4, paraphrased).

The modern church has become the Laodicean Church—the people's way, the people's will, and the people's thoughts. Very often, these are *seeker-friendly* churches that while trying to be friendly, go overboard catering to people more than to the Lord; they are *bless-me* clubs who think that God is a bell-boy waiting for us to petition Him with our list of wants or needs so He can jump to our service. Some modern music jams out selfishness and make feel-good promises to appease self. These self-elevated people have pampered egos that tell them God is overjoyed and honored to have them in His Kingdom. He is jumping up and down for joy because they are there. This seems to fit what Jesus said of the Laodiceans in Revelation 3:17a:

"I am rich, have become wealth, and have need of nothing"
He also said of the Laodiceans:

"I know your works, that you are neither cold nor hot ... because you are lukewarm and neither cold nor hot, I will vomit you out of my mouth" (Revelation 3:15-16).

Then Jesus lays out their true state of being by saying, *"[you] do not know that you are wretched, miserable, poor, blind, and naked"* (Revelation 3:17).

Do not think I am just an old out-of-touch man that is disgruntled by a new generation. What I say here is not meant to be critical, nor does it come from a critic's heart any more than Laodicea's rebuke from our Lord came from a critic's heart. It comes from a very deep concern for mankind's eternal welfare; the focus of tearful prayer and an agonizing burden for the lost. If there is no danger of falling into these Laodicean faults, then Jesus, through the Spirit would have no need to warn us of it today through Scripture.

This post-Christian gospel comes very close to what Paul warned us of when he spoke of *"a different gospel, which is not another [gospel]"* (Galatians 1:6,-7). Paul goes on in the same passage to say that some in the Church would *"pervert the Gospel of Christ."* Applied Psychology and Behavioral Modification is not a substitute for the real born-again experience in the Lord which is birthed out of true repentance, where the self-life gives way to the Christ-life. Otherwise, it becomes simply a newly energized self-life which teaches another Gospel. Paul was very specific about what our reactions should be.

The believer should have nothing to do with false teachers or another gospel. In fact, Paul said *"if anyone preaches any other Gospel to you than what we have preach to you, let him be accursed"* (Galatians 1:9). The very subtle *perversion of the Laodicean style is of the type that Jesus spoke about when He said that "if possible, even the very elect"* would be deceived (Matthew 24:24). Jesus warned us that the main deception of the last days would come from preachers and teachers who made the claim that Jesus is the Christ (Matthew 24:4-5). In other words it is often the preachers and teachers that fill our evangelical pulpits and believe that Jesus is the Christ, yet pervert the gospel into New Age selfhood.

It should be noted that the same promises made to the other churches still holds for those in the Laodicean Church. If they wake up and see the error of the Church, they will have opportunity to repent, for Christ is still knocking at their heart's door asking for entrance and fellowship (Revelation 3:20).

There is no other gospel, no other way to salvation, and no other forgiveness for sin, except through a broken spirit and crucifixion of self. Without the death of self and a new life in Christ, we remain lost to a voluntary humility and *will-worship* (worship of our own will), vainly puffed up in our fleshly mind, bound by the rudiments of this world and following the commandments and doctrines of men (Colossians 2:18-23).

Paul made it plain and simple by giving us the only way of living out the true gospel of Christ:

> *"I have been crucified with Christ; it is no longer I who lives, but Christ lives in me; and the life which I now live in the flesh I live by faith in the Son of God, who loved me and gave himself for me"* (Galatians 2:20).

THE CHURCH IN THE FINAL REVELATION OF JESUS CHRIST

Every promise to the churches is fulfilled in the final chapters of the Revelation. A list of these churches and the fulfillment of their promises may be found in the accompanying chart at the end of this chapter.

As stated earlier, the seven churches of Asia represent three distinct periods of time. 1) The actual churches of Asia in John's day. 2) Seven progressive periods of Church history from the early Church age to the present day. People that cannot accept prophetic scripture or grasp the foreknowledge of Christ, is unable to see the progressive fulfillment. Only those who have experienced the wonders of Christ's greatness can comprehend the marvelous prophetic insight that He has. 3) A third reality in the fulfillment of the Church Age promise. This includes all of the promises made to the Churches by Christ and have their ultimate fulfillment in the final days.

Each promise made to the seven churches of Asia and to John by Jesus, are fulfilled by the last Church in the day of Christ's final Revelation. Consult the following chart for these promises and their fulfillment in the End Time.

EPHESUS: Let us first take notice of the promise made to the Church at Ephesus in Revelation 2:7: *"To him who overcomes I will give to eat from the Tree of Life, which is in the midst of the paradise of God."* Keep in mind that the Tree of Life was sealed from Adam and Eve after *the fall* lest they eat of it and live forever in their sinful state. But now, since our Redemption through the blood of Jesus Christ, and having been promised eternal life by our Lord in the New Jerusalem, we may participate in eating from the Tree of Life. Revelation chapter two contains the promised fulfillment: *"... In the middle of its street, and on either side of the river,* *was the Tree of Life ... "* (Revelation 22:2). It bears fruit every month; a grafted tree with every manner of fruit for us. It is always fresh and the leaves are for the healing of the Nations which will be delivered from Satan and ruled over by those who were won to Christ by the missionaries of that country. We will all feast from the Tree of Life.

SMYRNA: Next, our Lord Jesus Christ promised the Church in Smyrna that *"he who overcomes shall not be hurt by the second death"* (Revelation 2:11). Revelation, chapter twenty tells us about the first Resurrection and how we *"shall reign with [Christ] for a thousand years ... this is the first resurrection"* also known as the Rapture of the Church (Revelation 20:4-5). Then we are told, "Blessed and holy is he who has part in the first resurrection. Over such the second death has no power" (20:6). Thus, the fulfillment of Revelation 2:11 is found in Revelation 20:6.

PERGAMOS: To the Church of Pergamos, the promise was made *"to Him who overcomes [God] will give some of the hidden manna to eat. And [He] will give him a white stone, and on the stone a new name written which no one knows except him who receives it"* (Revelation 2:17). The fulfillment is found in Revelation 22:2 where we are told that we will not only eat of the hidden manna mentioned in Revelation 2:17, but also fruit from the Tree of Life. Also, although a real city, the New Jerusalem is illustrative of the pure Bride of Christ who is promised a new name (Isaiah 62:2-3).

THYATIRA: To Thyatira the Lord promised power to rule over the nations with a rod of iron (Revelation 2:26-28). In Revelation 20:4, this is fulfilled in the millennial reign with Christ. He also promised the Morning Star—Christ, the Day Spring which came to us in Bethlehem, a light to the Gentiles, and the glory of Israel (Luke 1:78-79, 2:31).

Revelation 21:23 declares that *"the city had no need of the sun or of the moon to shine in it, for the glory of God illuminated it, and the Lamb is its light."*

SARDIS: To the Church of Sardis, Christ promised that *"he who overcomes shall be clothed in white garments"* and will not have his name blotted out of the Book of Life (Revelation 3:5). Also, Christ "will confess his name before [the] Father" (3:5). The fulfillment is found in Revelation 19:7-8 where the Bride is found dressed in pure white at the Marriage of the Lamb. And, in Revelation 20:14-15, Christ's bride—the church escapes Hell because their names were written in the Lambs Book of Life, and presented before the throne, confessed by Christ (Matthew 10:33).

PHILADELPHIA: To the Church of Philadelphia, Christ made the promise that they would be made a pillar in the temple of God; the name of God, the name of the city, and a new name would be written on them (Revelation 3:12). This promise is fulfilled in Revelation 21:1-5. The city of promise comes down out of Heaven, and God will dwell with them forever; there will be no more sorrow, pain, tears, or death. Revelation 21:25 promises no night time or going out. Heaven will be our eternal home with our beloved Lord Jesus, the Lamb (Hebrews 12:22).

LAODICEA: And finally, even to the backslidden and lukewarm Church of Laodicea, there is promise. Not all were lost, and Christ still sought to win their hearts (Revelation 3:20). He appealed to them to overcome this last treacherous generation and be open to Him. To the overcomers of Laodicea, He promised that they could sit with Him on His throne (Revelation 3:21). In Revelation 20:4 and 22:5 John shares the fulfillment of this promise. The saints reign with Christ on the throne throughout the thousand year millennium and all eternity.

THE COURT OF JUSTICE - THE THRONE ROOM

Passing over the bridge representing the Church Age or the stop-gap of Daniel's seventy weeks, and receiving understanding that the Book of Daniel is a prelude to the Revelation, we are ready to enter into the great Hall of Justice. There in spirit with John, we will be ushered into the presence of Jesus Christ our Lord on His throne, and follow Him through the saga of Redemption.

Therefore, we are now ready to consider the Pageant of Divine Justice which will begin after the Church age is closed by the Rapture of the Church. The pageant will include three acts, with scene after scene displayed before us. Although there will be frightening parts of its drama, most of the pageant will be thrilling to all believers who discern spiritual things. We will witness great applause and standing ovations as the curtain opens and drops at the beginning and end of each act. We will see what Paul spoke of when he said in 1 Corinthians 15:24-26:

> *"Then comes the end, when He delivers the Kingdom to God, even to the Father, when He puts an end to all rule and all authority and power. For He must reign till He has put all enemies under His feet. The last enemy that will be destroyed is death."*

Then, He shall usher in the Divine Redemption of all things (Acts 3:20, 21). With great joy, let us step into the great throne room of God and the Lamb, and witness each scene in the Revelation of Jesus Christ. Everything accomplished in this saga will be by the Lamb that sits on the throne, mentioned twenty-seven times in Revelation. It is He, a Lamb wounded as unto death.

Let us proceed to chapters four and five to see what is going on in Heaven. From our seats in the hall of Justice, we prepare to see the scenes of Heaven and Earth which give witness to the great final judgment of God almighty and Jesus Christ our Lords. Here we witness the final demise of Satan and the Dragon, and see the Rapture of the Church, the Return and glorious end of the promise to the Jews, and God's final redemption of the nations in our eternal home.

START WITH THE HEART

You can put Christ on a Pendant, around the neck to hang,
Or on a shirt or little tight skirt,
Or on a decal captioned with slang.
You can beat His beat to rock and roll, scream His name over a mike
Or walk like Him to talk like Him,
Or be His look-a-like.
You can hang Him on a crucifix, set Him on a mantle tall
Or paint His fame, put in a frame,
And hang Him on the wall.
You can boast a special gift from Him, call your church by His name,
And with pious works and dogma quirks,
Play the religious game.
You can call Him dude, daddio, or the big man upstairs,
Use His name, cry out and claim,
Or tack Him on your prayers.
You can stamp Him on your hand or arm to commemorate, at great cost,
But from the start He must be in your heart,
Or for all the rest ... you're lost.
"Many shall come in my name, saying 'I am Christ' and deceive many."

—Robert J. Smith '91

FULFILLED PROMISE

Beginning and ending of the Church

(Note to think about: Every promise to the Church is fulfilled in the last chapters of Revelation.)

PROMISE	FULFILLMENT
Rev. 2:7 Tree of Life in the midst of the Paradise of God	Rev. 22:2 Street, and on either side of river - Tree of Life (Eternal Life in Paradise of God.)
Rev. 2:11 Shall not be hurt by Second Death	Rev. 20:6 Blessed are those of the first Resurrection. The Second Death has no power over them.
Rev. 2:17 Eat the hidden manna. White stone and new name. Not 3:12 - where new name related to New Jerusalem.	Rev. 22:2 Fruit of the Tree (hidden manna) Rev. 21:18 Jasper, white, clear like diamonds Rev. 21:1 New Jerusalem and a new name. -see Isaiah 62:2
Rev. 2:26-28 Promise of Evangelism of all nations. Given to the church to rule and reign.	(Unrestricted fellowship) Rev 20:41 Thrones - live and reign with Christ for 1000 years. (Millennial Reign of Christ)
Rev. 3:4,5 Walk with Him in white, names written in Book. Confessed before the Throne	Rev. 21:1-5 A city of promise and God's presence forever. No more sorrows, pain or tears.
Rev. 3:12 Pillar in temple - go out no more. Name of God written - name of the city which comes down.	Rev. 21:25 no more going out. (Home in Heaven) Rev. 20:4 Throne-ruling and reigning
Rev. 3:21 Sit on Throne	Rev. 22:5 (permanent Position)

All of these are a manifestation of Jesus Christ in our lives. He is our Tree of Life, Water of Life (1) Our Resurrection (2) Our Hidden Manna (Bread of Life) (3) Our righteousness and redemption (4) He is King of Kings who will give us the world.

SEVEN CHURCHES OF ASIA
PROPHETIC FULFILLMENT

HISTORIC FULFILLMENT

Laodicea AD 1850 - Revelation

Apostate Church
World Council of Churches
The Ecumenical - rich, but poor
Compromised
-Only church with no promise or commendations.

Philadelphia AD 1750 - Rapture

The Missionary church
Revival - Open Door, Evangelism
(not like the great whore or adulterated church) but that little grows a lot. Only church with no rebuke. This is us, the revival Church.

Sardis AD 1517 - AD 1750

Restored and Reformed Church
Incomplete but pure.
Beginning of the exhortation to watch for His coming. Reformation with Luther, Calvin, etc.

Thyatira AD 590 - AD 1570

Adulterated Church
Given to the world - like Jezebel.
Those who call themselves by His name, but have seduced the church into adultery with the world. Only a few did not belong to adulterated Catholic Church.

Pergamos AD 312 - AD 590

Fornicating Church
Christianity married to Heathendom by Emperor Constantine - First universal (Catholic) Bishop. Settled in the world power prestige. This led to the dark Ages.

Smyrna AD 100 - AD 512

Persecuted Church
Late Apostolic - First and Second Century- Christianity - Nero's persecution. Christians driven underground.

Ephesus AD 33 - AD 100

Backsliding and Growing Cold Church
Apostolic Times
Age of the Agnostics.

SEVEN CHURCHES OF ASIA
PROPHETIC FULFILLMENT

FINAL FULFILLMENT

All of the churches represent elements in the final church at the end.

EPHESUS
Cold and backslidden.
Promise of Tree of Life to those who repent.

SMYRNA
Those who are persecuted and hanging on. Promises of Eternal Life to those who overcome.

PERGAMOS
Those who compromise their faith. Promise to be fed by hidden manna if they repent.

THYATIRA
A church of the world, but to the few - release from burden. Power over all.

SARDIS
Babes in Christ. Incomplete, but whole. Immature, but whole. Promise that names are written and will see the Lord.

PHILADELPHIA
Restored Church. Missionary zeal. Take the open doors. Hold fast. Promised to see the Lord.

LAODICEA
Apostasy - thinking material things are blessings of God.

CHAPTER 4

THE CHURCH IN THE COURT ROOM

Dr. Bob Pierce of World Vision once said: "Let my heart break with the things that break the heart of God." Certainly, as we enter into the judgment seat of God, our hearts must break for the penalty of sin upon wayward humanity. We must understand that neither God nor Christ takes pleasure in this judgment to come, for He said *"I have no pleasure in the death of one who dies, says the Lord, God"* (Ezekiel 18:32). And again in Ezekiel 33:11, He declares:

> *"As I live, says the Lord God, I have no pleasure in the death of the wicked, but that the wicked turn from his way and live, Turn, turn from your evil ways! For why should you die?"*

Keep this in mind as we enter Judgment. Both our Father in Heaven and His Son, Jesus Christ are always reaching out to save. They are in the redeeming business. As we proceed through the record of the coming days of judgment, let us not take pleasure in the death of the wicked; but instead, let our hearts break with the heart of God and Jesus our Lord for those who will not turn from evil. Especially as we realize that they have been deceived by Satan. Sin presents three problems for Christ and the Church: guilt, punishment, and correction.

The history of God's work in humanity shows that He has been long-suffering and patient, always willing to redeem.

Finally He is forced to judgment where He must judge both Satan and fallen humanity. Hell was made for the devil and His angels, but fallen humanity must share it with Satan and his angels because they joined him in his sin (Matthew 25:41). Remember, as we find our seats in the courtroom of Christ, the Lord is still *"not willing that any should perish but that all should come to repentance"* (2 Peter 3:9). His call for repentance and an invitation to turn to God throughout the seven years of trouble can be found throughout the seven years of tribulation. Even then, He is still willing to redeem.

The proceeding discussions will follow the general outline we have given before. We are back stage as far as the pageant is concerned. We are in Heaven by rapture where the world and its people cannot see. This entire chapter is happening in Heaven during the day of sorrows, preparing the world for judgment.

In chapters four and five, we see the court in session, the executor of our estate is chosen, and the *Demand for Justice*— conditions and requirements for our redemption is handed to the Lamb in a scroll. In chapter six, we see a foreview of what is to come. Chapter seven shows a seal of protection put upon the Godly before the Tribulation starts. And in chapters eight and nine, we see the first part of the Tribulation. Preparation taking place in Heaven for the last three and one-half years of God's wrath can be seen in chapter ten. And in chapter eleven, we see God's and Christ's last appeal to the world and the Jews through the two witnesses (Revelation 14:6). In chapter fifteen we see those who have overcome the beast and are kept from the last plagues. Chapter sixteen shows the Great Tribulation ending with Armageddon. Then finally, our redemption is completed in chapter nineteen and seven new things are revealed.

Take a look at the first thing John observes at the end of the Church Age in chapter four. He says, *"after these things I looked...*" (Revelation 4:1). After what? Obviously, he means the Church Age. Then there is a very clear call from Heaven. The Church is going to step from Earth to Heaven where a door is opened for them to transcend the dimensional barrier between the cosmic world out there and the material world down here. We will see our first view of heaven.

COME UP HERE (v.1)

The first words that we hear after the Church Age, is a call to Heaven. The first thing we learn is *"a door standing open in Heaven"* and we are going to get our first look (Revelation 4:1). There are more scientific ways to speak of this open door in our vernacular of today. It is interesting that three verses back, Jesus is shown standing at a door and knocking. We usually think of that door not as literal, but as a door of the heart. Now John is standing at another door, whether literal or cosmic, whether physical or metaphysical, we do not know. It most certainly had a spiritual change into a new dimension, for John said, *"Immediately I was in the Spirit"* (Revelation 4:2). We are sure that one of the qualifications for us to be translated is that we have to be *"changed"* for "flesh and blood cannot inherit the Kingdom of God" (1 Corinthians 15:50-51). We will all be changed from *"glory to glory"* for "we shall be *"like [Christ], for we shall see Him as He is"* (2 Corinthians 3:18, 1 John 3:2). John suddenly finds himself in another world where there are sights, sounds, and scenes that have never been experienced from our earthly dimension. He begins to describe what he is seeing in words and language that was designed for this world. So if his explanation leaves us puzzled at some things, we will understand, for the fullness of what He saw, will only be understood when we are standing there ourselves.

How many times we have longed for just a look into Heaven, but we are told that *"Eye has not seen, nor ear heard, nor have entered into the heart of man the things which God has prepared for those who love Him"* (1 Corinthians 2:9). What a wonderful moment it will be when first the curtain lifts and we get a view of what is going on in Heaven. These scenes give us a hint as to what we will see.

Also, we will "see Him whom we have never seen, but loved" (1 Peter 1:8, paraphrased). This song says it well:

> "What a day that will be, when my Jesus I shall see;
> When I look upon His face, the one who saved me by His grace…"

What an incredible thought! John is standing where we will literally stand soon, whether by Rapture or by death. How can I describe the grandeur and veneration which will surge through us unworthy mortals when we see Christ and the throne of the Father! Although no reference is made at this time about Him, we know He is sitting there at the right hand of God. How can we stand quiet in that surge of joy? I can hardly keep my feet under me just writing about it. There is an old spiritual song which attempts to capture the feeling one will experience:

> "Oh won't you sit down; Lord I can't sit down. Oh won't you sit down; Lord I can't sit down; I just got to Heaven, 'gonna look around. Who's that yonder dressed in white, must be the children of the Israelite. Who's that yonder dressed in black, must be the hypocrite a turnin' back. Oh won't you sit down, Lord I can't sit down. Just got to Heaven, 'gonna look around."

THE OPEN DOOR AND A LOOK INTO HEAVEN

Whether or not there is an actual door, we do not know.

However, we do find a definite division between the two dimensions of life in the universe. This is the scriptural way of saying that the invisible barrier between two dimensions of reality—the invisible world around us and the visible world we live in, will be opened. We do not know how it is opened and closed. However, what we do know is that those in the esoteric world of beings can cross the barrier from time to time. Angels come and go from Heaven. Christ crossed it occasionally and Paul was allowed across it to the third Heaven.

The first thing I think I will notice when looking into Heaven is all the busyness and activity. I have had some dread of going to Heaven if I am going to spend eternity lying around on a white fluffy cloud in pajamas, playing on a harp. First of all, I do not play a harp. Secondly, I do not sit around in my night shirt all day. And thirdly, I have no desire whatsoever to lie around on a fluffy cloud doing nothing. This dream about Heaven is almost as preposterous as the Muslim idea of Heaven and their seventy-two virgins. The world has always been confused in its perceptions of Heaven. I personally will be excited to find that there is going to be a lot to do when we get there.

Heaven is opened twice more; once to admit the witnesses who are also caught up in the Rapture and the second time to allow the return of Christ and His Church back to Earth (Revelation 11, 19). An opening is made for the Church to ascend again when the witnesses are called up, but not opened again until the Church follows Christ's return back to the Marriage Supper.

A door to that world is hinted at in the tenth chapter of Daniel where he is told by the angel Gabriel that he had been hindered for twenty-one days trying to get through from the esoteric world to bring the message, or the seventy weeks prophecy to Daniel. He was hindered by the Prince of Persia and would be confronted by the Prince of Grecia when he returns. Then, he mentioned that it was only by the help of Michael that he would be able to get back through. I know this is a strange insight, but it does hint that there is a door between the two worlds that is guarded by principalities, powers, and rulers of the darkness of this world (Ephesians 6:12).

THE TRUMPET: Scripture declares four times that a voice and a trumpet are calling *come*. Without question, we believe that this verse is a symbol of the Rapture of the Church before the Tribulation begins. We also find other evidence here of the Rapture of the Church.

The entire verse is clearly indicative of terms in other places that relate to the Rapture. John was immediately in the Spirit just as the Church will be when it is raptured. There is a voice, a trumpet, and a call upward. All of these signs match what we read in other texts about the Rapture (1 Thessalonians 4:13-16, 1 Corinthians 15:50). We also find hints of a bodily resurrection of the saints in many Old Testament texts.

The best understanding of Revelation comes by over eight hundred comparisons of Revelation alluding to the Old Testament text. It also contains at least two hundred, eighty-five direct quotes from the Old Testament. For instance, we may compare the Tribulation texts in Revelation to Isaiah 26:19-21. All of chapters twenty-four through twenty-Six are Tribulation texts. Zephaniah 2:3 is a little more subtle, but beyond question, refers to the Tribulation and the Gentile Church which is saved out of it. A "nation not desired" in this text is actually in Hebrew: *Goy*, or Gentiles. It refers to the Gentile Church hidden in God's protection while *the day of the Lord's anger* passes by. An amazing amount of background detail of the events of Revelation can be filled in out of related information found in the Old Testament. A close-up picture of our personal entrance into the presence of Christ is seen in Job 19:25-27:

> *"For I know that my Redeemer lives, and He shall stand at last on the earth; And after my skin is destroyed, this I know, that in my flesh I shall see God, Whom I shall see for myself, and my eyes shall behold, and not another."*

"Caught up," in 1 Thessalonians 4:16-18 is the same terminology used in Revelation 4:1 for *"come up here."* Both speak of the Rapture of the Church. It is also the same word used for the man-child that was *"caught up to God,"* and for Paul's transport into Heaven (Revelation 12:5, 2 Corinthians 12:2). We find it in Acts 8:39 to speak of the time when Phillip was caught away. How long did it take for John to reach Heaven and to be in the throne room? *"In the twinkling of an eye"* (1 Corinthians 15:52).

A TRUMPET

The *shophar* (ram's horn) was blown on many occasions in both the Old and New Testaments. It is always pointed to an announcement or warning. One will be blown from Heaven at the moment of the Rapture (1 Thessalonians 4:16). It is called the *Trump of God*. This trumpet is the last trumpet seen in 1 Corinthians 15:51-52 and contrary to a rather widespread teaching, has absolutely nothing to do with judgment. It is a call of triumph, not judgment. It is not the same as the last of the seven judgment trumpets described in Revelation.

There are several trumpets associated with Revelation and the last days. These include: the *last trumpet* to announce the Rapture of the Church before Tribulation; the *great trumpet* announcing the Lord's coming at the end of the Tribulation. Also, there are the *seven trumpets* which are judgment trumpets blown by angels that accompany various events during the first half of the Tribulation.

A THRONE WAS SET IN HEAVEN

I must pause here to speak of the throne. Heaven is a real place. Jesus said that He was going to "prepare a place for you" [then] will come again and receive you to Myself; that where I am, there you may be also" (John 14:3). Note that we are going to be ushered into the courtroom at the foot of the throne and will be received by our Lord Jesus Christ.

CHRIST GIVES US A SPECIAL INVITATION TO BE WITH HIM AT THE THRONE

As my late friend and mentor, Linfield Crowder used to say, "I think I am going to have a spell." Just to think that we poor sinful, but blood-washed mortals have the real hope of being received by our Lord at His throne. It is an overwhelming thought and causes excitement to our emotions. We can hardly help being overcome when we realize that John is seeing what we are going to see some day, and standing where we are soon going to stand. If we can grasp the magnitude of what we see, it is so awesome that we can hardly comprehend it. It so overpowers us physically and emotionally, that we break out weeping as when contemplating the reality of these marvelous scenes.

Only those whom Christ has recognized as His own and have a very intimate spiritual relationship with Him, are invited to this gathering at the throne to see His glory. In John seventeen, Christ established that special relationship in prayer by saying He had invited them to be where He was. Of course, He is at the throne and on the right hand of the Father. At first He is not made manifest, but He will be at God's special time and for His own special purpose (Revelation 5).

Those invited to be with Him are not of the world, but have a very special place in Him. They are made pure and holy through the words of truth (John 17:17). Then they will have another special relationship with Him because He said He was praying for them to be one with Him in the same relationship that He has with the Father. Just as Christ was one and the same with the Father, so are we to be one with both He and the Father. Therefore the Father, the Son, and the believer were all of the same heart and mind, making up a threesome in unity at the throne.

The throne of God and the Mercy Seat of Christ will be a central theme of Revelation. It is mentioned fifty-eight times in the New Testament, forty-three times in the Book of Revelation, fourteen times in chapters four and five alone, and seven times in the seventh chapter. The same word is used twice for the seat of the beast where the devil gives him a throne. It is used for Satan's seat, or throne in Revelation 2:13, but forty times it speaks of the throne of God and Christ. These are the ones standing in the court room near the throne, for it is for them that Christ made a request in prayer "that they also whom you gave to me may be with Me where I am, that they may behold my glory which you have given me" (John 17: 24). Now, because the Father loves Christ and Christ has requested our presence with Him at the throne, we find ourselves so graced immediately after the Rapture. It is necessary to ensure a personal relationship with Christ in order to be a privileged recipient at the throne.

Some occasionally have asked me how I know that Jesus is at the throne of God although He is not mentioned or immediately revealed. I know He is there for several reasons given in the Scripture. For instance, Revelation speaks of the *Man Child* which we know to be Christ. We are told that He, Christ, was *"caught up to God and to His Throne"* (Revelation 12:5). Then we read where Steven looked up into Heaven and saw "Jesus standing at the right hand of God." (Acts 7:55) But to me, the best thought is that He is there where

He has been since His ascension, seated on the Throne next to our Father in Heaven, and is making intercession for us. Romans clearly says that Jesus is "at the right hand of God, who also makes intercession for us" (Romans 3:34).

I am saturated with God's love just thinking of God's Son, Jesus Christ in Heaven. A further reason to be thrilled about Christ at the throne is that next to the throne is the actual, eternal Mercy Seat; the place where Christ presented His blood after His resurrection (Hebrews 9:12). Remember, Moses was to make the Tabernacle exactly as God patterned it in Heaven. That pattern was made like the throne room where we see John standing. Here, John is in the presence of our Redeemer. Remember, the Shekinah Glory was between the cherubim on the mercy seat, where the blood was sprinkled. Also, as the Temple was being sacked by Titus and the tenth army of Rome in A.D. 70, the priests saw the veil rent from top to bottom and Christ standing in the place of the Mercy Seat in the Temple. We are told that He is at the right hand of God making intercession for us. That is the very purpose of the Mercy Seat.

The eternal *mercy seat* reflected by its pattern in the Tabernacle, is the place in Heaven where the blood must have been applied by Christ, and was presented by our Lord after His ascension (Hebrews 9:12). It becomes a moment of brokenness and awe to the redeemed just to realize that His blood, like the blood of the Lamb, was placed on the mercy seat in the tabernacle in Heaven. It is significant to note that we are also in the courtroom of justice just prior to the sentencing of Satan and the world that he has influenced. To find the mercy seat still available to all those who will accept the blood of the Lamb when judgment is pending, and that the throne is still the Holy of Holies where we are offered mercy for our sin, is an exciting discovery. It demonstrates that Christ Jesus is still the merciful Savior even in the face of pending judgment. Mercy, love, and will for our salvation is further demonstrated as we consider God's promise through the rainbow (Genesis 9:12-13). Habakkuk 3:2 and Zechariah 7:9 both teach that Christ is always merciful in judgment. The rainbow communicates that by recalling God's love and mercy even in the flood.

A RAINBOW 'ROUND ABOUT THE THRONE (v.3)

At this judgment hour, the throne is still a place of mercy. Many are fearful as they read the book of Revelation. I fear they are dwelling too much on the negative and missing so much of the positive in the book. God's continued mercy and care is illuminated when we see the rainbow 'round about the throne and the color of emerald displayed. It would be a rainbow formed from the glory of God coming out of the midst of the throne. This is the only way it could be a complete rainbow—a full circle. The reason it is only half a rainbow from Earth's perspective, is that the earth cuts off the light and the prism is hindered. But coming out of the midst of the throne, it forms a full circle. The glory of God, which is pure white light, breaks into a three-sided prism and disseminates the colors of the rainbow. We see this rainbow present at the throne in chapter ten, which represents a time in the midst of the Tribulation when the *little book* of sentencing for Satan and his angels, is taken to be read. We will mention the rainbow in connection with the throne again in chapter fifteen, where we find its prisms of colors reflecting off of the *Sea of Glass*. The fifteenth chapter represents views from the throne room and temple at the beginning of the vials of the wrath of God, and tells us that Christ is still on the mercy seat making intercession, even for those in that late hour.

Green is a symbol of peace and serenity; and the rainbow takes us back to the last tragic judgment of God upon the earth. The pre-flood prophet, Enoch was plainly told that the world systems would be destroyed twice, once by flood and again by fire. After the flood waters had devastated the whole Earth, a rainbow was placed in the clouds to comfort Noah and his family. Imagine with me that Noah and his family who just stepped out of the Ark, find their world totally destroyed by what they thought to be an angry God, even though God was not angry, just broken. His Spirit could no longer strive with man. The flood became a necessity to keep man from destroying himself by the wiles of the devil.

As they look out of the Ark for the first time, devastation and carnage was everywhere. Imagine with me just what you and I would do if we were Noah. I know what I would do. The first thing would be to build an altar and send up offerings in an attempt to appease this supposedly angry God. That is just what Noah and his family did. Then imagine what Noah would feel like the first time a little thunder storm was threatening. I can hear him yelling at his family to head for the Ark and seal the door. He had no way of knowing when another flood was imminent, nor when God's anger would end, nor if there was even an end to His anger. The second thing I would do if I was Noah is to watch the sky very carefully for a sign of another flood. While Noah and his family were struck with fear and awe at God's judgment and wrath, God, in His mercy and grace came and comforted Noah who *"found grace in the sight of the Lord"* (Genesis 6:8).

God's answer to Noah's fears was to comfort them with promise. It has been said that God put a rainbow in the cloud. What great comfort and assurance the rainbow in the clouds must have been; it was a sign from God that He would not destroy the world again by flood. And what a comfort the rainbow is here in Revelation at the time of pending judgment and wrath. It continues to speak to us of the love of Christ and God's willingness to make peace with man.

I believe my point is understandable. God wanted to

assure Noah, his family, and the rest of humanity for all of time that in spite of the necessity of judgment, His great love and care remains. So, as John steps into the throne room where preparation was being made for a second pending judgment, comfort must have gripped him to see the rainbow around the throne and realize its implication. He is comforted by the reminder that even in this seven short years of judgment by fire, the throne is still a *throne of grace* and a *seat of mercy*. The throne Christ uses to administer the coming judgment contains a throne of Mercy (Habakkuk 3:2). Even in judgment, one can always *"come boldly to the throne of grace, that we may obtain mercy and find grace to help in time of need"* (Hebrews 4:16). Some people will need grace in the time of Tribulation judgment.

Take careful note that the rainbow is not seen *over* the throne. It is not a rainbow that reaches from side to side in an arch over the throne, but rather a rainbow 'round about the throne. It is a complete crowning circle. (See appendix for more thoughts on the rainbow from my dear friend and brother, Jon Hooper and his wife Billie.)

RAINBOW SETS THE TENOR OF THE JUDGMENT (v.3)

Suffice to say, God's real purpose is to bring peace and security to humanity. The rainbow tells us that even though there will be great Tribulation like never has been or ever will be again, He will not *"keep his anger forever"* (Matthew 24:21, Daniel 12:1, Psalms 103:9). Just as Jeremiah was comforted in the time of God's wrath upon Israel at the coming of the Assyrians, he assures us that God will not *"remain angry forever [or] keep it until the end"* (Jeremiah 3:5).

The rainbow around the throne sets the tenor of the judgment. It says to us that even the time of Tribulation is meant to bring peace, comfort, and assurance. (See the six-point-purpose of the Tribulation in Daniel chapter nine.) Even at this late hour, we are invited to the throne of grace where we can find the mercy of a loving Savior (Hebrews 4:16). Proverbs 20:28 says *"...by loving kindness He upholds His throne."* The *Jesus* of Revelation is still the same Jesus we know and love today; *"[He] is the same yesterday, today, and forever"* (Hebrews 13:8).

We tire of those who do not like the Old Testament God because they say He is mean and judgmental. They are like spoiled children who, when Dad has to correct them, think of him as a mean old Dad full of wrath and one to be feared. Oh, how wrong they are! They have missed the truth. They miss the fact that discipline is from the heart of a father's love, and for their own good (Hebrews 12:5, 6). As we study Revelation and walk through some of its short disciplinary moments, we remember the rainbow and look for Christ's mercy through the exploration of the text. It was the God of the Old Testament that put that rainbow there for Noah's comfort; there was a rainbow over the throne that Ezekiel saw (1:26); and the same God put a rainbow over the final throne of justice and judgment speaking of His love and mercy. When God proclaimed His name to Moses, He made it plain that even though our wayward sins demanded that He must visit the iniquity upon the wayward and in no way clear the guilty, His real nature is *"merciful and gracious, longsuffering and abounding in goodness and truth, keeping mercy for thousands, forgiving iniquity and transgression and sin"* (Exodus 34:6-7). The wrath of God and the Lamb is appeased for those who come to Him, even in the Tribulation hour, but wrath abides upon those who reject Him and refuse to serve Him (John 3:36). Have you ever contemplated how it must have broken the heart of God to slay those little lambs and flesh down their hides to make coats of skin to cover Adam and Eve in their sins? His love and pain for the sacrifice of His Son was shown in Abraham's pain when He was called to sacrifice His son, Isaac. Our Father is merciful even when Judgment is required. Moses heard Him proclaim His name as goodness and gracious and mercy (Exodus 33:17-19).

ONE THAT SAT ON THE THRONE (v. 2)

John declared in the Book of Revelation that *"one sat on the throne"* (Revelation 4:2). It was God sitting on the throne with the Lamb right next to Him on the Mercy Seat. This was the same glorified Christ as He saw in the first chapter, and the same fiery throne with wheels of burning fire that Daniel saw (Daniel 7:9). Then we read:

"We know that when He is revealed, we shall be like Him, for we shall see Him as He is" (1 John 3:2). This reveals that He is still the same Jesus as we know and love, and will still have that special relationship with Him.

In John 4: 3, John describes a short observation about Him. If we are not careful, we will miss another reference to our Lord and Savior, Jesus Christ. He was like jasper—pure white, and sardine stone—blood red. These stones were part of the priestly garments and the New Jerusalem. The white represents His purity. The diamond has prisms reflected in its cuts that form all of the colors of the spectrum. This might infer that the rainbow was formed from the reflection of Christ's beauty. The blood-red stone represents His death and sacrifice. It speaks of the blood that was presented here at the throne. It is the same Christ in glorified splendor sitting next to God, *"a lamb as though it had been slain"* (Revelation 5:6).

FOUR AND TWENTY ELDERS - THE CHURCH UNDER AUTHORITY OF CHRIST

The very next thing John noticed is the twenty-four elders. Twenty-four is the number of the priests' orders. It is also the number of Ecclesiastical wisdom, and the number of the seat in the Sanhedrin; the number of judges or jury in the highest court of the Jews. This is the Jury that will sit and judge in the high court of Heaven. We see how a jury around the court of Justice in Heaven matches what Christ told us our position would be when the judgment comes. These represent the Church under the authority of Christ.

They were sitting on seats all around the throne. This word *seat* in the Greek is *throne* and will be used five other times in the Book of Revelation. Once for Satan's seat or throne, twice for the beast's seat or throne, and twice more for the seat of the twenty-four elders.

These elders were sitting on thrones placed all around the throne of God and of Christ. The only time the elders leave their throne is first to bow in worship to the Lord, and to cast their crowns at His feet.

John sees *"thrones, and they that sat on them, and judgment was committed to them"* (Revelation 20:4). There is no question that those sitting upon the seats of judgment are the raptured saints. We will judge angels according to 1 Corinthians 6:3.

Jesus referred to these thrones when He told His disciples *"in the regeneration, when the Son of Man sits on the throne of His glory, you...will also sit on twelve thrones"* (Matthew 19:28). In 1 Corinthians 6:2-4, Paul informs us that the saints will not only judge the world, but also judge angels. Paul was no doubt speaking of this very throne. Therefore, it makes sense that we the Church, must be found seated here around the judgment throne. These are the self-same thrones from which the saints will judge, as is mentioned in Revelation 20:4. The end of the verse declares that "... they lived and reigned with Christ for a thousand years."

How else shall we distinguish these twenty-four elders as the raptured Church? Besides being the ones who sit on thrones of judgment, follow this trail with me:

1. They are dressed in white.
2. They wear crowns of gold.
3. They sit upon thrones.
4. They sing the song of the Redeemed.
5. Only the Church leaders are called elders.
6. All of these characteristics are included in the seven Churches.
7. We see the elders at the throne immediately after the Church age.

The last place we see them in Revelation is at the Marriage of the Lamb. Every place in chapters four and five, they are at the throne. In verses 7:11,13, 11:16, 14:3, and chapter nineteen, they are at the throne. This plainly shows that the Church will be caught up to the Throne, remain there during all of the Tribulation, and only return after Armageddon and the return of Christ. Chapters one through three and nineteen through twenty-two are all about the Church. None of the Tribulation chapters finds the Church on Earth.

8. Always the Church is seen in Heaven and Israel is seen on Earth, therefore these elders are not Jews. Israel and the Jews are not mentioned in the first three chapters dealing with the Church because it is Christ who is dealing exclusively with the Church in Heaven. The last seven years of Daniel's seventy weeks is designed to be the final epoch of Israel's history, but the gap in their history is for the Church Age (Daniel 9:23-27).

9. John, in writing to and about the Church, does not mention the Tribulation except to show that Philadelphia

would be kept from it. This shows that the Tribulation is not for the Church, and will not affect it.

10. They were called *Kings and Priests*. Only the Church has that distinction. They sing the songs of the Redeemed (Revelation 5:9).

11. Because of the Thrones they sit upon.

These are the eleven reasons why we can know these reference the Church.

They are not angels. Angels were not made of the dust of the earth and do not grow old, therefore they can be called *elder*.

They wear crowns. No angel has never been, nor ever will be crowned. Only the Church is promised crowns (2 Timothy 4:8, I Peter 5:4). These crowns prove also that they have been raptured at this time, for no crowns are ever given out until the Judgment Seat of Christ which is after the Rapture.

SEVEN SPIRITS OF GOD (v.5)

John saw *"a sea of glass, like crystal"* (Revelation 4:6). In Old Testament typology, this would be comparable to the laver which stood before the tabernacle and spoke of the sanctification necessary for entering into the presence of God.

Very closely related to the elders or the Church and also to John, is the fullness of the seven Spirits of God (Revelation 4:5, Isaiah 11:2-3). Naturally, our blessed Holy Spirit will be near the Church and present at the Revelation of Christ, for He speaks of Christ (John 15: 26). It was by Him that we were sealed (Ephesians 1:13, 4:30). Jesus our Lord promised us that the Spirit would "abide with [us] forever" (John 14:16). Therefore, it should be no surprise to find Him still with the Church around the throne in eternity and in the presence of the Spirit of God. Neither is it surprising that the Spirit's presence is often associated with lightning and thunder and voices. When John saw this lightening and heard the thunder, he probably looked up to reaffirm the presence of the rainbow. It was still there.

All of this adds to the mysticism of the throne, but mainly it lets John know that the sweet Holy Spirit is near. Through our long years of evangelism during the Church Age, He has always been a companion to every pastor, evangelist, and missionary who will testify to the wonderful companionship, presence and comfort that the Holy Spirit has been; not to mention His wonders, miracles, and power. The Holy Spirit's presence at Patmos was a comfort to John, and now as he stands in the awesome presence of the Throne with judgment pending, the Spirit becomes a support to him as well as to us. It is John's writings which best acquaints us with the coming of the Spirit, and His comfort, companionship and mission (John 14-16).

All of these signify the powerful presence of God at the Throne. We are shown here by the number seven that the Holy Spirit is in His fullness at the throne of Christ. The seven lamps burning again show the presence of the full Church as we know from Revelation, chapter one, and that these lamps represent the Church body and its angels, or pastors.

Along with Christ our Lord, the Church is standing in the fullness of the Holy Spirit in Heaven. We who know the presence of the Holy Spirit and His manifestations, are not fearful of His presence. We are comfortable in His outpourings. We have seen the promised "signs following;" we have witnessed the mighty miracles; experienced the infilling of His power; and have been set afire by His anointing (Mark 16:20). However, I think we can agree that we have never yet seen the complete power of His fullness. Someone said that the world has yet to see what God could do with one man who is totally in His control, completely filled with the Holy Spirit, and yielded to God's perfect will.

I have experienced His power in my life until I felt like I would explode. I have had His glory fill me until I begged for Him to turn it off. I have experienced His mighty anointing settle upon me while ministering, and watched Him flow over congregations like wind over a grain field. Please do not think I am boasting, for I speak of God's promise to us, the Church. Yet with all I have experienced and also heard of others experiences, I must say I have never known what it would be like to be in His fullness. John had to be in some form of a glorified body to be able to come into the presence of His fullness. If today just a little earnest or down payment of the Spirit makes us dance and shout, what would it be like to be in the presence of His fullness?

FOUR LIVING CREATURES (verses 5-7)

The rest of this chapter is taken up with the description and ministry of the four beasts. These are not the *therion* or ravaging wild beast used thirty-four times in Revelation, the same in Daniel seven which are the beasts associated with the dragon and the Antichrist. The word used for the four beasts is *zoa*, (zoon) simply meaning *animated with life*. These represent the created life on Earth. Four divisions are symbolized: Man as human kind; the ox as domestic animals; the Lion as wild animals; and the eagle as flying creatures. These were also seen by Isaiah when he entered the throne in Isaiah, chapter six. They are the cherub of scripture and the guardians of God's throne. They were the guardians of the *Tree of Life* in the garden and were stationed at Bab-el, the gate of God before the flood (Genesis 3:22-24). Therefore, as we interpolate them over from Old Testament typology, they are the guardians of the throne of God and the way of the Tree of Life which is now in Heaven (Revelation 22:2). They were a part of the décor of the holiest of all and spread their wings over the Mercy Seat above the Ark of Testimony, and the Ark was shadowed under their wings (Exodus 25:18-22). They symbolized guardianship over God's earthly throne.

From the Old Testament, we clearly see that before Lucifer's fall in his glorified state and before he became a dinosaur or dragon and a snake, he was *"the anointed cherub that covers"* (Luke 10:18-19, Ezekiel 28:14). That is, he was the guardian to God's throne. So this dragon that was evidently the power behind the beast and his government was once a living creature or one of these living beings who now have replaced him as guardians of the throne. For a rather detailed account of his original position and the reason for his fall, make a careful study of Ezekiel twenty-eight. These Cherubs have replaced Satan as guardian of the throne.

The number four may represent four types and not four in number. Ezekiel saw quite a large number of them in his view of Heaven as shown in the first chapter of his book. These four types also have some connection to the camps of Israel and represent their four standards. Judah was represented by the lion, Ephraim by the ox, the camp of Reuben by the form of a man, and the camp of Dan by an eagle. These were the same as the form of the Cherub in Ezekiel chapter one. They were no doubt involved somehow in the guardianship and protection of the camp of Israel during their long and dangerous wilderness trek. It would be no surprise to me to find that in some way, they represent the Jews or Israel at the throne of their Messiah.

THE BEASTS (living creatures, Zoa) START A GREAT PRAISE SERVICE AT THE THRONE (v. 8-9)

The beasts cried continually before the throne, "Holy, holy, holy," but as the living creature became overcome with praise to "The Lord God Almighty, who was and is and is to come!" an astounding thing happens (Revelation 4:8). In their reference to the coming of Christ in power and great glory, the praise began to reverberate all through Heaven. They started a vibrant praise service on the eve of judgment. Soon the Church and all the Angels, Seraphs, and Cherubs of Heaven began to shout.

I have witnessed this kind of spontaneous praise break out in church services and special assemblies of all kinds. It usually begins with someone who senses the presence of God and yields to the praise that, as Jesus said: "out of his heart shall flow rivers of living water" (John 7:38). Suddenly, out of one's inner-most being, begins to flow rivers of praise. And as this person begins to allow the Holy Spirit to flow through him or her, the hunger and thirst of others is stirred and awakened. Then there would be spontaneous praising until the entire congregation breaks forth in glorious praise. It all starts with one person.

This seems to be the situation at the throne. With Christ's presence, the mighty presence of the fullness of the Holy Spirit, the arrival of the Church into the throne, and with the living creatures so full of praise and adoration, the atmosphere around the throne must have been charged with expectation. Suddenly, an electrifying surge begins to flow over the whole crowd. John watched as the living creatures began to give glory and honor and thanks to Him that sat on the throne and worship Him that lives forever and ever.

They began making reference to Him that not only was and is present at the throne, but also to He that *"is to come"* (Revelation 4:8, 1:4, 8, 11:17). In other words, they were referring to His second Coming in power and great glory which would soon come. Another surge of joy and anticipation ripples over the crowd. The saints standing on the Sea of Glass until this time, are now so awe-stricken and overcome at having come into the throne room and hardly being able to say a word, they now catch the fervor of the four living beings in their praise. Then they begin to throw their crowns before the throne and rejoice in the ecstasy of the moment. Suddenly, all Heaven with the living creatures and the angels along with the Church, was lifting up Heaven-shaking praise and crying to Him that sat upon the throne (4:11).

> *"You are worthy, O Lord, To receive glory and honor and power; for You created all things, and by Your will they exist and were created"* (4:11).

Can you imagine it?! *"An innumerable company of angels"* and an enormous colossal of them throughout the immense universe, are joined by a great company of living creatures, and together with the Church of the Redeemed, make an earsplitting joyful noise of triumph to the Lord and His Majesty (Hebrews 12:22). Angels can shout in a way to shake all of the Heavens (Revelation 4:9, 5:11-14, Psalms 148:1-6, 1 Thessalonians 4:16). Just to hear the Church in jubilant praise here on Earth is an awesome experience. How John must have been animated beyond description to hear the angels, together with the living creatures joined by the Church, shake the pillars of Heaven in this gigantic anthem of praise. This is just one of at least seven great prayer meetings in Heaven during the Tribulation period of time.

THE EFFECT OF PRAISE ON THE DEVIL AND HIS CROWD

Who else could this praise affect other than those who ascribe to their Lord Jesus Christ the attributes due to Him. Have you ever thought what a soul- shaking effect these praise services in Heaven will have on the devil and his crowd? At this time, they are present, appearing as accuser of the brethren. Can you imagine what an effect this praise will have on Satan and His crowd of principalities and powers as they look on in Heaven? At this very time, they are making preparations to stand up against God and His Son, Jesus Christ (Psalm 2, Revelation 17:14, 15, 19:19).

We know in this present time that the more fervently we praise the Lord, the more we weaken the resolve of the devil and his crowd of Principalities and Powers who are the rulers of this present world (Ephesians 6:12). An example can be found in Jehoshaphat's choir whom in their praise and singing, discomfited the enemy. Just as the shout and songs of God's faithful brought the walls of Jericho down, in the same way our praises of triumph sends confusion and fear into the ranks of Hell. And just as the shout of an advancing army throws fear and confusion into the ranks of an enemy, our praise becomes a battle-cry in the ears of our enemies. Even in our present day, it lifts up Christ as the Captain of the Hosts of Heaven, declares our strength and power, and becomes a challenge to our own armies and their resolve. It also puts fear into Satan's camp. We will win more spiritual battles by singing and praising God and Christ than we ever could win any other way "for the weapons of our warfare are not carnal but mighty in God for pulling down strongholds" (2 Corinthians 10:4).

When we begin to sing our challenge to Hell in the name of Christ and declare that "the battle is not [ours], but God's" and "no weapon formed against [us] shall prosper," it makes the dark angels quake (2 Chronicles 20:15, Isaiah 54:17)! They begin losing their confidence in Satan to defeat God and His Christ. Our singing continues: "When the power of darkness comes in like a flood, the battle belongs to the Lord; He raised up a standard, by the power of His blood; the battle belongs to the Lord" (Lyrics by Jamie Owens-Collins). And then having made that clear declaration of our confidence in the Captain of our Salvation, we triumphantly sing right along with these verses in Revelation: "We sing glory, honor, power and strength to the Lord." Can you imagine what that does to the camp of the enemy?

This singing and praise will affect Satan and his Antichrist army as they challenge Christ at Armageddon. We will sing all the louder during Armageddon's battle as Christ *"with the breath of His mouth and ... the brightness of His coming,"* consumes and destroys the wicked one and his armies (2 Thessalonians 2: 8).

Remember in these scenes, Heaven is anticipating a campaign to completely destroy the devil, his Antichrist, and his cohorts. They are on the eve of the biggest battle in the history of the Universe. Revelation 12:7 tells us "war broke out in Heaven," and the old dragon—the old serpent, the devil, Satan—was cast out ... and his angels with him. I can imagine that the devil and his angels, already having suffered defeat, thrown out of Heaven and now here on Earth, are feeling fear as these court proceedings begin. He knows that his challenge to God and His throne are not going to materialize and He is doomed. His wrath will be terrible for a short season of three and one-half years.

This great crescendo of praise at the eve of battle not only sets our Lord in His proper place and encourages us the Church, but it rattles the ranks of the enemy, and weakens and discomfits Him. This kind of praise will accompany the actions of the Lord Jesus Christ throughout the rest of this Book. Oh, beloved, do not overlook these great crescendos of praise throughout the Book of Revelation of Jesus Christ as we proceed toward the final victory in Christ.

This is probably the only court setting you have ever heard of that started with and ended with such a great prayer meeting. How long it lasted we do not know. Was it an all-day prayer meeting or an all-night prayer service, or did it last on through the whole period of the Tribulation on Earth? It may seem as though it lasts throughout the Tribulation in-as-much as we note the many references to praise and worship throughout the Book of the Revelation of Jesus Christ. Whatever the case may be, it was this praise service that opened the court proceedings. Now in chapter five we watch as the court proceedings begin.

CHAPTER 5

COURT IS SET

As the curtain rises on Act One, we move into the main scene of the redemptive process which is shown to us in the Revelation. Our purpose is not to reveal any new things not yet seen, but to make the plain old things already seen. Revelation shows Christ's continued involvement with Israel and the Church. It shows the place that the Church plays in Heaven, and the work of the Lord with Israel still on Earth. It shows the final end and ultimate meaning of the *"Lamb of God who takes away the sin of the world"* (John 1:29)! Israel will realize the full meaning of their ritual of the sacrificial lamb which was very sacred to them throughout the centuries of temple worship. Seeing the involvement of Christ, the Lamb mentioned by this name twenty-seven times, helps the Church to realize the full meaning of the Jewish sacrificial ritual and their Messianic hope. It reveals to us why Jesus almost always referred to Himself as the Son of Man. We now see the Son of Man in Heaven, heir to the throne of David. The Lamb and the throne of David are very important to the hope of the Jews, both having their complete fulfillment in the Book of Revelation.

In the Book of the Revelation of Jesus Christ, we see the three covenants of God come together to be fulfilled as one. In the Covenant of the Law of Moses along with the commandments of God, Jesus plainly says that He did not come to destroy the law, but to fulfill it. The Abrahamic

Covenant is for the land, the city, and the Temple Mount. We also see the full meaning of the Abrahamic Covenant which was to be a blessing to the Gentile nations. Then we see all three covenants being fulfilled together in the Gentile church in Heaven. All of these covenants are working together with the Lamb to redeem the nations and the Jews out of the hand of Satan, and all of these entities are brought together in the New Jerusalem. The eternal nature of Moses' Covenant, Abraham's Covenant, and the eternal life of the Covenant of God with the Church, comes together in the New Heavens and the New Earth. This is another example of how an understanding of the Old Testament is so intertwined with Revelation.

Jesus our Lord, never directly claimed to be the Son of God but He allowed others to claim it. God called Him His Son. He said that Christ's works speak of His divinity. However, eighty-nine times He spoke of Himself as the Son of Man and admitted that on His human side, He was and is the Son of David.

In relating Himself to the Son of Man, Jesus picked up all of the cryptic references of this same term in the Old Testament, a term used to subtly symbolize the human side of the Messiah to come. Thus, He de-emphasized His eternal identification with God and emphasized His humanity. This placed Him in line to qualify as the Son of David and heir to His throne. Also, it presaged His title as King of Kings and Lord of Lords. It is the Son of Man who will return in power and great glory to accept the throne of the Millennial Kingdom on Earth. Paul saw it plainly and said that *"He made Himself of no reputation, taking the form of a servant ... humbled Himself and became obedient to the point of death, even the death of the cross"* (Philippians 2:7-8). This all speaks of His humanity. It was this sacrifice as the Lamb of God which allowed Him to have a name above every name, and by this means, He overcame Satan and gained the right to sit in judgment and take the Book.

THE SCROLL OF REDEMPTION AND THE LAMB

We will now follow the actual legal proceedings. Immediately the court opens by presenting the legal brief which will be the deciding factor in this case. We see the Judge and the Jury seated. The jury is the Church, representing the Sanhedrin of the high court of Heaven. We see the witnesses, the prosecutor, and the Executor.

We see the legal document that will state the case against the devil and the world which has fallen under His deception (Isaiah 14:5, Revelation 12:9, 13:14). We are clearly told that it is Satan who is behind the rebellion and deception that is on all nations. After His judgment and final sentence, as shown to us in the nineteenth chapter of Revelation, Satan enters Hell and we are told that the nation's leaders who are there already will say, "Have you also become weak as we? Have become like us" (Isaiah 14:10)? Isaiah 14:6 makes a startling statement: *"He who struck the people in wrath and with a continual stroke, he who ruled the nations in anger, is persecuted and no one hinders."* Then, verse twelve addresses the one which came into Hell and was met by many of those leaders of Earth who had been deceived by Him. The question is asked, how did it happen that you fell from such a high place (paraphrased)?

JOHN'S ATTENTION DIRECTED TO THE LORD - AND A BOOK IN HAND

Because this court session is a lot more than just a legal procedure, we find some very touching things going on, especially as it pertains to Christ and His future Bride—the Church. Be reminded that our purpose in this writing is to keep close to our Lord and His Revelation. We want to follow His activity throughout these writings. Too often He is the one who is ignored in the study of His own book. The Revelation of Jesus Christ shows Christ's involvement with the Church in Heaven and Christ's involvement with Israel still on Earth.

John's attention had been directed toward the great praise service taking place all around the throne, when something happening in the throne itself that caught his attention. Now he looks back at the throne and sees the right hand of God holding a scroll. He notices two things about the book. One, it has writing on the inside and outside; and two it is sealed with seven seals. Some scholars think it was papyrus sheets, written on each side. I feel it was a scroll rolled up. Either way, we should understand that it is a very significant and consequential book. In this instance it turns out to be a legal paper setting forth the court's position in the case to come before the judge and jury.

The seals were along the outer edge of the document. Each seal represents a condition which must be met to open the document and view its contents. We find a lot of evidence both in Scripture and in customs of the day, to indicate that this is a legal and authentically binding report. We understand that under Roman rules, all wills and estate warrants were sealed with seven seals.

We read in Ezekiel about a very similar book. Ezekiel is sent to testify on God's behalf to the exiles in Babylon and Persia. He was commanded to hear. Hear what? *"You shall speak my words to them"* (Ezekiel 2:7). Then he sees a hand, and in it *"a scroll of a book"* and it was *"spread [out] before me, and there was writing on the inside and on the outside"* (2:9-10). Ezekiel said that the contents contained *"lamentations mourning and woe"* (2:10). He was told to *"eat this scroll and go, speak to the house of Israel"* (3:1). Ezekiel said that the book in his stomach was bitter, but in his mouth it was sweet (3:3, 14). He was caught up in the spirit and found himself in the presence of the living creatures (3:12). One of the cryptic symbols of what would be revealed in the day of the Revelation of Jesus Christ is found here in Ezekiel.

DIFFERENT FROM THE BOOK IN THE TENTH CHAPTER

This is very familiar ground as we read these passages of Revelation. It compares in many ways to what we are reading in Revelation five, and also in chapter ten where we read of the *"little book"* (Revelation 10:8-10). We note that all of these books are official documents, handed out by God himself. The book in chapter ten however, is totally different from the one in the fifth chapter.

The *little book* in the tenth chapter was handed to John. John was not worthy to take the book in chapter five. The first was a legal brief, an indictment on the devil for his deception and devastation of the world, and His rebellion against God.

Revelation's tenth chapter is a divine decree with God's official signature. After the court action, there is an indictment, a sentence. Just before God's wrath in the last three and one-half years of Tribulation, the sentence is given. This is in contrast to the book before us in the fifth chapter which is not a decree, but instead a demand for justice placed in the hand of the prosecutor.

OTHER EXAMPLES

There are other Old Testament similitudes which gives us insight to the meaning and the contents of the book John saw in the hand of God. For instance; if we turn to Jeremiah chapter thirty-two we find some more familiar information. A piece of real estate which belonged to Jeremiah's family by inheritance had been lost by an uncle. This uncle sent word to Jeremiah that he is the one in the family who had the *"right of redemption"* and asks him to buy it back for himself (Jeremiah 32:7).

Upon paying the price to the lean holder of the property, Jeremiah said he was given the *"evidence of purchase"* or the Title Deed (32:11). It was "sealed according to the law and custom" (32:11). In other words, it was sealed and written on both the inside and out. The subscribing, or writing on the inside and outside of the book of the purchase was witnessed *"in the presence of witnesses"* (32:12). It was placed in an earthen vessel to be preserved for a long time when Jeremiah's possession would be witnessed again in the days of Israel's return and probably after the Assyrian invasion was over. In the fashion of unfolding prophecy, it also may refer to a greater fulfillment in the return of Israel in the last days (32:15). Archeology may someday dig up in Anathoth, or today's Amata, this evidence of purchase.

The Book of Ruth also gives excellent background concerning the redemption of the inherited promise. Naomi's husband died in Moab and she returned with her daughter-in-law to Israel. When Naomi found that Ruth had taken up with Boaz, she encouraged the relationship because Boaz was a kinsman and could redeem Elimelech's lost inheritance. The process of redemption by the goel, or *"Kinsman Redeemer"* is clearly illustrated for us there. We can go to Leviticus 25, starting with verse 23 and see where no inheritance was ever to be lost or sold. It can always be redeemed by the original family, as it is the Lord's land given to them by inheritance. In like manner and as it pertains to Revelation *"The earth is the Lord's, and all its fullness"* and He can redeem it as He wills. (Psalm 24:1, 1 Corinthians 10:28).

We know that *"all these things happened to them [in the past Old Testament times] as examples, and they were written for our admonition, on whom the ends of the ages have come"* (1 Corinthians 10:11). These comparisons compel as we try to understand the book that John saw in the hand of God.

It seems evident to the author that this book in God's hand, which will be placed in Christ's hand, has to do with the redemption of the earth, or the *"purchased possession"* in the final days of the Messianic Age (Ephesians 1:14). Jesus said, *"The meek...shall inherit the earth"* (Matthew 5:5). Since the whole book is about the revelation, or revealing of Jesus Christ and His return from Heaven at *"the times of restoration of all things,"* it seems logical and exegetically correct to assume that this book is the legal claim to all God has promised for both Israel and the Church (Acts 3:21). David said he could receive everything that God spoke in testimony and *"take them as a heritage forever"* (Psalms 119:111). They were taken from us and must be redeemed.

Information about the inheritance that Jesus is to redeem for both us and Israel can be found in several texts, namely 1 John 3:2, (Christ's power to redeem) Ephesians 1:13, 14, and Galatians 3: 16-18. For instance, when Jesus said "The meek would inherit the earth it was in agreement with the Old Testament promise (Matthew 5:5, Psalms 37:11, 22, Isaiah 57:13; compare Daniel 2:44 and 7:22-27).

There are two clear purposes for the Tribulation outlined for us in both the Old and the New Testaments. One, to punish the world and cleanse the earth from sin (See the 6 accomplishments of the Tribulation in Daniel 9:24). The second is to buy back from Satan that which has been usurped in the earth by his rebellion against God.

WHO IS WORTHY TO OPEN THE BOOK AND LOOSE THE SEALS THEREOF? (v. 2)

The question raises a challenge to the Hosts of Heaven. I am not sure it had ever been asked or considered as necessary.

God Almighty is the one offended and certainly worthy and able to dispel the ills of both the Satanic Kingdom and the transgressions of Earth. Had they ever quite understood the cryptic underpinnings of the plan for redemption? Had the angels understood it? Certainly Satan could only see through a glass darkly. Could he know that even before creation, a detailed record has been kept across the scope of time that recorded all of his offenses against God?

It is clear that the Jews, the sons of Abraham, only saw it in sketches. They had not understood the full impact of their ritual of sacrifice. They had not seen Christ's wounded-servant roll call. Only in Isaiah can any reference be found in the entire Old Testament which connects the Lamb with the dying Savior or Messiah (Isaiah 53). Their only vision of the Messiah was a Jewish King who would redeem their nation.

It must have been a jolt to the whole realm. Only the Church knew the answer, however, they did not know how it would work out. They only knew in advance that there was one who was, and is worthy. It would have to be Jesus Christ who alone distinguished Himself as the Savior and coming King.

We know in advance that Christ completed the plan of salvation on the cross when He cried "It is finished" (John 19:30)! The authority for Christ to take the book was complete on Calvary's cross. It became His right as the great shepherd of the sheep. We already knew what was declared that day *"Worthy is the lamb who was slain"* (Revelation 5:12). The church stood quiet in waiting for the revelation of their Savior while the rest of Heaven stood quiet in suspense as to what the answer would be, and *who* it would be.

The importance of the Book is made plain as we see an angel step forward and with a loud voice that rose above the thunderous sound of worship, challenge the worshippers and call them to pay special attention to what is going on at the throne. This angel was a direct representative of the Lord Jesus Himself.

In the court proceedings it has come time for an executor to be chosen who can execute the redemption of the purchase possession. You see, nothing is clearer in the New Testament gospel than the fact that the possession has been purchased. It already belongs to the Church and to Israel. It was purchased by the Blood of the Lamb and His sacrifice on Calvary. The price has been paid; it now must be executed.

There is one worthy in God's sight already sitting on the throne with God, but because of the challenge, Satan has offered to put himself in that place of honor (Hebrews 1:3). And because one third of the angels believed in and followed Him, God must clear these challenges to Christ's right of redemption. He has already been proven worthy of the title *Son of God* by the resurrection from the dead (Romans 1:4). By this Resurrection, He defeated all of the principalities and powers, placing Christ far above all of these heavenly powers and putting Satan's crowd to open shame when He was set on the right hand of God (Ephesians 1:20-23).

We know how those who oppose authority can raise all kinds of challenges to all legal sanctions. To settle Satan's challenge of Christ's rights to redeem and silence all opposition, these court proceedings in Heaven have to happen. Search must be made throughout the whole universe to see if anyone can claim that worthiness to step up and take the document of redemption. Satan and all of His angels were there and included in the search.

But, who is worthy? Throughout History, both in the realm of heaven among the angelic hosts as well as on Earth through the ages, hundreds of claims have been made for the Messianic place of redemptive right. To substantiate the worthiness of Christ alone, opportunity is given to all created beings in Heaven, Earth, and under Earth to come forth and show their claim of worthiness. What a privilege the Apostle John had—to be there when search was made and all of the self-proclaimed Messiahs who may have believed they were worthy throughout time were given opportunity to substantiate their claim.

WHAT MADE HIM WORTHY- WHAT WAS THE FINAL ACT OF REDEMPTION?

There was a final act on the part of Christ that clinched the plan of redemption. That redemption of not only man, but also of the Earth was not complete until Christ's final act. However, little is said about it and almost ignored. It is one of those secrets, or mysteries that is rather vague and we would not know about it except for the Book of the Revelation of Jesus Christ in Scripture.

There is an enigma in the blood sacrifice that was never made plain until the New Testament, and then it was brought to a clear understanding by these scenes which were before the Throne in Revelation: The blood sacrifice was well known and established as part of redemptions saga from the time of Adam, Seth and Enoch. When Adam sinned, God went to the flock and selected innocent lambs to be killed, or sacrificed, to cover Adam and Eve. In cryptic shadow, this act pointed forward to a time when a Lamb would come and who would take away the sins of the world. However, Israel, the Patriarchs, the Priests, or even the Jews quite understood the blood sacrifice and its full implication. They saw it as simply a way which God had established for their personal as well as national sins, to be taken away and atoned for. But they never made the application of it to the Messiah. They could not see the Suffering Savior and could not believe that their great King, the son of David would come in power and glory to smite the Gentile nations and usher in Israel's *Golden Age*.

Only in the shadows and types is this relationship hinted at. I think that we can say it was only enigmatically hinted at, and probably came closest to the surface of Messianic thought in the fifty-third chapter of Isaiah. Isaiah Himself, did not understand, and diligently searched His own writings. The Jews never could understand this chapter in Isaiah and still have not today. It is because they were and are still blind to a suffering Savior. Therefore, they never connected the sacrificial lamb to the man, the coming Messiah. This scene becomes an awesome revelation to every Jew. This is an amazing moment for all Jews. It is part of, and the beginning of Christ's revelation to the Jews. That is why John the Baptist's sudden statement at the baptism of Jesus was so startling, and almost ignored. No one understood the connection made between the Sacrificial Lamb and Jesus until John the Baptist at Christ's baptism, turned and said: *"Behold! The Lamb of God who takes away the sin of the world"* (John 1:29)! The Lamb of God is not mentioned in the other gospels. Christ is referred to as the Lamb of God only twice in John (John 1:29, 36, Acts 8:32, 1 Peter 1:19). We see that this concept was very new and vague to even the early Church, and it was not understood by the Jews at all, except to the Jewish converts. That is what makes this "Lamb as it had been slain" such a shocking revelation to everyone at the throne (Revelation 5:6).

As Jesus lived out His life, the Jews had not yet realized that the Sacrificial Lamb was actually connected to the Messiah, or a man. That is why the *Lamb of God* is never mentioned in Matthew, Mark, and Luke, but is forced upon our understanding by two references that only appear in John. In fact, it is only used four times in all of the New Testament. When we get to the Book of the Revelation of Jesus Christ, the Lamb is connected to Jesus. The title *Lamb* is used twenty-seven times, always referring to Jesus the Christ in Revelation. This makes the entire book an enigma to the unconverted Jews as well as the worldly mind. Part of the Revelation of Jesus Christ is the revelation of His connection with the Sacrificial Lamb of the Old Testament. What a revelation it was when out of the throne, and no doubt from the area of the Mercy Seat stood "a lamb as it had been slain" (5:6).

The connection between a human sacrifice and the sacrificial lamb of the ages is clearly and unquestionably made. When the Jews see this, the blindness in part will fall from their eyes and they will be converted by the thousands in the Tribulation period. However, a greater impact is made on the angels and upon Satan's host.

We now will follow the Lamb slain, from His resurrection to the throne in Heaven where He completed the final act of atonement. This part of His ministry was made plain but will not be realized until we see Him at the throne as a "Lamb who was slain" (5:12).

Right after the resurrection, Mary of Magdala came to the tomb. Jesus appeared to her there, and upon realizing who it was, she ran to embrace Him. He abruptly stopped her and made a mysterious statement. We ourselves do not understand Christ's next step in the redemptive act when He declared, *"Do not cling to Me, for I have not yet ascended to my Father"* (John 20:17).

What could He have meant by that? A few verses later Jesus met with the disciples and said to Thomas, *"Reach your finger here, and look at My hands; and reach your hand here, and put it in My side"* (John 20:27). There appears to be no problem at this time to touch Him. What is the answer to this puzzle? It is not a problem if we can see that the blood collected at the foot of the great altar after the lamb had been sacrificed, was not to be defiled by a human touch or anything else unclean until it had been carried to the Mercy

Seat and sprinkled there. Keep this in mind as we follow the Lamb from the Resurrection to the throne of God. Part of the sacrificial ritual of the Old Law was that the blood could not be touched until it was sprinkled with hyssop on the mercy seat.

We now go to Hebrews chapter one to follow the trail. Here Paul speaks of the Old Tabernacle and the blood sacrifice. Then He makes a startling bridge between the Old Testament sacrifice and the New Testament Lamb of God. First, He sets the stage for the transfer from the Lamb to the man, Christ Jesus:

> "...*who being the brightness of His glory and the express image of His person, and upholding all things by the word of His power, when He had by Himself purged our sins, sat down at the right hand of the Majesty on high*" in Heaven at the throne (Hebrews 1:3).

Then, in chapter nine of Hebrews Paul plainly connects the subject by writing:

> "*How much more shall the blood of Christ, who through the eternal Spirit offered Himself without spot to God, purge your conscience from dead works to serve the living God*" (9:14)?

Verse twelve gives the exact details:

> "*With His own blood He entered the Most Holy Place [in Heaven] once for all, having obtained eternal redemption*" by the presentation of His blood to God at the Mercy Seat in Heaven.

You see, beloved, it was the presentation of His blood to God in the heavenly tabernacle that made Him worthy. Hebrews 9:24 makes it abundantly plain:

> "*For Christ has not entered the holy place made with*

hands (i.e. not an earthly tabernacle), *but into Heaven itself, now to appear in the presence of God for us."*

I would like to have been there when He presented the blood; when He stepped from Earth into the throne room at the Mercy Seat in Heaven and presented his blood, unblemished to God. The enigma of the blood sacrifice is revealed as it is obviously connected to a man, the man Christ Jesus.

Hebrews 9:28 wraps this wonderful truth up and connects it not only to our salvation, but also to our hope at His second coming:

"Christ was offered once to bear the sins of many. To those who eagerly wait for Him He will appear the second time, [not to deal with sin], but [to bring] salvation."

Fast forward nearly 2000 years. The Church has just been raptured and is standing in the throne room waiting for Jesus to appear. They know who is worthy, for they have been following the Lamb. The title deed to their inheritance is in the hands of God and search is being made for someone worthy to take it. They know who is worthy, but He has not shown Himself yet. Then a voice from out of the throne announces that someone is found worthy. His connection to Old Testament cryptic enigma is pronounced:

"Behold, (be awestricken and amazed) the Lion of the tribe of Judah, the Root of David, has prevailed to open the scroll" (Revelation 5:5).

Christ's ancient connections clear back to the prophecy of Jacob, sets the stage for His cryptic appearance. As a lion He will conquer His enemies shortly, but right now, He has another image to fulfill. One of the elders of the church touched John, and in effect says "Hey John, you're missing it, look up" (5:5). John looks up from his weeping and records what he sees: *"In the midst of the elders, stood a Lamb as though it had been slain"* (5:6).

The Church understands. We have been preaching and teaching about the sacrificial lamb and its connection to Christ for nearly two-thousand years. The Jews, except for a few we know as the Messianic Jews, have not yet understood. But as He reveals Himself in the days of Revelation, they will know and be converted by the thousands, not to Christianity, but to Christ. They, along with the Church will understand Revelation 1:5: *"To Him who loved us and washed us from our sins in His own blood."* They are the ones, both Jews and Gentiles who *"come out of the great tribulation, and have washed their robes and made them white in the blood of the Lamb"* (7:14).

It is said of the Tribulation Jews that they *"overcame Him* (the Antichrist and dragon), *by the blood of the Lamb"* (12:11).

The same are those who escaped the hazards of the beastly kingdom because their names *were "written in the book of life of the Lamb slain from the foundations of the earth"* (13:8).

And, at the very eve of the Tribulation, they sing *"the song of Moses* (Old Testament) ... *and the song of the Lamb"* (15:3).

Beloved, Christ will still be our *"Lamb as though it had been slain"* clear into the New Jerusalem, and the New Heaven and the New Earth (5:6, 21:22, 22:1-3).

SEARCH WAS MADE

I have a vivid imagination and I will exercise it in the next few lines. I can imagine this great angel making the call which echoes through the universe, *"Who is worthy to open the scrolls and to loose its seals"* (5:2)? Verse three is short because it does not detail the next proceedings. However, there may have been quite a scene because anyone in Heaven, Earth, or under the earth in the sea or in hell, dared to step forward in their arrogance and lay claim. Great discussion may have taken place among the people in Heaven, Hell and from the earth, as to who might be worthy. Even though there may have been those who would venture a try at persuading the court of their worthiness, at the end of the search we are told that *"no one in Heaven or on the earth or under the earth was able to open the scroll, or to look at it"* (5:3).

Try to imagine that search. The first call was probably made to all of the angelic hosts:

"Michael, great captain of the host of God's armies; are you worthy?"

But Michael folds his wings about his feet in humility and submission, answering not a word.

"Gabriel, great messenger and chosen spokesman for God Himself, "Are you worthy?"

No Gabriel, you will not claim worthiness. Not a single inhabitant of Heaven would step up and claim the right. So then the search is moved to Earth.

"Abraham, father of faith, friend of God; are you worthy?"

Nay, Abraham would bow in contrition.

"David, the great King, worthy of an eternal throne; are you worthy?"

In the humility of Psalms, David would declare *"Bless the Lord, you His angels, who excel in strength, who do his word, heeding the voice of His word. Bless the Lord, all you of His hosts, you ministers of His, who do His pleasure. Bless the Lord, all His works, in all places of His dominion. Bless the Lord, Oh my soul"* (Psalms 103: 20-22)!

"How about you great Solomon, famous for your wisdom and prudence; are you worthy?"

Solomon would respond by referring to his final conclusion of the whole matter: *"Fear God and keep His commandments, for this is the whole duty of man. For God will bring every work into judgment, including every secret thing, whether it is good or whether it is evil"* (Ecclesiastes 12:13-14).

Not Paul, Peter, or James could step forward.

Even John, known as the disciple "whom Jesus loved," was sitting there watching the search (John 20:2). Would he step up and count himself worthy? Hardly! For among the writings of the life of Jesus, John was the only one who saw the eternal nature of Jesus and identified Him in his book as the Lamb of God (John 1:29).

Who of all you earthly messiahs and god-men who have gained great power among the people in claiming the right to redeem the human race and bring them into their millennium of peace and safety? For consideration, there would be Nimrod and Nebuchadnezzar.

Also there would be Cyrus, Darius, Alexander the great, Napoleon, and the like. What of the Pharaohs and Caesars? There would be emperors by the score who promoted themselves as god-kings with supposedly divine attributes, thereby fooling a whole history of generations. The rulers of the great Babylon, Persia, Greece, Rome; even the Holy Roman Empire with its holy Popes and Bishops could not claim the right. None of these could bring Paradise back. None among the great kingdoms and empires were found worthy.

Where are the distinguished philosophers—Plato, Socrates, Augustine, or Nietzsche? Where are their super-race and their Superman? Where is the existential who believes he can restore Paradise by indulgence? Out of all of this has come nothing but corruption and chaos. None were found worthy.

Where are the Islam Imams, or Caliphs and Clerics who are willing to destroy all heretics and lead the world into total apocalyptic chaos to bring its style of peace?

Where are the do-gooders of Earth now? Where are all those politicians who denied God His rightful place in society, and sought to set up their own version of the Millennium with *"peace and safety"* (1 Thessalonians 5:3)? They have voted God out of government, social and moral life, schools, universities, the political process, and even in many cases, out of the Church. Certainly none of these who are anti-church, anti-God is found worthy.

Where are all of the Bureaucrats and Government agencies who take the place of God in trying to *save* his world and perfect humanity? Where are the scientific gods who hope to lead us back to Paradise and believe, by medical practice, they can genetically manipulate us into Eternal Life, yet in the end, more diseases develop? Where are the inventors of gadgets and machines that only confuse and pollute? None of them will step forward. They have made their political and social brags; they have promoted their political and economic systems which they say would redeem if the rest of us would only cooperate. Where are the Humanists? They say we don't need God and Christ to perfect our race, and that they are far better able to run God's world than God Himself. Try as they may, they are also proven unworthy.

Let's make search among the New Agers and their promise of the Aquarian Age and the Golden Age through their Lord, the Maitreya—fifth Buddha. What of the occult secret societies with their world peace and council of wise persons? In all of their efforts to promote Lucifer as the real God, they have brought only confusion to their own ranks.

Our world is inundated with well-meaning goody-goods who say they have the answer to restore Paradise, but none of them will step forward to take the book, or scroll from Him who sits on the throne.

The search must include all of the leaders and designers of the host of *isms* in our day which promote their own brand of world peace such as Lenin, Stalin, and Hitler. And let's hear it for Communism, Socialism, and Fascism. How about them? They came close to destroying a whole generation with their own brand of peace. A call goes out to Mussolini, Tajo, and Castro. Step up now and answer to the King of the Universe! Where is the United Nations with its secretaries and diplomats? Are any worthy? The world is yet lost in spite of all of the efforts. Why can we not seem to get it together?

Nowhere among all the saviors of Earth, is found one who would claim the book and open its seals. None of the religious world or the Diplomatic world; the political world; the scientific world; the occult world; or even the do-gooders in the social sciences, could answer the call from the throne. What about under the earth where Hell has chided the Redeemed throughout history?

"Come on Lucifer! You have made your brags and pulled one third of the angelical hosts with you. You have subtly tried to organize your own world through the nations. Step up before the throne of the almighty God whose throne you promised to overthrow. Present yourself and your case against God and His Christ. Are you worthy? Step up here, face God, and take the book!"

Even Satan, in shame before his angels whom He lied to and deceived, stands awe-stricken and silent while the search is made, while those who had fallen into Hell by his deception mocked Him, the chief ones of Earth are raised up from their thrones and the kings of the nations say *"Have you also become as weak as we"* he that shook the nations (Isaiah 14:10)? No one in Hell can claim the right.

JOHN WEEPS BITTERLY

Among this entire vast crowd, no one dares come forth and face God and the Lamb with their righteous claims. No one can claim the rights of redemption of Earth and mankind. All of their promises were smoke-and-mirrors. No wonder John weeps. At this point it seems that all of his preaching and sacrifices of the ages is in vain. John, among thousands of others, paid a great price for redemption. He was boiled in oil and banished to Patmos. All seems loss!

Was it all to no avail? Was there no balm, no physician, or redeemer? Every nation, every government, every great leader, and even Christianity had tried to restore paradise. Until now in the court room, no savior had come forth. Our hearts break with John. I believe he knew that Christ would arrive, but did not know when.

Suddenly there is a commotion at the throne. Someone is moving to the forefront. Someone stands and moves toward the Father's outstretched hand. A great hush falls over Heaven. Anticipation fills the courtroom. Who would it be? Who would dare to make such a claim? Suddenly one of the elders of the Redeemed Church steps forward. Of course it would be given to an elder of the Church to bring hope to Heaven and to introduce Christ. It would especially be one of the churches leaders who would be selected to speak for the Lord Jesus Christ. His message is startling, like a high place in a sermon:

> "Do not weep. Behold, the Lion of the tribe of Judah, the Root of David, has prevailed to open the scroll and to loose its seven seals" (Revelation 5:5).

OVERTONES OF CHRIST'S COMMITMENT TO THE JEW IN TRIBULATION

The announcement of the angel not only pointed to the Redeemer as the Church would understand Him, but also carried overtones of the Messianic and Davidic covenant with the Jewish nation. It is worthy to note that the first identity of Christ was especially designed to connect Him with the ancient Messiah, who by earliest prophecies, would come from *"the Lion of the Tribe of Judah"* (5:5). He is not only the offspring of David, but the very root of the Davidic Kingdom to come.

We must pause and reflect on the fact that the Church has its first view of the Christ at the throne, and that view immediately calls our attention to His ancient roll as the anointed one of the Jewish nation to come out of the tribe of Judah. It also a harbinger heralding His soon coming work among the Jews during tribulation to build and establish their promised eternal kingdom of David.

Then Christ proceeds to be identified with the Sacrificial Lamb as well as the Lord and Savior, the Christ of the New Testament. We believe all of this was intended to tie together the sacrificial Lamb with the great King Messiah, a connection which the Jews had never made, and which blind-sited them, as we will explain later in this writing. From this point on, Christ identifies Himself with the Lamb throughout the rest of the Revelation.

John looked up from his weeping and declares, *"I looked, and behold ... in the midst of the elders ... stood a Lamb, as it had been slain"* (5:6).

A LAMB AS IT HAD BEEN SLAIN

As we have pointed out, who else would be selected to reveal the Lamb of God slain for the sins of the world? It should be no surprise to John, the one selected to record all of this, one who had spent his life revealing Christ. And who else would be more worthy to comfort John with the message of hope and point him to Jesus? It has been the mission of all of our elders for centuries during the evangelism of the world; to point the whole world to the Lamb and His sacrifice on Calvary, a Lamb slain.

He will forever be the Lamb of God. In the very end, connected to the New Jerusalem, and the New Heaven and New Earth, He is called the Lamb four times. Twice in Revelation 21:22-23, He is called the Lamb, the Temple and the Light of the New Jerusalem. In Revelation 22:1-3, He is on the throne. Oh, hallelujah!

THE LION OF THE TRIBE OF JUDAH

There is a cryptic image of the Lamb, as finally the Lion of the Tribe of Judah in Jacob's prophecy of the end-time for the tribes, and it is brought to our attention again here (Genesis 49:9). He is not only the *"Lamb as it was slain,"* but He is the Lion of the Tribe of Judah. Judah's whelp would be a conqueror that would rise up in the last days:

> *"The scepter [of the great king] shall not depart from Judah, nor a lawgiver from between his feet, until Shiloh comes; and to Him shall be the obedience of the people"* (49:10).

In the ancient Books of Scripture which we believe dates back to Adam, the concept of a Savior who began as the seed of woman (Virgo) and ended as a lion (Leo) was well known. Christ's final victory is seen as a roaring lion victorious over all of his enemies. I believe this is why Christ chose to identify Himself as the Lion of the Tribe of Judah here at His revelation. He first identifies with the hope of the Jew and the promise that is made to them. He identifies Himself with the seed of Judah and the Lion of that Tribe, prophesied by Jacob. Then He bridges the gap and comes to the Church and the New Testament where He is revealed as the Lamb that was slain.

Christ is seen as being full of wisdom and power, in the essence of the fullness of the Holy Spirit. Respectful fear and wonder must have consumed John as well as the silent and weeping Church, as Christ appears.

Oh beloved, if allowed to covet, I would covet the place where John stood. I would be there when the wounded Lamb of God revealed Himself before the throne in the presence of the Church. He has now come out of the cryptic shadows of Old Testament Messiahship and revealed Himself before all of Heaven and Earth. It would be wonderful to be chosen among the elders of the Church to make that eventful announcement to John the beloved. And what an eternal crescendo moment it would be when the Lamb, moved with all the compassion for the lost that had pressed Him to Calvary, and all of the love for the world which He was about to redeem, stepped toward the Father and took the Book from His right hand as declared in Revelation 5:7, *"Then He came and took the scroll out of the right hand of Him who sat on the throne."*

Oh beloved, I want with all of my heart to be there in Heaven some day when the Lamb takes the Book out of the hand of God. And I will be in the presence of the glorified Lord. Its symbolism means so much to me. You may be there too, by placing Christ in your heart and longing for His revelation. I can hardly wait until the time when, after the Rapture, we are gathered around the throne, and our blessed Lord and Savior takes the Book of our inheritance from the hand of the Father. No wonder we sing: "Oh I want to see Him, look upon His face; there to sing forever of His saving grace" (Cornelius, R.H.). No wonder we sing: "What a day that will be when my Jesus I shall see" (Hill, Jim). And, no wonder we sing: "I've a longing in my heart for Jesus, I've a longing in my heart to see His face; and I'm weary, oh so weary, as I travel here below; I've a longing in my heart for Him" (Masters, Dorothy).

We can understand John's weeping when we realize he has not yet seen the Lord. As far as I know, this moment at the throne will be our first glimpse of Him, "whom having not seen, you love; in whom, though now you see Him not, you believe, you rejoice with joy unspeakable and full of glory" according to the Apostle Peter's words (1 Peter 1:8).

I believe we are witnessing from Christ in Revelation the very time when the church and its elders, will first see Christ. It will be the time He steps away from His seat at the right hand of God; away from the Mercy Seat where He has been making intercession for us; where He presented His blood, without spot to God; and reveal Himself as the *"Lamb slain from the foundation of the world"* to redeem and restore all that has been taken from us (Revelation 13:8). Let me suggest that this is the beginning of the Revelation of Jesus Christ, for here begins His unveiling. First, He is revealed to the Church; later He will be revealed to Israel; and lastly, to the beast and the nations of the Antichrist.

ANOTHER HEAVEN-SHAKING CRESCENDO OF PRAISE

The rest of this chapter is given to a greater praise time than the one recorded in chapter four. The hosts of Heaven and the Church are silenced momentarily as the great angel cries with a loud voice, "Who is worthy to open the scroll" (Revelation 5:5). Of course, the Church knows immediately who is worthy, and when Christ takes the book, it will be the Church who first responds, breaking out again in praise. We have been used to responding in praise at every altar call, every sermon which exalts Christ, and at every evidence of His worthiness. We would certainly enter into instantaneous praise at this very worthy time. Revelation 5: 8 declares our response:

> *"Now when He had taken the scroll, the four living creatures four and the twenty-four elders, (the Church) fell down before the Lamb, each having a harp, and golden bowls full of incense,, which are the prayers of the saints."*

Can you see the familiar procedures here among the

saints? We are comfortable at falling on our face before the Lamb. We find ourselves there every time we worship. Singing is also very familiar to us as we worship. Of course, when we fall before Him, we always have the vials full of our prayers, which are a sweet-smelling savor to Christ.

And what a new song it will be when we sing at this Coronation:

> *"You are worthy to take the scroll, and to open its seals; for you were slain, and have redeemed us to God by your blood out of every tribe and tongue and people and nation. And have made us kings and priests to our God; and we shall reign on the earth"* (Revelation 5:9).

This time it is the Church that rises up and leads in the anthem of praise. Our praise catches fire throughout all of Heaven. Note that I am placing us in these scenes because of the Rapture, we will be there and take part. It is the promise of God and by the invitation of our Lord Jesus Christ. God the Father might have shouted, this is my beloved Son, *"let all the angels of God worship Him"* (Hebrews 1:6). The angels and the beasts, and the elders all joined in praise. What a prayer meeting that is going to be! We will be joined by tens of thousands, times ten thousands, and thousands and thousands of angels. And again, the old familiar song takes dominance:

> *"Worthy is the Lamb who was slain to receive power and riches and wisdom, and strength and honor and glory and blessing"* (Revelation 5:12)!

We never tire of singing praise and honor to our wonderful Lord as the Holy Spirit falls on us. Every creature which is in Heaven and on the Earth, and even Hell under the Earth (yes, so moving will this prayer meeting be in its exaltation to Christ, that even those in Hell will be moved) saying:

> "Blessing and honor and glory and power be to Him that sits on the throne, and to the Lamb, forever and ever ... and the twenty-four elders fell down and worshipped him that lives forever" (5:13-14).

When everyone else went home, the church was still there, lost in worship and praise, and awestricken in the presence of the Lamb.

Again, what do you suppose this challenge is going to do to Satan and His armies? As I have related before, this becomes a battle cry that shatters Hell's resolve. On the eve of his defeat, he hears a tremendous, victorious battle cry all over Heaven, and sees His cause begins to crumble, looking very small and unimportant. His angels will surely turn from Him at this point, for they have lost their faith in him, weakening their courage and resolve. Just after he is cast out of Heaven, he hears a loud triumphal voice, crying:

> "Now salvation, and strength, and the kingdom of our God, and the power of His Christ have come, for the accuser of our brethren ... has been cast down" (12:10).

No reason when Satan is cast to the earth, he will go with great fury, because he knows his time is short (12:12). But our triumphant Christ will encounter Him on every turn. Satan knows his time is up when he hears the Saints shouting around the throne, joined by the angels and living creatures.

What a wonderful Revelation we are enjoying as we consider this thrilling Book of the Revelation of Jesus Christ. AMEN!

CHAPTER 6

PREPARATION FOR JUDGMENT

"THE BEGINNING OF SORROWS"

Chapters four and five exclusively feature Jesus Christ at the throne in Heaven. This event takes place just after the Rapture. Earth is not mentioned in these two chapters. This takes place entirely in Heaven, therefore it is a *parenthesis*, or curtain closed as far as Earth is concerned. We will call chapter six, Act II, Scene I: The Pageant of Divine Justice.

CONTINUE THE SAGA OF THE LAMB AS THE LAMB OPENS THE SEALS

Chapter five ends with scenes in Heaven and chapter six begins at the throne, but brings us back to Earth. It will be important from this point on as we study The Revelation of Jesus Christ, to keep the events taking place on Earth, and those taking place over in the esoteric world of the Heavenlies clearly separated.

We continue the saga of *"the Lamb as it had been slain"* (Revelation 5:6). He has been found worthy as an Executor, to take the official court brief which documents the reason for the court case, and to open the seals. We must pause to notice that He is not only to be identified with the Lamb of God, but also to be the Lion of the Tribe of Judah, the Root of David. All of these emblems of redemption are said to have prevailed, making Him worthy to execute the case against the world, the flesh, and the devil.

All of this is so important in the long saga of God's plan of redemption. It began with the very first sacrifice of an innocent lamb to cover Adam and Eve's sins. It also shows that this Lamb standing in Heaven before the throne is a real earthly man, the Son of Man as Jesus referred to Himself. He is of the linage of Judah, Jacob's fourth son, and is of the House of David, the great King whose throne was to be restored in the last days and was to be everlasting. And notice, he is not only an off-spring of David, but he is a Root of David's house as well. It is very important for Him to qualify, not only as our Savior and Lord, but as the long awaited Messiah.

This brings the Old Testament promises made by God to Israel, together with the New Testament promises made by Christ to the Church, and in this one man is the final restitution of all things. It is the time that Israel will see the full impact of its sacrificial ritual as not only an act of atonement for the forgiveness of sin, but also a symbol of the Messiah and the blessing to the Gentiles that God placed in the Abrahamic Covenant. To this point, the Jews only understand the sacrifice to be atonement for their personal and national sins, and had not connected the sacrifice as representing their suffering Messiah, *"the Lamb of God who takes away the sin of the world"* (John 1:29).

It will also cause the Church to realize the impact upon its own redemption. This redemption is brought about by the Jewish sacrificial ritual as it is applied to the man Christ Jesus who, just as the Jewish sacrifice, took away the sin of the world. Oh beloved, there is such exciting depth in God's eternal Word and in the Book of the Revelation of Jesus Christ. Both the Church and Israel come into full realization of the impact of the Cross. No wonder great praise breaks out at the throne.

As we come to the sixth chapter of the Book of Revelation, we want to believe the humanist One World agenda that places its hope in human ability and effort, will bring the world to its final peace and safety, but without the help God or His Son, Jesus Christ. While championing the promise shown in Revelation, they disdain God and His Church, making every effort to cut both out of the plans for a New World Order. However, in reality, at the very time they are promoting peace and safety, sudden destruction threatens in every newscast (2 Thessalonians 5:1-3). Humanity faces its most terrifying hour. We have been promised by world planners a better world now for two hundred years, but rather than getting better, it is getting worse.

Even with all that the Church has been able to do through the Holy Spirit to convince men of sin, righteousness, and judgment to come, Satan has continued to persuade the whole world to rebel against God. He uses natural disasters, conflicts of culture, distress among nations, hate against Israel, and sin in general to make life absolutely miserable for the human race. The biggest battle of the ages is in the offing and yet we find Christ the Lamb still in the center of world events, warning us of coming disaster.

Satan has been allowed by God to effectively influence the World of Nations away from the true nature and purpose of the Lord. And, he has also influenced their attitudes toward Jesus Christ. They have been taught that Jesus was a great moralist, a great philosopher, a great teacher, and one to look back upon. But, they have not believed that He will yet bear great influence in their lives as a future coming King of Kings and Lord of Lords. Not being able to accept God's judgment to come on wayward nations, Satan has ignored that part of the truth, and therefore, they have suffered Satan's havoc caused by sin. With this lack of information, the worldly-minded have no understanding when they try to comprehend Revelation. They only see scary prophecy of future devastation, but do not see the real living Christ and His part to bring healing to the nations. They completely overlook Christ's part in the Revelation, and because some people in the Church too often follow the world's lead, they tend to overlook Christ as well, and fall for the hopeless end of the world spoof.

It will turn out good, even for the rebellious nations who have not yet realized that it is Satan who is leading them into the quagmire called Tribulation and Armageddon. When they realize that Christ is not a has been, but still very active and relevant in the cosmic warfare against Satan, they will move toward God. As sheep nations, they will begin to turn to God when they are taught the truth.

Satan is finally compelled to come out of His subtle hiding and forced to face the Lord openly (Revelation 19:19). The nations of people who have been deceived will suddenly realize that Jehovah is God (Psalms 83:18). And, Satan is a liar. I believe this revelation to the Nations is well represented by over 100 texts speaking of this final battle, and the saying found 85 times in the Book of Ezekiel alone, *"that they may know that I am the Lord."* When Satan is bound and His evil angels with Him, the nations will also turn to God. It is hard for us to conceive of such a sweeping conversion of the nations, but our mission work has not been in vain in these nations, and end-time prophecies by the score, support that hope. These include: Micah 4:2, Isaiah 66: 19 and 23, and Revelation 11:15. We will explore in detail the restoration of the nations in chapters 13-16.

THE OPENING OF THE SEALS

Once again, chapters six and seven are all about the Revelation of Jesus Christ. We must not fail to realize that even though He is not mentioned by name at the opening of each seal, from what we read in chapter five, we are plainly told that it is only He who is worthy to open the seals. Therefore, each of these seals will be opened by His hand through His Angel, or Messenger. No one except the Executor can open and execute official documents. These seals are the claims against the trespasser onto our estate and represent those things that have hindered the enjoyment of our full possession rights. Often in the Book of Revelation, just as in His earthly life-time, Christ Jesus slips behind a thin veil so that He is not readily recognized by those not looking for Him, but is easily seen by those who are. This should not be a surprise since Jesus said of His own departure to Heaven:

"A little while longer, and the world will see Me no more, but you will see me. Because I live, you will live also" (John 14:19).

The carnal mind searching the Book of Revelation will seldom see Jesus even when He is plainly manifest, because they are always interested in everything else except Him. Therefore, they certainly will not see Him when He fades into the background and is veiled. For those who are keeping Him in perspective, every "He" at the beginning of the opening of each seal, indicates His direct action throughout this chapter. He is named only in the first verse and the next to last verse, yet present at the opening of each seal (Revelation 6:16).

We have featured Jesus almost exclusively in the first five chapters, and Jesus will be featured in the next two. It is He who was in the midst of the churches noted in chapters two and three; He who was the object of worship in the fourth chapter; He who is opening the seals; and it is He who will seal the 144,000 on Earth, and the multitudes in Heaven in the seventh chapter. Anyone who knows Jesus as Lord and Savior and loves Him as friend and companion should surely not be fearful of the contents of Revelation. It is all about

Him and the impact He will have on our future lives. It is not all good for the rebellious world, but is all good and positive for those who know Him and have placed their trust in Him for their future.

Be reminded that I have shown in the chapter entitled *"Introduction"* that of the 404 verses in the Book of Revelation, 269 are all positive and supportive and without any hint of Judgment. Only 139 verses are involved with judgment and wrath. Two thirds of the book is about Christ and positive. When we finish chapter seven, we have dealt with all positive texts and very few verses about judgment. Even chapter six is only a warning of the things to come and is comparable to Jesus Christ's own words of warning in Matthew 24 which He called *"the beginning of sorrows, but the end is not yet"* (24:6, 8). I call these the *triggers to Tribulation*.

THE BEGINNING OF SORROWS

We see again that Jesus is the central theme of Revelation six and seven. The Tribulation and Armageddon are separate events from the *"beginning of sorrows"* which Jesus spoke of (Matthew 24:8). This chapter speaks of what Gary Stearman called the Pre-Pre-Tribulation sorrows. He believes that the four horsemen are not part of the Tribulation per se', but instead are harbingers of the coming Tribulation (Stearman, Prophecy in the News). Dr. Stanley Horton, an outstanding Bible expositor and Editor of Sunday School curriculum for nearly 40 years, agrees. They are signs and previews of what is to come. No actual part of the Tribulation has yet begun in this chapter. In these revelations, just as in Christ's teachings in Matthew 24, Luke 21, and Mark 13, we are simply being forewarned of what is soon to come.

Actually, we can say that our first exposure to these sorrows was shown to us as far back as the books of Ezekiel and Zechariah. We will explain this connection later. However, the clearest and nearest expose of these disastrous events came from the lips of our Lord during the Olivet discourse. We will mainly expound upon the connection between the twenty-fourth chapter of Matthew and the sixth chapter of Revelation.

THE FOUR HORSES AND MATTHEW 24

The conditions on earth that are causing the need for Christ's intervention in world affairs are listed here in cryptic symbolism. They are the seals that give us previews of what is to come; what Satan and His nations have in store for the world leading up to and including the first half of the Tribulation. The wrath of God in the second half of the tribulation does not come until the eleventh chapter.

There are comparable texts in the Old Testament which will help us to understand the four horses. In Zechariah 6:1-8, we have what appears to be the Old Testament counterpart to the horses in Revelation. The four horses in Zechariah match the four horsemen in Revelation in that they both show uncontrollable destructive powers in the hands of Satan, the God of this world. They are in the hands of four powerfully destructive angels who are the spirits of destruction as shown in Revelation 7:1-2. These four angels of the spirit of destruction are hindered from starting the Tribulation until the 144,000 are sealed on Earth and the Redeemed are seen in Heaven. They come forth from standing before the Lord of all the earth. Some believe this to be our God, but who is the God of all the earth? Satan is the God of this world, but Jesus is Lord of all the earth. Then there is the corresponding text in Ezekiel 14:13 where four punishments are spoken of. These four punishments also closely match the four horsemen of Revelation. When the land has sinned, God lifts His blessings and we fall prey to Hell's devastating work through ungodly and evil men.

THE FIRST HORSE: Even though the rider sits upon a white horse, he cannot represent our Lord Jesus Christ (Revelation 19:11). Never does Jesus set forth to conquer with the force of a bow. Nor does our Lord conquer at all. He only wins with love. The Antichrist will appear as the Messiah of Peace and Safety (1 Thessalonians 5:1). Daniel reveals this peace initiative by the Antichrist (Daniel 8:25, 11:21 & 24).

The lust for conquest has nothing to do with Jesus, but is rampant in the world. The World Order spirit of the Antichrist is depicted here. He is *"the Prince who is to come"* (Daniel 9:26). In the Matthew 24 discourse, we note that Jesus' answers His disciples inquiry of, *"When will these things be? And what shall be the sign of your coming"* (Matthew 24:3). Christ speaks of the Antichrist spirit: *"Take heed that no one deceives you. For many will come in My name, saying, 'I am the Christ' and will deceive many"* (24:4-5). He was speaking of the first horse that represents the spirit of the Antichrist in the world just prior to the Tribulation, and is referred to in many of Daniel's texts and also in the writings of Paul (I John 2:18, 22, 4:3 and 2 John 7, Daniel 7, 8; 2 Thessalonians 2:3-8). This Antichrist spirit brings spiritual confusion and lies to the Earth. It is interesting to see how this spirit in the end time will be a religion that uses the sword to conquer. Jesus, in his Olivet discourse as recorded in Luke 21:9 mentions terror. The greatest wars in our time are wars among religious groups, especially the Islam uprising that is spreading an Antichrist spirit all over world, and is conquering by the sword. I believe it is possible that the first seal suggest that the first hindrance to reclaiming our inheritance is going to be partly from Islam. It is also worthy to note that the only religion not involved in any kind of warfare is Evangelical Christianity.

There are worthy suggestions that this horse of war may even play into the Russian invasion of Israel which I believe will be at, or near the beginning of the actual Tribulation, and will excite the other wars in Israel during that same time. It may be what Daniel 11:44 speaks of when troubles out of the north and east will come against the Antichrist. It may be what causes the World Order to decide that a covenant with Israel over Jerusalem and the Temple Mount is necessary to bring world peace (Daniel 9:27).

THE SECOND HORSE: The second horse is a red horse. Jesus says that he has power to take peace from the Earth. This horse is red because he is bloody. It is prophesied here that terror, murder and violence, hate crimes, and an uncontrollable revolution will break out among men the world over, especially in the Middle East. Again, this is not the work of the Lord, but it is allowed to come upon wayward humanity by Satan because of their grievous trespass. The Lord came to bring peace, not to take it away. It is someone else that is taking peace from the earth, namely Satan. This fits perfectly with Christ's next warning in Matthew 24:6, *"you will hear of wars and rumors of wars ... these things must come to pass, but the end is not yet."* Again, he is not causing the wars, but they are a scheduled part of the last-day sorrows. It will be the struggle by the European World Order to bring the peace and safety. This will force them to submit to a demonic Roman prince and his consortium of ten kings to take action in the Middle East.

Most of these *"wars and rumors of wars"* are the result of what Jesus further gave us in Luke's version of this same Olivet discourse (Matthew 24:6). Jesus said that *"there will be signs in the sun, in the moon, and in the stars; and on the earth distress of nations, with perplexity, the sea and the waves roaring; men's hearts failing them from fear and the expectation of those things which are coming on the earth, for the powers of Heaven will be shaken"* (Luke 21:25-26). The original language says "the abilities which are in the atmosphere shall be released." Two atomic scientists have told me that this is a perfect description of an atomic blast.

Jesus speaks about the distress of nations in relationship to the second horse. As we continue to wrestle worldwide with the threat of nuclear war, stress increasingly grows among the nations. There are at least twenty-nine nations either with a nuclear bomb or else have the capability of building one, and some of those are rogue nations. We have come to the place where no nation in the world trusts any other nation. No one knows who is a trustworthy friend and who is a secret enemy. As trust breaks down, the level of stress goes up, so we not only have wars, but also rumors of wars that keep every nation nervously on alert. All of this is taking away from the earth, the peace and safety that the World Order of Europe and America through the UN, are striving so hard to accomplish. Interestingly enough, as we relate this stress of nations to the end time scenario and see it as a sign and a warning, we find that the word *distress* is actually the Greek word, *sunocho*, which literally means "pressing together, or gathering together out of fear." It perfectly reflects our world's attitude since WWII. In order to protect ourselves, we began organizations between states such as the UN, and also organizations within the organizations such as NATO. Now we have Warsaw, SEATO, CENTO, and others. Actually, there are ten major binding organizations of nations today. These groups of nations are pressed together out of fear.

The word *perplexity* is from a Greek word *Aporia*, which means "no way out or no answer." Of course, our high level diplomats and humanist dreamers would disagree that there is no way out, because they still believe they can manipulate the world into a One World Order of total peace and harmony. Surely we must thank them for their efforts, but Bible believers know the end of this age, and that there will be no way out until Christ destroys the Devil and sets up His Kingdom.

Next, Jesus said, *"the sea and the waves roaring"* (Luke 21:25). A natural understanding of this statement would say this means Tsunami's, but prophetically the language is used to indicate people, multitudes, nations, and tongues (Revelation 17:15). The term *roaring* indicates uprisings, riots, insurgence, revolutions, etc.

When we put together what Jesus said, we come up with a very interesting insight into these wars and rumors of wars, the red horse, and the evil angel to whom it is given to take peace from the earth. Nations in distress are growing weary and press together out of fear, but are finding no answers. Our efforts to democratize the world, especially the Middle East, is only aggravating the stress and encouraging insurgency against every organized government. Riots, rebellions, and revolution are everywhere. Somewhere, sometime, a nation is going to be forced into using the Atomic Bomb, and Tribulation will break loose. Peace is being taken from the earth even right now in our day.

THIRD HORSE: The third horse is a black horse. Everything about this horse indicates natural disasters that bring worldwide famine. This coincides perfectly with the next warning Jesus gives us in Matthew 24:7. There will be famines and pestilences—plagues and disease which are the natural aftermath of wars, especially nuclear war. There are also earthquakes and other natural disasters spoken of here, which cause the above and many other things that are not directly caused by man or by Christ.

We know by Scripture that man's wayward ways and his serious mismanagement of the earth lends to many of the natural disasters. It is political corruption that is causing starvation, and not because the land cannot feed its inhabitants. All of the aid that is sent to the countries of the world by the churches of the United States alone could effortlessly ease hunger. However, it is being stolen by corrupt leaders and never reaches the people. "Hurt not the oil and the wine" may indicate that there will be controls; and policies will be put in place to keep these sorrows from disturbing the luxurious living of the ultra-rich.

Jesus' warnings, or signs given in Matthew 24 and Luke 21, coincide with this black horse as more sorrows are forced upon us. These natural disasters again are not an act of God, unless you want to be specific as to what God you refer to—God Jehovah, or Satan who is the god of this world. The world cannot discern between their God--the God of this world, and our God—the one and only true God.

According to this world, all disasters are acts of God. They have not yet recognized that their god is a different God than ours, for they will not believe the Bible record. Satan has kept himself well camouflaged in the esoteric so that they who barely recognize the unseen world do not know him. "God told me to do it" is a catch phrase that has covered every kind of religious atrocity such as the Crusades, Pogroms, Inquisitions etc., to every excuse for murder, rape, incest, and the immoral and illegal. They all say that "God made me do it." It may be true, but it may have actually come from the god of this world.

I do feel, however, that the devil gets the blame for a lot of things that really comes from "old Ned." Someone once said that they found the devil crying and when asked why, he replied, "I get blamed for everything." Not to take away from the fact that the devil, when allowed by God, does use natural disasters to torment people. See the Book of Job where all kinds of natural disasters were worked by Satan, even to destroy Job's family.

There are also natural disasters perpetuated by nature.

Nature has certain natural processes set in order at creation and after the flood, which are not direct acts of God, although God can always change the course of nature for His use.

At a time when people were using the disasters of nature to debate this question, Jesus had some excellent insight. In Luke's gospel, referring to an act of political killings, Jesus said, *"Do you suppose that these Galileans were worse sinners than other Galileans, because they suffered such things? I tell you no; but unless you repent you will all likewise perish"* (Luke 13:2-3). Then Jesus refers to a very natural disaster; a tower fell during construction and killed eighteen men. Again Jesus asks the disciples if these men were sinners above all others. Take note that in no sense of the word does Jesus indicate, or even hint at these disasters coming from God. Things happen in this imperfect world. God must always allow disasters, but He does not cause them. The God of this world causes them.

Jesus said they would increase as we draw near the time of the end. We are certainly seeing an increase in natural disasters all over our world. These are the *beginning of sorrows*.

FOURTH HORSE: The fourth horse is a pale horse called Death. The term *pale* in the Greek is *chloros* which means *green* and translated that way everywhere else except here (Dake). Death rides a pale green horse, and Hell follows with him. Power was given to this fourth evil spirit to kill with natural disasters, hunger and death by disease, and wild beasts. It refers to great pestilences that follow war, especially nuclear war which clearly prophesied as part of the Tribulation time of trouble. In other words, the same as all these other horses, the results of all there disasters brings death and hell. We are encouraged here that it will only cover one fourth of the Earth, therefore the first part of the Tribulation will not be worldwide. It is our belief that this part of troubles will only involve the Middle East, and the current situation seems to support this thought.

There was a strange phenomenon recorded by MSNBC and carried on the web through YouTube under the title www.*Palehorserider.com*. While the MSNBC cameras were panning the riots in Egypt during January and February of 2011, suddenly a ghostly image of a pale green horse and rider appeared on the screen. He moved through the crowd from left to right and ascended upward toward the upper right side of the screen and disappeared from sight. As we have said, this image can be seen by going to the web site: www.*palehorserider.com*.

What to make of it is a bit enigmatic, but widespread opinion matched it with the fourth horse of Revelation. This horse was a warning of death, Hell, and destruction to come in the Tribulation. I do not feel it was a fraud or manipulation of film, as it was actually the worldwide report by MSNBC. It is not likely that they would manipulate the report in any way favorable to the Bible or prophecy. It very well could be an apparition sent by God to warn the world that these events, the Muslim Spring, are precursors to coming judgment.

Jesus used the word *pestilence,* meaning plagues. We have been suffering, or at least on the verge of suffering from all kinds of strange diseases. Then there are the earthquakes and their related Tsunamis in divers places. Other matching and related texts will mention violent weather, cyclones, and tornados.

Naturally someone could ask, "How are all of these related to the end times?" There is another thought that we should relate while talking about natural disturbances. There is a sense in which even the physical earth is affected by the end-time phenomena. Paul introduced us to this relationship between the physical earth and the redemption of the Church in the eighth chapter of Romans.

Paul said that even the old earth is groaning, travailing,

waiting (Romans 8:22). Waiting for what? He then connects this groaning and travailing directly with the time of our redemption (8:23).

There is a natural "groaning and travailing" of the earth itself. There are natural laws that have caused the old earth to be tired out. It is suffering from the breakup of the deep at the time of the flood; deep fissures in the earth's crust cause the plates to grind against each other and cause earthquakes. They are growing more frequent as the time of redemption of all things is at hand.

We can see that earthquakes were first caused by man's sin. Before the flood, Earth was perfect. It was not broken up nor shattered. When the *"fountains of the great deep"* were broken up at the time of the flood, the shell of Earth was shattered, causing great plates to grind against each other (Genesis 7:11). Natural forces are increasing agitation of the plates, and as the old Earth tires further, the plates are grinding more frequently and with greater force. Jesus, knowing all things and understanding the groaning of the earth in the last days resulting in the increase of earthquakes, relates their increased frequency to the days when He will be manifested and will manifest the Church. He is not causing this grinding of the plates, but foresees their frequency and warned us of the beginning of sorrows. We see now, that these disasters are not caused by Christ or God, but are allowed as the natural result of man's sin and the wrath of Satan. Like Satan's attacks on Job, they are allowed by God, but not caused by Him. According to Ezekiel, they are allowed because of a nation's grievous trespasses against God. They were only foreseen by Christ and are signs of the end of the age.

They are the things contained in the seals, which has and is taking away the paradise that God originally intended for us. They are things which must be broken in order to bring back our full inheritance. Peace cannot come until they are dealt with by our wonderful Lord, who asks that we trust Him, be patient, and wait for His coming.

After warning of these very things, Jesus plainly said that these were the "beginning of sorrows"(Matthew 24:8). Note again, these are not part of the Tribulation, which starts in the eighth chapter. Nor is it Armageddon, which comes later. They are however, presages, forerunners of those sorrows. As such, they are signs to us that the worst is yet to come. Therefore, we have these four things taken from us by Satan, that old Dragon:

1. Religious Truth 2. Peace 3. Prosperity 4. Health

A world saturated by Antichrist's lies, truth has failed; it has fallen in the streets (Isaiah 59:14). Truth is hard to find today. An earth covered with famine, and the world plagued by sickness with death riding the globe, are the things that Christ must deal with in the opening of the seals. How can Christ, either in His discourse on Olivet, or in His Revelation in the sixth chapter of Revelation, be any plainer?

OLD TESTAMENT HARMONIES OF THESE LATTER-DAY DISASTERS

FOUR SORE PUNISHMENTS ALLOWED BY GOD- Ezekiel 14:12-19

Ezekiel is given insight into the very matter of: *"When a land sins against me by persistent unfaithfulness, I will stretch out My hand against it"* (Ezekiel 14:13). This refers to the people of a nation and not the land itself; for the earth per se, cannot sin. It might be better understood by saying, "when any nation or people sin against me" rather than "when a land sins against me." We also note that the sin has to be to the stage of grievousness to warrant these sore punishments.

God is long- suffering, not willing that any perish, but that all come to repentance (2 Peter 3:9). These things are designed to bring us to repentance. The Book of Revelation calls on people to repent eleven different times, four of them during the Tribulation.

Then God says, *"I will cut off its supply of bread, send famine on it"* (Ezekiel 14:13). or *"if I cause wild beasts to pass through the land,"* (ibid v.15) or *"if I bring a sword on that land,"* (ibid v.17) *"or if I send a pestilence into the land..."* (ibid v.19). He is speaking of the same four sorrows represented by the four horses of Revelation. God said that our wickedness and trespassing can be so serious that if Noah, Daniel, or Job were there in that generation, they could but deliver their own souls.

FOUR HORSES OF ZECHARIAH 6:1-8

In Zechariah, chapter 6, we are shown four chariots with teams of horses coming from between two mountains of brass; and the colors of the teams of horses are comparable to the horses in Revelation, chapter 6. We are told that they are red, black, white, and bay. Zechariah says that these are *"four spirits of heaven who go out from their station before the Lord of all the earth"* (6:5). They are all destructive forces from destructive spirits.

We see these as the same four spirits that stand at the corners of the earth holding back the four winds of the earth (Revelation 7:1). And, we read in Revelation 7:2 that, to these four spirits or angels, it was given to *"harm the earth and the sea."* These are the Tribulation forces which are restrained until God seals His people on Earth. It seems there is a difference between the four horses of Revelation six and the four teams of Zechariah six, but there is also plenty of evidence that they are related in the long scheme of prophetic fulfillment, all of which we do not yet understand. These horses in Zechariah may represent the work of these spirits through time, whereas the four horses of Revelation six represent their final work to bring the pre-Tribulation woes or sorrows—the warning signs.

Some would question the comparison of these four teams of horses, and also question any relationship between Ezekiel's four, sore punishments to the four horses of Revelation. We can certainly allow that question. But when we understand that all of the things that were taught to these past generations were *"examples ... written for our admonition, on whom the ends of the ages have come"* and that most of the final days of man are already shown to us in the Old Testament, then the bridge is not hard to make (1 Corinthians 10:11). One of the great discoveries I have enjoyed through these sixty years of study, has been to find the hundreds of comparisons between the Revelation text and the Old Testament. As we have said, only by carefully considering Old Testament counterparts, can we understand Revelation because all Old Testament prophecy points and builds toward these final events of the Revelation of Jesus Christ.

NO TRIBULATION THROUGH THE 7TH CHAPTER OF REVELATION

In our view, there is no action in this Chapter as far as Tribulation is concerned. This is the pre-warning that humanity should be noticing, which is to warn them of the coming Tribulation. These are not ills placed upon the people by God. They are natural disasters caused by man's rebellion and directed by Satan in His last day frustration, because He knows his days are short:

> *"Woe to the inhabitants of the earth and the sea, for the devil has come down to you, having great wrath because he knows that he has but a short time"* (Revelation 12:12b).

In Satan's demonic hate for humanity as the objects of God's love, and now having realized that His plan to overthrow God and usurp total control of man is futile, he is causing all the *Hell* he can.

This is what Jesus warned us of in Matthew 24 when He listed the very same things that we see in the breaking of the seals. Each seal broken reveals what Christ must overcome to buy back our heritage and to bring back our paradise lost. In his book entitled, *Our Destiny*, Dr. Stanley Horton teaches that the sixth chapter of Revelation is anticipatory and shows what will happen, but nothing actually happens at this time. Everything is on hold until the 144,000 are sealed.

THE 5TH SEAL AND THE SOULS UNDER THE ALTAR - CRY FOR JUSTICE

Here, we hear the demand for judgment upon the wicked world, and who would be more worthy to press upon God and our Lord than the martyrs. This cry goes all the way back to the martyrdom of Abel who was killed simply because he sacrificed a lamb in atonement for his sins. He was killed by his ungodly brother, Cain who resented his true style of worship. His blood has been and still is, crying from the ground (Genesis 4:10; Hebrews 11:4). God seems to place the guilt for all blood that has been shed in murder upon the shoulders of every murderer (Matthew 23:35). The blood of all the martyrs are placed upon the Antichrist's great harlot of Babylon and its wicked money system (Revelation 18:24).

These are crying out for reconciliation and are asking *"How long O Lord, holy and true, until You judge and avenge our blood on those who dwell on the earth"* (Revelation 6:10)? The prayer of martyrs for Christ through all time must be heard and will be answered. The eleventh chapter of Hebrews gives us a brief insight into the suffering of the martyrs: *"And others were tortured, not accepting deliverance, that they might obtain a better resurrection"* (Hebrews 11:35). All of our resurrections are going to be glorious, but God has reserved an even better resurrection for these special people. They must include the tens of thousands who are suffering martyrdom today. There is such a heart-warming and beautiful similitude shared with us when we see that they are *under the altar*. We cannot miss the meaning. Again we must consider the Old Testament background for this observation. It was under the great altar where blood of the sacrifice was caught in a bowl and then carried to be used in the sprinkling of all holy things (Exodus 29:12; Leviticus 4:7).

It was the blood that redeemed us from sin. Every innocent lamb that died on the altar through the long weary years of temple work had their blood collected from under the great altar. This blood reached across the centuries to Calvary. It pointed to the Lord Jesus Christ and His atoning love. The cry of these martyrs' blood includes the blood of Jesus Christ.

And there is yet a cry from the altars of churches around the world. It is a cry for mercy. The Church does not cry for vengeance, but for mercy. However, the blood of martyrs does. God will eventually judge it as a cry for vengeance in response to the millions that are suffering martyrdom even today, from "those who dwell on the earth" (Revelation 13:14). There has been two million Christians martyred in the Soviet Union, six million Jews who were martyred during the Holocaust, and six million Christians have been martyred for Jesus' name since those days. Their blood cries out to the Lord, and is joined by the great multitudes of martyrs from the hand of Islam today.

The world has never been and never will be a safe place for the Jews or the Church. Oh yes, the blood of all of them is crying out from the ground, but there will be justice. The heart of God gets heavier by the day, and the cries of the martyrs becomes increasingly louder, but our long-suffering God waits in this time of judgment as He waited in the days of Noah (1 Peter 3:20). Finally it could be retained no longer and the world perished. Christ is *"not willing that any perish but that all come to repentance"* (2 Peter 3:9). The day of the Lord will come. Christ will soon destroy a powerful, destroying angel and bring wrath down upon everything and everyone who has persecuted His people, Israel and His Church. Live for Him as you can, die if you must, but as the song says, "until then," we must go on singing, loving, forgiving, winning, and rejoicing.

There will be justice in the earth, but *"though it tarry, wait for it; because it will surely come"* (Habakkuk 2:3). There will be a time when all wrong will be made right. The prophet Isaiah says that right now, *"justice is turned back, and righteousness stands afar off"* (59:14). However, Luke leaves us these words of our Lord:

> *"And shall not God avenge His own elect, who cry out day and night to Him, though He bear long with them? I tell you that He will avenge them speedily"* (Luke 18:7-8).

Jesus said even *"now is the judgment of this world; now the ruler of this world will be cast down"* (John 12:31).

It is well for us to remember as we study these texts in the book of judgment, that all judgment and the fulfilling of justice has been placed in the hands of Jesus, *"for the Father judges no one, but has committed all judgment to the Son"* (John 5:22).

As He hears this cry from the martyrs from under the altar, He is even then preparing to administer justice and judgment, even the judgment of that great day (Jude 6). These martyrs were told to rest. It is not easy to rest during troubling times, but it reminds us of Paul's very apropos admonition in 2 Thessalonians 1:4-10. After discussing all the glory in us, and our patience and faith in persecutions which will eventually bring the righteous judgment of God, verse five says that God will repay through the Tribulation, all those who trouble you (1:6). He then says He for the troubled to rest. We are and will be at rest when:

> *"... the Lord Jesus is revealed from Heaven with His mighty angels, in flaming fire taking vengeance on those who do not know God, and on those who do not obey the gospel of our Lord Jesus Christ. These shall be punished with everlasting destruction from the presence of the Lord and from the glory of His power, when He comes, in that Day, to be glorified in His saints, and to be admired among all those who believe"* (2 Thessalonians 1:7-9).

Thank our Christ for the rest with which we can have with the martyrs until and during the time of His Revelation and Judgment. Oh, thank God that during the Tribulation time, we will be with Christ and He will be exalted, and admired and glorified in His saints.

We are told that these were slain *"for the testimony which they held,"* but not for the testimony of Jesus (Revelation 6:9). They are evidently others not of the Church, possibly righteous Jews and Old Testament Saints, as well as Christians. However, the white robes are assurance that they will be joined with the redeemed.

Many have asked if these are Christian martyrs, and if so, why then are they not already joined in the Rapture? Are these the Old Testament martyrs who are not part of the Church but were slain for the testimony which they held? Where is this *altar* and where are they retained? The altar would probably be in the temple which is in Heaven. We will study the heavenly temple in chapter eleven comments.

They do not seem to be Christians, nor do they seem to be part of the body of Christ. The Church is already around the throne. As has been observed, the Church does not cry for vengeance. Our cry is for mercy. If our prayers were reflected here, we would be praying for the Lord to come. If we are saved, we love His appearing and would be praying for His coming Kingdom (2 Timothy 4:8). However, they have some relationship to the Church, because they are told to rest until "their fellow servants and their brethren, who would be killed as they were, was completed" (Revelation 6:11). This indicates that those yet to be killed in the Tribulation period were part of them. It is evident from this text that there will be salvation during the Tribulation.

HIDING FROM THE FACE AND THE WRATH OF THE LAMB

The sixth seal is open and suddenly we are able to look into the final tragedy which will be necessary to win back our inheritance and fulfill God's promise and Christ's purpose toward us and the Jews. We are seeing into the very near future, probably only days or weeks away at this point reflected in the writings. This is a preview of coming events that causes *"men's hearts [to fail] them from fear and the expectation of those things which are coming on the earth, for the powers of Heaven will be shaken"* (Luke 21:26).

Here again we see that the things in this chapter very closely resemble the signs of the coming Tribulation in the Olivet discourse.

All of this is Tribulation language taken from scores of references to the same time and event from the Old Testament Prophets. This is a world of leaders who have willfully rejected Christ and now realize our message has been true. Evidently by this time, these horrors will be so near that all of *"the kings of the earth, the great men, the rich, the commanders, [and] the mighty men,"* realize that their greatest efforts of peace and safety have come to no avail (Revelation 6:15). The dream of Islam's preparation for the coming of the twelfth Imam Mahdi, will have failed and total chaos will come. There is no stopping it at this point. All diplomatic efforts have failed and the only preparation for disaster is to hide and cry. Note that there is no cry of forgiveness for mercy. They are so hardened and set against Christ that they will not turn to Him, but there will be no place to hide. Even though the common people are mentioned, the main cry is coming from the leadership of our world, and it is these same categories of leadership who very soon will face Christ at Armageddon.

No mention of the Church is found here. We have nothing to hide in the face of Jesus, nor do we fear His wrath. And, we are not going to participate in it (1 Thessalonians 5:9).

STILL UNREPENTANT TO THE END

Note that, since our theme is "Christ" in the Revelation, somehow at this point the world will have realized that the wrath that is to come, is coming from their transgression of God's program for Israel and the Middle East, and it has offended Christ. They are hiding, not only from the great Tribulation disaster, but from the face and wrath of the Lamb. It is sad, but some people are not looking forward to Heaven or being with Jesus. Even at the final hour when judgment is evident and pending, they still are not repentant. It is amazing how hard and rebellious the human heart can get. People would rather the rocks and mountains fall on them than to face the Lamb.

We used to sing a song like this:
"And oh what a weeping and wailing, as the lost were told of their fate; they cried for the rocks and the mountains, they prayed but their prayers were too late."

They now see that Christ's judgment will be swift, unexpected, and unstoppable. They see the coming plagues of the fifteenth and sixteenth chapters. These plagues that are coming will be very similar to the plagues of Egypt, and they will have the awe of the darkness which surrounded the cross (Exodus 10:20-23; Matthew 27:45; Zechariah 14:1-7).

The sixth seal shows the parallels that we find all through the Book of Revelation. We see them that were already fearful for the days to come, but their cry represents a cry that will echo throughout the Tribulation. The final end of this crying will be clear down to the Battle of Armageddon at the end of the Tribulation. By the time Armageddon comes, their cries will have turned to blasphemy. They have been given opportunity all throughout the Tribulation to repent, but as they were not repentant in the beginning of sorrows, neither are they repentant in the end of sorrows. That hardness of heart has only grown harder, and now unrepentant. They still prefer to be killed, rather than face the Lamb, or Christ. Proverbs warns us about *"he that is often reproved and hardens his heart, shall suddenly be cut off and that without remedy"* (29:1).

There is more good news to report. Right at the time when the great Tribulation breaks loose and everyone at that time has come to know it, we are told that the four destructive angels who have been given power over the Tribulation times are held back and not allowed to let their dastardly wind blow on the earth. They are held at bay until another mighty angel comes from the East, and (Hello!) Jesus will return from the East. This angel has the *"seal of the living God"* in his hand (Revelation 7:2). All seals are in the hands of, and are administered by the hand of Christ. He cried with a loud voice to catch the attention of all spiritual, esoteric, and earthly forces, (every force to whom it is given to hurt the Earth) that they are to not *"harm the earth, the sea, or the trees, till we have sealed the servants of our God on their foreheads"* (Revelation 7:1-3).

No one but Christ could hold back all the forces of Earth and Heaven and especially the forces of Satan and Hell. This is another one of those *not-so-obvious* appearances of Christ's direct involvement. However, He is there in the person of an angel of the Lord's presence.

Thank God, even on the verge of Tribulation, Christ is still in control. The whole message of the Revelation of Jesus Christ is His eventual overcoming of all of Satan's wiles and the Tribulation time. Jesus said, "These things I have spoken to you, that in Me you may have peace. In the world you will have Tribulation; but be of good cheer, I have overcome the world" (John 16:33). PTL!

CHAPTER 7

HOLDING BACK TRIBULATION

SEALING HIS SERVANTS

In this chapter we will again find plenty of information to exalt Christ, just what we are looking for in our study of the Revelation. It may seem that we are giving extra prestige to Christ in this writing, but I am convinced we cannot over-do His exaltation, eminence, and grandeur. Because this book is all about His Revelation, we may assume that every part of it reveals Him. With all of our best efforts, and with all of our deepest research, we will never touch on the entirety of the glory that is due Him. We could never plumb the *"width and length and depth and height to know the love of Christ which passes knowledge; that you may be filled with all the fullness of God"* (Ephesians 3:18-19). Romans reaches for that depth:

> *"Oh, the depth of the riches both of the wisdom and knowledge of God! How unsearchable are His judgments and His ways past finding out"* (11:33).

I have no illusion that I could ever reach those depths in our exaltation of Jesus Christ. Christ must be all in all—Christ in the Church and the Church in Christ.

Beloved, I am impelled to remind you again, that at this

point in our study of Revelation, we have not yet encountered anything that should be scary, especially to anyone who knows and loves Jesus Christ and has placed their trust and hope in Him. We have been told about the beginning of sorrows. We have only seen a brief preview of coming Tribulation troubles and thereby simply have been warned of a time of sorrows to come. We have been shown that even at this late date just prior to judgment, Christ our Lord is still in control and all of our fears, if any, are unjustified. Still, Christ Jesus is caring for His children and He is showing mercy to those who love Him.

Four references to Christ are made in the seventh chapter of Revelation. In each case, He is keeping and sealing Jews from wrath, and walking among His beloved Church in Heaven where they are kept during the coming Tribulation.

PROOF THAT THE TRIBULATION HAS NOT STARTED

This again is proof that the Tribulation has not started, but is being held back from happening until God's anointed and protected are sealed from it. We have seen in the seals—what it has cost us and what we have lost, when Satan commandeered our paradise and took over our world. He stole the rights of Christ, destroyed our peace, our health, our wealth, and our environment. He has taken from us these things by His domination of the armies, kings, potentates, and political, economic and social powers of this world.

Notice that the seventh seal is not opened until the beginning of chapter eight. This chapter shows a curtain drop between the actions on Earth and events taking place behind the scenes in Heaven beyond Earth's dimension. The actual battle cry of the Tribulation does not start until the eighth chapter. This plainly demonstrates that these are events prior to the beginning of the seven-year Tribulation. These events are not on Earth, nor are they seen by the earth. This is more of the unseen events going on in the Heavenlies and surrounding the Judgment. These are events taking place between Christ and the four angels which are captains of destruction in Satan's kingdom. These are the ones who Paul spoke of as the *"principalities, against powers, against the rulers of the darkness of this age, against spiritual hosts of wickedness in the heavenly places"* (Ephesians 6:12).

According to the companion texts concerning the four horses, each of them in chapter six represents a spirit which goes forth before the Lord of the whole Earth (Zechariah 6:5). It can easily be postulated that this *god* before whom they stand, is the god of this world. Be that as it may (and there could be a legitimate question), these four angels are four spirits standing on all quarters of the earth, holding back four winds (destructive forces) that they not blow their destructive powers upon the earth until they are allowed to do so. These four angels may be the first four trumpeting angels who will blow their trumpets at the beginning of the Tribulation (Revelation 8:1). These four destructive forces or winds relate to the spirit of the four horses of chapter six.

Second Thessalonians 2:7 deals with this Tribulation time, the wicked one, and the mystery of iniquity involved in it. We are told that only He who withholds, will withhold until the right time. We can again thank God and honor our Lord Jesus Christ who is still in control and able to hinder or withhold these judgments.

GOD AND CHRIST NEVER OUT OF CONTROL

I cannot fully support the conspirator people, and even some Christian commentators who place so much emphasis on the inevitable takeover of an all-powerful World Order. Their writings and preaching dwells so heavily on the beastly systems that are without question developing in our present world, that they implicate there is just no controlling its inevitable takeover. Now I know, as most of us do, that Satan plans to totally rule the world through a World Order of his own style, using the Antichrist, whom Daniel calls the willful king (Daniel 11:36). We know that these plans have been in the making in esoteric circles of very powerful men and demons, and that they are trying to place man totally in control of this World Order. Their plans fit perfectly into the Beastly system exposed in chapter thirteen of the Book of Revelation. What is often left out of commentary, the preaching about this book is that certain men under Satan's control, have been trying over 300 years to build a World Order, but something just keeps holding them back, hindering them. (2 Thessalonians 2:7). It is we the church who are standing in the way of Satan's plans.

God and Jesus Christ are never out of control of these things. They will only allow a brief seven-year period of Tribulation trouble, and that only to deal with Satan and rebelling humanity and reveal their power and control to the Church and Israel. I will show that when we deal with the beast in the thirteenth chapter and relate these texts to the companion texts in Daniel, the Antichrist and His One World Order spoof will never be in total control and will only control part of the world. Our comfort and assurance is that our Christ, the captain of our salvation, is and always will be in control. He will withhold judgment until the right time and bring it to a sudden end at His discretion (Matthew 24:21-22). The term cut short means to bring to a sudden conclusion. The Tribulation will not be caused by God, but will be allowed after the rapture of His saints and the sealing of His faithful Jews.

Power and absolute control over these evil forces are explicitly given to us to understand. We read in the second and third verses of chapter seven about another angel, who has the power to command control by holding the evil spirits back until He releases them. He also has the power to seal or place the name of God in the forehead of those whom He chooses to mark for protection. This can only be Christ.

Here again is another one of several places in Revelation where Jesus chooses to hide His personal identity behind a veil of obscurity and appear as an angel of God's presence. There can be no doubt however in my mind that this is our Lord Jesus Christ. Who else has power over evil? Who else can withhold the devil and His forces? And who else has the seal of God in His hand to mark those that are His? We read in Paul's writings:

> *"Nevertheless the solid foundation of God stands, having this seal: 'The Lord knows them that are His,' and, 'Let everyone who names the name of Christ depart from iniquity"* (2 Timothy 2:19).

This seal or mark belongs to and will be placed upon all who are preserved by the Holy Spirit of promise which is *"the guarantee of our inheritance until the redemption of the purchased possession, to the praise of His (Christ's) glory"* (Ephesians 1:14).

THE SEAL OF PROTECTION FROM THE TRIBULATION GIVEN BY JESUS

We have an excellent example of this seal in two Old Testament texts. The first we will point out is the seal placed upon Cain. So much misunderstanding comes from a casual reading of the text in Genesis 4:10-16. Cain is called to account for his brother's blood and God places a curse upon him which he admits is very grievous. He pleads for some mercy in his fallen condition lest he and his whole race be wiped out. Our merciful God, even in the time of Cain's deserved curse, puts a seal of protection upon him:

"... therefore, whosoever kills Cain, vengeance shall be taken on him sevenfold. And the Lord set a mark upon Cain, lest anyone finding him should kill him" (4:15).

We find that Cain's mark, as so many have taught, was not a curse and had nothing whatsoever to do with Ham and Canaan, but was a loving mark of protection. So, here in Revelation at the final moment before the Tribulation, Christ lovingly places a mark upon His own. Some may say that these Jews, like Cain, have no right to God's protection, but Christ will choose whom He seals and whom will not be sealed.

There is a second example from the Old Testament text in Ezekiel. We find at a time when Jerusalem was doomed for destruction from the hand of God's judgment that men were sent out. Three bore the sword of destruction, and one carried the mark of God's protection. This man who carried the mark was told to:

"Go through the midst of the city, through the midst of Jerusalem, and put a mark on the foreheads of the men who sigh and cry over all the abominations that are done within it" (Ezekiel 9:4).

The slayers were instructed to slay everyone except those bearing the mark (9:6). By these examples all the way back to Cain, we see God placing a seal of protection upon those who He chooses to protect. In Revelation 7:2, Christ follows that policy just before the trumpets of Tribulation are blown upon the world.

This seal is reflective of an Old Testament text found in Ezekiel. There we read:

"As I live, says the Lord God, surely with a mighty hand, with an outstretched arm, and with fury poured out, will I rule over you ... I will make you pass under the

rod, and bring you into the bond of the Covenant" (20:33, 37).

He is speaking of "the time of Jacob's trouble, but he shall be saved out of it" (Jeremiah 30:7). In the Tribulation, Israel will pass under the rod, but God continues: *"...I will purge the rebels from among you, and those who transgress against Me"* (Ezekiel 20:37-38). The fury which will accompany the Tribulation will also be accompanied with the mighty hand and outstretched arm of God's protection on those who will be in the bond of the Covenant, and from whom by this fury, will purge the rebel and the transgressor. This *is* the exact purpose of the Tribulation.

Therefore the Tribulation is held back and nothing in the earth, sea, or even the trees (God is also concerned about the trees) *"till we have sealed the servants of our God on their foreheads"* (Revelation 7:3; see also 14:1). To hurt not is referring to the tragedies that will come with the blowing of the trumpets as told to us in Revelation 8:7-11.

THE REMNANT OF JEWS FROM EACH TRIBE SEALED AND KEPT DURING THE TRIBULATION

There are twelve thousand, or 144,000 Jews from each tribe. Twelve is the perfect number of selected authority—twelve tribes, twelve apostles, etc.

These are referred to as the servants of God (Revelation 7:3). They were not serving God at the time of the Rapture, or they would have been raptured with the Church. The Church is made up of both Jews and Gentiles. These will be saved in the revival referred to in Joel 2:28. They became servants of God after the Rapture and just prior to the Tribulation. We will speak more of their conversion in our comments in chapter twelve. Some have erroneously tried to teach that the whole Book of Revelation is allegorical. This false view of

Revelation actually began as far back as St. Jerome.

In order to accommodate the Popes of Rome, he was pressured to twist his idea of the Book of Revelation. It was the philosopher, Augustine however, who taught that Revelation should all be spiritualized. This has produced an "A-millennial" view; that is, to believe that Revelation is all in the past and has no futuristic or literalistic interpretation at all.

Chapter seven blows that theory all to shreds. It is indeed, very real and literal. These 144,000 are real people in our real world today who may not know it, but they have a great destiny. The *"multitudes that no man can number"* is very real, in a very real Heaven, with a very real Jesus (7:9).

THEY ARE SPECIFICALLY SAID TO BE JEWS

These are specifically said to be Jews. They are not Gentiles in any sense of the word, but are of the seed of Abraham and 12,000 from each Tribe of Israel. They are purely Jewish of a remnant that only God can mark and know. It is my persuasion that they are among the strictly covenant keeping Jews who are very serious about their relationship to the God of Abraham, and are keeping the commandments of God, even though they are mixed in with the commandments of man. They are Orthodox who observes the tradition of the elders. However, their hearts are pure and although they may be blind in part, they are true to what they know. The part of their mind that is not blinded by ritual and tradition of the elders is very well informed.

I am convinced that they are deeply Messianic in their persuasion, and are committed to studying the Messianic prophecies. They exist today, mostly in Israel, but may be found throughout the world. Some may be Orthodox and some may even be in the Sages, or Cabala, which is a strange and secret sect of the Jews. I am persuaded that I have met some of them in many of my trips to Israel and in association with the Jewish people, by the very essence of spirit that I sense when I am with them. Neither I, nor any man would dare try to identify them, either by certain sects or by individuals, but somewhere among the millions of Jews today there are 144,000 whom God has touched. God alone knows who they are and is preparing them right now to be the evangelists of the Tribulation time, and beyond to the Millennium. In addition to them will come two witnesses that will stand up to the Antichrist's Regime (Revelation 11).

We will visit them again later in our study of the Book of Revelation in chapter fourteen. Every reference to the Jews in the rest of this Book shows them always kept, protected, and blessed by God and by Christ. We will follow their path to the final day of Israel's glory under the throne of the Kingdom of David.

DAN'S NAME MISSING: The number chosen from all Israel at that time will be exactly 144,000, with 12,000 from each of the Tribes of Israel. The exception to this is that the tribes of Dan and Ephraim are missing. Joseph replaces his son Ephraim and Levi replaces Dan. Evidently at this time, Levi's work is done and will not need to be separate from the Tribes of Israel any longer. This is because the priesthood is dissolved and resides now in Christ, our High Priest. Ephraim will be included in Joseph and remembered (Jeremiah 31:20).

Dan is said to have leaped into obscurity from Bashan and disappeared from the Tribes of Israel (Deuteronomy 33:22). Dan dwelt in Lachish at the foot of Mount Herman with Bashan on the south flank of Herman. Today, it is the Golan Heights. Evidently, Dan migrated toward Damascus and northward where he mingled with Europeans.

The Tribe fell into gross idolatry, and was known to be completely corrupt. In Deuteronomy 29:18-20, God specifically pronounces a curse on the tribe that falls into idolatry and says that he would blot their name out of the records of Heaven. In 1 Kings 12:29-30, we have insight into the serious nature of the breach of Dan and Ephraim. It is said that the idolatry under Jeroboam, which split the Tribes of Israel into Judah and Israel, was centered in Dan and Ephraim.

It is interesting to follow Dan in the records. He is not listed among the tribes that returned from Babylon with Ezra, and he is not listed among the tribes sealed here in Revelation. However, he is listed back among the tribes in the Millennium (Ezekiel 48:30-35; Revelation 21: 12). Some would question whether his name would be found on one of the gates of the New Jerusalem, but we are specifically told that each would have a name of one of the twelve tribes of Israel. Israel is Jacob, and Dan is one of the twelve sons of Jacob.

We will visit them again later in our study of the Book of Revelation. Every reference to the Jews in the rest of this book shows that they are always kept, protected, and blessed by God and by Christ. We will follow their path to the final day of Israel's glory under the throne of the Kingdom of David.

THE TRIBULATION SAINTS IN HEAVEN AND ABOVE THE TRIBULATION

Now we come to more of the exciting, positive verses in Revelation. There is no worry or sense of fear in these scenes. They seem to be totally oblivious to any of the beginning of sorrows, or the Tribulation which is happening on Earth. They do not even seem to realize that a host of Jews has just been sealed from the Tribulation. What I am saying beloved, is that there is a place by God and in the presence of the Lamb, where all earthly cares and concerns are behind us. There is only joy and peace and praise in God's presence and in the presence of Christ, our Savior. Even David caught a sense of this peace when he said, *"You will show me the path of life; in Your presence is fullness of joy; at Your right hand are pleasures forevermore"* (Psalm 16:11).

Here in the presence of Christ is a *"great multitude which no one could number, of all nations"* (Revelation 7:9). They are in an extremely covenanted place that you and I can hardly wait to enjoy. They are *"before the throne and before the Lamb"* (7:9). They are clothed in white, already mentioned three times in Revelation 3:5, 3:18, 4:4, and will be mentioned again in 19:8. Just a comment: The way of salvation is always open and will still be there after the Rapture. It was offered to these people in their persecution and will always be open as long as Jesus Christ is Lord. To Jews and Gentiles alike it is always so, *"That whoever calls on the name of the Lord shall be saved"* (Acts 2:21). In every reference to the Church in Heaven, they are dressed in white robes. They also have *"palm branches in their hands,"* a symbol of great victory which was first mentioned in Psalms 118 (Revelation 7:9). It speaks of our future entrance into Jerusalem with the King, and repeated again at the triumphal entry of Christ into Jerusalem. Perhaps they are just practicing for another and greater triumphal entry to come when Christ again leads the armies of His saints through the Eastern Gate of Jerusalem.

Again, as in chapters four and five, they are joined by the angels in song. We should not be surprised that the angels are singing with the redeemed. We are told that they sing in Heaven every time one of God's redeemed is called home (Luke 15:10). And God said, *"let all the angels of God worship Him"* (Hebrews 1:6). They are joined with the elders and the living creatures, all who *"fell on their faces before the throne and worshipped God"* (9:11). And here we have a repeat of the great praise service we enjoyed in chapters four and five.

The singing of the redeemed with the angels here, in verse 15:2-3, and with the 144,000 during the Tribulation period

(14: 2); also, from the great cloud of witnesses in Heaven, which he can see and hear, will be so effective during the chaotic upheavals, that It will completely disarm the devil. As He fights His last battle against God and Christ, He becomes more and more exoteric in His hate and wrath. The Raptured saints, the martyred saints, the 144,000, and the two witnesses joined by the angels and living creatures in the presence of Christ, will raise such a victorious Heaven-rattling praise, that it will become a challenge to Satan's company. He and His armies will be completely discomfited.

Once again, where do we find Jesus in these very crucial days of His life? As always, He is found among His beloved people. He evidently has to go and come from His other involvements, but He always returns to fellowship with His people. Verse 7:17 shows Him feeding them and leading them into living fountains of water. It is the same Jesus whom we are told, that will eternally wipe all tears from our eyes. He is blessing them with that same touch.

WHO ARE THEY?

There is some variety of opinions as to who this multitude is and how they fit into the total scheme of things. Among the commentators and commentaries we find some difference, but not enough to take away from the basic concept. Whoever they are, they are definitely part of the great company of the Redeemed, who follow Jesus and the Lamb wherever He goes. They have the same spirit of love and praise as all other saints, and will enjoy an eternity with Jesus our Lord and Christ.

It is pretty clear from this text and others in this book, that they were killed after the Rapture of the Church (14:13, 15:2-4. 20:4). Evidently, they would not take the Mark of the Beast, or his number or name, for they were martyred (Revelation 13:15). It is also clear that they had been raptured, or they would not be in Heaven and before the throne. Further translation after the Rapture is imperatively mandatory to fulfill (6:9-11, 7:13-14, 19:8).

REDEEMED DURING THE GREAT TRIBULATION

Some of the best known prophecy teachers believe that this multitude in verse 9, are martyrs out of the Tribulation period. They are those that are spoken about to the souls under the altar, who would join the martyrs later. This interpretation is strengthened by the very clear statement that they *"[came] out of great Tribulation"* which is thought to be speaking of the Tribulation period (7:14). To strengthen this position, the only other uses of the term *"the great Tribulation"* is definitely speaking of the seven years of trouble (Matthew 24:21; Revelation 2:22, 7:14). This position is very legitimate. There are seventeen other uses of the word *Tribulation* which represent the great persecution that we go through in our regular Christian lives. However, this seems to refer to the great Tribulation of Revelation.

The problem I have with this interpretation is that I have a strong belief, and have clearly established it, that the Tribulation does not start until the eighth chapter. This shows these saints being sealed before then. Again, this could be a preview, but it is plain that these are already in Heaven.

PART OF THE RAPTURED CHURCH

Another strong position is that these are the same multitude that was raptured in chapter four. They are the Church—the body of Christ, shown sealed above and out of reach of the Tribulation. The only objection to this idea is again the term *great Tribulation*. The word *tribulation* is used seventeen times in the New Testament to speak of the tribulation we have in this world. And certainly, the Church has gone through very extreme persecution throughout all of its history. This wicked devil-led world does not love the Church and has no place for it here.

GREAT PERSECUTION IN LAST DAYS OF THE BEGINNING OF SORROWS

I want to postulate a third position. Could these be out of a great persecution time that is clearly prophesied right at the coming of the Lord for His Church; or possibly just after the Rapture and before the actual Tribulation starts? Could it be this is still in the period that Jesus spoke of as the beginning of sorrows, and the period projected by the fourth horse, which death and Hell followed?

Jesus specifically spoke of a terrible time of persecution and death during the time of sorrows, and said *"he who endures to the end shall be saved"* (Matthew 24:13).

Here are some previous verses showing that there will be great persecution and death during this time:

> *"Then, (during the times of sorrows) they will deliver you up to tribulation and kill you, and you will be hated by all nations for My name's sake. And then many will be offended, will betray one another, and will hate one another ... And because lawlessness will abound, the love of many will grow cold"* (Matthew 24:9-10, 12).

Now, I am sure these were not just casual words from our Lord Jesus Christ. Just as all of the rest of these disasters mentioned in the times of sorrows, certainly this warning should also speak to us.

TODAY'S PERSECUTION OF THE CHURCH BY WORLD ORDER, AND BY ISLAM

Jesus told us all along with these texts on pre-Tribulation sorrows that, *"this gospel of the kingdom will be preached in all the world as a witness to all the nations, and then the end will come"* (Matthew 24:14).

This has and is being accomplished today by our faithful witnesses around the world. Much of that witness is coming from within the nations themselves along with the witness of our missionaries. The spreading of the gospel into all the world where millions of very special Christians are in ministering and living in hostile nations, Christianity is persecuted for their witness.

We do not hear it reported on world news networks. In fact, persecution of Christians around the world is not only unreported, but is willingly covered up. For political convenience, religious persecution is ignored and hidden to the eyes of the world, especially where it involves Muslim persecution of Christians. Because we never hear of it, we are often ignorant of how serious it is. We are so tied to the news that we think if it is not heard it on the news, it is not happening. In many cases, not even our religious organizations can mention it out of fear of reaction against our people abroad.

Let me assure you that one of the greatest periods of persecution in the history of the Church is happening today. Tens of millions of Christians, especially in Islam nations, are being massacred, brutally killed, harassed, and driven into refugee camps with their possessions stolen. This is the very kind of persecution troubles that Jesus said He would keep us from. In the hereafter, we *"shall neither hunger anymore nor thirst anymore; the sun shall not strike them, nor any heat"* (Revelation 7:16). These are the kind of sufferings that even right now, millions of Christians are suffering all over the world, driven from their homes and divided from their families, shifting the best they can with little or no hope from the ungodly world which is ignoring them. These persecuted Christians during the time of sorrows which are spoken of, are going through great tribulation, and are probably the ones spoken of here in Revelation chapter seven.

WHOEVER THEY ARE, THEY ARE WITH JESUS CHRIST AND GOING TO THE NEW JERUSALEM-
and they are safe from the judgment to come.

My point is, that it is possible this multitude that no man can number, are those martyred right after the Rapture and before the actual Tribulation begins. I have no problem thinking that they may be Tribulation saints who were killed during the Tribulation, for I am fully persuaded that there will be conversions by the thousands all during the events that surround the rest of the Book of Revelation. And neither do I have a problem with those actually being added to the Raptured Church itself, because all that is said about them could clearly fit that category as well. However, I submit this last possibility for consideration. Be what it may, the wonderful message must not be lost in our inquiry for their exact identity. The fact is, whoever they are, they are part of the great redeemed throng who are around the Throne of God.

The glorious revelation is that Jesus Christ is still prominent in the story, and is again found faithfully caring for, and loving His Saints. It is also obvious that these with all the redeemed of the ages, are going to be led into the New Jerusalem where we are promised the same promises that are made here, *"... lead them to living fountains of waters. And God will wipe away every tear from their eyes"* (7:17).

This is one of those *meanwhiles* and parallels that will harmonize the Book of Revelation. The seventh chapter reaches all the way from before the Tribulation to the end of Revelation, and takes us to the New Jerusalem. While Hell is being destroyed and the world judged, Jesus Christ is busy among His people, preparing them for the New Jerusalem. All of this is *"so that I may rejoice in the day of Christ"* (Philippians 2:16). Hallelujah! Amen! PTL!

CHAPTER 8

EXECUTION OF JUDGMENT

FIRST HALF OF THE 7 YEAR TRIBULATION

PRELUDE TO THE TRIBULATION- ACTIVITY BEHIND THE SCENE IN HEAVEN

We have been behind the scenes and in Heaven throughout all of chapters four, five, six, and seven, while in an interlude as far as Tribulation action is concerned. We have been on hold since the end of chapter five and even up to that point we only have previews of coming events given as each seal is opened. Each time one is opened, it exposes the destruction of Satan and the things that Christ must overcome as He redeems what Satan has usurped from us concerning our inheritance.

Everything was put on hold, while in chapter six we previewed the sorrows to be brought upon us by the dragon, the devil, and his angry nations. The beginning of chapter seven shows us that behind the scenes, Satan's four demonic destructive forces were withheld from judgment until the 144,000 Jews on Earth were sealed, and also a brief view into Heaven. There we see the redeemed Church in Heaven in the presence of the Lamb and protected from the time of Tribulation. Those four destructive forces where bound and held in the Euphrates River, and not loosed until they were part the demonic deluge of chapter nine (Revelation 9:14). Continuing their destructive force, they make way for the

Kings of the East to cross the Euphrates River at Armageddon (Revelation 16:12).

Now, at the beginning of chapter eight, action on Earth is still on hold and the first six verses are again, scenes for the preparation of judgment in Heaven. All of the former actions from chapter four have been in Heaven and are preparations for judgment. No actual action has happened on the stage of Earth as transacted thus far to Earth's Tribulation, and will not until after verse 8:6. At this time, the first half of the Tribulation actually starts.

Meanwhile, while preparation for judgment has been going on in Heaven and behind the scene, the stress of nations on Earth has continued to grow and the threat of nuclear war is the main cause. Diplomacy is breaking down and the Middle East has grown more volatile. Israel has become isolated from the international community. Pressure on Israel has reached a breaking point; and on earth, violent weather has taken its toll. Earthquakes are increasing in intensity, and persecution against the Jews and the Christians have reached an all-time high. The time of the beginning of sorrows has come. They that *"[endure] to the end shall be saved"* (Matthew 10:22).

Soon deception, famine, pestilences, earthquakes, and violent weather will ride into the human scene, and death and Hell will have its heyday. (See Chapter 6 about the 4 horses). Peace will be taken from the Earth, and human failure will demand God's intervention if there is to be any hope at all (Matthew 24:22).

CHRIST OPENS THE TRIBULATION WITH INTERCESSORY PRAYER

The first three verses of chapter eight are again behind the scenes in Heaven. Action on Earth does not come until the end of the verse five. Here we are seeing Heaven's

EXECUTION OF JUDGMENT 243

preparation for the start of the seven years of the Great Tribulation known as the seventieth week of Daniel's vision. The curtain has been down on our pageant since the end of Act II in chapter six. The curtain is still down. All of this is in Heaven beyond the world's view. In verse five, the curtain goes up on what we will call, ACT III.

"HE" OPENED THE 7TH SEAL (v. 1)

Again, the first one we see and the one taking center stage as the leading character is Christ. We look again into Heaven where the scroll from chapter five is held in the hands of "a Lamb as it had been slain;" "the Lion of the Tribe of Judah, the Root of David." To those who are able to tie together all of the Old Testament Messianic texts and the promise of an eternal kingdom of David, these titles have great meaning with this description of Christ at the throne . They represent all of the eschatological hopes of the Jews and of the Church built on those hopes.

Who else is worthy to open the seals as shown in chapter five? Who else is the exalted angel of judgment in control of directing the seven trumpets which will announce the events of the first half of the seven years of Tribulation? God has handed all judgment to Christ (John 5:22). Who else can open the legal documents and make judgment about them other than the appointed Executor and Executioner, the one who fulfills the execution of the estate? With the opening of the seventh seal, the book is now open and the terms of redemption exposed. The first thing we see Christ doing is finishing his God-given task; the opening of the final seal, making final preparation to execute the judgment. As we will see, the seventh seal contains all of the seven trumpet announcements, and the seventh trumpet contains all of the vials, so in a sense, the opening of the seventh seal sets the whole scenario into action because it includes the seven trumpets and the seven vials to come. Who else as an intercessor, carries our prayers to God? Who else but the great High Priest can take coals from the altar and cast them to Earth? There is no logical doubt but that this great angel is Christ himself, or a Theophany or Epiphany of Him.

SILENCE IN HEAVEN FOR ONE HALF HOUR

Here is proof that women were not present at this time! Forgive me, but I have these lighter moments often, not really apropos. Now back to reality. The time of one-half hour must be from the earthly perspective, for there is no time in Heaven. What is the cause and reason for this silence in Heaven?"

It is the silence of *awe*.

It is so awesome and so fearful at this moment that no one can speak. The angels, the living creatures and the Church, all stand in awe. It is the beginning of the greatest time in human history. It is the beginning of the Great Day of the Lord, the beginning of the Revelation of Jesus Christ. It is the time spoken of since the ancient prophets began to foretell of that Great Day when the seed of woman would crush the head of the Serpent (Genesis 3:15). All of the Prophets, the Psalmists, the Patriarchs, and the Wisdoms have spoken of this Day. It has been the longing of every Messianic hopeful of the ages. It has been the subject I suppose, of no less than a million sermons and studies throughout the Church age. The prediction of it has cost countless thousands of lives, and mothers have wept over their slain. The blood of righteous martyrs has cried out in the ears of God ever since Abel's blood was shed in a religious argument. Every innocent lamb slain for sacrifice has added to the suffering, pointing to this time. All of this has built anticipation among the godly of the Kingdom of Christ. Now the throne is set, the Judge is seated, the Executor chosen, the Jews are sealed on Earth, and the Church is protected in Heaven. The time of *"restoration of all things"* has come (Acts 3:21). The brief has been placed on record, and Judgment is ready to start.

It is the silence of *expectation.*

What an overwhelming moment when seven angels, under the direct commission of Christ, step forward to sound. It is the time that all of the dreams and hopes of every Godly person has waited for. It entails not only the restoration of all things, but the long awaited return of our Lord and Savior, Jesus Christ.

It is the silence of *mourning.*

It is an awesome time for all of the Saints and the *knowing* Jews, but it is an awful time for the unsaved Earth and the regions of Hell. *"It is a fearful thing to fall into the hands of the living God"* (Hebrews 10:31). But at this juncture in time, it would be worse to fall out of those hands. Even though we rejoice, the Saints and the Angels still mourn the world's lost sinners and the cost of this hour.

It is the silence of *Anticipation.*

The time must have been from an earthly perspective and not a heavenly, for there is no time in Heaven. The thirty minutes of silence in Heaven must have seemed like an eternity. What is there about waiting and expecting that is breathtaking? However, God has been waiting through all of time with longsuffering and patience for this supreme moment, and has longed for it through the ages. Christ died in expectation of this time. The Church, those who have faithfully waited with expectation, especially those precious few who have given themselves to long hours, days, and years in study and prayer are in longing in anticipation of this hour.

It is the silence of *Reverence.*

It is reverence for the fact that they stand in the presence of Christ in His greatest hour. He is not yet revealed on Earth, only to those in Heaven. Now they wait in reverence as another angel steps forward from the throne.

The catastrophic events that are about to take place are so devastating that Jesus said it would be a time which never has been, or ever will be again. The devastation of the water of the flood, or the plagues in Egypt, or any other of the world's worst tragedies can never match it.

GREAT ANGEL WITH THE CENSOR AT THE ALTAR OF INCENSE

Another mighty angel steps out of the Throne. Here is another one of the many cryptic apparitions of Christ in the Revelation; another angel acting on His behalf. He is the only one who can take coal from off of the altar as the Great High Priest. He is only manifest to those of us yet on Earth that is looking for Him, but He is never seen by the ungodly. He told us very plainly in John, chapter fourteen that the world would no longer see Him, but that we would see Him (14:17). To those looking for Him, the language and setting of this passage is clear. Who else in all of the Old or New Testaments stands at the altar as our Great High Priest to make intercession for us? The prayer He is about to offer, is an intercessory prayer at the Golden Altar (Revelation 8:3). Paul left no doubt who is standing at the Altar of Mercy. He said:

"We have such a High Priest, who is seated at the right hand of the throne of the Majesty in the heavens" (Hebrews 8:1).

And in Hebrews 2:17 he says:

"...that He might be a merciful and faithful High Priest in things pertaining to God, to make propitiation for the sins of the people."

He further points out and encourages us in Hebrews:

"Seeing then that we have a Great High Priest who has passed through the heavens, Jesus the Son of God, let us hold fast our confession. For we do not have a High Priest who cannot sympathize with our weakness, but was in all points tempted like as we are, yet without sin" (4:14-15).

This Angel who holds the censor of intercession at the Mercy Seat in Heaven, is our Great High Priest.

OUR GREAT HIGH PRIEST AND INTERCESSOR

In Old Testament typology symbolized by the high priest, He came to the altar once a year with the blood of the Lamb to be sprinkled on the Mercy Seat and atone for our sins. In the same typology, he sprinkled incense on the Golden Altar in front of the Holy of Holies, which smoke ascending upward to God, represented the prayers of all the saints. All of this typology is perfectly reflected in this passage in Revelation 8:3.

It is so very significant and exciting to find our great High Priest is the same as always—*"yesterday, today, and forever"* and He is still making intercession for us (Hebrews 13:8). But here, just *before "the coming of the great and terrible day of the Lord"* we find Christ still atoning for us (Joel 2:31). He is still reaching out and offering prayer of intercession for those who are yet to be saved during the Tribulation. Some teach that by this time, all hope is gone and there is no mercy in judgment, yet He is continuing to call for repentance and offering forgiveness for sin. Even at the hour just before the Tribulation, He still says, *"whosoever calls upon the name of the Lord shall be saved ... [and] He is also able to save to the uttermost those who come to God through Him, since He ever lives to make intercession for them"* (Romans 10:13; Hebrews 7:25).

This act of atonement is meant to cover all that turn to Him during this great and terrible day of the Lord, but also to answer the cry of the souls under the altar, the martyred saints who cry for justice (Revelation 6:9). It is to bring about a final answer to all of our prayers of the saints for all time.

HIS INTERCESSION FOR THE TRIBULATION SAINTS IS ALSO PLEASING TO GOD

Revelations 8:4 gives us a beautiful Old and New Testament analogy. As Christ offers up the prayers of the saints as a sweet smelling savor to God, it wafts its way back to the throne where God is sitting, waiting for judgment and justice to begin. It is found acceptable and pleasing to God, the righteous judge. One of our prominent prayers since the Lord taught us to pray, has been *"Your kingdom come. Your will be done, on Earth as it is in Heaven"* (Matthew 6:10). He is about to answer that prayer. He cannot become King in His kingdom until He puts down all of His enemies (1 Corinthians 15:25). The Lamb prevailed in Heaven to take the Book. Now He must prevail over His enemies on Earth to win the war between Satan and God (Revelation 5:5). There are three enemies of the Lamb and the Church as well: (1) the beastly World System; (2) the harlot church (which has always opposed God's true saints); and (3) Satan and His hosts of dark ones in the esoteric world of devils and demons.

The prayers of the Saints throughout the history of the Church seem to be: "Come back, oh Lord Jesus, heal our world, bring back our paradise, and redeem our inheritance." The cry from under the altar seems to be the cry of the blood for revenge (6:10). The Church's cry is never for vengeance but for mercy and redemption, the cry of the saints is for the healing of our world (Acts 3:21). It is a blood-washed, blood-bought cry. So this intercessory prayer is for the lost in hope of salvation, even during the Tribulation.

TRIBULATION STARTS (VERSE 5)

Christ to this point has been the merciful High Priest, but now He becomes chief judge and prosecutor. Many of the churches today are not going to easily accept this side of Christ. As a merciful high priest yes, but as a judge and prosecutor, that's another story. I exhort the Church, and I encourage the "angels" of the churches (the pastors) to prepare folks for this side of the coming Christ, lest they become disillusioned or bewildered and lose their love for Him. Iniquity is abounding and the love of many will wax cold when they see a Christ who is now a blood soaked warrior (Matthew 24:12; Isaiah 63:3).

Christ now takes the same censor that had been the prayers of the saints, but which now becomes a censor filled with fire from the coals of the altar, and a symbol of God's righteous judgment upon the earth. These coals from off of the altar are also meant for cleansing (Isaiah 6:6-9). Isaiah had just cried out to God in confession of his sins and the sins of the society around him. This same angel took coals from off of the same altar in Heaven, and touched his lips and said "your iniquity is taken away and your sin purged" (6:7). We are to understand that the purpose of our great high priest in the coming troubles is not only to bring justice, but also to cleanse the earth of its sins (Daniel 9:24).

People on Earth, who have not been able to look into Heaven and see these scenes of preparation for judgment, will not understand what all of this implies. All of a sudden Tribulation breaks loose upon the worldly scene. Yet in Heaven, much commotion is created by the beginning of the Tribulation. There are voices of command, and Heaven's power is released, this being depicted by thunder, (God's voice) and lightening, (God's power). All of this causes an earthquake, which is the first effect of the seven years of Tribulation on Earth.

All of the warnings from Enoch—seventh generation from Adam, to Noah and Moses is a warning of the Tribulation (Jude 14, 15; Deuteronomy 4:30-31). Isaiah 2:19, 24:1, 3, and 6, and Revelation 19:20 all contain warnings. Jeremiah 30:7 and Daniel 12: 1-2 speak of Jacob's troubles; and the woes are described in Joel 2:1-2, and 15 along with many New Testament warnings. Matthew 24:21, 22, and 1 Thessalonians 5:3-11 speak the same warning. Revelation 3:10 promises to keep the Church from the same. The above text references are by no means exhaustive, but serve to remind us that this coming time of trouble is well established throughout the scriptures from the beginning.

All of the hate and wrath that has built up since Satan began His war on God and began using us as his *pawns in the game*, will be unleashed during this time. Eighteen times in the Book of Revelation, the word *wrath* is used. This includes the wrath of distressed nations (Revelation 11:18); the wrath of the false church (14:8; 18:3); the wrath of man (16:14-16); the wrath of the Lamb (6:16, 17); the wrath of Satan (12:12 and 17); and finally in the last three and one-half years, the wrath of God. All eleven times where the wrath of God is spoken of, are found from the eleventh chapter on, and are in the last half of the Tribulation.

Where are we today? The Church is breathlessly awaiting the Rapture. The world of distressed nations, in this period of no answer, is building in wrath toward each other, and trust even among friends is breaking down. Also, the economy nears fulfillment of chapter eighteen of Revelation. Any moment the wrath of the nations can and will break loose. The censor in the hands of Christ our great High Priest in

Heaven will be cast to the earth, and the Tribulation will start. If you love Jesus Christ and make the Rapture, you are safe. If you miss the Rapture, call upon Him in this time of trouble. Remember, He *"is not willing that any perish, but that all come to repentance"* (2 peter 3:9).

A WORD ABOUT THE TRIBULATION

For some that may be reading this and who are not familiar with the scriptural teaching of the Great Tribulation—its essence and its purpose let me take a few lines to explain what we are talking about.

If you will follow up on the references given above about the warnings of this time to come, they will quickly acquaint you with the basic concept which Jesus called *"a time of trouble ... such as has not been since the beginning of the world until this time, no, nor ever shall be"* (Daniel 12:1; Matthew 24:21). From the book of Daniel, we understand it will last only seven years. It is known as the seventieth of the seven year periods prophesied upon the Jews. It will accomplish these six outcomes, and all of them are an occasion for joy:

1. To finish and put down Satan, and by him all human transgression against God.
2. To make an end of sin.
3. To make reconciliation.
4. To bring in everlasting righteousness.
5. To seal up, or complete the vision and prophecy.
6. To anoint the Most Holy.

This seven year period will be divided into halves of three and one-half year periods. The first half will be the terrible tragedies prophesied in chapters eight and nine of the Book of Revelation. It will be caused by people and nations under the control of Satan. Satan has made six attempts to destroy the Jews, and during this coming seven years, through the efforts of the Antichrist, the beast will make his last attempt. This seven years will begin with an attempt to flatter the Jews with a covenant (Daniel 9:27). However, the covenant will be broken in the middle of the week.

The last half of the seven year period will be caused when God intervenes by cutting it short in order to spare the world of total destruction of the human race (Matthew 24:21-22). God will send Jesus Christ, who will be revealed to the world in His second coming. He will face down the angry nations and an angry Satan (Psalms 2:1-12). In the final scenario, He will face down Satan and His host of *"principalities, against powers, against rulers of the darkness of this age, against spiritual hosts of wickedness in the heavenly places"* at Megiddo in Israel (Ephesians 6:12). Afterward, Christ will set up the New Kingdom of a thousand year reign, and He will finish with the New Heaven and New Earth.

It is that terrible seven year time on Earth which is the subject of our study at this point. Its terror is only softened by the consideration of those six things mentioned above, which it is to accomplish.

We should make this point again as we have before, and refer to it several times. It is not the end of the world, nor the end of nations. The Sheep Nations must continue for another 1000 years and go into the New Jerusalem. God, at this time, will not destroy the earth. In fact He will never destroy it. He will only remove sin and unrighteousness from it and renovate it into a New Heaven and a New Earth. Turn a deaf ear to those fear mongers and just believe your Bible.

A GREAT UPHEAVAL (V.5, 6)

There will be no question in anyone's mind as to when the great Tribulation starts. Many terrible tragedies in the past have called forth the question by many of the unknowing as to whether that incident might be the beginning of the Tribulation. Friends, when it actually starts, and *"the day of the Lord will come,"* there will be no doubt or question that it has started (2 Peter 3:10). I have often said, "It will start with a bang." When the fire of that censor from off the coals of the great golden altar in Heaven hits the earth, it will reflect the end of the longsuffering of God, not for lost sinners but for a wayward and rebellious world. When God lifts his hand of restraint off of people, nations, and even Satan himself, what weeping and wailing there will be. Great upheavals and commotions will break loose from all corners of the earth, but mainly in the Middle East and Israel. All at once the best diplomats and politicians will be totally overcome and out of control of the situation.

I believe it will start with two overwhelming phenomena. One, *"a great earthquake ... as had not occurred since men were on the earth"* (Revelation 16:18). This earthquake may be one of several during the Tribulation, or it may be one singular earthquake. For sure, it is the one spoken of in the end of the times of sorrows as recorded in Revelation 6:12. As we move through the harmonizing of the Book of Revelation and see the same event happening simultaneously with many other events, and overlapping one another, we may discover that it is one and the same earthquake spoken of nine times in Revelation.

The second being a nuclear exchange triggered by some small incident, but quickly grows out of hand as the distressed nations experience fear of total annihilation (Matthew 24:22). Paul said it would come as *"sudden destruction"* on a world which had tried hard for *"peace and safety"* but without God or Christ's help (1 Thessalonians 5:3).

SEVEN TRUMPETS ARE PREPARED TO SOUND

Christ gives signal to seven angels ready to act on His

behalf from the throne in Heaven. The first four brings those devastating tragedies on the Earth as was recorded in chapter six, and are represented by the four horsemen. The next three are upon man and are called the three *woes* to be suffered.

The first four are administrated quickly in succession which could well mean that they happen all at once or at least in very close proximity. What is described here can easily be seen as in relationship to nuclear war. Ten texts in the Old and New Testaments clearly speak of what we know of as a nuclear blast. A list of these can be found in an appendix to this writing. I do not expect to dwell long on these seven trumpets and their devastation on Earth. Most people are well versed on these things from reading scores of other books.

Let's look carefully at what we are told here in Revelation 8: 6-12. In the first trumpet sound, great natural disasters occur including hail, fire mingled with blood upon the earth, destroying the trees, and the environment of Earth is disrupted. In a third part of the earth, a third part of the trees will be burnt up along with the grass. These were spoken of in Joel 2:30, following a great visitation of the Holy Spirit upon Israel. Take note that all of these perfectly describe what would happen to that part of the earth if an atomic explosion was unleashed. This is not said to be a world-wide event but only on one third of the earth. By other prophecies related, we are convinced it will be mainly in the Middle East and are nuclear.

When the second trumpet sounds, a burning mass is cast from the sky into a third part of the sea and becomes blood. It is common knowledge today that one of the results of the Bikini Island atomic blast was that the ocean waters around the site became like blood plasma. The creatures in this third part of the sea died, and all of the ships involved in this third of the sea, were destroyed. Again, these scenes are very reflective of nuclear disaster.

EXECUTION OF JUDGMENT

The third trumpet sounds and a great star (in appearance) fell from the sky, burning like a lamp. We can assume that it fell upon the same third part of the Earth, but this time affecting the waters contained in the rivers and fountains of the area. It may be significant to mention that today an exploding nuclear bomb from the air is considered one of the most effective ways to destroy.

The word *wormwood* means *bitterness* or *extreme inner suffering* and was applied to the Russian nuclear catastrophe at Chernobyl in the Ukraine. Many people died from this tragic event. It is of significant interest that the Russian word *Chernobyl* can actually be interpreted *wormwood*. Not that we think that incident has any direct fulfillment of this text, but it certainly is indicative of what is coming. I do not think it is perchance, and certainly, it is an eye opener.

The fourth trumpet sounds, and a third part of the sun and the moon were smitten. (Possibly nuclear dust and debris as the nuclear winds circle the earth seven times.) And a third part of the stars were darkened. Stars often represent the entities of the heavenly realm. We are told in Isaiah 24:21 that at this same time as the earth is made to stagger in its orbit, God will destroy *"the host of exalted ones."* Surely this means the evil angelic forces. Revelation 8:12 continues: *"a third of the day did not shine and likewise the night."* This is a bit of a puzzle, but it seems possible that the earth would be shaken in its orbit and its spin. In speaking of this very time, the Prophet Isaiah said, *"The earth shall reel to and fro like a drunkard, and shall totter like a hut"* (Isaiah 24:20).

It is said that the recent tsunami in Japan rocked the earth enough to cause it to wobble in its orbit and be disrupted in its spin, so we can imagine what would happen if nuclear holocaust would hit one-third of the earth.

Notice these Old Testament texts which are surely related to these Trumpets in Revelation:

Ezekiel 32:7-32: Here in the final years when the roll call of terrorist nations are listed, and God, through the strength of the terrible of nations brings destruction to these countries around about Israel, it is easy to see these events in proximity to Tribulation (32:12). This terror that they cause in the land of the living is no question, the war of terror which we are involved in today. And all that terror is caused by perpetuated hate against the Jews and the Land of Israel. These nations are the exact ones that are involved today.

Zephaniah 1:14-16: The events are set during the time of the return of the Jews to their land in the last days. God's determination is to gather all nations against Jerusalem. It is the time of God's judgment on all nations for their sin, and all this takes place when *"the great day of the Lord is near,"* and in the *"day of trumpet and alarm"* (ibid v. 14, 16).

Joel 2:1, 10, 30, 31: Again it is set in the day of the return of the Jews in the last days and also in the day of the trumpet (ibid 1, 15); A northern invasion (ibid 20); a great people and strong (ibid 2); and darkness, which smacks of thermonuclear destruction (ibid 30, 32). It is again over the deliverance of Jerusalem, and involves the gathering of all nations (ibid 3:2).

MOST OF THE TRIBULATION WOES WILL BE IN THE MIDDLE EAST

This thought may come as a shock to many, and may at first be rejected by some, especially those who have been caught up in the end of the world spoof and the all-powerful, world-controlling Antichrist. Certainly, there is scriptural evidence that He will have some influence over the whole world. It seems his control will be more in the religious area than any other, but there is also evidence that his control will be limited in the political arena (Daniel 11, 12). I ask you to hear me out and considerate it. It is not worldwide. This devastation is plainly said to be only on one-fourth of the earth. We draw from the many 100's of texts of the Old and New Testament which are comparative passages with the Tribulation to make this statement and conclusion. All of the last wars, including the war on terror, are prophesied to be fought in the Middle East, mainly in Israel (Ezekiel 33). It is also called the *"time of Jacob's trouble."* Jacob was renamed *Israel.*

THE TRIBULATION IS NOT WORLD WIDE THOUGH IT MAY AFFECT THE WORLD

We will note that according to these texts, about the first four trumpets of Tribulation, (and may continue into the next three trumpets of the three woes on man) is part of the Tribulation, and is not worldwide (9:15). These verses clearly state that it involves only one-third of the earth. I will comment along this line concerning the last half of the Tribulation later as we get into that part of the book which involves those years. However, there is much evidence that the first part of the Tribulation, at least the main part involving the wrath of nations and the wrath of man and the wrath of Satan, will not be worldwide. However, I am sure it will involve the rest of the world and will spread worldwide. However, we are told at one point that the great cities of the world will fall, so it will surely flow over into the world (Revelation 16:19).

I further suspect that this one-third of the earth will be mainly located in the Middle East, especially in Israel. This is evident in that all of the battles of the Tribulation, including the Battle of Armageddon, are fought in Israel and the Middle East. Here is one of the benefits of being able to tie together all of the Old Testament references which relate to this same time, and connect them into the Revelation. I will at this time only mention some of those scriptures that relate to the Tribulation from the Old Testament without elaborating on them. At a later time in this writing we will spend more time relating to them.

First, note that the location of the last four great wars which generally are accepted as part of the Tribulation, are all centered in Israel. (1) The battle of Gog and Magog which takes place on the *"mountains of Israel"* (Ezekiel 38:8); (2) The battle of Jehoshaphat to take place in the area just south of Jerusalem (Joel 3:2); (3) The battle for Jerusalem (Zechariah 12, 14); (4) The Battle of Armageddon which will take place in the Valley of Megiddo in Central Israel (Revelation 16:16). These texts, without question, place most of the Tribulation trouble directly in Israel. The allies of Gog are clearly Mid-Eastern nations—Persia (Iran), Libya, Ethiopia, and Togarmah (Ezekiel 38:5, 6). These are all Mid-Eastern countries which right now are locked in a mortal affront with Israel.

Second, note that all of the three and one-half years period mentioned in both Daniel and Revelation, have to do with the Jews and the Middle East. Please consult the Appendix for these details.

Also, God plainly tells us that Jerusalem will be an international burden to all nations, a cup of trembling to all nations around about her and the center of end-time events (Zechariah 12:3). A siege will be set by the nations of the world against Jerusalem. God will protect Israel during this Tribulation time (12:7). God will seek to *"destroy all the nations that come against Jerusalem" (12:9)*. These texts will serve simply to illustrate my point, but anyone even casually familiar with the eschatological prophetic texts of the end-time Tribulation, will know that this whole scenario of the end-time, revolves around the Promised Land, Israel, and its promised restoration of the Holy Land. This may be true of only the first part of the Tribulation.

We will find that as the nations in this part of the Tribulation find no solution, it will spread throughout the world. The wrath of God in the last half of the Tribulation, while still centered in the Middle East, will fall on cities and nations worldwide, and Armageddon will involve the whole Satanic version of the *World Order* and the *Prince to come* as well as His *Armies of the Nations*. However, at this point in our study of the first half of the Tribulation, we note that it only involves one-third of the earth. Later we will see that even in the second half of Tribulation (contrary to total-control theories), the Antichrist will not be unopposed and will not have complete control. Daniel's revelations of these last days of the *little horn* or the *Willful King*, i.e. the Antichrist, will show the Antichrist's weaknesses (Daniel 11, 12). Only Christ has total control. As we have shown before, the Antichrist is a *little horn*, not a *Big Horn* (7:8). Only Christ is a *Big Horn* and He is the star of these last days.

THREE WOES UPON MAN

We move to the next three trumpets where we are told that they will bring three woes upon mankind. Even though I am sure that the disaster of the first four trumpets will surely cause its woe upon man, the main effect of this time of trouble will now be turned to them in particular. Consider this statement as we move into the ninth chapter and the woes upon man.

The President of Bosnia, during the terrible times in Yugoslavia in the 90's, when asked by Jim Lehrer on the Jim Lehrer Show what he would attribute the terrible atrocities to that were taking place in Bosnia. He made such a significant statement that I think it is worth relating here. He said:

"There are affairs in the tides of men which unleash demons."

We will see an example of the truth and reality of this statement as we see the unleashing of Hell in all of its fury in the next chapter.

CHAPTER 9

THE HORDES OF HELL

"The words that I speak to you they are Spirit and they are Life" (John 6:63).

We come now face to face with one of the most baffling parts of the Book of Revelation. I must admit that this one chapter alone is enough to win the reputation for being scary. One thing that makes it most frustrating is that it brings us to a brush with the esoteric world of demons and devils.

Again, keep in mind that we came through seven chapters with nothing to cause us any fear, and even now for the Redeemed Church, these alarming event have nothing to do with us. We have *"[escaped] all these things that will come to pass, and to stand before the son of Man [in Heaven]"* (Luke 21:36). During the demonic release revealed in this chapter, only those who have refused to repent and will not allow Christ to protect them, will suffer (Revelation 9:20-21). Only those who live and love the devil's corruption will experience the result of this opening of Hell on Earth.

As we see thus far in Revelation and shall see more hereafter, the world and its sinful people are more and more allowing themselves to suffer an open Hell and an age of demonic activity. We repeat for emphasis the words of the President of Bosnia, "There are tides in the affairs of men that unleash demons."

Even though we are moving into one of those short parts of this Book which is scary, it still has a positive side. It certainly is not joyous; at least not to the worldly folks who have rejected Jesus Christ and rebelled against God's Word. They will soon find out that Satan is real. However, keep in perspective that this is all about Jesus Christ and what He must allow and what He must do, to put down Satan's rebellion and bring us into the Millennium. The demonic activities that are associated with Armageddon in the sixteenth chapter are the final end of this demonic onslaught that is revealed here in the ninth chapter.

Again, keep in mind that we came through seven chapters with nothing to cause us any fear, and even now to the redeemed, these alarming events have nothing to do with us. We have escaped these things, and now ready to *"stand before the Son of man"* (Luke 21:36). During demonic release, only those who have refused to repent and allow Christ to protect them will suffer (Revelation 9:20-21). And those who love the devil's corruption will experience the result of this opening of Hell on Earth.

OPENING HELL ON EARTH IS NOT SCARY TO THE DEVIL-LOVING SOCIETY

Our culture uses every means they can find to support demons, devils, occult practice, anything hellish, gruesome, violent, and immoral. From demonic exalting games on our electronic devices, to the stage décor for rock concerts and our appetite for occult movies like Harry potter, we see the constant vomit of Hell in our whole entertainment industry. With our lust for explicit, deviate sexual pleasures and the dirtiest levels one could imagine, you would think that this chapter, with its flood of the underworld into our society, should be reason for rejoicing among the worldly set.

It looks like it is going to be a delight for them, to have

Hell break wide open on our earth. This would surely be a reason for great celebration and rejoicing for most people. Read on! I don't think they will like it when they get it, but because that is what the world wants, that is what they are going to get.

Those of our world who choose not even to believe in devils and demon spirits and yet at the same time find entertainment in a devilish atmosphere where our society deals with them every day, are going to get a rude awakening very soon. During the opening events of the Tribulation, the dimensional door between Hell and the Earth which has been locked since Christ holds the key is going to be opened and a deluge of demons will escape into the atmosphere of the earth. Suddenly, that elite Ivy League crowd that has mocked our Bible beliefs is going to have the shock of their lives when they find themselves in a devil-worshipping world.

What sets so hard with the average intellectual and elite of our world, is that they have completely rejected the idea of devils and demons. The paradox of our society is that the influential set does not even believe in these esoteric beings, yet as we said, they cater to them in their entertainment world. These esoteric beings do not even exist to them. We must admit that our best information and understanding of Satan and His subtle work is very restricted._Without the Bible, we would not even know of His existence, and because the Bible's theme is Jesus Christ the Messiah and not Satan, the Confronter, we still have a very limited insight into his reality. In the ninth chapter of Revelation, we get a limited look into Hell. This invasion from Hell into the affairs of man will develop into full-fledged worldwide devil worship among those who follow the dragon and the beast. This includes those who take his mark, name, and number, and do not have the seal of God (Revelation 13:4). All of this is preparing a world to worship the dragon (13:3-4).

Why does Christ allow Hell's door to be opened? This question is not answered for us in the text, but its reality will be felt shortly. A world that worships Hell and longs for demons today, are actually forcing the door open. When it opens during the first part of Tribulation, they will get their fill. All of this mimicking of Hell and demons in our entertainment world as well as in books, magazines, CD's etc., is going to become reality. Let's see if they will enjoy the reality as much as they love to play with it. In every culture of the world, they are inviting Hell to flood the earth. We are told that they will not rejoice but be tormented (9:5). Verse six tells us that they will be so miserable, they will want to die, but cannot. Death will flee from them. It will be a time of woe for man. It does not appear that they are enjoying the reality very much.

We come now face to face with one of the most baffling parts of the Book. We must admit that this one chapter alone is enough to win the reputation for Revelation as being a scary book. One thing that makes it most frustrating is that it brings us to a slight brush with the esoteric world of demons and devils.

THE KEY TO THE BOTTOMLESS PIT

The bottomless pit is generally thought to be the center of the earth since, if you were in the center of the earth, there could be no further bottom, and every way you turned would be up. It is different from Hades, Gehenna, and Sheol, although they are related.

This pit is not Hades, or Gehenna, or Sheol. It is not the place of the wicked dead. It is not Tartarus, or the final Hell. It is however, a prison house of darkness where the demonic world waits the judgment. The demons that were in the Gadarene demonic, requested that they not be put in prison, but rather be allowed to go into the swine, saying *"have You come here to torment us before our time"* (Matthew 8:29)? These demonic spirits know that their time of judgment is coming. They are *"reserved in everlasting chains under darkness for the judgment of the great day"* (Jude 6). They will be loosed for five months at which time they will satisfy the world's hunger for demonic manifestation, and prepare the world for a visitation of Satan and His angels (Revelation 12:12). This will bring the whole world to demonic activity and devil worship, just as Revelation prophesies. This visitation of demons and Satan with his angels will open the world's minds to receive an occult Antichrist by bringing the critical mass and a paradigm shift so that the whole world worshipped the beast (13:4). At first, these demons will be esoteric, unseen and acting as tormenting spirits upon man. But later, some believe they will become visibly manifest, just as the fallen angels did before the flood.

An example of this kind of visible manifestations of angels is found in the Old Testament story of Abraham's visitation of angels, and the evil angels of Sodom and Gomorrah. When these demons and devils are loosed among men, society will fall to the level of Sodom. Jesus said *"as it was also in the days of Lot* (Sodom and Gomorrah) ... *even so will it be in the day when the Son of Man is revealed"* (Luke 17:28, 30).

With the Church gone in the Rapture and the wicked revealed and released, the devil will have full sway (2 Thessalonians 2:3). If any part of Revelation is scary, it is this part. The world is asking for a devil-controlled world and they will get it. No wonder they will be ready to cry *"Blessed is He who comes in the name of the Lord,"* just before Christ returns (Matthew 23:39).

In chapter nine, we see Christ who alone has the keys to Hell and death, opening up the pit and giving the world what they have asked for (Revelation 1:18, 20:1). A great star comes down out of Heaven. I suspect this is Satan as he is driven out of Heaven in the war between himself and his dark angels, and Michael and the host of God's army (Revelation 12:7-9, 12). Hell's pit is open by a key which Christ holds in His control. Satan is allowed to cut loose His dogs—demon hoards that have been locked up in chains of darkness ever since the flood (2 Peter 2:4, Jude 6).

By these revelations, we get to look into the esoteric world of demons and Satan's Hell, rarely allowed to see. Revelation joins the books of Daniel, Ezekiel, and Zechariah in exposing the other world. For reasons that only God knows, Satan has been allowed to operate in secret so he is never a suspect in the hazards he causes. Demons, by-in-large, have been locked up since Christ sent them back to the pit. However, according to the ninth chapter of Revelation, they will be allowed a short period of five months to torment men who do not have the seal of God (9: 4).

We have no doubt that those on Earth who have "the seal of God in their foreheads," include the 144,000 Jews of chapters seven and fourteen (Revelation 9:4). This hoard from hell and the sting of demons will not reach them, for they are protected by God by being *"nourished for a time and times and half a time, from the presence of the serpent"* (Revelation 12:14). When the dragon was cast out of Heaven and the door opened for him to come to Earth, His first persecution will be against Israel (Revelation 12:13-14). However, there will be others who have not taken the mark, the name, or the number, and that is the Tribulation saints who also will be kept from this onslaught of Hell.

There is a comparison of a mark in Ezekiel nine (9:4). When Jerusalem was to fall under siege, all of those who loved God and His city, and who sigh and cry for the abominations, were to be marked in their foreheads. When the angel of death passed through the city, he was not to come near anyone who had the mark upon their forehead. This may be a prophetic presage of this greater last day invasion of Jerusalem in Revelation. There will be those who Christ knows and has sent His angels out to mark, that have not submitted to the Antichrist, and who have come to know Christ during the Tribulation period. These will not be given over to suffer the sting of Hell during this time.

There is no torment like the torment of demons. Experiences with demons during the life of our Lord, testify to their horrors in the lives of people. Then, there are our own encounters with people who are, or have been, tormented by the demons all around us. This makes us know that there is nothing like it. The western part of the world, and especially America, has been protected from this kind of open hell by the predominance of the Gospel of Christ. However, as we continue to see the Gospel weakened and the predominance of demon-expression in our society, we will experience what this chapter reveals.

At the opening of the pit, there will be some natural phenomena. A great smoke as of a furnace covers whatever area is indicated here. I am not sure it is worldwide, although it could well be. This is a physical smoke because we are told it darkens the sun (9: 2). Joel 2:10 speaks of the same darkness, and there it comes in connection with an invading demonic army in the "day of the Lord" (2:1, 11). Further in chapter two of Joel, this demonic army is associated with a great invading army from the north, probably Gog and Magog (2:20). It is then possible that this invading army is connected to the invasion of Russia and Iran into Israel at the time the pit is opened. There is no doubt that these armies of the north are filled with demonic hate and power just as the armies that meet Christ at Armageddon are filled with devils.

This darkening of the sun is also associated with the invasion of the nations against Israel who come to the Valley of Jehoshaphat (Joel 3:15) and once again, this is in the day of the Lord (3:14, 15). In Matthew we find this same effect upon the sun and moon and stars, and again in direct correlation to the Coming of Christ and the great day of the Lord (24:29-30). It is said to be caused when *"the powers of heaven will be shaken."* The same words are used in Luke 21:26. I have been told by two atomic experts that the original language gives a perfect description of atomic fusion. "The abilities that are in the atmosphere shall be released; this again is in direct correlation with the coming of the Lord in His great day (Luke 2:27).

This was foreseen as part of the troubles to come in Revelation 6:12. It is preceded by a great earthquake which split the earth and great signs in the heavens (6:13-14).

I am not clear as to all the details which put the above texts together as a part of the phenomena of Revelation chapter nine, but since they are all connected with the day of the Lord and His coming, they have to fit in somewhere in the same time frame of the book of Revelation.

By connecting many texts that speak of the same time and, I believe the same event during the early part of the Tribulation, there will be a great shaking of the earth. The bottomless pit is opened to release great demonic armies of devils. The smoke of the pit, possibly related to nuclear phenomena, will be released upon the earth. The torments of these demons will last for five months, but their influence on the world to bring it to Armageddon will continue as they, like voices of frogs, call the Antichrist's armies to Armageddon.

What is probably not seen by the physical eye and what takes men by surprise, is what comes with the smoke. What here is called *locusts*, are loosed to torment men for a period of five months (9: 3-5). What they actually are, is a matter of speculation due to the fact that we have no criteria by which to determine their exact nature; for probably none of us have ever experienced an encounter with one. We have little knowledge or insight into Hell, its population, or its environs. They have been locked up in Hell all of our lives. Although we pick up some knowledge of their existence and nature as Christ deals with them, we are given very little revelation here on earth in any part of the scriptures to explain their exact nature of being.

I personally have in my library, nearly 150 books concerning the Book of Revelation. Many of their authors give us lengthy discourse on the nature of these locusts, trying to identify them. They are even thought to be war implements like tanks, or nuclear radiation. I will not venture to cover these speculations, which have been exhausted already and I do not care to try to out argue any of them, but I hardly think they can be put in any kind of physical capacity, especially if we compare them to the demon army of Joel chapter two. I believe that whatever they may be likened to will have to stay strictly in the esoteric dimension. The specific description of these demon beings in verses 9:7-10, is enough for us to know that they are demonic and not an earthy phenomenon. Their assignment is to hurt and torment people but not to kill them. This refutes any idea that they are tanks or nuclear radiation. They are much like those devil powers which God had allowed to torment Job. The fact that people will seek to die but cannot is enough to panic the soul of anyone who is taking these revelations seriously (9:6).

It does not really matter what they are and how we may identify them. Suffice to know that they are demonic and out of the pits of hell, especially since an understanding of them is not part of, nor is it necessary to the theme of this writing. I am only interested in Christ, His nature, and His direct involvement in all of these events. It is enough to know that He, for His own reasons, handed the key of the bottomless pit over to Abaddon, or Apollyon to be opened for five months.

I want to go back to the army in Joel chapter two for

another brief comment. I believe it can shed light on these beings and the army of them that comes out of Hell. This passage speaks of a strange army which has been a subject of much debate. Is it an actual physical army of men or is it an esoteric army of demons? Maybe it is both—men who are filled with demons. It is called God's army, yet its descriptions and actions are anything but a type of army from Heaven. This *god* may be the god of this world. I believe that Joel chapter two may be referring to this very same event in Revelation chapter 9.

Their king is called Abaddon. In Greek he is known as Apollyon. A chapter could be written on the historicity of these names and their relationship to the myths and legends of gods. He is the *angel* of the abyss and his name means *destroyer*. He is no doubt one of the legendary gods in the pantheon of Greek gods, who were and are the same as the *"principalities, powers, or rulers of the darkness of this age"* (Ephesians 6:12, paraphrased). They must include this Abaddon, or Apollyon. The name Satan carries with it the essence of a destroyer (Sattom or Saddam in Aramaic or Arabic). Abaddon of Apollyon may not be Satan personally, but of the same spirit and associated with Satan's work.

A WORLD INUNDATED WITH HELL

Without getting into any explanation of the details referenced in chapter nice, we can rightly say that this chapter represents and symbolizes the open door to an earthly deluge of demonic and hellish forces like has not been seen since the pre-flood, or Antediluvian Age. As we study the next few chapters we will see evidence of this open door to hell playing into most of the story-line through chapter nineteen. Demonic activity, hellish connections, and satanic influence will be everywhere. Examples to be mentioned in brief are the dragon of chapters 12 and 13; the false prophet and his mock miracles of chapter 13; demon spirits like frogs drawing the nations to confront Christ at Armageddon in chapter 16; the mystery Babylon in chapter seventeen; and the binding of Satan in chapter 20. These brief mentions of references to the activities of Satan and devils throughout the involvement of events to come, show the rather cryptic and yet plain invasion of Hell through an open door in the last three and one-half years of the Tribulation period. That invasion of demons, devils and the dragon probably started here in chapter 9.

HELL IS OPENED TO BRING A DEVIL SOCIETY

There contains every evidence in our society today that humanity is being prepared for, expecting, and actually desiring that invasion. We can see Hell mimicked everywhere we look. Even though humanity has made light of the reality of Hell, it will soon find that demons, devils and Satan's principalities and powers are nothing to trifle with.

Christ is holding back hell currently, but soon will give Satan the key. Let's follow the trail of the devil and His activities through the book to see this.

SEVENTH TRUMPET AND THE FIRST WOE TO MAN BECAUSE OF WICKEDNESS

As this chapter opens, we have the sounding of the fifth trumpet and the first *woe* on man. It starts right out with a most nerve-racking and hair-raising event that one can think of. What could be more terrifying than to open up hell on Earth which, like an artesian well when uncapped, would gush out upon society? But that's what we are reading here. The first part of the Tribulation will see an invasion of Hell. We do have to say however, that Jesus basically said, "You asked for it, you get it!"

Paul makes very plain the open invasion of demonic

forces in the last day:

> *"Now the Spirit expressly says that in the latter times some will depart from the faith, giving heed to deceiving spirits and doctrines of demons"* (1 Timothy 4:1).

For further study of the characteristics of the society that leaves God out and is given over to evil imaginations, see 2 Timothy 3:1-6 and Romans 1:28-32.

We have a world that is ripe and ready for Hell's takeover, just as we are told will happen in chapters 9-19 of the Book of Revelation. Those in our society that have played around the fringes of Hell, toying with and entertaining demons by playing games with them, would not at first think this a terrible thing. What they do not realize is that Satan and all of his imps have kept themselves well- camouflaged, playing the good guys such as *spirit-guides* and *familiar spirits*; or the spirits of the dead by mimicking our loved ones, etc. Therefore a large part of our culture today has been unknowingly friends and companions with demons. Consequently, the devil and his Imps have had, and are having themselves a hay day. In large measure, demons have become as acceptable as is ET. Of course, to anyone with Biblical savvy, he represents one of these demons.

As we have said, this exploitation of Hell among our present society can be no better illustrated than to consider what we call entertainment. The movie industry, the music industry, the games/gaming industry, along with many books and novels are almost all given over to the expose, images, language, and concepts of what is known as Hell in the Bible.

One of the signs designed to tell us that we are nearing the Day of the Lord, is that our society would be like *"the days of Noah"* (Luke 17: 26). We are told in the Book of Genesis that violence filled the earth, and *"wickedness of man was great in the earth"* (Genesis 6:5, 11). That violence and wickedness was the result of their evil imaginations (Genesis 6:5). These evil imaginations are included in all of our playwrights, television shows, videos, CDs, and most novels, etc. Almost every movie, novel, electronic game, television billing, along with many pop and heavy metal songs are products of a Godless and wayward generation of people whose imaginations are evil continually; who have rejected God and Christ, and are flirting with the devil. Their stages of performance are full of fire and strobe-light effects that demonstrate confusion and emotions out of control, just as is the case of demon frenzies. Not only are the imaginations of and thoughts of their hearts of those who produce these things corrupt, so must be the minds of those who choose their evil imaginations to enjoy as their kind of pleasurable entertainment.

Our music industry is almost body and soul, given over to Hell and its spirit. Songs regularly carry the Hell agenda of death, mutilation, gross filth, suicide, immorality, hopelessness, drugs, drunkenness, illicit sex, and every kind of debauchery you can name, including socialist politics. The sets on stage all depict Hell-fire and brimstone. As people gyrate to Hell's sounds, strobe lights flash fantasy and hallucination, and whip up the ungodly human spirit into demonic frenzy. Their music concerts differ very little from the old pagan demonic madness and mania. They seem to try to outdo each other to please Satan.

To add to their addiction of Satanic delusion, they soak themselves in the slop of drugs and actually seek hellish hallucinations that are demonstrated everywhere in the world where societies have opened themselves to devils. Their end is depicted in the last verse of this chapter where we see that they become so hooked on devil-delusions that they could not repent of the sorceries—the use and mixing of drugs.

Besides the entertainment world, which has become such a prominent part of modern life, there is the Church of

Satan that does satanic rituals and plays with devils in witch covens. Most electronic games are saturated with demonism. Humanity does séances, consult with fortune tellers, read horoscopes, and take counsel from the stars.

Many, if not most of the diplomats and bureaucrats of our nation confer with the occult. The White House and congress is obsessed with talking to wizards. Numerous occult consultants are on the payroll of an astounding number of our political and diplomatic leaders. Only one president in my lifetime that has not used someone in witchcraft as an advisor was Ronald Reagan. However, his wife was deep into the occult. People have asked me, "but what of George Bush? He was known to be a Christian." I cannot judge his Christianity; I can only tell you that he is a member of the *Skull and Bones* of Yale University. Anyone who has done any earnest footwork will know that the *Skull and Bones* is deeply wrapped up in secret occult societies and very Satanic in its practices.

If you have visited the United Nations, you will know that it is true what I am saying. The UN is saturated and given over to occult and demon influence. The basement of the UN is filled with various New Age headquarters and offices showing that the pseudo-religious base of the UN is occultic, New Age thought. World Servers, World Servers for the World We Choose, the Counsel of Wise Persons, and many other cosmic organizations are stationed there. Prominent among them and one of the most powerful publishing companies in the world is the Lucis Trust. At one time, the Lucifer Trust and financed the beginning of the League of Nations, however, when many objected to the name Lucifer and the US would not join because of that name, it was changed to *Lucis* which means the same, *light-bearer*. The only God you will find there is a statue of Zeus at the door of the General Assembly.

One of the most influential elements in today's world is called the *New Age* movement. It is worldwide and bears tremendous influence on the leaders of the nations of our world. Their vortex centers are all over the world and carry powerful influence on people who have rejected Christ. They admit openly that they are led by Lucifer. (I have recently written a book which will be published soon under the title, *Simulations of the Second Coming*; it details the devilish, satanic nature of the New Age Movement.)

Another aspect of our manifest, devilish agenda is our worship of Mother Nature. Through the ecology movement, this is nothing but old Babylonish Paganism. We need to expound on that influence in our world. I do not speak here of genuine and honest environmental concerns for which the EPA was designed, but I speak of the hostile takeover of the EPA by Devil-led ecologists who seem to worship creation more than the Creator.

Sacrifice of cats and dogs, and even human sacrifice from time to time, is found in our nation. In Santa Cruz a few years ago, a young girl was found hanging on a grave and evidence showed plainly that she had been used as a sacrifice by devil-worshippers.

I am aware that this sounds like a wholesale condemnation of our present generation. It is not intended to be, but I will admit that I have no allegiance whatsoever with the demonic side of our society, and I can say without reservation that God and Christ has none either. The world has asked for more of Hell, and according to the revelations in this chapter they are going to get it.

Our world, outside of the circles of influence by the Church, is almost entirely given over to various forms of devil worship, and is opening the way for an occult world leader who will receive *"his power, his throne, and great authority"* from none other than the dragon himself (Revelation 13:2). We must see that the beginning of this demon-possessed world to come, will begin right here in the first half of the Tribulation when, because of the world's lust for demons, Christ delivers up the key to open the bottomless pit, allowing Hell to vomit on the earth. I know I have been quite repetitive, but this is so heavy on my heart and I want to repeat for emphasis. My heart bleeds, as does the heart of the rest of the Church and the heart of Christ, for people so lost in the devils delusive world, especially when we read what the outcome will be for them.

As the first few years of the Tribulation progresses, Satan will gradually become more and more obvious. Soon, a critical mass will be reached, and a paradigm shift will take place. Society will openly slip into a devil-saturated world—the worship of the dragon (Revelation 13:4). This is the world that Jesus Christ is coming back to redeem.

We made reference to the President of Bosnia in our closing of the last chapter. Let me return to that statement as a summation to these thoughts concerning an invasion of Hell on Earth. The President of Bosnia said when asked by Mr. Jim Lehrer to what he would ascribe the atrocities to, going on in Bosnia at that time? He gave a simple but profound explanation:

"There are tides in the affairs of men which unleash demons."

The scene where demons are unleashed in Bosnia was further described like this:

> "Blood trod upon the heels of blood. Revenge in despair meant revenge at midnight. War betrayed war. Deceit deceived deceit, lie cheated lie. Treachery mimicked treachery, perjury was strengthened by perjury. The Sword of Justice read with ultimate and unrepentant wrath. Blasphemy arose with

hideous blasphemy, curse loved and answered curse, drunkard stumbling over drunkard, fallen husbands returning each from the others bed and meeting the other returning from his bed. Thief stole from thief, robber running from robbery knocks down a robber coming. Lewdness, violence, hate met mercy weary from forbearing."

This is the description of a totally corrupt society that we are heading towards on a worldwide scale as soon as the Church is gone in the Rapture. It is the description of a world given over to demon possession: *"And then the lawless one will be revealed"* (2 Thessalonians 2:8).

Revelation says, *"For they have shed the blood of saints and prophets, and you have given them blood to drink, for it is their just due"* (16:6). This somehow comes close to describing a world without the presence of the Church, and one given over to an open Hell and the wicked one (2 Thessalonians 2:8-9).

FIVE MONTHS AND THE WORLD IS HOOKED (9: 10) (Possibly 5 months before Armageddon.)

It is easy to reason from what we know of demon powers working in our world today, five months of the open door policy where demons by the hordes are tormenting people to the place that they want of die and cannot, that the world would give in to Hell in fear and misery. A demon manifestation is a very fearful experience to the unsaved and the lost.

By the time these horrible experiences worldwide had gripped mankind, we would find widespread confusion, fear, and demon possession like we have seen in the primitive areas of Africa, South America, and in the Islands of the Pacific. People held in total fear and will do anything the demon-possessed witch doctor says. They will be ready to worship the devil. It is easy to see how a world who did not like to retain God in their knowledge could be given over to a reprobate mind, and en mass, to *"[worship] the dragon who gave authority to the Beast"* (Revelation 13:4).

We have described here, a world given over to devil-worship. It would be much like the antediluvian world who was completely controlled by the Nephilim of old. Whole societies and entire armies totally demon possessed and controlled by the dragon. These demonic principalities and powers will have taken control to work their ill on humanity. That is the world of the pre-flood; it is the same world of demon control described for us in Revelation. Jesus said that *"as it was in the days of Noah, so it will be in the days of the son of man"* (Luke 17:26).

No wonder Jesus said that by the time it comes for Him to return for His bride, the people of the world who know He is coming will be crying *"blessed is He who comes in the name of the Lord"* (Matthew 23: 39).

The above is a brief warning to the Church until Christ comes to Rapture us. Living in this kind of age so saturated with Hell, we can easily allow our own soul to become cauterized, or made insensitive to these things. Paul used this same analogy when he said some would "[have] their own conscience seared with a hot iron" (1 Timothy 4:2). The more we allow ourselves to be part of this kind of a world, the less sensitive we are to spiritual things.

TIME OF TROUBLE (v. 12)

Chapter nine continues to describe in cryptic symbolism, what is involved in the time of trouble--the seven years which men and Satan have brought upon themselves. It represents part of the first half of the Tribulation period.

The last three trumpets are three woes specifically listed here that will come on the human race for their refusal to obey God and honor Him and His Son, Jesus Christ. This chapter of demonic power upon man is a *woe* that is to come upon man.

The term *woe* brings with it a frightening thought. *Woe* comes from *oual* in the Greek, and is counterpart to *owy* or *oweeee* in Old Testament Hebrew. It has been adopted by our English language in its original form.

There is some base in our cry "ow, it hurts," but here it represents the most forlorn, agonizing, hopeless, and helpless empty cry known to man. It is mostly used to express the cry that rises up on a battlefield where the wounded lay fallen and are dying alone in extreme agony of both body and soul. Thank God for the Rapture of the Church and the sealing of the righteous, all of which will spare us of these terrifying events. Those who think they might go through the Tribulation had better read these texts carefully and with consideration. You may be saved in Tribulation, but it will be by passing through all of the *woes* of the day. Such an experience will be so unnecessary, especially since there is such an easy way to escape, and not by suicide (Revelation 9:6).

ARMIES FROM ACROSS THE RIVER EUPHRATES (v. 13)

At the sound of the sixth Trumpet—the second *woe* of man; the rising of the Kings of the East. We have another one of those rare looks into the throne room and again we are pointed to Christ at the Golden Altar before the Mercy Seat (9:12-13). We are drawn back to this scene in Heaven to remind us that even in the blackest days of Earth's history, in the midst of an invasion from hell and worldwide devil worship, the great altar of intercession is still there. It is enveloped in the smoke of incense, which is the prayer of the saints. Because of His mercy, Christ the Great Intercessor is still available to whosoever will call on the name of the Lord.

We may remember the four angels to whom it was given to hurt the earth and which were withheld from acting in verse 7:2. Here again, we are reminded that even these angels are under the control of Christ who bound them there. We were not told in chapter seven where they were positioned, but now we are told that they stand on the border between the east (Orient) and the west (Occidental) division in our world. The great River Euphrates for millenniums has been known as the dividing line between the east and the west.

The Euphrates is also recognized as the eastern border of the Middle East, the territory of Shem, Noah's son, and also the prophesied border of the promise to Abraham. The Millennium borders of Abraham's promised land will reach to the Euphrates River in Iraq (Genesis 15:18).

The drying up of the Euphrates adds understanding to this same event (Revelation 16:12). This is one of those parallels, or *meanwhiles* found throughout the book. In chapter nine, we have the actual beginning of the gathering of the world of nations, and the armies of the nations which finally come to Armageddon. Hoards from Islam are gathering around Jerusalem, Israel, and the Holy Land at this time; and the armies of the nations including Gog and Magog of the Russian consortium, are looking toward Israel. Now the kings of the east are gathering, possibly in opposition to Russia, to prevent a hostile takeover of the Middle East, even though they themselves covet control of this area (16:14).

In the '60s, I remember marking the day when China announced to the world that it could deploy an army of two million. It is incredible that even today, we have a mighty nation just across the Euphrates River which has been poised and waiting for the right hour, day, month, and year to invade the Middle East. Its number of fighting forces is *"two hundred million"* men (9:16).

It is my persuasion that this army may possibly be the same one as described in Joel, chapter two. This may be the actual human side of the army, whereas Joel may describe the demonic side of the army. Their descriptions are comparable (Joel 2:3-10, Revelation 9:17-19). They are both described in the *"Day of the Lord"* which puts them in this very place in Revelation (Joel 2:1). It is interesting to note, that we are uncertain whether this is an actual army of men, demons posing as men, or possibly both? Joel describes his army by saying they would not be wounded if they were run through with a sword. That makes them something other than human. The description of this army in verses 17 and 19 certainly begs the question whether they are human or humans possessed with devils. The symbolic expressions definitely lean toward demonic.

Without being dogmatic about it either way, and having consulted scores of books and writings by many of our most respected scholars, I will render a position. I suspect that this is a further and fuller expression of an invasion from an open Hell upon the earth. They are demonic forces, or at least men completely demon-possessed, as Satan makes his final all-out assault on Israel and the Holy Land. Verse eighteen seems to tie in description this army to Joel's army, and to this demon invasion by "the fire and the smoke and the brimstone which came out of their mouths" (9:18). This definitely alludes to demonic and dragon-like creatures that are still in the form of men like the Antichrist.

An example of an army of men completely possessed by demons can be found in Josephus's insight into the tenth army of Rome under Titus, when they destroyed Jerusalem and the Temple in AD 70. It is said that Titus did not want the Temple destroyed, and gave orders to the same wishes. But Josephus says that suddenly the whole Roman Army in Jerusalem became *possessed* and went into an uncontrollable, demonic frenzy. Not even Titus or his captains could control them. In a demonic fit, they tore down the Temple stone by stone, all the while, killing and mutilating. Therefore, it will be comparable with this army from the east of Euphrates. This may be a combination of the Orient forces all the way from China, Japan, Russia, and Iran who are possessed with open demonism. They have already given allegiance to the dragon for millennia, so it is not hard to imagine their total devotion and obedience to the dragon during the Tribulation. It is clear from Revelation 16:12 that these armies are part of the beast's kingdom that will fight against Christ at Armageddon. It is also clear here that they come to this battle by the allurement of demons (16:13-14).

One thing we know, they will be given power to slay a third part of mankind, and meanwhile wreak havoc, such as startling details of the elite's plans to diminish the human population by 90%.

NO REPENTANCE

This chapter ends with sickening finality. We see it fulfilled here like it was foreseen by the kings, the rich and great men, and chief captains in verses 6:15-16; those who would rather die than turn to Christ.

What a hurtful thought that is, especially to those of us in the ministry of Jesus Christ, who spend our lives appealing to men and women, young people and children, to come to repentance. The very fact that repentance is mentioned, presupposes that there was both invitation and opportunity to repent. We can find in chapters 11, 12, 14 and 16 that there are still opportunities offered by angels who preach the good, for the continued chance to be saved. Even right up to the pre-Armageddon time in chapter fifteen and during the plagues or vials, there is offered a chance to repent. Unfortunately, only blasphemy and rebellion ensue (16:9).

We are told that the *"rest of mankind, who were not killed by these plagues, did not repent of the works of their hands"* (9:20, 16:11). Those that we spoke of at length earlier, of a society which is saturated with Hell, continued to worship devils and money. The last verse is revealing of our generation, as it reveals the very indictment we made earlier of a society that rejects God and Christ, and chooses to follow the devil: *"and they did not repent of their murders or of their sorceries or of their sexual immorality or their thefts"* (9:21).

THE DEVIL AND THE DRUG CULTURE CONDEMNED

As we study verse twenty-one a bit closer, we discover a startling relationship of this verse and the elements of our present drug-saturated society. Four things are listed from which the ungodly would not repent, even in the face of certain judgment: (1) Murder - it is the epitome of our world today; (2) Sorceries - the word in Greek is *Pharmakeia* which means mixing and use of drugs, and speaks of our drug culture today; (3) Fornication - all kinds of illicit sex; once again, is an example of our world today; (4) Thefts - an interesting thing to note is that all of these tie together with the drug trafficking of today. Theft to feed one's drug habits is rampant in our cities today. It is *Pharmakeus* that has as its prime motive for use in illicit sex. And most of the thefts and murders are linked to the trafficking and use of drugs. It is worth mentioning is that the most unrepentant of all people are drug traffickers. I believe that the part of our society most vulnerable to Hell's onslaught, are those in the drug trade. The closer one gets to demonic control, the more difficult it is to repent. The heart gets so hardened that if stops feeling guilt or conviction.

We will encounter the unrepentant several more times in the story of the Tribulation (6:15-16, 16:9, 11). If they would only repent of their sin, they would even at this late date, be forgiven, and although it may cost them martyrdom, that would be much preferable to an eternity in Hell. Chapter nine ends with the sting of the serpent. This chapter has been the scariest part of the entire book. The beast, the false prophet, the mark, name and number, etc. cannot hold a candle to demon possession and satanic control.

In chapter ten we will again move out of the earthly scene back into the other dimension—Heaven. The curtain is closed on Act III, and we will witness some more behind-the-scenes preparation for what is to come. While we are back in the Heavenly scene, we will tie together companion texts and share what must be happening in Heaven with the Church during this part of the Tribulation, happening on Earth.

I will not be on Earth during this time, and hope that you will not be there either. So, where do we plan to be and what will we be doing? In the next chapter's comments, we will find answers to these questions. Our promise is that we may *"escape all these things ... and stand before the son of man"* (Luke 21:36). There is an old song known so well to most of the Church; it tells the story:

"Oh there's going to be a meeting in the air, in the sweet, sweet bye & bye, And oh, I want to meet you over there in the land beyond the sky;

Such singing you will hear never heard by mortal ear, 'Twill be glorious I do declare;

When God's own Son will be the leading one, at the meeting in the air."

(Author unknown)

CHAPTER 10

THE LAST 3 1/2 YEARS OF JUDGMENT

In this chapter we see the scene shift from this old trouble-torn Earth and its plague of Hell, back to Heaven, and John sees Christ who is still in the midst of His Church.

Again, we have the *curtain fall*. These behind-the-scenes events in the tenth chapter will take place between the first half of the Tribulation and the second half. We are preparing for the final three and one-half years of the seven-year period of judgment which will end at Armageddon. We will see the total collapse of Satan's kingdom along with three enemies of the Lamb—the Antichrist Kingdom, the Harlot Religious System, and the World Economy.

We will have several *meanwhiles* in this Act. On the outline, this part of the book is called, *THE PARTICIPATORS IN JUDGMENT.* They are: 1) The two Witnesses; 2) Israel in Tribulation; 3) The beastly One World System and the Roman Prince; 4) The second beast which we believe to be the actual *Antichrist;* 5) The last plagues on the Armies of the Nations; 6) The Harlot Church; and 7) The World Economy. We will see Judgment performed upon each of these simultaneously; therefore a *meanwhile* will come between each of them.

This is another one of those chapters where there is no direct mention of any trouble or violence. It is a positive chapter that takes place in Heaven. It shows us activities in Heaven and not on the Earth. We are excited to see the rainbow still about the throne telling us that God still wills peace and safety, and He promises not to destroy the earth and the human race any more (10:1). This rainbow dispels any idea that it is the end of the world and the demise of the human race. The message is similar to the Christmas story—"on earth peace, good will toward men" (Luke 2:14)!

Throughout this chapter, we pause in our observations of the events on Earth. The curtain closes and we have an interlude. We are again going to be given insight into that other world and to Christ, the Exalted One.

Holocaust is taking place on one-third of the earth, where demons have been loosed, thermonuclear war ensues, and angry nations turn against angry nations. An angry devil has turned His anger toward Israel, using angry men in an angry world to inflict havoc upon each other. Satan is full of wrath and playing his last hand (Revelation 12:12). On Earth, the wrath of nations and the beginning of sorrows are going ahead, accelerating and leading into the final judgments upon a wayward world. But in Heaven, we visit the temple and the throne room again.

In Heaven, far above all principalities, powers, and rulers of wickedness wreaked on the earth, Christ is still among His Church, and His Church is still in the presence of the Lamb—the one that is leading them and feeding them (7:14-17).

We tend to get so involved with what is happening on Earth, *where "men's hearts [are] failing them from fear and the expectation of those things which are coming on the earth,"* that we lose a sense that Heaven is at peace during this time (Luke 21:26). In what activities is the Church involved while up in Heaven the Tribulation ensues on Earth?

THE ACTIVITIES OF THE CHURCH IN HEAVEN

In order to keep up with the full scenes, I would like to depart from the text for a time and give some insight into the activities of the Church in Heaven while the Tribulation takes place on Earth. This will be another *meanwhile*. Chapter seven gave us a glimpse of *"a great multitude which no one could number"* from every nation (Revelation 7:9). They were seen in Heaven and they were seen around the throne, same place they were in chapters four and five. They were in the presence of the Lamb, who is of course, our Lord Jesus Christ (7:17). We have been tracing the activities on Earth but now let's track the Church during the same period of time.

It is again from companion texts in both the Old and New Testaments that we can track the activities of the Church in Heaven during this time. While Christ is partially involved commanding the war against sin and Satan on Earth, His main interest is His beloved saints who surround Him in Heaven. We will now see what comparable texts tell us about the Church and Christ during this time.

THREE EVENTS IN THE SKY

There are three events predicted by our Lord in His Word, which out of necessity must take place at the time of the Tribulation. This is the only time they can fit into the sequence of prophecy. Each one takes place after the Rapture and in Heaven. You may want to consult the chart, at the end of this chapter, called *The Harmony of Revelation;* note the *Church in Heaven* and these three events are shown on the chart. These events have to take place in order to prepare the Church for its next part in God's and Christ's plan of redemption. The three events include: 1) the Reception where we will meet Christ; 2) The Judgment Seat of Christ, (The Bema, or Court of Awards); and 3) The Marriage Supper of the Lamb. Revelation 19:7 says *"the marriage of the Lamb has come and His wife has made herself ready."* How has the Bride made herself ready? She—the Church has participated in these three events in the sky. Let's briefly speak of these three marvelous events taking place in Heaven during the Tribulation on Earth.

FIRST: MEET THE LORD - THE RECEPTION

Part of the Revelation of Jesus Christ entails the time when Christ is going to meet His saint's, one at a time and in their order (1 Corinthians 15:23). This is such a thrilling reality for those who love Him, for we are going to see Him face to face and hear Him speak to us individually. Peter said it best: *"[Him] whom having not seen you love"* (1 Peter 1:8). Those with only a casual relationship with Christ, and then only for *religious purposes* will not experience the thrill at the prospect of this meeting as those of us that have waited with a yearning, unspeakable through the long valley of life. In my worship, I have often sung alone to Him:

"I've a longing in my heart for Jesus; I've a longing in my heart to see His face; And I'm weary, oh so weary, as I travel here below; I've a longing in my heart for Him" (Masters, Dorothy).

Suddenly, over there just beyond the Rapture, and probably after we have seen Him in the impersonal business of taking the scroll and opening the seals, we shall be ushered into the presence of Jesus Christ and see Him face to face (1 Corinthians 13:12).

Let's stop for a moment in our worship of Him to see what scriptural base we have for this hope. Paul told us plainly that part of the Rapture process was going to be that we would meet Christ We will be caught up in the clouds to *"meet the Lord in the air, and thus we shall always be with the Lord"* (1 Thessalonians 4:16-17).

For so long we have loved and labored for Him, most of the time feeling very incompetent and unworthy. However, He does not see us like that. He longs for the day when we will be with Him as His Bride, just as we also long for that day. His high priestly prayer to the Father shows us His heart's sentiment:

> *"Father, I desire that they also whom You gave Me may be with me where I am, that they may behold my glory which you have given Me"* (John 17:24).

This is the time that, not only are we glorified in Him, but He will be glorified in us:

> *"... when He comes, in that Day, to be glorified in His saints and to be admired among all those who believe"* (2 Thessalonians 1:10).

What a time that will be when two lovers meet. It is illustrated in the time when Joseph introduced himself to his family after so long an absence, with much crying, hugging, and rejoicing; and the family's eyes were opened to behold him, and they also found such elation In His presence. Also, when we meet Jesus face to face and behold Him far beyond the starry sky, we will experience *"joy inexpressible and full of glory"* (1 Peter 1:8).

Jesus plainly tells us that He is preparing a place for us, and that He will *"come again and receive [us] to [Himself] that where [He is] there [we] may be also"* (John 14:1-3). This verse is most thrilling to me. This will be a personal reception by our Lord to each one of us. Here is the beautiful scenario; first we will be *"caught up,"* then we will *"meet Him;"* we will be with Him and *"we shall be like Him, for we shall see Him as He is"* (1 John 3:2). It will be an exciting and abundant entrance into His presence; a rich and wonderful welcome into the King's presence and into the Kingdom of Christ (2 Peter 1:11). It will be at the Groom's dinner just prior to the marriage, when He receives His Bride, and the bridal party and the Bride all meet the Bridegroom after a long absence.

Somewhere in Heaven, no doubt near the throne, there

is a reception center prepared. After Christ starts the wheels rolling toward justice and judgment, He will turn His attention back to His Bride who has just arrived in Heaven. It will take a while, as each of us personally hears Him communicate about our lives lived for Him. And finally He beckons each one into the reception hall. You think we are choked up now as we anticipate it; just wait until we actually hear Him speak peace and love to us.

SECOND: THE JUDGMENT SEAT OF CHRIST- THE BEMA OR COURT OF AWARDS.

> *"For we must all appear before the judgment seat of Christ, that each one may receive the things done in his body, according to what he has done ..."* (2 Corinthians 5:9-10).

This is not a criminal court. We will not be judged for our sin at this court. Those were all taken care of on the cross. When we are taken up in the Rapture, all of our old nature is left behind. Remember, our sins have been blotted out by the blood of Jesus Christ and remembered no more (Isaiah 44:22, Psalms 103:12). We have already been judged as sinners. This will be our judgment as stewards. We are not on parole, but instead pardoned.

We are not saved by any works that we do, but after we are saved by grace through faith (Ephesians 2:8). We will be placed in the Kingdom by our works as a servant. When He comes this second time, it will be *"apart from sin, for salvation"* (Hebrews 9:28). In other words, He is not coming this time to judge us for our sins, but to bring us salvation.

The word "Bema" is the Greek word for the judgment seat of Christ and a court of awards. For instance, it referred to an athletic awards event and also an awards banquet for giving out military honors. All the Saints must all appear before the court of awards to receive what we have done for

Christ Jesus (Matthew 16:27, Galatians 6:7). All of the good we have done in Jesus' name will come up for examination. Crowns will be awarded. These crowns are given out after the Rapture, therefore at the Bema, *"to every one according to his work"* (Revelation 22:12). If we fail, our crowns could be taken and given to someone else who did the work for us (Revelation 3:11).

It will be a time of accolades with joy when we rejoice with those who rejoice. We will be rewarded for how we lived (2 Corinthians 5:10); how we fought the good fight of faith (1 Timothy 1:18, 6:12; 2 Timothy 2:3); how we overcame (Revelation 2:26); how we pleased God (2 Timothy 2:4, 5); and if we have been found faithful (1 Corinthians 4:2). We should strive to please Christ and master our Christian walk (1 Corinthians 9:25, 2 Timothy 2:5). None of this has any part in our salvation, only our service to Him.

We will be rewarded for how we built our lives. Those that build good solid lives with the best materials will be rewarded, but those who, although saved, did not take heed to what kind of life they build will suffer loss, yet they themselves will be saved so as by fire (1 Corinthians 3: 9-15).

It will be a time of humbleness and thankfulness; not a time of selfish pride. We will be especially humbled and appreciative when we find that our sins will not be mentioned. As Paul so wonderfully informed us in Timothy:

> *"... nevertheless I am not ashamed, for I know whom I have believed and am persuaded that He is able to keep what I have committed to Him until that day"* (2 Timothy 1:12).

Beloved, do you understand that? Christ, who has *"wiped out the handwriting of requirements that was against us"* and who has covered and cancelled our sins with His blood, will keep silent about our sin and failures, those we have committed to Him when we stand before Him in that day (Colossians 2:14). Oh, Hallelujah! Do you know Him as your Lord and Savior?

At this judgment, the great recording angel will take out the book of our record, and open it to our name. There he will prepare to read our record on earth, but will quickly see written across each page reads, "Cancelled by the Blood of Christ." How will you react in that moment when you see how real this salvation is?

All of these prepare us for the third event, which will be in the stage of preparation during the first half of the Tribulation and will take place at the end of the Tribulation.

THE MARRIAGE OF THE LAMB

"Let us be glad and rejoice and give Him glory, for the marriage of the Lamb has come, and his wife has made herself ready" (Revelation 19:7).

This world below is scheduled for massive upheaval. Right up to the time of the Marriage Supper of the Lamb, the beast kingdom, the great harlot, and the world economy are being destroyed. By this time we have just witnessed the destruction of the beast and his cohorts, and the complete collapse of the world money system. But in Heaven, one of the greatest praise services recorded in the Book of the Revelation of Jesus Christ is taking place. The only place where we find the word *Hallelujah* in the New Testament is in the nineteenth chapter of Revelation, just after the collapse of Babylon and before the Marriage Supper of the Lamb: . When we come to the nineteenth chapter, we will enter into a lengthy discussion of all of the procedures of this marriage and the marriage supper. For now we must consider the amount of preparation that must be made. Those preparations will be going on in Heaven while the Tribulation rages on Earth.

Many relative Old Testament Tribulation texts can be

found in Isaiah 24 - 26. It is not hard to recognize Tribulation language in these chapters. The Marriage Supper takes place right after the Great Tribulation. For instance, Isaiah 24 shows us that this is the time when Earth is empty, wasted, and turned upside down (24:1). The earth is defiled by its inhabitants who in turn, *"are burned and few men left"* (24:5-6). Now these are the scary portions which certainly predict the Tribulation. As we read these three chapters in Isaiah, we find the same formula for positive and negative verses that are also in the Book of Revelation. Let us be reminded again that in Revelation itself, there are 404 verses; 269 of them are positive and supportive, and only one-third—137 are negative. That figure holds true for these Tribulation texts. Over two-thirds are positive. They declare that in spite of the Tribulation on Earth, the Church is still praising the Lord in Heaven.

For instance, in Isaiah we are startled to find people singing in the fire of judgment: *"They shall lift up their voice, they shall sing; for the majesty of the Lord, they shall cry aloud form the sea"* (24:14). Verse 16 says, *"from the ends of the earth, have we heard songs."* These songs are rising from the fires in which *"the Lord will punish on high the host of exalted ones* (Satan and his ilk) ... *and the kings of the earth"* (24:21). Isaiah 26:12 definitely places these things in the day of the Lord and in the Tribulation when those who praise the name of the Lord say He is doing great things during the Tribulation.

Chapter twenty-six tells of the time when Israel, the Church, and Christ, will come through the gates of Jerusalem. It is one of our great memory verses of comfort:

> *"You will keep Him in perfect peace, whose mind is stayed on You, because he trusts in You"* (26:3).

This promise is written as a benefit during the Tribulation. We are also told that,

> *"When your judgments are in the earth, the inhabitants*

of the world will learn righteousness" (26:9).

Isaiah 26: 19-21 are the most exciting. Here, associated with the Tribulation and detailed in the Book of the Revelation of Jesus Christ, we find the Rapture clearly related:

"Your dead shall live; together with my dead body they shall arise. Awake and sing, you who dwell in dust ... [for] the earth shall cast out the dead."

Isaiah then speaks of these resurrected saints as being hidden in God's chambers a little moment, *"until the indignation* (another term for the judgment of Tribulation) *is past. For behold, the Lord comes out of His place to punish the inhabitants of the earth for their iniquity"* (26:20-21).

The point is that while the Tribulation is in full force upon the earth, the raptured saints are above it in Heaven, singing and praising the Lord.

What else are they doing during this time in Heaven?

A MIGHTY ANGEL (10:1)

From Heaven, comes another mighty angel. This is another example of the cryptic expressions of Christ that we find throughout Revelation. Christ appears under His own name many times throughout the book, but more often He chose to remain enigmatic, and appear as an angel of the presence of the Lord. It is apparent that the angel is the same as the Lord Himself.

In the appendix, we will enter a lengthy study of angels which actually represents the presence of the Lord (Isaiah 63:9). For instance, Jacob wrestled with an angel, but we know it was the Lord, for he said "I have seen God face to face" (Genesis 32:30). It cannot be doubted that this angel is the Lord Himself, both by the description given of Him and by the things He does.

THE LAST 3 1/2 YEARS OF JUDGMENT

Just as the first half of the Tribulation is finishing and the second half is beginning, we see Him again in control of all things. At the beginning, He is our *"Advocate with the Father"* (1 John 2:1); He is the great possessor of the churches and our great prophet (Revelation 1:12-16); He is the great high priest as He presents His blood in Heaven (5:9); He holds the seal of the Living God (7:2). He is our soon-coming *"King of Kings and Lord of Lords"* (19:16). We see the progression of His status: from Intercessor, to Prophet, to High Priest, to King. And, He is the Ruler of Heaven and Earth; the Executor of our estate with an open Book in His hands after all the seals are broken, all the conditions are met, and He hands the final decree to John. Now, He takes total control after man and Satan has had their say; then He roars like a lion. I am always comforted, no matter how bad my plight, just knowing that Jesus is in control.

The world is not so thrilled at this time, for here Christ is plainly their Prosecutor. The world will take a beating in order for Christ to correct them. It reminds me of the story about a boy that was taking a spanking from his father. The father in his frustration said, "I think the devil has got a hold of you." The little boy looked up and said, "I think he has too, Dad." The world is soon going to find out that it is the devil that has a hold of them. But, Christ is going to break his power and make him turn the world loose.

However, to the Church, He is not our Prosecutor, but the Executor of our estate, and our Redeemer as we shall see by the actions that take place as this Mighty Angel steps forward from the throne.

We will make another observation here. It seems that the longer John gets into his recording of the Revelation of Jesus Christ his concept of Christ grows larger and more impressive. As he followed Christ through the Church Age, then saw Him as the crucified Lamb, watched him take the book, break the seals, and ride the crest of the first half of the Tribulation, Christ has become greater and more powerful in his eyes. Here in chapter ten, Christ has to be a Mighty Angel, Hercules in John's sight (10:1). He is so large that he can stand with one foot on the earth, probably at the Holy Land, and the other foot on the sea, possibly the Mediterranean. In cryptic symbolism, He is growing in might and in power.

THE RAINBOW ABOVE HIS HEAD (v. 1)

The rainbow is a symbol of God's love and protection. It is emblematic of God's promise never to totally destroy the human race again. It reminds us that His purpose is still peace and safety. It is refreshing to find that our Lord Jesus Christ is always with us, *"even to the end of the age"* (Matthew 28:20). Here in the middle of the Tribulation, God wants to remind us that His covenants and promises still hold true, and He will not allow a total demise of the world.

A LITTLE BOOK OPEN (v.2)

Just as the scroll placed in the hands of Christ in chapter five, began the first half of the Tribulation, this little book opens the last three and one-half years of the Tribulation. We note that the book is open, whereas in chapter five, it was closed with seven seals. We see by verse seven that the seventh seal is being opened, so the book from chapter five is now opened. The seals have all been broken and the book lies open for all to see its contents.

It is a smaller book now, only the Title Deed which is the actual statement of ownership, remains. It also contains the proclamation and sentence of Satan and his cohorts. This is the open Warrantee Deed showing God's and Christ's ownership, and our interest in the claims. We have interest in it because we are *"an heir of God through Christ"* and *"joint heirs with Christ"* (Galatians 4:7; Romans 8:17). We will enlarge on the little book, as it is spoken of later in this chapter. It is bitter-sweet. It is bitter because of the sentence of Hell, and sweet for its proclamation of our claims to the inheritance. It is sweet to the redeemed, but it is very bitter to the world and those who are required to administer judgment.

THE ROAR OF THE LION OF JUDAH (verse 3)

All that is recorded next involves Christ as He makes an open proclamation of ownership and lays claim to the territory. Here is further proof that this is Jesus as "He set His right foot on the sea and His left foot on the land" (Revelation 10:2). He shouts with the voice of triumph, as the voice of a victor like when *"a lion roars" (as the Lion of the tribe of Judah to get the Jews attention.)* (10:3). Angels are never given authority to command. Only Christ has the authority over Hell according to Matthew: *"All authority has been given to Me in heaven and on earth"* (28:18).

The *Lamb of God* has now become the *Lion of the tribe of Judah* who will break every chain, and give us the victory (Revelation 5:5)! Hallelujah!

We are given several comparative texts in the Old Testament. Jeremiah prophesies about this very time of the Tribulation. The roar he mentions in verse thirty takes place as the fourteenth chapter is in progress:

"The Lord will roar from on high, and utter His voice from His holy habitation; He will roar mightily against His fold. He will give a shout, as those who tread the grapes against all the inhabitants of the earth" (Jeremiah 25:30; Revelation 14:16-20).

Amos 1:2 says, *"The Lord roars from Zion;"* Joel 3:16 uses the same words. This *roar* is probably a presage to the day He roars from Zion in Revelation fourteen; the lion is the king of all beasts, and when he roars, all of the beasts tremble. At this time, Christ is the King of the beast of Revelation. *"As a lion* roars ... so the Lord of Hosts will come down to fight for Mount Zion" (Isaiah 31:4).* This is the same *lion* here that we see in Revelation 10:3. His roar makes all the beasts head for what I used to call their *fraidy-hole*.

THE SEVEN THUNDERS (verse 4)

Psalms twenty-nine speaks of the seven thunders of God's voice. As He roared, seven thunders echoed back. I have read much speculation concerning these thunders by those who try to outwit God, or for sensational purposes, try to impress us with how close they are to God and show us how He reveals things to them that none of the rest of us can know. In my opinion, we are not supposed to understand or speculate as to who the seven thunders are or what they articulate. If Christ had wanted us to know, He would have revealed it.

If I am to comment at all, I would suspect that this was a private conversation between Christ the Son and God the Father, concerning the warring Host of Heaven who were preparing for the final battle at Megiddo. It is probably classified the same as a high-level secret—the strategy of attack. Christ will make the final proclamation and claim ownership of the inheritance, which had been usurped from Him and us. Since Christ has now assumed ownership of the inheritance from the usurper, the final battle is planned. Christ our Lord has boldly laid claim to Earth, and He does not share his strategy with Satan.

It is of interest that immediately after this secret meeting, the declaration is made *"that there should be delay no longer"* (10:6). Time is up for Satan and the final battle between God and Satan is set.

This mighty angel which is no doubt Christ, stands on the inheritance with one foot on the sea and one on Earth, lifts His hand to heaven and makes a pledge, a covenant, or an official decree (10:6) He is claiming back what has been lost, as we were told throughout the Old Testament Messianic prophecies and in the books of Ephesians, Colossians, 1 and 2 Peter, and others which all speak of our inheritance with the Saints of Light. We have read of the time of restoration of all things, and the restitution in the fullness of time when the cup of iniquity has come to the full. This is the time of their fulfillment.

The decree is made before God and all of the hosts of the universe, that there will be no more time given to the enemy.

NO MORE TIME--SATAN'S TIME IS UP (10: 6)

This is not the end of time. Time continues through the rest of Tribulation, and on into the Millennium. Time will continue as long as earth remains (Genesis 8:22; Psalm 89:36-37). In fact, there are no prophecies in the entire book that are more timed than the events of the next three and one-half years. This decree from Christ that there is no more time simply says to Satan that he has been given plenty of time to make his claims good. He has not taken the throne away from God, or built a better world than God made. Satan will be given no more time to work his wiles on Earth.

MYSTERY OF GOD IS FINISHED (verse 7)

The *"mystery of God would be finished, as He declared to His servants the prophets"* (Revelation 10:7); and everything prophesied in all of the Messianic predictions is finished. It is to say: "Satan, It's all over; the jinx up; the chips are down; no more longsuffering with you, no more chance, no more grief from your folly; you're finished!"

God is not going to keep His activities and His kingdom secret any longer. The mystery of the Kingdom, the mystery of the bride, and other mysteries will all be exposed.

This is why we are told that there is war in Heaven.

Michael and the angels fought against the dragon and his angels. Satan did not prevail, neither was there found a place for them any more in Heaven. And when the Devil sees that he is cast down to the earth, he is full of wrath, for he knows he has but a short time left. (Revelation 12:7-12)

Of course, He knows that from this proclamation of Christ. The decree is set and He will have only three and one-half more years to finish his war on God, Christ, the Jews, the Church, and the World. We understand that this little open book is a Decree Proclamation and is the opening shot which opens up the final war with Satan on Earth. From here he faces the wrath of God eleven times. We understand that time wise, this means from the middle of the week when he sits in the temple and declares that he is God, to Armageddon where Christ *"will consume with the breath of His mouth and destroy with the brightness of His coming"* (Revelation 10: 8; 2 Thessalonians 2:4, 8).

Satan's challenge to God and His chance to occupy God's throne or Christ's place on the Temple Mount is all over. He is through as the *"accuser of our brethren"* and as the leader of dark angels. He is humiliated and abased so that all of His followers, as he enters into Hell, will ask him, *"have you also become as weak as we"* (Isaiah 14:9, 10)? Satan made brags and promises like Hitler, Mussolini, and ToJo did, all of which could not fulfill their promises, but were willing to destroy the world in trying. So it is with Lucifer.

MYSTERY OF GOD SHOULD BE FINISHED (verse 7)

All that God in Christ has planned through the ages is complete including our preaching and teaching, and our burden for the gospel and shame for the name of Jesus. The sixty years that I have labored together with the Church to validate Christ's claims and to reveal the mystery of God, is over. No more nights in prayer, no more anguish over the

Church, no more tears and sorrow for the lost, and no more bouts with the devil. The mystery of God, the Church, and the esoteric battles with Hell are finished.

Let me mention some information that I have shared before, but is so relative at this point: the Tribulation is a fulfillment of the seventieth week of Daniel's prophecy. It is from that prophesy found in the Daniel chapter nine that we get much of our information to complement the Book of Revelation. The last seven years was to be God's final consummation of His whole plan. This seven years, which we call the Tribulation was to accomplish six very positive outcomes. These outcomes show us the final finish of the mystery of God. It is to be finished on His people Israel, and upon the Holy City (Daniel 9:24). If we want to know how deeply Jerusalem is involved in this final battle, read carefully the prophecies made about Jerusalem in the book of Zechariah where Jerusalem is mentioned over eighty times. Once again, keep in mind that the Tribulation is meant by God and Christ to: 1) Finish the transgression; 2) Make an end of sin; 3) Make reconciliation for iniquity; 4) Bring in everlasting righteousness; 5) Seal up, or finish the vision and the prophecy; and 6) Anoint the most Holy.

These are certainly a part of the mystery of God that will be finished. God will complete them as He winds up the Tribulation. We should carefully study the implication that accompanies them in light of the final days of Tribulation and the setting up of the earthly kingdom of Christ.

BACK TO THE BOOK (10:7)

Now our attention is brought back to the book. Christ, holding the open book of our claim to rights of inheritance and standing on our claimed property, makes the proclamation of ownership and takes possession. Now He calls John's attention to the book. John is told to take it from the hand of Christ, the Conqueror. John, willing to take it, said *"Give me the little book." And [Christ] said to [me], 'Take and eat it up'"* (10:9).

Now, all has been placed back in the possession of Christ who has secured it for us and will soon yield it back to God (Ephesians 1:10; Colossians 1:16-18; 1 Corinthians 15:24-25). The right of possession was paid for by Christ, but now we are to share in the reclamation of it. This command reminds us of an Old Testament counterpart found in Ezekiel 2:8 and 3:1-3. To Ezekiel, it was a book of proclamation, and now to John, it is the same. Both were told that as they devoured the book, it would be sweet to the taste like honey, but in the stomach it would be bitter. It is bitter for its judgment proclamation, sweet for its proclamation of the inheritance.

It is a symbolism of our part in the process of redemption. Just as we take the Bible in hand and begin to devour it, it is sweet to us as we study. But when we must make it the proclamation of Christ to a wayward and sinful world, many times it becomes bitter to us. Sometimes when we proclaim our rights and stand with Christ as He claims our borders, we have to pay a price. Our preaching of Christ is mostly sweet, but it becomes bitter to our inner man when we must speak of Judgment to come.

JOHN TO PROPHESY TO MANY PEOPLE (v.11)

Christ said to John that he would again prophesy to many people. To John, this was a sign that somehow he would get off of Patmos and return to active ministry. He did return as a pastor of the Church at Ephesus, and died later of old age. Some people have stretched this verse to say that John would not die but would live through the Church age and be one of the two witnesses of the next chapter. I have not been able to find that hidden in this verse. John was only told that he would survive Patmos; and that his ministry with the testimony in his hand—the Book of The Revelation of Jesus Christ—was not over. There would be more sweetness and bitterness before the mystery of God was finished.

Now we enter into a discussion of one of the most revealing and exciting chapters in the continuing saga of the Revelation of Jesus Christ. We have found Him in every chapter and we will also be looking for Him in the chapters to come.

CHART OF THE HARMONY OF THE REVELATION

The Church in Heaven

- (Meet the Lord)
- Three events in the sky (Marriage Supper)
- (Court of Awards)
- Things that are to come

Second Coming of the Lord Chapter 19
With the saints - (Jude 14, Zechariah 14:9)

Chapter 20 - The Kingdom Age - The 1000 year Millennium
Hell Destroyed - Earth and Heaven cleansed
Chapter 21, 22 The New Heavens, Earth & New Jerusalem

God's wrath

| Chapter 7 |
| Chapter 9 |
| Chapter 11 |
| Chapter 12 |
| Chapter 14 |
| Chapter 16 |
| Chapter 18 |

3 1/2 yrs

Pause - Chapter 10 - Scene in Heaven

Man's wrath - Satan's wrath

| Chapter 6 |
| Chapter 8 |
| Chapter 11 |
| Chapter 12 |
| Chapter 13 |
| Chapter 15 |
| Chapter 17 |

3 1/2 yrs

Tribulation Time - 7 years

Chapter 4 & 5 — Preparation for Judgment in Heaven
Rapture of the Church

Chapters 2 & 3 The Church age - The things that are

CHAPTER 11

CHRIST, THE TEMPLE AND THE WITNESSES

ENTRANCE TO LAST HALF OF THE TRIBULATION
7TH TRUMPET PREPARES TO SOUND

Chapter eleven continues the interlude that began with chapter ten. The seventh trumpet will not sound until after the two witnesses have finished their testimony and have been caught up into Heaven (11:15). It is however, preparing to sound in the seventh verse of chapter ten when the declaration was made that *"The mystery of God [is] finished."* The events of chapter eleven, verses one through fifteen take place between the preparation to sound, and the actual sounding of the seventh trumpet. The second *woe* of man was in the sixth trumpet, and the third *woe* of man comes with sounding the seventh trumpet.

Strangely enough, the third *woe* of man comes with the declaration of Christ's Kingdom (11:15). The sounding of the seventh trumpet will include all of the events of Revelation up to the coming of the Lord Jesus Christ in chapter nineteen. At that time, the second *woe* will be over and the third *woe* upon man will begin. The third *woe* must then cover the entire last three and one-half years of Tribulation. The curtain is still closed and there is a hold on reporting the action of the Tribulation on Earth. During this time, we are still seeing some events that set the stage in Heaven for the Great Tribulation—the last three and one-half years, and the wrath of God.

The seventh trumpet may begin the second half of the Tribulation period. This period will cover all that is reported in the twelfth through the eighteenth chapters. All of these facts and the events accompanying them will take place simultaneously, and will happen within three and one-half years of time.

I will try to put it together briefly as I see it. Allow me and my colleagues to study these thoughts and develop more details of the scenario. This is intended to be studied as a general idea. While the beast's concept of his One World Order is expanding its control over a world shattered by the chaos of the first half of Tribulation, it will compromise the Temple Mount with a covenant to try to settle the Jerusalem problem and strife taking place over it.

A Temple will be constructed on the Temple Mount, but the hate of the Beast toward Israel under the Dragon will cause a breaking of the Covenant. The West Bank remnant and other of the Jewish faithful will have to flee into the wilderness of Edom. The demon-controlled armies (the dragon under the beast) will continue to pursue them. The beastly kingdom will expand to some great control over their part of the earth, but will have trouble with the north and east, and probably the kings of the east. He will not be able to subdue Jordan because of the protection of God over the refugees from Israel (Daniel 11:41).

In the battle over the Jews in hiding, Christ in person, or possibly by angels will evangelize among the Remnant and at least 144,000 will be converted. The Antichrist will win by flattery, much of Israel by convincing the secular Jews that he is the Messiah. He will plant his palace on the south end of the Temple Mount and set himself up a throne, declaring that he is God.

This will be the final straw for Satan and the Antichrist. The mystery of God is finished and time is up for Satan. The seventh trumpet declaring the establishing of Christ's Kingdom will sound from Heaven (11:15). Christ will proceed to Jerusalem via the Mount of Olives with 144,000 Jews from the refugee camp in Jordan (Isaiah 63:1). He will overcome the Antichrist and declare His Kingdom. Antichrist will retreat to his world center, probably in Babylon where He will prepare to meet Christ at Megiddo. He and his world army, who are filled with satanic demons, will be defeated at Armageddon, and Christ will cast him and all his cohorts into the pit.

With this general outline in mind let's begin with chapter eleven's commentary.

TEMPLE TO BE BUILT

Our attention is called to a temple in heaven which is the pattern of one that must be and will be built on the Temple Mount, starting at the beginning of the first half of the Tribulation. Daniel 9:27 pre-supposes a temple on the Temple Mount in order for sacrifices to resume. Out of world chaos from the time of sorrows, prior to the actual Tribulation, I believe the international community will allow the building of this temple as part of the covenant confirmed with the Jews, just as Daniel prophesied. This is an earthly Temple and must be distinguished from the Temple in Heaven which we will see opened on several occasions starting with the nineteenth verse. It is also mentioned eleven times during the next few chapters. See Appendix for further study on the earthly and heavenly temples.

We will see four different temples in the rest of the

book, including: The new earthly temple on Mount Moriah in Jerusalem which will be built at the beginning of the Tribulation; the millennial temple which will be built by Christ at His coming; the Temple in the New Jerusalem which is Christ; and the temple in Heaven.

All of the references to a temple in the Book of Revelation will be made from this point on. None of these refer to the Millennial Temple which Christ will build at His return as He sets up His 1000-year Kingdom (Zechariah 6: 12). The Millennial Temple is detailed for us in Ezekiel 41 through 48. However, in the New Jerusalem there will be no temple, for the Lamb is the Temple.

There are two references to the temple to be built in the Millennium on Mount Zion, but not in the New Jerusalem. This remains an enigma. All of them are found in relationship to the last three and one-half years of the Tribulation which is the same as the period of the wrath of God upon the Antichrist and His Kingdom. These two references in chapter eleven will be the only reference throughout Revelation to the earthly temple on the Temple Mount in Jerusalem. No doubt, however, it will be to this temple which Christ shall come to when He visits Zion (Revelation 14:1).

THREE AND ONE-HALF YEAR SCENARIO IN DANIEL AND REVELATION

There is a most exciting and telling scenario in the prophetic texts, which by a careful study, could yield a wealth of information to tie together Daniel's foresight into, and also take away from, the enigma of the last days, especially the last three and one-half years of the seven-year Tribulation. The scenario is slightly cryptic, comprising of one of those rather secret mysteries of prophetic fulfillment, yet very discoverable with some detailed observation. It is what we will call *the 3½ year scenario.* It is of a purpose that the Lord leaves much of the Book of the Revelation of Jesus Christ in analogues, as we said in the introduction. An analogue, meaning it is designed to be studied, contemplated, and researched.

The three and one-half years are mentioned ten times in scripture; five times in Daniel and five times in Revelation. All of them relate to the Antichrist's reign and to Israel in the last half of the Tribulation. This alone can show plainly our position that Daniel is in fact the stop-gap to the Revelation. We now will see how Daniel and Revelation are tied together by the *3 ½ year scenario*.

One of the timing concepts tied to the Tribulation and so clearly established in both the Old and New Testament texts (especially in Daniel and Revelation) is the *3½ year scenario*. It will give us a good background for the eleventh through the nineteenth chapters. If we will take a moment to study this synopsis, it will become clear that this period of time is the best documented in all of Scripture. It will be necessary to study this scenario to be able to properly understand the rest of the Book of the Revelation of Jesus Christ, and God's schedule for the rest of the Tribulation. A detailed list of the texts mentioning the *3½ year scenario* can be found in the Appendix.

To understand it, is an absolutely necessary to understand the last half of the Tribulation. The seven-year Tribulation period is the most time-controlled period in all of prophecy. While most prophetic predictions are generally predicated to certain signs and often rather general events, the seven years of the 70th week of Daniel has very specific timing.

This is one of the reasons that the Rapture of the Church must take place before the Tribulation starts, because if it was to take place during the Tribulation, it would be a timed event. However, we are told by Christ five times in the texts, that it is an imminent event which means, it can happen any time and we are to watch for it not knowing when it will come.

The study of the 3 ½ year plot alone, is so exact and complete that through understanding its place in prophecy, it can synchronize the whole Old and New Testaments' insight into the last half of the Tribulation. Every mention of the *3½ year scenario*, whether in the form of "a time, times and half a time"; or 1260 days; or 42 months are harmonious with the last years of God's wrath, and all of them have to do with the last days of Israel and the Jews. This scenario alone shows that God's ultimate motif of all prophecy was to arrive at this final consummation.

CONCERNS OF ALL THE JEWS IN THE LAST THREE AND ONE-HALF YEARS

All of the Old Testament that mentions the three and one-half year time-frame are found in the following verses: Daniel 7:25, 8:14, 9:27, 12:7, and 12:11. Each of these verses concerns the *little horn* and his dealings with Israel and their temple during the last days. In like manner, note that all of the New Testament references, with the exception of a hint of it in Matthew 24:15, are found in Revelation 11 – 13: verses 11:2, 12:6, 14, and 13:5. All are concerning the Antichrist and his dealings with the Jews of the Tribulation period. The beast is the counterpart to the Little Horn of Daniel's writings. So perfectly coordinated are these texts from writings nearly 600 years apart, that we cannot doubt the inspiration of the prophetic texts.

In every case from Daniel and Revelation, it refers to the last half of the Tribulation, and all are in reference to the Antichrist, or the beast and his dealings, with his persecution of the Jews at that time. Therefore, it has great significance for the Jews during the tribulation.

COURT OF TEMPLE LEFT OUT

According to Daniel 9:27, the Antichrist will defile the

Tribulation temple. This is just like we find in the eleventh chapter of Revelation. When John is measuring the temple, he is told to *"leave out the court ... given to the Gentiles"* for three and one-half years (Revelation 11:2-3). The *"abomination of desolation"* spoken of by the prophet, Daniel speaks of the time when the beast sets himself up in the place of Christ in that Temple, showing himself to be God (Daniel 9:27; Matthew 24:15; 2 Thessalonians 2:4). Ezekiel 42:20 explains how that the court was profaned by the priests when they would not set a difference between the holy and the profane; between the clean and the unclean. God hid his eyes from the court when the ministers would not set the difference. Selah!

It is of interest to note that the Dome of Omar on the Temple Mount today sits in the very place of the Court of the Gentiles. It is this abomination which causes spiritual desolation, that is, the departure of the presence of the Holy Spirit and all spiritual blessing.

COVENANT IN THE MIDST OF THE WEEK (DANIEL 9:27)

It is from this text in Daniel that we get the seven-year time frame set for the Tribulation, with a covenant to be made with the Jews over Jerusalem. This covenant will be made at the beginning of the Tribulation. It will be broken in the middle of the seven-year period, and then will be set up—the Antichrist setting himself up as God in the temple. Here we see clearly the dividing of the last seven years into two halves of three and one-half each.

BLASPHEMY

In Daniel 7:25, we find the Antichrist in the days of the little horn and the ten kings—the beast of Revelation and his ten horns, speaking great things of blasphemy against the Most High God, and changing the times and laws. This power will be given unto him over the Jews and the Temple Grounds for a *"time and times and half a time"* (Daniel 7:24, 25). All scholars agree that this speaks of one year, two years and one-half of a year. This fits perfectly with what we are told of the blasphemous beast of Revelation (Revelation 13:5).

2300 DAYS - 6 YEARS AND 110 DAYS

Daniel follows through with further information about the same, as he shows the sanctuary to be polluted and the sacrifice taken away for *"two thousand three hundred days; then the sanctuary shall be cleansed"* (8:14). Twenty-three hundred days is just short of seven years (6 years and 110 days). Thus, Daniel sees even the time that the covenant is in force, as part of the total time of the pollution of the temple. The Antichrist will have control of the Temple Mount under a covenant made with the Jews for most of the full seven years, but he will break the covenant in the midst of the week and will commit the abomination that makes desolate in the sanctuary, with His presence for the last half of that time (Daniel 9:27).

Matthew 24:15 and 2 Thessalonians 2:4 tells us that the abomination will take place when the Antichrist sets himself up in the temple as God. This all correlates with the cutting off of the two witnesses in Jerusalem (Revelation 11:3) and the beginning of the persecution of Israel, when Israel will flee for three and one-half years (Revelation 11:3). Jesus helps us to see this relationship to the Abomination of Desolation and the fleeing of the Jews, and the beginning of the Great Tribulation in Matthew 24: 15-22.

Daniel 12:7 tells us that Israel's persecution would end in a *"time, times and half a time"* and the Jews will receive all of the things that have been promised to them. This time-frame fits perfectly with the extent of time of their hiding and

God's protection on them. According to Revelation 12:14, this remnant of the Jews will be nourished and kept from the face of the serpent for *a "time and times and half a time."* In Daniel 12:11 we are told that from the taking away of the daily sacrifice in the tribulation temple in Jerusalem, and the setting up of the abomination, there would be one thousand two hundred and ninety days, thirty days longer than three and one-half years to the end of the beast's reign (Daniel 9:27). It will take thirty days to make the transition from the kingdom of the Antichrist and the kingdom of Christ.

Again, except for the extra thirty days, this matches perfectly with Revelation 13:5, which says that the beast would continue for forty-two months, or three and one-half years. Evidently, it will take thirty days to make the transfer from the Antichrist's kingdom to the Kingdom of Christ. Daniel even adds another forty-five days, making a full seventy-five days from the fall of the Antichrist's kingdom at Armageddon, to the setting up of the Kingdom of Christ (Daniel 12:12).

In Revelation, the three and one-half year term begins with the last half of the Tribulation, which starts in the eleventh chapter. It is also chapter eleven that first introduces the term, *"the wrath of God"* which will be used ten more times for a total of eleven times during the last three and one-half years (Revelation 11:18). This last three and one-half years also represents the time of *God's wrath*, as well as the *great day of God Almighty* and the *Lord's Day* which will bring a head to all of the *Law and Prophets* and the *New Covenant's* prophetic promise.

These facts show beyond question that the last half of the Tribulation begins with the events in chapter eleven.

In conclusion to the 3½ year scenario, all references to 3½ years are connected to the Antichrist's persecution of the Jews during his final reign; and all of them are related to the last half of the Tribulation period and to the wrath of God. Only by tying the book of Daniel together with the book of Revelation through the 3½ year scenario, can we clearly see and understand the meaning of the temple and the two witnesses in chapter eleven, the persecution of the Jews in chapter twelve, and the hate of the beast toward Israel in chapter thirteen. It also shows us the meaning of the visitation of Christ and the 144,000 to Mount Zion in chapter fourteen. We can see why the last four wars of the Tribulation and the final battle of the ages, is fought in Israel on Mount Megiddo, as told in chapter sixteen.

God scheduled all of this for the last 3½ years of this age, and He made it very clear by timing it perfectly. The ten times in which the 3½ year period is mentioned in scripture, shows us that it is the most important period of time on God's future time schedule, and that is because it deals with Israel's final restoration. The Church has already been redeemed and is in Heaven.

We can also see through this same 3½ year scenario, how much more clearly Revelation is explained by fitting its prophecies into Daniel, Zechariah, Ezekiel, Isaiah, and others as well. This is because every Messianic prediction has to be tied directly into the final Revelation of Jesus Christ, and the great day of God Almighty, namely *The Lord's Day which* lasts the full 7 year period. The 2300 days relates to the full week of years, both the first and the last 3½ of Tribulation. Evidently the Antichrist will continue his pollution of the Temple for the best part of the last 3½ years until his abominable seat is destroyed by Christ and His coming to Zion.

With these things in mind—the concept of the outline of the book, and the 3½ year time line, we see plainly the beginning of the wrath of God and the great Day of the Lord—We will return to comments on chapter eleven.

CHRIST, THE TEMPLE AND THE WITNESSES

With these things in mind—the concept of the outline of the book, and the 3½ year time line, the beginning of the wrath of God and the great day of the Lord to begin—we will return to comments on chapter eleven.

THE MEASURING OF THE TRIBULATION TEMPLE (v. 1)

To measure the temple shows a scriptural pattern which means to prepare for construction, just as you would draw up a set of blue prints that give all of the measurements. Ezekiel was told to measure the millennial temple in chapter forty-four of his book.

After addressing John about the little book in chapter ten, Jesus hands John a reed to measure the temple which is to be built on the Temple Mount in the near future. Evidently, the Temple Mount and the temple to be built there, is a very important part of that *Book of Decree*. The decree of promises must start with what happens on the Temple Mount.

On every one of my thirty-four trips to Israel, I have personally been on the Temple Mount and viewed most of the temple instruments which are already prepared; and which reside in the Temple Mount Museum in Jerusalem today. We are told that the finances to build the temple have already been raised. Donated by a Russian Business man, a great solid-gold Menorah at a cost of over a billion dollars stands just outside the Temple Institute as a testimony that that temple will be built in the near future. The *temple faithful* say that it can be built in three years. This fact fits perfectly with the 3 ½ year schedule which is given to us in scripture (Daniel 9:27).

The reason that it comes into focus here, is it represents activities that will result from the covenant made at the beginning of the seven-year period, the last seven years, or the seventieth week of Daniel's vision, and the issues that will ensue when the covenant is broken in the middle of the seven years (Daniel 9:27). It is a rebuilt temple that plays a very important part in the seven years of the Tribulation.

Daniel's question to the angel Gabriel was to know what would be the end of the Jewish nation, and their hope of a new temple. Gabriel gave this prophecy about the last seven years. These show that the Jews are and will be a very vital part of the Revelation of Jesus Christ (Daniel 9).

COMPROMISE OF THE TEMPLE MOUNT

The book of Daniel gives some details about the Antichrist's abuse of the temple and his covenant made over Jerusalem to flatter the Jews (Daniel 9:27). Evidently, both the liberal and the secular Jews will receive him as the Messiah, and believe in his covenant over Jerusalem. It appears that he will compromise the Temple Mount by giving the south end and the old Crusader Palace to the Christians while keeping the central part, or the court of the Gentiles, for the Muslim Dome of the Rock; and he will give the north end to the Jews to build their temple.

It is interesting that this very situation is pending in the current affairs of the Middle East today. Since 1948, when the State of Israel was born, the UN has not known what to do with Jerusalem. It was decided by the General Assembly of the UN to be called *Coeptus Septrum*, meaning a body separate. The entire world is to be one body—Globalism, but Jerusalem is supposed to remain a separate body. The plan is for it to be an international city owned by no one, but administered by the three major religions involved—Judaism, Islam, and Christianity. The Temple Mount is to be shared by these three faiths. The Scripture is vague on this topic; however, the World Order diplomacy is pushing for it today. The arrangement sounds good from the human, diplomatic standpoint, but it is not pleasing to God or according to His promise for the Messianic age.

The seven-year period of time actually starts with a covenant made over Jerusalem and the Temple Mount (Daniel 9:27). It is to be a decree which allows the Jews access to the Temple Mount, and to begin their daily sacrifices again. The daily sacrifice was cut off in AD 70 when the Temple of Herod was destroyed by Titus and Rome's tenth Army. No Jews, and only limited Christian activity, have been allowed on the Temple Mount since the State of Israel was established in 1948. The Arabs totally dominate the Mount. They control it through the State of Jordan. Even Christians are forbidden to pray, teach, or in any way comment about their faith while on the Temple Mount. One Jew, Prime Minister Arial Sharon, went on the Mount in 2001 and it caused the four-year Intifada, which cost 1000's of lives. If any man could come up with a solution to Jerusalem today he would be hailed as *Mr. President Planet Earth*. Mr. Kissinger introduced that thought years ago. The world is just waiting for that covenant over Jerusalem today.

In the near future, after some terrible crisis in the Middle East, the international community is going to realize that peace will never come until they treat the Jews fairly in their claim to the Temple Mount. A covenant will be signed to allow Jews access to their temple place. The Arabs fear that this place where the Jews would want to build their new temple is on the very place where the Arab *Dome of the Rock* sits today, and that it would have to be torn down. However, recent studies have shown, and in my own research which I have proven to my own satisfaction, that Solomon's Temple actually sat on the north end of the Temple Mount, directly west of the Eastern Gate.

If the new Temple was built there, it would place the Dome of the Rock exactly where this prophecy in Revelation eleven allows it to stay. We read here that while John was measuring the temple for construction, he was told by our Lord Jesus Christ to leave out the court which is without the temple, and do not measure it. The current location of the Dome of the Rock is what is known as the *Court of the Gentiles* and would sit on the south side of the temple. Take note of this: The Arabs declare that it was to be left out and given to the Gentiles. For three and one-half years. Once again, our *3½ year scenario* appears.

This fits other prophetic patterns that indicate just what World International diplomacy is working toward today. In the final settlement over Jerusalem, they hope to negotiate an arrangement, or covenant which will compromise the Temple Mount by dividing it between the Christians, Jews, and the Muslims. The idea coming out of the UN is to give the place of the old Crusader Castle which was built for the king of Jerusalem (now called the Al Aqsa Mosque), to the European Christian community, namely the Catholics. Also, they would give the center of the Mount where the Dome stands, and also the court of the Gentiles to the Muslims so they could keep their sacred Dome. This would allow the Jews to build their Temple on the very sight of Solomon's Temple, which is straight west of the Old East Gate and north of the Dome of the Rock.

This gives good insight as to why the Temple comes into focus at this point. The city of Jerusalem continues to be *"trampled down"* by the Gentiles for forty-two months (Luke 21:24). This would be during the last half of the Tribulation. Here again is the *3 ½ year scenario*. These prophecies fit perfectly with the world scene as we know it today.

We do well to understand that the international community in their dealing with Israel and the Temple Mount, does not desire to either promote, or offend local religions, but to work out difficulties in a way that would complement the World Order's agenda. The part they do not understand is Satan's involvement in these affairs. By not discerning His esoteric influence, they do not realize that disaster is pending. When a compromise is acceptable to the Jews, Muslims, and Christians, they will feel their goals have been reached. Imagine their disillusionment when the World Order leader, the very one that they have chosen, moves his headquarters, probably from Iraq, to the Temple Mount in Jerusalem and sets himself up as God. This also fits the present plan of the Muslim Brotherhood to unite the Shiite and Sunni factions, do away with the present borders of nations in the Middle East and bring together 10 nations of the Turkic peoples and revive the old Ottoman Turkish Empire and put there 12th Imam in the Temple in Jerusalem. I have not been able to put this together with the prophetic plan (see Appendix for details). This is inspired by the Treaty of Izmir made on September 14, 1996 between 10 Turkic nations.

WORLD ORDER BEING FORCED TO PAY ATTENTION

The Church is being forced to look toward the Middle East and the Jews are being forced to drift back to their homeland in the Middle East. The World Order personified by the UN does not want to deal with the Middle East, Jerusalem, or God, but they are being forced to pay attention. Why is the world being forced to be put in jeopardy just for the sake of these desert places? There seems to be an impetuous, impulsive, almost reckless energy driving the forces of the world toward the very scenario we find in Revelation. We are being forced to turn our attention back to the land, and to the God of the Bible. The trend is clear; the tide is coming in. The Intelligence Digest Editor-in-Chief, Joseph de Coursey Jr. makes a powerful proclamation by saying,

> "I am convinced that what is happening in the Middle

East is bringing the world to its last battle. I know nothing about the Bible. I draw my conclusion from the data we gather for the Digest."

OUR LORD'S INTEREST IN THE TEMPLE MOUNT

This chapter opens and closes with the Temple. The question must be asked, "Why does the Temple that is to be built on the Temple Mount in Jerusalem come into focus here at the beginning of chapter eleven? And why does the chapter close with the temple in Heaven?" The answer is obvious when considering Daniel's prophecy of the last seven years. As we shared earlier, chapter eleven records the beginning of the last half of the seven-year Tribulation, and the temple plays an important role in the three and one-half years. These references to a temple are about an earthly temple on the Temple Mount.

None of the further References to a Temple will refer to the Millennial Temple which Christ will build after the Tribulation and after His Second coming, which is detailed for us in Ezekiel 44 through 48. Nor do they refer to the Temple in the New Jerusalem (Revelation 21:22). There are a total of eleven references in Revelation to the Temple in Heaven (11:19, 14:15, 17, 15:5-6, 16:1, 17). All of them are found in relationship to the last three and one-half years of Tribulation, or the period of the wrath of God upon the Antichrist and his kingdom. The reference in chapter eleven is the only one throughout Revelation to the earthly temple on the Temple Mount in Jerusalem. It is mentioned here because the controversy of Zion and the issue of the Temple Mount, and a future Jewish temple on Mount Moriah are, and will be key issues in triggering the Tribulation.

What interest would our Lord Jesus Christ have in the Temple of the Tribulation? We must ask this and remember that it is He who is dictating these things to John. Why would He turn His attention to what is going to happen on the Temple Mount and a Covenant of the last day?

We remember that our Lord is always very interested in the temple and its ordinances. He said, *"Do not think that I came to destroy the Law or the Prophets. I did not come to destroy but to fulfill ... [for] not one jot or tittle will by no means pass from the law till all is fulfilled"* (Matthew 17-18).

In contemplating His interest and connection to the latter-day Tribulation temple on Mount Moriah, I submit the following:

1. The Temple will be where He visits to deliver it from the Antichrist (Revelation 14:14-16).

2. The Temple Mount will be the place from which He will reign in His earthly Millennial Kingdom (Revelation 20:4-6).

3. The re-establishing of the sacrifice is all about Him. He is the sacrifice, and Israel will come to recognize this.

4. Any action against the Jews, their sacrifices, and their Temple will be taken as an action against Christ Himself and His Father, God. However, when the Temple on Moriah is polluted again, this time by the Antichrist sitting on *his throne* claiming to be God, the Jews will realize that the sacrifice is no longer necessary for, in the evangelizing of the 144,000, they will finally see that the Sacrificial Lamb was truly a symbol of Jesus Christ, the man, *"who takes away the sin of the world"* (John 1:29). What a revival this will bring among the converted Jews. I doubt that they will mourn the broken covenant and the sacrificial ritual being broken, in their exuberance for finally clarifying and exposing the enigma of the meaning of the sacrifice—a man, Christ Jesus the Messiah.

5. It is very possible, however, that the hate of the Antichrist against the covenant and the sacrifice as revealed in Daniel 11:28-31, will be a key factor in the beginning of God's wrath toward him and his entire World Order Kingdom.

6. We may also see that the turning of the Antichrist against the covenant and the causing of the sacrifice to cease, will force the Jews to reconsider whether the sacrifice is necessary. This would give opportunity for the converted Messianic Jews, possibly even the two witnesses, to show that there is no longer any need for a sacrifice. The fulfillment of the sacrificial lamb is in the Lamb of God, Jesus Christ, and He is right there among them. Some major change is coming among the remnant of Israel, especially those who have fled and are protected by God in the wilderness (Revelation 12:14). It is clearly stated that they *"have the testimony of Jesus Christ"* (12:17).

One of the reasons that many of the Old Testament details are not repeated here, is probably because the Book of Revelation was not written for non-Biblical people, but for those with a background in the whole Messianic texts of the Old Testament, and assuming that they know enough to research the Old Testament Messianic texts, putting them together with the Revelation texts.

TWO WITNESSES (v. 3)

In connection with the measuring of the soon-to-be built Temple on Mount Moriah, two witnesses appear on the scene. That they are real human beings is beyond question, although they perform angelic or God-like feats; then they die like other men, and probably have not tasted death before.

WHO ARE THESE TWO MEN?

There is a lot of speculation as to whom they are. They must be known from antiquity as they are prophesied to come nearly five centuries before John writes of them, and before Christ reveals them (11:4; Zechariah 4:2-3). A study of Zechariah four will add to our understanding of these two witnesses and their purpose.

There are several prospects as to who they are. There are four most prominent candidates: one is John himself, but I think his qualifications are very weak. Elijah is a second candidate as he probably ranks high in qualifications. Moses is a third, but if you rely on very questionable tradition, he does not fit the bill. A fourth is Enoch who is a good possibility.

There are a few requirements for any man to qualify: 1) He must be a prophet; 2) He must have never died, because *"it is appointed for men to die once"* (Hebrews 9:27); 3) He must still be alive and standing before God in Heaven since Zechariah wrote his book; 4) He must be a man who represents extraordinary power with God and bears a strong witness.

I believe that there are only two men who could meet these conditions: Enoch and Elijah. They both stood strong and alone against a wicked world; they both prophesied judgment upon a wicked world; and both were raptured having never died. These two men can surely qualify for the title of *"anointed ones who stand beside the Lord of the whole earth"* (Zechariah 4:14). Other Bible scholars favor this view. For a list of them, refer to *The Apocalypse,* by E.A. Lowmaster (173-175).

These two were prophesied of old. To better understand the two witnesses and the synopsis which ties them to the Temple Mount, we will need to consult the first mention of them in Scripture. Revelation 11:4 points us directly to prophecies in the book of Zechariah, chapter four. There we find the following reference to the two prophets referred to as two olive trees and the two candlesticks *"who stand beside the Lord of the whole earth"* (Zechariah 4:12-14).

In Zechariah, a man with a measuring line is sent to measure Jerusalem for reconstruction (2:2). We are told in that day that, *"Jerusalem shall be inhabited as towns without walls, because of the multitude of men and livestock in it"* (2:4). It is an amazing thing to see what God and Christ are doing in Jerusalem. Who would ever think it could be? Just over half a century ago, no one except Bible readers would ever believe that Jerusalem could rise to a status where its affairs would shake up the whole world. Before the turn of the 20th Century, it was nothing but a heap of rocks and rubble from 27 fallen cities that had been destroyed in the past. Very few people lived there and most of them were poor. Today we see the city that Zechariah spoke of as a sprawling metropolis of towns without walls.

If you wish to know what God intends for Jerusalem and the Temple Mount during the last days, Zechariah is the book to study. Verse by verse, the Old Testament Book is being directly fulfilled today. Its message is simple, God is *"returning to Jerusalem"* (Zechariah 1:16, 17).

Forty times, Jerusalem is mentioned by name in the book of Zechariah; six times in the first chapter and three times in the second chapter. By putting together what is said about the Temple Mount and Jerusalem in the book of Zechariah, and the sequence of events in Revelation, we get good insight into the last years of the Jews in this present age. All of these activities mentioned in Revelation about Jerusalem and the Temple, are found prophesied and paralleled in Zechariah. Many of the details left out in Revelation can be filled in by comparing Zechariah's prophecies of the *Day of the Lord.*

Jerusalem's final status is clearly given to us in chapters twelve and fourteen of Zechariah, where Jerusalem is to become a *"cup of trembling"* to all nations round about, and a *"burdensome stone"* to the whole world (12:2-3, King James Version). The *"day of the Lord"* referred to in verse 14:1 is a direct reference to Revelation, and it is said in that day, Jerusalem will be under siege by *"all the nations."* According to verse four, Christ will come at that time, and *"His feet will stand on the Mount of Olives"* and then come to Zion, which is exactly fulfilled in Revelation (14:4). We see then, that Zechariah and Revelation have much in common, and when Christ with His 144,000 comes to Zion, Jerusalem will be under siege.

In another interesting comparison between Zechariah and the fourteenth chapter of Revelation, we see a prediction that there will be a Tribulation temple constructed during that same time. The rebuilding of the temple at the return of Israel from Babylon becomes a direct prophetic example of the building of the final Tribulation temple associated with the return of the Jews in the final day. The difficulties in the building of this Tribulation temple, is reflected again in that it will be built in troubled times but *"not by might nor by power, but by My Spirit, says the Lord of hosts"* (4:6). The *mountains* refer to the resistance against its construction; and this resistance will be brought down, and a covenant with the World's Leaders over Jerusalem and the temple will be made (Daniel 9:27). The bringing forth of the headstone is already prepared and will be brought victoriously to the Temple Mount with shouts and dancing, and singing *"grace, grace to it"* (Zechariah 4:7).

The foundation will be laid and it will be finished, and the Jews will "know that I am the Lord," says God. The *temple faithful* have tried on a number of occasions in recent years to bring the headstone to the temple grounds, but have been turned back, not by Muslim people, but by the IDF (Israel Defense Forces) of Israel.

After some extreme crisis, the World Order will make a Covenant with the Jews and allow them to build their temple. Then, the headstone will be set. The reference to the two witnesses of Revelation eleven has its introduction then in Zechariah, four. It is interesting to note that these two anointed ones are in direct relationship to building a temple, so we can know that the two witnesses spoken of in Revelation chapter eleven, are also in relationship to a temple which is spoken of here (Zechariah 4:14). It clearly prophesies that a temple will be built and finished by the time of Christ's visit (Revelation 14).

Zerubbabel's second temple was built when the Jews returned from Babylon and Assyria. But again, we cannot miss the comparison in this prophecy and how it becomes a pre-sage to the building of the temple in the Lord's Day. Therefore, the Spirit of God carries us with long strides across the long ages from the event of building a Temple in Zerubbabel's day to the future time when again a Temple will be built during the Lord's Revelation. The *"not by might, not by power, but by My spirit says the Lord of Hosts"* is to be fulfilled in larger fashion in Revelation eleven, as we see the mighty power of the Spirit of the Lord prepare the way for Christ's coming by humbling the kingdom of the beast at the hand of these two witnesses.

The two witnesses, are said to be *"the two anointed ones, who stand beside the Lord of the whole earth,"* and are called to witness in Jerusalem during the last three and one-half years of the Tribulation (Zechariah 4:14; Revelation 11:3-4). I believe in addition to their witness here on Earth, they will have tremendous intercession power before the throne of God during this same time as it is said that they *"stand by the Lord of the whole earth"* (4:14).

They will be protected by Christ throughout the last half of the Tribulation. As the Spirit of Christ works through them, they will be Christ's evangelists, and many Jews will be saved and encouraged. They will be a great encouragement especially to the Jews in exile that had to flee from the West Bank and Judaea (Matthew 24:16). As they stand by the God of Earth, they will call down the plagues from Heaven upon the Antichrist's kingdom just prior to Armageddon. I believe these plagues are the same ones spoken of in Revelation fifteen. The Devil, who is on a rampage *"because he knows that he has a short time,"* will begin a great persecution of the Jews, starting by killing these two witnesses in Jerusalem (11:7, 12:12). Then he will send out his armies with the intent to slay the protected Jews in the wilderness (12: 12-16). The death of these witnesses can only happen when they have finished their testimony (11:7).

We now see how the Spirit of God could look down through time and see an event that could never have been conceived of by people in John's day. However, an all-knowing Christ could see perfectly and without any fanfare, reporting it just as it will happen in our day.

TWO WITNESSES KILLED AND RAPTURED (v.7-12)

The bodies of the two witnesses will lie in the streets of Jerusalem, "then those from the peoples, tribes, tongues, and nations will see their dead bodies three days and a half days" (11:9). Here is a direct reference that can be nothing else but the world link of satellite TV which is so common today. News media of the world can and will download these scenes live directly from Jerusalem, Israel.

Note how far the world will drift into critical mass and the paradigm shift toward a total world worship of Satan. With the Church gone for over three years, the world will shift so far into universal devil-worship, that it will have a hey-day in celebration because of their deaths (13:4, 8). They will even have gift exchanges and parties galore (11:10).

Why? *"Because these two prophets tormented those who dwell on the earth"* (11:10). The preaching of Christ is always a torment to willingly blasphemous and rebellious people.

At that very hour, there was a great earthquake *"and a tenth of the city fell ... seven thousand men were killed, and the rest were afraid"* (11:13).

CAUGHT UP

Now watch this! *"After the three and a half days the breath of life from God entered them, and they stood on their feet"* (11:11). Suddenly, the Spirit of Life comes into the two prophets, and they stood up right before a breathless world who is watching on worldwide television. These witnesses hear the same voice of Christ as the Church heard in chapter four: *"'Come up here' and they ascended to Heaven in a cloud, and their enemies saw them* (11:12). The world will be familiar with this type of *catching away* since the Church will already have been raptured a few years before. Talk about Christ having a sense of humor; what a joke that will be on a devil-stupefied world! They heard the same voice as the Church heard at the time of its Rapture (4:1).

GREAT EARTHQUAKE IN JERUSALEM (v. 13)

I am convinced that the earthquake is probably the same one that will take place when the feet of Christ touches Mount Olivet, as recorded in Zechariah 14:4 (11:13); because we are immediately told that the remnant—those Jews who fled into the wilderness, was afraid, and gave glory to God: *"The kingdoms of this world have become the kingdoms of our Lord and of his Christ, and He shall reign forever and ever"* (Revelation 11:15).

We see this very same scenario in Zechariah 14:9:

"And the Lord shall be King over all the earth. In that

day it shall be—the Lord is one, and His name one."

Christ's presence on Zion will convince the world that He is the King of Kings.

ANOTHER CAMP MEETING IN HEAVEN (v.13 & 16-17)

While the people of the world are having a holiday, another camp meeting breaks out in Heaven, praising Christ for His power, and that He has set Himself to reign at the declaration that He is King of all the earth (11:16-18). They are already celebrating the homecoming of the witnesses and also Christ's victory and Kingship, even before the final battles are won. So just before we turn back to the earthly scenes of chapter twelve, we will look toward Heaven, where a great praise service ensues. Back on Earth, all of this stirs up the Antichrist's devilish notions and shakes up the entire world, setting the tenor for Armageddon. It is set just after the second and third woe is declared upon man, whom now recognizes that the trouble comes from the hand of God:

> *"The nations were angry, and Your wrath has come, (they recognize this as God's hand) and the time of the dead, that they should be judged..."* (11:18).

Psalm two closely parallels this verse where the nations rage against God's plan to put Christ on David's throne in Jerusalem. God will *"destroy those who destroy the earth"* (11:18).

This is speaking of the final judgment of those in the second death. But up in Heaven during this time as we have shown in the previous chapter, it is time for the Judgment Seat of Christ, and for rewards to be given to the servants of Jesus Christ, and the saints (Bema) that fear Christ's name (11: 18; 2 Corinthians 5:10).

(Note: In my opinion and many others, our modern-day environmentalists are destroying the earth more than anyone else.)

TEMPLE OPEN IN HEAVEN (11:19)

We will now consider the temple that *"was opened in Heaven"* (11:19). We started this *time out* with the temple in Heaven and we end with the temple in Heaven, to remind us that Christ is still in total control as He sits on the Mercy Seat in the temple, making intercession for all of His Earth-bound saints (10:1, 11:19).

The temple represents to us an assurance of God's presence among us. The Lord Jesus Christ is once again, encouraging us to know that God's plan is still intact, and the temple representing His abiding presence, is still open in Heaven. Here we see the *ark of His covenant* in Heaven (11:19). This will be important to remember as we come to chapter fifteen and see the vial of judgment coming from the open temple in Heaven. The ark of the Old Testament tabernacle has now become the ark of Christ's Covenant, representing His *will and testament*. It is Christ's will and testimony which will be enacted upon us very soon, as it returns our inheritance back to us and to Israel.

This is a sentence involving lightening, voices, thundering, and great hail, are terms which bring our attention back to the Tribulation hour. They are terms associated with divine justice and judgment. Natural disasters are always a part of God's judgment process.

This judgment is upon angry nations that in satanic wrath, would *"destroy the earth,"* but for Christ who knows how to mingle mercy with judgment (11:18).

As the prophet Isaiah points out that He is:

"God of Israel, the One who dwells between the

cherubim, You are God, You alone, of all the kingdoms of the earth. You have made heaven and earth" (37:16).

Psalms 80:1 and 90:1 make reference to Him sitting among the Cherubim's, shining in His strength.

Christ, as shown in the open temple in Heaven, is at the Mercy Seat between the Cherubim's (Revelation 11:19). The temple is shown as open to indicate that God has not forgotten either His covenant with Israel, or His promise to the Church. It is still a seat of mercy for those who are repentant, but will be a seat of judgment for the blasphemous. It will again be shown open just prior to Armageddon (Revelation 15:5-6). Out of it comes the seven angels with the vials of judgment.

The nations are soon to meet the *"weapons of indignation"* in the *"day of the Lord"* which will *"break in pieces"* and *"destroy the kingdoms"* that try to steal Israel's inheritance; and those who have sought to *"destroy the earth"* (Isaiah 13:5-6; Jeremiah 51: 20; Revelation 11:18).

We see Christ still in the temple as the Great Intercessor before the throne of mercy. His purpose is to show mercy on all who repent; to spare the earth from satanic hate and destruction; and to save humanity from total and complete annihilation (Matthew 24:21-22).

The temple is spoken of fourteen times during the last 3 ½ years, while the throne is mentioned only eight times. The throne seems to be the center of action for the first half of the Tribulation, but the temple in Heaven is the center of action during the last half. This is to remind us that God in Heaven, through Christ's presence on Earth, is in control of all of these events which are out of the temple in Heaven, and represent Christ's purpose of salvation, restoration, redemption, and reformation. His purpose is to return Israel to its glory, and to redeem the nations for Christ's Kingdom.

Remember, while these things are taking place on Earth, some of the Jews may be martyred for the testimony of

Jesus, even though 144,000 of them are *sealed* and under the protection of Christ (Revelation 12:11, 17). Meanwhile, the Church is above all of this and busy around the throne in Heaven, making preparation for the Marriage Supper of the Lamb. Revelation declares that the Bride has *"made herself ready"* (Revelation 19:7).

Chapter twelve will show us more of the saga of the Jews in the last days and give further insight to the plight of the Jews under the Antichrist in the Tribulation.

CHAPTER 12

ISRAEL IN THE TRIBULATION

CHRIST AND THE JEWS IN TRIBULATION

Chapter twelve in the Book of Revelation gives us another meanwhile that we have spoken of. While the first half of the Tribulation is in progress, with all of the natural disasters and wars among the angry nations; and while the covenant over Jerusalem is in force; and while the Temple is being built and the two witnesses are in charge; while the Jewish faithful are busy preparing to sanctify the new temple and all of the instruments, and begin the daily sacrifice again; and while the Arabs and their terrorists' schemes having been stayed for the time, are now willing to compromise the Temple Mount with the Jews and allow the Al Aqsa Mosque to be used by the Christian Catholics and the Orthodox, the Jewish plight has just begun.

At the close of chapter eleven, we see the temple in Heaven and the Ark of the Testimony in evidence. Remember, the top lid of the Ark is the mercy seat where Christ sits in intercession. Christ's presence in the temple before the Ark of the Testament shows He is still very much in control. A *testament* is a will, and the Ark before Him recalls all of the promises and covenants made from Abraham and Moses. His intentions for the Church, the World, and the Jews, will be administered by Him in His estate as the Executor of His own will. The little book in His hand in chapter ten, spoke of the legal decree by which He will act. His testament was ready for probate at His death, and now it is to be revealed before all of the benefactors. It is always accompanied by God's great power and authority (11: 19).

The Apostle Peter says in that He has bequeathed to us *"an inheritance"* (1 Peter 1:4). An inheritance is not something you work for; it is something that is handed to you by the will of the testator. Christ has bequeathed to us a place in His kingdom by the blood of His testament. Peter said it is waiting for us in Heaven. It is *"incorruptible and undefiled"* and unending; and that it is *"reserved in Heaven for [us]"* and He will be *"revealed"* (1:4-5). This is the promise that Christ is ready to win for us, after He has defeated all of the enemies of God's Kingdom.

There is a worm in the apple! When judgment opens up to us the realities hidden in the spiritual world, I am afraid that the whole world, including much of the church will be surprised that there is one entity from whom the whole world is taking their orders. While Christ is building and establishing His Kingdom, Satan is busy building his kingdom among the lost people of this world. It is his kingdom which will be destroyed. In this chapter of Revelation, He is revealed and exposed more than anywhere else in the Bible.

Satan, the ancient protester of God's and Christ's will, is set to go all out to block any final fulfillment of the Testament. Through His protégé, the beast who was introduced in the chapter eleven and expounded upon in the thirteenth chapter, and who will play a prominent co-star role throughout chapter nineteen under the power and authority of the dragon, Satan, is setting his plan to break the covenant made over Jerusalem and unleash a major onslaught against the Jewish nation. However, remember that the Jews are a major benefactor in Christ's will and testament. Speaking of the Jews, he said, *"inasmuch as you did it to one of the least of these My brethren, you did it to me"* (Matthew 25:40).

DON'T LOSE SIGHT OF JESUS CHRIST WHILE WE WATCH HELL AT WORK

Don't lose sight of Jesus Christ while we observe some of the work of Hell through the beast. All the time that Satan tries to finish his dirty work, Christ is very active in the esoteric. He is still the Executor and Redeemer of the estate, and the oil and light of the candlesticks (Zechariah 4:2; Revelation 11:4). Also, He is still the sealer and protector of the remnant of the Jews during the coming 3½ years of the Great Tribulation. Very quickly, after the Beast, or Antichrist breaks the covenant over Jerusalem which gave Jews the legal right to build their temple, Christ will bring Satan and His Kingdom to full judgment (Daniel 9:27). Remember, Satan has no more time to work His wiles, and only a very short period to vent His final anger against the Jewish people and Christ before He is destroyed.

ISRAEL IN TRIBULATION

In this twelfth chapter of Revelation, we are going to witness the plight of the Jews, especially the remnant of refugees who must flee during the last half of the Tribulation. In my opinion, one of the great oversights of so many who write and expound on the Book of Revelation, is their preoccupation with the co-stars of the story like the beast, false prophet, harlot, the 666, etc. and their tendency to forget the two main stars in the plot. Namely, they do not see Jesus Christ in His proper role, and they almost always overlook the Jews in their final days. Because of the overriding Replacement Theology theory so prevalent throughout Evangelical Churches today, they do not properly relate the Old Testament Messianic themes to Revelation. And, they do not know how to intercalate them into the final part of the story, so they miss the best of Christ and His part in the Revelation scheme. They also overlook the part played by the Jews in those final promises. They relate all of these references to the Jews, with the Church.

Also, because we are so negative in nature and the scary part is what most of our reading crowd want to read about, we dwell on those sections of the Book rather than upon its theme and main motif.

WHY ISRAEL IS OFTEN OVERLOOKED IN REVELATION

Oversights of Israel are made possible because of at least three misconceptions.

1. As related above, Replacement Theology has played a prominent position in the Church and its concept toward the latter time of Israel and the Jews for the past 400 years.

    This extremely erroneous concept is far more prominent and widespread among the Evangelical churches than previously recognized. It is almost universally taught and allowed to dominate our thought in a great number of our Bible Institutions today. As I have said, it is an oversight just generally accepted without really giving it any thought. In error, it cuts Israel and the sons of Abraham, both Jews and Arabs, almost totally out of the end-time promise. This chapter is generally seen as allegorical in which the Church has inherited all of the promises that were made to Israel.

    This causes the Old Testament prophets to be

interpreted almost entirely as allegorical, making every prophecy, prediction, and promise written to the Jews, now to be written to the Church in a metaphorical way instead of literally written about the Jews. Thereby, they are usurping Israel's actual future place in God's plan. Their premise is the same as that taken by Jerome, Luther, Calvin, and others of the reformation who taught that because the Jews crucified Christ, they were cut totally out of promise, causing all of the promises to go to the Church now.

With this idea in heart and head, these well-meaning custodians of God's Word have given impetuousness to a horrible error and do not see the Jews' and Israel's literal part in the Book of Revelation.

In case there are those who are not familiar with the term *Replacement Theology* and its influence on our attitude toward the Jews, I will share a little more of the history and damage done to basic doctrine that *Replacement Theology* has inflicted upon the Church and its sound interpretation of prophecy.

It began with Jerome, who translated the Scriptures into Latin to favor the Catholic Popes. The Popes were promoting the idea that the Catholic (Universal) Church was now the inheritor of all of the Jews' hopes and promises. Since the Jews had failed to recognize their Messiah and God cursed them and scattered them throughout the world, they were to assimilate into the Gentile nations and have no more future in Christ's kingdom.

With this basic doctrine and attitude toward the Jews, they were thought to be a cursed people with no rights, and all of the Messianic prophecies and promises now belong to the Church. As penalty for crucifying Christ, Israel and the Jews had no place in the future kingdom, and therefore did not appear in the Revelation of Jesus

Christ. It seems almost as if Christ holds a grudge against them and has cut them out of His kingdom. According to these commentators, the many verses of Old Testament prophecy which relate to the Jews, were actually cryptic and symbolic terms and are now to be seen as belonging to the Church.

Even Martin Luther whose anti-Semitism was used by German leadership to foment the Holocaust, Calvin, and Knox were very strongly Anti-Semitic in their day, so the attitude prevailed in the Church until the outpouring of the Holy Spirit and the beginning of the Evangelical Church in the early 1900's. The idea that Israel and the Jews were no more considered a part of God's and Christ's future plans, and that all predictions and promises were assumed by the Church, has allowed for gross misunderstanding if not deep deception regarding the end-time events. With this concept widely taught and promoted in the Church, naturally very few understood the Jewish part in the Book of Revelation of Jesus Christ.

2. Consequently they fail to see the role of the Jews in the final days and especially as depicted in the Revelation of Jesus Christ.

Christ's love and concern for His people—the Jews, are largely misunderstood. Certainly, the Jews by-in-large, failed to recognize their Messiah when He came; and yes, they did have a role in His Crucifixion. But let us not forget that Rome had a far heavier hand in Christ's Crucifixion, so why do we not place the same curse on Rome and the Roman Church? And yes, the Jews were scattered throughout the world in Diaspora, but they were never cut off entirely from the Kingdom. Jesus said, *"Father forgive them, for they do not know what they do"* (Luke 23:34). Paul taught us very specifically in Romans, chapters 9 through 11, about the plight of the Jews after the Crucifixion. He said that the Holy Spirit gave Him great heaviness and sorrow for the outcast Jews. He reminded us that Jesus came from their stock by promise when He said, *"My heart's desire and prayer for Israel is that they may be saved"* (Romans 10:1).

They were cut off and grafted in, but we were not to boast ourselves against them. Then He brought us right down to the final days for the Jews. He pointed us right to the time of the Revelation of Jesus Christ. When the Gentile Church was complete comes into Heaven by Rapture, then:

"... all Israel will be saved, as it is written: 'The deliverer will come out of Zion, and He will turn away ungodliness from Jacob" (Romans 11:25-26).

Paul concluded with Romans 11:33:

"Oh, the depth of the riches both of the wisdom and knowledge of God! How unsearchable are His judgments and His ways past finding out."

As we study the Book of Revelation we must remember that the Christ and God His Father are far beyond our understanding. We can only assemble His Word in its proper perspective and leave the rest to Him. One thing is absolutely clear. He has not cut off Israel and the Jews from their heritage and promise. I want to be burdened with the burdens that burden the heart of God, and if Christ is burdened with the Jews and Jerusalem, I want to be burdened with them also, and I want to understand their last days under the plan of God and Christ.

3. They fail to assimilate the Old Testament Messianic

prophecies into the Revelation of Jesus Christ and therefore miss all of the covenants and promises to be fulfilled in the Jews and Israel in the last days.

Because the theme of the Revelation is Jesus Christ and His second coming at the *Day of the Lord,* the book specializes in assimilating most of the Old Testament Messianic prophecies with the events taking place there.

And because most of the Messianic prophecies are cryptic in nature and rather hard to understand, and their secrets revealed only to those who know Him and respect His name, even the majority of the Jewish Sages, Rabbi's and Scribes miss part of the message. There was and is only a few in Israel who are students of the last-day role of the Jews and their Messiah. The Messianic prophecies are not meant to be understood by most people including the Jews, but were written in such a fashion that only those who look for Him will find Him and only *"the wise shall understand"* (Daniel 12:10). This text in Daniel is speaking specifically about the last days and of the Antichrist and his relationship to the Jews. In other words, this is exactly what is revealed in the Book of Revelation. Those Jewish scholars that still reject Jesus Christ as the Messiah are partially blind and cannot see the Christ in Revelation, just as many of the scholars in Christ's day could not see the more than 109 Old Testament prophecies which He fulfilled in His life, because they could not accept the concept of a suffering Messiah (Isaiah 53). Even today, they cannot accept a time of *Jacob's Trouble* which reveals Israel's sufferings before they are able to accept Jesus Christ. It leaves them totally blind to the meaning of Revelation. But we who are stewards of the Word must not overlook their part. We must search diligently to see their relationship to the events of the *Day of the Lord*.

4. Because they do not understand the cryptic nature of the Old Testament Messianic prophecies, they are not able to see and discern the cryptic nature of Revelation. Christ has chosen to keep Himself hidden in mystery all through the Old Testament and also in the Book of His Revelation. Only those who give careful prayer and consideration of the Messianic secrets are able to understand how to assemble the insights of the Old Testament with the symbolic and cryptic expressions of the Book of Revelation to get the whole picture. Therefore, the place of the Jews in the last days is largely overlooked by most readers and students of the Revelation of Jesus Christ.

Therefore, because the Jewish scholars by-in-large, do not want to accept the true message of the Revelation of Jesus Christ, and because a bulk of Christianity for reasons mentioned above do not want to see the Jewish part in Revelation, little is written about their place and their plight during the coming days of trouble. However, by considering the whole motif of Old Testament prophesies, we must confess they have a very important role in the last days. Here we have two whole Chapters exclusively about the Jews and their place and plight during the Tribulation. By comparing and incorporating Old Testament texts which prophesy about the same time as the events written in Revelation, we find a very fascinating expose' of the final days of the Jews.

CHAPTERS 11 AND 12 ARE ABOUT THE JEWS

My point is to leave no misunderstanding that chapters 11 and 12 are not metaphorical about the Church, but are clearly about Israel and the Jews in the last days, and carry a major part of Old Testament ideology contained in eschatological and Messianic terms. These eschatological concepts are brought forward to the end and represent the final days and complete fulfillment of the Abrahamic promise. If the Jews and Israel have no future place in the kingdom of Christ, why are these major themes so clearly expressed in these two chapters and matched by scores of texts in the Old Testament which complement them? And why is the building of their temple so promised in Daniel chapter nine and brought to our attention here? The temple is not a Christian concern. If the Jews have no future in the end-time events, why are 144,000 (12,000 from each tribe) particularly singled out for mention? And why are the names of the twelve tribes of Israel placed on the gates of the New Jerusalem? Why do the stones of the breastplate of the priests garnish the foundation of the city? Why is it called the Bride of the Lamb? The lamb was strictly a Jewish concept until it became incorporated into the literacy of Christianity. And why is the city of New Jerusalem full of cryptic, Messianic, Jewish concepts?

Most, if not all of the praises, verbiages, and thoughts contained in the 12th chapter, have their base in the Old Testament, and concern the Jews. Therefore, in order to understand them, we must find their counterpart in the Old Testament, and fit what is said there into what is taught here. If the Jews, Jerusalem, and the temple burden Christ's heart, then that is what I want to be burdened with (Psalms 126:1-6, 122:6-9). These Psalms show us the burden of God and Christ for Jerusalem in the days of Israel's return, and that is today. That's why these chapters and their companion texts are of great interest to me.

OLD TESTAMENT IDIOMS AND THEIR CONCEPT IN THIS CHAPTER

An *idiom* is meant to express a language particular to a person or group, or it is an expression with special meaning.

Old Testament Messianic language is expressive of a certain person with a special meaning. It is often Cryptic, shrouded in symbolism and mystery, and designed to be understood by only those who devote themselves to its study. So it is with much of the language expressed in this chapter. We will now look at it phrase by phrase.

Revelation 12:1 connects with the prior thoughts in the former chapter. There we were shown angry nations who were destroying the earth. While this terrible tragedy of the first half of the Tribulation is happening on Earth, we notice that an earthly temple is related to the temple in Heaven. It is my opinion that the last verse of verse 11:19 should have been the first verse of chapter twelve, for there is a direct connection between verse 11:19 and verse 12:1; the temple in Heaven and a wonder in Heaven—a woman clothed with the sun.

The ark of the testimony is seen in Heaven, a reminder especially to the chosen people to whom this chapter particularly relates, that the Old Testament covenants are still valid by the authority of old-time prior decrees. While war is going on in the earth as a counterpart to that war, there is a theater of another war being prepared in Heaven, and it deeply involves the ancient Biblical people of Israel. In this chapter a lot of ancient cryptic symbols, not wholly understood by the Jewish scholars or the Christian commentators are coming to light.

THE WONDER WOMAN IN HEAVEN (v.1)

"There appeared a wonder in Heaven" (12:1). The Greek word *semeion* means a miraculous sign which leaves one astonished and carried away in amazement. Something about this *wonder woman* is so amazing that she leaves even Heaven astonished let alone the scholars and commentators. This is what Heaven thinks of Israel. Who is she, and what is she a miraculous sign of? She is a far cry from the *mystery Babylon* woman of chapter seventeen. While that entity is covered in darkness, confusion, and abomination, and full of the blood of the saints, this woman is clothed in light, like the brightness of the sun. That is God's view of Israel.

This is not the Church, nor is it Mother Eve as some believe. There are many reasons why we can say this. None of the cryptic and symbolistic patterns fit either of these interpretations. We will discover that this is Israel, Abraham's seed as we see in the Revelation. This is what Heaven thinks of Israel.

Now we are led into some cryptic symbolic expressions in which we are totally lost if we do not have the ability as given by the Holy Spirit to discern this symbolism which comes from Old Testament types and shadows. This present idiom takes us back to the very first book of the Bible where most of the basic concepts were formed. The reason the book is called Genesis, is because it is the book that records the original *coming into being* of things. Like *genetic* which means relating to, or determined by the origin and development of things. All of the idioms and concepts (the cryptic meaning of things) began in the book of Genesis.

In Genesis 37, we read where Joseph had a dream that seemed to have very deep prophetic overtones. He saw the sun, the moon, and eleven stars bowing to him (Genesis 37:9). His father and mother were astonished at the dream. His father said, *"Shall your mother and I and your brothers indeed come to bow down to the earth before you"* (37:10)? And his father rebuked him. Nevertheless, something in Jacob's heart made him remember and ponder the dream. History would eventually prove its exact accuracy.

However, as often is the case, the Holy Spirit was inclosing this story and dream in cryptic prophetic typology. Out of Israel, and one of the twelve sons, or stars was to come the

Man-child of Genesis 3:15; the very *Man-child* that is to be revealed in the last days.

It seemed like just an isolated incident in a family concern, but something deeper was aloof. The Holy Spirit saw into the genetics of this family, into the DNA of the seed of woman who would eventually destroy the dragon (Genesis 3:15). In the seed of Israel and his wife were the genetics of a race of people who would endure the ages and be the body of people that would bring forth the *Man-child of fame*. All the way from that promise in Genesis 3:15, the human race began to look for and expect a *Man-child* who would be the Savior of the world—the Dragon-slayer. He is bringing to us the mystery of His own life and history.

THE WONDER OF ISRAEL AND THE JEWISH PEOPLE

This is an astounding and amazing cryptic expression that represents a great bulk of Old Testament idiom, to show us that this body of people would and did, in *"the fullness of time,"* bring forth God's Son, the hoped for and promised *Man-child* of old (Galatians 4:4). One of the absolute wonders of history, are the people of Israel. King William Frederick IV was once asked to give an absolute proof of God's existence. He thought for a moment, and then said simply, "the Jewish people."

When we consider the history of this race of people who began as refugees from Iraq, a wanderer of the wasteland of the Middle East, we begin to see why she is a marvel and a wonder. It is amazing how they built the Ethos as slaves in Egypt, and survived seven attempts at their total demise by the most powerful Empires of history. How they have survived the Diaspora for 2000 years, lived through the Pogroms, the Holocaust, the Inquisitions, and worldwide anti-Semetics, and then returned to rebuild their own nation after 2500 years. All of this is nothing short of an absolute miracle. No wonder King Frederick rightly said, the greatest proof that God exists is the existence of the Jewish people.

As we study God's miraculous care of the Jewish people throughout the Old Testament, and the wonder of their existence today, even with all of their blindness to Christ and their multiple sins, we begin to understand that they are an astonishing body of people, astonishing even to Heaven. In the genes of Israel, resided he who Balaam could discern when he cried out, *"The Lord his God is with him, and the shout of a king is among them"* (Numbers 23:21). They represent God's marvelous faithfulness in completing His plan to bring Jesus Christ to Earth and preserve His heritage until the full consummation of the plan and promise are fulfilled. What a wonder is Israel and her *Man-child*.

From my book, *Jerusalem, Rushing Toward the Midnight Hour*, I quote,: "With Sinai in their souls, and the memory of the Shekinah in their hearts, they are again forcing a wayward world to come to grips with the eternal design of their existence." (Copies may be obtained from author.)

Israel then, is represented in symbolic language as a woman in labor ready to bring forth a child, all through the prophetic images of the prophets. There are Messianic Psalms that depict Israel as a pregnant woman. We see it depicted in the Christmas texts of Micah 4 and 5: "be in pain, and labor to bring forth, O daughter of Zion" (4:10). In the Christmas saga, not only is Mary in labor, but so is the whole nation of Israel in labor to bring forth the *Man-child*. In Jeremiah 15:10, Israel is shown as a woman who was born well, but her son is a child of great sorrow and grief, and becomes a contention to the whole earth, just as we see in Revelation 12. Both Jeremiah and Revelation speak of the *Remnant* that would be protected and saved (Jeremiah 23:3; Revelation 12:17).

In Isaiah concerning the final days of Israel in prophecy, Israel is seen as a mother in labor to bring forth her child (66:7). There is a *"voice from the temple! ... the voice of the Lord"* (ibid v.6). A voice cries out, *"Let the Lord be glorified, that we may see your joy, but they shall be ashamed"* (ibid v.5). Then it speaks of Israel (Zion) travailing and miraculously bringing deliverance of *"a male child"* (ibid v. 7) Even Israel giving birth to the Gentile Church, is viewed as part of the wonder and awe of Israel's travail (Isaiah 54:1).

There are more examples which can be found in the Old Testament to illustrate Israel's image as a pregnant woman bringing forth the promised *Man-child,* but let these examples suffice to show that this wonder-woman in Heaven is none other than the wonder-people of Israel.

ANOTHER WONDER IN HEAVEN, DRAGON-PATRON SAINT OF THE EAST (v.3)

This verse is a major revelation that needs to be carefully considered. Because Satan, the serpent, that old dragon who God said is the most subtle of all of the created beings, has been allowed to keep himself totally esoteric, makes this verse most revealing. He is well hidden, but only to the earthling. He is not hidden to inhabitants of Heaven or to the Saints on Earth. A little study about this strange being who plays such a major role in the whole Bible saga, and yet is seldom recognized, will help us understand much of the final outcome of things as recorded in Revelation. He is the dinosaur of ancient worlds now gone.

Even in this end-time disclosure, he is nearly obscure, although he is a major mover of the events divulged in Revelation. The dragon is spoken of thirteen times in Revelation as a symbol of Satan. No creature is so hidden in cryptic secret as this dragon. It takes some study of both what the Bible reveals of him and what ancient antiquity (especially in the Orient), tell us about Him. That old piercing and crooked serpent must have found good seed-bed for his wiles among the descendants of Cain, who left the Garden of Eden in Babylon, (today's Iraq) and inhabited the east (Isaiah 27:1). The culture of Cain was open to worshipping the dragon and giving him the prominence he desired when rebelling against God (Isaiah 14:12-23). He and the snake are the patron saint in all of the eastern culture. Soon the whole world is going to pass a critical mass and make a paradigm shift toward devil worship under the regime of the beast (Revelation 13:4).

In Satan's rebellion in Heaven, he was so influential and persuasive, that he pulled a third of the angels into rebellion with him (Revelation 12: 4). In the Orient, he is seen as exactly what is said of him in Revelation, chapter 12. He is depicted everywhere in the east as a great red dragon hidden in symbolism, snorting fire, piercing and crooked, working his wiles on that whole society. In the west, we haven't fallen for His cryptic symbols, but treated him only as a myth. He has certainly had a hey-day in our immoral, sinful, and rebellious society. It is a fact that, although He has remained well hidden to the average worldly people, he certainly is openly manifest in our culture to those who understand what the Bible tells us about him.

However, Satan is no stranger to Heaven. We should not be surprised in this text to find Him there. The book of Job shows him as coming and going from Heaven to visit and *"going to and fro on the earth,"* then returning to Heaven to meet with the angels before the throne (Job 1:7). It is said that he comes to the throne of God as our *"accuser of the brethren"* (Revelation 12:10).

Why is he called another *"wonder in Heaven"* (12:1)? He is evidently another miraculous sign that leaves Heaven astonished and amazed. What is the wonder of him and how does he astonish Heaven, leaving it amazed? It must have been a total shock to all of Heaven's inhabitants, so devoted and submissive to God, to find one of their own, to be so proud, arrogant, and rebellious. Then, when one-third of the angelic hosts followed his arrogance and rebellion, it certainly must have been a shocker. When God gave him a set amount of time to prove himself and his claims, it was surely an awesome time in Heaven. They, like us, are still wondering about him and his host.

To tie him in with his many images in Revelation, he is said to have seven heads and ten horns. These heads and horns represent past kings and empires, and shows us his deep connection to these world powers, always playing his part behind the scene (see Daniel 10 for an insight to this truth). This shows us exactly who he is and who his political ally will be. This is the same beast of the chapter thirteen which turns out to be his earthly representative, under His power. (Revelation 13:1-4). He will be very active in the background of all of the events from chapter 11 through chapter 20, where Isaiah 27:1 will be fulfilled: The Lord will *"slay the [dragon]."*

It is this red dragon who is behind the world's hate for the Jew and for the Man-child, Christ. Satan, through Herod, was not only ready to slay Him at birth, but has been seeking the destruction of not only the *Man-child,* but the Wonder Woman, Israel, as well (Revelation 12: 4).

A MAN-CHILD—CHRIST OUR LORD (v.5)

It astounds many of us who spend a lifetime contemplating the prophetic message of the Bible, how absolutely naive some people can be, and how they can miss the absolute obvious. It certainly seems that way to me concerning this subject. How do so many miss the manifest meaning of this *Man-child*? They would have to be totally blind to Old Testament themes in prophecy, not to see the patently and unmistakable idioms which represent none other than Jesus Christ.

What other *Man-child* of such fame came from the seed of Israel? Who else is the only one who would sit on the eternal throne of David in the last days? Who else would rule the nations with a *"rod of iron"* (Revelation 2:27, 19: 15)? Who else in Israel or in all of mankind, is clearly seen as the promised Child, who Satan wanted to destroy the minute He was born? Who else do we know of that was caught up unto God and His throne? This *Man-child* is none other than Jesus Christ, the Lord. If you are really looking for Him in the Book of Revelation, there are a few places He is not hard to find.

Ancient cryptic symbols that reach back to Eve and the promised seed can be found in ample supply. They go all the way from the earliest records, to cryptic signs in the Heavens which are as primeval as Enoch's day, speaking of and reflecting on Genesis 3:15. This *Man-child* has been known through antiquity as the hope of the world and its Redeemer. Virgo, and her virgin-born son, the *Man-child* who becomes the great Dragon-Slayer" and Serpent-Fighter," make these symbols in Revelation 12, rich in antiquity. This whole chapter reflects the ancient hate between the seed of a woman and Satan, the dragon. Satan, through the ages, has sought to corrupt every woman in the hopes of spoiling God's promise of a pure virgin birth and an uncorrupted seed who would be the promised *Man-child*. Thanks be to God that a pure virgin was found, and a pure seed came, in spite of Satan's war against God's plan and promise.

There is some strong persuasion that this *Man-child* is the Gentile Church. Such an idea shows just how far off we can get when our premises starts with a falsehood, i.e. Replacement Theology mentioned above. Because those who believe the Jews have no place in the future kingdom, in order to justify their position, become totally blind to obvious truth.

Another strong idea is that this *Man-child* is the 144,000 Jews of chapters 7 and 14. Again, what a stretch some will go to try to be sensational in their discoveries. There is nothing plural about the Man-child. He is singular all the way. Those who cannot ascertain the symbolic language of Old Testament Messianic prophecies are lost in this chapter, because it reaches clear back to Eve, and is a fantastic synopsis of Israel's history and place in God's economy.

TO DEVOUR THE CHILD AS SOON AS HE WAS BORN (v, 4)

One of the prime identifying factors that this *Man-child* is in fact the cryptic image of this ancient dragon laying wait near the pregnant Israel, with the purpose of devouring the child as soon as He was born (12: 4). This image has a history of fulfillment. We see this best exemplified at the birth of Jesus Christ in Ephrata near Bethlehem. It has been recently discovered in the Fields of Boaz and Ruth, near the Grotto where the temple lambs were nurtured, and where an inscription in the floor of a 1st century Byzantine Church, the words, "Jesus was born Here" is found.

When Herod first heard from the wise men about Christ's birth, and because the wise men did not return to report His location, Herod had all of the babies two years and younger killed, thus hoping to be sure that Christ was slain right after birth and before He could gain notoriety (Matthew 2:16).

A beautiful part of this portion of the story causes the Jewish believers to look back into ancient antiquity for some prototypes which had been part of the prophetic enigma ever since Jacob and Rachel. Matthew's record reaches back and brings to our attention, an incident which had developed a stigma among the Jewish Messianic sages for ages. Matthew 2:17 sees this as a fulfillment of one of those mysterious symbols that pointed to the end time. He said it was *"fulfilled,"* or a prophecy spoken of by Jeremiah, and relates to the incident where Rachel died in childbirth and the tears were shed over 1700 years prior to Christ's death (Jeremiah 31:15). The question then arises, what connection does her sorrow in childbirth have to do with the birth of Christ?

In this enigmatic symbol, Rachel seems to become a type of the woman with child travailing in birth, which is Israel pregnant with Christ (Revelation 12:2). While the Babylonians were on Samuel's Mountain, six miles north of Jerusalem (called Rama) sorting out the Israelis worthy to be transported to Babylon and others who were judged too influential to be left in Israel, they were taken on the mountain of Samuel and slaughtered by the thousands. The cry that went up from this sorrow caused Messianic people to see it as Rachel, i.e. Israel, *"weeping for her children"* who were not (Matthew 2:18, Jeremiah 31:15).

In Matthew, the Holy Spirit catches the same symbolism of old, where we saw Rachel as a type of Israel weeping for her children. When Herod killed all of the babies in Bethlehem two years old and younger, he was under the influence of Satan, the dragon, in his efforts to destroy Christ at birth. The symbolism of Israel as a woman in travail at child-birth has many references in the prophetic texts (Micah 4:9-10, Isaiah 66:8-9).

It is this age-old Old Testament prototype which is brought to our attention in Revelation 12:4, to make us once again aware of Satan's hate for the Christ, and His everlasting vigil to try to destroy Him.

THE REMNANT OF ISRAEL- FLIGHT INTO THE WILDERNESS

Revelation 12:6 continues in this absolutely astonishing synopsis of the history and place of Israel in God's plan. Here again we find need to resort to Old Testament Messianic prophecies to understand this verse. It is also clearly referred to by our Lord Jesus Christ in his Olivet discourse. According to Jesus, the remnant of Israel will have to vacate their homes in the West Bank when a covenant between the Antichrist and Israel is broken in the middle of the seven-year Tribulation by the *"abomination of desolation"* (Matthew 24:15). Most likely, their troubled existence was settled for the seven year duration of the covenant, but the peace was shattered for them when the Antichrist breaks that covenant.

The beast, or Antichrist, will first come to the world scene as a man of peace, with hope of *"peace and safety, but sudden destruction will come upon them"* (1 Thessalonians 5:3). Three references in Daniel show His claimed peaceful purposes (Daniel 8:25, 11:21, 24). He will make a *peace covenant* with the Jews and Arabs, which will be slated for 2300 days or just over six years. During that time he will use flattery to turn many Jews from the covenant: *"They (of the Jewish people) who know their God shall be strong, and carry out great exploits"* (11:32). The Antichrist will find a great amount of resistance to his actions, for the Jews during the Antichrist's days, *"who understand among them, shall instruct many"* (11:33). *"And some of those of understanding shall fall to refine them, purge them, and make them white, until the end of the end"* (11:35). Thus we have the Jews plight during Tribulation, clearly stated by Daniel, and agreeing perfectly with Matthew 24 and Revelation chapters 11 - 12.

During this period, by use of *"flattery"* among the secular Jews, the Antichrist will appear to be Israel's long-awaited Messiah (Daniel 11:32). These are the Jews *"who forsake the holy covenant [and] ... do wickedly against the covenant,"* the one made at the beginning of the Tribulation, and encourage the Antichrist to break it (ibid vs. 30,31).

Many details about this period of time before and after the breaking of the covenant, can be garnered from Daniel chapters 8, 11, and 12. For instance, we are told how He will, by peace, destroy many (8:25). What a strange paradox! It is said that He will "destroy wonderfully." (ibid vs. 24) The same verse says that under the guise of peace, He will *"destroy the mighty and also the holy people,"* supposedly the Jews (8:24). And in Daniel 11: 30, we are told that after making a covenant with the Jews, *"he shall return and show regard for those who forsake the holy covenant."* I surmise that *this holy covenant* is not the one he made with them. It could hardly be called *holy*, and it is never called as such. I believe that the *holy covenant* is the covenant of daily sacrifice in the temple. Daniel 9:27 says that the Jews will immediately build their temple on Mount Moriah and begin the daily sacrifice. This shows his total disdain for the crucified Christ, the Lamb. When the devil comes down with wrath, and incarnates the Roman prince as a con for his evil purposes, he will cancel the covenant, stop the daily sacrifice, and set himself up as God in the Holy of Holies. This is his indignation against the holy covenant. More details can be gained by a careful study of Daniel chapters 7, 8, 11, and 12, keeping them in relationship to the Book of Revelation and the beast's activity toward the Jews. All of the above scenarios agree perfectly with Revelation.

Daniel spoke of the breaking of the covenant with the Jews and setting up the abomination that makes desolate in the holy place (Daniel 9:27). Jesus brings this same text to our attention when He refers to it as an occurrence, just after the Church is complete and is caught up in the Rapture (Matthew 24:15). Christ then instructs the Jews of the West Bank (Judaea) to flee into the wilderness (24:16). This is during the beginning of the Great Tribulation (24:21). The correlation of Matthew 24:16 and Revelation 12:6, is absolutely astounding. Again it is said that the time of their hiding will be "one thousand two hundred and sixty days," or

ISRAEL IN THE TRIBULATION

3 ½ years (12: 6).

It may seem to the reader that we have lost our way and strayed from comments on the Book of Revelation of Jesus Christ, but we are endeavoring to show the marvelous background to chapters 11 and 12 that Daniel adds to these texts. Before we return to chapter 12, we will garner a few more details that can be learned from the Old Testament about Israel's plight during the Tribulation. This need for the Jewish inhabitants of Judaea and east Jerusalem to flee, is very near in the offing today. We see the whole international community, including America's president, trying to force Israel to give up the West Bank and east Jerusalem, to a people who have no vested interest historically in those areas.

This event which forces those settlers into a wilderness place will be very vexing to the heart of God and our Savior, for it is a prominent theme in the Messianic prophecies. Daniel tells us that Jordan, Edom, Moab, and Amman will not fall under the domination of the Antichrist (Daniel 11: 41). This represents what we know of as the country of Jordan today. It is conjectured that this escape from the Antichrist may be due to this country's kindness to the Jewish outcasts; the wilderness of southern Jordan around Petra—the rose red rock city of the giants, Bozrah in Teman, and in the area where Moses struck the rock, bringing water to the thirsty multitude, will be their place of protection by God (Isaiah 63:1; Habakkuk 3:3). This all coincides with Revelation 12:14. Their sojourn in Jordan will be 3½ years, just long enough to miss the last half of the Tribulation. Several rather cryptic texts may be studied to reveal this as the hiding place during the last 3½ years of Tribulation. We will not take the time and space here to make a detailed study of the sojourn of the remnant of Israel in Jordan, but I will make a few short comments.

In Isaiah 16:1, the Lamb will be sent from Sela (Petra)

to Zion. The daughters of Moab will meet the wandering Jewish outcasts at the Fords of Arnon, where they will be hidden (ibid v.2). Jordan allows the outcasts to stay in Moab (southern Jordan) until the spoiler is gone, for they are told that the *"extortioner, [or Antichrist] is at an end"* (ibid v. 4). It then speaks of their return when the throne of David will be established (ibid v.5). Note in Revelation 14 that the Lamb will bring with Him the 144,000 to Mount Zion to take back the Temple Mount and make way for David's throne.

Psalm 60 prophesies a time when the outcasts of Israel will be in Moab and Edom, over which God will *"cast [His] shoe,"* a symbol of His protection (60:8). Then the strong will cry *"who will lead me to Edom?"* where they will receive help from trouble (60:9).

It is my persuasion by these texts and many others, that Christ in His return, will first reveal Himself to the remnant of Jews in Jordan, including the 144,000, who are hidden and protected by God in the wilderness of Zin, namely Petra and Bozrah. Isaiah 63:3 describes Him coming from Bozrah with blood on His apparel. We are told that is where He will begin to tread the winepress (Revelation 14:19). He will walk the borders of the terrorist nations named in Ezekiel 32, and conquer the Temple Mount, driving the beast out of the temple area and then come to Mount Zion. On the way, His feet will stand on the Mount of Olives and from there He will meet the beast at Megiddo (Zechariah 14:4-5).

WAR IN HEAVEN

"And war broke out in Heaven…" (Revelation 12:7).

Here we come to another *meanwhile* in the sequence of events. All of the prior verses have been esoteric scenes and cryptic symbols which form a synopsis of Israel's history and her involvement down through the ages, with this great dragon in Heaven. The story of Israel and the great dragon brings us right down to the end of the last half of the Tribulation and the remnant of Israel's final deliverance, with the destruction of the great dragon—Satan.

We now return to Heaven and see a war going on there, while these Tribulation events and Israel's persecution by the great Dragon, is taking place on Earth. This period of time is very intense, because not only is Christ entering into His final overthrow of all demonic and satanic forces here on Earth, but at the same time, He has directed His great angel, Michael to cast Satan and his angels out of Heaven. Michael is said to be the leader of Heaven's host, and the prince which stands for the children of Daniel's people—Israel (Daniel 12:1). A cosmic war is going on in the sky while a time of trouble like never has been nor ever will be again, is transpiring on Earth. I hope you can get the implication. It is the Battle of the Ages, the long anticipated war that will change not only the earth, but will liberate all of Heaven too, from anarchy and rebellion. It is Christ's greatest hour. It is His glorious revealing when He comes in power and great glory.

It is said of the Devil:

> "... but they did not prevail, nor was a place found for them in Heaven any longer. So the great dragon was cast out, that serpent of old, called the Devil and Satan, who deceives the whole world; he was cast to the earth, and his angels were cast out with him" (Revelation 12: 8-9).

The war seems to be concerning Israel and the Jews, since it is mentioned in that context.

Jesus saw it and spoke of Satan falling *"like lightening from Heaven"* (Luke 10:18). The powerful fallen ones, (Nephilim) will be manifest on Earth with Satan. The Esoteric will become Exoteric (revealed) and be seen and known as those powerful principalities and powers, which have ruled the darkness of this world for millenniums of time (Ephesians

6:12). Many of Lucifer's plans and the manifestation of these powerful rebels from God's kingdom, is spoken of in Alice Bailey's book, *The Externalization of the Hierarchy.* Through the Millenniums, Satan has concealed himself and worked in secret through demon activities and the occult secret societies, or through the Luciferian New Age. Now, he can no longer conceal himself, but will be plainly seen for whom and what He is (Revelation 12:12).

REJOICING IN HEAVEN, WOE TO THE EARTH

At this time, when Satan is cast out, Heaven declares:

"Now salvation, and strength, and the kingdom of our God, and the power of His Christ have come" (12:10).

Ever since Lucifer rebelled sometime in the ancient past, there has been a hindrance to God's plans and purposes, and trouble before the throne of God, for the *"accuser of our brethren"* has appeared there regularly to bring charges against us (12:10). God has always had to deal with the results of Satan's accusations, as he accused not only us, but God and Christ both day and night. Heaven has not been at rest. For how could there be any peace with the accuser of the brothers there? Now the Kingdom of God is free and the "power of His Christ" can be fully revealed:

"Therefore rejoice, O Heavens, and you who dwell in them" (12: 12)!

It is going to be a glad time for all dwellers of Heaven, including we who may have recently made our home there. It is another story for those on Earth:

"Woe to the inhabitants of the earth ... for the devil has come down to you, having great wrath, because he knows that he has a short time" (12:12).

This *woe* begins the second *woe* upon man and brings on the first vial of wrath (16:2). All of chapters 13 through 16 are inclusive of the seventh trumpet and the third *woe* of man.

We may have to stretch our imaginations a bit to realize what it means when Christ our Savior gets rid of that old accuser who accuses us day and night before the throne of God; and except for Christ's intercession for us, we would have no hope. I am sure all of us realize that we have each committed enough sin to pave our way to Hell, and that many of the devil's accusations are true. What a terrible time it would be to stand before the Judgment Seat of Christ and have to answer for all of our transgressions against God and His law. Hallelujah, the accuser will be cast out and our sins washed away from the books. It will be for us as it was for Paul in his faith when he said:

> *"... for I know whom I have believed and am persuaded that He is able to keep what I have committed to Him until that day"* (2 Timothy 1:12).

Whatever we have asked Jesus to forgive us for, and have placed it in His care; and no matter what the accuser has said, when the time comes for Christ to confess us before His Father in Heaven, He will keep it to Himself. Praise the Lord forever, Amen! Let's make sure we have repented and given everything to Jesus Christ our Lord. No wonder Heaven breaks out into a crescendo of praise. You probably won't be able to hold us down when that happens.

As the devil, who has been *"the prince of the power of the air,"* is driven down to the earth, he has great wrath because he knows his time is up (Ephesians 2:2). The time between when he is cast out of Heaven and his final demise, will be 3 ½ years. During this short time the world will be demon-dominated and ruled by the dragon:

"... and all the world marveled and followed the Beast. So they worshipped the dragon who gave authority to the beast" (Revelation 13:3-4).

It will be easy for the devil to dominate the world with the Church gone and the righteous Jews in hiding. We are the only ones who know Him and are hindering His coming (2 Thessalonians 2:7).

I suspect that Christ in the exercise of His great power and authority over all of the principalities and powers and rulers of the darkness of this age, will cause the whole creation to groan and to be filled with a horrible conflict during this 3 ½ years (Romans 8:22). This terrible upset will affect both Heaven and Earth. With the wrath of Satan in all of his final fury against all humanity including the Jews, and with the wrath of God against Him, we will see the worst ravages of war and evil corruption that the world has ever seen. This conflict will involve all of the nations and individuals who submit to the beast by the mark, name, and number. We are told about these in chapters 13 and 14.

These wars and persecution against the Jews on Earth, which dominates our news today, are only a reflection of the war that is going on in Heaven. While there are major onslaughts against the Jews, Jerusalem, and the Temple Mount here on Earth, there is a great battle in the esoteric and cosmic world between God and Satan, Heaven's hosts, Hell's hosts, the good angels, and the fallen angels; and we are getting the fallout of it on Earth.

I know the Church is gone during this time, because if it was here and given power over Satan's powers as it has been given to us, we would still be hindering. However, we will be gone and the wicked one will be in power (2 Thessalonians 2:7-8). It will be a wonderful time for the Church to be in Heaven above the fray.

SATAN'S FINAL ONSLAUGHT AGAINST ISRAEL, AND ISRAEL'S FINAL VICTORY

Satan knows he will have to face Jesus Christ the Lamb of God, at Armageddon, and he knows that his defeat is sure, but he cannot control his hate for the Jews. He turns immediately upon the Jewish nation:

> *"Now when the dragon saw that he had been cast to the earth, he persecuted the woman who gave birth to the male child"* (Revelation 12:13).

It is remarkable to note that the beast, or Antichrist, is not mentioned in this chapter. However, he is mentioned in Revelation 11:7 where we see that it is he who is filled with, and under the power of, the one named *Abaddon* (11:7, 9:11). This same *Abaddon* ascended out of the bottomless pit and began to persecute the witnesses in Jerusalem, eventually causing their deaths.

It may be that the beast was first under the power of one of the angelic principalities and powers who worked for Satan himself. However, now in chapter 12, no mention is made of the beast being directly involved with this onslaught on Israel, only the dragon. Yet we know that Satan, an esoteric being, must be working through some protagonists on Earth. All of our attention is now drawn to the hidden world of spirits, and to the dragon in the Nether World. All of our insight leads us to see into that other world to help us understand, that behind all of this is that great Red Dragon, Satan, who set out to destroy Abraham's blessing through a son ages ago, and has persecuted his seed ever since.

We begin to see the real reason behind the hate of the Jews. By pointing us directly to the source of anti-Semitism, it removes all of the political, social, sectarianism, and ethnic issues and implications, opening our eyes to the real, but hidden source of persecution against the Jews. By the revelations given to us in this chapter, we are left with no doubt that it is all coming from Satan as he whispers his guile into the hearts of lost humanity.

It turns out after all that the idea of a real being in a real esoteric world has a real hate for the seed of Abraham. It becomes clear that this enemy of Israel is not a religious fantasy, but factual, plainly showing all of his hideousness in this chapter. The hate against Israel throughout the ages has not been directly because of a problem in the family of Abraham, but has only been used by a hateful being whose motives are to unseat Jesus Christ as Lord of this world, and usurp His rightful place on the throne. It is obvious by this chapter in Revelation, that he sees the destruction of Israel and the Jewish people as a defining event in his cause.

WAR BETWEEN CHRIST AND THE SERPENT IN THE WILDERNESS

From Revelation 12: 6, where Israel's flight into the wilderness was first introduced, we now return to the details. The woman—Israel, now represented by a chosen remnant, is given some help in her flight. Two wings of an eagle are provided for her transport into the wilderness. Some have boldly suggested that this is an air-lift for them, but that does not seem to fit with other companion texts where their exit seems to be by foot.

Jesus was clear about their means to get to the hiding place. He said they were to immediately vacate the area of Judaea, the West Bank (Matthew 24:16-18). Every consideration is given to the weak and needy in this flight. Verses 19 and 20 give every indication of a trek across the land. Isaiah's mention of them meeting at the *"fords of the Arnon"* suggests foot travel (16:2). Therefore, I do not see it as an air-lift.

However, it is possible that the two wings of an eagle could well indicate America's assistance in the flight. These Jews will be clearly warned by the witnesses and by ministering angels not to take the mark, name, and number, and not to follow this false Messiah, the Antichrist (Revelation 14:9-10). At some time during this period, *"all Israel will be saved"* (Romans 11:26).

An evacuation route has been secretly designed, not so much that the Israeli government is acting on these prophecies in Revelation, but that the diplomatic atmosphere makes it very obvious that they may need an emergency contingency set up for the settlers of Judaea. The route which has been laid out goes down through the wilderness of Zin, across the Aquaba at the Vail of Sidon (Sodom) into Edom, and ends at Petra. Again, we are told that this remnant in south Jordan will be under special care from God and that their sojourn there will only be for 3½ years (Revelation 12:14). It is interesting to note that the same rock Moses smote and water gushed forth, is still pouring out water, and is enough to take care of the remnant of Jews that will be there.

The cryptic analogies and symbolisms of the Book of Revelation are never more impressive than in this chapter. A beautiful example is verse 15. Evidently, where we put verse 15 in our occidental western words of expression, we would say that the devil, or serpent working through his armies of the nations such as NATO, and their head officer—the beast, sent a large detachment to root out the Jews in south Jordan. Then with boots on the ground, they flooded the theater at Petra and Bozrah. With Oriental, poetic verbal impression mingled with moods and passionate feelings, we read this eloquent, imaginative expression of vivid graphic insight into the actions of Satan and his hate toward the Jews. It is *"waters ... like a flood"* which came out of the serpent's mouth *"like a flood"* (12:15). How poetic is that? It's almost as if we can see right into the heart of the old dragon, for "out of the abundance of the heart his mouth speaks" (Luke

6:45). By this means, he expresses his vindictive nature and blasphemous oath against them. He gave orders to his army of blasphemers who had the mark, the name and the number, to sweep the Remnant of Jews totally away in a deluge of power. We can see this same blasphemous vengeance coming from the little horn suggested in both the eighth and eleventh chapters of Daniel.

Again, we have graphic symbolism coming from the Old Testament. It was in the days when Moses was trying to lead the people into the Promised Land. A similar rebellion of the beast was inspired by Korah, Dathan, and Abiram. Moses called for all that were on the Lord's side to separate themselves from the camp of these rebels. As Moses lifted up his voice to God, the Bible records that:

> "... *the earth opened its mouth and swallowed them up, with their households and all the men with Korah, with all their goods. So they and all those with them went down alive into the pit; the earth closed over them, and they perished ...*" (Numbers 16:32-33).

Wow!! What a comparison. The whole bulk of the beast's demon-possessed army filled with the spirit of the dragon, perished in a great earthquake. This is the same old dragon which will perish with the beast and the false prophet (Revelation 20:2).

Was it the same earthquake that split Mount Olivet in two at the touch of the feet of Jesus only a short fifty miles away? Was it the same as in verses 6: 16, 8:5, and 11:13? Is it the same as the *"great earthquake as had not occurred since men were on the earth,"* when Jerusalem was divided, and the great cities of the nations fell (16:18)? Was it the one that brought down Babylon the great?

This defeat of the dragon in the wilderness of Jordan only served to heighten the resolve of Satan's beast against the rest of the Jews who were still in Israel. We have learned through the Middle East conflict of our day, that hate with malice cannot be appeased. Both Daniel and Revelation show his terrible wrath against the people of the covenant. Daniel speaks of his entrance into the Holy Land. He came to destroy the State of Jordan, but it escaped out of his hand (Daniel 11: 41). For 3½ years, he will carry a campaign against the holy people—the Jews (not the Church, for we are in Heaven waiting to return). However, *"all these things shall be finished,"* or ended (Daniel 12:7). The wonderful truth is that *"he shall come to his end, and no one will help him"* (Daniel 12:45).

VICTORY OF JEWS IN THE WILDERNESS — CONVERTED TO CHRIST (13:17)

This chapter closes with another marvelous revelation which we want to remember, as it will affect a portion of the rest of the study. Although we do not know how many, but at least a remnant of the Jewish people become openly what we might call Messianic Jews (Revelation 12:17). It may be necessary to note that many Jews today who have turned to Christ, do not desire to be called by this name.

Whatever they choose to be called, one thing is evident in this verse, they all have accepted Jesus Christ as their Messiah, as well as their Lord and Savior. They *"have the testimony of Jesus Christ,"* but they also keep the old covenant of commandments. They will not be committed to all of the tradition of the elders, i.e. the 620 or so of the traditional Jewish religion, but will still be committed to God's written law.

What a procession that will be when I believe, they will be brought to accompany the 144,000 with Jesus on Mount Zion (Revelation 14:1).

Beloved, we need to associate Jesus Christ behind all of

these esoteric scenes, because it is He who is the *Man-child* caught up to Heaven from where He is protecting His own, and delivering them from the dragon. Remember:

> *"They* (these Jews with the testimony of Jesus Christ) *overcame him* (the devil) *by the blood of the Lamb* (Christ*) and by the word of their testimony [of Jesus], and they did not love their lives to the death"* (12:11).

This verse is also used by those of us who are not facing the Great Tribulation, but in context, it is speaking of the Jewish people who face the dragon and his onslaught against them in the Tribulation. It is also the last verse in the Bible which makes reference to the shed blood of Christ, the first being mentioned by Christ Himself at the last supper:

> *"For this is My blood of the new testament, which is shed for many for the remission of sins"* (Matthew 26:28).

THE OVERCOMING BLOOD OF CHRIST THE LAMB

There are 43 other references to the blood of Christ in the New Testament. All of the references to the sacrificial lamb and its shed blood in the Old Testament is said to be direct references to the blood of Christ. All of them are symbolic, and types of the blood of Christ. However, the Jews were never able to make the connection between the sacrificial lamb and the Messianic King. They could never understand a suffering Messiah. That is why John's statement at Christ's baptism was so startling when He said, *"Behold! The Lamb of God who takes away the sin of the world"* (John 1:29). This is the first clear statement which ties together the sacrificial lamb of the Old Testament with the Christ of the New Testament.

Here are several more revealing texts about the blood of Christ. They are interesting in the light of this text about the Jews of the Tribulation, and their new knowledge of the blood of Christ and their Old Testament lamb of sacrifice:

1. The innocent blood—Matthew 27:4
2. The precious blood—1 Peter 1:19
3. The cleansing blood—1 John 1:7
4. The washing blood—Revelation 1:5
5. The purchasing blood—Acts 20:28
6. The redeeming blood—Ephesians 1:7
7. The shed blood, price of salvation—1 Peter 1:18-19
8. The justifying/redeeming blood—Revelation 5:9
9. The peacemaking blood—Colossians 1:20
10. The sanctifying blood—Hebrews 13:12
11. The everlasting covenant blood—Hebrews 13:20
12. The New Testament blood—Matthew 26:28
13. The remitting blood—Matthew 26:28
14. The covenant blood—Hebrews 10:29

"The innocent blood, infinitely precious blood, perfectly justifying blood, always cleansing and fully sanctifying and completely acceptable blood to a holy God for our redemption" (Dr. Henry Morris, *Days of Praise*, June 22, 2012).

> "When you are in distress, and all these things come upon you in the latter day, when you turn to the Lord your God, and you will find Him if you seek Him with all your heart and with all your soul" (Deuteronomy 4:30).

At the end of days, you shall return to the Lord your God, who will remember these words (4:30-37, paraphrased).

We are told in these verses that God, at the end and during the Tribulation, will not forget Israel, and also that He will remember: 1) The words He has spoken; 2) The covenant He made with Abraham about the land; 3) All that He had promised when they came out of Egypt; and 4) The conquest of Canaan that He gave to them because He loved their forefathers. During their great anguish in the end-time, they will turn to God Jehovah, call solemn assemblies for fasting and prayer, and find that their great God Jehovah is actually Jesus Christ (Joel 1- 2).

ISRAEL BLINDSIDED

Some of the great enigma that surrounds an accurate understanding of the Book of Revelation, is partly the fault of misunderstanding by the Church and partly the blindness of the Jewish Sages. Early in the Church age, and even up to this very time, both the Church and the Jews were blind-in- part. All through their Old Testament record, the Jews had a serious blind-side. This fact is clearly stated by Paul and put in perspective as to its relationship to the gentile age when Paul said that the Church should not be ignorant of this mystery that *"happened to Israel until the fullness of the Gentiles has come in"* (Romans 11:25).

That blindness will end when the Gentile Church is brought into Heaven at the Rapture. At that time, Jesus Christ will set out to cure the blindness among the Jews of Remnant in the wilderness, and we believe it is exactly that which the Book of the Revelation of Jesus Christ is mostly about, as we shall seek to demonstrate in this writing.

HOW THE JEWS FAILED TO ACCEPT CHRIST- THREE BLINDNESS'S CURED IN REVELATION

In the Revelation of Jesus Christ, He will not need to reveal Himself to the Church, for the Church has already received Him and they are in Heaven with Him. However, He will need to be revealed to the Jews and to the Satanic Nations who have rejected Him.

In my observations, there are three major elements of the Jewish religion that has caused their "blindness in part."

1. The Jewish sages, in their contemplation of the Messianic Prophecies of the Old Testament, were never able to associate the Sacrificial Lamb that was meant to take away the sins of the world, with the man, Messiah.

    A suffering Messiah, a servant Messiah, humbled and humiliated, could never fit their image as the great King in David's stead. So they "despised and rejected" Christ when they saw Him "stricken and afflicted, they esteemed him not," for there was "no beauty in Him that they should desire Him."(Isaiah 53:1-4) They completely misunderstood Isaiah 53. When Christ came, they would not believe the report (ibid v.1) and could not believe their coming great King would first shed His blood for their sins.

    Another plain revelation they should have seen, was the connection between the Sacrificial Lamb and the Messiah as a man. They could have, and should have seen, at Abraham's attempted sacrifice of Isaac; that God was making a clear connection between the Messiah and the Sacrificial Lamb that takes away the sin of the world. (Genesis 22) When Abraham said, "My son, God will provide Himself a sacrifice, and in this very mountain we will see it" or "it shall be provided."

    That's why He first appears as "a Lamb that had been slain" and calls Himself "the Lamb of God" 27 times in

Revelation. This was for the opening of the eyes of the Jews.

2. They trusted in the Laws of Moses rather than the Covenant of Abraham. Abraham's Covenant was based not on keeping the Law to become Righteous, but upon "grace through faith," for "Abraham believed God and it was counted unto Him for righteousness" (Genesis 15:6). Not only so, but Abraham's Covenant did not teach them to build a ridiculous and meaningless ethnic religion of 633 laws which isolated the Hasidim from the world, separating them from the hated Goy (or Gentiles). Abraham's Covenant taught that they were to be a testimony of the saving love and grace of God and the Messiah to the whole world. Christ will cure this blindness when He reveals Himself to the Jews during the Wilderness experience.

3. Rather than isolate themselves from the world, they were to become evangelists in the world, to spread the good news of their Messiah's redeeming grace. When that mission was rejected and the Jews of the New Testament could not receive it, Paul and Peter and all the apostles turned to the Gentiles to fulfill the Abrahamic Covenant. The Church was injected into the promise of Abraham. Blindness in Israel will continue until "fullness of the Gentiles be come in" (i.e. complete and raptured). At that time, "all Israel will be saved" (Romans 11:26). The answer will be when Christ reveals Himself to them in the Wilderness during the Tribulation. All three of these blind spots in the Jewish faith will be healed at Christ's 'revelation' to them, when He comes to "reason with them." This will be the time when they receive the "testimony of Jesus"(Revelation 12:17).

THE CHURCH IS BLIND-SIDED BY REPLACEMENT THEOLOGY

As mentioned earlier, the Church was blind-sided by a serious error of understanding. Late in the 1st Century A.D. when two major Jewish revolts against Rome were instigated, the anti-semitic spirit was actually started by defective Jews themselves, who defected from Jewry to Roman sympathy and spread anti-Jew venom. This did great damage to the reputation of the Jews. For instance, Josephus in writing about the Jewish Wars of A.D. 70 and A.D. 135, himself a Jew who had defected from the armies of Israel and became a lackey for Rome, called his fellow Jews of the rebellion, Sicaarii, or dangerous men. He said that they were "slaves and scum," and a "spurious and abortive off-spring of our nation" (Jewish Wars 5.443). The title "semite" has as its root "smitten," or "to kill." To be semitic was to be of a race to be destroyed.

Comparable passages from the Dead Sea Scrolls were also critical of so-called "renegade Jews" of that time. The Community Rule, Jewish manual of discipline, called them "Sons of Darkness, full of wickedness and lies, haughtiness and pride, falseness and deceit, cruelty and abundant evil, and ill-tempered and folly."

This anti-Jew attitude was picked up by early Church fathers such as Augustine, Jerome, Hippolytus, and Origen. By their theology, the Church had become the only future interest of the Lord, and the sole proprietor of the inheritance of God's blessings and promises. The Jews had deeply offended God by crucifying His Son. Therefore, they had been cut off from all future blessing and had forfeited their future heritage in the promises in the Messianic prophesies. From the crucifixion of Jesus Christ and hence-forth, according to this theory, they had no place in the future promises, thus no place in the Revelation of Jesus Christ. All of the Old

Testament Messianic promises were assumed by the Church.

This theory known as Replacement Theology was believed especially by the Catholic Church leaders, but also by other leading Church authorities. Each of them had much to gain by the belief that they were the sole inheritors of all the Messianic Prophecies. It was basically an Augustine System of eschatology. He was obligated to the Roman Church to enhance their claim that a new covenant replaces the Old Mosaic Covenant and gives all the promises now to the Church. It was believed by early fathers, and also Protestant Christian leaders such as Luther and Calvin who picked up the same persuasion, believing that the Jews were completely expelled from future blessing or any part in the coming of Christ. The Jews were expected to amalgamate into the Gentile nations and become equal parts of the membership of the Gentile Church. This teaching became deeply ingrained into all Christian doctrine, thus the overshadowing basis of Evangelical and Nominal Church interpretation. Therefore, all of the Old Testament blessings and promises were taught as allegorical and metaphorical, taking away from the Jews and giving it to the Church. This has created deep and lasting confusion, misunderstanding, and the conventional teaching of the Church has tried to fit all of the promises made to Abraham, Isaac, Jacob, and Israel into a Christian eschatological interpretation of The Revelation of Jesus Christ.

This is the historic background of the separation, and largely the cause of hate and animosity between the Jews and parts of the Christian community today.

For our subject concerning Christ in the Revelation, it is our opinion that this doctrine known as Replacement Theology has completely distorted any rational understanding of the Revelation of Jesus Christ. By removing the Jews and Israel from any part of the last days, the whole concept of the Book has been seriously distorted. We will take a brief moment to explain this conclusion and reasoning.

THE CHURCH HAS NO PART OF THE TRIBULATION

I believe by careful observations, we can surmise that most of Revelation is not about the Church at all. The first three chapters depict the Church age up to the Rapture. From that point on the Church is in Heaven around the throne. In Revelation the Church is never seen on Earth again until the 19th chapter when it returns with Christ in the Millennium. It is always seen in Heaven and at the throne. In all of Revelation's activity during the next seven years of the Tribulation period, the Church has no direct connection with those events since they are not on Earth much.

Therefore, none of the details taking place on the earth from chapters 4 through 19, have anything to do with the Church. During the period of the Tribulation, the Church is actively involved with Christ in Heaven. Three events will take place in Heaven: 1) Each of the saints will personally meet the Lord; 2) the Judgment Seat of Christ (Bema—Court of awards) will take place during this time; and 3) the Marriage of the Lamb will take place. At the end of Tribulation and after Armageddon, the Church will return with Christ to rule and reign with Him through the Millennium. Again, for emphasis, none of the events of the seven years of Tribulation or Armageddon will involve or affect the Church what-so-ever.

Who then, is involved in the Tribulation? Who are the participants on Earth during the seven year Tribulation? It seems clear to me that they will be the Jews along with the unsaved people who missed the Rapture, and of course, the ungodly nations that are under the power of the great dragon—Satan.

MOST OF CHRIST'S WORK AND HIS PERSONAL REVELATION IN THE BOOK, IS TO AND FOR THE JEWS

If none of these events have anything to do with the Church, whom do they concern and for whom is Christ writing? By giving careful interpretation to these chapters, it becomes obvious who it is that is mainly involved in the Tribulation period. It is first of all about the Jew, God's chosen people. In anticipation of what the Rabbis call *Jacob's Trouble,* some have been heard to ask if the Lord would choose someone else.

Chapters 7, 11, 12, and 14 are given entirely to the final days of the Jews. Even chapter six can be closely compared to Matthew 24, which was written to Jews about Jewish questions concerning the time of the rebuilding of the temple, and Jewish troubles, or Tribulation at the end-time. The fifteen chapter can be seen featuring the converted Jews out of the Tribulation and their involvement with the temple in Heaven. By these texts, we also see emphatically the devil's hate for the Jews and for Israel, and His last effort to annihilate them. Christ's protection of them during the Tribulation and His revelation of Himself to them, are major themes in the texts, showing us that the Tribulation is mainly for the Jews, the unsaved at the time of the Rapture, and the ungodly nations.

Here are two examples of these texts:

In the Old Testament and even among many Jewish teachers today, the Tribulation is known as *Jacob's Trouble*. Jeremiah, chapter thirty definitely relates to the regathering of Israel in the last days (30: 3). Verses 30:5-9 speak of terrible suffering called *"Jacob's Trouble"* (30:7). It then says that Israel (Jacob) will be saved out of it and comes into the re-established kingdom of David. The rest of the chapter speaks of Israel's deliverance when God deals with the world

ISRAEL IN THE TRIBULATION

of nations (30:11).

Another example of Old Testament prophesies speak the same truth. Daniel's 70 weeks, which is 70 weeks of years, or 490 years, are said to be *"determined for your people,* (the Jews) *and for [Jerusalem] your holy city"* (Daniel 9:24). This Prophecy given by the great angel Gabriel, to Daniel, plainly shows that the last seven years (i.e. the Tribulation) will be the final days of God's dealings with the Jews. The Angel Gabriel will then give six positive outcomes that will come out of the Tribulation, all aimed at concluding the Jewish Messianic hopes. (Daniel 9:24-27).

Since the 70 week prophecy involves the time of God's dealing with the Jewish Nation and the last week, the 70th, being the last 7 years of God's dealing with the Jewish nation, it is plain to see that the 7 years of Tribulation in the Book of Revelation, positively involves God's dealings with the Jews. It is also significant that each of the final wars during Tribulation will be fought in Israel. Therefore, all of these chapters (6-18) are the Revelation of Christ to the Jews and to the nations. Remember, Christ has already been revealed to the Church. Revelation, chapters 8, 9, 13, 16, 17, and 18, are Christ's judgment of the Gentile nations, the separating of the sheep and goat nations, and the bringing of righteous nations into redemption and favor during the Millennium.

It is in the general conventional interpretation of chapters 7, 11, 12, and 14 that the Replacement Theology has been most devastating in the basic understanding and interpretation of The Book of Revelation. By this theory, the 144,000 and the two witnesses are understood to be the Church; the Rapture of the two witnesses is the Rapture of the Church; the building of the temple is the building of the Church; the wonder woman in Heaven is said to be the Church; the Church is the overcomer spoken of in Revelation 12:11, and the persecution against the remnant is against the Church.

Here we have a major misunderstanding, for it is supposed that the Church flees into some wilderness. This idea of the Church fleeing is contrary to any serious consideration of the Church in the last days. Never is the Church seen as fleeing under any kind of persecution. We are an army with banners, marching always forward to evangelize the world with the gospel. Never in the image of the Church in the last days, can we find any indication of them fleeing. Because of Replacement Theology and our unclear teachings of prophecy, many people believe that those who have fled to some wilderness place, taking their water and guns, are waiting out there for years, expecting the Tribulation Jesus to come (Matthew 24:15-20; Revelation 12).

The very serious and erroneous ideas projected by removing the Jews from any part of Revelation are evident. The fact is, most of the activities in chapters 7- 14 are all about the Jews. Chapter 15 is mostly about the Jewish Tribulation saints gathered with the Church in Heaven, and most of them will be Jews. It ends with a very Jewish image of the heavenly temple filled with the same glory that filled the old tabernacle and Solomon's temple in Jerusalem. These images are more about the Jews than about the Church. We must not miss the close tie to Jewish hope and cryptic symbols all through chapters 20 and 22 of Revelation.

It is of exceptional interest that these redeemed Jewish converts out of the Tribulation, together with the Church in Heaven around the throne, are singing both the Old Testament *"Song of Moses"* along with the *"Song of the Lamb"* (Revelation 15:3). Are they singing some of the songs that we are now singing which address Christ as the Lamb?" Or such as Redeemed and saved by the blood of the Lamb? Or are they singing a brand new song? Of this we cannot be certain, but we are sure that they are singing the *"Song of Moses."*

SINGING THE PROPHETIC SONG OF MOSES

By singing this ancient song, they are bringing prophetic subjects into reality. Interestingly enough, Moses sang of the Diaspora and prophesied of the re-gathering of Israel in the last days. He told how they would return in unbelief and corrupt their ways, and how evil (great trouble) would befall them from the hand of God. This would take place in the latter days, or last days of their history. This last day prophecy relates these texts directly to the Book of Revelation which is all about the last days. By the Jews own commentary on these verses, they believe this to be *"Jacob's Trouble."* Again we find, as we found above, that the Tribulation is mainly for the Jews, by our teaching as well as by the Jews themselves. It will be during their latter day return that sorrows come upon them (Daniel 12:1-2).

THE SONG OF THE LAMB

And last, we must recognize the close correlation between the image of the Lamb and the Jewish culture during the Tribulation. The idea of the *"Lamb of God which takes away the sin of the world"* would have less meaning to Christians, except that we are able to pick up its significance from Jewish rituals and symbolism (John 1:29). It is largely for the purpose of impressing the Jews that Christ calls himself the Lamb 27 times in the Book of the Revelation of Jesus Christ. Part of the Revelation of Jesus Christ in the Tribulation time has to be His Revelation of Himself to the Jews as their Messiah, as well as the Lamb of God in His relationship to their ancient ritual.

Jesus in His birth, life, death, and resurrection, perfectly fulfilled to the letter, hundreds of prophecies found in the Messianic prophecies of the Old Testament as we have shown earlier. Still, the Jews were blind to Him being their Messiah. He was the perfect pattern of all they were to expect. What was it that blinded them? Why were they not able to know

Him as the Redeemer they had been waiting on for so long? It certainly seems that whatever it was, will have to be clearly revealed to them in the Revelation of His great day.

How the Jews could miss all this evidence was explained above. It becomes a strange alchemy to realize that even though all throughout their religious history, from Adam and the blood sacrifice of Abel, and especially from the Tabernacle era, they were extremely committed to the ritual of the Sacrificial Lamb. They knew very well that without the shedding of blood, there would be no remission of sin. Once a year, in the Jews' most sacred and cherished event, on the Day of Atonement (Yom Kippur) by the hand of the High Priest, a lamb was sacrificed upon the great altar. Its blood was carried into the holiest-of-all, and sprinkled on the Mercy Seat. That sprinkling atoned for the sins of the nation. The needs of a sacrificial lamb and the sprinkling of its blood for the remission of sin were deeply stamped upon every Hebrew's conscience. Their respect for this slain lamb, which takes away the sin of the world, ever overshadowed all they knew about their relationship to the great God who came down to them and shook Sinai; who uttered His voice and gave them the Law.

It seems almost incredible that so few of them would be able to recognize Him *"when the fullness of the time had come* (that exact time marked by Daniel's 70 week prophecy), *God sent forth His son* (the Messiah), *born of a woman, born under the law"* (Galatians 4:4). It is the studied opinion of thousands of Bible scholars, that Jesus certainly fulfilled all the law and prophets concerning the expected Messiah. His word to the Jews of His day was, *"You search the Scriptures* (only the Old Testament was available to them at that time), *for in them you think you have eternal life; and these are they which testify of Me"* (John 5:39). Just before His ascension, Jesus sat with the disciples and beginning with Moses and all the prophets, *"He expounded to them in all the Scriptures the things concerning Himself"* (Luke 24:27). It is no doubt to the author that Jesus opened up to His disciples, the connection between Himself and the Old Testament sacrificial lamb, yet the disciples were able to grasp only a part of what He taught them. Certainly, the Jews around Him could not accept that connection.

I would like to propose a thought which may explain why they were not able to match Him up with the promised Messiah, even though there was so much evidence supporting His claim.

RITUAL *OVERSHADOWED* THE *FORESHADOW* OF REALITY

Could it be because their ritual had overshadowed the reality which was meant to foreshadow the reality of His coming? The Old Testament sacrifice was to foreshadow the New Testament sacrifice, not to overshadow it in ritual. They made the same mistake that hundreds of churches make today. They let the ritual of the earthly and worldly symbol *overshadow* the reality, rather than foreshadow the truth. The Jews could never see the Messiah, Savior of national Israel, King and Lord, Royal apparent of the throne of David, as a suffering Savior. The Lamb took away their sin, but Messiah would take away their reproach and redeem them back into kingdom status, but the great King could never be a suffering Savior, so they thought. It seems that they never did make the connection: the Man Messiah with the Lamb that takes away their sin.

This is the reason they pursued stoning Christ for blasphemy, and rejected His every claim to Messiahship, while at the same time, admitting that He would suffer and die in humility and shame. How could their great king and redeemer of the nation ever suffer at the hand of the Goy—Gentiles? Therefore, mentally, emotionally, and spiritually they could never make an association between the great Messianic person with the lamb of sacrifice. And, we must give them credit. All of the prophets saw the Messiah, not as a suffering Savior, but as high and lifted up, a conquering King.

Moses saw Him High and exalted in Sinai and the burning bush. Ezekiel saw Him in His glorified state, as did Daniel. Only Isaiah seems to dare present Him as a suffering Savior; although at first he saw Him *"high and lifted up, and the train of His robe filled the temple"* (Isaiah 6). He later presents Him as a suffering servant. It was hard for Isaiah to dare speak out from under the *overshadowing* ritualistic image of Messiah in his day, and yield to the inspiration of the Holy Spirit, catching the *foreshadowing* of a real image of the Great One. The Jews did not understand his writing, and still do not today. However, in the Tribulation they will come to the full understanding of *"the Lamb of God who takes away the sin of the World"* (John 1:29).

ISAIAH WRITES OF THE SUFFERING MESSIAH

Isaiah's writing of the suffering Savior can be found in the 52nd and 53rd chapters of his book. Isaiah is said to be the writer of the New Testament, and the Church age in the Old Testament. Chapters 50 through 66 are largely about the Church as well as the Jews, in the last days.

Starting in Isaiah 52:14, note how hesitant he is to introduce a suffering Messiah. He admits that many will be astonished at his teachings concerning the Messiah as marred in his body more than any other man. Then in verse 53:1, he continues to note their astonishment and questions whether any of his peers will be able to accept what he writes: *"Who hath believed our report? And to whom is the arm of the Lord revealed?"*

Who can believe this and who can see this revelation, he asks? Then he speaks of the Messiah's lowly estate. He would grow up as a tender root out of dry ground (53:2). Roots that grow up without water are very weak and have little chance of growing strong. The Messiah also would have nothing attractive about Him that the Jews would desire (53:2).

Now Isaiah really shocks them with what is impossible for them to believe: that the Messiah and great King would be *"despised and rejected by men"* (53:3). He would be *"a man of sorrows and acquainted with grief"* and the Jews would hide their faces from Him (53:3).

Now Isaiah begins to get into language that I believe the Holy Spirit intended to introduce the Jews to the idea that this Man, the Messiah and suffering Savior, was indeed related to the Lamb of God which takes away the sin of the World:

"He has borne our griefs and carried our sorrows; yet we esteemed him stricken, smitten by God, and afflicted ... " (53:4).

And throughout the next several verses, there is more language which can be associated with the sheep, and the Suffering Lamb. He was *"led as a lamb to the slaughter"* (53:7). When you make this lamb of slaughter an,

"offering for sin, [God will] see the travail of His (the Lamb's) *soul, and be satisfied"* (53:10-11).

It is said that the travail of this suffering Savior,

"brought as a lamb to slaughter [will] justify many, for He shall bear their iniquities" (53:7, 11).

He would,

"[pour] out His soul unto death" and make intercession for *"the transgressors"* (53:12).

What a wonderful revelation this was over 700 years

before the Messianic Lamb would actually suffer at the hands of sinners to bear the iniquity of many. If Jews would have considered Isaiah's insight, and intercalated it into the other Messianic prophecies, what a difference it would have made in their nation when Jesus Christ was born. It would have brought them out from under the *overshadowing* of ritual, and brought them into the *foreshadowing* of reality.

All of this is nearly impossible to accept for the Jewish mind which was and is steep-deep with Jewish concepts, making them unable to peek out from under the *overshadowing* of ritualistic miss-concepts and see the *foreshadowing* of reality to come, so that they could hardly believe Isaiah's report. Even today, if you engage a Jewish teacher with this text in Isaiah 53, they will show quickly that they do not understand it and really do not want to consider it. It will take the Tribulation—their fleeing into the wilderness, and the Revelation of the Lamb as we see in the Book of Revelation, to finally convince them and bring them into right relationship to the Lamb of God. This is indicated in Revelation 12:17 where it speaks of these Jews hiding in Edom, and coming out of there with the *"testimony of Jesus Christ"* (12:17).

All of this helps to explain how they could be blind-sighted, or as Paul stated a *"hardening in part has happened to Israel"* (Romans 11:25). I propose among other things, that they had allowed their own hope of national exaltation, pride, and self-interest, to blind them in at least one eye, to the whole truth and purpose of their rituals. They lost sight of the real purpose for which God designed their religious liturgy, and became devoted to their own piousness, instead of to God's plan. It is like so many Christian religious practices today where we are blind-sighted by devotion to the ritual rather than to its real meaning. Our religion *overshadows* its own *foreshadow* of reality. The Jewish leaders allowed their ritual to *overshadow* the *foreshadow* of reality. They could see the need of the suffering Lamb to take away the reproach of their sins, and they could see the mighty Messiah, the hope of their nation, but they could not put them together and see a suffering Savior to take away sin; one who would also be the conquering Messiah who would bring them into David's eternal kingdom. It will be in the days of the Tribulation that they will finally see the Lamb.

All of this blindness opened the way for the Gentile Church to be born, and it is that Church which will be moved out of the way before God turns back to deal with the Jews during the Tribulation (see Acts 15:15-16). God rebuilds the kingdom of David by bringing the Jews into right position during the Tribulation and incorporating 144,000 converted Jews to accompany Him to Mount Zion (Revelation 14). Then the Nations will be brought into promise as was the purpose of the suffering Lamb from the beginning: (Acts 15:17).

"That the rest of mankind may seek the Lord, even all the Gentiles who are called by My name, says the Lord who does all these things" (Acts 15:17).

Even for the Church, the full impact of the *"Lamb of God who takes away the sin of the world"* will be pressed upon them at the throne (John 1:29). The first time they see our Lord in Heaven, will be when John (after weeping bitterly for lack of anyone to open the book) said he looked up, "and behold ... *[there] stood a lamb as though it had been slain"* (Revelation 5:6). Even though this term had only been used four times in all of the New Testament, the Church came into full understanding of the reality of this connection between the Old Testament sacrifice and the New Testament reality. It will be forcibly pressed upon the Church at the Rapture. This truth was pressed upon John the Baptist when He saw Jesus coming to be baptized, and suddenly, caught by the Spirit of Revelation, said, *"Behold! The Lamb of God who takes away the sin of the whole world"* (John 1:29). He uses the term once more and only two other times, is it written in the entire New Testament.

WHY CHRIST REFERRED TO HIMSELF AS THE LAMB 27 TIMES

Let us bring a close to this dissertation by bringing the subject to what we believe will be its final significance. The purpose of Christ referring to Himself as the Lamb 27 times in the Book of the Revelation, is the fact that He is dealing with the Jews in most of the Revelation. Therefore, in order to bring them into full acceptance of Himself as the Messiah, He will need to convince them that He is their sin-bearer, as well as their great Redeemer. He will accomplish this sometime during this Tribulation period. I believe it will be when He reveals Himself to the Remnant in Edom. There, He will come to plead with them, ie. He will present a legal claim before them. When they suddenly grasp the full impact of Him as both their Lamb that takes away their sin, and the great king that is ready now to plead their cause before the whole world, a revival will break out and *"all Israel will be saved"* (Romans 11:26).

We can see Israel's conversion to the Lamb by noticing that this remnant returns with *"the testimony of Jesus"* as the 144,000—the Redeemed, coming up to Mount Zion *"[following] the Lamb wherever He goes ... being first-fruits to God and to the Lamb"* (Revelation 12:17, 14:4).

In the Tribulation period, the Jews will find their blind-side while driven into exile. They are going to come out from under the *overshadow* cast by their ritual and see the *foreshadow* of reality. At this time, they will realize why they could not see Jesus Christ as both their sin-bearer and their great coming King as the same. They will see Him as the Church has already seen Him—as He is.

ISRAEL IN THE TRIBULATION

The Revelation of Jesus Christ continues throughout the remaining chapters of the book, with Israel seeing the total disarray of Gog and Magog on the Mountains of Israel, the West Bank (Ezekiel 38,39); watching the multitudes that gather in Jehoshaphat, destroyed (Joel 3); witnessing Christ's coming to Zion with 144,000 converts and defeating the Armies that come against Jerusalem (Zechariah 12, 14); and defeating the Antichrist and his demon-inspired armies at Megiddo, will be reassuring to the Jews. Then, there is the setting up of David's kingdom with the 144,000 in leadership roles, and with a resurrected David as their King. The New Jerusalem, their eternal city on Earth with the eternal New Jerusalem of the Church, hovers in the sky on the sides of the North (Psalms 48:2). All will convince them of the total fulfillment of their hopes and dreams in the long-awaited Messiah.

It is always the Lamb that fights for the Jews and Israel in the Tribulation and during the time when Satan takes his best and last shot at their destruction. It is the Lord who shortens the time for the elect's sake (Israel is the elect). He will not have to shorten time for the Church's sake, for they will be gone in the Rapture (Matthew 24:22). It is the remnant of Israel who is fleeing from the onslaught of the devil, the dragon, of whom it is said that they (the Jews) overcame Him by "the Blood of the Lamb and by the word of their testimony, and they did not love their lives to the death" (12:11). For a sense of Israel's repentance, see Appendix.

ARMAGEDDON NOT FOR THE JEWS DEMISE

It is certainly not, as the extreme left of both America and Israel have widely propagated, that Christians teach Armageddon is the final demise of the Jews. Nowhere do either the Bible nor the prophetic teachers and expounders teach that Armageddon is for the Jews demise. Where do we even find that the Jews as a people, or even the State of Israel, will be involved in the Battle of Armageddon? The secular state may be, but not the remnant that will be hidden.

First of all, no Christian who supports the state of Israel and the Jewish state teaches that the Jews are the target of Christ at Armageddon. Neither do we teach that the Jews as a people and Israel, as a nation, will even be involved at Armageddon. The Jews have their part in the Tribulation, but not in Armageddon.

A careful reading of the biblical record of the battle at Megiddo clearly shows that the targets of Christ and His armies from Heaven will be the Antichrist's kingdom and His sorties (Revelation 16:10). This includes those who have taken the mark, name, and number, and therefore have joined with the Antichrist and His pseudo-World Order. The Armies of the nations are the kings of the whole world who are full of spiritual darkness and are drawn by demons to the alliance with the demonic world of that time; those who refuse to repent and blaspheme God (Revelation 16:9-13).

In fact, it is a clear teaching of Revelation that this consortium of people and nations will be the enemies of Israel and will be actively seeking their demise, and not the Christ whose full Revelation will come when He appears on Zion and at Armageddon to defeat these enemies of Israel and the Jews. It is true we teach that the Jews will go through the Tribulation as *Jacob's Trouble* but they will be protected through it and delivered out of it.

A recent documentary on the History Channel, had a week of the most gruesome and fearful speculations imaginable from every science and persuasion of thought of academia, as to how the world could end. It was entitled the familiar Armageddon. We must persuade our friends and Christian companions as well, that such a view of Revelation is totally and completely misleading and unacceptable. We must teach that the Book is about our Lord's purpose for the end of this age. Certainly He who loved the world and gave Himself for that love, is not out to destroy it. The only destruction among the people will be those who have taken the Mark of the Beast and given themselves over to the Antichrist and the Dragon, and their purposes. In this writing I hope to show a more positive outlook.

The worldly, fleshly and natural mind cannot begin to understand the Book of Revelation, for it can only be *"spiritually discerned"* (1 Corinthians 2:14). All of the intellect stored up in the natural mind, even the greatest of degrees from Ivy League schools, can never suffice to understand spiritual things. Paul was very insightful in this matter when he said, they are *"always learning but never able to come to the knowledge of the truth"* (2 Timothy 3:7). I submit that these will need a spiritual experience from the Holy Spirit in order to understand not only the Book of Revelation, but the whole message of the Bible as well. I also submit that it will even be helpful for Christians to develop some spiritual growth and maturity before trying to understand what they hear, read, and keep from the prophesies of this book (Revelation 1:3). Even those who have spiritual discernment and understanding may find it a bit confusing if they regularly fail to see Jesus and His purpose in every part of it.

Just as Jesus comes to us today in an esoteric way through the presence of the Holy Spirit, He also appears in the Revelation through the presence of one of the seven spirits of God. This is the complete essence of the Holy Spirit. Only those who are spiritually discerning can behold Him. Jesus taught us in John 14:17 that the world itself cannot receive the Holy Spirit. Since His resurrection and ascension, He can only be seen through the Holy Spirit. Therefore, the world cannot see Him. Only those led by the Holy Spirit can discern His presence throughout the Book. A new convert not yet accustomed to impressions in the Holy Spirit, may have some difficulty.

It is still all about Jesus Christ and His Revelation

While chapters 11 and 12 are about the Jews, Jerusalem, and the temple in Tribulation; and while these things have been taking place from Israel's perspective, we will now turn our attention to the beast and his version of the World Order. That is, the kingdom of the beast, the false prophet and his control over the nations and the economy. We shall insert another *meanwhile* between chapters 12 and 13.

Our central purpose has been to search for Jesus Christ and His Jewish people, and to premiere their special place in the end-times, and the Revelation of Jesus Christ.

CHAPTER 13

THE BEAST AND HIS WORLD ORDER

ACT IV SCENE IV

TRIBULATION—THE BEAST AND THE ANTICHRIST

(For an alternative approach about an Islamic Antichrist and an Islamic world order see the Appendix under the subject.)

We have spoken at length about the beast and his relationship to the Jews during the Tribulation. This is the same beastly system that was responsible for the death of two Jewish witnesses in chapter 11, the effort to kill the *Man-child*, and the onslaught on the Jewish remnant in chapter 12. It is the same beastly system under the devil that broke the covenant with the Jews at the half-way mark of the Tribulation (Daniel 9:27). It is the same beast that will appear again in chapters 14, 15, 16, 17, and 19 of Revelation.

Chapter 13 profiles the Tribulation from the standpoint of the beast, the false prophet, and the political World Order under the leadership of a Roman prince. Christ will profile for us Satan's earthly cohorts: the beast, its Roman prince, the Antichrist (or false prophet) in whom he will incarnate with himself. We may inject another *meanwhile* because the actions of this World Order System and its head, along with the Antichrist and his version of the One World Order, will be a part of the action in the next six chapters of Revelation. This One World Order and its Roman prince, has been a main actor with the dragon in the last two chapters, and it is profiled in this chapter. The International Community of Nations is quickly moving toward being taken over by the beastly system today.

THE RISE OF THE BEAST AND THE ANTICHRIST OVER THE WORLD ORDER

During the first half of the Tribulation, while nations rise against nations and kingdoms against kingdoms, and while there are wars and rumors of wars as angry nations seek to destroy one another by the violence of these conflicts, one-third of the earth is destroyed (Matthew 24:6; Revelation 8:6-12, 11:18). The World Order will be working very hard to gain global control and set up the beastly system, by putting their man in power, and to establish his control over the world, bringing its promised peace.

They seem to be well aware that there can be no peace in the world until the Jewish problem and the turbulence in the Middle East are settled. Today's malignity against the State of Israel will continue right on into the Tribulation period as we have already seen in chapters 11 and 12. The European powers, along with America, will be pushing the UN agenda for World Control. Their effort to dominate and control the Muslim world is backfiring on them all over the Middle East. The West Bank problem and Israel's existence will continue to be in jeopardy.

Out of the chaos of the first half of the Tribulation, the UN and the Global Leaders will see a need to compromise on the Israeli question, and negotiate a *peace covenant* with Israel. Also, out of the chaos and near destruction of the world, (Matthew 24:23-4) a European king most likely from the old Merovingian line of occult kings will arise as an Imam Mahdi, or the Messiah. He will gain control by peace and flattery, and will set himself up as a New Age master that controls the World Order and the Global System, which is the beast that rises up out of the *sea* of peoples.

He will gain command of the NATO forces and the control of the IMF, which is the World Treasury (Daniel 11:43). Pressure will continue upon Israeli. Israel will become more and more isolated and the world agenda will demand that Israel get out of the West Bank and Golan Heights, and allow a Palestinian State with east Jerusalem as its Capitol.

He will continue the effort to destroy the Jewish State. At least two of the four major wars against the Jews will be fought during this time, and out of the devastation of those wars will come a covenant with Israel over Jerusalem. In the covenant provisions, a Jewish temple will be allowed to be built on the north end of the Temple Mount and the ritual of sacrifice will be re-instituted. I imagine that the world powers will later discover the demonic nature of their man, but it will be too late for them to back out. By then, the whole world (in the absence of the Church) and the loosing of demons and devils, will have crossed the critical mass toward devil worship, and made a Paradigm shift into total worship of the dragon (Revelation 9, 13:4).

It will be the middle of the week, or half way into what we know as the seven-year Tribulation, however, the World Order (or the Community of Nations) will not recognize their beastly satanic connections as such, until this European Prince teams up with a second beast out of the earth from the pits of Hell. He will be a devil-possessed and a radically demon-possessed man. His demonic revolutionary nature will cause him to become very fanatic religiously and very militant in his use of power. He will force worship of the World Order and its Roman King. Out of the pseudo-religious base of the UN and its New Age Occultism, he will force dragon worship, or worship of Lucifer as God. He will gain power as the first beast does by peace and flattery, but by his occult demon power, we will fascinate the Lucifer-worshipping New Age Globalists with "signs and wonders, like calling fire down from Heaven. When he breaks the covenant with the Israeli and stops the daily sacrifice in the newly built temple, He will set himself up as God, and probably will make the old Crusader Castle his palace (Daniel 9:27; 2 Thessalonians 2:4; Matthew 24:15). That fanaticism is revealed to us in chapter 12. All of this will be with the support of his new version of the revamped UN World Order and the EU with its Roman prince.

This will be the status of the world in Mid-Tribulation. All current events on the world scene point to this very scenario today.

CRYPTIC SYMBOLISM FROM THE OLD TESTAMENT

We will of necessity, have to spend some time in the history and Old Testament background of the beast. However, I do not plan to spend much time there. Frankly, it is because most of the books written on the Revelation of Jesus Christ go to great lengths and do a good job of exposing and explaining these things. Under separate writing, I am putting together a whole book on the background of this beast. However, since the subject of this writing is Christ in the Revelation, I choose not to be side-tracked on what I believe are minor and not major roles in this Revelation. Many people have gotten so fascinated and caught up with the beast, the false prophet and its 666, Mystery Babylon the Great and other things, which I fear have undermined and overlooked the main star of the book. It is my intention to remain focused on Christ.

The beast that is introduced to us by our Lord Jesus Christ in earlier chapters and is featured in this one is not a new feature in the saga of divine justice. He is a long time enemy of God and His plan in Christ. The dragon introduced here is introduced as *"that serpent of old called the Devil and Satan,"* (Revelation 12:9). Christ means to portray for us exactly who he is in the cryptic symbolism of the Bible. He is the power behind the Old Empires morphed and mutated in a mutant form of the beasts spoken of in Daniel seven, but merged into one (13:1-4; compare with Daniel 7:1-3). We will now follow his crooked, slithery trail with just a brief synopsis of his character and development through time, as exposed to us in Scripture.

WE ARE NOT TO IMAGINE OR SEE AN IMAGE, BUT TO CATCH THE IMPRESSIONS

As we try to imagine a beast with seven heads and ten horns, we get nightmares. But, we are not to imagine a physical form, but rather catch the impression intended. Again, in all of the cryptic symbols given, God does not intend for us to see visions of the physical forms of these things. However, we are supposed to think deeper and find the impression or meaning intended.

The eastern Oriental mind understands impressions, poetic metaphor, and abstract symbolism better than the western occidental mind, which is short on the poetic and metaphoric impressions and long on the physical side of life. The western mind has to physically see, while the mid-eastern mind wants to feel, or to be impressed with meaning.

The Bible is an eastern book written by eastern men with a Syrian mindset. The prophetic texts are best understood by those who seek deeper meaning than just a physical image. In some ways those who have endeavored to visualize these beings portrayed in Revelation have not helped us, for we have attempted to make meaning out of the physical features, rather than follow the imagery back into the esoteric mysteries behind these depictions, and find their real, deeper meaning.

For example, the term *beast* is not meant to conger up an actual *beast* or animal that we will face, but to receive the impression that this World Order System will be terrible, fearful, ravaging, and destructive, just as the historic empires and world governments historically have been. In the Scriptures, God depicts imperial powers and governments as *ravishing beasts* throughout history, especially as the Gentile world powers have related to Israel and the covenant people. This impression is plainly shown in Daniel and consummates itself in Revelation. Whatever the *beast* symbolizes, he was a ravaging beast alive in Daniel's day, and all through the ages of the empires. And now, he still exists in the end-times, therefore, he could not be a man.

We should not look at this as a beast made up of four different animals, but understand that each of these animals represent the characteristic of four great empires. We should try to imagine an animal with seven heads, but as we have shown, a system which has morphed and mutated from four empires into one with the same characteristics; and will yet mutate into seven throughout the rest of the Revelation. This is not a physical animal, but an end-time empire headed by ten powers in the person of ten Kings. The Antichrist's One World Order will be headed by an amalgamation of ten kings out of the occultic side of European society.

DOCTRINE OF THE DRAGON

Nearly every culture on Earth has in its history, some form of dragon worship. In South and Central America, we have *Quetzalcoatl*, the feathered serpent of the Aztec and Inca cultures. He is especially popular in the Far East where they have been dominated by a dragon culture for over 4000 years. This dragon has had them mesmerized as the image of their *Patron Saint* and presents himself as the old dragon in all forms, shapes, and doctrines. In India and the islands, he has mutated into the python-type, and cultured the snake concept of the Hindu religion. These are only a few samples of the dragon culture throughout the world. He is none other than the snake, or dragon of Eden. He is an esoterical being who has lost his glory and is ever in pursuit of its return. His dreams of returning to the power he once had. Temples, statues, and carvings of all types are dedicated to him, expressing every human whim. There can be no doubt that he is the *Patron Saint* of the world harlots, the old whore of Revelation 18, and the peoples of the world's prime deity. His physical side is seen in the great dinosaur culture which depicts a strange culture of dragon and serpent-type creatures of Satan's nature.

Then we have the Zodiac. The Bible tells us that its language has gone throughout the whole earth. In it we have Draco, Hydra and Serpens the serpent, along with Cetus the Sea Monster, and Scorpio the Scorpion. These images cover one-third of the Heavens. Also, all of the hero images in the stars signs are known as snake killers, dragon slayers, and similar images. Since these images in the heavens go clear back to ancient times, it shows that whatever their original meaning was meant to be, the stigma of an ancient serpent and its divine slayer, is well established throughout all of history. From the overwhelming themes in the stars which mimic the Bible story, it is very likely they were initially an original Gospel developed by Seth and Enoch, before their corruption by Nimrod and Babel.

This dragon of Revelation is no doubt, related to the ancient snake. Thirty-one times in Scripture, he is called *Nachash*—identified in Genesis 3. He is also identified many times in prophetical texts (Isaiah 14:29, 27:1; Amos 9:3; Jeremiah 8:17, 46:22). The dragon, *drakon* or *dracula*, is named twelve times in Revelation; the devil, *diabolos* 5 times;

and Satan eight times. The beings found in Revelation 12:9 and 20:2 are all one and the same. This accuser is mentioned in opposition to Christ, the Jews, and the Church 25 times. He is very prominent in the saga of the Revelation of Jesus Christ. Remember, this Beast and His kingdom is esoteric.

He of course, starts his appearance and begins to show his subtle character in the Garden during his encounter with Mother Eve. There the whole nature of his rebellion against God and Satan's deception of man is clear. He begins to lecture Eve on how unfair God is and how He wants to prevent them from knowing everything. He says that we can become gods, which is exactly what his own heart's desire is (See Isaiah 14:12-13). He played on the emotions of the woman. He questions God's Word, thereby sowing doubt; He questions whether they will really die; He begins to sow in their conscience the idea that they could be like God knowing both good and evil, i.e. carnal knowledge. He appeals to their earthly appetites and desires: the lust of the flesh, and the lust of the eye, and the pride of life (1 John 2:16).

We can appreciate the fact that the devil is always in every generation, subtle above all other created beings. However, we can also recognize him for his predictable subtlety, as we see here from his first appearance on Earth and right on through to his last days. We find that he is far too clever for his own good. His own cleverness and self-interest will destroy him.

The saga of Satan continues and becomes more evident at *Bab-el,* the *Gate of God* where his subtleness takes on public political perspective. It represents Satan's extreme hate for the God that put him out of the Garden and placed the cherubims to guard the gate (Genesis 3:24). Building on that hate and the basic lectures in his very beginning, he was able to influence a whole society with his philosophy under Nimrod at Babylon. The people's fear of the God that brought on the flood made them easy prey to Satan's teaching that Adoni was a mean God while Satan was the good guy. It was natural for a rebel like Nimrod to allow the devil to influence and make him the real Redeemer.

Satan's rebellion continued to build through his behind-the-scenes influence on the great empires of the Middle East. Four of them are illustrated through the great image of Nebuchadnezzar's dream. They were Babylon, Persia, Greece, and Rome. His influence on these old empires is shown in the seven heads of the beast (Revelation 13:1). His hate for the promised seed of woman who would bruise his head, was evident from the beginning in the disdain shown toward Israel and the Jews from the very beginning of the Empires (Genesis 3:15). Every empire tried to annihilate the Jews and Israel in order to stop the coming of the *Man-child*.

His latest appearances will be in his hate and death of the two witnesses of chapter 11, and his pursuit to kill the Christ-child and his campaign against the Jews in chapter 13.

Throughout the era of our time, these great powers have been struggling with other powers in the Middle East, always with the same hateful disdain of Israel and God's plan for Palestine.

However, as we see developing right before our eyes today, these great powers are mutating, or morphing further into one great empire, which is made up of the characteristics of all four of Daniel's beasts, to comprise what we know as the One World Order (Revelation 13:1-2). We have seen three efforts to re-establish the Holy Roman Empire in the three military Reich's of Germany (Reich, meaning *empire* in German). The Nazi party was known as the *3rd Reich*. The fourth effort to resurrect Rome has the same purpose, only upon an economic conquest rather than a military insurgence.

Today, it is the old empires of Daniel's image and the four beasts of Daniel seven which have mutated into one worldwide philosophy of governance. They are the great political/social/eco system with a pseudo-religious base rising up out of the nations of Europe, America, and the UN made up of all tongues and peoples, and striving for great powers and controls in the Middle East. It is the Imperial Systems of a World Government rapidly spreading its control through the UN, "by the effort of the Supranational Sovereigns, the International Elite, and the World Bankers" (Quoted from David Rockefeller's talk at the National Press Conference in Washington, D.C. 1997).

TEN KINGS WITH NO KINGDOM AS YET

There is also further mutating in the fact that Satan's efforts are no longer represented by great empires, but by ten kings who have no kingdom as of yet.

These never represent ten nations, but rather ten individual kings. All five of the references to them, found in Daniel 7 and 8, and also in Revelation 16 and 17, tell us that they are kings. The effort of Satan is now resident in these ten European kings who *"have no kingdom as yet, but they receive authority for one hour as kings with the beast. These are of one mind, and they will give their power and authority to the beast"* (Revelation 17:12-13).

We can now see that the beast is one of the heads of an age-old Satanic-led imperial system of world power, whose desire has always been to dominate the whole world with its control. Seven heads have passed in history by the time this beast, or *8th head*, rises up in the form of what we have identified as the One World Order, or the New World Order.

At the head of it is a Greco-Roman prince; a political/eco wizard who will try to push the New World Order to full fruition. Not able to comprehend the Luciferian/Satanic plot behind this World Order, and in frustration of the World Order over its failed policies as evident in the first half of the

Tribulation, He will be open to teaming up with a second beast—the false prophet, and the actual Antichrist who will usher in the full and open policy of the devil.

CHRIST'S REAL ENEMY- NOT THE NATIONS, BUT THE DRAGON, SATAN

The reason that they appear briefly here in the latter days of Christ's Revelation, is to show us that this world will be wrestling with these world powers and the final World Order under the Antichrist, and to make us aware of the real issue. It is not the nations and people involved, but the principalities and powers in the esoteric world of cosmic warfare that is the real foe of Christ, and the real enemy that He will deal with at Armageddon.

All of this is a continuation of the historicity of the beast as he emerges in the end time. In Daniel, he has only ten horns, because the seven heads are yet future in his day. The Empires are the heads, the Horns are ten kings that will arise out of the Old Holy Roman Empire—the 7th head (Revelation 17:9-12). There will be a resurrection of the 7th head now past. Then, the beast's One World Order becomes the 8th head and goes into perdition.

As we have shown, it is significant to observe again that the nature and character of this beast is made up of all four of the great empires of Nebuchadnezzar's vision and of the four beasts which strive upon the Great Sea (Daniel 2, 7:2-8; compare Revelation 13:1,2) In Daniel, the head beast is the little horn, who remains rather cryptic in the shadows, and it typifies the coming beast. However, in Revelation he is made manifest by coming to the forefront in world affairs.

The same four spirits (winds) mentioned in Revelation 7:1 are the same four spirits that strived upon the Great Sea (the Mediterranean) throughout history, and we see them continuing to strive in the Middle East to form the beastly imperial system today (Daniel 7; Revelation 17:7-18). Already, the world is wandering after this system of governance, and inadvertently following the satanic lead to formulate the final World Order under the Antichrist!

A SYNOPSIS OF THE BEAST'S KINGDOM

The thirteenth chapter of Revelation is in no way a complete treatise of the beast and his kingdom, nor is intended to be. It is only a synopsis of Satan's last-day effort to expose himself and his plan for world domination. Our Lord expects that those who search for the whole story, to be cognizant of all of the related texts of the Old Testament; especially those texts which deal with this same beast as the little horn and the blasphemous king of Daniel 7 and 8. He would expect us to tie in Paul's insight into this beast as the wicked one of 2 Thessalonians, chapter two. The introduction mentions that the book is purposely written in analogues, i.e. the enigma meant for study and analysis, or a mystery to be solved. As we have already shown that a consideration of all of the related texts in the eschatological prophesies must be compared. However, we will briefly comment on the Lord's *short story* in this chapter. Let's see what the Lord has to tell us of this last day expression of Satan's final effort to establish His kingdom.

Revelation 13:1 immediately places him in a clear prophetic profile. Again, we are taken back to Daniel 2 and 7:7, 24 where a lot of information is given to us about this latter-day beast. Revelation 17:12 makes it clear that these ten horns are ten kings, not kingdoms which will arise out of Europe in support of a European prince who is the little horn of Daniel 7 and 8. These kings represent the kingdom, or governmental system which will be used by the Antichrist.

The 4th beast of Daniel 7 does not have 7 heads, but does have the 10 horns of the beast of Revelation 13. However, as we compare the four different beasts that make up the beast

THE BEAST AND HIS WORLD ORDER   401

of Revelation 13, we see that they are comparable to the 4 beasts in Daniel 7. Also, they are all said to be part of the character of the beast in Revelation 13. This tells us that they are the same beasts, but the 7 heads had not yet come to completeness, as we will explain below. It does show that this beast in Revelation is made up of the social/economic/governmental essence of the old empires.

As to the 7 heads in John's day, 5 Empires were fallen; one is Rome and one is to come. We believe the 7th head was the Holy Roman Empire, which existed for over 1000 years from AD 800 to AD 1800. The 8th is out of the 7th and will be the beast of the 13th chapter of Revelation, shown by the fact that it goes into perdition, or hell and judgment (Revelation 17:10-11).

The 7 heads are not necessarily men, but the first 4 are empires as they are seen in Daniel; i.e. Babylon, Persia, Greece, and Rome. Each of these Empires has a man who is well-known as its head, i.e. Nebuchadnezzar, Cyrus, Alexander the Great, and Julius Caesar. So at the head of the Beastly System will be a man, but not the Antichrist per se'. The empire was the *head*. We can only understand the 13th chapter by comparing symbolism with Daniel, and also by comparing it with the 17th chapter where we have a more complete explanation of these things. There we clearly see that the heads are empires and not a man per se. Five of them have passed into history (fallen) in John's day, and one is Rome, and one is to come. The "Holy Roman Empire" and the 8th kingdom of the beast, is to come out of the 7th , i.e. out of the whole gamut of empires shown in Daniel. This empire is the final end of the 4th empire, and the 4th beast of Daniel 7. For those in the prophetic circles, we usually think of it as the resurrected Roman Empire, or more perfectly the resurrected Holy Roman Empire. Actually, both the Roman Empire and the Germanic Holy Roman Empire are still existent today in the European Union and in the two long legs: the western Roman Church and the Eastern Orthodox Church. A world leader, depicted by the little horn of Daniel 7 and the Roman prince of Daniel 9:26 will eventually be chosen by the UN and other international community leaders to lead this 8th head of imperialism.

A word of explanation on the Roman Prince of Daniel 9:26. After the death of the Messiah, the "people of the Prince" will destroy Jerusalem and the Temple. This prophecy was fulfilled in A.D. 70, just less than 30 years after Christ's death. The Roman 10th army under Titus destroyed the Temple and the city of Jerusalem. Therefore we can conclude that the Prince to come will be a Roman Prince, probably of the lineage of Titus.

After all of these Empires demise, and through the efforts of the Holy Roman Empire and the Catholic Popes, the Empires influence on the world scene gradually grew through the Middle Ages and morphed into four great powers striving with each other in the Mediterranean area (Daniel 7). We are told that these beastly empires' characteristics are represented by the four beasts of Daniel: 1) like a Leopard; 2) with the feet of a bear; 3) with the mouth of a lion; and 4) is great and terrible, with ten horns (Revelation 13:2; Daniel 7:2-7).

From this information, we may deduct that the beast is not strictly a man for the following reasons: No man has existed throughout the time of these five fallen empires, or the one that existed in John's day; neither is there any man who will exist through the long years of the Dark Ages and come forth in the final days of the 7th Empire, and on into the 8th; nor is there a man who can be ten kings. But both the heads and the horns of this beast can very clearly represent what we have seen develop in the world system of government today. Whatever this beast is, he existed in an earlier form in the days of Daniel.

THE POLITICAL ECO-SYSTEM TODAY; THE ONE WORLD ORDER

When off course, any administration of government soon becomes identified by the man at its head and his policies. It is important to understand this fact. It can be established by comparing what is said with Old Testament symbolism. He is one of the 7 heads. Five of these heads are exposed in the Old Testament and a 6th was in existence in John's day (Revelation 17:10-12). A seventh was to come, which I believe to be the Holy Roman Empire, and an eighth (the Antichrist's kingdom) is to come out of the seventh. There have been seven World Order empires which sought to destroy the Jews and set up a New World Order. Trying by the world's people under Satan, this beast will be the 8th one to accomplish a One World Order without God and His Son, Jesus Christ. They want to accomplish what God and Christ has promised in Revelation. It is going to take the world-shaking Tribulation and Armageddon to accomplish it.

Today they are the great political eco-system with a pseudo-religious base rising up out of the nations of Europe, America, and the UN, made up of all tongues and peoples, and having great power and controls in the Middle East. Again, it is the Imperial Systems of World Government rapidly spreading its control though the UN, by the effort of what David Rockefeller called the "Supranational Sovereigns, the International Elite, and the World Bankers" (quote from Mr. David Rockefeller, spoken at the National Press Conference in Washington D.C. 1997).

CAN WE KNOW AND IDENTIFY THE ANTICHRIST?

Speculating as to who the Antichrist might be is one of the great side-tracks involved in the study of Revelation and one that takes us far off from the theme of the writing. Because of carnal man's negative nature, we tend to be more interested in devilish and demonic themes than about spiritual things. Therefore, it is easy to get caught up in all of the spooky, spiritual side of Revelation. We tend to want to know about the ghoulish and mysterious, rather than to know about Christ. We know a lot about the Antichrist; not from the Scriptures, but from sensational speculation. Scriptures only speak of the *spirit of Antichrist* four times in John's epistles. However, from Scripture we are made aware of the beastly system that the Antichrist will be the head.

We are told in Daniel that he will come out of the Grecian/Roman peoples and out of an occult system of kings in the last days which very likely will be the *Royal Blood Cult* of kings that exists today in Europe (Daniel 8:23). Daniel's few sketches of him as the little horn, shows him not to be the normal run of politician or diplomat, but a very occult and weird demon-led man, just as Revelation shows Him to be. Paul also shows his occult nature, as he will come working the works of Satan with cultic *"power, signs, and lying wonders"* (2 Thessalonians 2:9-10).

In this same text, Paul plainly tells us that we will not know the Antichrist, "that wicked one," before the Rapture takes place. Only after the Church, who has been actively hindering his appearance, is taken out of the way through the Rapture, then he will be revealed (9:6-9). He is probably breathing air today, but neither we, nor the world can know him until the Church is gone. We can only know Him in the trappings of the systems that are developing to bring him to power.

We can spend so much energy and time looking for the Antichrist that we fail to keep our eyes on and our interest in Christ, who is the one to be revealed in Revelation. We should stop looking, because not until we are gone, will he be *"revealed in his own time"* (2 Thessalonians 2:6). Therefore, I am not looking for the Antichrist. I am looking for the Christ, the real star of the end time; I'm not looking for the little horn, I'm looking for the Big Horn.

We should keep in mind that the Antichrist is only active for a short time—3½ years, and even in those few years, he is never in total control. It is Christ who will set up an eternal kingdom, and we shall live and reign with Him for a thousand years.

It seems as though Christ disappears and is not evident in the 13th chapter, but his is far from the truth. It is because the 13th chapter is focused on and is a short synopsis of the short-lived beastly system that will open the doors for the Antichrist. Christ's involvement with the beast is not made plain in Revelation, but it is made very clear in Daniel. Christ's main involvement in Revelation is with Satan and the dragon.

However, in every reference to the beastly system in Daniel, the kingdom of Christ comes to the forefront (Daniel 2:44, 7:17-18, 27, 12:10-13). Daniel 11:45 says that he, the Antichrist *"shall come to his end, and no one will help him."* It is very plain who will help him come to his end. No man or government of man will bring his demise. It will be Christ by his Revelation that will destroy the domain of the Antichrist and make way for the set-up of Christ's eternal kingdom.

BEAST—NOT A MAN, BUT AN IMPERIAL SYSTEM RULED BY A MAN

These empires are tied together in the mind of God and in the plan of Satan. He who sees the hearts of man and Government, can discern the *"thoughts and intents of the heart,"* and can see the very nature of these governing bodies (Hebrews 4:12). He knows that they are all tied together by the philosophy of Satan. Each empire builds on the foundation of the preceding empire, and each has expectation of becoming that final big world government, or the first world system. Satan is trying to rally his forces again to produce a peaceful world, a Millennium if you will, but of His own style and of course, without God or His Son, Christ Jesus.

Just as Satan has been laboring through the godless nations to build His Kingdom without God and Christ, Jesus Christ has been building His own Kingdom. While Satan's Kingdom represents the "Mystery of Iniquity" (II Thessalonians 2:7) Christ has been working on the "Mystery of Godliness." (1 Timothy 3:16, Ephesians 2:4, 5, 5:32, Revelation 10:7) Those mysteries are becoming manifest by the Revelation of Jesus Christ. If we clarify this it makes the rest of Chapters 13 and 17 easier to understand.

I am persuaded that it was not a man who had a deadly wound that was healed, but it was an empire. This fits the history of the Roman Empire to a "T." The Roman Empire existed until the 4th and early 5th centuries A.D. It was then almost wounded to death, but survived and healed by the resurrection of the Holy Roman Empire, which dominated history for the next 1000 years, from Charlemagne in AD 800 to Napoleon in AD 1800. Therefore, it is a historical fact that the Roman Empire *"was, is not, and yet is"* (Revelation 17:8).

Today we look for the resurrected Holy Roman Empire resident in ten kings of the Roman royalty, to come to the forefront with the One World Order's selected *Mr. President of Planet Earth* (Quoting Henry Kissinger). There may be a man who suffers death and is resurrected, but I have reservations about it. In my opinion, Revelation makes it plain, that the *head* that was wounded unto death is one of the empires which were *heads* of history. It has been suggested that it was of the seven heads and becomes the 8th head, or imperial system (17:8, 11).

It seems that a man becomes so embedded in the system

that at the end, he represents the whole system, just as dictators or regimes today finally become personification of the empire. Revelation 19:20 seems to indicate that a person is recognized as the system, but it remains that the beast described in Revelation 13 and 17, cannot be only a man. It is evident that the Antichrist's World Order will be ruled for a short time in the last part of the Tribulation. It is the second beast described in Revelation 13:11, and it may be he who is spoken of in Revelation 19:20. We will expound on this second beast later in this chapter's comments.

His beastly system has already appeared in Daniel 7:1-8 and 17-28. It has also been spoken of twice in the Revelation. Once in chapter 11:7, where the One World Order under their Antichrist system, destroys the witnesses in Jerusalem. Again, we see this beastly system under the Antichrist in verses 12:3-4, where it is shown as the historic enemy of Israel and the *Man-child*, Jesus Christ; and where the world armies set out to destroy the remnant of the Jews. Even though the word *beast* is not used, we know it is this same worldwide system mentioned in chapter 13. Here, the dragon is made synonymous with the beast in that he is described as having seven heads and ten horns. Again, whatever the beast symbolizes, he was alive in Daniel's day and all through the ages of the Empires, and exists in the end times.

THE ONE WORLD ORDER HEADED UP BY THE ANTICHRIST

It seems that evil triumphs for a short duration after the devastation of the first 3½ years of the Tribulation. The World Order System becomes very vicious, and the door of Hell is open to flood the world with dragon worship or Satanic worship. Revelation 13:4 seems to indicate such, but what we actually see here is not directly the worship of a man, but a worldwide devotion to the One World Order, the 8th *head*.

I think we can see that as far as the people of the world are concerned today, they are amorously in love and fascinated with the idea of Globalism. Our schools are saturated with its influence on students; our government institutions are totally global; and the critical mass of society has been reached by this beast of Globalism. I would be condemned if I spoke negatively about it. This beast depicts Gentile rule of the earth. It will be headed for the short duration of the last 3 ½ years of the Tribulation by the false prophet or 2nd beast, which we call the Antichrist. I inject here that I am not intending to suggest a wholesale condemnation and rejection of the global system of government, but simply what Satan will do with it through his ten kings and Antichrist for that short period. Therefore, we as a world are already worshipping the international Globalism.

It is true that a global system is and will be necessary, but it will be dangerous to humanity until Christ sets up the real One World Order under God during the Millennium kingdom.

BLASPHEME (Revelation 13: 5) THE WORLD ORDER VENUE TODAY

The very essence of the little horn and the Antichrist beastly systems shown to us in Daniel, Revelation, 2 Thessalonians, and other places in the texts of Scripture are represented by and in our international community today. They are earth-worshippers, Mother Nature worshippers, and animal or beast worshippers. They "worshiped and served the creature rather than the Creator" (Romans 1:25). They worship the God of cosmic forces (Daniel 11:37). The word *force* here is not worldly or military force, but a word depicting inner strength, such as the New Age cosmic powers. They already worship dragons; i.e. dinosaurs. They are money worshippers, anti-God, and they worship man as

God (Daniel 11:36, 37). All of this prepares them to fall right into the world that is predicted and shown us in the day of the Revelation of Jesus Christ. These New-Age Globalists will readily accept a man who claims to be God, sitting on the Temple Mount; worshipping the devil, and working miracles by the powers of Hell. They are blasphemous toward God and Christ, do not want Christ or God to rule over them, and find no fault with those who blaspheme.

It is also plain that our public might have already, or almost already, passed the point of critical mass and made the paradigm shift to total Devil worship, and would readily accept the occult Antichrist. Case in point: note the craze over Harry Potter, a totally demonic and Devil-inspired story; accolades the witches and their covens with demonic possessed people, with a devil enhancing them. Also, look how the public rushes to devour any movie or entertainment which has to do with the occult, devilish themes, or ghoulish and violent drama. Is it not strange that they find leisure in participating in these devilish expressions? They flock to music concerts which perform on stage with sets designed to enhance Hell, and in every lyric, carry the devil's agenda and swoon to his moods. It is strange, that with all of this devil-expression in their phobic worship, they still do not believe in a personal devil. Satan has done a great job with His subtle deceit!

These *One-Worlders* today are also anti-Israel, and are given over to Satanic anti-Semitism (Daniel 11:32-34). Proof of this is the total anti-Israel stance of the UN and nearly every nation they represent. In every resolution that concerns the State of Israel, over 97% vote against Israel every time.

PEACEMAKERS MAKE WAR

These are peacemakers. Their main theme is that they will bring peace to a war-torn world. We respect their good intentions, but they make the mistake of trying to bring peace without the *Prince of Peace*. By his policy of peace, the Antichrist *"shall destroy many in their prosperity"* (Daniel 8:25). What a paradoxical statement that is! However, it reflects our peace efforts today where more people, especially in Israel, are being killed by the peace efforts, than are being rescued. Peace efforts have taken more lives than war these days.

SATAN AND THE DRAGON AND THE WORLD ORDER TODAY

In this chapter we see a world sold out to Satan and given over to dragon-worship. It's a world that allows its leaders to blaspheme God and Christ, and all that dwell in Heaven. At this point in time, Satan, having been defeated in Heaven and cast out to the earth, injects his venom into the people of Earth toward not only God and Christ, but to all of Heaven's hosts (13: 6). A prime example of that world of blasphemy is embodied in the Arabic writing that circles the Dome of the Rock on the Temple Mount, where in defiance of God and His Son Jesus, is declared over and over, "God has no son, God has no son, God has no son." From Daniel's expose' of Satan, I have dubbed him *Mr. Big Mouth* because Daniel says of this little horn:

> *"... the king shall do according to his own will: he shall exalt and magnify himself above every god, shall speak blasphemies against the God of gods ..."* (Daniel 11:36).

Paul profiles the same spirit of the wicked one:

> *"... who opposes* (all that is sacred) *and exalts himself above all that is called God or that is worshipped; so that he sits as God in the temple of God, showing himself that he is God"* (2 Thessalonians 2:4).

We have the spirit of Antichrist in our world today. The Tribulation saints that have come to confess Christ and refuse the mark, number, and name of the World Order or beast, will be hated, and will draw his venom also (Revelation 13:7-8). The whole world, all whose names that are not written in the Book of Life of the Lamb from the foundation of the world, will worship this hellish, demon-inspired Godless World Order (13:8).

About the only people today who will allow any criticism against the international community (World Order) and all of its control over our lives, are the saints in the Churches of born-again believers where pastors and teachers regularly expose the nature of this beast among us today. We are forced to submit to all forms of control, which encroaches on our lives and keeps us from speaking out against the World Order.

Not only does the world benefit right now by submitting to the world community in our buying and selling, but also in many other areas of our lives. There are advanced technologies which make it possible to *mark* us today. One thing that must be considered when we think of the encroachment of the World Order is the control over every aspect of our lives by technology. We are and will be traced not only in buying and selling, but in every aspect of our lives. Increasingly, we submit to these controls for we have no choice. The governments of the world can know all about us and it has increasingly become acceptable to us. We know it is common knowledge that nearly every detail of our past and present is encoded on our credit cards and web outlets. We talk about privacy, but there is no such thing. Every bank in the world system knows everything your local bank knows. Even though businesses deny it and say they do not share your private information, they do sell their clientele names and information to the highest bidder. We are already drawing the disdain of this satanic beast and the devil behind Him. Therefore, if any man has an ear to hear, let him hear; he had better be listening! I will not enter into a lengthy discussion of these technologies, for the reader can find detailed expose' of them in many books and other sources. It is communicated to us in virtually every headline around the world today.

THE SECOND BEAST IS NO DOUBT A MAN
(Revelation 13:11)

Now in this writing, we depart from most of the standard teaching of the Book of Revelation of our day. In doing so, I do not intend to criticize or challenge any of the worthy commentators, all of whom I have great respect, and many of them I have referred to and even quoted during this writing. I depart simply because in the years of study and contemplation of the Book of Revelation of Jesus Christ, I have not been able to answer many of the questions that are presented in the following standard interpretation of these texts about the beast and false prophet.

Please allow me to present what conclusions I have arrived at and the reason for my departure from former teachings. They may be subject to further study as truth is systematically revealed to us by the Holy Spirit

Most teachings and writings about the first beast and this second beast, present both as being male gender. As I have already shared, it is my persuasion that the beast is not a man per se, although there is probably a Roman prince of the occult bloodline of Christ as the president over it. The first beast is an imperial system of world government, the 8th head. Remember, the heads are Empires, or governmental systems of a world-wide nature. All of the information given to us shows him to be one of the ancient historical heads.

This second beast coming up out of the earth from Hell has no information written about him that relates him to or makes him one of the 7 heads, or even indicates that he is a head. Every impression of this beast indicates that he

THE BEAST AND HIS WORLD ORDER   413

is a man, an individual; the exact fulfillment of the willful king of Daniel 7 and 8, and the *wicked one* described in 2 Thessalonians 2: 3-12. At a point where the world order or community of nations have run aground by chaos on the world scene, are completely frustrated with opposition to their plans, and open to any help, this demonic, occult-man, incarnate of Satan himself and of cosmic religious persuasion, comes out of demonic woodwork, or Satanism. He will be a practicing member of the *"craft,"* a man of *"fierce countenance,"* and a miracle worker (Daniel 8:23, 25 *King James Version*). He probably comes from the ten super occult *Kings of the Blood of Christ*, deeply imbedded in European culture.

By his signs and wonders, he will impress a world that will accept a religious leader who works wonders (2 Thessalonians 2:9; Revelation 13:13). My mentor Pastor used to say that even today, if the Antichrist came to this valley, stood up on a pinnacle, and called fire down from Heaven, the valley would not hold the Christian people, let alone the worldly people who would gather here to bow down and worship him. The world will be led into deception by the wonder-working, miracle specialist (2 Thessalonians 2:9-11). The world will be allured and seduced by his charm. He will fascinate a world that is already enchanted and beguiled by Satan, because He is Satan incarnate. The devil will possess Him.

His miracles will include giving life to the image of the beast, possibly by television or some type of holographic picture (Revelation 13:15).   Daniel says that he will *"understand sinister schemes"* and by this, he will fascinate and mesmerize the world's lost people who are always mesmerize by the mysterious (Daniel 8:23).

The Roman Prince, which heads the beastly system, may be from among the political, diplomatic core of the world, but has not been known on the public scene. He is totally demonic and by the power of witchcraft and Satanic force, pulls a devil-worshipping world under His hypnotic draw. His power will not be necessarily political or economic, but demonic with persuasion over a devil-worshipping world (13:4).

Notice how close the world is and has been drawn to Satan. Dr. Henry Spaak, Secretary General of NATO, speaking of the already frustrated World Order folks a few years ago, expressed their disappointments by saying,

> "What we want is a man of sufficient stature to hold the allegiance of all people and to lift us out of the economic morass into which we are sinking. Send us such a man, and be he God or devil, we will receive him."

This second beast is certainly that sort of man with all of Satan's subtle deceptions that they are looking for (2 Thessalonians 2:10). He will appear after the first half of the Tribulation. The One World Order, the world's hope for a savior, has failed to bring peace; with war, and famine and social chaos widespread, and natural disasters everywhere, they will be grasping for a man to put their last hope in, even a deeply-occult man who claims to be God. They look for a worker of miracles from of some extra-terrestrial out of the stars by cosmic vortexes of force and power. If such a man were to appear right now, the whole world would follow him, not even caring whether he is God or the devil. All of them, except for the born-again Church, will go crazy and follow Him. Demonism, which we saw begin in chapter nine; will flourish into an all-out devil worship, expressing their devotion to this man.

We saw a sample of this in the 2008 election of Mr. Obama, whether he saw himself as the Messiah, or more likely the Imam Mahdi. That phobia began circulating worldwide. This man began to hold the world spellbound and build world-peace around him. As mentioned earlier,

Obama made a speech in Berlin at the altar of Zeus, better known as the Seat of Satan. Then he had a replica of the Seat of Satan built in the Denver Stadium where he made his acceptance speech. It wasn't long until he had discouraged that fervor, but the fact that it took hold in such a worldwide move, shows how ready the world is to worship him.

HORNS (POWERS) LIKE A LAMB (CHRIST) BUT SPEAKS LIKE THE DRAGON

The Antichrist has characteristics that makes flattered Jews and Christians, who have a form of Godliness but no power, believe that he is Christ (2 Timothy 3:5). Here is the basis which allows us to call him Antichrist for he will mimic Christ and claim to be God's incarnate crucified Son. However, if we are spiritually alert, we will recognize that his speeches and policies are still Satanic. Horns are indicative of power, and he seems to have the power of the crucified Lamb. He speaks like, and lectures with the same deceptive doctrines as the dragon.

Satan knows all too well that if he is to be successful in beguiling the world after him, he is going to have to look like the Lamb (Revelation 13:11). In Isaiah, we read *"and in that day,"* there would be seven women, i.e. Church groups who would say, *"we will eat our own food and wear our own apparel; only let us be called by your name"* (4:1). There are seven major Christian cults today which are doing their own thing, but call themselves by his name. The Antichrist knows that the only way he can seem authentic is to look like Christ the Lamb. Horns are a sign of power, so he claims Christ's miracle working power, and He claims to come in the name of Christ's peace. In every way, he mimics Christ.

Since the World Order was not able to totally eliminate religion, although they tried to do so for 40 years after the UN was born debunking it as the *opium of the people,* they decided to develop a world religion that looked like Christianity, but was saturated with New Age simulations. They realized that any successful attempt to pull religion into their camp as a useful tool would require using Christ in their deceitful end.

"If anyone has an ear, let him hear" (Revelation 13:9). All religions in the world's Ecumenical World Church Movement have just enough Christianity in them to inoculate people from catching the real thing. They look like the Lamb; they have horns, or power like a lamb; they have the likeness of Christ; but they speak like a dragon's religion. Only those who are spiritually aware can "discern between *"the thoughts and intents of the heart,"* and know the truth (Hebrews 4:12; Bob Smith, *Lectures of Lucifer*).

Isaiah prophesied in metaphoric images when he said that in the Day of the Lord, there are false religions awash today that spread their own doctrine. They appear in the apparel of Christians, but just use His name to add legitimacy to their claims. The World Ecumenical Church has the horns of Christianity and feels good like the real thing by using his name, but it is of illegitimate birth. It has the look of the Lamb, but if you listen to it for a while, it has nothing of the real Christ at all. This anti-"Christ" does not receive his power from God, but from the dragon who gives him his power and great authority (Revelation 13:2).

I can speak with some authority and insight, as I was selected in 1986 as one of three delegates to represent North America at the First World Council on Religious Liberty under the auspices of the United Nations, which convened in Ottawa, Canada. I soon realized that I had been called to one of the founding councils of the World Church. I saw in their council sessions very little of Christ and a whole lot of the dragon. In fact, I found them showing respect for every religious persuasion, but a total disdain for Evangelical

Christianity and Judaism.

The name we have given the second beast of Revelation 13 is the Antichrist, but I believe it is slightly misleading. The scriptures do not indicate that He is against Christ, but is a pseudo-Christ—a fake. He comes in place of Christ or in Christ's stead, since the World and the Church thinks Christ is so long overdue. Satan has always had a substitute waiting in the wings because he does not know when Christ will return and is willing to substitute his own version of Christ at the right time. Only the Holy Spirit within the true people of God would be able to make the distinction. His speaking or lectures will be the same old deceptions that satanic people have fallen for ever since Eve.

Even the Jews, along with carnal Christians, will fall for his flatteries which may indicate that he is of, or reportedly of Jewish extraction (Daniel 11:32).

We notice in this text in Daniel that there will be those who will not fall for his lies. Those of the Jewish culture as well as awakened Christians, "shall be *strong, and carry out great exploits. And those of the people who understand shall instruct many; yet for many days they shall fall by sword and flame, by captivity and plundering*" (11:32). They will be helped *"with a little help,"* but will suffer under this man and his world system (11:34). This is a clear reflection of the Tribulation Saints. These texts agree perfectly with Revelation 13:15, for *"... as many as would not worship the image of the beast [is] to be killed."*

There are people who will be startled into the realization that Christians were right after witnessing the Rapture of the Church, and they will turn to Christ during the Tribulation. These will refuse to follow the Antichrist and turn away from the mark, name, and number (15:2). They will turn many to righteousness and do exploits in the name of Christ (Daniel 11:32-33).

It is this second beast who will impose these identity symbols. He will force all people under his domain to worship the World Order and its authority, and demand that they submit to its demands. Just as the World Order beastly system of that day has received its power from the dragon, this man will receive his seat and great authority from Satan himself. Those who will not submit to worship him will be hampered in every part of their lives.

All people of the world, rich and poor, great and small, bond and free, who receive the identification mark, specifies that they have sold out to the devil's control. They must not only identify with the Antichrist's World Order, but with the man himself by taking his *name* in their foreheads and hands. And to show his further occult connection, there is a mysterious occult number attached to the whole scheme, which again shows that they who submit to these things fall under demon-control. Those who will not receive these identification symbols will be killed.

I will clarify that this does not mean you are taking the Mark of the Beast today because you are being forced to live in a society which is already falling in love with the World Order. Because '666' appears in several places, does not mean it is the Mark of the Beast. Only when it is connected to the number of his name will the world will need to be concerned. There is now no actual *number of his name* evident, or a mark that represents the beast. That will not come until the Antichrist is evident, which will be after the Church is gone. However, we can even now resist the spirit of Antichrist, and show our disapproval of the UN and its World Order.

COMING PERSECUTION IN AMERICA

Many people may not be aware, but secretly in the echelons of government, there have been programs set up to identify those who resist the World Order. Already, some are being challenged to show support to the global program or be marked as social rebels. It is said that they who resist Globalism are unsettling the hope of the world. Those preaching the evilness of a coming World Order are tagged by the elite as anti-social and counted worthy for disdain.

In his book *Earth in Balance*, Al Gore condemns all who resists the global effort and says that anyone who preaches prophecy is unforgivable. It is rumored that Bill and Hillary Clinton tried to initiate a program called *Operation Megiddo* to mark all that believed Revelation, and were teaching mockery and resistance to the government programs. We are said to be part of the radical right, like the white Aryans and pseudo-Nazi groups. We are anti-government radicals, so they say. The day may come in America when we will be imprisoned simply for preaching prophecy.

There is another sense in which government subsidies are preparing folks to depend on being *marked*. By identifying themselves as U.S. citizens, they are told that they will be taken care of. Eventually, to get these *entitlements*, one will have to belong to the *party of the beast,* and depend on the name of the beast, the World Order. They will have to be a legal member of the party with the numerical stamp of approval—the mark, name, and number.

This guy who looks and acts like the Lamb, but has the agenda of the dragon, will come in as a peacemaker according to Daniel, and will persuade by flattery. He will gain great advantage because of a chaotic world and the wrath of nations caused by the collapse of the world economy. He will act like a good guy and socialize everything, including the market place, food, and medical care. Then, the ungodly and the unaware will see this mark as a mark of hope. This is similar to how people saw all the social support programs under President Roosevelt in the 1930's. They would fall for anything to avert suffering in a time of chaos.

We do not know what the mark actually is. Speculation is rampant and every sensationalist has his version. I have listed over 125 different ideas about the nature of the Mark of the Beast offered in the past. We do not know exactly what it is, but we know its results and see its possibilities in dozens of technological and scientific inventions today. Add the occult diminution to its possibilities and you have a great mystery.

There are four forms of identity which ties the participant into the whole scheme. They must sell out to the world image, and they must sell out to the world eco-political system by taking its mark, and worship the dragon and his system. They must be totally submissive to the man himself by taking his name, and identify with the occult by taking an occult number. None of these have anything to do with our own numbers (credit card, etc.), or any mark of our own, but it has to do with his mark, his name, and his number. Let's quit running afraid and becoming superstitious of the technological systems which simplify our world. Yes, those systems will be used by the Antichrist, but they have nothing to do with beastly control, until he himself imposes it. According to Chuck Missler, there are 33 names of the beast in the Old Testament, and 13 different names in the New Testament. These names are listed by permission in the Appendix to this writing.

Since ancient times, the Luciferian (Illumines) has had a system of secret and mystic numbers. A search of those ancient symbols reveal that the 666 is the number of Lucifer himself, his ancient occult, and mystic meaning supposedly understood only by the highest initiates of the craft—Masonic above the 33rd degree, and Rosecrans or Pierre de Zion. Alice Bailey and Madam Blavatsky have done extensive work on this. Those who have no background or knowledge of the Bible have absolutely no clue as to these symbols, for only the Bible offers any insight into Satan and his system of deception in the world.

THIS POWER AND CONTROL ONLY PARTIAL, AND ONLY FOR 3 1/2 YEARS

Many people become totally fearful and hopeless as they read about these things. These are the people who fall into the world's mode of worry-mongering, and who listen to the sensational loving ministries of the gloom and doom type. They are also those who benefit monetarily from keeping people in fear but who do not read their Bible carefully, and have come up with the idea that Satan will have all control. They believe he will destroy everyone and everything, which would be a World Order with total and complete control, and nothing we can do to prevent it or get out from under its awesome control.

May I remind you that the Bible teaches of no such world, and the Book of Revelation does not leave that kind of woe-be-gone gloom and doom end. The Book of Revelation shows just the opposite. One thing we learn from following Christ in the Revelation is that He is never out of control and Satan never has the upper hand.

We must also remind you again that the born-again, Christ-honoring Christian, will not be here to suffer these things. The time-frame for this strict control will only be the last half of the Tribulation, and Christ will come in His revelation to the world, defeat this World System and its head, the Antichrist, and in 75 days, set up a Millennial reign on Earth (Daniel 12:12).

Evidence from Old and New Testament prophesies very strongly show that those who are left after the Rapture, will find hope for salvation during this time; howbeit, probably by Martyrdom. We will see this plainly in chapters 14 and 15.

I also want to encourage you that this reign of the beast and false prophet will not be in total control over every part of Earth, and of every individual. For years I have rejected the idea taught by many, that this time is out of God's hands, and that Christ has no control over it; that this World System will be universal and absolutely unavoidable. I am not a gloom and doom preacher. I am a teacher of Christ's gospel of good news to all that will receive it. There will be those who will receive salvation even in the time of Tribulation.

None of the writings and teachings of Christ, Paul, Daniel, Zechariah, or any of the prophets, and especially the Book of Revelation, will support such a theory of total control by the Antichrist. There will never be a time when Christ has no control; that idea is preposterous. He is the Lord of glory, the great *I AM*. All power and authority has been given to Him, even over principalities and powers over the darkness of this world.

Also, there are many texts that show that the World System and the Antichrist have only limited control. For instance, the 11th chapter of Daniel clearly teaches us that during the reign of this little horn, or wicked king, there will be those who do know their God and will teach, persuade, and lead others out of the World System. They will be highly successful in their evangelism and *"carry out exploits"* (Daniel 11:32). To exploit means to put to good use their advantage and to advance in spite of opposition. The NIV and AMP say they will *"firmly resist."*

This plainly paints the picture during the Tribulation as relating to the saved Jews and the Tribulation saints. We must know that Christ and all Heaven will be backing them up and cheering them on. Let me quote Daniel 11:31 and 32 from the NIV:

> *"His Antichrist forces will rise up to desecrate the temple fortress and will abolish the daily sacrifice. Then they will set up the abomination that causes desolation. With flattery he will corrupt those who have violated*

the covenant, but the "people who know their God will firmly resist. Those who are wise will instruct many, though for a short time they will fall by the sword, or be burned or captured or plundered. When they shall fall, they shall receive a little help and many who are not sincere will join them. Some of the wise will stumble, so that they may be refined, purified and made spotless, until the time of the end, for it will still come at the appointed time" (Daniel 11:31, 32).

Their strength and testimony can be seen in the two witnesses of Revelation chapter 11 and in the refugees' resistance to the world armies of the Antichrist in Revelation chapter 12. We see Christ in total control; and in chapter 14, He comes to Mount Zion. He brings plagues down upon the beast in chapter 15, and defeats the Antichrist's kingdom in chapters 16-19. Beloved, be well assured that there will never be a time when the Word of God and the Gospel of Jesus Christ is powerless. Even in the Tribulation, they will *"[overcome] him by the blood of the Lamb and by the word of their testimony"* (12:11).

As pertaining to the limit of the Antichrist's control, we read in Daniel 11 where Jordan escapes his power (Daniel 11:41). This fact shows that Christ is still in control, inasmuch as Jordan (Edom, Moab and Ammon) is the place of the protected Jewish remnant. We are also told that He exploits several countries like Egypt, yet "... news from the east and the north shall trouble Him" (11:44). Evidently Russia and China will resist, and they will both invade the Middle East (Revelation 16:12). However, when the Antichrist plants the tabernacle of his palace in the glorious Holy Mountain (the Temple Mount in Jerusalem), such a backlash will come from not only Israel, but also the world, for *"he shall come to his end, and no one shall help him"* (Daniel 11:45).

So my friends, do not let the fear-mongers of our world

or sensational preachers of the prophetic scheme, throw you into despair. Do not see these verses as forever and totally hopeless. Christ is still in control and will bring the beast, the Antichrist, and even Satan to their end in just 3 ½ years. It will happen at Armageddon, and none will be able to help him (11:45). His total and complete destruction, along with the beastly World Order System, will bring an end to the devil's control of the world, and Christ shall reign as King of kings and Lord of lords. We shall see this very fact as we open the next chapter.

As we begin the next chapter, our vision is taken away from these short-lived horror scenes, lest we have our attention diverted too long, from the One who is the star of the show—the real Redeemer, and not this imposter. While the world's attention is diverted to the powerful economic/political/religious system, it is not aware of the great things in the making and the things taking place in Heaven among Christ, the Lamb, and the Church. In chapter 14, we turn our attention back to Christ as we see Him coming in all of His glory, and putting an end to all.

CHAPTER 14

THE REAL REDEEMER COMES TO ZION

"BEHOLD HE IS COMING ... AND EVERY EYE WILL SEE HIM" (Revelation 1:7)

This chapter opens with scenes that take place on Earth. They are exciting themes, including the first direct reference to the Revelation of Jesus Christ on Earth. Once realizing the importance of the themes, it will strike us with awe. *"I looked and behold, a Lamb* (Jesus Christ) *standing on Mount Zion"* (14:1).

This chapter joins chapter seven where the 144,000 Jews were sealed, for these are the same 144,000. What possible significance can we find when in the midst of the woes of the earth, the beast, and the false prophet, when suddenly Christ and the Jews show up on Zion?

How exciting to be shown a great celebration where together with Heaven's orchestra and the Church in Heaven, Jews are singing a new song. Along with the songs that reflect the Old Testament Covenant of the law—the song of Moses, these Jews are singing the song of the Lamb (Revelation 14:2,3). It is likely that these same Jews will be among the Saints redeemed in Tribulation and singing just before the plagues come in chapter fifteen. They are followers of the Lamb, redeemed from the earth, and the first fruits of God and the Lamb (14:4). And, more exciting yet, they hear a solo voice from Heaven like the roar of many waters (or the Voice of Thunder). It is possible that Christ Himself in a solo voice, possibly as a narrator, accompanies the orchestra from Heaven with the combined voices of the Church and the Jews. These are scenes that we can only imagine. One thing is absolutely sure—Christ is shouting to get everyone's attention because some great things are about to happen. We cannot treat lightly or pass over quickly, the event of the Lamb coming to Zion. Old Testament Messianic texts are full of this event; a great day for Israel.

MEANWHILE

To remind us of our outline and the sequence of events, we will visit the *meanwhiles* again. Up to this point in our study of The Revelation of Jesus Christ, or at least since the seventh chapter, Jesus Christ has been somewhat hidden behind the preparations and process of judgment. However, evidence of His presence and control are everywhere, with much of it hidden backstage behind the scene in Heaven. The eighth chapter features Christ opening the first part of the Tribulation. Chapter nine shows Christ handing the key to the pit to the angel who opens the door of demons, allowing Hell to vomit on the earth. Meanwhile, in chapter ten, Christ takes the book and brings us to the final decree of judgment with the sentence levied against Satan and the Antichrist system of the World Order. It shows us Heaven's preparation to execute the *Book of Inheritance*.

Meanwhile, chapter eleven begins the last 3½ years by the measuring of the temple for construction, which is a right given to the Jews by a covenant. This measuring is for construction and building of the tribulation temple, not the millennial temple as in Ezekiel, chapters 40-48. We see the rebuilding of the temple finished at mid-Tribulation. It brings us insight into the compromise of the Temple Mount to be accessible to the three major monotheistic religions: Judaism, Christianity, and Islam. It also brings us to the time when the Antichrist will break the covenant with the Jews and set himself up as God. The witnesses begin to preach the gospel of the Kingdom and call down plagues on the Antichrist government, but are put to death by the World Order beast.

Meanwhile, chapter twelve shows the same time-span and the Tribulation from the standpoint of the Jews in the Tribulation. It shows the Antichrist's hate and campaign against the Jews during the last half of the Tribulation (Daniel 11:30-31). The Antichrist, under power of the dragon, cuts off their daily sacrifice and drives the West Bank settlers into the wilderness (Daniel 9:27; Matthew 24:15). It also shows us Satan's ancient hate for Christ, his anti-Semitic disdain for the State of Israel, and how Christ will swallow up the World Army which has been sent by the Antichrist to destroy the Jewish remnant who are in hiding. The martyrdom, or two witnesses near the close of the last 3 ½ years probably brings Christ and the 144,000 Jews to Zion.

Meanwhile, chapter thirteen shows us the Antichrist system of the One World Order during the last half of the Tribulation, and its Satanic base. It covers again the same time-span of the 3 ½ years, but makes us acquainted with the beast and the Antichrist, and their effort of world control. All of this is the last half of the Tribulation period, covered from various scenes in the drama of judgment, and happening simultaneously in a short time. Chapters 11-13 contain four different *meanwhiles*.

To recap for clarity, the first half of the Tribulation is in progress: meanwhile, the Jews are building their temple and setting up the daily sacrifice; meanwhile, the witnesses are preaching the kingdom and harassing the Antichrist with plagues; meanwhile, the beast's hate for the Jews and Israel forces some of Israel's remnants to flee into the wilderness of Edom, and the World armies in their pursuit of the remnant into Edom are destroyed; meanwhile, the World Order is strengthening its power and control through its leaders—the Roman Prince and the False Prophet, which I believe is the Antichrist. The Roman Prince represents the political side of the World Order, and the false prophet represents the eco/religious side, but still in full support of the political side. During this time, Islam will continue its belligerence toward Israel, and through the Islam Brotherhood set plans to possess the Temple Mount and set their 12th Imam there. All of this precedes the manifestation, or revealing of Jesus Christ which we see in chapter fourteen.

I believe, along with Henry Spaak, Secretary of NATO, that the world community will be anxious for a powerful charismatic leader in the midst of world crisis. By the time the first half of the Tribulation is in progress, and the four horsemen of devastation are riding rampant all over the world causing a pending total collapse of the World Order, that the world will readily accept this man of sin in a desperate effort to find someone powerful enough (as Henry Spaak said) to pull them out of the morass they are in. Only too late will they realize their error in selecting this second beast for leadership, when they come to realize that he is demon-controlled and Satanic in all of his policies.

By a careful reading of Daniel, chapters eleven and twelve, I believe the world community, at least Asia and the far east, will quickly turn on the Antichrist. Daniel shows us that troubles out of the east and north will cause him to react in great fury, and his inability to bring Jordan into his power will frustrate him. His failure to destroy the Jewish refugees in South Jordan will bring a final blow. Daniel tells us when he reaches a total wipeout diplomatically and politically, he will *"come to His end and no one will help Him"* (Daniel 11:45).

His end will come when Christ and the 144,000 come to Zion. The world powers have dropped Him and now His last desperate effort will be to gather what support he can get from the demon-possessed rebel kings and leaders of the world, and try to make a show of strength against the Lord who will meet him at Armageddon.

That will be at the time that only his *select* will stand against Christ at Armageddon, and "*the mystery of God*" will be finished (Revelation 10:7).

DAY OF THE LORD

In considering Christ's coming to Zion, we must mention the *Day of the Lord,* or *the day of the Revelation of Jesus Christ*. It is a cryptic term from the Old Testament messianic prophecies that is the general motif of the Book of Revelation. This motif, or central theme of the Old Testament, is also found in the New Testament and serves as the foundation of the Revelation. His coming to Zion is the Day of the Lord.

It is not possible to understand the Book of Revelation of Jesus Christ without a working knowledge the Old Testament and the *Day of the Lord* in Old Testament prophecy. The seven years of Tribulation are the day YOM, or cycle of the Lord. As we have said, there are over eight-hundred references to the Old Testament in Revelation and over two-hundred, eighty-five direct quotes in Revelation from the Old Testament. Jesus said:

> "You search the scriptures, for in them you think you have eternal life; and these are they which testify of Me" (John 5:39).

At the time this passage was written, there was no New Testament Scripture, only the Old Testament text. Therefore, it is easily assumed we were instructed to search the

Old Testament to find Him. We will study namely *The Day of the Lord*, the *Lord's Day*, or *that day* , the *Revelator*—Jesus Christ. John, the writer of Revelation would assume that those studying the Revelation would be as literate to the Messianic undertone of all Scripture as the Jew would be. For Gentiles not trained in the study of the Torah and the Prophets, it takes a more effort to understand the full application of the term *The Day of the Lord*. Time and space in this writing will not allow for an in-depth, comprehensive study so we will research it for a brief time only. See Appendix for a detailed discussion of *The Day of the Lord*.

THE SEVENTH TRUMPET BEGINS TO SOUND

As we enter chapter fourteen, we come out from behind the scenes which have taken place during the curtain drop. It will be important that we put each chapter in perspective to the seventh trumpet.

We now enter into the time when the seventh trumpet sounds and the seven vials of the wrath of God will begin to be poured out (10:7, 11:15, and 16:17). It is very important that we see the seventh trumpet from chapter ten, getting ready to sound. However, it does not sound until chapter eleven with the announcement of Christ taking charge of the nations of the world. It is not finished sounding until the sixteenth chapter, when the vials of the wrath of God begin to pour out, and when Christ comes to defeat the Satanic forces that control the world.

We can see the behind-the-curtain interlude by noticing that all of these scenes have taken place while the seventh trumpet is preparing to sound. The preparation began back in Revelation 10:7-10 with the opening of the little book:

> *"... but in the days of the sounding of the seventh angel, when he is about to sound, the mystery of God would*

be finished, as He declared to His servants the prophets" (10:7; namely Daniel in the 70 weeks prophecy).

When the seventh angel sounded, there was a great proclamation from the temple in Heaven saying, *"The kingdoms of this world have become the kingdoms of our Lord and of His Christ, and He shall reign forever and ever!"* and immediately following, the nations are full of wrath (11:15, 18).

This proclamation may possibly be made from the Temple Mount or on Mount Zion at the arrival of the Lord.

The final reference to the seventh trumpet is in verse 16:17. As the seventh trumpet period comes to an end with the final vial of wrath, "… there came a great, mighty voice out of the Temple of Heaven from the Throne saying, *"it is done!"* What is done? The mystery of God is finished. It seems then, that the seventh trumpet announces the final finish of the mystery of God, and at its final sound, declares that *"it is done!"* (16:17). So with this scenario, chapters 10 through 16 contain the final acts of God in the seventh trumpet to finish His work between the declaration, *"the mystery of God would be finished"* and the final end just after Armageddon, *"It is done"* (10:7, 16:17).

I believe that the *mystery of God* probably refers to the whole redemptive plan of God, which started at the fall of Satan before the world began. It has to do with the entire esoteric battle between God and Satan and his fallen angels, whose purpose was the thwart God's plan to put His Son as the Redeemer of mankind on a throne in Zion, hinder God from bringing that Son into the world through a chosen people Israel, and redeeming the whole human race by Him. God's plan was then to Return Israel to Jerusalem and Zion, Rapture a Gentile Church, and redeem the sheep nations out of the hand of Satan. It is a mystery because most of this battle between God and Satan is esoteric, that is unseen and unheard, where even Christ's part in the battle is not apparent to the earthly people. Revelation is the expose of the final end of that battle at the Revelation of Jesus Christ and His part in finishing that battle.

The time for the last battle with Satan is over. The war that started in Heaven when Satan and 1/3 of the angels fell was now coming to a close. It had been fought all through the ages and brought death and devastation throughout the whole of history. Satan had been kicked out of Heaven and going about the earth, full of wrath (12:9). He came to an end of his worldly power when he found that he was not God and was run off of the Temple Mount. Now, his final time at trying to dethrone God and destroy God's son, Jesus Christ, has failed. His angels now know that he is a fraud, and along with them, are headed to the bottomless pit. It is done!

The sequence we want to notice here is that beginning with the decree of the little book in chapter ten, the final end begins to come. From the decree of that book, the mystery of God is finished. Satan, knowing he has but a short time, namely 3½ years, will turn his fury on the Jews and the Christians of the Tribulation time. That fury or great wrath of Satan will eventually bring him against the great wrath of God at Megiddo or Armageddon. It is when the 7th trumpet sound announcement has been made in Heaven that He is finished and *the kingdoms of the world are the Kingdoms of Christ and He will reign over them forever* (Chapter 11:15). I believe that the reign on Earth begins right here in Revelation 14, with His return to Zion with 144,000 Jews.

THESE ARE JEWS AND NOT PART OF THE CHURCH

Along with Christ, there are 144,000 Jews that have been sealed from judgment, and I believe they are among those protected in the wilderness. I am persuaded that they will be a part of the throng that will escape into the wilderness when the Antichrist sets himself up as God in the temple, and the great persecution against the Jews and Israel begins (Matthew 24:15). They will gain the *"testimony of Jesus Christ"* while there (Revelation 12:17).

There are some who have tried to imagine that this 144,000 are actually Tribulation saints and Gentiles of the Church. It is believed that they will not mind getting left behind to go through the Tribulation because they will be *sealed* from the dangers and woes of it. My friends, I exhort you to study more carefully before you leave yourself open to such hope. These texts make very plain that these are Jews—12,000 of each tribe of Israel, sons of Jacob.

They are not of some supposed lost tribes which are either British Anglo-Saxon or Americans. Plainly, they are Jews of the blood and seed of Abraham. Those who have fallen for the British/Israel deception, or the Replacement Theology delusion, do not believe that the Jews have any part in Revelation or in the final restoration of all things. They readily debunk the idea that these are Jews, because to them, the Jews have been cut off and replaced by the Church.

The Seventh Day Adventists see them as a part of their number representing the most faithful. These would then be Gentile Christians. The Jehovah Witnesses include only the *overcomers*, these 144,000 among their believers.

Beloved, all of these make one obvious error in their spiritual blindness. Revelation declares beyond question that these are Jews. There is not a Gentile among them.

THE LORD AND 144,000 ON MOUNT ZION

In chapter fourteen we pick up the activities of Christ and what He is doing during this time of the beast. The crowning thought here is this: while the world is caught up and mesmerized with the Antichrist, his beastly system of world control and His miracles and personification of Christ in the midst of their plans, they will soon be introduced to the real Christ in His glorious Revelation. It seems the first place the world will see Him will be on Mount Zion, the very place where God the Father has promised Him a throne. I believe this is the opening scene of Christ's actual public Revelation. What a commotion this will create in the whole world, especially among the Jews of the Diaspora.

ANTI-CHRIST FACES THE REAL CHRIST

It is my persuasion, as we try to correlate all that is told to us of these same days about the Antichrist and his reign as shown in Daniel 8:11-25. By the time of Christ's appearing on Mount Zion, the Antichrist will have moved his headquarters from the center of the World Order, possibly in Iraq or Babylon, and relocated it on the Temple Mount in Jerusalem where he:

> *"who opposes and exalts himself above all that is called God or that is worshiped, so that he sits as God in the temple of God, showing himself that he is God"* (2 Thessalonians 2:4).

This will lead to a time of cleansing the sanctuary of this wicked ruler:

> *"He shall even rise up against the Prince of princes; but he shall be broken without human hand,"* or without help, and *"he shall come to his end and no one will help him"* (Daniel 8:25, 11:45).

We now take a slight diversion at this point to see the sequence of events that have taken place. After the time the Antichrist seems to have brought peace in the Middle East between Islam, the Jews, and the World Order, he makes a covenant with the Jewish Nation concerning Jerusalem and the Temple Mount, then breaks it in the middle of the seven years of Daniel's *"70 weeks of years"* prophecy.

The prophecies found in Daniel chapters eight, eleven, and twelve fill in many of the gaps not revealed to us in Revelation. I believe they are left out by the Lord to force us to study the Old Testament comparable texts. We are told in Daniel eight of a very weird and scary occultist megalomaniac, known as the *willful king* who, coming from among the ten kings of Rome, will gain power by his seeming superpowers and extra-sensory perception. He will be a person given his own free will with no restraint, probably because the world will be in such a mess that they will not dare oppose this man, hoping that his supernatural power will, as Dr. Henry Spock said, "pull us out of the morass we have gotten into; be he God or devil, we will receive him" (Dr. Spock, former Secretary General of NATO; speaking before the yearly conference).

He will *"exalt and magnify himself"* (Daniel 11:36) until, by the time he sets up his palace in the Holy Mount in Jerusalem, will be accepted by a world flattered by his narcissist tendencies, commonly received in today's culture. He will not care for family, his heritage, or any God, and will fulfill the New Age expectation of the coming one as a god-man.

However, not all of the world will follow Him. He will have troubles from the east and north, tidings out of the north and east will trouble him, and he will not be able to bring Jordan into his domain. It is said in Daniel 8:25 that he will come face to face with the *Prince of princes* which is of course, Jesus Christ. As we have said, he will probably be driven off of the Temple Mount by the approach of Jesus Christ and the 144,000 Jews. He will flee back to some safe place and begin a terrible onslaught against the Jews (Revelation 12). He will later face Christ at Armageddon, which we read about in Revelation 19:19.

FEET ON MOUNT OF OLIVES

We have been taught that His first appearance will be when His feet stand on Mount Olivet, and that might very well be. He may cross Mount Olives on His way to Mount Zion. There is some controversy here as to whether Mount Zion means the Temple Mount or what is known as the *Hill of Zion* to the west and near David's Gate, or *Lions Gate* a short distance west of the Temple Mount. It probably means the whole area from Opel up to the Temple Mount and across the valley to David's gate and Zion, where the Jews dwell today. It is sure however, this appearance on Mount Zion with 144,000 Jews will be only a short time before His appearance at the final battle of Armageddon and the defeat of Satan.

In Revelation fourteen, Christ does not return with the Church because it is still in Heaven, but instead, returns with the 144,000 Jews. These are not Gentiles, as we have said, but Jews from each of the twelve tribes with the exception of the tribe of Dan. We should not confuse this appearance with His Return with the Saints.

CHRIST THE LAMB, THE SON OF MAN (VERSE 1)

Here, He calls Himself the *Lamb*. Christ prefers to be symbolized in Revelation as the Lamb of God, rather than exposing Himself by name. This is one of the cryptic enigmas of prophecy, and is responsible for missing this reference to Christ, including the carnal and unbelieving, as well as the half-blinded Jews.

It is easy to overlook Christ in the Revelation. First of all, too many are not looking for Him, and second, He seldom names Himself by His proper name. Some people do not understand the meaning of the Lamb and how it relates to Christ in the end-time. Christ almost always refers to Himself in His earthly sojourn as the *Son of Man* (89 times). He never exalts Himself! The *Son of God* is used less frequent, and only occasionally would He allow anyone to call Him the *Son of God*. Many times He requested that no one call Him the Son of God, even when it was at the threat of His life. Pilate was urged to put Him to death because they accused Him of *"[making] Himself the Son of God"* (John 19:7). He never answered them. In other words, even in facing death, He did not claim to be the Son of God. Was it that He was not the Son of God? Oh no! He, in His meekness and humility, just preferred to identify Himself with men, calling Himself the Son of Man. This name for the Messiah was used throughout the Old Testament Messianic texts and Christ needed to identify Himself with that term. He only called Himself King of kings after He defeated Satan at Armageddon.

Jesus simply said that His works would declare who He is. Therefore, He addresses Himself as the Lamb. This same humility shines through in all of His appearances in Revelation. He seldom ever identifies Himself other than in humility and meekness. In His strong acts of judgment, He is always obscure. He will be forced by the context to allow Himself to be called the majestic name of *"the Lord of lords and King of kings,"* a name used only one other time in the New Testament and only twice in the Book of Revelation (Revelation 17:14, 19:16). Yet, for ascetic reflection, He is called the *Lamb* 27 times in the Book of the Revelation of Jesus Christ. He continually points us back to His humblest hour of *shame* on the Cross and the price He paid for the right to redeem us.

However, Paul says that at the right time, in the *Day of the Lord, He* will in all of His glory, show who He is:

> *"... which He will manifest in His own time, He who is the blessed and only Potentate, the King of kings and Lord of lords, who alone has immortality, dwelling in unapproachable light, whom no man has seen, or*

can see, to whom be honor and everlasting power" (1 Timothy 6:15-16).

The Church, Jews, and Christians that are converted during the Tribulation, know who He is, but He will choose the time when He reveals to the World who He really is.

The Antichrist and the world of rebellious nations will soon understand that He dwells in a light that no man can approach when He destroys them *"with the breath of His mouth and ... the brightness of His coming"* (2 Thessalonians 2:8).

THE LORD COMES TO MOUNT ZION WITH 144,000 JEWS

What a marvelous thing we are reading. All of the 144,000 have been preserved without exception. Not one has defected or been lost. Jesus has not lost even one of those whom the Father has given Him except Judas, the son of perdition (John 17:12). We the Church are preserved in the same manner, but we are not represented here. These select Jews are preserved and protected by God during the Tribulation and will become evangelists of the Gospel of the kingdom during the Millennium, and warriors in the last battles (Revelation 7).

Even though He is called *Lamb* by name on Mount Zion, it is without question, the Lord Jesus Christ. Christ will come to Mount Zion and the Temple Mount at the very time when this imposter, the Antichrist has set up His tabernacle and palace there, usurping the Holy Place for a throne and claiming that He is God. While Hell has been working to set up its plan for Mount Zion, Heaven has been busy formulating and preparing to finish God's plan and implement it on Zion. All of the prophetic texts reveal to us the very truth that is enacted here. The whole drama of the ages finally centers in and consummated on Mount Zion. There are scores of texts in the Old Testament Messianic prophecies which tell of the Messiah the Lord, coming to Zion in the last days.

Right in the midst of what Hell, the dragon, and Satan believes, is the great day when they hear rumors of an approaching army of Jews from Edom (Isaiah 63:1). Suddenly, the Lord appears in all of His glory and power on Mount Zion, shattering the mesmerism of the world's fascination with the beast, and according to Isaiah, *"no one will help him"* (Daniel 11:45).

We read in Psalms 133:3:

The Lord *"[descended] upon the mountains of Zion"* (Psalms 133:3).

In Zechariah 8:3, we read"

"I will return to Zion, and dwell in the midst of Jerusalem. Jerusalem shall be called the City of Truth, the Mountain of the Lord of hosts, the Holy Mountain."

The Lord will not have to get a permit from the Jerusalem authorities of the beastly government seated there; or the WAQF, the present Jordanian Authority over the Temple Mount. He will not have to seek Israel's permission or get approval from the UN, USA, Europe, or NATO. He said,

"I am zealous for Zion with great zeal; with great fervor I am zealous for her" (ibid 8:1).

The Lord is furious because of the battle over Zion today!

Jude said that Enoch prophesied these same things in his day. Although this is probably later when He returns to Armageddon with the Saints, it does show His anger and jealousy over the ungodly host of the Antichrist:

"Behold, the Lord comes with tens of thousands of His saints, to execute judgment on all, to convict all who are ungodly among them of all their ungodly deeds which they have committed in an ungodly way, and of all the

harsh things which ungodly sinners have spoken against Him" (Jude 14, 15).

Acts 15:16 puts Christ's coming to Zion and His purpose for coming, in full perspective. Quoting the prophet Isaiah, it declares that:

"After this I will return and will rebuild the tabernacle of David which has fallen down (i.e. his homeland, his kingdom and his place of worship etc.). *I will rebuild its ruins, and I will set it up, so that the rest of mankind may seek the Lord, even all the Gentiles who are called by my name"* (i.e. the Church, who will come to worship on the Temple Mount.

The Old Testament covenant closes with this event, for in Malachi we read:

"The Lord, whom you seek, will suddenly come to His temple" (3:1).

He will appear on the Temple Mount at the sight of the temple built there. His return to Zion is an oft-mentioned promise in the prophecies. Isaiah sees this event that was spoken of in Revelation 14:

"The Redeemer will come to Zion" (Isaiah 59:20).

Isaiah chapter 60 must be read in context to the Lord's visit to Zion. It is the time prophesied at Israel's return. "And they shall call you the City of the Lord, Zion of the Holy One of Israel" (Isaiah 60:14). Here all of Jerusalem is called Zion. *He "declares in Zion the vengeance of the Lord our God, the vengeance of His temple"* (Jeremiah 50:28). This possibly refers to His immediate coming to Armageddon:

"So the multitude of all the nations shall be, who fight against Mount Zion" [for] the Lord shall *"fight for*

Mount Zion and for its hill" (Isaiah 29:8, 31:4).

Isaiah 37:31, 32 says that it will be the *remnant* that escaped out of Mount Zion and fled, and would be involved in the deliverance of Zion. We will identify this *remnant* later in these comments.

Even James and Peter in the book of Acts say that God *"first visited the Gentiles to take out of them a people for His name"* (Acts 15:14). Then, He will return to build again the dwelling place of David. I believe this is speaking of the place of David's throne (Psalms 69:35, 102:16). In doing so, He will fulfill what Paul said in Romans 11:26 after the Gentile Church has been gathered in:

> *"And so all Israel will be saved, as it is written: the deliverer will come out of Zion a Deliverer, and will turn away ungodliness from Jacob."*

It is told in Jeremiah that from Zion, the vengeance of the Lord will be declared (50:28). Christ's coming to Zion is mentioned in Amos 1:2 and Joel 3:16, as well as seven times in the first two chapters of Joel. We read in Joel:

> *"The Lord will also roar from Zion ... the heavens and earth will shake; but the Lord will be a shelter for His people ... so you shall know that I am the Lord your God, dwelling in Zion My holy mountain"* (3:16-17).

This could well be the same *roar* spoken of in Revelation 10:3 where the Lion of the Tribe of Judah roared when Christ put one foot on the earth (probably on Mount Zion) and the other on the sea, while holding out the book of decree of ownership (5:5).

From these companion texts in the Old Testament intercalated into Christ's visitation to Zion, we see that He comes in vengeance to fight the nations at Zion. He will roar at the nations who gather there to fight (Zechariah 12,

14). We are shown from Isaiah's writing that it would be the Remnant who had to flee to the wilderness, that would assist in the fight, and salvation and deliverance would come out of Zion. He will begin the construction of the throne of David that was broken down.

Paramount to all of these promises, the deliverance of Israel and the nations of the world will begin right here at His campaign with the 144,000 Jews on Zion. He has come to set up His kingdom in the stead of David. I believe that somehow, the 144,000 Jews will be the founding fathers of the establishment of the kingdom of David in the Millennium (see Micah 4:1-4 quote from Isaiah 2:1-4). It is my persuasion that this whole text is enacted from Zion and the Temple Mount, beginning with Christ's visit to Zion with 144,000 Jews depicted here in Revelation 14. From the New Living Translation, I quote:

> *"This is a vision that Isaiah son of Amoz saw concerning Judah and Jerusalem: In the last days, the mountain of the Lord's house will be the highest of all—the most important place on earth. It will be raised above the other hills, and people from all over the world will stream there to worship. People from many nations will come and say, "Come, let us go up to the mountain of the Lord, to the house of Jacob's God. There he will teach us his ways, and we will walk in his paths. "For the Lord's teaching will go out from Zion; his word will go out from Jerusalem. The Lord will mediate between nations and will settle international disputes. They will hammer their swords into plowshares and their spears into pruning hooks. Nation will no longer fight against nation, nor train for war anymore"* (Isaiah 2:1-4).

This is indication of universal peace with not military academies or camps in existence. They will all be closed down

(The Living Bible). I have visited the present-day Temple Mount more than 20 times and let me assure you, the above situation does not exist there at this time. These 144,000 Jews, including their Jewish Christ, would not be allowed on the Mount today. Gentile Christians are allowed to walk over the Mount, but not allowed to lecture, pray, or comment while on the Mount. We must in silent awe, walk across it. I assure you, circumstances are about to change. Revelation 14 describes the first thing that is going to happen when the Lord comes to Zion—there will be a great prayer and praise service with combined Jews and Christians.

Nowhere else does this scenario of last day prophecies fit the revelation! The full impact of this prophecy will be realized after Armageddon, but here, only a brief time before Armageddon, the conquest of Mount Zion and the Temple Mount, begin the Lord's campaign of conquest.

All of these texts and many others describe many circumstances related to Christ's coming to Zion in Revelation 14.

A NEW SONG: THE JEWS ARE JOINED BY THE CHURCH IN PRAISE

Christ, with the 144,000 Jews, is joined by the Church which is still at the throne in Heaven. Together, in Heaven and from Earth at the very sight of Zion and the Temple Mount, they all lift up a great chorus, sounding like the voice of thunder and a great *Niagara Falls*. They are joined by the orchestra of Heaven. A New song is given the 144,000 which no one else, not even the Church could sing. Like the song of Moses, it represents an expression of these particular Jews and their place in Christ, just as our songs reflect our position in Christ. What a crescendo the songs will be, when both the Church and the Redeemed Jews, sing together. I have heard it in the King of Kings Church in Jerusalem, where the

Gentiles and the Jews come together for worship.

One of the great experiences of my life came, when during one of my 35 trips to Israel, I visited the Western Wall at the beginning of Shabbat. Gathered there are pilgrims from virtually every nation. They were singing from the ramparts around the walls, or the plaza. Every tongue is represented as they sing. Sometimes the whole body of the Redeemed Church will recognize a song or chorus, and all join in singing, each in their native tongue. That alone will set your soul on fire and *bring down the glory* as we used to say. The deep emotions of the scene brought tears of joy.

Just as the sun drops behind the profile of Jerusalem and the Western Hills, and to add to this crescendo of song from the Church universal, out of the Yeshiva's (school of the Priests) will come the Jews, arm in arm, dancing as they descend onto the plaza. The Jews, in their expression of praise, try to out-sing the Christians, and the Christians try to out-sing the Jews. Then the Jews voices blend with the Church, and what an anthem of praise is created. This is the scene described here in Revelation 14, only magnified about 1000 times over.

THIS IS NOT THE TRIUMPHAL ENTRY

I do not believe this represents Christ's *triumphal entry* which will come after Armageddon, when with His Bride, returns to Jerusalem to set up the millennial *honeymoon.* That Triumphal Entry when Christ, with the redeemed goes through the gate, will be some time later at the end of Armageddon and after the Marriage of the Lamb. We see in Revelation 14 that the Church is still in Heaven and does not accompany Him in this campaign. There is no Gentile in this entourage. This is not a coronation of the king, but rather a war campaign (a military advance) coming into a battle theater, and involves the remnant of the Jews and not the Church. However, the Church would certainly rejoice with them.

REDEEMED FROM THE EARTH

We are plainly told that these 144,000 Jews have been redeemed from the earth, just like the Church is redeemed. They do not come out of Heaven as if they were the Church; they are still on Earth, sealed in chapter seven, converted to Christ, and have a very distinctive place in Him (Revelation 14:4). They are pure and undefiled before God spiritually (just as all of the redeemed are cleansed from sin), having been washed in the blood of the Lamb. They have the same position in Christ as the Jews in chapter 12, where it is said *"they overcame him by the blood of the lamb"* (12:11). They will *"be like Him for they shall see Him as He is"* (1 John 3:2). What a day that will be! I am a little tired of fighting this old sinful nature. We are like Pogo once said: "We have seen the enemy, and he is us." Thank God at this time, both the Church and these Jews are beyond sin.

These Jews are pure because of their relationship with Christ, the Lamb of God who takes away the sin of the world. Many ask when these Jews were converted to Christ. There had to be a time of evangelizing and revelation among them at some point. We will look into that later.

WHO WILL ASCEND UNTO THE HOLY HILL?
(Psalm 24)

There is a Psalm written by David which, although it has general purpose, the Holy Spirit may have inspired Him to write lines that point to this very event. He asks the question:

> *"Who may ascend into the hill of the Lord* (Zion)? *Or who may stand in His holy place* (at Holy of Holies before the Ark" (Psalm 24:3).

The Hill of the Lord is this very Zion, and the Holy Place is this very Mount. The Psalm gives the conditions needed to come to this Holy Place. David answers in a very prophetic way. We must note that they are ascending—coming up from somewhere. It specifically refers to the *ascent* by which the Jews approached the holy hill from Ophel, but it includes anyone who approaches the hill while Christ abides there. Any time that we come into the presence of the Lord, and especially in the days of His exaltation as King of kings and Lord of lords, these rules would apply:

"He who has clean hands and a pure heart, who has not lifted up his soul to an idol, nor sworn deceitfully. He shall receive the blessing from the Lord, and righteousness from the God of his salvation" (24:4-5).

These words are very close to what we are told about the 144,000. These were Jews who were made righteous in Christ; pure in heart; undefiled with a mouth of guile, and without fault before the throne of God. They followed the Lamb wherever He goes. They are pure like the first fruit offering that was offered before the Lord (Revelation 14:4-5). I believe these 144,000 are being prepared by God today among the world's Jewry.

Don't ever let the devil or anyone else say that it is impossible to be *"not [have] spot or wrinkle"* (spiritually) in these closing days of time (Ephesians 5:27). Both the Church in Heaven and the 144,000 Jews were just that, here in the midst of the Tribulation.

SPIRITUAL VIRGINITY, NOT SEXUAL VIRGINITY (14:4)

They are *virgins*, free from idolatry and spiritual fornication. They are not inflamed with worldliness and its guile. Dake comments that if taken literally, they would all have to be women. But the sentence before says they have never defiled themselves with women. They therefore would all have to be men. This demonstrates that it is not speaking of a literal sexual virginity.

It speaks of spiritual virginity, not sexual virgins. However, they are sexually pure as well since they *"were not defiled with women"* (Revelation 14:4). This passage is not suggesting that our marriage relationship is impure, for that is not the teaching of Scripture whatsoever. In fact, Paul rebuked those who abstain from marriage for spiritual purposes, except for fasting (1 Timothy 4:3; 1 Corinthians 7:5). Further, he taught us plainly *that "marriage is honorable among all, and the [marriage] bed undefiled"* (Hebrews 13:4). First Corinthians teaches *"If you do marry, you have not sinned"* (7:28). Certainly marriage cannot be put in the bracket of sin, and marriage does not defile a man with a woman or a woman with a man. Don't ever let the filthy-minded world try to put you in the same mold as the sexually impure because of your marriage relationship. The marriage relationship is as pure as our relationship with Christ (Ephesians 5:25, 32-33). However, be assured that *"fornicators and adulterers God will judge"* (Hebrews 13:4).

I remember counseling with a certain couple during my pastoral days. As I listened to their excuses for the trouble in their marriage, I got a shock in my spirit. It came when the husband suddenly burst out in total frustration and near tears saying, "I was once one of the 144,000 until I got married and lost my salvation." I immediately looked over at the wife and my heart sank with her broken heart, as she bowed her head in shame and tearfully apologized by saying, "I'm sorry I caused him to lose his salvation by marrying him." What a travesty! Pardon me as I give expression to this in my *farmer* lingo, "hog wash!" How easy it is to read into Bible texts what it does not say, when led by our own ignorance and superstition.

What is meant here is more perfectly reflected in what Paul taught us in Second Corinthians:

"I have betrothed you to one husband, that I may present you as a chaste virgin to Christ" (11:2).

These Jews had become chaste virgins in their relationship to Christ even though they were not part of the Bride of Christ. They are saved individuals who have not polluted themselves with the idolatrous and immoral world; neither have they polluted themselves with the Great Whore of chapter seventeen.

I want to comment however, that even though this is not speaking of sexual defilement, it does hint of a special blessing reserved for those men who keep themselves in sexual purity by remaining absolutely undefiled with women before marriage, and remain absolutely true to their marriage.

THE BEGINNING OF THE GREAT GRAND FINALE' OF THE BOOK

I think many writers and commentators on Revelation have treated this portion of the book far too lightly regarding their fascination with the beast, false prophet, 666, and others in chapter 13, and the vials of the wrath of God in chapter 15. They are in danger of missing one of the great, grand finales of the whole Book, as well as the climatic conclusion to all of the Messianic prophecies which culminate with Christ's return to Zion.

There are at least nineteen Old Testament Messianic texts which speak of this very event—when Christ the Messiah comes to Mount Zion. It is mostly called the *Great Day of God Almighty* or the *Day of the Lord.* Let us briefly emphasize more of these texts.

For instance, Psalm 2:6 tells us that God sets His King (Son) on His throne in Zion. Isaiah speaks of the event in Revelation 14, where the Lord will visit Zion and fight against those nations that fight at Mount Zion (29:6-8, 34:8; Zechariah 14). Isaiah 52:7-10 speaks of when the Redeemer comes to Zion. Joel talks of the trumpet being blown when the Lord comes to Zion in the middle of Tribulation language that matches the context of Revelation 14, proclaiming the Lord will roar out of Zion and declare *"I am the Lord your God, dwelling in Zion"* (2:1, 3:16-17). Zechariah 8:3 confirms Revelation 14 where it says, *"I (Christ the Lord) will return to Zion."* These comparative texts bring us back to our theme of *The Revelation of Jesus Christ*, and I believe it is possible that this is the first actual event of His earthly Revelation to the world.

When speaking of Christ's Second Coming, we do not speak of the Rapture, but of His second appearing to the world; that is, His *Revelation*, or *Revealing*. His second coming to this world covers all of the events in seven years. It seems He will be revealed to the world when He first appears on the Mount of Olives, and then immediately preceding to Mount Zion where He unseats the Antichrist. He will then walk the borders of the Holy Land to make proclamation against the ten enemies (Ezekiel 25-32); clears the resistance in Jehoshaphat and around Jerusalem (Joel 3); and deals with the Russian/Sino/Islamic invasion, and finally meets Satan, the Antichrist, and his world armies at Armageddon. All of this will take place in the last 3 ½ years of the Tribulation, in *The day of the Lord*, and within the seven-year period.

I am of the persuasion that this appearance on Zion will be near the end of the last 3½ years and probably within a year or less of Armageddon. It may entail the 75 days that Daniel mentions at the end of the Antichrist's reign (Daniel 12:11-12; 1260 days or 3½ years from 1,335 days equals 75 days).

Four wars will be fought in Israel, and each will be an extension of the other. They will take place after the Jews have fled near the end of their time of protection. When the armies of the Antichrist have come in as a flood to destroy them, Christ will appear in Bozrah to fight their battle (Revelation 12:15-16; Isaiah 63). We will enlarge on and detail this in the second half of the comments on this chapter.

THREE HEAVENLY MESSENGERS WITH A THREE-FOLD MESSAGE

Further evidence shows us that there will be evangelism still going on during the Tribulation. Those who teach that the Holy Spirit leaves earth at the Rapture of the Church, and believes that there is no more salvation after that have not read the Book of Revelation carefully enough with the mind of the Holy Spirit. Besides that, they probably do not understand the nature of the Holy Spirit who is omnipresent. They also forget that Jesus Christ is the *"same yesterday, today, and forever"* (Hebrews 13:8). That means He is still Savior and Lord in Revelation and in Tribulation as well and will never be found anywhere, at any time without the Spirit.

We have already seen the two witnesses working in chapter eleven. If they are not witnessing and preaching Christ's coming kingdom, then why are they called *witnesses*? They will share their testimony of Christ until the Holy Spirit raptures them into Heaven. Then, there is no question that the 144,000 are commissioned as witnesses and surely carrying the gospel message with them since they are said to *"have the Testimony of Jesus Christ"* (Revelation 12:17).

Now, we come to understand that there are three more angels preaching three very strong gospel admonitions. These evangelistic sermons are preached in conjunction with Christ's appearance on Mount Zion.

It is declared that angels, God's messengers are doing the preaching. I will not comment at length, on what is meant by *angels*. Sometimes, they are angels of the Lord's presence, and the presence of the Lord Himself. Sometimes they are heavenly beings with a mission and a message. If this is so, then this is the first time that actual heavenly-being angels are ever commissioned to preach. Preaching is commissioned to us, the Church. Sometimes they are men with a message who are called angels like the seven stars spoken of in chapter one.

It is very possible that the preaching here is not by actual angels as we understand, but by human messengers like the angels or pastors of the seven Churches. It is also possible that these messages were the preaching of the two witnesses of chapter eleven. If so, we can certainly see why the beast and the Antichrist were upset with them and felt they had to get their message stopped. All of these messages are a direct confrontation to the beast and the Antichrist.

The message of the first angel was the message of the everlasting gospel of good news. In the midst of the Tribulation to come, they were supposed to *"Fear God and give glory to Him, for the hour of His judgment is come"* (Revelation 14:7). The second message was a warning that the World Order and its economic system would soon fall. They cry out, *"Babylon the great is fallen, is fallen ... for all the nations have drunk of the wine of the wrath of her fornication"* (18:2-3).

The third message really rancor the Antichrist and his cohorts in the One World Order. A loud voice proclaims from the Temple Mount:

> *"If anyone worships the beast and his image, and receives his mark on his forehead, or on his hand, he himself shall also drink of the wine of the wrath of God ... and he shall be tormented with fire and brimstone in the presence of the holy angels and in the presence of the Lamb"* (14:9-10).

The important thing is not who does the preaching, but what the meaning of the message is as it relates to the events that are taking place at the time. These messengers are sent with very strategic and current messages for those people who are under the beastly system of a One World Order at a time when the Antichrist is working his signs and wonders, and calling the world to submit to the first beast and his World Order. These people are threatened with force to take the mark, the name, and the number of the beast.

The signs of the soon-coming of Christ in His Revelation, and His appearing are everywhere, but the nation's leaders are set in rebellion against His anticipated coming to sit on the throne. They are determined to get the whole world to worship the beast and the dragon who give him power (13:4). These are redemption messages preached to the Tribulation people. Verse six starts this subject, but is still vitally connected with Christ and His appearance on Mount Zion.

THREE POWERFUL MESSAGES OF ADMONITION
MESSAGE NUMBER 1

With Christ's personal appearance on Mount Zion, I am convinced there will be great multitudes of both Gentiles and Jews who will turn to Christ from all over the world of nations where the gospel of Christ has been preached. They are exhorted by an angel with the everlasting gospel and cry out:

> *"Fear God, and give glory to Him, for the hour of His judgment has come"* (14:7).

I am convinced that the coming of Christ to Zion will cause one of the greatest revivals among both the Jews and the Gentiles that the world has ever seen. I know plainly by the texts relating to Christ's visit to Zion, that it will perpetrate the greatest worldwide *Alyia* (return) of all time.

All of these people as well as others, who are converted to Christ and alive at this time, are in dire need of enlightenment, admonition, and instruction, because there will be a lot of mass confusion, along with deep deception. Jesus said in Matthew 24:24 that if possible, even the very elect would be deceived. Thessalonians tells us that during the last days of the Tribulation and while the Antichrist is working his signs and wonders, and his One World Order is in control, there will be such a strong delusion that masses will tend to believe a lie (2 Thessalonians 2:11). Such deep persuasion by the international community will lead to Hell and damnation.

Added to these things, we know that the next 3½ years are going to be a defining time for the entire world.

It is possible that even the 144,000 Jews will need clarification about the events at hand. So, along with Christ's appearance with the 144,000 on Mount Zion, come forth some powerful admonitions from Heaven. There are three separate and compelling messages, each deal with life-altering decisions that every individual must make concerning the events to come in the last half of the great Tribulation. Even now as we face the very near coming of the Lord and the time of the Tribulation upon the earth; when the One World Order is being forced upon us and the International Community is forming the policies and conditions that we read about in the Revelation, we need these admonitions also. It would be well to let Christ speak to us today and prepare our hearts to *"escape all these things that will come to pass, and to stand before the Son of Man"* (Luke 21:36).

Revelation 14:6 speaks of the *"everlasting gospel"* that will be preached. First, we note that it is the *Gospel*, the same word we use continually to caption the *Good News*. It is hardly imaginable that any gospel could be preached without its subject material relating to the good news of Christ Jesus. Paul said that there is no other gospel, only one (Galatians 1:6-9). Paul said plainly that if he himself, or even an angel from heaven—anyone should preach another gospel, let him be accursed. It has to be the same Gospel of the grace of God with forgiveness, without which it could not give promise of Eternal Life, or Christ would not have used the word *Gospel*. Second, it is the *everlasting Gospel*, initiated by Christ and no different from the gospel that we preach every day. Our gospel includes eternal life in its promises.

A call goes out, no doubt with the support of the 144,000, to the Gentile world that is being duped by the Antichrist, and to the Jewish citizens of Israel, Jerusalem, and the Temple Mount. It is a call that points them to the great Creator God, which both Jews and Christians can accept.

"Fear God and give glory [only] to Him" (Revelation 14:7).

In the face of this pseudo-God sitting in the holy place claiming to be God, the call is made that they *"fear God and give glory to Him for the hour (time) of His judgment has come"* (14:7). Then, in order to clarify what *God* they were supposed to worship, the message continues, *"worship Him who made heaven and earth, the sea and springs of water"* (14:7). It is a call to come back to the Creator of Genesis. This is a direct challenge thrown in the face of this pseudo-god and Antichrist, who is seeking great power.

It is certainly apropos for the preachers of the time to call the world's attention back to the one, true God. Where will the Evolutionists, the Naturalistic Scientists, New Age Gaia worshippers of nature and earth, and the animals be at this time? There is a judgment for those who would not worship the God who has made Himself well known by the things He has made (Romans 1:19-28). This call is to every man and woman of the day; a call to turn away from these deceptions promoted by the international community under the Antichrist, and go back to worshipping the God of Genesis. We must turn away from the pantheon of Gods that the world worships and refuse to open our minds to accept such a man/god as the one who will be leading our world in that day.

MESSAGE NUMBER 2

Equally apropos for the preaching of the day, will be Christ's warning to the people through the angel messenger, who are tempted to sell out to the World Order or Community of Nations, to not base their hope on the world economy. The big selling point today that rivets the people of the world to the New World Order is the continual promise of peace and prosperity tied to the world bankers involved in the IMF *(International Monetary Fund)*. Very shortly, all nations will be forced into a world money system in the form of SDRs (Special Drawing Rights from the IMF). This Babylon is the same as found in chapter 18 and plainly represents the world economic order:

> *"Babylon the great is fallen, is fallen ... for all of the nations have drunk of the wine of the wrath of her fornication"* (Revelation 18:2-3).

This message is to encourage the nations and peoples of Earth to understand that this World Order is going to collapse, and Babylon is going with it. A careful study of chapter 18 will convince us that whatever else Babylon may represent with its many mysterious connotations, it is in the final analysis of the embodiment of the world economic system. Its fall is also spoken of in chapters 16, 17, and 18. We will explore its full meaning as given to us in the scriptures when we comment on chapter 18.

MESSAGE NUMBER 3

While these messages from Christ are being shouted from the housetop, and no doubt over every major television outlet and the World Wide Web (www), a third message is forthcoming. With a loud voice, Christ in the sermon of the messenger comes to warn them:

> *"If any one worships the beast and his image, and receives his mark on his forehead or on his hand, he himself shall also drink of the wine of the wrath of God, which is poured out full strength into the cup of His indignation"* (14:9-10).

Brothers and Sisters, that is strong preaching! I do not know what the future of a large portion of the Church will be if they reject strong negative preaching today and will not hear a good old-fashioned "Hell, Fire and Brimstone" message like this one, and who despise those who preach the same. That may be why those that are hearing this message probably missed the Rapture and are still around for the Tribulation. They must not *"despise prophecies"* and listen this time to the message of truth (2 Thessalonians 5:20). For to reject, as even in our day, will bring eternal negative consequences:

> *"... and he shall be tormented with fire and brimstone in the presence of the holy angels ..."* (Revelation 14:10).

Now that would be bad enough, but what would be sheer *Hell* is the next part"

> *"... and in the presence of the Lamb"* (14:10).

When those who have folded to the pressure of the beast (His mark, name and number), have to face Christ who paid the price for their sin and rebellion, knowing that all they would have had to do was to receive Him—*"the Lamb of God who takes away the sin of the world,"* will be the worse torment one can imagine (John 2:29). And then to realize that even at that late hour, Christ was still in the redeeming business. Even in Tribulation, the hand of redemption is reaching out to all who will refuse the Antichrist—his mark, name, and number.

Christ is calling them to turn to Him and receive Him, the Lamb who appears on Mount Zion to make Himself manifest, and drive the beast from the Mount (Revelation 6:15-17). They fear the wrath of the Lamb, because the great day of His wrath is come on Zion (by all of these other texts from the Old Testament above). There is no rest in an eternal Hell (14:11).

THE BLESSED DEAD

Revelation 14:12-13 has been read at thousands of funerals throughout time and has comforted us in the time of bereavement, and rightly so. However, placed in context, it is a verse taken from the third message of redemption for the Tribulation saints who will face death for refusing the Antichrist's mark, name, and number (13:16). It is written for the admonition of those who suffer death after this. The reason that it can be used for us at funerals today is that it carries the same gospel hope in Christ as it does for the Tribulation saints. Just like today, if these Tribulation saints die in the Lord, having received Him as Lord and Savior, they will have rest. Those that are martyred, henceforth, or after that will also be at rest, while those of their worldly companions are suffering in an eternal Hell. As always, their works will follow them into the day they must give an account to God.

And *"here is the patience of the saints"* (14:12). What does that mean and how does it fit into the context? John was instructed to write to those who would refuse the mark, name, and number, and face martyrdom. No doubt they would have copies of the Book of the Revelation of Jesus Christ, and probably have been well instructed in its pages as they were facing that very time. They will read of the Lord's encouragement to be patient in Tribulation. They will be reminded through the Word that we were to joy in Tribulation because we were counted worthy to share in Christ's suffering. We are told that with much Tribulation, we enter into the kingdom of God. Jesus told us, "In the world you will have tribulation; but be of good cheer, I have overcome the world" (John 16:33). We see then that Tribulation is not an unexpected commodity of our faith. His message, while dealing with very serious circumstances and consequences, gives us encouragement in three ways: 1) Be patient in Tribulation; 2) Keep the commandments of God; and 3) Keep the testimony of Jesus. The mention of the commandments of God may indicate that many of them are Jews.

They would then be directed to Revelation 14:13:

"Blessed are the dead who die in the Lord from now on. Yes, says the Spirit, that they may rest from their labors, and their works follow them."

This verse is a comfort and a blessing to us this side of Tribulation, but think what an encouragement it would be if you were facing execution and martyrdom. James exhorted us to, *"be patient, establish your hearts, for the coming of the Lord is at hand"* (James 5:8).

TWO HARVESTS

After witnessing the wonderful event of Christ on Mount Zion with the 144,000 and hearing the heart of the gospel that will be preached to those receptive in that day, we now turn to the ultimate results of reception or rejection of the gospel message. As this chapter closes, Christ clarifies the two harvests which anticipate the Hope and Judgment of the world and of each of us individually.

THE FIRST HARVEST (V. 14-16) CHRIST REAPS HIS HARVEST

There can be little speculation about who is involved in

this first harvest and what that harvest is. A very recognizable language, with which we are familiar, is used here by Christ to help us recognize Him. He is sitting upon a white cloud, and He is *"One like the Son of Man"* with a crown of gold (14:14). All of these leave no doubt. This is not the Antichrist on a white horse, or any other imposter. This is Christ, the Son of the living God, who identified Himself 89 times by the term *Son of Man.*

John is directed to remember the first Rapture when the Lord appeared for His saints. This is one of the verses used by those adhering to the mid-Tribulation rapture, and no doubt, it speaks of the coming of the Lord in the clouds to receive His saints. Everything about verses 14-16, speak of the reaping of a harvest from the Church.

However, there are some major differences in these verses from what we know about the Rapture of the Church. Nowhere is the Rapture of the Church likened unto a harvest of the earth. Nowhere is the Rapture likened unto a harvest using a sickle or weapon of brutality, and nowhere is the Rapture likened unto thrusting in a sickle to harvest us from the earth. This is a violent act during a violent time, in which it appears that these were snatched up out of great Tribulation.

It is my persuasion they are saints who have found Christ at a very violent time, having suffered great unrest, and are harvested out of martyrdom. These are they, whom the souls under the altar were to wait for in Revelation 6:11, and are those who appear before the throne just prior to the Battle of Armageddon (Revelation 15:1-3). Also, the time of *this* Rapture was known, unlike the Rapture of the Church.

A cry comes out of the Temple in Heaven; a cry to Christ Himself. You see, the exact time of the Rapture was not known to anyone, not to the angels, nor even the Son of Man—Christ Himself, but only to God. But here in this passage, the time is known. Christ waits for the Father's signal. A loud voice out of the temple in Heaven cries, *"for the time has come for You to reap ... and the earth was reaped"* (14:15-16).

This reaping does not seem to be a peaceful Rapture as it was for the Church, but Rapture associated with violence. At the Rapture of the Church, nowhere is it indicated that there would be a sharp sickle thrust into the earth. In fact, we are told of a glorious *catching away*—Rapture. In this passage, these are ripped away in violence.

MID-TRIBULATION RAPTURE OF TRIBULATION SAINTS

Now, there can be no question that this speaks of a Rapture, but what Rapture and when? Here they seem to be killed, but immediately changed and taken to Heaven. Is this a reminder of the Rapture that took place in chapter four? I doubt it. At this time, the Church is around the throne being led and fed by the Lamb. Is this a mid-Tribulation Rapture? That is a possibility. Those who use these verses for proof of a mid-Tribulation Rapture may be correct, but it cannot be the Rapture of the Church, inasmuch as the Church has been seen many times in Heaven before this time.

Is this a mid-Tribulation Rapture of the Tribulation saints? This Rapture is associated with violence, probably martyrdom. We will see these in Heaven at the beginning of the next chapter.

There have been many raptures in Scripture up until this time: 1) Enoch (Genesis 5:24); 2) Elijah (2 Kings 2:11); 3) Christ Himself (Acts 1:9); 4) Old Testament saints at Christ's Resurrection (Matthew 27:52); 5) Rapture of the Church (1 Thessalonians 4:16-17); and 6) The Rapture of the two witnesses (Revelation 11:12). Therefore, to accept another rapture or two, would not be out of the question. However, it would have to be after their martyrdom. It could very well be those spoken of in Revelation 15:2-4 who are Tribulation Saints, and are found around the throne in Heaven on the Sea of Glass, singing and shouting and preaching the message of the Kingdom. They were probably referred to also in Revelation six as the ones who the anxious souls under the altar had to wait for, to join them in martyrdom.

Also, it certainly could be those spoken of in chapter seven, *"a great multitude which no one could number"* (7:9). They came out of the Great Tribulation and have washed their robes in the blood of the Lamb. Are they separate from the Raptured Church or are they part of it? Are they part of the Bride of Christ, or are they friends at the marriage? It seems to me that the Bride would not be called servants and would not be destined to stay around the throne, but will accompany Christ in His return. I believe these are the same Tribulation saints who "overcame him by the blood of the Lamb and by the word of their testimony, and they did not love their lives to the death" (12:11). These are probably the same that were at the throne at the beginning of chapter 15. They are those converted by the great revival and pulled out of the fire; a harvest out of the earth during the Tribulation.

THE SECOND HARVEST, THE HARVEST OF THE WICKED

This second harvest in Revelation 14:17-20 is far different, as is the harvester. Again, the cry from Heaven indicates that this harvest is still controlled by God, in Christ. It is Christ in the temple who is giving directions to what we familiarly call the *Grim Reaper*, or the *Angel of Death*, possibly the fourth horse of chapter six. Orders are given to another angel from the altar. Remember those martyred souls crying for vengeance from under the altar? Here we see that their cry has the force of destructive fire, the element which God will use to judge the ungodly world.

Remember that they were to rest a little while until joined by their fellow servants and other brethren who would be killed just as they had been. This will be fulfilled in the first harvest above. The second harvest represents what the souls under the altar called for. It is a harvest to avenge them of their blood by judging the wicked world, which through the centuries, have taken their lives in martyrdom. The time has come for them to be avenged of their blood.

Their cry motivates the Grim Reaper of Death and the sickle is thrust into the ungodly world (Jude 15). he wine press of the wrath of God which was referred to by Christ as He comes out of Bozrah, speaks of Christ's judgment upon the nations and its World Order over which He will reign *"with a rod of iron"* (Revelation 12:5, 14:8, 10, 19; Isaiah 63:3-4). It is also the same wine press referred to in Joel:

> *"Put in the sickle, for the harvest is ripe. Come, go down; for the winepress full, the vats overflow—for their wickedness is great. Multitudes, multitudes in the valley of decision! For the day of the Lord is near in the valley of decision"* (Joel 3:13-14).

This speaks of those who were part of Babylon; who took the mark, name, and number, and who would be "... tormented with fire and brimstone in the presence of the holy angels and in the presence of the Lamb" (Revelation 14:10). They would be those who suffer the wrath of God spoken of in Revelation 15:1, 7, 16:1, 18:3, and 19:15. There are eleven references to *"the wrath of God,"* and all of them appear after the eleventh chapter of Revelation. All are involved in the last half of the Tribulation. The wrath of the Lamb, the wrath of the nations, and the wrath of the devil are all involved in the first half of the Tribulation.

The eleven mentions of *the wrath of God* begin in chapter 11, just after the Antichrist's campaign against the witness (and I believe at the same time of the insurgence against the Jews in chapter 12), at the same time of the anger of the nations, and probably at the same time of Christ's appearance on Zion. After this, there are ten more mentions of *the wrath of God*. The last 3½ years are going to be the time of God's wrath when He finally and completely fed up, and fires away.

THE TIME OF VENGEANCE IS COME

I know it is hard for us to comprehend the wrath and vengeance of God and Christ, but I would not be true to Christ, the writer and composer of the Pageant of Divine Justice, if I did not cover it in its entirety. So I must tell you that the time of God's vengeance is come; the cup of iniquity is full; and the transgressors have come to their full. The *Grapes of Wrath* does not originally refer to the sins of Clark Gable and Scarlet O'hara, but to the sins of the whole world for all time.

Vengeance belongs to the Lord. The day of grace is over, not for the repentant, but for those who are unrepentant as we will see in Revelation, chapters 15 and 16. Every prayer and every cry which has been placed before the throne has come up into the ears of the Lord. Isaiah 34:8 declares it as the day of the Lord's vengeance. Joel 3:12-13 put it in relationship to multitudes gathered to make war against Jerusalem and God's Son, when Christ is set to judge the heathen round about Jerusalem. Isaiah 35:4 says that He will come with vengeance; and Isaiah says, *"for the day of vengeance is in my heart"* (63:4). Luke says *"for these are the days of vengeance, that all things which are written may be fulfilled"* (Isaiah 21 & 22). And Joel speaks of this very time by saying:

> *"Put in the sickle, for the harvest is ripe. Come, go down; for the winepress is full ... for their wickedness is great"* (Joel 3:13).

As we have mentioned, the cup of iniquity in the world is full; the transgressors have come to their full; and the grapes of this world which are full of wrath are harvested and will be treaded out in the winepress of God's anger.

This is Christ's war against a wayward, unrepentant, and rebellious world which begins with His appearance on Zion, continues with Him walking the borders to put down terrorist nations, and ends by facing Satan with his cohort the Antichrist, and his armies of the nations at Megiddo in Israel (Ezekiel 32).

He will then Judge the nations, some as *sheep nations* to be with Him in the Millennium, and some as *goat nations* whose leadership will be destroyed (Matthew 25:31-46).

To illustrate how that Christ's appearance on Mount Zion is a war campaign, we may note the last verse of this chapter which sums it all up. The *"winepress"* of judgment against all nations is *"trampled"* outside of Jerusalem proper (Revelation 14:20). Christ meets the multitudes gathered round about Jerusalem (Zechariah 14:1-4; Joel 3:1-3, 9-12). It will be as bloody of a campaign as the one just previously at Bozrah. It is this battle, not Armageddon, that speaks of the blood running down the gullies to the horse's bridles outside of Jerusalem (14:20).

TRODDEN OUTSIDE THE CITY (14:20)

The last verse has very important insight as it relates to the whole scenario of *The Day of the Lord*, which signifies the time between the Lords coming *for* His saints at the Rapture, and coming *with* His saints in judgment of Satan and the wayward nations. This is another Old Testament cryptic symbol relating to God's laws and how they are applied here at the end-time:

"And the winepress was trampled outside the city…"

This law, or practice, ordained by God from the beginning of the tabernacle period which began at Sinai, was practiced to separate the spiritually clean from the spiritually unclean. According to Dr. Henry Morris, in his very wonderful daily devotional entitled *Days of Praise* (July 5, 2011), there are thirty references to activities that took place outside the camp.

All of the accepted practices were in or around the tabernacle which was placed in the center of the camp. The custom of doing some things outside of the camp, were designed to keep the Tabernacle area from being polluted with the unclean. Anything dangerous to the people's health or spiritual welfare was taken care of outside the camp. I will mention only one group that was to be stoned outside of the camp. They were the blasphemers (Leviticus 24:14). Certainly, this is the practice that is symbolized here in verse twenty. The Antichrist is a blasphemer, and was in the company of a society of blasphemers that makes up the *community of nations* today (2 Thessalonians 2:4; Revelation 13:6, 16:9, 11, 21). All of those nations and individuals who will suffer the wrath of God and who will be *trampled* down in God's vengeance outside of the city of Jerusalem were to suffer *outside the city* and are called blasphemers. We read extensively about their blasphemy in coming chapters.

Another prevalent practice of Old Testament custom reflected here, is the fact that all of the bodies of the sin-bearing animals which had been sacrificed for sin offerings, were burned outside of the camp (Hebrews 13:11). Because they carried the sins of the people, they were considered unclean and taken outside of the city for burial. In Christ's time on Earth, they were taken outside the walls of Jerusalem to be burned.

Can we miss the significance of this verse? It certainly brings into focus, our own Lord and Savior Jesus Christ, who bore our sins and carried our sorrows in His own body on the cross (Isaiah 53:4, 12). Now, note how this very fact about Him as a sin-bearer is carried over into the subject of Christ in the Revelation. Hebrews 9:28 states:

> "So Christ was offered once to bear the sins of many. To those who eagerly wait for Him He will appear a second time apart from sin for salvation."

He appears in cryptic symbolism in this verse, for we remember that He was taken outside the walls of Jerusalem, *"outside the gate"* and suffered the cross (Hebrews 13:12). As a sacrificial body, unclean for having carried our sins, He was crucified outside the gate, and because He carried our sins, caused Him to be *polluted.* Bearing our sins made Him unfit to be honored in the city. Selah!

He is joined by all of the sinners and blasphemers who will be trodden down outside the city gate of Jerusalem. It is said that He "made His grave with the wicked ... because He poured out His soul unto death, and He was numbered with the transgressors" (Isaiah 53:9, 12). I weep while sharing this for the humility and brokenness of my Lord and out of a grateful heart for His wonderful love. He is still the Lamb that had been slain for us (Revelation 5:6).

Now we are encouraged to join Him, die out to the self-life, and give ourselves a living sacrifice for Him. I think it probable that the battles to free Jerusalem which will take place at Christ's visit to Zion will be fought outside the perimeters of Jerusalem.

All of the texts dealing with these battles have them happening outside the walls of Jerusalem (Joel 3: 9-17; Zechariah 14:1-5). The valleys will run to the horses' bridles with the blood of the blasphemers and the rebellious. If God allowed His own Son to spill His blood for their sins, do you think He will require any less of these sinners? Christ declares of the unrepentant sinners: (Revelation 16:6) "You have shed the innocent blood of the saints and prophets" so

(Revelation 14:20). God has given them blood to drink. In other words, they thirst for blood in their wickedness and God is requiring their own blood in sacrifice.

It all began at Mount Zion, and it all will end on Mount Zion. We will continue comments on the next section dealing with the fourteenth chapter.

We are continuing our discussion of chapter fourteen, where Christ our Lord depicts Himself as the Lamb, coming to Mount Zion with 144,000 Jews— 12,000 from each Tribe. As the seventh trumpet *"is about to sound,"* we see our Lord turning His attention to Israel, the temple, and events which concern the Jews in the last days (Revelation 10:7). Chapters eleven and twelve are exclusively about the Jews. Chapter thirteen is another *meanwhile* which simply describes the beast and his companion, the Antichrist; we see both in chapters eleven and twelve. Chapter fourteen turns our attention back to the Jews and Mount Zion. In the last chapter, we related many texts from the Old Testament Messianic scriptures which presage Christ's visit to Mount Zion.

It is only as we begin to assimilate many of the prophecies of the Old Testament into these texts of Revelation that we see that the Revelation of Jesus Christ has much to say about Israel in the last days. We begin to realize that even though three whole chapters are almost exclusively about Israel, the temple, and the Jews, there is much more about Israel's future. Many, who as we have shown through a very serious error, taught throughout Evangelical Christianity known as Replacement Theology that the Jews were cut out of God's promise, therefore all promises to Abraham, Israel, and the Jews now belong to the Church.

The Book of Revelation is sketchy regarding all that the Old Testament has to say about Israel's last days, yet we find plenty of evidence of the promise to Abraham, Israel, and the Jews in Revelation. We will have to intercalate many references from the Old Testament to complete the story. In this part of our discussion of chapter fourteen, we will continue to zero in on many texts from the Old Testament which show us much about the Jews in the last days, their beloved promises, and how this all ties in with Jesus Christ.

REVELATION AND THE JEWS

I have a theory as to why our Lord chose to leave the prophecies of the last days concerning the Jews and Israel, largely out of His Revelation, and leave them in the shadows to be searched out by the faithful. With the Lord's perfect insight and foreknowledge of the future, He could certainly see the climate of today's political scene. God knew that in order to save some havoc against the Jews and some persecution against Christ's beloved people, it would be wise to hide their future in mystery just as He hid those promises in cryptic symbolism all through the Messianic texts of the Old Testament. Satan has certainly used the hope of Israel to his advantage.

The gross misunderstandings of Bible promises which Replacement Theology has created in the Church, and the anti-Semitism caused by it throughout the world, has not only created disdain for Israel and the Jews in the Church, but has been used against Israel by her enemies. Any suggestion that would place Israel at the head of nations and not the tail in the last days, would hint of the Jews control over the Temple Mount. The future Kingdom of David ruling over the Middle East, and expanding the State of Israel to what has been dubbed *Greater Israel*, placing its borders from the River of Egypt to the River Euphrates, would further inflame the world against the Jews.

People of the world who do not know the true nature of God and Christ are suspicious of these promises. The world is somewhat aware of the promises that God's blessing upon Abraham's seed, would bring the Jews to the head of the world in a future era. Because most of the unsaved world is very resentful of that promise, and since the modern day humanists and their UN are set to fulfill those promises by their own ingenuity without Christ and God, they certainly resent the challenge against their plan. Any hint that the world will someday be ruled over by Christ and the God of the Jews, has raised all kinds of ire and anti-Semitic sentiments among the nations. The Church, with its attitude that makes the Gentile Church the real Israel of the last days and all of us—Abraham's seed has only added to the world's anti-Semitism.

I realize that my plain teaching from the scriptures about Israel and the last days flies in the face of worldly thinking. However, I would rather be true to God, Christ, and His Holy Word than try to please the world. Thus, I will proceed to be very direct and clear about the future of Israel and the Jews.

The very justifiable effort that brought about the first Jewish Congress in 1898, was simply an effort to find a homeland for the scattered and persecuted Jewish people of the world. It was turned into a political football field by the anti-Semitic rebels of the world. The purpose of the Jewish Congress however, was not secret and subtle, but open and honest. It was simply an effort to find a homeland for beleaguered Jews. However, there was and is a secret group of Jews in secret societies, just as there are Gentiles in secret societies that teach, plan, and look for the days promised by the Lord through the prophets, when Israel will be honored again as the spiritual leaders of the world. This promise is misunderstood as a diabolical conspiracy by the Jew-haters of the world and is being used to malign all Jews. Just as the radical Islamic terrorist groups are causing world reaction against all Muslims, the secret actions of a few Jewish fanatics, has caused a world reaction against all Jews. See the Appendix for further details on the cause behind anti-Semitism.

If the whole scheme of God's plan through Jesus Christ is for Christ to eventually rule the world with a *rod of iron*, openly and directly connected with Jewish efforts to have a homeland for their people, we can easily see how hateful world leaders could use that to wreak havoc upon the Jewish people. Of course, anti-God secular leaders would resent any hint that Gentile rule of Palestine would end and that the Holy Land would be given back to the Jews. God promised to give that land to Abraham and his seed forever, but they were to bless the whole world. However, it is ironic that to this point in history, Abraham never owned any part of it except for a plot in which to bury his wife Sarah and eventually himself. Jesus said in Luke 21:4 that the Gentile control of Palestine will continue until the time of the Gentiles are fulfilled.

The whole theme of Revelation is to show the end of the time of the Gentiles and the setting up of Christ's Kingdom when He will return Zion, Jerusalem, and the Temple Mount to the Jews as promised. The whole purpose of the last battles fought in Israel (Jehoshaphat—Joel 3; Jerusalem—Zechariah 14:1-4; Gog and Magog—Ezekiel 38, 39; and Armageddon—Revelation 16), are fought to return the Holy Land to Israel.

WHY ISRAEL HAS BEEN CUT OUT OF OUR UNDERSTANDING OF REVELATION

As we see now the reason why the complete story of the final plan for Israel is cryptically hidden in the Book of Revelation, and nicely tucked away into the Messianic prophecies, is so that only those who Love God and Christ and are willing to search the Messianic texts, can find the plan and understand God's redeeming purpose. As we have said before, in order to get the complete picture of events in the last 3 ½ years of the Tribulation and leading up to the

Millennium preparation, we will have to glean it from the Old Testament prophecies.

Since Israel's place in the Tribulation hour and the restoration afterwards is left behind the scenes, it forces us to fill in the gaps from the Old Testament. The Jews' place in these last days and their special relationship to their Messiah is hidden in the Messianic prophecies, making Israel's future only understood by students of the Old Testament texts who can intercalate those texts into Revelation.

Both the Jew and Gentile have been half-blinded to the full realities of Christ's future Kingdom. Replacement Theology has blinded the nominal churches and also to a large extent, the Evangelical Churches from including Israel in the final days. To justify this grossly erroneous heresy, they have made all of the mention of Jews (144,000) and Jewish terms (Zion, Jerusalem, the Temple, etc.) as allegorical, speaking to and of the Church. As we have said, the Jews are half-blinded by the fact that their traditions have kept them from fully realizing the Messiah's rightful place in their history and future by keeping them from seeing Jesus as their suffering Messiah and the Lamb of God in the end-time. Jesus, calling himself the Lamb 27 times in the Book of Revelation, appeals to the Jews, who of all people should understand the sacrificial Lamb. However, they were only *cut off* for a time because they did not associate the suffering Messiah to their concept of the conquering Messiah. The Church was grafted in, but when the Church is gone, the Jews will be grafted back in and *"all Israel will be saved"* (Acts 15:13-17; Romans 11:25-26). This great event of the salvation of Israel takes place during the Tribulation years, but is cryptically hidden from the text of Revelation.

To correct these two errors in our thinking, and to give us a true understanding of Israel's place in Revelation, it will be helpful to pause and intercalate into our discussion the Old

Testament's clear prophecies of Israel's part in the Tribulation period, and the restoration to follow.

THE LORD WILL COME TO HIS TEMPLE

One of the most evident signs from Heaven that shows a subtle appeal to the Jews during the Tribulation is the many mentions of the temple in the last chapters of The Revelation of Jesus Christ: four times each in chapters 11 and 15, once in chapter 14, and two times each in chapters 16 and 21. Just the mention of the temple tends to conger up deep and moving feelings and dreams for any religious Jew. It is important to notice that as we move into the last 3½ years of the tribulation, part of it which is normally thought of as *"the time of Jacob's trouble,"* the temple both on Earth and in Heaven come into play 14 times (Jeremiah 30:7).

Only a casual glance at the Old Testament record and Israel's history, will tell us the importance of the temple in Jewish thought. Just to mention the temple calls up sentiments of moving spiritual experiences, and leaves a sense of, and a longing for God's holy and eternal presence. To the religious Jew, the temple always represents the presence of God. To the Church it awakens memory of Christ.

The early history of Israel sets the pattern for worship at the Temple. The songs of Israel, expressing Israel's deepest sentiments, has prophetic overtones as they speak of the awakening of our soul toward the Lord after finding and worshipping Him in the temple. Even during the Diaspora, in the days when there was no earthly temple, for 2000 years the Jews worshipped toward the temple site in Jerusalem. While remembering their ancient habit, they recalled Psalmist's words, *"I will worship toward Your Holy Temple"* (5:7). They still believe Psalm 11:4, *"The Lord is in His holy Temple."* The temple has always been a stereo-type, representing the presence of the Lord. Experiencing God or Christ's voice out of the Temple in Heaven is a regular occurrence in the last chapters of Revelation. This *"voice from the temple"* was prophesied in Isaiah 66:6. This verse is preceded by *"we may see your joy"* and I believe prophesies His appearance on Zion in Revelation 14. Micah prophesies that the Lord would witness against them from His holy temple (1:2).

It is plainly told in Old Testament prophecies that the Lord will return and build again the earthly temple. For instance, Zechariah says that *"He will build the temple of the Lord"* (6:12, 15). And Malachi 3:1 declares He *"will suddenly come to His temple."* The famous prophetic chapter, Matthew 24 answers questions about the rebuilding of the Temple. It is mentioned 116 times in the New Testament. All of this shows how absolutely centric the temple is to the liturgy of the Jews and to the spiritual sentiments of the Church as well. Also, we are told in Isaiah 44:28 that a temple would be built at the Lord's return.

This demonstrates how Christ subtly begins to appeal to His own race, as well as to the rest of those who have not taken the mark, the name, and number of the beast. Some will take the mark, name, and number, but many will not. We often dwell on those who do, but forget about the many that will not and will be evangelized and brought to faith in Christ by the two witnesses and by the Lord Himself as He speaks out of His temple in Heaven and on Earth.

THE REVELATION OF JESUS CHRIST—A NEW MEANING TO THE TEMPLE

One of the great enlightenments that must come to the Jews in the Revelation of Jesus Christ is to see there will be no need for the old use of the temple after Christ is made manifest to the 144,000 Jews. At some time during their banishment to the wilderness, Christ as their sacrificial Lamb will be made plain to them, for they will have *"the testimony of Jesus Christ"* (Revelation 12:17). Christ will teach them all about the meaning of sacrifice, and how it relates to Calvary and His death, burial, and resurrection. He will expound to them all the scriptures of the Old Testament which speaks of Him, as He has already expounded to the Church (John 5:39, Luke 24:27, Acts 8:35).

Why did they have to search the scriptures to know Him? It is because of the enigmatic nature of the Messianic texts. Christ will reveal Himself to these Jews in Tribulation. The temple will take on a whole new meaning to the Jews of that day. It will mean to them the same as it does to the Church today.

There are many other subtle, but easy-to-see signs of the part that Israel plays in the Tribulation and in Christ's ministry to the Jews during *the time of Jacob's trouble.* By pulling some of the related Old Testament texts into our study, we can see what happens just before Christ's feet stands on Mount Olivet and prior to His appearance on Mount Zion (Zechariah 14:4). I believe the central theme of the Revelation of Jesus Christ actually begins here in Revelation, chapter fourteen.

CHRIST WILL COME TO ZION

"The Lord ... will suddenly come to His Temple" (Malachi 3:1). Often while preaching, I say, "Mark it down, hide and watch, our Lord will come to Zion." God said in Psalms, *"I have set My king on My holy hill of Zion"* (2:6).

This is a well-prophesied event. Zechariah clearly prophesies this event in chapter eight:

> *"Thus says the Lord of hosts: I am zealous for Zion with great zeal; with great fervor I am zealous for her. Thus says the Lord: I will return to Zion, and dwell in the midst of Jerusalem. Jerusalem shall be called the City of truth, the Mountain of the Lord of hosts (Temple*

Mount), the Holy Mountain ... Thus says the Lord of hosts: Behold, I will save My people ... [and] I will bring them back, and they shall dwell in the midst of Jerusalem. They shall be my people and I will be their God, in truth and righteousness ... [hear] in these days (Days of restoration of Israel and Jerusalem, which is the days of Revelation's prophecies) these words by the mouth of the prophets ... that the temple might be built" (Zechariah 8:2&3, 7&9).

See also Isaiah 59:20, Acts 15:14, Romans 11:26, and Amos 1:2. Each passage listed substantiates the Jews and Israel's place in these events in Revelation.

The excitement of His appearance on Olivet and then on Mount Zion, will surely shake the world and unnerve the Antichrist who has been working his miracles and trying to impersonate Christ and God. It will cause a mass-reaction by the World Order (the Beast) that will be covered by the major media of the world, and it will affect an immediate reaction from the Antichrist. It will also cause the great persecution against the Jews and Israel as recorded in chapter 12, and the greatest Alyia (return) yet among the Jews of the Diaspora.

I am absolutely fascinated by what His activities will potentially be prior to this appearance on Zion. What activities placed Him together with the 144,000 before their combined entourage to the Temple Mount and to Zion? What does the Old Testament Messianic texts tell us and how do they enhance what we are studying in the Revelation. Oh, this is so exciting I can hardly sit still to write about it!

We are most familiar with the prophecy in Zechariah 14:4, that declares Christ's feet will stand on Mount Olivet. The angels said to the disciples the day He ascended from the Mount of Olives:

"This same Jesus, who was taken up from you into

Heaven, will so come in like manner as saw Him go into Heaven" (Acts 1:11).

We are not so familiar with His feet standing on Mount Zion.

Christ will come to Mt. Zion when the whole world of armies (armies of the nations such as NATO) will be in siege against Jerusalem. It will be in *"the day of the Lord"* (Zechariah 14:1). That is comparable to the days of the same fulfillment in Revelation. He will come when the Lord has gathered all nations there for His own purpose (14:2) ...

"then the Lord will go forth and fight against those nations ... " (14:3).

From across the Kidron Valley, He will plead with them: *"on account of my people"* (Israel) ... *[for] they have also divided up My land* (West Bank)" (ibid; Joel 3:2).

"And in that day His feet will stand on the Mount of Olives" (Zechariah 4:4). How exciting it must have been for John, who was certainly privy to all of these Scriptures and their meanings, to suddenly be turned away from the worldly scenes of the beast and, as he said, *"Then I looked, and behold* (excitement), *a Lamb standing on Mount Zion, and with Him one hundred and forty-four thousand ... "* (Revelation 14:1). Is the Revelation as exciting to us today as it was to John? As we study these texts, are our souls jumping with excitement and amazement? It is as if we are in Christ and Him in us!

We see by these texts that His feet touching Mount of Olives, is directly related to His coming to Mount Zion.

What a moment that will be for the wicked entourage of the beast, the Antichrist, and all the worldly servants of the Antichrist, who have set Him up as god, to suddenly see *the* real Savior and Christ appear. What a shock when they see Him appear on Mount Zion with 144,000 Jews.

THE REAL REDEEMER COMES TO ZION

HOW DOES THE LORD AND THE 144,000 JEWS GET TO ZION?

How Christ and the 144,000 got to Zion and what took place just before it may be a source of some discussion. We can only depend on the Old Testament texts to give us the clue. I will express my honest opinion from 50 years of detailed research into the Messianic prophetic scriptures of both the Old and New Testaments. Many Bible scholars are aware of His feet touching Mount of Olives, and assume that is where He will first appear. This may be true. However, if He was coming from southern Edom as I believe the prophetic texts will show, He would necessarily pass over the Mount of Olives on His way to Mount Zion. There are many texts that must be considered in relationship to His return and His first appearance that suggests this scenario. We will explore them next.

Isaiah 63:1-4 is preceded by several chapters which unquestionably are Second-Coming texts and relate to the return of the Jews to the Holy Land in the last days. I will touch upon the chapters around Isaiah 63 to show the context it is in. We read in Isaiah 59:20 an Old Testament counterpart to Revelation 14:1:

> "The Redeemer will come to Zion, and to those who turn from transgression in Jacob, says the Lord."

By this text He seems to especially make contact with the repented Jews, possibly the remnant. The rest of secular Israel, moved by flattery to reject the holy covenant, will be left to honor the Antichrist (Daniel 11:30-32). Then, chapter 60 tells about Israel restored in the last days and the help they will receive, and have already received, from the Gentile Church. Chapters 61 and 62 continue the general theme of the restoration of Israel and its involvement with the Redeemer. These are all last-day Messianic texts.

Isaiah 62:1 shows the messianic purpose for Jerusalem and Zion, and verse 11 speaks of His coming with work to Zion. Just after He comes through the gate of Zion, the Lord is said to make an announcement to the whole world, "[saying]

> *"Surely your salvation is coming; behold, His reward is with Him, and His work before Him"* (Isaiah 62:11).

In the very next chapter, speaking of the Lord who has just returned to Zion, the question is posed:

> *"Who is this who comes from Edom, with dyed garments from Bozrah?"* (Edom is another name for Petra, a part of a three-city complex in Edom) He is *"glorious in His apparel, traveling in the greatness of His strength"* (Isaiah 63:1).

Christ answers the question with:
It is *"I who [speaks] in righteousness, mighty to save"* (63: 1).
Verse two asks another question of Him:

> *"Why is your apparel red, and your garments like one who treads in the winepress?"*

And again Christ answers,

> *"I have trodden the winepress alone ... for I have trodden them in My anger, and trampled them in My fury; their blood is sprinkled upon My garments, and I have stained my robes"* (63:3; compare Revelation 14:20).

It is beyond question that at some time, there is to be a slaughter in Edom and around Bozrah. It is also obvious that the slaughter is the work of the Lord Himself. How interesting that in Revelation 14, His appearance on Mt. Zion is followed by texts that relate to the harvest of the earth, resulting in a great wine- press of the wrath of God being trodden (14:19-20). Christ's answers are what we find at the end of chapter fourteen in verses 14:10 and 18-19 as it relates to Isaiah 63:3.

I can find no other place in the scene of the last days to put these texts unless they are in classic cryptic form, describing His deliverance of the Jews in Edom and Bozrah, and His coming to Mount Zion afterword. The grand conclusion of all things; the restitution and restoration of all things seems to begin here on Zion.

It is my persuasion that Jesus will first appear in Edom to the Jews in exile. The prophet Ezekiel makes this very plain. In the midst of the Return and the Tribulation text of Revelation 12:14, he speaks of Israel by saying:

"And I will bring you into the wilderness of the peoples" (20:34).

When He comes to the remnant of Israel in the wilderness, He will manifest Himself by pleading with them. The term is *shaphat* is Hebrew meaning to plead a legal and logical position in court. It can be best understood that the Lord strives to convince them that He is their Messiah and the Sacrificial Lamb. Ezekiel 20:35 says that He will plead with them face to face. Interestingly, Ezekiel, chapter twenty mentions the *wilderness* ten times, indicating a particular well-known wilderness in which Israel was judged.

There is another puzzling text, but when put it into the above scenario, it makes perfect sense. Habakkuk says:

"God came from Teman (just a few miles from Petra), *the Holy One from Mount Paran"* (3:3).

These verses describe the Lord as He led them out of Egypt through Paran (Sinai) to Teman—Southern Jordan just a few miles from Petra. This is possible, but the texts seem to be using that part of the Exodus as an allegorical symbol, or ensample of the coming of Christ in the last days. However, I will show later how it refers back to the beginning of their trek in the wilderness when they came out of Egypt.

Nothing in these texts suggest that He is speaking of the present time or any connection to Egypt, but rather the context clearly shows that He is speaking of a former time that relates to a future time, a visionary time to come: (2:2-3).

> *"Then the Lord answered me and said: Write the vision and make it plain on tablets, that he may run who reads it. For the vision is yet for an appointed time; but at the end it will speak and it will not lie. Though it tarries, wait for it; because it will surely come, it will not tarry"* (2:2-3).

The interesting thing is that these verses are in the midst of a future Tribulation and Millennium in Habakkuk 2:2-4, 2:14, and 3:3-6:

> *"His glory covered the heavens, and the earth was full of praise. His brightness was like the light; He had rays flashing from His hand, and there His power was hidden. Before Him went pestilence, and fever followed at His feet. He looked and startled the nations. And the everlasting mountains were scattered ... His ways are everlasting."* These are tribulation texts.

Habakkuk 3:2 is an interesting plea as it could apply to the very Tribulation period:

> *"Revive Your work in the midst of the years! In the midst of the years make it known; in [the time of your] wrath, remember mercy."*

It is the work of our Lord in Revelation and the time of Tribulation that brings Israel and the Jews back to full heritage and the renewal of all of the promises to them. We will see all these things fulfilled that have been promised to Israel and the Jews. Tim LaHaye, in his *Prophecy Study Bible,* says that this will be fulfilled at the time of Christ's coming. There must be some sense in which Christ will come by Sinai to Teman and Petra. There He will visit with and instruct His special people before he leads the 144,000 of them to Zion.

Some say that these texts are poetical and allegorical, not literal, but that is one of the great interpretive errors of our time. Many believe that everything in the Old Testament is seen as allegorical and not literal, but prophecy teachers teach that we must take everything literal unless plainly shown to be allegorical.

In contemplating the whole motif of Old Testament Messianic Prophecy, it seems absolutely normal that Jesus, who has already raptured the Church, would first reappear on Earth to the righteous remnant of the Jews who are protected by the seal of God in their foreheads, and who are present for their Messianic stand.

Let us consider Isaiah 34:5-8. Most commentators admit that Isaiah 34 and 35 belong to the Messianic texts of the last days and are set in Tribulation tones; that they have to do with the *Day of the Lord.* Just as other texts have already related, it is the day when God gathers around Israel, the nations of the world for judgment (34:1-3). All of verses one through seven of Isaiah 34, are clearly related to the Tribulation texts of Revelation. Verse eight brings us to the controversy of Zion.

This text may reflect some detail of the Lord Jesus Christ's first encounter with the Antichrist and the *armies of the nations.* It certainly speaks of the same gathering of nations as in Zechariah 14:1-4, Joel 3:1-3, and Zephaniah 3:8. It is the time the Lord will utterly destroy them. It will be the same time as the *"signs in the sun, in the moon, and in the stars"* (Luke 21:25; compare Isaiah 34:4). It seems to be the same time as the war in Heaven (Revelation 12:7). Here we are told that there will be such a shake-up throughout the Heavens, that "my sword shall be bathed in the Heaven" (Isaiah 34:5). The war in Heaven seems to be carried down to Earth where Satan has come (Revelation 12:12). He seems to have brought the battle right to the Jews in Idumea--region south of Judea, and upon the armies of the nations who have come in pursuit of the Jews (Isaiah 34:5). The Battle of Edom from which the Lord comes to Zion, is described in verse six, and called the *"sacrifice in Bozrah, and a great slaughter in the Land of Edom,"* or Idumea (63:6). Verse eight ties it in to Revelation 14 when it says, *"it is the day of the Lord's vengeance, the year of recompense for the cause of Zion"* (34:8)

Our interest at this point is to once again, notice the mention of a slaughter in Idumea—Bozra. It is connected to His appearance on Mount Zion, with the 144,000. Bozrah is a companion city to the Rock City of Petra—identified in chapter twelve, as the place where the remnant of Israel will flee to *"her place"* as if there was a certain place prepared for her (Israel) for protection during the Tribulation. We are sure that the Lord would not cause a slaughter of these Jews whom He is protecting. Who then are those multitudes slaughtered in Bozrah, Petra, and Teman?

It is logical and seems to fit the pattern of the whole scenario of these texts, that the multitude to be slaughtered down in Edom is the flood of *armies of the nations* which the devil sent to destroy the outcasts, and who we are clearly told about in Joel 3, Zechariah 14, and Revelation 12:15-17. According to this Scripture, when the serpent—dragon realized that these Jews have escaped his control, he becomes wroth and sent his armies to make war with them (Revelation 12: 17). However, a great earthquake came to help by swallowing up the armies. A similar event happened in the same wilderness place, to Korah and his rebellious cohort

(Numbers 16:32).

There to the exiled in Edom, Christ will reveal Himself as the Messiah to the Jews by expounding to them all of the Messianic texts and showing how He fulfills each one. For the first time in mass, this great Remnant of Israel will see that the Old Testament sacrificial lamb was actually depicting the Messiah personally in His servant's roll, when He suffered and died. The Jews, by their blindness, have never been able to make that bridge/connection between the lambs slain in the tabernacle with its blood sprinkled on the altar, to the man-Messiah, the King. For that reason, all texts in the law and the prophets which made that tie, have been a puzzle to them. Seeing Christ appear in His Revelation glory and coming to deliver them in the form of a Lamb, will convince and lead them to conversion. At least we know these 144,000 Jews are converted to Christ. Revelation 12:17 says that these Jews in hiding will *"have the testimony of Jesus Christ."* This probably refers to the whole company of the Jews in exile. Paul said that after the Gentile Church has *"come in,"* then *"all Israel will be saved"* (Romans 11:25-26).

When the crisis hits, and the Antichrist cuts off the daily sacrifice and defiles the temple by sitting in the Holy Place and setting up the *"abomination of desolation,"* declaring Himself God; and with all of the proselytizing by the two witnesses of chapter 11, and the angels in verses 14:6-11, there will be a mass conversion among the Jews worldwide. They realize they have no need of the sacrifice any longer, for the *sacrifice that takes away sin* is here among them in person.

His coming to Zion would cause a worldwide Alyia (return) as awakened and converted Jews will come in mass to Israel. The airways will be overwhelmed with Jews returning to their ancient homeland when they hear that the Messiah has appeared on Mount Zion. The only Jews not moved by it will be those strictly secular Jews whom the Antichrist has deceived by flattery (Daniel 11). This can only happen when the Gentile powers of Satan have broken off from the nations of the world (Isaiah 2:1-4, Micah 4:1-4).

MOUNT ZION

All of the mountains of Moriah, including the Temple Mount and the Western Mount across the Tyropoeon Valley where the Jewish headquarters are located, are known and have been known throughout the ages as Mount Zion, or Sion. We could be accurate in suggesting that Mount Zion can include all of the land of Moriah in an area of several mountains. On one of these mountains, Abraham offered his sacrifice to God (Genesis 22:2). In cryptic symbolism, Mount Zion probably includes the whole of Jerusalem, including the Temple Mount, the area of David's gate, and the Jewish section of Jerusalem. Abraham came up from the area of the Philistines through Hebron and to the mountains of Bethlehem. There he could look across and see Ophel, Mount Zion, and the Temple Mount, all of which encompassed the land of Moriah. Christ's appearance put Him in sight of the whole area from Ophel, the Temple Mount, and the hill of Zion where the Jewish quarters in Jerusalem are today, and where you can see easily from the top of Mount Olivet.

THE PROPHETIC ENIGMA OF ZION (SION TO THE GENTILE WORLD)

It may be worth explaining a little about the meaning of Zion, or Mount Sion—the New Testament Greek, and its place in the enigma of prophecy. Zion, as first used in 2 Samuel 5:7, seems to be purely an earthly place in Jerusalem that David took for his capitol: "David took the stronghold of Zion (that is, the city of David)." However, when we consider

THE REAL REDEEMER COMES TO ZION 485

many of the old traditions, we see that already in Abraham's day it had a mystic and enigma about it. It was already a very sacred place to God. A man named Melchizedek, the priest of the Most High God was there. He had no father or mother, no end of life etc. He was a heavenly being if not the Lord Jesus Christ Himself. My book, *Jerusalem* (21 Century Press, Springfield, Mo.), gives a detailed explanation of the old traditions of Zion.

There are ancient records showing spiritual activity in this very place, and give us the reason why God chose Moriah as the place that Abraham should sacrifice his son. David's choice was led of God because it was the place where God had chosen from the beginning of the sacrificial ritual, to put His name there. Zion is mentioned fifty-nine times in the Old Testament and seven times under the New Testament name (as we find here) where the Greek counterpart *Sion* is used.

We will not give a detailed study of the morphing or progressive change in the enigma of the word Zion as it would be a complete subject within itself; but we will give a brief synopsis as it relates to the importance of the final days of fulfillment and the Revelation of Jesus Christ. Thus, there is a cryptic enigma which accompanies the term in Scripture.

As the term is progressively used in relationship to the prophetic future of Jerusalem and the Temple Mount, it begins to take on the essence of all Israel and the Jews. It appears to represent the throne of David and especially the final days of his eternal throne. It then progresses to indicate the final hope of all Israel and the fulfillment of all the promises to the seed of Abraham. Today, it is a term used for political efforts to restore the State of Israel and has become the embodiment of the *Return of the Jews* and represents the beginning of the Return back to the Holy Land. The First Zionist Congress convened in 1898 under the direction of

Theodore Herzl and as indicated by name, it became political Zionism (See Appendix for details).

Sion, then, is not only the name of a place in the earthly Jerusalem, but is also a cryptic term which represents all of the hopes and fulfilled promises to the Jews and their pursuit of its full manifestation. In a special spiritual connotation for the New Testament Saints, it came also to mean the fulfillment of the expectation and manifestation of the Church. In reality, the Church is only an extension of the promise to Abraham and therefore, a part of the Jewish heritage, and not a replacement of it. Romans 11:26 reads that a *"Deliverer will come out of Zion;"* and in Hebrews 12:22, the Church is said to:

> *"But you have come to Mount Zion and to the city of the living God, the heavenly Jerusalem, to an innumerable company of angels."*

Its enigmatic symbolism then moves all the way from a one-time obscure place in Old Salem, to the New Jerusalem of dreams.

Christ, with the 144,000 on Zion, and Heaven opened to show us the Church in Heaven. Heaven and Earth together, all sing chorus with the Jews in Zion. I can't wait to be there! My original mentor pastor, Rev. Kenneth R. Schmidt, used to say, "Heaven and Earth just kissed and I was right in the middle of the smack."

Christ's coming to Zion at the time of the Antichrist's possession of the Temple Mount, brings into focus what is called in prophecy, *the controversy of Zion.* The cryptic enigma will be cleared up and the mystery solved when Christ returns to Zion, sits on the throne of David, and reigns in His earthly Kingdom. He will also settle *the controversy of Zion.* It would be well for us to study that subject as we try to comprehend the total meaning of His appearance on Zion.

CONTROVERSY OF ZION

The prophet, Isaiah give valuable and interesting insight in the Tribulation context, declaring that the final rage of nations and God's wrath upon them is the *cause of Zion*:

> "For it is the day of the Lord's vengeance, the year of recompense for the cause of Zion" (Isaiah 34:8).

This very subject brings the prophecies and the Book of Revelation of Jesus Christ into present day relevance, because most of our international quagmire is controversy over the Temple Mount and Jerusalem, or Zion.

This verse is clearly prophetic and eschatological, pointing to the ancient and present circumstances that are in back of the very events enumerated for us in Revelation fourteen. Christ has returned to settle the controversy over Zion, and He comes in vengeance and recompense against a world order which has haggled over Mount Zion for years. Throughout our lifetime, the UN and most of the two-hundred plus nations chartered with it, have been in defiance against God and His plans and purposes for Mount Zion. Their defiance is not necessarily against Israel, but rather God's plans for Mount Zion to be the throne of Christ and the center of His Kingdom. They will not realize that it is Satan. It is the end of a continuing saga of Satan's rebellion which has been from the beginning. Christ will force a rebellious world to submit to God's plan for the Temple Mount and Jerusalem.

Clearly, in the prophetic Messianic texts, and even today we see that there has been a particular dispute over the Temple Mount, causing a deep altercation over this elevated spot in Jerusalem. The quarreling and bickering seems to be a stigma that involves an argument over who is the rightful owner and who is the king worthy enough to sit on the throne there. In November of 1947, when the UN was partitioning Palestine, and they came to the subject of who should own and control

Jerusalem and the Temple Mount, they could not decide who it belonged to. They finally decided that it would belong to no one and called it *Coeptis Septrum*, meaning a *body apart*. It would be no-man's land. All the world would be one and Jerusalem separate. Since that day no one has owned Jerusalem.

The real reason behind this age-old controversy is not always evident. Much of the debate and rivalry has taken place beyond the reach of carnal minds, and in the esoteric world of Satan and God. The lie that gives reason for the controversy is an effort to usurp the rightful ownership from God, Israel, and Jesus, heir to the throne.

I am persuaded that Satan clearly understood what God said to Eve when He gave her the sketch outline of her future and Satan's seed (Genesis 3:15). Although, neither Eve nor the snake understood the details or time frame, they both knew that what was said had set a rivalry between a coming Redeemer from the seed of woman and a counter rival from Satan's offspring. According to Isaiah fourteen, Satan's first desire is to take over the throne of God and therefore, the throne of Jesus Christ, which has been promised to Him from eons of ages past. God's choice of location for the throne of Christ is Mount Moriah in Jerusalem. Lucifer wants Christ thrown out and wants to set himself on that throne, which he has tried to do as part of the back-drop of Christ's appearance on Zion. Each of the seven heads of the Beast in Revelation thirteen represent one of those Empires which have tried to destroy the Jews and set one of their own on a worldwide throne under Satan's direction, and the eighth will be in existence at the time of Christ's appearing (Revelation 17:11). If Satan is allowed to sit unchallenged on a throne in the Temple Mount, he would defeat God in His purpose. It is Satan who has set the world against Israel and Zion.

As Satan is the *god of this world* and therefore controls the actions and attitudes of the nations, He has caused great strife over the Temple Mount from the beginning of its history. He has hindered everything God and His chosen people have attempted to do on the Temple Mount, in Jerusalem, and around the world in every generation. He has polluted and destroyed two temples built by the Jews, and a third one which he is destined to pollute with his abomination of desolation (Matthew 24:15). Satan threatened genocide for the Jews six times through the empires of the Gentiles and a seventh time is in the offing, near or immediate future. It is Satan, working through anti-God, anti-Christ nations such as Iraq (Babylon), Iran, Syria, Jordan, and Egypt who want the extermination of the Jews and possession of the Temple Mount through the termination of the state of Israel.

An age-old contention has seethed over the mountains of Moriah since man's earliest involvement there and is a major dispute still today. It is even now an incentive to enrage the nations and for the world of diplomats today, it defies an explanation. Only a correct reading of the Revelation of Jesus Christ and its key in all of the Messianic prophecies, can we begin to explain the *cause of Zion* today.

ARMAGEDDON AND THE CONTROVERSY OF ZION

It is over Zion, the raging nations of the end time will dare enter war with God and His Son (Psalms 2:6). In this passage we are forewarned that the nations of the world will shake their fists at the coming Christ, declaring that they will not have Him rule over them. They will *"take counsel together, against the Lord and against His Anointed, saying, let us break Their bonds in pieces and cast away their cords from us"* (Psalm 2:2). These texts clearly show a *World Order of Nations* in the last days, shaking their fists in the face of God and Christ in defiance over Zion. Christ and God will get fed up with this Controversy of Zion soon, as the events in Revelation Fourteen show.

These texts are prophecies of this event in Revelation fourteen. This is the day when Christ appears to the face of the wicked one sitting on His throne in the temple, the same temple where the final war is set (2 Thessalonians 2:4). The drums of Armageddon begin to beat there. When Christ arrives suddenly, the World Order will send its armies like NATO to try to preserve the Antichrist, even in the face of the returned Christ. However, Christ will prevail and the Antichrist with his beastly order will be sent back to their original headquarters, which I propose will be in Babylon or Iraq, because God is setting the stage for the fulfillment of Psalms 2:6, *"Yet I have set My King upon My holy hill of Zion."*

This first confrontation of Christ and the Antichrist will be the opening volley that leads to the Battle of Armageddon. In the leadership of a very demonic man filled with the rebellion of Satan against God and His Son, the world order will muster the armies of the nations to openly confront the coming of Christ.

The Battle of Armageddon has been grossly misunderstood by those who contemplate it with a carnal mind. It is not the end of the world; it is not some cataclysmic disaster that destroys the whole world and all mankind; and it is not even a war between nations. It is a select army of all nations under the demonic Satanic leadership of the Antichrist, in open defiance against Christ when He returns with His Saints. Under the leadership of a very demonic and devil-possessed man, filled with the rebellion of Satan against God and His Son, who will muster the armies of the nations to openly confront the coming of Christ (Zechariah 14; Joel 3).

It will not be a conventional war nor an atomic war, but a *star wars* confrontation between the cosmic powers of Heaven and Hell. Christ will destroy Antichrist with the words of His mouth and the brightness of His coming (2 Thessalonians 2:8). This is not conventional warfare.

I believe the cause of Zion ends with Christ's coming to Zion with the 144,000 Jews and the ensuing three and one half years to Armageddon. I believe the Controversy of Zion ends at Christ's coming to Zion with the 144,000 Jews and the final assault on Satan and His cohorts at Armageddon, which will end the conflict. As we have shown, this *cause of Zion* is one of the great enigmatic and cryptic themes of Old Testament prophecy, and warrants a far more detailed study than we can give in this writing. However, I will give a brief resume' of the subject.

OUR CURRENT WORLD EVENTS ARE FULL OF THE CONTROVERSY OF ZION

This is the final solution to Jerusalem and the Hills of Moriah. There are thirty Psalms which deal with Zion, (or Sion) and all illuminate the destiny of Zion as the place of God's throne which He has promised to His Son in the stead of David. This is why it is in such controversy today. It is evident that our world is shaping up just as prophecy foretells. The end-time battles in the Middle East all take place in Israel. These battles include: Gog and Magog, Jehoshaphat, and the battle for Jerusalem and Armageddon. The final battle will be in the Holy Land, and it will bring those armies of the whole world who have given themselves to satanic influence and to the kingdom of the Antichrist, to fight against Jerusalem and the Temple Mount.

Today, Jerusalem is a *"cup of trembling"* and *"a very heavy stone for all peoples"* (Isaiah 51:22; Zechariah 12:3). The whole issue is over Mount Zion.

Satan and his crowd of Antichrist cohorts are defying the Jews today, and in doing so, they are defying God and His plans for Christ and Zion. Our current events are full of this controversy. It is the subject of the final solution between the

Palestinians and the State of Israel, especially over the final status of Jerusalem. Will it be what God and Christ plan, or will it be what the UN decides?

The issue will not be settled until this incident recorded in Revelation 14—when Christ in His return, comes against the Antichrist on Mount Zion. Then the prophecy in Psalms 126:1 will be fulfilled *"when the Lord brought back the captivity of Zion,"* and also Psalms 69:35, *"for God will save Zion and build the cities of Judah, that they may dwell there and possess it."*

I believe that Islam will accept the Antichrist as their 12th Imam Mahdi until He moves onto the Temple Mount and claims to be God. I know of nothing that would cause the world's biggest Jihad, or Intifada (uprising) in the world or in Islam, than for someone to sit in a holy place of Allah, claiming to be God.

This is the beginning of the end as portrayed for us here in Revelation 14; that Christ our Lord, together with the redeemed of Israel, comes head to head with Satan incarnate in the Antichrist. The Antichrist will retreat to other places where he musters his troops and meets Christ for the final time at Armageddon. This great campaign is preceded by a great time of praise involving Heaven's redeemed Gentile Church and Earth's redeemed Jews.

Christ's coming to Mt. Zion will make a great impact on the Jewish leadership that dwells on Mount Zion. In chapter 15, we see Christ's plans to totally end this war between Satan and Himself that has affected the Jews and the Church. The two great redeeming forces in this world will be the Jews and the Church, standing together against this ungodly resistance to God's plan for Zion and total redemption of His people, Christ's Bride and the Earth itself.

EDOM AND THE REMNANT TO BE SAVED

I have always been intrigued with the many mentions of

THE REAL REDEEMER COMES TO ZION

a *remnant* in the prophetic Messianic texts, and how most of the time a remnant was part of the last days. Adding to that connection, a careful study of Messianic texts together with the history of the Jews will reveal that there has always been a rather secret and enigmatic side of Israel that was never outwardly apparent, and yet existed as a *remnant* alongside mainline Israel. I will not elaborate on this for it is a study all of its own, but I will mention it enough to tie it in with our subject.

Especially since the first temple was destroyed and the house or kingdom of David began to ebb away in public consciousness, there was a very small group of the family of David who were enamored with the promises of a worldwide eternal kingdom upon his throne. These began to take on special oaths and vows, continued to keep themselves pure by the law, and were especially alert to any sign of prophecy being fulfilled. They became rather tight societies and seldom made themselves public as to their vows and beliefs.

When the captivity of Babylon came, many of them were carried into Babylon. They lived in this foreign country as quiet, rather secret groups, believing that the time would come after 70 years, as the prophet Jeremiah had said, that they would return to Israel, build the temple again, and the Messiah would come. By the Messianic prophecies they knew that he would be born of a virgin lady of Israel, or the House of David, so they kept their lives pure to be worthy by special consecration as those who would be the heritage of the Lord and King. They were known as the Nertzer, or the Nertzerenes (in Greek, the Nazarenes). The Nertzer was the *branch*; that is, the branch of the House of David that would bring forth the Messiah; they were called the *Remnant* and believed themselves to be the remnant spoken of so often in prophecy. I also believe that these were known as the remnant in prophetic *Messianic* texts.

THE PROPHETIC REMNANT

There is little doubt that in the last days there will be a remnant saved. It is also clear that they will flee from Judaea and Samaria, or the West Bank to the wilderness, to go *"into the wilderness to her place"* (Revelation 12:14). The time is made clear by Jesus in Matthew 24:14. It will be during the time spoken of by Daniel the prophet. It will take place midway in the seven-year Tribulation when the *abomination of desolation* is set up in the holy place of the Temple Mount in Jerusalem. That is when the Antichrist sets up his palace and throne on the Temple Mount, and claims to be God (2 Thessalonians 2:4).

At that time, the Antichrist will set out to destroy the settlers of the West Bank and they will flee to the wilderness into her place, there to be protected and nourished by God for 3½ years. The beast, or the world armies under the influence of the Dragon, will pursue them. However, an earthquake will swallow them, just like happened to Korah and his rebellious crowd (Numbers 16:31-33). These who *"keep the commandments of God,"* had been converted and discipled in Jesus, and had *"the testimony of Jesus Christ"* were called the remnant (Revelation 12:13-17).

One of the most certain facts of the prophecy, and yet an enigma towards many, is that they will be hidden in the wilderness of Edom. The place is said to be Petra, but Petra is only one of three famous cities in that area; another is Bozrah. The prophets make quite a case out of it. In several seemingly unconnected places they say that the place of hiding would be in Edom, and Bozrah is mentioned. It is in the center of the area that includes Teman, Kedesh Barnea, the Wilderness of Zin, and others.

For years I have struggled as to why the case is so plainly made that it would be in that particular place? I have a conviction after six decades of contemplation in the prophetic texts, that God never does anything casually. He has a reason for every minute part of His revelation. For instance, why is Edom in the area of Petra and Bozrah called the wilderness? Also, what would be the activity among them down there for nearly 3½ years? I have wondered if during that time many of them will be converted to Christ and will come back to Zion with a testimony.

I have also contemplated what connection they might have to the 144,000 Jews that return with Christ to Mount Zion (Revelation 14). In the nighttime of December 5, 2012, I went to bed with these deep questions on my heart. Half asleep, I asked the Lord to help me understand why they were sent to what seemingly was a special place, *"her place"* in the wilderness (Revelation 12:14). I could not understand why this place in Edom was so special. Suddenly, the Lord impressed me that I should look again at Ezekiel, chapter 20. I got up and went to my desk and looked up the reference.

My study markings were all over the chapter for I had contemplated its meaning many times before. I noticed how I had circled the word *wilderness* nine times in the chapter. I wondered why the Holy Spirit, through the Prophet Ezekiel, emphasized *wilderness* so many times. Suddenly, a connection began to form. As I carefully read the surrounding information to these nine references to the *wilderness*, I discovered that it appeared to be about a place where Israel had especially angered God with their rebellion on their way out of Egypt and on the border of the Promised Land. I thought, "Is God is sending them back to the place of their rebellion, when they were cursed to wander in the wilderness for forty years?" It said He would *"plead [His] case with [them]"* there; and He would *"make [them] pass them under the rod, and … bring [them] into the bond of the covenant"* (Ezekiel 20:36-37). I recognized this term as a standard practice of a shepherd, who in numbering his sheep and accounting for them as they came into the fold, would bring them through the narrow gate, and sit on the side with his rod extended over them, counting as they passed one by one, under the rod.

So it seems that God, in Christ, will number the remnant and place them under protection in the Middle East for that 3½ years. There, just like Jacob returned to Bethel, this remnant of Israel would return to the place of their rebellion and sin, and there be reconciled, redeemed, and discipled in Jesus Christ.

At first, I thought my idea was a bit farfetched and wondered if any other commentator would see the same as me. So I picked up the *Dakes Annotated Reference Bible*, and there under comments on Ezekiel 20:35-38, I found his notes teaching the same thing. I will refer to some of them and see how this prophetic text relates to Revelation, chapter twelve.

Dake tells us that this text refers to the woman, or remnant who escapes the beast by going to a place prepared for her. Here, she is protected for 3½ years from the dragon and the beast. Some have tried to make this the Church, but nowhere is the Church ever told to flee. However, Israel, or the remnant of Israel, is spoken of many times as fleeing into the wilderness of Edom and speaks often of a remnant fleeing to a place in Edom prepared for them (Ezekiel 33-44; Isaiah 16:1-5, 42:11-13; Hosea 2:14-23; Revelation 12:6, 13-16; Matthew 24:16).

Three times the text repeats in Ezekiel 20, what is stated over 85 times in Ezekiel: *"that you may know that I am the Lord your God."* Why is there a question to the Jews that He is Jehovah? Is it possible that this is when they discover that Jesus is Jehovah? Verse 44 says that He will *deal*, or reason with them. They will know that He is Jehovah when He begins to reason with them, i.e. work with them, show them, deal with them, execute His work in them, perform and prepare them and accomplish, keep and finish His Word to them.

He will prepare them to serve Him in His Holy Mount (20:40); He will plead with them *"face to face"* as He pleaded with them when they came out of Egypt, indicating that it was in this same place (20:35-36); (Note that it will be a face to face personal encounter) He will cause them to be accounted for by passing them *"under the rod"* (20:37); He will purge away their sin (v. 38); He will "bring them into the bond of covenant (20:37); and when they return to Israel and the temple Mount, no rebel will be among them (20:38). This strongly indicates that Jesus Christ will work among them to bring them into full relationship with Himself and prepare them to serve Him in the Temple Mount in Jerusalem.

Most commentators see Ezekiel 20:35-40 as a later day event which is presage of the children of Israel coming out of Egypt and the days that Moses pleaded with them; yet, they rebelled in this very spot in the wilderness. God is bringing them back from the Diaspora in the midst of great violence to again plead with them and deal with their rebellion. Here, according to some commentators (Dake and Kiel/Delitzsch), He will reveal Himself to them as the Messiah, the suffering Savior of Isaiah 53, and the Lamb of God.

"HER PLACE" IN THE WILDERNESS

We tie all of this into the Revelation. It was *"her place,"* a special place prepared for them; it would be in the place—Kadesh Barnea where they first rebelled against Him under Moses, and sentenced to 40 years of wandering in the wilderness. A study of this Wilderness of Zin, of Teman, Bozrah, and Petra (all from which Christ would come to Zion) shows all to be in less than a 30-mile radius of Kedesh Barnea. In over 100 texts, this same wilderness is featured as a place of many activities in the Old Testament era and simply called *the wilderness* as if readily understood which one is being spoken of. This wilderness is less than a ten days' journey from Paran of Mount Sinai.

When Israel under Moses came to Kadesh near the famous spring *Bered,* the border of Canaan, the place where Hagar saw the angel and where Abraham and Isaac dwelt, they camped there and sat the tabernacle down. The original name was *Rithmah,* but later changed to *Kadesh* (holy, or sanctuary) in order for the Bible record to indicate the place where the Tabernacle was placed for most of the forty-year wandering in the dessert. From here, one rebellious act after another are recorded as committed by the people of Israel and their leadership; *Bered,* later called the *"fountain of judgment,"* or *Meribah*, the *place of strife* because of the rebellion committed there. It was well known as the place where Israel strove with Moses and God, and the place where Israel was judged.

This is also the same place where ten spies were sent out and upon returning, turned Israel's heart from entering the promise land. It is the place of murmuring against Moses; the place where Moses lost his temper and struck the rock, and told by God because of it, he would not enter the promise land with the people; and it is the place of Korah's rebellion and those who followed him.

It becomes very clear to me that there is a definite tie between the one-hundred references to wilderness in Moses' day and the wilderness spoken of by the prophets where the remnant of Israel will flee according to Revelation, chapter twelve and Ezekiel, chapter twenty. (See appendix for more on this topic.)

In this famous wilderness place noted for rejection and rebellion, God will plead with them, prepare them, work with them, and put them under *"the bond of covenant"* (Ezekiel 20:37). Commenting on *"the bond of Covenant,"* Kiel and Delitzsch translates this new covenant as saying, "I will bind you to me and myself to you in a new covenant." They go on to say it will be a bond of fetters; true, but these fetters will be a bond of love.

He may even send the two witnesses to disciple them. Then, He will put them under the rod and count out 144,000 of them to accompany Him in His campaign to the Temple Mount to dislodge the Antichrist and set up His Kingdom. They may be the founding fathers of the Kingdom of David under Christ. From warfare with the Antichrist armies He will come from Edom, in the area of Petra and Bozrah, with blood stained garments where He has trodden down the winepress (Isaiah 63:1, 3; Revelation 14:19). It will be *"in the day of [His] vengeance"* and in the year of His redemption of His people (Isaiah 63:4).

I believe He will come out of Edom with the 144,000 Jewish converts to set up His Kingdom on the Throne of David. It is very likely that King David of old will be resurrected, and accompany Him as well (Jeremiah 30:9).

Let us proceed to chapter 15 where immediately upon Christ's ascension to Zion, we see preparations being made in Heaven for Armageddon and the Lord's final battle with the beast and his Antichrist.

CHAPTER 15

THE LAST PLAGUES AND JUSTICE EXECUTED

SIGNS IN HEAVEN

This is a most marvelous and exciting chapter. Even though it carries the presage of coming tragedy for those who have been unwise enough to join the beast's kingdom, it gives us insight into Heaven, hope in Christ for a better world, and salvation for those who will hear the gospel, even during the Tribulation.

We find in chapter 15 another one of those totally positive chapters. There is no wrath or judgment in the whole chapter. The wrath of God is mentioned in verse one, but only in passing as 7 angels out of the temple in Heaven prepare to deliver the 7 vials of plagues upon the Antichrist's kingdom. These plagues will generally only affect that part of the world, namely the Middle East, where the Antichrist's kingdom is centered (Revelation 16:10, probably Syria, Iraq and Iran etc.).

The scenes in this chapter will only be understood by the redeemed, and those who perceive the esoteric world, for they all take place in Heaven. The opening scenes happen around the same throne room we saw in chapters four and five. The first reason for rejoicing is our insight into Heaven where we see the redeemed saints out of the Tribulation, at the throne. This chapter opens at the throne in Heaven and ends with the tabernacle in Heaven. What is the relationship between the throne of judgment and the open tabernacle of testimony in Heaven? This will be very important in understanding the chapter.

Far above all of the strife on Earth, above the Beast and beyond the plagues that were called down by the two witnesses of chapter 11; above the preparation to pour out the vials of the wrath of God which comes out of the temple in Heaven, there is a land not affected by any of this. That is where we see the Church of the Redeemed during all of this time. They are with Christ around the throne and in the temple in Heaven. As these events of wrath unfold, we will be glad we overcame the world and placed our trust in Christ.

We are still in an interlude between the seventh trumpet and the first vial. The curtain of the pageant of divine judgment is still down, and we are seeing preparation for the final judgment behind the scenes. This whole chapter lets us see into the heart of Heaven just before wrath is released upon the Antichrist and his kingdom. Beloved, we must cast our sentiments with the kingdom of Christ and not overburden ourselves with the fate of the ungodly and rebellious world, especially that part of the world that forsakes God's wisdom and God's way, and rebels against Christ. While the world is unrepentant and rebellious, we have come out of the world and are found among the redeemed, those whose hope is for a far better world to come with the kingdom of Christ.

Before Christ leads us through scenes of the horrors of God's wrath upon a rebellious world portrayed in chapter 16, He first wants us to turn our attention toward Heaven, for we must never forget that Heaven is always in the background of earthly activity and Christ is always the master of the situation. Christ will never allow the devil to have complete control. This will not be the end of the world, or the end to the human race, because God will shorten the time (Matthew

24:23). And, there will never be an Antichrist that is all powerful, and beyond Christ's control.

SCENES IN HEAVEN AND THE TEMPLE OPENED

In verse one; a great and marvelous sign is working in Heaven while the seven angels are making preparation for God's final onslaught against Satan's wayward kingdom. This preparation is evidently awesome, even to the inhabitants of Heaven. We the Church are awestricken because we have preached and taught about these events all during our ministry on Earth. Here we see those very events in preparation. We have tried to warn a wayward world, but seemingly to no avail. However, Christ wants us to catch the celebration that is going on in Heaven at that time.

"Then I saw another sign in Heaven" (Revelation 15:1). *"Another"* must refer back to a prior sign that we saw in Heaven in chapter twelve. The first was a wonder woman representing Israel, and the second great sign was a wicked red dragon ready to devour Christ at His birth. However, this great sign in Heaven in verse one is said to be not only great, but marvelous. This *"another"* ties us back to chapter twelve and shows again the *meanwhiles* in the text.

We marvel at the longsuffering and patience of God and our Lord Jesus Christ, which have put off this judgment for so long; we marvel that the judgment is initiated in the temple in Heaven; we marvel that the first scene we see, is the seven angels preparing to unleash the plagues on the Antichrist's kingdom on Earth, which were called for by the two witnesses at Jerusalem (Revelation 11:6); we marvel at the great victory celebration that is taking place at the throne of God in Heaven, as the martyrs in chapter twelve claim the victory. They are the ones who were harvested in the first harvest of chapter fourteen, and the ones who:

"... they overcame Him (the Beast) by the blood of the Lamb and by the word of their testimony, and they did not love their lives unto death." (12:11)

They were the final Jewish martyrs of a long history of martyrs. Take note that they are not victims, but overcomers washed in the blood of the Lamb who was martyred for their testimony. Like Paul and the apostles, all of the martyrs throughout history in both Old and New Testaments, and also the Church since Christ's death and resurrection, have loved not their lives unto death. One of those rejoicing martyrs whose blood has been crying out for retribution, is the Lord—*"the Lamb as though it had been slain"* (5:6). Oh yes, Christ our Lord feels comfortable among the martyrs who rejoice. He overcame by His own blood and testimony, and loved not His own life unto death.

Instead of mourning with the world, Christ turns our attention Heaven-ward, and we rejoice with Christ and the saints in Heaven.

We are still in the interval between when the last trumpet prepared to sound, and when it was decreed and declared that the *"mystery of God would be finished"* (10:7). We marvel that the final end of the Great Tribulation will bring such marvelous accomplishments. This finishing of God's mystery refers back to the six things to be accomplished by the Tribulation as was given to Daniel by Gabriel (Daniel 9:24). We enumerate them again:

1. To finish the transgression (of Satan and His angels)

2. To make an end of sin

3. To make reconciliation for iniquity

4. To bring in everlasting righteousness

5. To seal up the vision and prophecy

6. To anoint the most Holy

These are the things which are the purpose of the Tribulation and those things which will finish the mystery of God. The seventh trumpet actually sounds in 11:15 when the announcement is made from Heaven:

"The Kingdoms of this world have become the Kingdoms of our Lord and of His Christ, and He shall reign forever and ever!"

This is the final end of the mystery of God, when at the end of the Tribulation and the Battle of Armageddon, finishes Satan's transgression and puts His Son on the throne of David in Zion (14:1). It is then that He cries with a loud voice out of the temple and declares, *"It is done"* (16:17)!

After the Tribulation and Armageddon, the seventh trumpet is finished and another declaration is made from the temple in Heaven declaring, *"It is done!"* Armageddon had finished God's plans and mystery, by putting down Satan and the rebellious unrepentant world of nations.

For the world, it is the third *woe* of man, and the declaration that the kingdoms of the world are become the kingdom of the Lord, excites the wrath of the nations (11:14, 18). With the Church and the temple in Heaven, it is a great victory, and another great praise service breaks out among the Church and the redeemed Jews out of the Tribulation, around the throne in Heaven. This praise time may be another mention of the same praise time found in verses 11:16-17. We need to go back to chapters 11-14 to pick up the background of chapter 15.

The first four verses of chapter 15 are a refreshing breath of air after having to view details about the beast, and the Antichrist, and their political agenda for a One World Order which the Antichrist will abscond from the world's efforts to bring about peace. The problem with the world government's efforts is that they want to create a prototype of Christ and His promised Millennial kingdom without the real Christ or the real God. They do not understand that when they leave out Christ and God, they eliminate the only power that can withstand the old dragon and Satan. By denying God's power, they open themselves up to Satan's control, who takes them *"captive ... to do his will"* (2 Timothy 2:26). Therefore, in the crisis of the first half of the Tribulation, the World Order people become desperate for strong leadership and are easily persuaded to turn power over to a miracle-working genius believing him to be the promised coming Christ.

They could not understand with their natural minds, that when they give power to a demonic person, they open the door to a flood of demons, and soon all the world is worshipping the beast or his version of a One World Order (Revelation 9). Then, aliening with him inadvertently, *"they worshiped the dragon"* (Revelation 13:4). We remind ourselves here of the statement Henry Spaak, Secretary General of NATO, made to the International Community of Nations (UN) requesting that they "send a man of sufficient stature to be able to hold the world together and get us out of the morass we are in." He then said, "Send us such a man and whether he be God or Devil, we will receive him."

I am also bound to repeat the statement of the President of Bosnia what he said to Jim Leherer on his TV program. Jim asked him to what he attributed all of the terrible atrocities going on in Bosnia and He simply stated a profound insight:

"There are tides in the affairs of men which unleash demons."

Therefore, welcome to the Antichrist with world support. When the world opens up the tides of devil worship, it will unleash demons that will cause a greater atrocity than Bosnia saw during the recent war in Yugoslavia.

Chapter thirteen presages this very scenario and chapter

nine shows us what a demon-infested world will be like. Chapter 14 shows us God's answer and solution to the matter of Christ coming to Mount Zion. The great *I Am*, the *Alpha and Omega*, the *Beginning and the End*, whose name is *Wonderful, Counselor, Mighty God* and *Prince of Peace;* and yes, our *Lord* and *Savior Jesus Christ* is sent to Mount Zion in Jerusalem to begin His campaign to unseat the Antichrist's control, by first unseating him from his throne on the Temple Mount.

ANOTHER POWERFUL PRAISE SERVICE IN HEAVEN

Chapter fifteen shows us about the great victory celebration in Heaven just before the final onslaught against the beast and the dragon, Satan. While the world is getting itself deeper into an Antichrist demonic trauma, Heaven is on a different agenda. The case for destroying the devil's work through the beast and his One World Order is growing ever stronger as more martyrs come to Heaven with their cry of vengeance upon their blood (Revelation 6:9-11). The justice they cry for will come in the next chapter when the 7 vials of wrath are poured out.

Before the wrath of God is poured out on an ungodly and rebellious world, Christ wants us to rejoice with Him over another group of the redeemed that recently comes into Heaven. They are a group who were to be added to the martyred souls under the altar in chapter six. These souls were crying for vengeance upon their blood, and were told that they must rest awhile and wait for others who would be martyred in the Tribulation. Whether by Rapture or more than likely Martyrdom, we do not know, but they are in Heaven with the Church. Their presence has completed the sacrifice to be made for our faith. Having been victorious by *"the blood of the Lamb, and by the word of their testimony, they loved not their lives unto death"* (Revelation 12:11). They create no small stir among the company around the throne, because an immediate anthem of praise welcomes them to Heaven. The angels also rejoice at new souls added to Heaven's number.

These recently redeemed people will probably include recently converted Jews to whom Christ has revealed Himself, and which have been saved during the Tribulation. It would not be any of the 144,000 Jews, for they are still on Earth and with Christ on Mount Zion. Paul saw this day and commented upon it in Romans 11:12:

> *"..think how much greater a blessing the world will share later on when the Jews, too, come to Christ"* (*Living Bible*).

It is said of this multitude of Martyrs that they received victory over the beast, his image, his mark, and the number of his name (Revelation 15: 2).

Oh what a day it will be to the Jews when this old devil who has persecuted and harassed them all of their history by deceit of the nations, will no more be able to lie to them about the Jewish people, and about Israel:

> *"Satan, who deceives the whole world [about the Jews]* (12:9) and *"deceives those who dwell on the whole earth,"* (13:1) will now *"deceive the nations no more"* (20:3).

Christ rejoices over every Gentile convert in Church history, but I assure you, He is especially joyous to see His own people come to the knowledge of Himself. Therefore, this praise service must rise to even a grandiose crescendo. Remember, Christ Himself was a Martyr, a Lamb that had been slain.

Here is another of those continuous prayer and praise services that seem to be going on all the time among the saints and the inhabitants of Heaven. I am deeply impressed and thrilled at how many of these are reported throughout the Book of Revelation, as recorded in chapters 4, 5, 7, and 11. Also, there will be another great praise service which will take place after the final victory over Babylon, and after the victory over the whole kingdom of Satan and the dragon. It is recorded for us in Revelation 19:1-4.

Those who do not love the Lord and are not attracted to praise and worship miss the whole impact and intent of these praise services as they read the Revelation of Jesus Christ. There are also many Christians who do not practice praise and are not accustomed to this kind of praise service, who would also be very uncomfortable in such an atmosphere of praise. That is why they only see the *scary* parts of the book of Revelation. However, those of us who spend our lives in praise and worship to God, find services like this very comforting. We do not attend these services because it a religious thing to do, but because we love Christ. I think we can safely make the assumption that as in other praise services reported throughout Revelation, the Lord Jesus Christ was present when these new converts are welcomed into Heaven. He is still leading and feeding His beloved redeemed:

> *"For the Lamb, who is in the midst of the throne will shepherd them and lead them to living fountains of water"* (7:17).

THEY SING THE OLD AND THE NEW SONGS

It seems each group that gets *saved* and comes into the presence of Christ, has a new song; for example, the 144,000 on Mount Zion singing in the presence of Christ. This prayer meeting in Heaven is probably still on-going from the visitation of Christ to Mount Zion. Remember, these are singing on the Sea of Glass which is the floor of the great throne room of justice, the very same location as the one upon which the Church and heavenly hosts were singing in chapters 4 and 5.

Just as we write new songs at each new adventure in the Church today, they also have written some new songs which commemorate this great event of that time. However, they also sing some very old songs. For instance, they sing the *Song of Moses and of the Lamb*. The *Song of Moses* was one of triumph over Egypt and Pharaoh, and is especially apropos here for the plagues that will come on the Antichrist and his associates. These plagues will resemble the plagues that came upon Egypt for the purpose of freeing God's people from the bondage of Egypt (Exodus 15). Likewise, the *songs of the Lamb* celebrate His triumph over the kingdoms of this world and of a victory soon to be won over Satan and all of the enemies of God and man. Paul said that at this time, that Christ:

"... Having nailed it to the cross ... disarmed principalities and powers, [making] a public spectacle of them, triumphing over them in it" (Colossians 2:14-15).

This triumphal throng made up of the Old Testament saints—the Jews—the Church of the Redeemed—and all the converts and martyrs of the Tribulation, point out in song how great and marvelous the Lord God almighty really is; and how just is the judgment He is about to administer. Like the 100+ songs written during the revivals of the early 1900's, these songs spoke of victory and a victorious Rapture. He is called the *"King of the Saints,"* a new song (Revelation 15:3). Christ has emerged out of obscurity to show up the false messiah; these new songs epitomize the grandeur of the real Messiah: *"Just and true are Your ways, O King of Saints! Who shall not fear You, O Lord, and glorify Your name? For You alone are holy. For all nations shall come and worship before You, for Your judgments have been manifested"* (15:3-4). We note that these are not in any way, frustrated or fearful of the Antichrist and the coming Armageddon. Their only fear, or respect now, is toward the Lord in their midst.

These new songs which are sung by the new arrivals in Heaven are songs that also anticipate the Second Coming of Jesus Christ. They speak of a time after Armageddon when all nations shall come and worship before Him (Isaiah 2:2-4; Micah 4:1-4; Zechariah 14:16-21). Their songs reach beyond Armageddon and foresee the great victory that Christ will soon win.

Coming out of the throne room in Heaven, these songs make two declarations. They declare Christ's coming in victory over the nations; and they declare His soon-to-come assumption of the throne of David as King of kings and Lord of lords. It is after this great time of praise that Christ turns our attention from the throne room to the temple of the tabernacle of the testimony in Heaven.

SEA OF GLASS MINGLED WITH FIRE (v. 2)

Those obtaining victory over the beast, are found on the same Sea of Glass witnessed in the fourth chapter, except the glass is now mingled with fire. That fire is said to be mingled with blood when it is cast to the earth (Revelation 8:7). I believe the best explanation of fire on the floor of the throne room comes from a comment made in the *Dake's Annotated Bible*. It tells us that the fire is probably something like the Aurora Borealis—Northern Lights, a reflection of the sun off of the ice field of the North. Therefore, light is reflected from the great floor of the Heavenly Throne which is made of transparent glass. It is probably the prism of light reflecting from the *"fiery stones"* which have been taken from Satan, (Ezekiel 28:14) and given to the *"saints in the light,"* and will be displayed in the New Jerusalem (Ezekiel 28:14; Colossians 1:12). Also, it may be a reflection from the glorified Son of God in the midst of His beloved Redeemed. However, I believe it could also be something else.

THE RAINBOW IS STILL SPEAKING PEACE

The appearance of fire on the glass floor may come from prismatic colors produced by the glory of God proceeding from the center of the throne and producing a rainbow above and around the throne of God. Oh yes, the rainbow is still there, although it is not mentioned here. It is and always will be, a decorative part of the throne of Christ and will still represent God's grace and peace.

The same Shekinah glory that has always accompanied God and Christ, as on the Mount of Transfiguration, is coming out of the center of the throne. It is preceded by light which breaks into the prism of colors and forms a glorious rainbow. With no earthly hindrance, the rainbow would be a full circle around and about the throne. This prismatic reflection upon the glass floor would then be a reflection of the mirror of the glory of God. It is emanating from the glory which forms the aura of light which Christ dwells, lighting the whole area and causing this glittering effect on the Sea of Glass (Revelation 21:23). The light is said to be so glorious that no man can approach it.

TEMPLE AND TABERNACLE OF TESTIMONY IS WIDE OPEN

Again, the Old Testament is brought to our attention. Without the understanding of the entire Old Testament motif of the tabernacle, we are lost in understanding this chapter. This again is suggesting more of the cryptic enigma of the Messianic prophecies fulfilled in Revelation. Only those

THE LAST PLAGUES AND JUSTICE EXECUTED 513

dedicated to *keep* this book will understand. In verse five we are introduced to further mysteries of the Old Tabernacle in the wilderness, which was made after its pattern in Heaven. We are privileged now to actually see that pattern in Heaven, from which the old tabernacle was taken. When God in the post-flood era, set out to establish a covenant relationship with man and begin the process of redemption through the nation of Israel, He set up a meeting place where He could put His name.

THE MERCY SEAT IN HEAVEN

A special place in the tabernacle had to be protected from the pollution of the world; a sanctuary set aside and closed in from man, yet available to an ordained high priest who would atone for sin and cover judgment with the sprinkling of the blood of a sacrificial Lamb. This inner-sanctuary contained an *ark* to shelter the symbols of His right, and to judge the sins of mankind. Covering the ark of judgment however, was a mercy seat upon which the blood was sprinkled after Christ ascended to God, symbolizing His coming sacrifice for the sins of the world (Hebrews 9:14 and 24). All of this is set in cryptic symbolism. It was to be completely separated from carnal man, and placed in a mystery understood only by those who love and respect God and His Son, Jesus Christ.

We are reminded in this text, and we are privileged to see it in Heaven—the temple, or whole sanctuary which contains the holiest of all, the Holy of Holies. The ark of the testimony of God can also be found inside the temple. Placed inside of that, are the two tablets of law written by the finger of God, and testifying of the reality of the unseen God and the surety of His promise and covenant.

A testimony is an attestation, a sworn statement under oath, and a declaration and assertion of truth. This Book of the Revelation of Jesus Christ is the testimony of Jesus

Christ, therefore, it is an attestation sworn under oath, which declares and asserts Christ's eternal truth (Revelation 1:2, 9, 11:10, 19:10). We see here in the tabernacle, an attestation of Christ's fulfillment of the old covenant which has been preserved for us in our knowledge of the Holy of Holies and the ark of the testimony of God. It again asserts and declares the truth of what we are reading in these texts. This final consummation and final conclusion of the controversy of Zion is clearly stated in a decree from God Himself; a testimony of His faithfulness to His promise. He will yet put His king on the throne in Zion and Jerusalem (Psalms 2:6). This will be the proof of His attestation. Although the ark is not mentioned here, we can assume its presence from earlier reference. When we saw this temple in Heaven opened once before, the ark was there at that time (Revelation 11:19).

LOCATION OF THE ARK OF THE COVENANT

There has been an ongoing saga as to the location of the ark at this time. We note that in the long detailed list of the temple instruments carried into Babylon as recorded in Jeremiah 52:17-23, the ark is not mentioned. Tradition suggests that Jeremiah, along with the priests, may have hidden it before the invasion and destruction by the troops of Babylon, in 586 B.C.

Several places for hiding the ark have been suggested. I will not comment further on this subject although I have some strong evidence as given me personally by the Chief Sephardic Rabbi and also archeologist, Vendal Jones years ago. I have a picture of what is said to be the ark, which I am not privileged to show. I do not know where the ark is kept today for sure, but I do know that in the post-Rapture time and during the Tribulation, it will be in Heaven, for we are plainly told so.

It is of particular interest at this point, that the Holy of

Holies and the Ark are not hidden behind a veil any longer. We recall that at Christ's death on the cross, the great veil in the temple was *"torn in two from top to bottom"* (Matthew 27:51). The veil was meant to hide the ark from being seen by anyone except the high priest, and then only once a year. The symbolism of the open temple and this torn veil is meant to show that the way of God through Christ is wide open now, and anyone can witness God's eternal testimony.

Here we are excited to see that there is no longer a veil between the sanctuary and the testimony of God, for the temple was thrown wide open, and there before all people, was the tabernacle of the testimony of God (Revelation 15:5). It shouts at us from Heaven that we are redeemed by the blood of the Lamb and have a covering for sin which covers not only our sin, but also shields us from God's judgments. We need not fear or be terrorized by the coming judgments of God's wrath.

The implication is plain. Finally, after eons of time, the final testimony of God is about to be made manifest. What God affirmed when the tabernacle was built in the wilderness is to be fulfilled in the next short time.

SEVEN ANGELS OR MESSENGERS OUT OF THE HOLY OF HOLIES IN HEAVEN

We must not overlook the significance of the Mercy Seat and its symbolism both in the past and here in chapter 15. It is important to note that these angels came from the Mercy Seat and from the presence of Christ, our Intercessor.

THESE "ANGELS" WERE MEN, SOME OF THE SAINTS

It is fascinating that the seven angels who were given the seven vials of wrath, came from the place of the Mercy

Seat which covered the ark of the testimony in the heavenly temple. They did not come from the throne of justice, but from the temple. Verse six seems to support the fact that they were men; their appearance recalls the garments of the saints, clothed in pure white and their breasts gird about with gold, seems to suggest men.

They are coming from the throne of mercy again to demonstrate that even in the time of God's intense wrath upon the rebellious world, mercy is still mingled with wrath:

> *"Renew [your work] in our day, in our time make them known; and in wrath remember mercy"* (Habakkuk 3:2, *NIV*).

The new songs epitome the grandeur of the real Messiah and His mercy, even in the time of His wrath.

The *"golden bands"* girding the breast described in Revelation 15, is reflective of our Lord (15:6). It was the saints who were clothed in white linen (Revelation 3:5, 18, 4:4, 7:9, and 19:8). One of the saints was appointed to show John the mystery of the great harlot and the beast that carried her (17:1). Another was commissioned to show John the city of the New Jerusalem (21:10). When John had seen these things, he fell down on his face to worship the messenger, but was told not to do so, as he was just a man, one of the prophets, a fellow servant, and one of the brethren (Revelation 19:10, 22:8-9).

Why were these vials of judgment given to the saints to administer? I believe it was because we have been commissioned with Christ, to judge the world (Revelation 20:4). He told us that we would work with Him in this judgment. The Apostle Paul said:

> *"Do you not know that the saints will judge the world"* (1 Corinthians 6:2)?

And again:

"Do you not know that we shall judge angels" (6:3)?

Why do the vials of judgment come out of the temple, and what is the relationship between the throne in verse 15:1 and the wide open temple in verses 5-8? I believe Christ our Lord wants to signify for us the holiness and righteousness of God's wrath. In chapter 19, when the final judgment is fulfilled in the fall of Mystery Babylon, they praise the Lord saying:

"... true and righteous are His judgments" (19:2).

Isaiah has a very interesting observation about this very time of Judgment:

"When Your judgments are in the earth, the inhabitants of the world will learn righteousness" (Isaiah 26:9).

We must discover that the judgments of God on the earth during the Tribulation period are just and right, and are not just the wrath of an angry God out of control.

It is also worthy to mention, that even though God and Christ have been forced by the willful rebellion of men to commit the wayward world to judgment, He is still the Savior of the world. And although great wrath will be poured out on the Antichrist and His rebellious nations, Christ still sits on the mercy seat above the ark as a covering for the world's sins. Even at this late hour, there is an extension of mercy to those who choose to repent. We will see this call for repentance in chapter 16. It is in keeping with all of the prophetic utterances of God in the whole scheme of redemption, that the judgments should come out of the temple and from the mercy seat. The book of Hebrews declares:

"Therefore, He is also able to save to the uttermost, those who come to God through Him, since He ever lives to make intercession for them" (Hebrews 7:25).

I believe this verse tells us that there will never be an end to His mercy, and that He will forever sit in that position, making intercession for us. We know that part of His ministry in the whole of the Millennium will be to sit in the seat of mercy and administer justice to the host of people in the Millennium. We know that He will be involved with judging the sheep and goat nations, and that mercy will be part of the judgment of the sheep nations in allowing them to enter the Millennium, in spite of weaknesses from the deception of Satan (Matthew 25:32).

Also, He is not willing that any should perish even in the last judgment:

> *"The Lord is not slack concerning His promise ... but is longsuffering toward us, not willing that any should perish but that all should come to repentance. But the day of the Lord will come ..."* (2 Peter 3:9-10).

One of the four living ones, who we have seen before as guardians of the throne of God, is given the privilege of handing out the vials of wrath to the angels.

ANGELS ACTING UNDER THE DIRECT WILL AND AUTHORITY OF CHRIST

Again, it is very significant that these plagues representing the judgment of God do not come from the throne of God, but from the temple of God. I believe that God and Christ are making a very clear point by this strange fact. These judgments are not only legal retributions for crimes rendered, but are spiritual affirmations of a righteous judge who is trying the case because of offenses committed against the character of God. I believe there is a very significant truth in a shell of Godly mystery revealed to us in this chapter. It is the relationship between the throne and the temple.

Paul taught us to observe equally the goodness and the severity of God. To lessen one at the expense of the other is to throw our concept of God out of balance. The throne speaks of the severity of God. It represents God's holy justice. Standing next to the throne of justice in Heaven, is the temple and although it does not lessen the concept of severity, it puts emphasis on the mercy of God and His age-old plan to redeem mankind by the blood sacrifice sprinkled there. Remember, the blood of Christ was presented there and sprinkled on the mercy seat of Heaven. It was Christ's final act in completing the plan of atonement when He actually appeared before God the Father at the Mercy seat of Heaven with His own blood, once and for all (Hebrews 9:12, 9:14). This briefly explains the difference between the throne of judgment and the temple of mercy shown here in this chapter.

The *Ark of the Covenant* represents a holy God who does not condemn men for sin, but has made a contractual agreement. It is an attestation, confirmation, and voucher for the official authenticity of God's covenant. A decree from Heaven has been made concerning the answer to man's sin.

The ark is a witness to the judgment of God, and the reasons for that judgment. Within the Ark is: 1) The *law* which Paul says is actually ordinances against man in that it reveals his sin; 2) The *manna* which reminds them of how they received their daily food when they became critical of God's provisions and asked for *flesh*, or meat; for their complaint, God gave them *flesh* to eat, but many of them died in a curse; and 3) The *Aaron's rod* reminds them of the rebellion of Korah. After the earth swallowed Korah and his associate—Dathan and Abiram, the people continued to murmur. They felt that Moses was being prejudice, and that one of them had as much right as the others to serve in the tabernacle. Moses had each Tribe bring a rod to lie before the Lord in the Tabernacle, saying the rod that would bud by the next day would be God's choice to serve in the Tabernacle. The next morning, Aaron's rod representing the Levites was in full bloom, so Levi was chosen and the sign was meant to stop the murmuring and stop rebellion. Numbers 17:10 records the story:

> "*The Lord said to Moses, bring Aaron's rod back before the Testimony* (Ark), *to be kept as a sign against the rebels, that you may put their murmurings away from Me, lest they die.*"

All of the articles in the Ark were reminders of man's rebellion against God, and were instruments of God's judgment. The Mercy Seat was designed to represent God's forgiveness, overshadowing man's sins and rebellion, as the blood of the Lamb was sprinkled there for a covering.

Ruth Specter, with the *Rock of Israel* suggests that these three articles in the Ark represent God's answer to the sin and rebellion of man, covered by the Lord on the Mercy Seat. The *Law* speaks of Him as the Way, which we fail to keep; the *Manna* speaks of Him as the truth, which we fail to recognize; and the *Rod of Aaron* represents life, which in our rebellion, we fail to appropriate His gift of eternal life. Therefore, all of these condemn man. Without the covering of the Mercy Seat and the blood sprinkled upon it for our sins, the Ark would have been a judgment throne.

I am sure there are those who will criticize this thought and think I am stretching the imagination to see Christ in these vials, but I tell you, since I met Christ and have come to know Him so well and so personally, I believe what I share here is in perfect keeping with who He is and how He acts in judgment. As we have shared before, all of God's judgments and acts of correction in man's affairs always come from the Mercy Seat which was designed to be the place of the meeting of God with man to reconcile his sin. I am fully persuaded that even though Christ is not mentioned here, these angels are direct representatives of Him.

None other would be given power over God's judgment. The Scriptures clearly declare that all power over Satan and his angels was and is given to the Son, Jesus Christ. Ephesians makes it very plain that God has placed all things under Christ, both on Earth and in Heaven, *"not only in this age but also in that which is to come"* (1:21). Jesus said, *"all authority has been given to Me in Heaven and on earth"* (Matthew 28:18). He also said *"I give you the authority to trample on serpents and scorpions, and over all the power of the enemy"* (Luke 10:19). Luke 9:1 declares that Christ gave His disciples *"power and authority over all demons."*

These vials are also the subject of Revelation 16, and are the last vials full of the wrath of God to be poured out on the enemies of God. They are used by Christ who will *"put an end to all rule and all authority and power. For He (Christ) must reign till He has put all enemies under His feet"* (1 Corinthians 15:24, 26).

With these texts before us, it is not hard to see that it is actually at Christ's own bidding and authority that these angels who come out of the temple are acting directly under Christ. His purpose is to fulfill all that the prophets have said, and put down all enemies both in Heaven and on Earth, in order to bring in the Kingdom of God. His purpose is not destructive, but redemptive whenever and wherever it can be. He must destroy the Antichrist and his version of the World Order Kingdom, and Satan or the dragon that has authorized and empowered the beast and the false prophet, to bring bondage on all humanity. Once Christ has put down all power and authority in Heaven and on Earth that resists God's kingdom, *"He delivers the kingdom to God, the Father"* (1 Corinthians 15:24).

It is clear then, that these vials of the seven last plagues of the wrath of God are directly under the supervision of Christ Himself. Remember as we study these texts that it was Christ's mission and purpose to lift the wrath of God off of us if we would come to Him and allow Him to cover our sins. These angels would never have been given one of these vials if their preaching had been heeded. But for those who would not heed, they had the heartbreaking task of taking one of the vials:

"... *full of the wrath of God who lives forever and ever*" (Revelation 15:7).

GENTILE WORLD POWER DESTROYED; GOD'S CONTROL RESTORED THROUGH CHRIST

God is not set out to destroy the nations, but He has three covenants that must be fulfilled in the *Day of the Lord*: 1) With the Church, to take out of the Gentiles, a people for Christ's name—a bride for Christ; 2) With the Jews, to return and build the tabernacle of David that has fallen down—return the Jews to full favor in their promised land, and to set His Son on David's throne; 3) With the Nations, to redeem the nations. It was his purpose in the Gospel that the residue of men, the *sheep nations* left after the judgment, and all the Gentiles might seek the Lord upon who's name they are called (Matthew 25:31-32; Acts 15:17).

The *"times of the Gentiles"* must come to a close according to both Christ and Daniel, whom Christ quotes (Luke 21:24). The whole prophecy of Daniel shows the empires of this world beginning with Babylon, are in control of the Holy Land until the power of the final eighth Empire is broken, thus ending the *times of the Gentiles* (Revelation 17:11). This is not the end of the Gentiles, but only the end of their time of rule of the world and over the land of Israel. Jesus said that *"Jerusalem will be trampled by Gentiles until the times of the Gentiles are fulfilled"* (Luke 21:24) These judgments, including the Battle of Armageddon are designed not to destroy the nations, but only to break the control and power over the nations that still insist on keeping control of Israel and the Holy Land.

God has made promise to the children of Israel which must be fulfilled. He promised to give the Holy Land, the City of Jerusalem, and the Holy Mountains, including Mount Zion, to Abraham and His seed forever. And with these coming vials of judgment, He will do that very thing. Just as He broke the power of the dominant Empire of Egypt by the plagues of Moses, He will break the power of the World Order under the Antichrist to free Israel again. This is the only way Christ can bring Israel back to full inheritance, and bring the Church as the Bride of Christ back to the Millennium Kingdom. This is obvious today.

The main purpose of this is to put Israel and the Jews in their rightful place. However, He will have to break the pride of Israel as well as the Nations, to do so. My perspective is this: if God cannot and does not fulfill His promise to Abraham, how can I trust Him to keep His promise to me? He has promised me eternal life, and I, like you and like Israel, are depending upon absolute reliability of His promise.

GOD'S GLORY FILLS THE TEMPLE OF HEAVEN JUST BEFORE JUDGMENT

In the last verse of chapter 15 we have another awe-inspiring scene from Heaven. Just before the righteous judgments of God are poured out on an unrepentant world, we witness an awesome sight in Heaven; a sight that men have only been privileged to see twice in the whole history of God's program among men. It is a stunning and awesome theophany; a visual manifestation of the great creator-God of the universe, manifested to the glory of Christ, coming down to make Himself known to men. So great is the awesome presence of God and Christ, when He comes out of obscurity and manifests the fullness of His glory, which it is impossible for mortal man to stand in His presence. He only comes in His fullness at high and holy times. Twice before He in Christ, fills the tabernacle with an *"unapproachable light"* (1 Timothy 6:16).

As recorded in Exodus, Moses had just finished setting up the Tabernacle in the wilderness, when suddenly:

> *"... the glory of the Lord filled the tabernacle. And Moses was not able to enter the tabernacle of meeting, because the cloud rested above it, and the glory of the Lord filled the tabernacle"* (40:34-35).

And once more, at the dedication of Solomon's magnificent Temple on Mount Zion, or Moriah, it is recorded in

> *"It came even to pass, when the trumpeters and singers were as one, to make one sound to be heard in praising and thanking the Lord, and when they lifted up their voice with the trumpets and cymbals and instruments of music, and praised the Lord, saying: 'For he is good, for His mercy endures forever,' that the house, the house of the Lord, was filled with a cloud, so that the priest could not continue ministering because of the cloud; for the glory of the Lord filled the house of God"* (2 Chronicles 5:13-14).

He was manifest at the dedication of the wilderness Tabernacle when His Shekinah came down in a pillar of cloud and fire to sit upon the Mercy Seat between the cherubim. There His glory was still hidden behind the veil.

He again manifested Himself at the dedication of Solomon's Temple, again with fire and smoke, or cloud, and there He is hidden behind the veil.

The glory came down upon the Church on the day of Pentecost and *"filled the whole house where they were sitting"*

(Acts 2:2). And the glory will come down again upon Israel, here on Earth during the Tribulation. The Prophet Joel says:

"Then you shall know that I am in the midst of Israel, and that I am the Lord your God and there is no other. My people shall never be put to shame. And it shall come to pass afterward that I will pour out My Spirit on all flesh; Your sons and your daughters shall prophecy, Your old men shall dream dreams, Your young men shall see visions; And also on My menservants and on My maidservants I pour out My Spirit in those days.. And I will show wonders in the heavens and in the earth" (2:27-30).

Friends, you who are excited about the revival that the presence of the Holy Spirit brings when He comes into the midst of His people, will find this exciting news. Both in Heaven among the redeemed around the throne, and here on Earth among the faithful of Israel, just before judgment and Armageddon, there will be a spontaneous and simultaneous outpouring of the Shekinah Glory of God. The glory came down right at the time when the anointing of the Holy Spirit filled the entire old tabernacle right at the time that the singers and musicians and their music blended into one. In that atmosphere of ecstasy, God came down and dwelt among them. So powerful was His presence that all human ministries had to cease.

According to Revelation 15:8, we find the temple *"filled with smoke from the glory of God and from His power,"* happening on Earth in Israel at the same time it is happening in Heaven. While the Church, along with the redeemed Jews in the presence of angels, begin to lift up their voices with the orchestra of Heaven, the glory of God and His power fell in the temple of Heaven. This great outpouring of the Holy Spirit must have overflowed onto Earth, for right when there were pillars of smoke from the wrath of God on the rebellious people of Earth, that same glory filled their midst in Israel and a great Pentecostal revival broke out among them (Joel 2:28). At this same time, the glory falls in Heaven. If you cannot get excited about what we are showing you here, you're too dead for us to help you.

Who, of human extraction, can be found worthy to stand in His awesome presence? Many times we have witnessed just such a visitation upon our worship service; the harmony and unity of spirit seem to increase. And suddenly, in the middle of praise, the power and presence of God would come down so we could not continue with the service. Musicians were stilled, no preaching could be offered. All had to step aside while the glory of God swept over the congregation like wind across a grain field. Wave after wave of God's glory would fill His people. We could not and would not have tried to stop it. Many times it was midnight, and sometimes in the late hours of the morning when the glory lifted. Oh yes, my God is real for I can feel Him in my soul!

For a third time, God manifests Himself at the opening of a temple, only this time it is the temple in Heaven (Revelation 15:5, 8). No veil now separates the holiest place from the people. The holiest of all places is wide open, so that not only an especially sanctified high priest, but all who are washed in the blood of the Lamb, and especially sanctified in and by the Spirit, can now enter into the full presence of God. It came when all of the congregation of Heaven, the Church, the living ones, and the new converts were singing the songs of Moses and the Lamb. As described above, all of Heaven must have experienced the glory of God's presence just as we have.

Right before the most crucial time in history, when the awesome judgment of God was about to fall upon the earth, God reassures us that He is the same God, Christ is the same

Savior and Lord, and they are in control and want to bless us in the Spirit. There is nothing God would rather do than be able to *"pour out [His] Spirit out upon all flesh"* (Joel 2:28). I am sure He enjoys His outpourings as much as we do.

Wow, how is that for a commentary on what is supposed to be one of the scariest chapters in the Revelation of Jesus Christ?

Out of that glory of the temple scene and from the Mercy Seat, comes the command to the angels holding the seven bowls of the wrath of God, to pour out their plagues upon the Antichrist, the beast (World Order of Nations) and armies who have taken the mark, name, and number, and who are gathered against Christ and His armies at Megiddo in Israel. This tells us that even the wrath of God is coming out of His theophany and is still part of His holiness and righteousness. The world cannot accept his wrath as part of His mercy, but we the redeemed can. Only the saints and angels can see that it is for the world's good that He destroys blasphemous rebellion, and sets up the Kingdom of Christ on Earth.

Chapter 16 will show us how God, in His mercy and in faithfulness to His promises to both Christ and Israel, and to us the Church, finally rids our world of these rebellious angels and men. By doing so, we can enjoy a Millennium of peace and health in the presence of Christ our Savior, and Israel can come to the full blessing of their beloved Messiah.

CHAPTER 16

A QUICK CONCLUSION

EXECUTION OF THE WILL - THE WRATH OF GOD

If life is a bowl of cherries, this chapter is the bowl of *vial* pits.

A little boy awakened in the night and found he was thirsty. The house was dark and still and the kitchen was downstairs. He called out to his father who was asleep in the next room and said, "Dad, I'm thirsty." In a sleepy voice his dad said, "Well go on down to the kitchen and get a drink, you're a big boy." The little fellow stood at the head of the stairs looking down toward the dark kitchen. He called out again to his dad, "But Dad, its dark down there." His father answered, "It's all right son, you know what the kitchen is like and where the water is. Besides, you don't have to be afraid, God is down there."

The little boy thought about it for a moment, and then his dad heard him say, "Now God, I know you're in there, but if you move, you'll scare me to death."

Our point is this: God is moving in this dark world and it seems to the unsaved that God is sitting in the dark, trying to scare the world to death. The rest of us who know God, and know Jesus Christ as our Savior and our coming Lord, although we may be a bit apprehensive at times, we are not afraid, for *"we know that all things work together for good to those who love God, to those who are called according to His purpose"* (Romans 8:28). Jesus said, *"See that you are not troubled; for all these things must come to pass, but the end is not yet"* (Matthew 24:6). We also know that our loving Savior has given us a way of escape during times of tribulation, given to us for our own good:

> *"Watch therefore, and pray always that you may be counted worthy to escape all these things that will come to pass, and to stand before the Son of Man"* (Luke 21:36).

What a terrible time it will be for those who are alive and remain here to face this last 3 ½ years, especially these last days and hours, when we realize how easy and painless it would have been to have taken the resurrected Christ at His word and accepted His *escape*. I am speaking of those worldwide who had heard the gospel and refused to repent of sin and to come to Christ. Can they yet be saved? The answer is yes; *"Jesus Christ is the same yesterday, today, and forever"* (James 13:8). But will they repent? It is very doubtful. We are told that most will not.

The Spirit of God through Jesus Christ warns us in this very late hour. (There was a warning of these same plagues in Revelation 14:10) The chance to repent is still open. These plagues are coming out of the temple, not the throne of judgment, and from the Mercy Seat of Christ. Zechariah recorded God's attitude in judgment: *"Execute true justice, show mercy, and compassion ... and in wrath, remember mercy"* (Zechariah 7:9; Habakkuk 3:2).

Revelation 16:9 tells us that most of those left for Tribulation were so hardened in sin, that they "blasphemed the name of God who has power over these plagues; and they did not repent and give Him glory."

I share this with tears and a broken heart, along with thousands of ministers, missionaries, and dear Christian witnesses who have spent a lifetime trying to tell everyone we know that there is an escape clause in our Gospel of Salvation for them. Unfortunately, most today do not have the capacity or will to repent.

THE SCARIEST PART OF REVELATION

These plagues come only on those who gather out to the world to the "Seat of the Beast" (Revelation 16:10). This location may very well be in Babylon or Iraq, on the Euphrates River. Just as the 10 plagues were only in Egypt and did not affect Israel or anyone else, and were meant to deliver God's people, so these plagues will be directly on the Beast, and are meant to redeem those who will hear. Repercussions will be felt in the whole world as well, but darkness will be on the headquarters of the beast like the plague of darkness that fell upon only Egypt (16:10). Plagues are weapons of God (Jeremiah 50:25).

Where does Jesus Christ show up in this part of the Tribulation and what part does He play in these events which lead up to Armageddon? He gave us a hint. In Matthew 24:21-22, Jesus warns us of the Tribulation to come, therefore every Bible reader and they who hear, are plainly forewarned of a time like never has been or ever will be. The good news is that it will only be for a short time, and will be cut shorter than planned, for He said:

"... but for the elect's sake (Israel) *those days will be shortened"* (24:22).

The word shortened is *Koloboo* which in the Greek means *"to bring to a quick and decisive conclusion."* Christ will be busy making these days shorter than they would have been had He not had mercy on the elect; Israel will be taking the blunt of Antichrist. He will be busy making it shorter that it would have been had He not had mercy for the elect—Israel who will be taking the brunt of the Antichrist.

As we enter into some of the more tragic episodes in the book, remember that we must keep our minds positive or we will lose track of Jesus Christ in the middle of scary circumstances.

While the ungodly imperial fabric of Earth's society will be destroyed by Christ, the peoples and nations themselves, which Christ called *sheep* nations, will be spared; of course, at Christ's own pleasure, and will enjoy the Millennial Age. We must remember that the wrath of God is not on the nations of the world per se, for He sent His son to redeem them. "For God so loved the world that He gave His only begotten Son, that whoever believes in Him should not perish but have everlasting life" (John 3:16). Christ died for them and sent His called, chosen, and faithful followers into the entire world to evangelize them. But, *"he who does not believe is condemned already, because he has not believed in the name of the only begotten Son of God"* (John 3:18).

I will never forget the late David Wilkerson, after a very disturbing sermon about the judgment of God upon sin, leaned into the microphone and loudly proclaimed, "Don't be scared, GOD HAS ALL THINGS UNDER CONTROL!"

Yes we can, and we do find and identify Christ in this chapter. We will encounter Him over 40 times in Revelation; He is mentioned by name 13 times and 27 more by the title *"The Lamb."* In the midst of the worst of storms in the world's history, we can be sure that He will be there. Even now as it will be then, we have found that it is in the darkest time of our lives that we find Jesus somewhere in the shadows of Armageddon if we look for Him, shining more and more to a perfect day. A chorus comforts us:

> "Standing somewhere in the shadows you'll find Jesus, He's the one who always cares and understands. Standing somewhere in the shadows you will find Him, and you'll know Him by the nail prints in His hands" (E. J. Rollings).

SEVEN PLAGUES SENT FROM THE TEMPLE IN HEAVEN (1-17)

These plagues represent the wrath of God upon an already select group of people, namely the Armies of the Nations and the Beastly Kingdom. I believe the plagues come mostly on those nations that fought against Jerusalem. This may represent those who fought in the last four great battles: 1) The battle of Gog and Magog (Ezekiel 38, 39); 2) The Battle of Jehoshaphat (Joel 3); 3) The battle for Jerusalem (Zechariah 12, 14); and 4) The battle of Armageddon (Revelation 16). All of these battles may be at the same time, or very closely allied, and all accumulate at Armageddon.

In chapter 15 we have already commented on the reason for these plagues that come out of the Temple and not the throne of judgment. We believe this is a very significant fact which shows God and Christ are making a major point. The judgment is of course, generated in the courtroom at the throne. That is where the prosecutor won His case, and the sentence was made. There the world and Satan was condemned. But when the final plagues are administered, they come not from the throne, but from the Mercy Seat in the Temple where Christ makes intercession for us, the Jews, and for the world. It comes therefore out of the heart of God, in love for His people and His Kingdom (15:1).

In a sense, these plagues are an answer to the cries of the blood of the martyrs under the great altar, from the place where the blood of sacrifice is collected (6:9, 10). We observe that the martyrs had to wait a little while until other martyrs joined them, before vengeance was administered. God is about to bring final deliverance and redemption. Like with the plagues on Egypt, He is going to set His people free, restore ancient persecuted Israel, and return the Earth from the domination of Satan back to the sons of Adam, for the "meek ... shall inherit the earth" (Exodus 7-11; Matthew 5:5).

The first plague—verse 2 (Same as chapters 6 and 9)

When the first plague is poured out, we see a noisome and grievous sore developed upon men, but note: here is the pestilence of chapter 6, and the torment of chapter 9. It was not upon all men, but only on those who had taken the mark, the name, and the number of the beast. It is morally and spiritually selective, just like AID's is generally selective. It causes bleeding; ulcerated and open sores that will not heal (16:2). Those who submitted to the beast's mark, name, and number were not living in hope of Christ's coming, but placed their trust in the Antichrist's version of the World Order's *peace and safety* of the day.

This is very important to note. It does not follow the idea of an all-powerful beast and Antichrist whose control falls on all mankind. Daniel 11 shows us that the Islamic/Sino/Soviet Block will trouble Him. Some will refuse to join his kingdom. There is the chance that they will be martyred, especially the Jews who *"know their God"* (Daniel 11:32). Never-the-less, the plagues of wrath will not fall on those who refuse to be marked by the Antichrist (14:9, 10).

The second plague—verse 3 (Same as verse 8:8)

The sea becomes as blood plasma. This is probably very comparable to nuclear fission, based on what we learn in

Revelation 8:8-9. We note that it only affected 1/3 of the earth and sea, and I suspect that this plague is again limited to only the area under the control of the Antichrist, probably in the area of the Middle East.

The third plague—verse 4 (Same as verses 8:10-11)

This judgment covers their beloved ecology where the rivers and springs also become blood. Here again, this plague is very comparable to verses 8:10-11. Not only was the sea is affected, but also the rivers and springs of water become too bitter to drink. In chapter 8, it was only occurred upon 1/3rd of the earth.

God's judgments are right and holy-verses 5-7

The angel, who is a man from the redeemed and raptured Church in this case, makes an observation that is worthy to note. He first testifies that these judgments from God are justified. All that we have learned thus far, especially from chapters 4-16, have been litigated, and are just and right. He then observes that it comes upon a world that is blood-crazy and violence-crazy. In all of their lives of violence, the ungodly world has reveled in blood and shed innocent blood. Now God is giving them blood to drink. I think of our blood-thirsty entertainment society and the viewers who sit mesmerized before the movie and television industry, gloating after blood. Even their games are filled with blood. Its blood they want and that's what the entertainment industry gives them. They have loved blood, so God is going to give them blood (16:5-6). *"Be not deceived, God is not mocked; for whatever a man sows, that he will also reap"* (Galatians 6:7).

Can we then be harsh with God because He also gives them what they crave and demand?

We have satanic covens where teens sleep in coffins and drink each other's blood. We have registered over 200,000 witches, many of them in Washington D.C. to service government officials. We have another 8 million unregistered but practicing witches, fortune tellers, prognosticators, etc. We have 800 different divisions of satanic cults, many of them registered under the status of *churches, but* most of them deal in sacrifices of blood –animal and human. (Statistics from Tom Horns, *The Ghost Busters*)

My family and I, and most of our Christian friends, do not watch a single one of these gory feasts and I hope if you do, you will take seriously what the Spirit is saying about it. We do not take part of, nor show interest in any kind of occult activity. The best way to defeat the devil before his demise is to stay out of his territory.

The third plague—verses 4-7 (Same as verse 8:9)

Again we have the plague poured out on the rivers and fountains of water which turned to blood, like the plague of Egypt when the Nile water became blood. The angel of the curse upon the waters justifies God by this praise:

"You are righteous, O Lord, The One who is and who was and who is to be" (16:5).

Note that there is no question regarding who exactly is being praised. It is someone called *"Oh Lord"* and then *"who is and who was and is to be."* It is therefore, specifically the Lord Jesus Christ being praised for these plagues.

"… for they have shed the blood of saints and prophets, and You have given them blood to drink. For it is their just due" (16:6).

Those who were under the altar crying for vengeance seem to agree:

"And I heard another from the altar saying, 'Even so, Lord God Almighty, true and righteous are Your

judgments' " (16:7).

These saints who are pouring out the vials, are remembering their preaching about these things, and even while judgment is being poured out, are having to testify the truth of God's righteousness and mercy in judgment right in the presence of the Lord Jesus Christ and the Holy Spirit who anointed them to preach this same message while on earth. The message that we preach today will still be true at that time.

The fourth plague—verses 8-9 (Same as chapter 12, and verse 8:12)

Here again, this plague is comparable to verse 8:12. Jesus said there would be signs (disturbances) in the Heavens (Luke 21:25). A third part of the sun, moon, and stars are smitten. The day shown only for a third part of it, and the night also. The rotation of the earth was changed by some mighty force, either nuclear or an awesome earthquake.

Here at last, is the *true global warming*. The prophetic Word of God says it is surely coming. And we notice that it is not caused by the changing climatic conditions on Earth. Nor is it the results of the exhaust from automobiles or coal plants. It has nothing to do with carbon dioxide emissions. It is not caused by the *footprint* of industrial revolution or emissions from power plants. In fact, the great hosts of scientists who insist the above is not so, are right after all. It has nothing to do with our *carbon footprints* or any other activity of man. It will be the result of solar activity on the sun. It is a celestial phenomenon clearly prophesied in God's Word and a sign of the soon Return of Christ. It is caused by a solar flare. Nothing is said of the glaciers melting, but I am sure that will be a part of it. Drought, famine, and violent weather may accompany it.

"For behold, the day is coming, burning like an oven" (Malachi 4:1).

This is the judgment upon wicked sinners, but the text continues:

"You shall trample the wicked, for they shall be ashes under the souls of your feet on the day that I do all this, says the Lord of hosts. But to you who fear (respect) My name, the Sun of Righteousness shall arise with healing in His wings" (4:3, 2).

Isaiah, among others, makes mention of this event in Isaiah 30:26:

"The light of the sun will be sevenfold ... in the day that the Lord binds up the bruise of His people and heals the stroke of their wound."

And how do the ungodly respond? They are said to be unrepentant blasphemers (Revelation 16:9). They are incontinent—unappeasable. Such will be the defiance of man toward God; they have taken on the very spirit of Satan himself.

These are the same as spoken of in verses 6:15-16. Thus, the reaction of men on the earth is to become increasingly bitter against God and Christ. They become open blasphemers, cursing both God and Christ. However, remember that Jesus told us if anyone spoke a word against either God or Christ, they could be forgiven. Therefore, forgiveness is still an option, even at this late hour. However, we note that even when they know God and Christ, they only grow harder and more calloused in their heart. The Bible clearly warns us that the more we reject God and Christ, the more our conscience is seared and it soon becomes impossible for us to repent. They were given a chance to repent many times, but continually refused (Revelation 9:20-21). We are warned of the tragedy of refusing to repent:

"He who is often reproved, and hardens his neck, will suddenly be destroyed and that without remedy" (Proverbs 29:1).

Paul shows God's heart toward people who are often reproved. (Titus 3:10)

"... after the first and second admonition, turn away, (leave them alone) for they sin and they know it."

Those in the beast's kingdom hardened their hearts when they took the mark, name, and number. Now, even in the face of God's ultimate and final judgment upon sin, they are full of malice and envy; they shake their fists in the face of God and blaspheme His holy name. They would not, or could not repent and give Him glory.

The fifth plague—verse 10 (upon the seat of Satan, or the beast)

Like the plague upon Egypt which only affected the house of the king, the fifth plague brings darkness and confusion only on the *seat of the beast*—Antichrist's kingdom. Wherever the base of his Kingdom is by then, this plague hits it. I do not believe by this time that he is seated on the Holy Mount. Jesus and 144,000 Jews would never leave him there. He was driven off of the Mount when Jesus Christ visited there as we saw in Revelation 14. From a host of other texts that I have expounded heavily upon in my book, *Post Saddam Iraq in Bible Prophecy*, I am inclined to believe that he will set up his international office and place of operation in Old Babylon where the World Monetary unit will be set up on its own base in *Shinar* (Zechariah 5). Wherever his seat or place of governance is, this plague will be poured out there (Closely relates with verse 8:12).

Again, the people are totally unrepentant. I believe that

when they took the *Mark of the Beast*, they were fully knowledgeable of what they were doing, and blindness fell upon them, the Holy Spirit departed from them, and they were filled by the darkness of devils, unable to repent. It was so terrible that they gnawed their tongues in pain. They continued to *"blaspheme the God of Heaven ... and did not repent of their deeds."* (16:11). We will speak at length later of repentance.

The sixth plague—verse 12

The Euphrates River comes back into play in verse 16:12, proof again that there are many *meanwhiles* and that these events overlap each other. Back in verse 6:12, the sixth angel with a trumpet blows the warning when the sixth seal is opened, giving us a pre-curser of this very event in verse 16:12. At the end of the 6th chapter and verse one of the 7th chapter, four angels of evil and destruction are bound in the great Euphrates River. The river is generally accepted as the boundary, or the border between the Occident and the Orient of our world. These angels bound in the Euphrates River were not loosed at that time to cause any destruction. They were still bound so that the 144,000 could be sealed, and they are still bound here in the days of the plagues, loosed only to make preparation for when they will be loosed to *"harm the earth, the sea, or the trees"* (7:3). These are also comparable to chapter 8. They were to prepare for a certain hour, day, month, and year to slay a third part of men. They numbered 200 million.

Now we see the hour, the day, the month, and the year that they were preparing for. It is interesting to note that they were bound at the 6th seal, and loosed at the 6th vial, or plague. It is also very interesting that these kings of the east are mentioned by name here as part of the Antichrist's armies that meet Christ at Armageddon (16:14). They are here mentioned in association with demons and devils. They were mentioned there in texts that talked of Abaddon and Apollyon, and the great devil infestation that began when the door of Hell was opened to allow a deluge of demonic activity on the Earth (Revelation 9).

Evidently the Eastern Society, which had already given itself to the worship of the dragon, was a fertile seed-bed for this last day devil-led kingdom of the Antichrist. They seem to do well under Apollyon of chapter 9 when the unclean spirits come out of the mouth of the dragon, mouth of the beast, and out of the mouth of the Antichrist and false prophet. (16:13) They find again fertile ground to draw this great company of over 200 million to Armageddon.

The word of Christ leaves us no doubt who and what leads them. They are led by spirits of devils working miracles, which go forth to all kings and leaders of the world to draw them to Armageddon and the Great day of God Almighty. Demons and devils find their expression through the mouth of this European prince and the Antichrist as they breathe out wooing from the world headquarters of the World Order of the day.

UNREPENTANT

Unrepentance, a theme that Christ wants us to notice, is one of what we have labeled the seven deadly sins. It can be a sin of the mind, spirit, or emotions, but when we harden our hearts and refuse to repent, it becomes *a sin of the soul*, and that is part of our basic character. The great Philosopher Philo of Alexandria, while studying the life of Esau, observed that "the sins of the soul are nearly, if not entirely, incurable."

These sinners of the world like Esau, *"who found no place for repentance,"* have by this time, become so hardened in their sin and attitude, that it has reached their souls and become part of their character (Hebrews 12:17). They cannot repent.

We recall back in Revelation 6:15-17 that we were first

introduced to the unrepentant in the Tribulation and Revelation. They would rather the mountains fall on them than to face the Lamb in His wrath. They were not at all inclined to repent. At first it amounted to only a few in the world, but now it has become standard actions and attitudes.

In chapter 9 we see a special class of the unrepentant, which a few years of our world's society, it is said of them that *"they did not repent of their murders or of their sorceries or their sexual immorality or their thefts"* (9:21).

We may note that they were the drug culture of the day. Sorcery comes from the Greek word *pharmakeia* and simply means to mix and apply drugs. *Phar* is from pharmaceutical, and *makeia* in the Greek, is to mix or make. This is a culture which has only appeared in the last few decades. We may also note that all of the other mentioned crimes and sins of which they are unrepentant, are all part of and companions of the drug industry and culture: murder, fornication, illicit sex, and thefts. In our world, many times it is the political people and governments who lead in the drug traffic.

In Revelation 16:9 and 11, the unrepentant are associated with the Antichrist's kingdom of mighty men (military) and kings (political and social leaders) who are epitome of the raging nations of Psalm 2. They are in rebellion against Christ and His plan to sit upon the throne of David in Zion. The nations (UN) take counsel together against the Lord and against His anointed one who is Christ. They declare that they will not allow Him to reign over them, so they cast of His control and break His restraints (Psalm 2:2-3).

The book of Revelation says *"they blasphemed the God of Heaven ... and did not repent of their deeds"* (16:11). As usual, unrepentance is always part of rebellion, and this word is epitome of our present society.

Today you seldom hear anyone speak of repentance or rebellion. No action of either adult or child is ever called rebellion. No one outside of the Church is ever expected to repent. Sadly enough, this is true of our soft-soap preaching today. Repentance, rebellion, and making things right with God are supposedly leftover words from a primitive religion. Yet, rebellion and unrepentance have been at the zenith of our world since the 60's, 70's, and 80's. Those drivers of a new society were children and youth who wanted to throw off the old generation and bring to birth a new one with no control or restraint. Now, those same youth are adults. They are the *boomers* that allowed rebellion to become the criteria of their society; the hippy-yippy-yuppies of our adult generation who make rebellion their norm. They were raised in a society of unrepentant rebellion. Even many grandparents have adopted the spirit of the age. Most of the churches of chapters 2 and 3 (excluding Smyrna and Philadelphia) were called upon to repent, but many of them have refused to teach and preach the truth. Often, they will not teach the true Word of God from the Bible, only a version that does not say what God said, but says what we want Him to say. It is not a true gospel; only a watered down version which caters to our self-interest with no sense of righteousness, truth, or conviction. They are in complete rebellion against God and Christ, and any suggestion of repentance is offensive to them.

These are the ones who will feel comfortable with the mark, name, and number. They will rejoice when the two witnesses are slain, lay in the streets, and are mocked; when the world takes a holiday in celebration of the death at the hands of the global community—UN. They consider them relics of the old society and old religions. They will gather in the face of Jesus Christ and the holy angels at Armageddon, and blaspheme and mock God and Christ until fire comes down from Heaven and consumes them. Only the wrath of God knows how to preserve the righteous and bring the ungodly to judgment. Second Peter 2:5 says *"God did not spare the ancient world."* Only the fire of God can cleanse a wayward society, renovate the bad, and preserve the good. In *"these times of ignorance, God overlooked [sin], but now commands all men everywhere to repent"* (Acts 17:30).

ARMAGEDDON—THE RAGE OF NATIONS AND THE WRATH OF GOD

Revelation 11:18 first introduces us to the *angry nations*, their wrath against God, and the wrath of God in return. What will make the short 3 ½ years of the last half of the Tribulation, and especially the few months at the end, so very troubling to the world of unrepentant sinners? It will be, as Jesus Christ said, *"a time of trouble, such as never was since there was a nation"* (Daniel 12:1). It will be caused by the extreme animosity that has built up between two rivals—God and Satan. Remember, the nations of ungodly men are only the pawns in the game. It is actually a rivalry that has been building up since Satan, as the God of this world gained control, or was given control of the Gentile nations. It is Satan who has kept them stirred up against God, the Church, and the Jews all through the millennia; and all because they are part of God's plan to overthrow the devil and redeem the world to God and to His Son, Jesus Christ.

The intensity of the final wars and conflicts in that rivalry will be because Satan has been cast to the earth, and is full of wrath because he knows his time is short (Revelation 12:12). In his extreme wrath, he will have accomplished whipping the unsuspecting nations into demonic frenzy against Israel, Christ, and God Himself (16:14). It will be a world that set itself against God and opened itself to satanic power.

As mentioned earlier, the President of Bosnia said to Jim Lehrer when asked to what such horrible atrocities in Bosnia could be attributed to, and he said, "There are tides in the affairs of men which unleash demons." With the Church gone in the Rapture, this will be a society that has willingly stepped out from under the protection of God, and without realizing its subjection to Satan, has opened itself to demons.

PERILOUS TIMES

When God, through Christ, sets out to bind Satan and His fallen angels, and force the nations to come under Christ's control, the fallout of this war will affect our world. Like in all wars, there are always casualties among the innocent. All societies will feel its impact upon their people and upon their land.

This will create in the end-time, societies of the world in perilous times, spoken of by Paul to Timothy. We are talking about nations, and nations are made up of people. National trends will have their effect on social ethics, and the hate, rage, and rebellion of these kings and rulers will create perilous times among the people. The word for perilous times is *chalepos* and can best be described as *raving madness; furious with violent insanity*. And when you go down the list of characteristics in society that the furious and violent insanity will generate, it certainly will be demonstrated in the last day society. Paul tells us of these dangerously fierce times his letter to Timothy, just as we find them described in Revelation, chapter 16.

> *"But know this, that in the last days, perilous times will come: For [people] will be lovers of themselves, lovers of money, boasters, proud, blasphemers, disobedient to parents, unthankful, unholy, unloving, unforgiving, slanderers, without self-control, brutal, despisers of good, traitors, headstrong, haughty, lovers of pleasure rather than lovers of God, having a form of godliness but denying its power. And from such people turn away"* (2 Timothy 3:1-5)!

Second Timothy tells us of these dangerously fierce times spoken of Revelation, chapter 16, and he follows through with verse 13:

> "But evil men and impostors will grow worse and worse, deceiving and being deceived."

This is a picture of the society created by Christ-rejecters, and it is the society that will result when the world worships the dragon, and when the door of the pit is opened and demons run rampant all over society. We see this kind of world developing today. Increasingly, we see our society flirting with demons and becoming a seed-bed for every kind of debauchery, insane depravity, and beastly depravity, imaginable.

Transfer these attitudes and characteristics into the world leaders and you can see the possibility of their rejection of, and their rebellion against Christ. However, this insane rage against Christ is not the end. The final outcome is recorded in the next four chapters of Revelation. It is plainly and simply stated in book of Psalms:

> "He who sits in the heavens shall laugh; the Lord shall hold them in derision. Then He shall speak to them in His wrath, and distress them in His deep displeasure" (Psalm 2:4-5).

It is no wonder God can laugh at their destruction. In spite of their hate, rage, and threats, He proceeds to bring these kings and rulers to account at Armageddon, and in the end, it will be according to the pattern of prophecy and the promise made to Abraham and Israel, as well as the whole world:

Revelation 16 is a disclosure of that *wrath* and *displeasure* spoken of here, and how God will *distress* (anger, annoy, irritate, and enrage) them. He will make Satan, his angels and his ilk—beast and Antichrist, the laughing stock of all Heaven. Even the people of the earth will turn on him, for Daniel records his final end, and as mentioned before, *"he shall come to his end, and no one will help him"* (Daniel 11:45). Fire from inside of his being, will devour him (Ezekiel 28:18).

The Tribulation will be limited in scope. It will most likely affect *some of the world* with a great impact; although it will most likely affect *the entire world* to some degree:

1. Only a third part of the earth and sea, although its ravages will be felt worldwide.
2. It only involves the blasphemous in the Antichrist's kingdom.
3. It falls on those who have not repented in their rebellion.

It is redemptive in its purpose. Refer to Daniel 9:24 to review the six results of the 7th week. Those who are rebellious always reject the acts of God's judgment and see every tragedy as a reason to blame God—an *act of God* they claim. Only the redeemed can see the redemptive purpose of God's discipline.

In spite of their hate, rage, and threats, He will proceed to bring these kings and rulers to account at Armageddon, and in the end, *"Yet I have set My King* (Christ Jesus) *on My holy hill of Zion"* (Psalm 2:6).

The outcome of Armageddon will bring to an end to the Tribulation period.

It will also close the times of the Gentiles; that is, the time that the Gentile Imperial System that has ruled the world clear back to Babylon, will end. Jesus said "the times of the Gentiles [would be] fulfilled" (Luke 21:24). That is the Imperial Empires ruling over the world in general, and Jerusalem and the Holy Land specifically. With the Gentile powers coming to a complete failure and are broken down, and with Satan bound, Israel will come back to her full strength. The center of the world will be in Jerusalem, and King David will reign with the twelve apostles.

THE ROMAN PRINCE AND THE WORLD ORDER MEETS CHRIST

We must pause to consider the Roman Prince over the beastly One World Order. As the nations rage against Christ, and the demonic effect on society causes these perilous times, the head of the Global community—the Roman prince, will become involved. He has probably already been reproved by the two witnesses from Jerusalem who have tried to reason with Him. We find several references in texts that without doubt, refer to the Tribulation time which speaks of God and Christ's efforts to *"plead His case"* with the nations, especially those who have a controversy with Zion (Jeremiah 25:31). Joel 3:2 shows God pleading with the multitudes that gather at Jehoshaphat regarding the West Bank problem.

Since God always uses His servants on Earth to do His pleading and to serve His warnings, there would be no better ones to use than the two witnesses in Jerusalem. Then the *prince* and his World Order Government will experience God's wrath by the plagues that are also called down on the kingdom of the beast by the witnesses (Revelation 11:6). The subjects of the beast will be like old Pharaoh of Egypt during the plagues which were sent to set God's people free, and awaken him to the reality of Moses' God. Instead of repenting, He rebelled and hired magicians to encounter the miracles of Moses and Aaron. So the Roman Prince and head of the World Order beast will seek out a demon possessed, occult man—the second beast and Antichrist, to assist him in his quest for World Order. This *little horn* king relies on the Antichrist's false prophet—the 2nd beast who looks like the Lamb, but speaks like the dragon, and calls down signs and wonders to counter the plagues of the Witnesses. Even after hearing the everlasting Gospel of the kingdom preached, he repels (14:6-7). In spite of the signs and wonders worked by the Antichrist sitting in the temple and calling himself God as He mesmerizes the prince and the World Order who worship the Global Governance and the dragon that empowers them, the Antichrist will have to flee both the temple compound and Jerusalem when Christ appears. The World Order and its prince will have no choice but to back off of their demands over Jerusalem and the Temple Mount. He will then muster the world armies, such as the NATO troops who are swept into his kingdom by flatteries and committed to the Antichrist, and meet Christ at Armageddon.

Let me clarify my attitude toward Globalism and the One World Order. I do not intend to leave the impression that I am, or that all Christians should be totally again the UN and the Global World Order that is developing today. It is the only hope that a war torn world has, as far as their human efforts go, to ever hope for an orderly world. Two serious mistakes are being made however: 1) they have rejected God and Christ; and 2) They do not realize that their rejection and rebellion against God and Christ leaves them wide open for the devil and demons to use them. It is only what Satan and the Antichrist will do with the One World Order for a very short time, and at the very end of this age, that is troublesome to us. The world's leaders cannot and will not accept what the Bible shows us about these esoteric powers that are working behind the scenes. We can only understand it as we clearly see it in God's Word.

JERUSALEM INTERNATIONALIZED

We read the final outcome from Micah 4:1-4 (paraphrased from the *Living Bible,* Isaiah 2:2-4):

"In the last days, [the days of the Revelation of Jesus

Christ], Jerusalem and the Temple Mount will become the world's greatest attraction, and people from all nations will flow there to worship the Lord Jesus Christ. 'Come' everyone will say, 'let us go up to the mountain of the Lord, to the Temple of the God of Israel. There He will teach us His laws, and we will obey them, for in those days the world will be ruled from Jerusalem. And the Lord will divide among the nations, and settle all international disputes, all the nations will convert their weapons of war into implements of peace. Then at the last of all wars—Armageddon, war will stop and all military training will end. Oh, Israel, come, let us live in the light of the Lord, and be obedient to His laws and His ways."

When the cosmic wars between God and Satan end, and Satan and His angels are bound (20:1-3); when the goat nations are cast out with them (Matthew 25:41); and when Christ sets up His Kingdom and rules over the sheep nations from the throne of David in Jerusalem, we will have peace from all war, and Jerusalem will truly be the International City which God intended it to be. We see then, that Armageddon will not be the end of the world, but will be the birth of a new world in a new age!

In the plaques, or vials, the world is going to experience the Wrath of God, but let us be reminded that this wrath is not coming out of the throne of judgment. We are told that it is coming out of the temple. We have already shown that the mercy seat is a part of the throne and these plagues are coming from angels out of the temple. Therefore, they are coming from the mercy seat. God's wrath is always mingled with mercy. Habakkuk 3:2 prayerfully proclaims, *"Renew [your work] in our day, in our time make them known; in wrath remember mercy" (New International Version, 3:2).* And Zachariah declares, *"Execute true justice, show mercy and compassion"* (7:9).

When our forefathers were debating the establishment of our new nation, and having just signed the Declaration of Independence, Benjamin Franklin addressed the Chair by saying, "Sir, I have been watching that sun upon the back of your chair and trying to decide whether it is a rising sun, or a setting sun. I believe, sir, it is a rising sun." When we contemplate these plagues, remember they are marking a rising sun and not a setting sun over the world. Angels from the temple in Heaven visited Philadelphia that day to mark the birth of a new nation. So these angels are marking the birth of a new kingdom, the Kingdom of Christ our Lord. (Ronald Reagan spoke of an angel's visit to Philadelphia.)

THE GREAT *I WILL* NOW MEETS THE GREAT *I AM* AT ARMAGEDDON

As the Tribulation progresses, Israel increasingly becomes the major point of agitation. The nations' anger at one another will eventually turn toward Israel because, as is the current atmosphere among the UN nations, Israel is supposedly the cause of all of the world's problems. Anger over the West Bank will bring it all to a final head (Joel 3:1-2).

Because God has shown great patience with Satan through the centuries in allowing him to take his best shot while he is trying to make good his plan to dethrone God and control the world, God has called *time* (Revelation 10:6). The cup of iniquity and the sins of the transgressors have all come to a full, and the time for the *restoration* and *restitution* of all things has come (Acts 3:21). God's wrath has reached a vengeful level. The clash between Satan and his *raging nations*, and the patience of the great God and Creator of the universe, has run out. The clash between wayward men and their Creator is going to be horrific. Satan, who said *"I will...I will...I will,"* (Isaiah 14:13) will meet the great Creator God who is the *"I AM;"* and when the great *I AM* meets the great *I Will*, it will be the clash of the ages (Isaiah 14:13; Exodus 3:14).

The thing we must keep in mind as we consider the battle of Armageddon is that the nations have come under God and Christ's wrath because of their part in Satan's rebellion. And those who have taken the mark, the name, and the number, and have become associated with Satan's rebellion, have to go down with him. Christ said Hell was prepared for the devil and his angels, but wayward nations—the goat nations must be turned into Hell along with the esoteric powers they followed.

We are plainly taught that in the *Day of the Lord*, one of the acts of Christ in the day of His Revelation will be to dethrone Satan, the great dragon. Isaiah leaves us no doubt about it:

> *"For behold, the Lord comes out of His place to punish the inhabitants of the earth for their iniquity ... In that day the Lord with His severe sword, great and strong, shall punish Leviathan, the fleeing serpent, Leviathan that twisted serpent; and He will slay the reptile that is in the sea"* (26:21-27:1).

We see here that Christ will slay Satan, but the people who associate with him will also suffer, and all of this happens in *That Day*, or *The Day of the Lord* in Revelation.

The rage of the nations against Christ and His plan for a Millennial Kingdom has already been whipped up to that fervor. The longer this present Mid-East problem goes on, the more the rage of nations rises to an infuriated pitch. In the second Psalm, we read about that seething anger which will grip the nations as we draw near to the time of Christ's return.

The question is raised in Psalms 2:1, *"Why do the nations* (heathen) *rage, and the people plot* (imagine) *a vain thing?"* What do they have to rage about? It doesn't seem that it is

A QUICK CONCLUSION

against one another. The answer is given in the next verse. They get together in vain counsel and whip up each other's anger against God and His Son. Although they do not know that the source of their anger against God and Christ, is coming from a very subtle esoteric being who is constantly injecting his vindictive hate into their hearts. They discover that their counsel is always contrary to God's plan and Christ's purpose. The result is found in Psalms:

"The kings of the earth set themselves, and the rulers (political and diplomatic persons) take counsel together against the Lord and against His anointed" (2:2).

Their anger and rage is against God and His Son. Although they would never admit it today, that is exactly where the nations of the Middle East and the International Community are directed. It is not actually against Israel and the Jews, but against God and Christ's claim to the Temple Mount and Jerusalem.

Let's take a look now at the outcome of their conspiracy against God and Christ. Psalms says: (ibid v.3)

"Let us break Their (God and Christ's) *bonds in pieces and cast away Their cords from us"* (2:3). What bonds and what cords? It is their plan to bring the world under their control and set up a kingdom which will rule the nations.

We are living right now in this prophesied time. Since 1947 when the Jews returned to the Holy Land, great rage has been building up, not only toward the State of Israel but toward the plan and purpose of God for the land, the city of Jerusalem, and the Temple Mount. The UN and its World Order patriots, have voted against God, Christ, and the Jews unanimously on every resolution concerning Israel and her existence (nearly 50 times), even though it was by their own mandate that the State of Israel exists. By following the Muslim agenda, in essence these nations are saying to God,

Christ, and His people the Jews that, "we will not have their bands of restraint upon us; and we will not be controlled by their cords." They want to give Jerusalem and the Temple Mount to their God, Allah.

Since the gospel of Christ has been preached in every nation for a witness, thousands in these nations have accepted Christ and are among the redeemed. However, these kings and rulers who have not accepted Christ have hardened their hearts against Christ. Led along in the delusion of the World Order and its false promise of peace and prosperity, they have set their hearts against any idea that this Jewish Christ will ever rule over them, especially the Muslim nations who are hard set against Jesus Christ returning to rule over them. Their rejection of Christ is clearly stated, since around the upper part of the Dome of Omar on the Temple Mount in Jerusalem, over and over this phrase is repeated: "God has no Son; God has no Son; God has no Son." The same rage is building in Europe as the Muslim society increasingly takes control over the European Union. America is in danger of the same thing, although the strength of the church community and our favor for the Jewish State of Israel is a hindrance to Satan's hate at this time.

This rebellious rage among the Christ-rejecting leaders of the world has risen to a fervor pitch. When Christ appears on Mount Zion and proceeds to free the Holy Land of these rebellious elements and their terrorist hold on the world, their uncontrolled rage will rise up against the conquering Christ. Remember that by then, the world will be given completely over to worshipping not only the World Order's 8th head of the beast, but will be worshipping the dragon himself. They will rise up and challenge Christ. Thus, the rulers set themselves against the Lord and His Anointed" (Psalms 2:2). With all of this, the case in Judgment has gone against the world and the devil.

A PLACE CALLED ARMAGEDDON

I have stood at Armageddon at least 30 times; lectured there, and listened to the late Doctor Linfield Crowder lecture on the precipice of Megiddo, overlooking the plains of Esdraelon, the sight of the Battle of Armageddon to come. I have tried to give our pilgrims a sense, or feeling of the great battles that have taken place there in the past, and the One that is to come as shown to us, not only in the Book of Revelation, but in many of the Messianic prophecies in the Old Testament.

We are quickly made to know that it is not a visionary imagined place, and not a cryptic symbol, but it is a very real place. Even though the battle depicted here has been portrayed in many places with many various expressions, and has been a visionary part of many Prophets' insights; it will in fact be a very real battle between very real enemies. The enemies that will meet there are not those who normally appear in flesh and blood and involve real people from the nations, Kings, and mighty men, still the main battle will not be a conventional war. Even though they have always been a part of an esoteric world—beyond our sight and hearing, nevertheless they will at last become materialized.

If we read with insight and discernment, we will find nothing in these verses to indicate that this involves all of the people and nations of the world, but only a select group out of those nations who have given themselves over to the kingdom of the beast by taking a mark, name, and number (Revelation 16:2). They are those in rebellion against God and His Christ, and refuse to give Him glory (16:9). They are blasphemers and haters of both God and Christ (16:11). And, they are of a kingdom of darkness, cursing Him who has sent the plagues (16:10). This then, proves that they are of the beast's kingdom, for these plagues are only poured out on the seat of his power (16:10).

NOT END OF WORLD

It is almost universally believed and accepted by the unbelieving and ungodly world that Armageddon represents the end of the world, the end of man, or the time when all life will cease to exist in a nuclear night and the earth will drift off into a universal dark hole where all humanity will be part of an eternal soup. I assure you, as I have before, that those who have these notions have not seriously read the Book of the Revelation of Jesus Christ.

In July of 2009, the History Channel broadcast a documentary they called *Armageddon*. Night after night they postulated on one of the ideas of the totally lost world of experts who know not God, Christ, or Their power and purpose. Night after night a mostly unaware audience watched as one after another Earth-ending tragedies was displayed with masterfully deceptive dramatics. I am sure someone made a lot of money with that display of nonsense, but there was not a thimble full of truth about Armageddon in the whole week's features.

Their prerogative is to postulate about many scenarios as to how total destruction could possibly come and the "end of the world" could happen. They may think what they will, but it must not be associated with Revelation or Armageddon. Asteroids left from the Big-Bang , Cosmic shooting Galaxies or one of 500 NEOs (near earth objects) which NASA has been tracking, may crash into the Earth in 2029. Or it could be some secret tool of a rogue nation or a stray nuclear bomb, or a catastrophic natural disaster like the flood which they will not believe in, may wipe us out. Or the sun may be darkened by a Gama Ray Burst, or worldwide volcanic ash, or Bio-terror, or a Red Tide which would cause the seas to become blood, poisoning all water with algae toxin. And of course, climate change has to be considered.

We are not making light of the possibility of any one of

these tragedies to happen, but we are mocking those who, for a credible excuse, uses Armageddon of the Bible to add credibility to their speculation. It shows absolute and total ignorance of the reality of the event that is shown us by our Lord and Savior Jesus Christ in the Book of Revelation.

By-in-large, these experts are people who do not accept as credible, any ideas of the possibility that there is a real God out there; or even angels and Satan or devils. Therefore, they could not begin to understand what a living Christ, who rose from the dead and dwells at the right hand of a living God, has to say. And, here is where they cannot begin to understand what Christ shows us and tells us about this final battle at Armageddon.

With all due respect, let me ask the reader to completely wash their mind of all you have heard from an ungodly and unknowing world, and make an honest and careful study of what the same man that walked the trails of Bible Land, and rose from the dead has to say to us; and what understanding Christ meant for us to glean. One must read the Book to know the man.

THE PROSECUTION WINS; THE EXECUTOR DECREED THE SENTENCE

The prosecution has won; the Executor has decreed the sentence; and the execution of the world is before us. From here on, we will see the three great hindrances to Christ and His people put down: the political World Order, the Religious World Order, and the Economic World Order. After that, we will see Satan's kingdom collapse and he will be bound during the time of Christ's kingdom on Earth; i.e. the Millennium, the New Jerusalem, and the New Heaven and Earth.

As a further discussion about the plagues and the wrath of God, we give you several assurances. The plagues and the wrath of God do not fall on all of the people of the world, necessarily. It is especially hard for us to believe that nations could actually rise up against the coming Christ. We must realize that by-in-large, it is not the people that are rising up against Christ, but it is the kings and rulers of the nations. It is the political *despots* of this world, and the diplomats, who are rising up against Christ. It is even harder for us to accept, but at that time, Christ will be openly manifest in the flesh, thus the nations are fully knowledgeable that it is the resurrected and returned Christ which they are fighting against.

However, to believe the message of the Revelation of Jesus Christ is exactly what the last battles are all about. It is not about the end of the world; that is Satan's lie to distract us. Nor is it about the destruction of mankind, although that possibility will exist (Matthew 24:22). It is about Christ's return to destroy the sins of the nations and bind up the rebellious iniquity of Satan, so that Christ can establish His kingdom on Earth without Satan's interference. This is what the nations are enraged about—they are against Christ.

When the disciples asked Christ just before His ascension: *"Will You at this time restore the kingdom to Israel?"* it was the promised Jewish Kingdom of the throne of David they were asking about. Their question demonstrated the hope of the coming of His kingdom. That is what Revelation is all about. It is about breaking the power and control of the Gentile world kingdoms and restoring the Kingdom of Christ who will sit on the throne of David.

BEHOLD, I COME AS A THIEF

The fact that this verse, spoken by Christ, is found right in the dead center of the Armageddon texts has caused some to assume that Jesus is coming at the end of the Tribulation period, inasmuch as Armageddon is most likely to be at the end of the 7 years. It does seem to match fairly close to other texts that indicate the Rapture. For instance, in Revelation 3:11, Christ declares *"Behold, I come quickly!"* And in 22:7, He again declares, *"Behold, I am coming quickly! Blessed is he who keeps the words of the prophecy of this book."* We find the same promise in both verses 22:12 and 22:20 where Christ says: "Behold, I am come quickly! ... Surely I am coming quickly." Obviously, if we use the placement of the statements to relate to a time frame of their fulfillment, we have four Raptures taking place at four different times; one during the church age; one in the middle of Armageddon; one after the new heavens and new earth; and another at the very end of Revelation. Surely all of them, and possibly none of them, can necessarily relate to the events taking place at the time of their presentation. A little study of these texts may help make sense of its enigma.

First of all, I believe that each of these statements are simply a declaration or affirmation that supports the hope of the Church, the hope of Israel, and embodies the whole theme of Revelation, which is, of course, all about His Coming and the Revelation of Jesus Christ. His Second Coming is stated in verse 1:7 and reaffirmed throughout the whole book (3:11, 16:15, 22:7, 12, 20). I believe that it is reaffirmed three times in the last chapter to alert us to the fact that His Second Coming is the end of the Revelation.

In verses 22:6, He reaffirms that all of *"these words are faithful and true. And the Lord God of the holy prophets sent His angel to show His servants the things which must shortly take place."* It is not something that has been added by the angel himself, or that anyone else has added, but it is truly the Word of God and has been spoken as a direct quote from the authority Himself—Jesus Christ. It points out the subtle, but clear distinction between the Lord Himself and the details of His revelation. He is the Revelator and at the same time, He is the Revelation. In each case, it is the Lord

Jesus Christ Himself that is speaking. All through the Book, it is obvious, that even though the angels are carrying the message, it is Jesus Christ that is dictating to and through them. But when it comes to the affirmation of His Revelation or His coming, He speaks in the first person. It is clear that the angel is repeating what Christ has said, therefore, the angel speaks in first person in the name of the Lord.

So impressive was this angel speaking in the first person, that John becomes confused. He thought the angel was actually Christ Himself, because he spoke in the first person as if he himself was Christ. So John fell on His face before the angel to pay him homage, as if he were the Lord. But the angel saw that John was confused and had misunderstood, and quickly made it clear that he was not the Lord by introducing himself:

> *"See that you do not do that. For I am your fellow servant, and of your brethren the prophets, and of those who keep the words of this book. Worship God"* (Revelation 22:9).

Notice how quickly anyone in the Church—the body of Christ rejects receiving any glory to himself, giving it all to Christ our Lord who is the head of the body. This angel was a saint out of the multitude that was dwelling in Heaven.

In verse 22:12, after describing to us those who will not be found in Heaven, Christ shows us who will not be in the New City (21:8, 22:11). He repeatedly reaffirms Himself as the object of our faith during all of this troubled time, and it is still He who is the Alpha and Omega, the beginning and the end, the first and the last. He is still Lord, to the glory of God the Father (1:8). He is the same one who introduced us to Himself at the very first of the Revelation, and we surely should not stray very far from Him who is the very essence of all of the Revelation. He said in Revelation 1:7 that *"He is coming with clouds"*, and in 1:8 says, *"I am the Alpha and the*

Omega, the Beginning and the End." So we find Him in the beginning and He is still the same in the ending. (see Lange's commentary on Revelation by Schaff) In verse 22:20, He sums up His testimony. He forces our attention back from Armageddon, the beast, demons, the dragon and the armies of the Antichrist, and brings it back to the theme of the Revelation. He makes an all-corroborating and all-embracing affirmation, *"Surely I am coming quickly"* (22:20).

Oh yes my beloved friends; mark it down, hide and watch, tack it on your refrigerator, put it in your mind, and be sure, for He said *"I am coming,"* and it will be suddenly! John responds spontaneously, *"Amen* (yah, shore, you bet cha'). *Even so, come, Lord Jesus"* (22:20)!

DIVIDE THE SHEEP NATIONS FROM THE GOAT NATIONS

Isaiah 34:1-2 leaves no doubt that there will be actual physical nations involved and some of them will be destroyed. Jesus said in Matthew that when He *"comes in His glory"* to sit upon His throne, He would gather the nations, and separate them into sheep and goat nations (25:31-33). He further said in verse 34 that the sheep nations would be taken into the Kingdom prepared for them.

In 25:41, He speaks to the goat nations saying, *"Depart from Me, you cursed, into the everlasting fire prepared for the devil and his angels."* These verses inform us that the nations, who were not a blessing to the Jews and Israel, will be destroyed. No doubt, they will be the same nations that will gather to fight against the Lord at His coming. The rest of the nations will go on into the Millennial Kingdom. Zechariah plainly says:

> *"And it shall come to pass that everyone who is left of all the nations which came against Jerusalem [from the*

battle of Armageddon] shall go up from year to year to worship the King, the Lord of hosts, and to keep the Feast of Tabernacles" (14:16).

The nations that gather at Megiddo will be nations, kings, and mighty men who are soldiers of the armies of the nations. They will be nations and leaders already given over to the worship of the beast and worshippers of the dragon. These nations will not only hate Israel and the Jews, but they will hate God and blaspheme Him for the plagues which have come on the seat of the Antichrist. Therefore, like all who hate or even rebel against God, will be subject to demons and evil spirits which the Devil takes captive at His will (2 Timothy 2:26). The Apostle Paul points out the seriousness of rejecting God by saying:

"And even as they did not like to retain God in their knowledge, God gave them over to a debased mind, to do those things which are not fitting" (without the ability to properly judge right from wrong) (Romans 1:28).

DEMONS, DEVILS AND EVIL SPIRITS

We are told that they will be drawn, not by any political or economic or military cause, but by demons coming out of the speech of the dragon, or Satan. (Revelation 16:13). Verse 14 explains:

"For they are spirits of demons, performing signs, which go out to the kings of the earth and of the whole world, to gather them to the battle of that great day of God Almighty."

The unsaved and the worldly that do not even believe in demons, devils, and Satan, totally ignore these verses, relegating them to the trash-bin of religious superstition or old wives tales. Therefore, they completely miss the meaning and true nature of Armageddon. They will be gathered at Megiddo and destroyed, not by any suggestion of military warfare, but by the great voice coming out of the temple that causes lightning and thunder, and a great earthquake on the seat of the beast and the whole world; *"a great earthquake as had not occurred since men were on the earth ... and the cities of the nations fell. And great Babylon was remembered before God"* (16:18-19).

ARMAGEDDON IS WAR BETWEEN TWO ESOTERIC BEINGS, GOD AND SATAN

It has real fleshly participators, Jesus and the Antichrist, and there are kings and armies of the earthly realm. But, its real combatants and powers are in the Spirit realm. We read carefully what the Holy Spirit teaches us about the things to come. This is the final battle of a war that has been going on in the heavens since the beginning of time, and has had its fall-out on the earth, and among nations and people. However, the time is coming soon when *"neither shall they learn war anymore"* (Micah 4:4).

From whom and from where have we learned war over the centuries? The answer is, from the same Satan, demons, devils, and evil spirits who will summons the rebellious nations to this final war at Megiddo. It is hard for the average worldling to believe that such great people as those ruling the nations, could be so easily given over to demonic powers, but it is the morbid reality of what is coming.

WAR TO END ALL WARS

Our sincere, but godless leaders said that WWI and WWII were to be the wars that ended all wars, but we have had over 85 major insurgencies since then.

If we read the Bible, we know that the last war will not necessarily be a world-wide war, but a local war at the Hill of Megiddo in Israel, and will involve the world armies of the beastly kingdom who gather there. It will for sure be the war that ends all wars. From there they will learn war no more as Micah states. The reason is obvious; Satan and His evil angels will be defeated and immediately thrown *"into the bottomless pit"* (20:2-3).

The battle of Armageddon will not be fought in a conventional way. Atomic weapons will be used in the Tribulation by rogue nations, but not at Armageddon. Christ will not need bombs, tanks, or any other item to fight His battle. He will *"consume [them] with the breath of His mouth and destroy with the brightness of His coming;"* this is all that will be necessary (2 Thessalonians 2:8).

Our prayer for Armageddon should be what David prayed in presage of that time:

> *"Pronounce them guilty, O God! Let them fall by their own counsels; cast them out in the multitude of their transgressions, for they have rebelled against You"* (Psalms 5:10).

Someone is always asking me if we, the Saints will fight in the Battle of Armageddon. My answer is a firm "No!" Christ just brings us with Him to give us a great show. He doesn't need us to fight His battle. He will not use bombs and tanks because He doesn't need them. We will get a ring-side seat to watch the greatest *Star Wars* that one will ever see. You talk about fireworks brother; watch this celebration!

BACK TO THE TEMPLE IN HEAVEN

The seventh or last vial of the wrath of God is a bit intriguing. It is tossed into the air and as it comes raining down, the voice of Christ out of the temple of Heaven shouts to a war-torn world declaring, *"It is done"* (16:17)! The mystery of God is finished. All of the enigma of the cryptic symbolism from the beginning is all over and fulfilled. Then we will understand all of the mysteries of the dark sayings.

Hallelujah! Every one of my beloved prophecy teachers and colleagues who have spent their lifetime burning the midnight oil and praying and struggling to understand, will be released from the burden, and will truly know, "we will understand it better by and by" (Charles Albert Tindley).

Coming back to the temple which has watched over all of the events of chapters 15 and 16, we are reminded again, that in all of the chaos on Earth, the Lord Jesus Christ from His position as intercessor on the Mercy Seat in the Temple is still in charge and overseeing all of it. The *great harlot* of chapter 17 and the economic debacle of chapter 18 will be destroyed in the Battle of Armageddon along with Satan their mentor. (see verses 18:18-19 where Babylon—both the harlot and the Economic structure fall) Christ will come from Heaven with the armies of Heaven to meet the dragon and Satan in the final battle. It will be between Heaven and Hell; between right and wrong; between good and bad; between righteousness and unrighteousness; between light and darkness; between God Almighty and the want-to- be God Almighty--Lucifer; and between Christ, the true *king apparent/heir* for the Throne of David, and the Usurper of the throne. Some of His great power is exemplified in verses 18-21: thunder and lightning, and earthquakes such as never have been before, so mighty and so great. Islands in the sea and mountains will change; there will be extreme weather upsets and hail stones weighing a talent, or about 100 pounds.

ONE MORE REMINDER OF THE MERCY OF GOD

In the plaques, or Vial of the Wrath of God, the world is going to experience the Wrath of God, but let us be reminded that this wrath is not coming out of the throne of judgment; it is coming out of the temple. We have already shown that the Mercy Seat is a part of the throne and these plagues are coming from angels out of the temple. Therefore, they are coming from the mercy seat. God's wrath is always mingled with mercy (Habakkuk 2:3; Zachariah 7:9).

Again, for emphasis: When our forefathers were debating the establishment of our new nation, and having just signed the Declaration of Independence, Benjamin Franklin addressed the Chair saying, "Sir, I have been watching that sun upon the back of your chair and trying to decide whether it is a rising sun, or a setting sun. I believe, sir, it is a rising sun." When we contemplate these plagues, remember they are marking a rising sun and not a setting sun over the world. Angels from the temple in Heaven visited Philadelphia that day to mark the birth of a new nation, and these angels are marking the birth of a new kingdom, the kingdom of Christ our Lord. I believe these things show a *rising sun* on a broken and confused world.

The nations of the world are being polarized by the Gospel today. Some are coming to Christ, others are rejecting Him. Which side of the threshing floor are you being driven by the wind of the Holy Spirit? Consider this poem I call:

SIFTING AND DRIFTING

"The harvest is past, the summer is ended,
and we are not saved" (Jeremiah 8:20)!
Behold there is a sifting throughout the land,
Threshing floor cleansed, fan laid to hand.
'Tis the fan of the Spirit, stirring every soul,
A holy wind is blowing, sweeping each to his goal.
On the one side the grain, into the garner it goes,
On the other side the chaff, and judgment woes.
And where will you be at the setting of sun,

When harvest is over, and the threshing is done?
Robert J. Smith, '87

You are being sifted today, and drifting to heaven or hell, depending on how you are responding to the wind of the Spirit of God. It is our hope and the will of the love of Christ that you are being swept in to the kingdom of God by the events that currently plague our world.

CHAPTER 17

THE WORLD CHURCH

THE JUDGMENT OF THE GREAT WHORE

Two old cowboys around the bunk house in winter, bored stiff, decided to go ice fishing. They had never tried it before, so they bought one of those power augers and went down to the ice. One watched while the other was boring away in the ice. Suddenly a voice came right out of nowhere saying, "There ain't no fish underneath that ice." Well, you know cowboys and they are not going to be told anything, so he kept right on drilling. Again the voice came right out of the sky, "I said, there ain't no fish underneath that ice." They looked up in the sky, then at each other, and went right on drilling. Finally, louder and absolutely persistent, the voice came again, "I said, there ain't no fish underneath that ice." The old cowboy shut down the auger, looked up to the sky and said: "Is that you God?" The voice came again and said, "No I'm not God, but I am the manager of this here ice rink and I tell you, there ain't no fish underneath that ice."

Well, we do have a point and a reason for telling this story. When we open the Bible, we want to hear from God. In all of this study in Revelation we are not interested in hearing what the ungodly or carnal scholars have to say. However, we are very interested in what God through Christ is telling us. Much of it is hidden in mysteries or riddles to which we must find the key in order to understand its cryptic message. What God, through Christ, wants us to know is well worth the study, research, and doing our homework. The keys are available and plain, if we look for them. Most of the keys to the cryptic symbolism are well exposed in Old Testament ethereal shadows and types. We have said that the Book of the Revelation of Jesus Christ is purposefully written analogous. It intentionally forces the separation between the real believer and the casually curious, by forcing us to *"[search] the scriptures daily to find out whether these things were so"* (Acts 17:11).

We admit that of all the chapters in the Book of the Revelation of Jesus Christ, this chapter and the next will be the hardest to explain. The reason is simply this: we are told up front that most of this chapter is a *mystery*. It is almost totally symbolized in cryptic mystery and written analogical, i.e. written to be analyzed. However, one thing is helpful; God is not the author of confusion. There are very clear and definite keys to understanding all cryptic and symbolical writings in the Bible to be found by those who are like the Bereans who searched the *"Scriptures to see if these things are so"* (17:11). Therefore, with the help of the Holy Spirit and Jesus Christ who is revealing Himself in this Book, let's make a careful search of the cryptic symbolism that we can find in the Scriptures and compare it with chapter 17.

THREE ENEMIES OF THE LAMB

Over these next two chapters, we have more *meanwhiles*. Chapters 17 and 18, are going to inform us about two other parts of the beastly system and its One World Order. These will both *fall* at Armageddon. We will also see the fall of the three enemies of the Lamb in these chapters. The first is the beastly political system of chapter 13. In chapters 14,

THE WORLD CHURCH

15, and 16 we see how Christ deals with this devilish latter-day system, to control the world. In chapter 13 we have the political machine led by the dragon, and in 14 we see Christ coming to Zion to face down the beast and its Antichrist. In 15 and 16, Armageddon puts an end to the beastly system.

In chapter 17 we see the religious harlot, the One World Order's ecclesiastic One World Religion, and its ancient connection to the first occultist pagan religion of Babylon with two heads. We see a Religious/political system like the Holy Roman Empire where the Pope and the Emperor are equal in power. And we see the beast with its Roman prince and 10 kings; and as a second head, we see the second beast—the Antichrist, destroyed. The demise of this Mystery Babylon was foretold in chapter 14:8. The collapse of the World Order Economic System which was in control of both of the heads of the Beastly System happens in chapter 18. It is what will be left of the present Economic World Order which is currently in its death thralls.

Thus, we have a *meanwhile*. All of these are destroyed at Armageddon simultaneously: the beast and the false prophet, together with the Economic world structure. These three—the *political beast*, the *religious beast* and the *economic beast*, are all part of a worldwide system of international, or global control which will be under the dragon, or Satan._

A GLOBAL NETWORK OF RELIGIOUS CONTROL

First, we are shown the *whore*, a rather gross term to use in a religious setting, but it is meant to illustrate just how offensive this system is to God in its Global setting. Here is a global, religious system with its roots going back to ancient times and controlled by the political powers of the day. It is in close ally with the beastly system of the World Order upon whose back it is riding. Its power is actually coming from the esoteric *dragon* who gives to the beastly World Order *"his power, his throne, and great authority"* (Chapter 13:2). Part of this power, throne, and authority is with the great *whore*. As we have said, here are two of the three enemies of the Lamb exposed for us in cryptic symbolism. The third will be exposed in chapter 18, namely, the *One World Economic System*. They are shown to be a global, political, economic and religious system designed and empowered by the dragon—cryptic symbol for Satan, all in opposition and even in spiritual combat, with God and His Son, Jesus Christ.

The actual power behind these three elements of the Gentile World is well hidden from the godless, the carnal, and the lost. Their spiritual eyes are blind and their ears are deaf; their minds are darkened and their consciences seared with a hot iron, and they cannot see or hear what the Spirit says to the Church (1 Corinthians 2:14). To them, all of this cannot be bad because it is coming from a human effort to bring in world peace, and they cannot see or discern that there is a vial and diabolical influence underneath it. To the Church, the godly—those who have an eye to see and an ear to hear, all of this failure of human effort to bring in the Millennium is also good news, and I will show you why.

The contrast between the believer's and the non-believer's attitude toward this and the next chapter, can be seen in their response to God's judgment on these elements of the World Order. When worldly people see God's judgment upon these three enemies of God and Christ, they fall into dismay and anguish. It is because their entire hope and social interest is built upon earthly wealth and pleasure, and upon the hope of this global system:

> *"And the kings of the earth, who committed fornication and lived luxuriously with her will weep and lament for her, when they see the smoke of her burning, standing at a distance for fear of her torment, saying, Alas, Alas, that great city (financial system), Babylon, that mighty city!*

For in one hour your judgment has come" (Revelation 18:8-10).

The response of the Church and the godly around the throne is found in Revelation, chapter 19 when they see the fall of this World's Systems, and they rejoice and praise God for His judgments:

"I heard a loud voice of a great multitude in Heaven, saying, 'Alleluia! Salvation and glory and honor and power to the Lord our God! For true and righteous are His judgments, because He has judged the great harlot who corrupted the earth with her fornication; and He has avenged on her the blood of His servants shed by her. Again they said, Alleluia" (19:1-6)!

It is interesting that their worship is the same as we heard in chapter 5, just as if that worship was also in anticipation of this very event taking place in chapters 17, 18, and 19.

The only record of the term *Hallelujah* in the New Testament in the Greek form, *Alleluia*, is found four times after the fall of Babylon; and the Beast's version of the One World Order has fallen. They rejoice at the demise of the Gentile World Order and its allies, the World Church and the World Finance System.

A WICKED WOMAN SITTING UPON THE RED DRAGON

Quickly, we are introduced to some entities hidden deep in Old Testament cryptic symbolism and subtly kept from surfacing during the long years of paganism. We know that this worldly system is wicked for it is called a *whore*, or *harlot*. Now, the Bible is frank, but not filthy. Its purpose is to reveal sin, and not to propagate it. It only exposes the filth of the world and has a redeeming moral value and purpose. This is a term we do not like to use, but Christ wants to shock us into realization, that what may seem on the surface to be a Church—a religious entity of good works and intentions, is really a very wicked esoteric abomination. It hides in its real purpose, because Satan knows people would never fall for his plan if they knew what its real purpose was.

CONTRAST OF TWO WOMEN

> "The Book of the Revelation of Jesus Christ has a great part to do with two allegorical and metaphorical women" (Chuck Missler).

This *harlot-woman* is in stark contrast to the woman revealed in chapter 12. That woman that comes from Heaven is not arrayed in worldly wealth, but is arrayed with light with the moon under her feet and crowned with 12 stars. Abomination and filthiness is not mentioned about her. Nothing is said of her or her child being in any favor or friendship with the world and its governmental systems. She and her child are both hated by the dragon, and she is protected by God from the face of the Dragon; she is shrouded with light.

In contrast, the woman of chapter 17 comes from a wilderness out of the people of the earth, (17:3, 15). She is a product of the earthly peoples and not from Heaven. She is called a *whore*, a term used for spiritual idolatry and adultery. She is very offensive to God and His people. She is a drunkard and her drink is the blood of the saints, or martyrs of Jesus, so she is a part of the terrorist consortium. She commits spiritual adultery with the powers of the world. She is not bringing forth a man child who will be a savior to the world. She is full of darkness, decked with worldly wealth, riding on the back of the dragon's beast; she is not hated and pursued by the beast like the woman in chapter 12. She is said to be abominable and filthy (17:4). Also, she is shrouded in cultic and demonic mystery.

This wicked woman is not meant to represent a sexual sin, but to reflect its spiritual nature. It is something in the religious world that is pleasing and honored in the world, but abominable and nauseating to God and Christ; we'll see why as we further explore its stated characteristics. We will also discover why God judges her so harshly, and why that, even the World Order of the Antichrist turns on her and destroys her, although they are companions in the same delusion (17:16).

It is interesting that one of its little harlots, (Islam), so hated The World Economic System, they attacked the World Trade Center. She is cryptically understood to be the false bride of Christ; as a religious body she commits spiritual fornication (2 Corinthians 11:1-4). It is supposedly a Christian church organization, but is actually a very worldly entity, which she cohabits outside of her relation to Christ.

VERY WORLDLY: She finds intimacy with the world. We as Christians, are forbidden to love the world, but she is a very worldly church which intoxicates the inhabitants of the world with her riches and wine of spiritual adultery (1 John 2:15-16; Leviticus 20:5-6; Jeremiah 2:20; Ezekiel 23:7). Her idolatries include a close relationship to the political system of the World Order.

PURPLE AND SCARLET: It is wrapped in royalty and decked with great riches.

RIDING THE BEAST: It is a worldwide union of Church and State. It is riding on the strength of the beastly global system of world government. This is the same beast as we have seen consistently involved with all facets of last-day drama (11:7, 12:9, 13:1-4, 14:9, chapter 16, 19). It is the beast with 10 horns out of Daniel's prophecies, and now with 7 heads, which enigma will be cleared up in this chapter. Here, the beast is again a red dragon like he was in chapter 12, representing a bloody system.

FULL OF BLASPHEMY: She will fit right in with the crowd at Armageddon.

GOLDEN CUP IN HER HAND: The *golden cup* in her hand definitely ties her to the old Babylon's Pagan system of worship as mentioned in Jeremiah 51:7. This woman with a golden cup in her hand is found as a symbol of Nimrod's idolatry all throughout the world and in every ancient culture. Everywhere the little harlot religious systems have developed as the abominations of the whole Earth, and which this occult pagan Babylon has mothered, it can be found. It represents the filthiness of her fornications worldwide.

WATERS: She is a worldwide religion that controls many *"peoples, multitudes, nations, and tongues"* (17:15).

MYSTERY: She is mysterious, cryptic, enigmatic, terra-incognita, obscure, arcane, baffling, and puzzling. That pretty well describes the world religions.

The reason they are mystic is described in the next few paragraphs. Satan was said to be the most subtle, or cunning of all creatures (Genesis 3:1).

THE LUCIFERIAN BASE OF THE PRESENT WORLD ORDER OF GLOBALISM

I am sure that many will take serious offense to my suggestion that *Globalism* today is a very deeply diabolical system. Many of the world's peoples, especially its diplomats and politicians, but also our professors and teachers; and many of our churches and preachers sincerely believe Globalism is an innocent effort to avert war, bring hegemony to our world's ethnics, and in the end, bring *"peace and safety"* (1 Thessalonians 5:3). Few of them are aware that its institutions have had a demonic, diabolical base that can be traced in hundreds of writings, records and civic/social expressions. If they *are* aware of that fact, it doesn't seem to matter to them. From its inception, the League of Nations and the United Nations have been deeply involved with Luciferianism. All of what I have said here can be documented adequately. Satan, the master deceiver and father of all lies, sees to it that his part in the World Order is kept out of public consumption. For sake of brevity here, we will only give a synopsis of the subject.

Esoterically, behind the world political, economic, and religious systems is a real devil—Satan. This may be shocking to many: Satan and his connection to the One World Order can be well documented and traced. What we say will immediately be thought to be a direct affront to the UN, to all accepted knowledge, and all academic and social status. Any criticism of the Global Community or the International Community—Globalism, is not acceptable and will isolate people from the world's social circle, because these global systems are deeply worshipped in the essence and spirit of our times. The worship of the dragon, or Lucifer, is clearly prophesied in chapter 13:4. Our political, social, religious, and economic world, worship at his altars. I will show enough evidence to plainly establish this fact.

Everyone has suspicions that there is an enigma about the UN, something hidden that only tends to sneak toward the surface occasionally and then is quickly suppressed and pushed back into the *no-no* world. On the surface it seems to be a human service organization with its NGOs (non-governmental organizations) growing at an alarming rate. Like an octopus, it has tentacles all over the world and in every facet of our affairs. People continue to trust it, politicians court it, and diplomats romance and worship it as something good and necessary, even though they know that it has its ethereal side. In God's eyes, they worship it (Revelation 13:4).

Globalism is also the accepted doctrine of our whole governmental education system. Every student is now, and has been for five decades, deeply indoctrinated with its concept. We can say without question that elite professors from the Ivy League Universities are by-in-large, worshippers of Globalism.

Globalism may have some good and is certainly not all bad. However, I do not share that opinion largely due to my knowledge of prophecy and especially the Book of Revelation. It is in the Scriptures alone that we are made aware of its satanic base. We mostly dislike it for we know what the devil will do with it as Christ reveals to us in Revelation. Therefore, what I will share does not come from an uninformed alarmist, a fear monger, or a gloom and doom preacher hung up in conspiracy, but from knowledge of what Christ has given us to understand about the beastly world system of the last days. I will add to what the Scriptures show me with what I have observed in my own experience. I have personally discovered the simple truth that lies behind these chapters in Revelation as it relates to our present world. What I say can be quickly proven by facts, even from much of my own personal investigation, plus a visit to the UN. I will only give you what I know firsthand.

There is no question that the UN came into play after the failure of an earlier effort for world hegemony at the end of the First World War which devastated both America and Europe. Leaders began to realize that war was becoming increasingly more dangerous to man's survival. Out of this concern was born the *League of Nations* which proved to be a failure when the Second World War ensued. This war was even more fearful, devastating, and threatening to man's survival. Therefore, another organization was designed with the purpose of stopping all wars. It was called the UN, or United Nations, with headquarters in New York.

One of the great factors in the failure of the League of Nations was that America would not join it, even though like the UN, it was conceptualized and organized in the United States. And, there was a reason.

From the start, it was well known that the finances that paid for the founding of the League of Nations came from the *Lucifer Trust*. These monies were largely earned by the international sales of Alice Bailey's books; books that became so popular universally that they out-sold the Bible for several decades, and became the bible of the New Age Movement which was just beginning to surface at that time.

At the time of the forming of the League of Nations in 1923, there were enough politicians and social leaders who were biblically literate, thus wanting nothing to do with anything that had connections with Lucifer. They knew that if it was financed from occult money, it surely had deep roots in the occult. They were right in their assumptions. What was not well known on the surface in those days was that the New Age Movement really existed or that it had become very powerful in the world of Secret Orders and Occult circles, and based in *Luciferianism*. It was deeply influential in the founding of the League of Nations. From its inception, Globalism was born out of the occult world. A study of the many occult and secret societies reveals that the background of many heresies grew out of the Masonic order of Hiram's and Solomon's temple. Especially notable is the *Illumines* which began on May 1, 1776. Since then, the secret world of the occult societies has been awash with the idea of a New World Order. Worth mentioning is the Madam Blavatsky Theosophy.

Little do most of us care as long as it stays in the Secret

Orders, but when it begins to seep out into public policy, it becomes a real concern. The fact is, it not only seeps out into public policy, but has become its main pseudo-religious base. We will show this as a fact a little later in the writing. This is puzzling to world planners who, not even believing in God let alone a devil or evil spirit, didn't even notice the secret society's World Order agenda, nor did they care. They only saw their grandiose plans for domination of all people.

They do not understand why such a great and worthy effort as is supposedly represented by this Global System, should have its roots in Occultism. Also, it ought to be a puzzle to the rest of those people who do not even accept God's existence let alone a real devil. Because they are Bible-illiterate, they do not see the esoterical side of history. Therefore, they think these occult roots are not worthy of consideration.

Because these global plans of the occult fit so well with the hope of humanistic manipulators of society, they ignore the occult side of Globalism and, as shown in Revelation, they lock arms with the occult hope of a New World Order thinking them to be harmless, and a good partner. In doing so, they fall right in step with Revelation's great esoteric Mystery Harlot and began to let her ride along on the World Order beast. From the very start, they allowed the headquarters of many of these occult societies to be housed right in the basement of the UN and become the pseudo-religious base of the World Order. I do not believe it was without design, but in the heart of those who gave the land and the money to establish the United Nations. I believe it came by design from the philosophies of those who designed the League of Nations. Why have they not exposed these things to the public? Surely you don't expect Lucifer to expose his plot to destroy all order and rule the world from Hell!

As a fact, Globalism has a long history of riding along

THE WORLD CHURCH

with the occult religious harlotry. We are shown here that this Mystery Babylon goes way back in antiquity, even as far back as the first murder of Abel, by Cain his brother. The blood of every murder has been a plot of the devil who resides in this beast (18:24). It is part of Satan's original rebellion and can especially be traced all the way back to Babel and ancient Babylon, thus its name, *Babylon the Great*. It was exposed in the Tower of Babel, in an effort by rebellious Nimrod to bring the world under a World Order. Each empire of Nebuchadnezzar's Image was a new effort of the *god of this world* to arrive at a World Order, and each of them was steep deep in occult. It is the spirit behind the heresy of the Gnostics and almost surfaced in the Crusades and their cultic chiliastic interpretation of the Millennium. The Merovingian kings of France, who were conceived of the Crusades, were deeply influenced by the *Cult of Mary* and her son, supposedly a son of Jesus Christ. These *Kings of the Royal Blood* believed that they were of the blood of Christ and had a misconceived idea that the *Royal seed of Mary* should create the millennial reign of Christ. The *Priory de Sion* (secret society to protect Christ's and Mary Magdalene's sacred bloodline) and the *Templars* came out of it. The New Age people are amorous about the idea of a One World Order. Most all of the secret orders are filled with teaching about a Global Community, but what of the UN?

THE UN AND OCCULTISM

One visit to the basement of the UN building in New York, and one immediately realizes what the pseudo-religious base of the UN is and where its impetuousness comes from. The concepts, precepts, and ideology of the UN seeps up from the basement to the halls of the assembly above where an image of Zeus ordinates the entrance to the General Assembly. I will just name a few of the offices that I saw, and some of the people I spoke with on my visit there in the early 80s.

When I first visited the UN, I found the offices of the *Lucis Trust* in the basement. It was originally known by the name of the *god* who inspired those who brought it into being. It was originally called the *Lucifer Trust* when it financed the League of Nations. The name *Lucifer* did not set well with Bible-believing Christians, so it was changed to Lucis Trust after so much reaction to the original name. Both words are from the same root word *Lucifer*, which means *light holder or light giver.* This name can be found in Isaiah 14:12 as the personal name of God's arch-enemy, Satan.

Along with the Lucis Trust, I found the headquarters of the *World Servers*: the *World Servers for the World we choose*, the *World Council of Wise Persons,* and various other planetary movements that have been responsible for many peace and environmental movements. They, along with Share International and the Findhorn Institute of Moray, Scotland, are all base organizations of the New Age movement and very busy components of the pseudo-religious precepts and ideologies of the UN. These are all responsible for the world-wide Gaia worship of Mother Earth and the pagan Babylonish worship of the female Goddesses, along with animal worship (Romans 1:20-28). They are all leading organizations in the highly Luciferian Occult New Age movement—the pseudo-religious base of the UN. All of them are steep-deep in old Babylonish Paganism. They are working at an ongoing evangelism, spreading their philosophy and ideologies throughout the entire UN worldwide organization. Revelation 17:2 shows us the intoxication of the devil inebriating the whole world with its Babylonish fornication. I have written a book called *"Simulations of the Second Coming"* which documents this whole deception.

All of the weight of evidence that can be found and documented in our present time plainly shows the devil's direct involvement in the Global System and its base at the UN. No one should be offended to find my expose' of the very existent fact; and that this fact is fully revealed and substantiated in our real world just as it is prophesied in Revelation, chapters 13-19. There we find a system which permeates the whole world with the dragon and devil-philosophy, and causes all that follow those concepts to take a mark, name, and number, and track with Satan through the end-time drama. As we get into this chapter, we will see that it is full of Luciferian and satanic enigma.

MYSTERY BABYLON, MOTHER OF HARLOTS AND ABOMINATION OF THE EARTH

This system of religious harlotry is identified by Christ, who alone can see perfectly into the esoteric world of demons, devils, and Satan, and see its base in the idolatry of Nimrod's Babylon. It is represented in an occultic impressive image of a woman, personification of the goddess worship that came from Semiramis, wife of Nimrod who after Nimrod's death through whoredom, produced a son named Tammuz. She said he was virgin-born, and promoted him as the resurrected Nimrod. This began the mother/child goddess *Queen of Heaven* cult movement that swept the world and became an Antichrist fakery of Mary and the Christ Child.

They knew well from an old universal knowledge born by the promise of God to Eve, that there was coming a great One, a Savior. From the beginning, they depicted Him as a virgin-born son epitomized in the Star sign *Virgo* and her virgin-born son in *Bootes*. Semiramis promoted herself as that virgin with a son. It caught the imagination of the world willing to mimic the real truth. This is the background of this woman in Revelation 17 who is called *"MYSTERY BABYLON THE GREAT, THE MOTHER OF HARLOTS AND OF THE ABOMINATIONS OF THE EARTH"* (17:5).

THE BLOOD OF THE MARTYRS

One of the first things that Jesus Christ wants to catch our attention with, is that this ancient Antichrist system of worship is drunk, but she is drunk with the blood of the saints—the martyrs of the ages who were killed for truth and their testimony of Jesus (17:6). Interestingly enough, She is in common with the great economic system of Chapter 18, as it is said that:

"And in her was found the blood of prophets and saints, and of all who were slain on the earth" (18:24).

It is evident that both this devilish false religion and all of its Harlots the world over and through the ages, have always been hand and glove with the world economic orders of their day.

Let us pause now for a moment of silence, and remember the tens of thousands of martyrs even in our time that have been, and are being, massacred by cruel religions. The cry of the blood from under the great altar of sacrifice, is mounting as it comes to the ears of the Lord in Heaven (6:9-10). One day it will be avenged by the wrath of God upon these wicked religious systems which have joined the Armies of the Nations, to war against the Lord and His Christ.

This is a great mystery which we can hardly understand. Only Christ, who sits in heavenly places, along with God our Father can track all of the blood that was spilled and still hear the cry of the blood of Abel and those on forward. Whatever we can make of these truths, this harlot represents an ancient spiritual harlotry and fornication from the beginning. The cry of the blood of martyrs (Christ Himself one of them) rises to God in Heaven from under the great sacrificial altar which we see in chapter 6. Even today, seldom observed by our news media and driven by *political correctness*, are literally *tens-of thousands* of Christian martyrs filling unmarked graves. God and Christ can and will mark every one of them.

MYSTERY BABYLON AND THE GOLDEN CUP

The harlot is very wealthy from her courtship with the kings of the world much like the Laodicean Church, the Catholic Church, Buddhism, Hinduism, and others who court the World Government Systems.

Significantly, she has a *golden cup* in her hand, and it is full of abominations and *spiritual* filthiness of her fornication. This symbol comes directly from the mysteries of old occult Babylon. This symbol is well understood to everyone in John's day—the first century, and it is full of Old Testament symbolism. Now, let's research more about the cup in her hand.

Names in the Bible often reveal character and her name is very reflective of her character. She is called *Mystery*, a riddle and a puzzle to the world and to the Church. She is not openly understood by the world's media, the elite, or world-shakers. Very little about this religious system is on the surface of current events, but can be researched in most commentary documents of the past.

I believe some have wrongly taught that she depicts the Catholic Church. No doubt, the Catholic liturgy reflects a lot of the characteristics of this Babylonian religious cult. But what we are shown here is far more inclusive than just the Catholic Church, for it is said to be part of a system throughout the ages long before the Catholic Church began. It includes all false, religious, and occult abominations the world over, which can be shown to emanate from the Babylonian rebellion. It can be shown that every major religion in the world, even the Far East religions, can be traced back to Babylon, and too much of Catholicism as well.

We note that whatever she is, she has deep roots in Babylon mysticism, so we will have to do a little background in old

Babylonish paganism to understand. The city of Babylon has long passed from prominence in our world's thoughts, although it has existed continuously since Nimrod and the Tower of Babel. However, its pagan religious system has not diminished its impact on the world.

The word *Babylon* comes from Babel, (Bab-el) meaning *"a false way to God."* It was so named because it was built at the gates of the Garden of Eden (Genesis 3:24). It was the place where huge angelic beings guarded the gate of Eden up until the days of the flood, to keep man, angels, and Satan from returning to the Tree of Life. Satan, very offended that he was cursed and not allowed back in the garden, hated God and was able to breed hate in the hearts of post-flood people who ignored God's plan for their redemption; he hated the God of the flood, and started their age-old deception at those gates. That gate stood there until the flood. In the post-flood era, Nimrod built a city and a tower near that gate of the garden and started a deception which took all of the prophetic plans of God and Christ, and perverted them to a substitute system of Cain's type of religion which was based on good works (Genesis 11:4). They perverted the ancient gospel, which prophesied a future Redeemer as told in the stars. Nimrod surrounded the top of the Tower of Babel with a perverted idea of the circuit of the Heavens, and they became the Zodiac, a false interpretation of the old *Gospel of Adam*. This false gospel became inbred into the whole world, and in every culture and kindred. Although its names in religious circles were many, it was basically the same ideology.

1. It was at Babel, the first foundation of the *World Order* was conceived (11:4-6).
2. It was at Babel that the first foundation of a *World Economy* was conceived.
3. It was at Babel that the first idea of a *World Church* was formed; an Ecumenism was conceived.

4. It is Babel that is much alive today, first in the *Mysteries and Secret Orders,* and now emerging as a full-fledged religious/political/economic *System of Globalism.*

In these present-day elements, Old Babylon is very much alive and all of it is cradled in mystery. We note here, that in some mysterious sense, Babylon and its ancient Pagan System of worship is credited with and said to be responsible for, all of the religious harlotry in the whole world today (17:5). Somehow, she mothered it. We see here in Revelation 17 that that old *"Babylon the Great"* is coming to its full mutation in our time. We are told that the cup of iniquity is full and all of the world's harlot religions will *come home to roost* in a worldwide ecumenical effort inspired by the second beast, who will and is teaching the world to wander after, and worship the beastly system of the World Order (Daniel 8:23; Revelation 13:2-4, 11-15).

Let us now observe and study what we are told about the beast upon which she is riding. The symbolism is obvious. The fact that the evil religious system is riding on the back of the scarlet-colored beast, we know then it is the same beast we have been studying in several texts.

THE BEAST, THE SEVEN HEADS, AND THE TEN HORNS (vs.7, 8)

This is a very familiar being to all who are acquainted with Daniel's prophecies. In Daniel the heads are shown in the empires of the Great Image of chapter 2, but are not shown by description. We will explain. The 10-horn-monster of the last days in Revelation 13:1-2, is clearly shown in Daniel 7:7 and strongly suggests that it is the 10 kings from which the little horn will emerge (Daniel 7:8, 8:9). The rest of Daniel 11 and all of chapter 12 speak of the 10 horned beast's end-time effort to destroy the Jews and inhabit the Temple

Mount, and thus thwart God's effort to put Jesus Christ on the Throne of David.

We have given a synopsis of this beast in our comments in chapter 13, and we will refer again to these chapters in Daniel at this time, as we detail further this 7-headed beast with 10 horns. The Global overlords are having difficulty understanding why the Nation of Israel, Jerusalem, and the Temple Mount is such an issue in the world and why it continues to come to the forefront of international concerns. It appalls me that such otherwise sharp and knowledgeable people will not read a few pages of their Bible, which clearly exposes the reason. Satan and his angels are determined to destroy the Jews and possess the Temple Mount. How wise the world planners would be to quit ignoring the evidence of the devil, the dragon, and evil powers, which are evidenced all around us in the real world.

GENERAL OVERVIEW OF THE BEAST IN HISTORY

First, the Lord gives us an overview of the beast through time as only He could give having existed from the beginning and understanding Satan's rebellion since the start. Satan has ascended out of the bottomless pit and will, at Christ's victory over him, go into perdition (Revelation 19:20).

WOUNDED UNTO DEATH, YET LIVES (v.8, 13:3)

The Lord reminds us of this enigmatic view of the beast as having been wounded unto death, but revived and lives again. It has been taught that this was a resurrected man, but my spirit has rejected this thought. There is only one resurrected man, and that is our Lord Jesus Christ.

For many years I tried to see this resurrected beast as a man, but good exegetical interpretation would not allow me see it that way. How could it represent a man only, since its heads clearly represent empires of the Gentile world as depicted by

Daniel's interpretation of Nebuchadnezzar's image? Therefore, this beast has to be some entity which has existed since the days of Nebuchadnezzar. This interpretation of the heads is made clear in chapter 17. Seven mountains upon which the woman sits does not refer to the 7 mountains of Rome. How can we exegetically compare them to 5 mountains in Rome that are fallen, one mountain in Rome that existed then, and one mountain of Rome that is coming (17:10)? It makes no sense at all which mountain of Rome fell and which one is to come! On the contrary, these mountains are political and military mountains of history; the high places of world rule through the great empires of history.

When we relate them to the Empires of the Gentiles which were depicted in Daniel, chapters 2, 7, 8, 9, 10, 11 and 12, it makes absolute sense. By John's day, 5 of these empires had fallen: Nimrod's Babel, Assyria, Babylon, Persia, and Greece. Some say that Egypt was the first. However, careful study has shown that Egypt was actually part of Nimrod's Babel. He built a worldwide Kingdom in his day.

ROME WAS WOUNDED UNTO DEATH, YET LIVED (V.8)

The *one* that is, or existed in John's day would be Rome; and one which was to come would be resurrected. A cross analysis of Nebuchadnezzar's great image in comparing them to history's great empires of the Middle East, shows us that the 4th Empire, which by comparing other texts in Daniel 7 and 8, existed in two long legs—the Western Roman and the Eastern Orthodox, clear down to the end where they reappeared as a 10 King confederacy which was smashed to pieces by the rock cut out of a mountain without hands (Daniel 2:45). This rock turns out to be our Lord Jesus Christ who immediately set up His Kingdom which *"shall stand forever"* (Daniel 2:44).

We are taught that Rome would be wounded as unto death, yet lived, and in the end, re-emerge as another kingdom embracing 10 kings, one of which would be the *little horn*. By historical fact, Rome was resurrected in the form of the Holy Roman Empire, which existed and controlled the world for 1000 years. (AD 800 to AD 1800) Out of it, yet in the future, comes the 8th which even today, is thought of among the royalties of Europe, to be the resurrected Germanic Holy Roman Empire. Three attempts have been made to resurrect it. They are known as the first, second, and the third Reich (Empire). They inspired two World Wars in Europe with Germany, the present seat of the Empire.

TWO-HEADED BEAST (chapter 13)

This dual leadership is seen in the woman—the pseudo-religious head, riding on the back of the beastly system and its Roman prince.

In my opinion, the Holy Roman Empire is in fact, the 7th head. The old Roman Empire in all reality, was wounded near to death before Charlemagne started the Holy Roman Empire in AD 800, which in a sense, was Rome resurrected. Under Otto, it later became known as the *Germanic Holy Roman Empire*. The old empire died and rose again.

It actually existed with two heads. Its political head was, of course, the Roman Emperors. Its second head was the Popes of the Roman Church. This duel head, being raised up again, more perfectly reflects what we see here in Revelation in both the 13th and the 17th chapters. In chapter 13 we see these two heads as personified in the beast as the political head; and the second beast, the False Prophet and, I believe, the actual Antichrist, as the pseudo-religious Pope who has horns like a lamb (looks like a lamb), but speaks like the dragon. He looks like the real Christ, but in fact, his policies and dogma are those of Satan. He works his religious wiles on humanity through miracles and deceptions.

EIGHTH TO COME FROM SEVEN, THE KINGDOM OF THE ANTICHRIST (vs. 10, 11)

It is made plain that the beast of Revelation and his Kingdom would be the 8th coming out of the 7th and would be the last Kingdom (Antichrist's kingdom) of the Gentile rule before the Lord destroys the whole system by hurling Himself into the ten toes at the feet of it, and sending it to perdition (Daniel 2:44).

TEN HORNS ARE NOT NATIONS, BUT CLEARLY "KINGS" (v.12)

Now we come to a clarification of the horns. To get the complete story, we must consult Daniel. The ten horns are ten Kings. Every time they are mentioned in prophecy, they are said to be kings. They are never nations or divisions. Much confusion could be saved and many side-tracks avoided if our prophetic teachers would simply read their Bibles and consider all of the related texts before they go into some sensational interpretation.

It becomes convenient to see them as nations if we would take the easy way out, since on the surface there are no longer any kings. Europe formed what at first was a Ten-Nation Confederacy, so it became convenient for many prophetic teachers to jump to a conclusion at what was obvious to them, the fulfillment of the 10 kings. This conclusion was easy since there were kings back then, but no Kings now in leadership of the EU. I have held to the text and said all along that these have to be Kings. A careful reading of the texts in Daniel 2:44, 7:24, 8:23, 11:36, and Revelation 13:1, 16:14, 17:12, 16, will show that they are kings and never nations.

I have consistently taught for over 50 years that these

would be Kings emerging from Europe, devastated after the fall of social democracy, and *"who have received no kingdom as yet"* (17:12). I have often been challenged on this. On one occasion, I was challenged by a brother minister who said, "Oh, come on Smith, the only kings left today is the king of hearts, the king of diamonds, the king of clubs, and the king of spades." I laughed and said, "I see you know more about cards than you do about your Bible." No insult intended.

Let's examine every place these 10 are mentioned in the prophetic texts. These kings are first mentioned in Daniel, chapter 2. They are the 10 toes of the great image (2:41, 43). Nebuchadnezzar was shown *"what will be in the latter days"* (2:28). Verse 40 shows the fourth beast (Rome) to extend by two long legs to the last days and down to the toes (2:41). Then in the 44th verse, we see that these 10 kings will be broken and the Lord will set up His Kingdom. Note, it says *"in the days of these kings"* (2:44). It then goes on to say that the destruction would consume all of these kingdoms. I could concede that these 10 were *kingdoms* from this verse, except all of the other references say *kings*.

Go to Daniel 7:24 where again, the 10 horns are being addressed, and we are told that 10 *kings* would arise. Again, when they are mentioned in Revelation 17, they are *kings*. In verse 10, and twice in verse 12, they were *kings* and they would receive power as *kings*. We must assume that God knows better than us what they are, and He specifically calls them *kings*.

So, we are looking for 10 kings to arise out of the seventh head, the Holy Roman Empire, and out of them will arise a Roman prince who will be the actual one who breaks the covenant with the Jews, bringing on the *"abomination of desolation"* (Daniel 9:26-27; Matthew 24:15).

From Daniel, we know he is to be a Roman prince, for it was to be the people of this prince who would come and destroy the city of Jerusalem and the sanctuary in the days that the *"Messiah shall be cut off, but not for Himself"* (9:26). It was the Roman Prince Titus, son of Vespasian of the Flavian Royal House, who destroyed the temple in AD 70. These are the people of the prince who are to come and head up the beast of Revelation. He will be of the House of Flavian.

KINGS WITH NO KINGDOM AS YET

There is another specific that is given to us about the 10 kings. It is said in Revelation that they are *"ten kings who have received no kingdom as yet,"* but would *"receive authority for one hour as kings with the beast"* (17:12). For many years, we knew that there were in existence, kings—heirs of the old Holy Roman crowns, but who had no kingdoms at this time. They were looking for a time when their crown and authority as kings would be restored.

Then one day while waiting in Amsterdam for a flight to Greece and then on to Israel, I noticed a copy of the *London Times* in a rack nearby. I purchased one and was casually looking through it when my heart gave a leap and my eyes widened; I felt an elation I had not enjoyed for some time. There was a copy of the *Telegraph*, a small magazine insert like our *Parade*. On its cover, I saw this headline, *"KINGS WITH NO KINGDOMS,"* and I recalled Revelation 17:12:

> *"And the 10 horns which you saw are 10 kings who have received no kingdom as yet, but receive authority for one hour as kings with the beast."*

Inside this edition of the *Telegraph*, were listed 26 kings who were *apparent*, i.e. they were in waiting. They were mostly kings of the Royal Blood, said to be of the bloodline of Christ. They were still counted as Kings, even though they had lost their thrones when in the 19th century, King Charles was ousted and the Holy Roman Empire gave way to a present democratic-socialist Europe. The highly secret and occult organization called the *Priory de Sion* is said to be the *kingmaker* organization and determines which of the kings of a certain blood line will be the king when democratic socialism fails, and when the Holy Roman Empire is revived.

One of these days, in the first half of the Tribulation, when the World Order of the UN and the Democratic Socialism system of Europe breaks down during the chaos of Nuclear war, these kings without kingdoms (at least 10 of them) will *walk in* just as Mussolini said that he did, and take over the old throne rooms of their fathers. They will take again the scepter of power and will take their cue from the Antichrist, who himself has just *walked in* and taken power for a short time. However, they will rule but for a short part of the last 3 ½ years of the Tribulation when they will be replaced by the true and only King of kings, and Lord of lords. His throne room in Heaven has never been vacated. He still rules the reigns over the world and will rule over the coming Millennium and beyond.

When the Empire returns, according to these prophecies, it will return with one of these kings as the *little horn* of Daniel, who will be a Roman prince among these highly occultic *Kings of the Blood*. This is a deeply satanic cult built on a lie, that Jesus married Mary Magdalene and produced a baby boy. Mary is supposed to have migrated to South France in the Lorraine area, and this blood-line was supposedly propagated from this supposed son of Jesus. This is all a horrific lie of course, but it is strongly believed by much of Europe and fits perfectly into the Antichrist, occult prophecies that tell of a beastly order to come. It is just the kind of lie that Satan would deceive the world with for the purpose of setting up a false Christ, and a King in Jerusalem.

Verse 13 tells us that these kings will be united in their

submission to the *little horn,* the beastly One World System, and its head who is the Roman prince, or king. He will be one of those in the bloodline, and comes up among them. They will give their strength and power to the beastly One World Order System under the duel head—the Roman prince and his false prophet, the Antichrist (17:11-13). They are known today as the kings of *royal blood*—blood of Jesus.

A strange paradox develops when in 17:16, we read that this European consortium of kings will actually *"hate the harlot"* and turn on her, destroy her, and confiscate her wealth. It is not so strange when we understand that the UN and the World Order has always hated all religion and tried to destroy it for years.

WAR WITH THE LAMB

What an audacious and insolent move for these kings to make, but realize that they are totally and completely lost in their demonic, Luciferian occult belief, and persuaded by Satan and demonic spirits to think they are in fact, of Christ's bloodline. To them, this *Lamb* that appears on Mount Zion is just another Jewish imposter, and with the 144,000 Jews, it just looks like another Jewish Zionist effort to take over the world. It will be easy for them to believe this lie, for they have bought into all of the anti-Semitism of the day, and have been trained in the satanic lie called "the Protocol of the Learned Elders of Zion." This was a perversion of the "original writings of the sect of the Illuminate" which can be viewed in copies received from the London Museum. It sought to lay the whole blame for the World Order concept on the Jews, taking it away from the real source—satanic-occult lies.

These bold audacious anti-God and anti-Christ occult men, schooled in anti-Christ occultic beliefs, have no conscience or allegiance toward the true Christ and the God of the Bible, but are of the Luciferian worshippers. So to make war with this Jewish Christ is no matter to them.

What they have not understood is that this is a no-play Christ. This is the real King of kings and Lord of lords. The armies that are with Him are the Called, Chosen, and Faithful of God's Kingdom. This beastly system and its head—the little horn, and its false prophet—a false Christ, will gain the support of the whole world of *"peoples, multitudes, nations, and tongues"* (Revelation 17:15). The plan is well along today, and it will be able to affect the critical mass, causing the paradigm shift spoken of by the cults and the New Age Movement. The whole world will follow the beastly system of the One World Order, and they will *"worship the dragon* (Satan) *who gave authority to the beast"* (13:4).

It is the same masses of people that Jesus spoke of when He said that there would be *"distress of nations"* and *"the sea and the waves roaring"* at the end times (Luke 21:25). He saw the mass uprisings and human insurgencies that we are beginning to see today. Starting with the *Arab Spring* and the overthrow of the Egyptian government, it has spread throughout the Middle East and moved into Europe where great masses are demanding an overthrow. It has moved into America where huge crowds march against Wall Street and Washington. The seas of peoples, multitudes, nations, and tongues are rising on the tides of democratic (Democracy means "the rule of the rebel") *Mob Rule,* and they are certainly roaring (Revelation 17:15; Luke 21:26). This is just one sign of the stress that is upon the Nations as we near the time of the end. There seems to be a spirit that is moving the whole world against all established governments, seeking to overthrow all political, religious, and economic order. And, as painful as this may seem, it is in perfect fulfillment of what prophecy tells us would happen as the way is made for the setting up of a rogue kingdom, and finally the real kingdom of Christ or David, "in which righteousness dwells" (2 Peter 3:13).

THE GREAT WHORE FORMULATING UNDER THE U.N. IN OUR DAY

This great World Religious Order has had its impetuousness given to it by the World Order concept all the way back to ancient Babylon and the dominance of its political/religious/economic consortium. Even before the modern day movement toward The New World Order, ecumenism has been closely allied with the world power of the former times. Now in these last days, as prophesied here in Revelation 17, we see the heyday of the glory and power of this World Religious Order. The World Church finds that the very dragon which was their means of power and motivation is turning against them. Since this *harlot* is a rogue Christian religion, it begins to be held in disdain and contempt by the World Order.

It is a fact that the UN has always disdained all religions. They are building their own religion based on the pseudo-religious concepts of the Luciferian New Age movement, seeping up from the basement of the UN. It is the worship of man, or humanism, and will welcome a man who claims to be God (2 Thessalonians 2:4).

I have personally dealt with this Antichrist attitude for years, and have written an expose' of the New Age movement. I was invited to be one of three ministers to represent the North American Continent at the first *Council on Religious Liberty* under the auspices of the UN's NGO organizations, which convened in Ottawa, Canada in July of 1986. I realized quickly that I was participating in a council, not to deal with or encourage religious liberty worldwide as I was told, but in actuality was and is a movement to destroy all religion by merging all faiths into one worldwide religion; ironically, the very religion that inspired the Church of all Nations in

Washington D.C. That church, built with billions of our tax dollars is dedicated to the World's six major religions. With my knowledge of Revelation chapter 17, I realized I was seeing the old mother harlot call in all of her little harlots worldwide, to formulate the great Mystery Babylon, or the World Church.

At that time, the UN for 40 years had sought to quiet all religious disturbances in the world, thinking that religion was the opiate of the people. (Communist doctrine) In other words, religion as a whole was drugging and dragging people into the hallucination of superstitious lies. Every effort was made secretly by the UN to destroy all religions. Consequently, they did not want to deal with the Buddha/Hindu problem, or the Irish/British problem, or the Jewish/Arab problem. However, in reality they found out they were going to have to deal with religion.

Through their NGO organizations, they began to try to destroy all religion and formulate their own style of worship of man as his own God, by merging all religions into what they called the *Ecumenical World Order Church*, a church made up of all religions worldwide, but perverted into a religion of man. In so doing, they began to formulate just what is prophesied here, a World Church, riding on the back of the political/economic World Order. It is an attitude toward religion that allows them to exist as long as they are under the great beastly World Order rule. To fit into the pseudo-religious base of the UN, which we have shown to be the New Age Humanistic view, they have to accept man as his own God and formulate his own World Kingdom. It is this very attitude of world religious discipline that will allow an Antichrist to believe he is God and presume to set himself up on the Temple Mount as the coming *god-king*.

Do you understand how all of this perfectly fulfills what The Revelation of Jesus Christ tells us about the very last days?

All of this is to say that the very scenario we read about in Revelation 17 is developing in our world today. The time of the great beast and the whore riding its back, is now upon us.

THE NEW CHRISTIANIZED OCCULTISM
SEDUCING SPIRITS-DOCTRINE OF DEVILS

We have long watched nominal Christianity drift away from fundamental Bible truth into a socialized gospel of do-gooders, thinking our service to the community is Christianity. It has been this apostate diversion of Christianity that has been the basis of the Ecumenical Movement which now is the New World Church philosophy; the hope of uniting all religions of the world in a compromised unity to bring peace and safety to our world. The ecumenical form of Christianity has since 1986, mutated into a harmonious relationship with the New Age Movement, picking up its mystic sense of spirituality, and creating a whole new meaning to the Christian experience. It blinds the spiritual experiences of Christianity (for example: the born-again experience, the baptism in the Holy Spirit, the miraculous, and the sanctification experience) with the ancient old mysticism of occult eastern idolatrous religion. The result is a Babylonian type self-help religion of good works that is in essence an occult Christianity. The *born-again* experience is now behavioral modification; sanctification is self-improvement; the Holy Spirit baptism is empowerment. Naturalist medicine is divine healing; Yoga is spiritual meditation, and so on. In fact the great Babylon, the world religion of all faiths, actually becomes an occult perversion of apostate Christianity, a false type of the Bride of Christ.

THE GREAT RELIGIOUS WORLD CHURCH
DESTROYED BY THE WORLD ORDER

In Revelation 17:16, we read one of the most enigmatic,

puzzling paradoxes we can ever read, even in these texts of puzzles and mysteries. We would never expect the turn of events which would allow the fulfillment of verse 16. The World Order which encouraged and birthed the World Religion, would in fact turn on her, strip her of her wealth and power, consume her, and burn her with fire. However, when we think back on what we have just exposed about the World Order's hate and disdain for all religions, we can begin to understand how this very scenario could develop under the Antichrist who will hate all religion:

> "*Then the king shall do according to his will: he shall exalt and magnify himself above every god, shall speak blasphemies against the God of gods, and shall prosper till the wrath has been accomplished; for what has been determined shall be done*" (Daniel 11:36).

The World Order, after world chaos, turns its power over to the cultic Roman prince, and the Antichrist who is setting himself up to be God, quickly moves against all religion. Daniel makes this plain.

Paul adds to this very fact by writing in 2 Thessalonians:

> "*... who opposes and exalts himself above all that is called God or that is worshipped, so that he sits as God in the temple of God, showing himself that he is God*" (2:4).

The book of Daniel further exposes this coming Prince and his attitude toward God and religion:

> "*And in the latter time of their kingdom, when the transgressors have reached their fullness, a king shall arise, having fierce features, who understands sinister schemes. His power shall be mighty, but not by his own power* (his power, seat and great authority given by the Dragon); *he shall destroy fearfully, and shall prosper*

> *and thrive; he shall destroy the mighty, and also the holy people,* (the Jews). *Through his cunning he shall cause deceit to prosper under his hand; And he shall magnify himself in his heart. He shall destroy many in their prosperity. And he shall also stand up against the Prince of Princes, but he shall be broken without hand,* (that is without human strength) *but by the Prince of peace, Jesus the Christ"* (8:23-25).

I have taken the liberty to inject the parenthesis into our writing in order to show the exact correlation of Daniel's prophecies about this coming Antichrist and what is said of Him in the Revelation of Jesus Christ.

With these texts in our consideration, it is not difficult at all for us to realize that the beastly World Order, in support of their head man, will turn on the religious whore and all of her harlots steal their wealth, destroy their influence, and completely get rid of them in order to set himself up as God.

GOD AND CHRIST ARE STILL IN CONTROL

Now note in verse 17 who is said to still be in control: God, through Jesus Christ:

> *"For God has put it into their hearts* (the 10 kings) *to fulfill His purpose, to be of one mind, and to give their kingdom to the beast, until the words of God are fulfilled"* (Revelation 17:17).

This great religious system has ruled over the kings of the earth throughout the ages and still ruling in our day, but is now destroyed by the kings of the earth.

In a sense, chapter 18 is a continuation of this chapter inasmuch as the beast and the great whore are in control of the World Economic Order by this time, and will lament the destruction of Babylon and her great hold on world finance.

In connection with chapter 18, read James, chapter 5. Now follow us into another *meanwhile* to see the destruction of the final three enemies to Christ's coming Kingdom.

CHAPTER 18

FALL OF THE WORLD ECONOMY

A simple bit of advice:

"Keep your income above your outgo, or your upkeep will be your downfall." Anonymous

How can such great riches come to nothing in one hour? (Revelation 18:17).

The book of James touches upon the woes of the rich who are affected most by the fall of the World Money System:

> *"Come now, you rich people, weep and howl for your miseries that are coming upon you! Your riches are corrupted, and your garments are moth eaten. Your gold and silver is corroded, and their corrosion will be a witness against you and will eat your flesh like fire. You have heaped up treasure in the last days. Indeed the wages of the laborers who mowed your fields, which kept back by fraud, cry out; and the cries of the reapers have reached the ears of the Lord of Sabaoth. You have lived on the earth in pleasure and luxury; you have fattened your hearts as in a day of slaughter. You have condemned, you have murdered the just"* (James 5:1-6).

We are made aware in these scriptures about the world of finance which *"has become a habitation of demons, a prison of every foul spirit, and a cage for every unclean and hated bird"* there is (Revelation 18:2). This is not speaking of actual animals or real birds. As this chapter makes very clear, there is a deep Satanic spirit in back of the money.

There is an evilness of demons and devils connected to money. An article I read in the *Christian Science Monitor* many years ago was entitled *Money Made Mysterious*. It traced the history of fiat money back to Babylon and the evil god of Mammon. Jesus Christ said all money is unrighteous and therefore evil. However, we must make friends with the mammon of unrighteousness, but not fall in love with it, for that *"is a root of all kinds of evil"* (Luke 16:9; 1 Timothy 6:10). Mesmerism with money is a sin. The more we study about it, the more we realize that there is more than just a cryptic meaning to the above passage in James. Money systems certainly seem to be the haunt and habitation of devils and foul spirits and every unclean thing.

This chapter begins with a very hard-hitting statement of fact. Very few in our world, even among the Christian community, are willing to accept this condemning analysis of the World Economic Order. And certainly, none of the financiers involved in world banking and trade will welcome this observation from God's Word. However, the author fully concurs with it and believes it to be so. Because our world monies are by-in-large controlled by people who do not believe in devils, demons, foul spirits, or even in Satan himself, they do not see the esoteric and hidden side of the World Systems. We will know their truth and reality when all these prophecies come to pass as revealed by Heaven. Only then will all the saints rejoice over her fall.

We should clarify the difference between world finance and Christ's attitude toward our personal finance. Neither what I say here nor what Christ condemns, has anything to do with our personal monetary needs. We must maintain a good attitude toward wealth, and for the sake of our family and friends, seek to make money, spend it wisely, store it up for future needs, and be liberal in caring for the needs around us. There is nothing wrong with making money unless we fall in love with it, and as long as we control it and it does not control us.

What we are talking about in this chapter has nothing to do with personal business or finance. We are not even talking about honest corporate enterprises or those who head them. The *rich* these texts above address attention to is not in the upper crust of our tax brackets.

Those merchants involved in commerce, and enterprises necessary for our support and survival are not what God is condemning in this chapter. Christ is revealing to us a money system far beyond our everyday commerce. They are far bigger than our tax codes. These world financiers and money controllers pay no taxes, nor do they answer to any government. In fact, through their cartels, they finance governments. We are talking about a handful of men who control the world finance, but who are never exposed to the common people, never a feature story on the news, and never allow their picture to be taken. We know only a few by name. We are not privy to know where they live, or what their income is.

We will be addressing the One World Economic system that is a prototype of systems which have financed the empires. As far as America is concerned, our part began when the FRS (Federal Reserve System) was established in 1913 and is revealed in Brzezinski's world finance book entitled *Between two Ages*. This book, backed by Rockefeller money, paved the way for the beginning of a World Economic Order by formulating the Trilateral Commission which sought to blend together the stock markets and commerce of three leading orders: the US, the EU, and Japan. Since that time, it has expanded into the G26 and a world-wide financial control.

THE THIRD ENEMY OF THE LAMB, AND CHRIST'S COMING KINGDOM

The above verses in the book of James, adds to the weight of condemnation against the World Order Economic System of the last days. Here again, this is not talking about the rich, but about that secret few of the ultra-rich that David Rockefeller speaks of in his private circles of finance as the "Supra-national Sovereigns."

As we get into this subject, I have some encouragement for those who are in Christ's Kingdom, who live by God's care, and put their personal finances in God's hands. We will learn that God's economy does not depend on the World's economy.

Once again, we are experiencing another *meanwhile* inasmuch as this fall of the world's economic structure, is probably simultaneous with, or at least directly related to, the fall of the first two enemies of the Lamb; namely, the political One World Order of the Antichrist and the One World Order Ecumenical World Church (Revelation 13, 17). Babylon the Great represents the 3rd enemy of Christ as He prepares to set up His Millennial Reign on Earth. The political beast and the Antichrist will be driven out of the Temple Mount when Christ and the 144,000 come to Mount Zion (Revelation 14). However, that will not be the end of the Beast's reign. The beastly World Order under its Roman prince, along with the Antichrist with his ten-king confederacy will continue to spread his influence for a short time, except over Edom, Moab, and Ammon, which will escape His control (Daniel 11:41).

Mystery Babylon will continue for a short time, but will be hated by the 10 kings of Europe's occult—*kings of the blood,* and will be destroyed by them, and their great worldwide assets will be taken (17:16-17). The fall of both the political beast and the religious beast, was foretold in

Revelation 14:8 and was there associated with the coming of Christ and the 144,000 Jews to Mount Zion. The time of the fall was foretold in 16:19, and associated with Armageddon. The collapse of the world's financial system comes to us as the final fall of Satan's control of the world in chapter 18.

This is the final scene in the *Pageant of Divine Judgment*, in the 4th Act entitled *Participators in Judgment.* Others participating include Israel; Jerusalem and the witnesses; the beast and his global government; and the Harlot Church along with the world economic structure—Babylon.

An outline of chapter 18 could be this:
Verses 5-7: Judgment of Babylon
Verse 8: The plagues (same as Ch.16)
Verse 9: Her suitors
Verses 10-11: Her wealth, God of mammon
Verse 15: Merchants bewail
Verse 16-19: Mourning of the world
Verse 20: Rejoicing in Heaven
Verses 22-23: Her desolation
Verse 24: Her total guilt

CONDEMNATION OF THE GREAT GENTILE WORLD - MODUS OPERANDI

We come now to the condemnation and destruction of the great Gentile World Imperial domination by empires as shown in Nebuchadnezzar's dream, in Daniel, chapter 2. A political idea of a One World Order or an empire of world control, and a world money system of finance, along with a religious pagan worship system, would be part of world control that began with the Golden Empire of Babylon. The political and religious side of the World Order is supported and financed by the Economic Order. These three elements make up the main factors that control our lives, our civic and religious structure, and our government style. All of these, in the understanding of God's Word and which can also be demonstrated in actual history, began with Babylon. The systems that developed the great *golden empire* of King Nebuchadnezzar in Babylon were the basis of all of the empires to follow, each building upon the foundation of the first. The essence of that system has been carried down through the ages of successive empires, and continues today in the Trilateral Commission, The Council on Foreign Relations, the IMF, the G28, and other associated institutes of Global control.

Babylon, both as a city and as a Pagan System of governance, economy, and religion, is mentioned six times by name and several other times by inference in the Book of Revelation. It is second only to Jerusalem in the frequency of time mentioned in Scripture. Jerusalem itself is mentioned by name over 800 times and many other times by titles and other references. Babylon is mentioned 256 times by name and several other times by other titles. Of course, Babylon is deeply involved in the Book of Daniel, as all of the events in that book took place in Babylon, or was at least related to Babylon. Is of great importance and should be of interest to us that it is mentioned six times in Revelation.

JUST JUDGMENT FROM HEAVEN (v.1)

"After these things," that is, after the fall of political and religious Babylon, we come to God and Christ's dealing and destruction of economic Babylon. Some might question our suggestion that this economic system is also part of the enigmatic or Mystery Babylon. These verses tell us plainly that it is. All of the cryptic symbols and mysterious impressions left by what is told to us in chapters 13-18, are enigmatically tied to Old Babylon. That is where Satan began His scheme to take over the world.

FALL OF THE WORLD ECONOMY

TIME OF GOD'S VENGEANCE

The prophets said that this would be the time of vengeance. Over and over again the prophets speak of these last days as being the time of God's vengeance. For two thousand years, God has been patient and longsuffering:

> "..not willing that any should perish but that all should come to repentance. But the day of the Lord will come..." (2 Peter 3:9-10).

Isaiah 61:2, 63:4, and Jeremiah 51:6 point to the last-day events saying that they will be the day of God's vengeance. Isaiah 59:17, Ezekiel 25:17, and Micah 5:15 warn us that in the day of His coming will be in vengeance. In the Gospel of Luke, Jesus confirms these scriptures when he says:

"For these are the days of vengeance, that all things which are written may be fulfilled" (21:22).

Jude 14 and 15 solidifies these texts:

"Now Enoch, the seventh from Adam, prophesied about these men also, saying, 'Behold, the Lord comes with ten thousands of His saints, to execute judgment upon all, to convict all who are ungodly among them of all their ungodly deeds which they have committed in an ungodly way, and of all the harsh things which ungodly sinners have spoken against Him."

The cry will be heard of the martyrs to avenge their blood (Revelation 6:10); and God declares, "vengeance is Mine, I will repay" (Romans 12:19). Revelation 18:24 brings us to this very scenario:

"And in her (Mystery Babylon) *was found the blood of the prophets and saints, and of all who were slain on the earth."*

The saints rejoice, because in her destruction, is vengeance for all that they had suffered and all the miscarriage of justice that has corrupted the money systems of the world throughout the ages.

She has been a polluted system since the beginning. In her is not only the blood of all the martyrs slain for Jesus' name, but this world economic system is polluted with the adulterated practices of the political world, and it can hardly be argued that politics the world over are essentially corrupt. It is impregnated by occult practices, Antichrist and satanic corruption, beastly ambitions and practices, and tainted with selfishness and greed. It is infiltrated by the military/industrial complex, trafficked by the Mafia, drugs and the drug cartels, sexual deviation, and the manufacturing of filth. Jesus called all money the *"unrighteous mammon"* and filthy lucre—*"greedy for money"* (Luke 16:9; Titus 1:9).

CHRIST PRONOUNCES THE FALL OF BABYLON

"Another angel [comes] down from heaven" (Revelation 18:1). The rest of the verse tells me that this is again, Jesus Christ represented by an angel, the angel of the Lord's presence, called so because He has a message to deliver to us. It is said He has *"great authority"* and the whole earth will be "illuminated with His glory. And He cried mightily with a loud voice" 18:1-2). All of these terms relate to Christ's coming and to His Revelation. Jesus told us that His coming would be *"as the lightning comes from the east and flashes to the west* (all around the world), *so also will the coming of the son of man be"* (Matthew 24:27). He then places the *light* in this passage in exact perspective with Revelation 18:

> *"Immediately after the tribulation of those days the sun will be darkened, and the moon will not give its light (possibly because of the brighter brilliance of His glory);*

the stars will fall (i.e. possibly "go out") from heaven, and the powers of the heavens will be shaken. Then the sign of the Son of Man will appear in heaven, and then all the tribes of the earth will mourn, and they will see the Son of Man coming on the clouds of heaven with power and great glory" (Matthew 24:29-30).

I am persuaded that this is another cryptic symbol of Jesus Christ in Revelation.

BABYLON—CITY AND SYSTEM (V.2)

As we study the subject involving Babylon, again, like the study of the beast, we have some difficulty and cause for very careful scrutiny to determine whether a given text is referring to the literal physical Babylon, or to a cryptic symbolism of a pagan religious practice and a modus operandi (how something works) of global finance and governance, all of which had their origin at Babel. These three are often interchangeable and the literal meaning of the terms in a given text must be understood by the message it seeks to communicate.

The idea that the literal physical city of Babylon should be restored in the last days has been the subject of much theological debate. However, there are sections of prophetic texts that certainly indicate that this is so. An erroneous idea that Babylon was destroyed in the past has been widely published, but it cannot be established by historical facts. Babylon as a city has never ceased to exist.

When the Persians conquered Babylon, they simply stole into the city via the water system, broke up Belshazzar's drunken party, and took over the city. It continued on as a capitol for the Persians. Alexander made it the capitol of his Eastern Empire as Napoleon thought to do. It was the center of Babylonian Judaism for 500 years, and largely a legacy of Daniel. Seven Jewish universities existed there at different times. Peter preached there, and it existed as part of the Roman Empire. Since the reign of Saddam Hussein, the old ancient city has been largely restored and made into an International Cultural Center under the UN's UNESCO (United Nations Educational, Scientific and Cultural Organization; specialized agency of the UN). The literal city still exists about 35 miles southwest of Bagdad and near the ruins of the old ancient city and tower.

However, the prophecies involving Babylon go far beyond and deeper into cryptic mystery, than just the actual physical city. The background of these two other meanings can be substantiated. Nimrod, in establishing Babel and its tower, intended to establish a totally separate world kingdom from what God had planned (Genesis 10:8-10, 11:1-9). To do so he set up his own political, economic, and religious systems. Of course, he was under the direct power of satanic influence, just as we find the Babylonish system in Revelation under the dragon's influence.

Satan had the same design for overthrowing God and His plans for His Son, which was a kingdom on Earth. Therefore, out of Babylon came a global system of political/economic/social and religious ideas, that has basically driven the successive empires and the *"times of the Gentiles"* ever since (Luke 21:24). Babylon shows up through the prophetic texts in all three esoteric systems representing the world system of politics, economy, and religion, and is reflected in all of the references to Babylon in Revelation. A more in-depth discussion of Babylon can be found in my recent book *Post Saddam Iraq in Bible Prophecy.* (CSNbooks.com. or contact the author) (see Appendix) The city and its religious system of good works patterned after Cain's religion, is representative of man's attempt to achieve by culture, self-improvement and character modification, what God intended for man and his culture to be. It is a substitute for God's remedy for the fallen nature with a complete new birth through His Son, Jesus Christ the Lord; something that God says must happen before we can ever see or be part of the kingdom of God. Through man's knowledge, we try to modify the old man, or by character improvement, to bring about a substitute for God's born-again experience in order to side-step God's plan. Its final expression is what we call *humanism*, the improvement of man through human ability and effort. The results are Mystery Babylon, mother of harlots, and abomination of all the earth. The political, religious, and economical Babylon is corrupted by man's lack of conversion to God's way:

> *"For all the nations have drunk of the wine of the wrath of her fornication, the kings of the earth have committed fornication with her, and the merchants of the earth have become rich through the abundance of her luxury"* (Revelation 18:3).

RICH WITH HER DELICACIES (v.3)

This is not speaking of the many entrepreneurs and business people who have prospered by their ingenuity and commitment to hard work in providing for the needs of people. Therefore, this is not a wholesale condemnation of free enterprise.

This is speaking of those whom David Rockefeller called "supra-national sovereigns, international elite, and world bankers; a society of the ultra-super rich. As we have shared above, they are seldom ever named or appear in any media. There is never a photo opt. Their finances are beyond any scrutiny because no one can find out their status. They pay no taxes and claim to be citizens of the world. We are told that there are approximately 300 who rule the world through the intrigue of the world economy.

I believe they may be pointed out by the finger of God and exposed in their secret hiding, behind lies and falsehood (Isaiah 28:14-22). Here is a society of men who are called *scornful*. Not that they display scorn, but in God's eyes and in the eyes of men, they are scorned because of their disdainful rule (28:14).

This is not the Jews for they have not ruled Jerusalem since AD 70. They live in secret comfort and luxury. It is said in Revelation that the evil spirits causing destruction were not allowed to *"hurt the oil and the wine,"* symbols of richness and luxury (Revelation 6:6). In other words, they have an agreement with Hell and Hell is not to disturb their luxury when the *"overflowing scourge"* comes on the earth (Isaiah 28:15).

I believe this *"overflowing scourge"* is related to their final end; what God calls the consumption, or final consummation of things. It is shown to come to Earth after the Antichrist breaks the covenant (Daniel 9:27). We learn in this text in Daniel that it is a determined sudden end. In Isaiah 28:22 it is a completing of the plan determined on the whole earth. These men believe that they will escape it. They have an agreement with Hell, (they are followers of Lucifer as all of the pseudo-religious side of the UN) and they have an arrangement with Hell that they and their cartels will not be affected by the *"overflowing scourge"* that is coming. They have secretly hidden themselves in lies and falsehood (Isaiah 28:15). However, verse 17 says that there is coming a judgment that will dig them out, expose their lies and falsehood, and disannul their covenant with death and Hell by an *"overflowing scourge"* connected with the final quick end of judgment from God (28:18). Everything they lived by and lusted after will be gone at the fall of the World Economic System. God will not only destroy their haven of rest but expose this international den of thieves. Let us read and study

Ezekiel 28 more carefully.

BABYLON THE GREAT—AN ANCIENT GLOBAL SYSTEM

To show Babylon's close tie to the political and religious sides of this beastly World Order, and it's involvement in features of the past few chapters, we find the presage of its fall in Revelation 14:8-10, where the language used in verse 10 has a definite defining relationship to Babylon the Great. All of this is directly related to the coming of Christ to Zion, and in 16:19, the fall of which is part of the defeat of the beast and Satan at Armageddon. Its fall is related to the fall of Jerusalem and the rest of the cities of the world.

That this economic system is involved globally can be seen by such phrases as 1) The political: *"kings of the earth"* (18:9); 2) The economic: *"merchants of the earth"* (18:11; and 3) The cultic religious: *"become a habitation of demons, a prison for every foul spirit, and a cage for every unclean and hated bird"* (18:2). Not that its physical environs are inhabited by such beasts, but its soul and spirit is full of Hell. Its connection with *"BABYLON THE GREAT"* can be seen in the language of verse 3 where, by her fornication with the kings of the earth and merchants of the earth, they have gotten rich from her (17:5).

These three elements of our earthly life: the political, religious, and economic powers have been the oppressive influences which have played havoc upon humanity. They must be dealt with before God can restore man to the dream world He intended for them. He *"puts an end to all rule (political), and all authority (religious), and power (economic). For He must reign till He has put all enemies under His feet"* (1 Corinthians 15:23-24). These enemies have been enumerated for us in Revelation. His victory over death is also part of the great victory of The Revelation of Jesus Christ.

This economic system is part of an age old system and goes back to the beginning. This can be seen through its economy and religious practice that, according to these Bible texts, have been responsible for every murder since Abel (18:24). It also has been associated with all of the empires as shown in its relationship to the 7 heads. It will also be associated with the coming 8th head, i.e. the World Order beastly system of the Antichrist (17:10-11). Its world influence is Global; this can be seen in the statement: "all the nations have drunk of the wine of the wrath of her fornication," i.e. its political and religious harlotry (18:3).

Latter day Babylon stands for all times in all ages, godless civilization, culture, politics, society, and governmental systems including: global, national, and municipal. Babylon symbolizes the materialism, humanism, commercialism, and imperialism of the world. It makes a show of the pretentious spirit of the affluent and a mockery of their extravagance. It exposes the world's insatiable thirst for Imperial control and monopolies. It sees the arrogance of a world system of finance that believes it can never be challenged or destroyed in its strength and affluence. This is why it is such an awesome reality when it suddenly collapses in one hour.

FIVE GREAT SURPRISES FOR WORLD LEADERS

There are five great surprises that will come to the world's leaders as they enter into Eternity. These surprises are mentioned in this chapter of Revelation:

1. That the real power and authority behind world finance from its beginning at Babel is Lucifer, or the Devil. They actually know this because of their connection to the Luciferian occult entities which form the base of the World Order in our real world. However, they have not taken this seriously. (See Isaiah 13, 14:16-19;

Ezekiel 28:19 which speak of the world's leaders and their surprise when they find this out.) Isaiah chapter 13 and verse 14:22 ties the fall of Lucifer to the fall of Babylon and this study in Revelation.

2. There has been, and is in existence in an esoteric world, a secret modus operandi of International Finance and Wealth which operates through men who are beyond public scrutiny and are tied together in a close-knit, relationship to Lucifer. This system financed and controlled the nations and created by powerful world controlling beastly empires. In essence, they created the One World Order and its methods of operations.

3. That history has not been a random and perchance evolutionary process of political and economic power, but has been a planned, purposeful conspiracy of Lucifer and His principalities and powers to control the world, destroy Christ and God's anointed people and thwart God's plan.

4. That the underlying of all the world systems of finance at its very roots, is a pseudo-religious system, based upon Lucifer's doctrine which was propagated in the Garden of Eden, and whispered into the soul of man through the world's religious perversions.

5. That religious perversion has actually been at the core of all economic and political powers throughout the ages. Luciferianism has been a fact throughout the ages, but only the most spiritual and discerning among God's people, have been able to discern its presence.

6. That the statement of Christ is very true, *"the love of money*

is the root of all kinds of evil," especially in those circles of satanic intrigue which we identify as the Economic World Order. The concepts shared here are believed and understood only by Godly people, who have been *"[guided] into all truth"* by the sweet Holy Spirit who, we are told, will *"tell you things to come"* (1 Timothy 6:10; John 16:13).

The world does not know, believe, or accept these concepts. No media, elitist, politician, or worldly leader will ever believe that God would look on their political institutions as a beastly government; or that He would see the great religions of our world as great beastly harlots or their humanistic and humane efforts to be shrouded with wickedness. They certainly would not believe that the power behind their work is an evil spirit or that there is a powerful evil principality inspiring them. They will not allow our Lord Jesus Christ to teach them that there is a *god of this world* who is *"the prince of the power of the air"* and who is diabolically and dialectically opposed to the God of Heaven and to our Lord (Ephesian 2:2). It is this *god* that is their god, and it is he who is the strength behind the nations. However, some of the men in these Escalon's of power have a suspicion of Satan being present.

AFRAID OF SOMETHING, SOMEWHERE

Consider a statement made by President Woodrow Wilson which can be found in his book, *The New Freedom*. He seems to have recognized this diabolical esoteric power behind the nations and their financial institutions, as well as their commerce and manufacturing organizations, but would not call it by its Biblical name, when he said:

> *"Some of the biggest men in the United States in the field of commerce and manufacturing are afraid of*

something. They know that there is a power somewhere, so organized, so subtle, so watchful, so interlocking, so complete, and so all pervasive, that they had better not speak in more than a whisper when they speak to condemn it" (also quoted by Pat Robertson in *The New World Order*, p. 95).

He was probably referring to that enclave of secret rulers of power and finance, but seems to recognize an esoteric force behind them.

For those of us who read the Bible, the Book of Revelation of Jesus Christ, and other prophetic texts know what that *something* is; where he dwells and what his power is that is so "organized, so subtle, so watchful, so interlocking, so complete, and so all pervasive." He is the original rebel and key adversary of Heaven—Satan himself.

We can easily follow the trail of this economic Babylon by some rather hidden agendas under way in a secret side of European politics. These are plans to bring back the Germanic Holy Roman Empire as it was in the days of Otto. This is actually the underlying cause and obscure facts about the last few centuries of history. These plans have nearly surfaced in the real cause of two World Wars with Germany. (Called the 2nd and 3rd Reich, or Empire; efforts to restore the old Reich or Empire) There are over two dozen kings of the old Empire in waiting to receive a kingdom when these plans are complete. They expect this will happen at the collapse of the Social Democratic failure soon to come in Europe. All of this fits perfectly into what we are told in prophecy.

Two efforts were made to bring back the Empire; both of them failed and are off the record. The third effort was made more public and came under Hitler and his Third Reich. A Reich in German is Empire. The supra-national sovereigns financed both sides of the conflicts with the design to bring the whole world under their control of an Empire of their making.

With the failure of the Third Reich, they have put together a Fourth Reich known as the Fourth Reich of the Rich.

Deciding that their dreams of the Old Empire coming back to power by military or political efforts have been futile, they have been working on a new effort to bring it back by a worldwide economic process. As we have said, its first step was the Trilateral Commission, an economic consortium between the U.S., European Union, and Japan. This eventually resulted in the G7 and now the G28, and at this point through the IMF, the World Bank, etc. who have for all practical purposes, accomplished putting together the Great Economic Babylon described in Revelation 18. We believe that out of this will come the 8th head, or the final *resurrection* of the Roman Empire.

We doubt that any normal thinking person can deny that the world is at this point, controlled financially by a worldwide, One World Order Economic Babylon. Every nation in the world is in debt over its head to this World Economic Order. All that is necessary to bring the World under control of the supra-national sovereigns is to call in the debt, which for all practical purposes would be to crash the economy of the world. America and Europe are bankrupt and only surviving even now on debt to the World Order of economic moguls. The Political/ Religious/Economical beast is just about here. The *"kings with no kingdoms as yet"* are in waiting (17:12). All we wait for is the total crash of the world economy, and the beast and the dragon (Satan) will be given control for a short 3 1/2 years. As Dr. Henry Spaak, Secretary General of NATO, said:

> *"What we want is a man of sufficient stature to hold the allegiance of all people and to lift us out of the economic morass into which we are sinking. Send us such a man, and be he God or devil, we will receive him."*

AVOID HER AS MUCH AS POSSIBLE EVEN TODAY (v.4, 5)

This is a message for any Christians who might be left on Earth, and especially to the Jews at the time of her destruction, and does not affect the Church because it is at this time, already in Heaven. However, it is wise to avoid the World Financial Order as much as possible, even today.

I believe that what we see here is a system of world finance which does not necessarily need to directly affect our personal finance. In this chapter, what will be destroyed are not all finances on all levels of the economy, but only a system of world finance. It only partially affects our personal finance, and less if we will keep ourselves out of debt and solvent from the banks in our personal life and business. There are finances that operate on a separate base which are only partially affected by what goes on in international finance, depending on how much we are able to keep our personal affairs outside of the world scene.

Our Lord Jesus Christ has an economy that operates, without, and in spite and independent of, this world's money systems. It operates on faith in God, hard work, and individual ability to meet and supply a need, and wise fiscal responsibility. This system of finance goes right on in spite of what the world's economic picture is doing. David said, "I have been young, and now am old; yet I have not seen the righteous forsaken, nor his descendants begging bread" (Psalm 37:25). Jesus said, *"But seek first the kingdom of God and His righteousness, and all these things shall be added to you"* (Matthew 6:33).

ONE DAY, ONE HOUR

I won't take a lot of time boring you with the details of the crash of the economy that is shown in chapter 18. Verses 9 through 19 shows us the world's kings, merchants, and shipmasters, all of whom by this time, have become totally dependent upon a system of world finance, and cry out:

> *"Alas, alas, that great city, in which all who had ships on the sea became rich by her wealth! For in one hour she is made desolate"* (18:19).

It is not news that they will be pulling their hair, ripping their cloths, committing suicide, and suing each other. Oh yes, this world will be in total chaos. We are experiencing in all countries today, some of the reactions caused by a small scale world financial crisis, but think of the uprising of total collapse.

Four times we are told that this great wealth that has been built up by the "Supra-national Sovereigns and the International Elite, and the World Bankers" (David Rockefeller's term, 1997), will collapse in *one day* or *one hour* of time (18:8, 10, 17, 19).

Now a puzzle is raised. It is one of those enigmatic mysteries associated with these last day prophecies. The question is raised by these world's financial moguls: "How can this happen in one hour?" At first it seems such a ridiculous thought, and certainly gives the mockers of Bible prophecy cause for their scoffing. But before we get too critical, we need to take a good look at the nature of today's World Finance.

I have puzzled over this statement for 50 years, knowing that God's Word is absolutely accurate and never misses future truth. But how could such a massive worldwide economy collapse in one hour? We have had to come to our present age to understand this *one hour, one day* scenario.

Today, it is a fact that our whole world economic system of money is built mostly on electronic transfer. All of that transfer takes place by computer. Therefore, we are told that at least 93% of the world's money is on the computer database and therefore it literally only exists in cyber-space. It is no longer on paper or hard copy, but exists on the worldwide web. Therefore, it is possible that it could totally collapse in only one hour.

Suddenly, this one day/one hour prophecy becomes very real. We had a taste of this one hour crises in the Y2K scare. It never happened, but it could have. As another example of how it could happen, can be imagined in the fact that one atomic bomb exploding 300 miles in the air over Washington, D.C., New York, or other economic centers, could cause an EMP (Electronic Magnetic Pulse) to happen. This could and probably would, cause a magnetic disturbance that would destroy all computer data base, and 93% of the records of all of our financial wealth would be gone. Certainly there would be backups, but that would have to be recovered and reinstalled, causing a tremendous blip in our systems. Personal properties and real estate ownership would still exist, but would have to be proven. The vast inter-relationships of international corporations, the shares each have in each other, and the proof of those shares etc., would have to be searched and reinstalled.

Jesus made reference to this disturbance in Luke 21:25, when He said, *"Men's hearts [will fail] them from fear and the expectation of those things which are coming on the earth, for the powers of heaven will be shaken."* Literally, the powers that are in the atmosphere shall be released. Atomic scientists tell us that this is a perfect description of Atomic Fusion. *"Men's hearts failing them"* is referring to the same reaction that is shown to us in Revelation 18:

> *"The merchants of these things, who became rich by her, will stand at a distance for fear of her torment, weeping and wailing"* (18:15).

No wonder they "threw dust on their heads and cried out, weeping and wailing..." (18:19). We see how the insight of

God personifies the system and uses the term *her* to relate the system to the harlot woman depicted in chapter 17. Verses 22 through 24 shows further how the world will lament as it describes the total chaos in society which will ensue at this worldwide collapse of the economy.

But remember, those of the body of Christ, who belong to Him and whose names are written down in the *Lambs Book of Life* will be caught up above this foray. These verses describe the social morass during the Tribulation and which will be afterward, until Jesus comes. There is one thing for sure, by the time He comes they will be ready for Him. In Matthew 23:39, Jesus says:

> *"For I say to you, you shall not see Me no more till you say 'blessed is He who comes in the name of the Lord.'"*

CARRIED EASTWARD TO SHINAR OR BABYLON

There is a strange prophecy in Zechariah, chapter 5. It certainly fits into this part of the Book of Revelation, and has to do with economic Babylon. Zechariah was one of the captives carried into Babylon, and he writes from there. His book speaks of the Lord's return to Jerusalem and to His temple, speaking of course, of Zerubbabel, Ezra, and Nehemiah's return in their day to build the second temple and restore Jerusalem. However, laced into the fabric of the hope of the return from Babylon to Jerusalem, lies presage of the latter-day return. We see the comparison of these texts in chapter 2 as it talks of the two olive trees being the two anointed ones who stand before the Lord of all the earth, which Jesus Christ pointed to and spoke of these two witnesses (Revelation 11:4-10). Chapter 3 of Zechariah ties the theme as Revelation 11, 12, and 14; speak of the Lord's return to Zion and Jerusalem. Chapter 4 of Zechariah speaks of the two witnesses of Revelation 11, and chapter 5 tells

FALL OF THE WORLD ECONOMY 625

about the transfer of the World Order unit of International Exchange, moving eastward to Babylon (Shinar). Chapter 6 has the 4 horsemen which ties into Revelation 6, and so on. Zechariah, chapter by chapter, parallels Revelation, and is fulfilled in the State of Israel and the Jewish return.

Now, let's direct our attention to the chapter 5 of Zechariah. Two visions have come to Zechariah. They speak of the interests of Israel moving to Babylon in the foreseeable future of Zechariah's day, which certainly was fulfilled, in that the center of Judaism moved to Babylon. But as we have said, there are predictions of a far greater scope hidden in cryptic symbols here in these texts, all of which point us to very specific revelations that come to us in their final stage of fulfillment. Christ reveals them to us in the Revelation. Let's look closely at the context of Zechariah, chapter 5. A flying scroll is seen, and an explanation reveals that it is a curse which falls on the whole world (Zechariah 5:3). It will be put in the house of liars, thieves, and consumers; consumers, not as we who buy things, but in the sense that they are taking from others' unearned and undo profit, and consuming the wages of the working class on themselves (5:4; James 5:1-6).

The second vision is related. The angel said that Zechariah should notice where it is flying to and why (Zechariah 5:5). It is now likened to an ephah. This ephah has something to do with the whole earth (5:6). In those days, the ephah was a standard measure of exchange between people and nations. It was worth a little over a bushel of grain, and everyone traded with its measure. So we have a measure of International medium of exchange moving somewhere.

This International measure of exchange is said to be a curse to the whole world, and has a very heavy weight covering it which indicates that it is a heavy weight on the whole world (ibid 5:7). In cryptic symbolism it is called a *woman.* She is sitting on this measure of exchange. She is called *"wickedness"* (ibid v. 8). Now we have the picture. An International medium of exchange unit is a great weight to the world, and has a strange woman sitting on it and flying through the air. It is being taken somewhere. Verses 5:9-11 allow us to look into a strange airline flight. We see the International Exchange unit lifted up by the wings of a stork, which has very strong pennons in its wings; therefore, it can carry a very heavy weight. It is carried to Shinar, or Babylon (Iraq) where they will build it a house and set it upon its own base, or foundation. We hear rumblings today of a move by the International Community to collapse all the monies of the world and use the Dinar (Iraq's or Shinar's money) as a base for international finance. Some sort of action by the World finance will create World Money soon.

How does this all fit into Revelation 18? Note that it is a unit of monetary exchange that is used by the world economic system, which is the subject of chapter 18. Also, note that it is likened to a woman, which we see in cryptic symbolism in Revelation 17 and 18. This great worldwide economic system is called by the feminine gender over and over in chapter 18. She is called *wickedness* and a *curse*. She is clearly likened to a heavy weight upon the whole world. So in cryptic symbolism, I believe it is easy to identify the ephah with the harlot and her evil system of world monetary exchange.

Where is her house and foundation to be moved to? The land of Shinar is its destination. Shinar is the old name of the land of Babylon, today's Iraq. In some strange sense, which we will probably only understand its full meaning in the day of its fulfillment, a strong economic base for international exchange will be moved to Iraq, or Babylon—old Shinar. I believe the name Shinar is used to remind us of the first worldwide monetary fiat money to be used and it began in

Babylon—Shinar in Nimrod's days (Genesis 10:10; Daniel 1:2). Dakes' Annotated Bible has this to say:

> "The ephah was a unit of international trade and if there is one thing for certain, Babylon will be the center of activities in the East during the last days of commerce, religion, and politics. It will become the capital of the Antichrist."

This answers why Babylon is brought back to our attention and mentioned six times as related to the last 3½ years of Tribulation. Satan, who has sinister plans for the world hidden in the institutions he started in Shinar at the gate of the wrong way to God (Bab-el, a false way to God), returns there to finish his dastardly deeds.

All pagan, heathen religions, as well as the fiat money system of exchange, and the political will to conquer the world, grew out of Nimrod's Babylon. It was all a mystic system of mysteries, and contained the element of rebellion against God as it does today, because it came from the heart of Satan, whose rebellion against God was externalized at the Gate of God (Isaiah 13:17-22). We read here the same language as in Revelation 18:2 and Jeremiah 51:60-64. The Antichrist will probably come from Babylon to meet the Lord at Megiddo, and the final end of Satan's rebellion will center in Babylon.

To lend further evidence of the International World Order's plans to bring in a world money system, consider the front cover of the *Economist Magazine* for January 9, 1989. Depicted there is the old *Phoenix Bird*, a symbol of resurrected Rome, rising out of the fires of the burning up of all of the world's monies. On its head is the crown of the Holy Roman Empire and around its neck is a medallion representing the New World Money, and it's marked 2018. The picture is captioned with, "Get ready for a World Currency."

THE CHURCH AND HEAVEN'S REACTIONS TO THE FALL OF BABYLON

It is no wonder Heaven and the Church and all of the Apostles and Prophets are rejoicing over her fall. It will be replaced by Christ with a pure and righteous system. In the meantime, we must make friends with the mammon of unrighteousness—money. Notice who is rejoicing now: first the Heavens, which would include the Church, the angels and the living creatures; then the apostles, and finally the prophets (Revelation 18:20).

This will be the attitude and spirit of the Kingdom of God upon the collapse of the world economy and the demise of the last three enemies of the Lamb. But, note verse 20, and then turn to the first seven verses of chapter 19 to catch the attitude and spirit of the Church, and the people of God in Heaven at the collapse of Babylon:

> "*Rejoice over her, O heaven, and you holy apostles and prophets, for God has avenged you on her*" (18:20)!

Babylon's destruction is so complete that it is depicted as having a millstone hung around its neck and cast into the depth of the sea. It would no longer finance domestic life, entertainment, the pomp of society, or marriage bliss. And one reason for rejoicing is that, there would be no more drug trafficking (18:23). We are not told what the Millennium's financial structure will be, but we can be assured it will take care of every facet of our lives without the waste, graft (political corruption), greed, and corruption of the World Order. Drugs are hard to stop because of the deep inroads of the World Order made by its involvement in the illicit money exchange in the world drug market.

The final fall of Babylon is foretold in Jeremiah 51:54-64. The things that we read in Revelation 18:21-23 were prophesied by the Word of God to Jeremiah in detail, like we read here:

"After these things I heard a loud voice of a great multitude in heaven" (19:1). Here is the Church of the Redeemed; the Bride and Bridegroom, and all the friends of the Bridegroom, along with the living ones, and the redeemed Jews, especially the 144,000. And what is their reaction to the fall of Babylon? The only record of the use of the word *"Hallelujah"* in the New Testament can be found in Revelation 19, and it is all in response to the collapse of Mystery Babylon the Great. Our praise is due to God, because:

> *"He has judged the great harlot who corrupted the earth with her fornication; and He has avenged on her the blood of His servants shed by her"* (19:2).

This verse shows us to be absolutely correct in tying together the great Mystery Babylon, the spiritual whore of the 17th chapter, and the economical Babylon of the 18th chapter.

Chapter 19 is the great final blessing that shows the result of the end of all this corruption that is a part of Satan's world through his control of the ungodly and rebellious nations.

CHAPTER 19

OUTCOME OF CHRIST AND ARMAGEDDON

RECEIVING THE PROMISED POSSESSION

Two adolescent boys from a Christian home were giving their mother problems, so she decided to send them for a session with the Pastor. She called him and made arrangements for them to meet. The Pastor, being a discerning fellow from long experience, requested that they meet one at a time, beginning with the younger.

The time came and the mother brought both boys to the office. The younger boy was sent in to meet the Pastor. The Pastor was a very large Viking type fellow. He studied the boy for a long period of time without a word. Suddenly, he said, "Where is God?" The little boy just sat there staring at him, so he asked again, "Where is God?" The little fellow jumped up, ran out and by his mother and brother, out the door and down the street toward home.

It worried the mother so she suspended the older boy's appointment and followed the younger boy home. The older one found him hiding in the closet up the stairs. "What in the world is the matter?" he asked. The little fellow looked up with traumatic fear in his eyes and said, "Oh brother, they've lost God and they're blaming it on us!"

Friends, as we view the final end in the Book of the Revelation of Jesus Christ, I think there is no time to lose our relationship with God and Christ. The world has lost God and is trying to blame it on us.

As we have been thinking of the whole drama of Revelation as a theatrical production, we have designated Chapters 19 through 22 under the title of Act 5 with 4 scenes, the final act in the Pageant of Divine Judgment and the final result of the Revelation of Jesus Christ.

We have also moved out of the *meanwhiles* for there is no parallel to this chapter. These events are the conclusion of all that we have been through to this point. It is the grandest of the grand finale. When we reach this point, it's all over except the shouting. And, although there are references to chapters 19 - 22 in all of the other chapters, especially from chapters 2 and on, these events do not parallel any of the others. We are now going to witness what the:

"Eye has not seen, nor ear heard, nor have entered into the heart of man the things which God has prepared for those who love Him" (1 Corinthians 2:9).

With this verse to consider, I doubt that even the half is told to us in these chapters. I also doubt that we can begin to imagine what these days will be like. Just as we are getting over the shouting for the complete destruction of the beast, the harlot, and the economic morass our world has been in, we are allowed to see the dragon and Satan with his angels bound and cast into the pit for 1000 years. As if that wasn't enough, we are called to the Marriage Supper of the Lamb. Some time in this preparation, we will be introduced to the throne room, and with great humility and feeling of unworthiness, we are shown our throne.

We have barely caught our breath when we look up and watch the New Jerusalem coming down from God out of

Heaven, adorned as a Bride for her Bridegroom. Oh Lord, strengthen me, as I will need a new body, soul, spirit, and heart to handle it.

THE CONSUMMATION OR COMPLETION

This *Act* will be called *"The Consummation (or completion) of the Inheritance"* with a subtitle *"Receiving the Promised Possession."* The *will* has been read and executed by its executor Jesus Christ, and He brings His bride to receive their inheritance.

In these next four chapters, we will be dealing with what the scriptures have called *"the dispensation of the fullness of the times"* (Ephesians 1:10). After eons of ages since the beginning of time and the first promise, we finally come to the fulfillment of all the expectations foretold by the prophets, both for the Church and for Israel.

It also brings to an end what Jesus called *"the times of the Gentiles"* (Luke 21:24). This is the end of the great Empires—Babylon, Persia, Greece, and Rome; the Gentile rule over the world as well as over the Holy Land, and their persecution of Israel. We have seen these empires morph into a One World Order made up of a mutated form of all of them combined. (Compare Revelation 13:1 with Daniel 7:1-4) In Daniel 2:44-45 we see as Daniel saw, a rock which no doubt is Jesus Christ, crashing into the feet of the Gentile World System. Then the whole World Order of Gentile power comes tumbling down at the feet of Christ to end *"the times of the Gentiles"* (Luke 21:24). That will be the result of Armageddon.

In the time-line of this chapter, we will study the events that take place between the Fall of Babylon—the final part of the World Order at Armageddon; that is, the fall of the beast's kingdom and the setting up of the Millennial Kingdom of Christ. This will be about 1,335 days according to Daniel

12. The European prince, the Antichrist and false prophet will fall at Armageddon. The details of the fall of the men involved, the Romans prince or little horn, along with the false prophet, the second beast (what we believe to be the Antichrist) will be shown in this chapter.

The beast's kingdom with its European prince will fall at Armageddon. The details of the fall of the men involved, the Roman prince or little horn, along with the false prophet, the second beast (what we believe to be the Antichrist) will be shown in this chapter (Revelation 19:20).

We now come to the final end and see the purpose for all that has passed. Remember, all of the horror and terror that we have studied takes place in only a 7-year span and most of it in the last 3½ years (42 months, 1260 days). According to what the angel told Daniel, there will be 75 days to set up the Kingdom of Christ and come to the coronation of the Great King inside the Eastern Gate. *"Oh I want to be in that number, when they crown Him Lord of All"* (E. Abdel). The earth mourns the loss of its prized possession, but Heaven rejoices at the end of the false Church, a fiat economy, and a beastly political system.

A loss to the world is a gain to Heaven. Christ *"puts an end to all rule and all authority and power"* (1 Corinthians 15:24). The world's political, economic, military, and religious systems are moved out of the way so the Millennial Kingdom and reign of Christ can come.

The seven seals have been opened and all conditions have been met for our inheritance in Christ; the seven trumpets have laid claim to our promised possession in Christ; and the seven vials have put down Satan's rule, won the war, and ended the conflict between Heaven and Earth. Also, Christ has returned to Zion. The last victory was the fall of Babylon the Great, and her religious and economic fiat (Revelation 16:19). That old harlot, mother of all of the abominations of the earth, and Satan who begat her (which has distracted the world from the true Bride for centuries) is revealed. The triangle love affair is over, so now the true Bride of Christ can be given in marriage with honor. All Heaven and Earth, Jews and Gentiles, angels and seraph, have come to see the wedding take place. The great victory of Christ and the Church with the Jews as guests is shown in the praises that continually go up to the throne and the temple:

> *"Alleluia! Salvation and glory and honor and power to the Lord our God! For true and righteous are His judgments"* (19:1).

We see now that Christ and the Father were right all along!

A GREAT NUMBER - MANY PEOPLE

By this time, there has been a great multitude gathered which no one could number of every nation, kindred, people, and tongue (7:9, 19:6). Verse 19:9 pronounces a blessing on all of those that received an invitation to the *"marriage of the Lamb."* Great excitement builds as the saints from every age and every time, both Old and New Testaments along with pre- and post-Tribulation martyrs, gather at the banquet hall in Heaven. It recalls for us the innumerable times we have participated in the gathering of family and friends at a marriage feast: the joy, the good will with laughter and tears, renewed acquaintances, and memories.

Oh, what a time that will be when old friends, ministry associates and missionaries, business partners, and beloved church members, meet again. And what of family: brothers and sisters, Dads, Moms, Grandma's, Grandpa's, children, aunts, uncles, cousins and others come together to celebrate the Marriage of the Lamb.

"Oh there's going to be a meeting in the air, in the sweet, sweet by and by. And oh, I want to meet you over there, in the land beyond the sky. Such singing you will hear, never heard by mortal ear, 'twill be glorious I do declare. When God's own Son will be the leading one, at the meeting in the air" (Old Immortal Chorus).

And what of that moment when He breaks the bread with us in the Kingdom? It will be the first time that we, His disciples have broken bread with Him since the night before Calvary when He said to His disciples:

"Assuredly, I say to you, I will no longer drink of the fruit of the vine until that day when I drink it new in the Kingdom of God" (Mark 14:25).

He spoke of a feast He will have with us, and then said we would sit on thrones:

"I bestow upon you a kingdom, just as my Father bestowed one upon me, that you may eat and drink at My table in My kingdom, and sit on thrones judging the twelve tribes of Israel" (Luke 22:29-30).

GREATEST CAMP MEETING EVER (v. 1-6)

Revelation 19:1-6 allows us to attend the last great camp meeting before the Millennium. The marvelous vision of Handel's *Messiah* will be enacted as Heaven with its angelic host, and Christ our Lord joins the Church and the Jews in Heaven—the redeemed yet on Earth, and the sheep nations left after Armageddon. All will join in the greatest anthem ever, crying *"Alleluia ... Alleluia ... Alleluia"* (Revelation 19:1-6; Greek for Hallelujah, Hallelujah, Hallelujah!).

OUTCOME OF CHRIST AND ARMAGEDDON

Handel wrote:

> "Hallelujah, Hallelujah, for the Lord God omnipotent reigns, Hallelujah, Hallelujah, for the Lord God omnipotent reigns."

And another old song of the Church comes to mind, *When the Saints go Marching In:*

> "Oh Lord, I want to be in that number, when they sing, I've been redeemed; and when they march around the throne; and when they crown Him Lord of all" (Anonymous).

This great Camp Meeting will initiate a practice that will continue throughout the Millennium. It is recorded in Zechariah:

> *"And it shall come to pass that everyone who is left of all the nations which came against Jerusalem shall go up from year to year to worship the King, the Lord of hosts, and to keep the Feast of the Tabernacles"* (14:16).

BLESSED ARE THE PEOPLE WHO KNOW THE JOYFUL SOUND (Psalms 89:15)

The Old Testament is very specific about this time, when Christ with His Saints, return to Jerusalem. There never has been and never will be again a triumphal march like the day that the King comes through the Eastern Gate, and His saints with Him. As Doctor Henry Morris reminded us in a *Days of Praise* pamphlet, a joyful sound was heard when He created the earth (Job 38:4, 7); and when Christ was born (Luke 2:10-14); and again there is a joyful sound when one repentant sinner comes home (Luke 15:7). Psalms 89:15 refers to the joyful sound of Israel ascending the steps from Ophel to the temple grounds at a Holy Day celebration, which was so glorious that the Queen of Sheba, when she heard it, said *"the half has not been told"* (1 Kings 10:7). Returning to her kingdom, she sold all she had and returned to Jerusalem to be part of that glorious crowd that worshipped there. But nothing can compare to the glorious shout, the joyful sound of Christ and His Church—the Bride, as they make their way from Heaven to the Great Gate in Jerusalem. If we were not changed, our hearts would burst within us for joy. That joy is reflected in many texts, but I am thinking of the one from which a great chorus was written that speaks of our coming to Zion in the return. It closely follows Isaiah 51:11:

> *"Therefore the redeemed of the Lord shall return, and come with singing unto Zion, and everlasting joy shall be upon their heads. They shall obtain gladness and joy, and sorrow and mourning shall flee away. Therefore the redeemed of the Lord shall return with singing unto Zion, and everlasting joy shall be upon their heads."*

THE MARRIAGE OF THE LAMB - THE BRIDE HAS MADE HERSELF READY (v.7)

The guests are all present, including the saints of all the ages who are not part of the Bride, and who are friends of the Bridegroom; angels and seraphim all stand waiting for the revelation of the Bride.

There are two revealed in the Revelation. One, of course, is the Lamb, or in this case, the Bridegroom. Romans 8 tells us that it will also be the time when the bride is revealed, for it will be the time of the manifestation, or *"revealing of the sons of God"* (the Church) (8:19). All creation has been waiting for this moment when the bride as well as the bridegroom, is revealed. There is a lot of speculation about just what group, or which individuals will be in the Bride of Christ. For the first time ever, we will all know exactly who they are, Nevertheless ... *"the Lord knows those who are His, and let everyone who names the name of Christ* (takes that name as in marriage) *depart from iniquity"* (2 Timothy 2:19).

THE BRIDE MADE HERSELF READY (V. 7)

This, of course, is speaking of the time of the wedding, but there is another factor important to us today as we yet wait for the Rapture. Are you ready? An old song used to rattle our conscience as it was sung: "Are you ready, are you ready, are you ready for the Judgment Day?" Well we are not worried about Judgment Day since our sins have been covered by the blood of Christ. But there is a time coming that is another important time of judgment, and that is the time of the Rapture. Are you ready? Have you departed from iniquity?

One day I was waiting for my flight at an airport and watching the incoming flight depart, I observed two women. Now, before you jump to conclusions let me finish the story and give you my purpose for watching them. They were both waiting for either their husbands or boyfriends to disembark, or at least the love of their lives. One was decked out to a "T" making herself presentable for her lover. She stood as close to the gate as they would allow, and on tip toes looked over the head of the departing passengers, anxious to get the first glimpse of her lover. No doubt she was anxious.

The other was sloppy in dress, casual in demeanor, with no sign of anxiety or excitement for the appearance of her supposed lover. Rather than standing at the gate waiting, she was lazily slouched in a chair in front of the Television. She seemed unaware that the plane was unloading, and her friend would soon be appearing. She was absorbed in some ridiculous comedy show. The question came to me, "was she really ready to meet him?"

Suddenly the first lady saw her lover, she screamed and danced around, and suddenly ran down the hall to meet him, throwing herself into his arms. No doubt she was excited to see him. I watched the other lady as her man approached. He had to look for her to even find her. Finely he spotted her and slipped up behind her, bent over and kissed her on the forehead. She turned and frowned at him, pushed him away, indicating she did not want to be disturbed from her program. The first couple went down the walk-way arm in arm while the other couple, when they finally started toward the luggage area, just slouched along, she with no seeming interest in him, and he broken-hearted and exasperated. Hello! I need not preach on this story; I think you can catch my implication. But let me ask again, "Are you ready?"

We celebrate the marriage at the marriage *gamos*, Hebrew for marriage supper. This great praise service will initiate the marriage procession of the Bride with Christ when the Bride is made ready and manifest (or is revealed to the world):

> *"For the earnest expectation of all creation eagerly waits for the revealing of the sons of God* (the Church)" (Romans 8:19).

MYSTERY OF CHRIST AND HIS CHURCH

Proverbs 30:18-19 tells us that there are four things too wonderful for us to understand: *"The way of the eagle in the air, the way of a serpent on a rock, the way of a ship in the midst of the sea, and the way of a man with a virgin."* All personal relationships between a man and his wife are a mystery that no one else can understand except them. It is a total mystery to the rest of us (Ephesians 5:32).

So it is with Christ and His Church. Only Christ Himself knows who the members of His body—His Bride are. There are plenty of hints, and we can make some good guesses, but in finality, no one knows who the Bride is and who members of the Bride are until they are called out and made manifest at the Marriage Supper of the Lamb (Romans 8:19).

I have often said that we will have three surprises at the Marriage Supper of the Lamb: 1) Who is there that we did not expect to be there? 2) Who is not there that we certainly expected to be there? and 3) That we ourselves are there! Only Christ knows those who are in love with Him. Paul said:

> *"For I have betrothed you to one husband, that I may present you as a chaste* (pure) *virgin to Christ"* (2 Corinthians 11:2).

Paul said that the mystery of Christ had been kept secret from the beginning of the world, but made known to us and revealed only at the coming of Christ (Romans 16:25; Ephesians 1:9). And:

> *"… eagerly waiting for the revelation of our Lord Jesus Christ, who will also confirm you to the end, that you may be blameless in the day of our Lord Jesus Christ"* (1 Corinthians 1:7).

That is when He will confirm us as part of the Bride and present us to His Father. Christ will "receive" His Bride and, together with His Bride, will be revealed, or be made manifest in all of His glory:

> *"And if I go and prepare a place for you, and if I go and prepare a place for you, I will come again and receive you unto myself; that where I am, there you may be also"* (John 14:3).

The Bride has made herself ready by her life of discipleship on Earth. Christ, together with His Bride, will be totally victorious.

We note that the Marriage of the Lamb takes place probably in Heaven, before Christ's return to Earth. We will also note that the Bride, the Church, is coming with Christ out of Heaven so she must have been in Heaven.

We are told that Christ will return *"with ten thousands of His saints"* (Jude 14). How did she get to Heaven and when did she enter? The answer is very clear in Revelation 4:1. She has been in Heaven ever since she was invited to *"come up here,"* and she is seen in Heaven throughout the time of the Tribulation.

After the marriage of the Lamb, Christ and His Bride will return to take ownership of the Promised Possession and the Inheritance of the Saints in Light, which Christ has prepared for us (19:1-7). We will enjoy a honeymoon with Christ in His 1000-year kingdom reign. This period of time will involve the events between Revelation 19:1 and 20:3. It takes us from Armageddon to the setting up of the Millennial Kingdom. That time-frame is probably represented by the extra 75 days on the end of the last 3 ½ years of the seven-year period of the wrath of God (Daniel 12:6-13):

"Blessed is he that waits, and comes to the one thousand three hundred and thirty-five days (1335 days after the end of the war and the binding of Satan)*"* (12:12).

Daniel is told that from the time that the *Abomination of Desolation* is set up in the middle of the seven-year period in Daniel 9:27, it will be 1290 days (ibid 12:11). That is 30 days past the 3½ year period. Then Daniel is told that those who wait for day number 1,335 will be *"blessed"* (12:12). It is another additional 45 days to the setting up of the Millennium and the *"[anointing of] the Most Holy"* (9:24). This is the inauguration of the Lord Jesus Christ as shown as the 6th and last blessing at the end of the Tribulation. It will take 75 days between the fall of the beastly kingdom and the setting up of the Kingdom of Christ.

This period includes the great praise camp meeting

service in Heaven (19:1-6). At the end of Armageddon and after the Millennium Kingdom is set up, the Marriage of the Lamb takes place in Heaven (19:7-9). Also, the earthly return of Christ with His saints in glory, to Jerusalem and the Temple Mount will take place (Isaiah 25:6-9). There, we will eat at His table in His Kingdom which is the Inaugural Banquet (Luke 22:30). He will then take the throne and accept the kingdom, and seat His Bride next to Him (19:11-16). There are some great things that will take place in Zion and the Temple Mount at that time. He will destroy the *veil of deception* that has been over all nations, and the rebuke of His people—the Jews, will be broken, and death will be swallowed up in victory.

This is almost too overwhelming to comprehend, that I scarce can take it in. The seals have been opened and all the conditions for inheritance have been met (Revelation 6, 8). The *Book of Sentence* has been opened and the sentence meted out against the imposters (10, 13-18). Satan's short time is over and the mystery of God is finished. It is done (15-16, 19:20).

Now we will follow closely the afterglow and glory of the victory of Christ and His Bride.

FULLNESS OF TIME - RECEIVING THE PROMISED POSSESSION AND INHERITANCE

The afterglow of Christ's great victory over Satan and his version of the World Order is known as the Dispensation of the fullness of time." (Ephesians 1:10) This time is when we receive our full inheritance and several different, but related things will take place (Ephesians 1:11-14):

1. *Christ will bring a full Restoration*—Restoration of Earth, to conditions as they were in the beginning before the fall of either Satan or man; and conditions as God the

Father and Christ the Son had intended them to be in the beginning. A habitable earth like a paradise of Eden, was envisioned by the God-head, to be a place for the kingdom of the Son and His subjects among men.

2. *Personal restoration*—We ourselves will be restored to our original state as we were before sin and rebellion entered our lives. We were originally not naked, but were clothed in an aura of light, which reflected the glory and brilliance of God and Christ. The human race lost that aura and we discovered that without it, we were naked. Now only a slight resemblance of that aura dwells on our skin until we die. When we are complete in Christ at the restoration of all things, that aura will be restored to us as a covering of full brilliance, i.e. *saints in light*. We will have no need of light, for *"the Lamb is its light"* (Revelation 21:23). We will speak at length of this when we comment about our state in the New Jerusalem.

3. *Christ will bring a full restitution of all things* (Acts 3:19-21)—Restitution differs from restoration in-as-much as restoration has more to do with physical things. Restoration means to renew or to put back as it was; to repair or put back in original condition. All of this is a physical thing. Restitution means to lay it to rest, or to redress a situation rather than renew something; to indemnify, recompense, or repay legally; a reimbursement.

    Therefore Christ, in His redemption process will both restore the physical earth and restore us to our original form, but will also redress and repay all of our legal claims, and reimburse us for our losses.

4. *Christ will also bring full Redemption*—He will complete the whole of the plan of God for redemption. For instance, since Satan fell taking two thirds of the angels with Him and then becoming involved in the fall of

man, it was necessary to devise a plan of redemption for man. That plan will be finished when Christ returns in His Revelation, as shown in this book. *"Now salvation, and strength, and the kingdom of our God ... have come"* (Revelation 12:10). We have been saved from sin by the blood; we are being saved and sealed from self by the Holy Spirit; we will be saved from Satan and His rebellion at the return of Christ.

5. *Christ will make Reconciliation*—A careful study of 2 Corinthians 5:17-21 will help us realize the impact of this reconciliation, both on Earth and in Heaven, as well as in us. The Word indicates that there has come a rift, or very hurtful separation, between two people. There is deep hurt on both parties and in heartbreak and loneliness, they long to work it out and be friends again. There has been a lack of communication between friends, business partners, family, children, siblings, husband and wife, and neighbors far too long. All of them live in heaviness every time we see or think of the other person.

That is precisely the separation that has come between us and our maker, God. We must realize that the breach has not been caused by anything on God's part. It is all on our part:

"But your iniquities have separated you from God; and your sins have hidden His face from you, so that He will not hear" (Isaiah 59:2).

God and Christ are as hurt as we are. They long with broken hearts to resolve the breach caused by our sins and iniquities. Their great hearts for our reconciliation is shown in that: (John 3:16)

"He gave His only begotten Son, that whoever believes in Him should not perish but have everlasting life" (John 3:16).

No one has to tell us that we have plenty in our own lives that has offended a holy God, let alone how we have often offended precious friends and relatives. Before I came to know God through the love of Jesus Christ, I thought of him as kind of a mean, old dictator who just sits around on high, striking out at all of us because he hated us; that mean old God of the Old Testament. But I found that through the reconciliation of Christ, God is really a loving God who cannot tolerate sin in His sinless universe. He has purpose and design for a trouble-free universe for us to help him administrate. It will be so wonderful throughout the ages to come to be part of a universe where there is no loss of close friendship between us and God, as well as between each other. There is no joy like the joy of true heartfelt reconciliation. Oh, how sweet is the wonder of reconciliation. I don't know of any experience as joyful and accelerating as to be part of, or witness real heartfelt reconciliation. I suppose it may be one of the most exciting experiences in Heaven as well as here on Earth. We are told that the angels rejoice when one sinner comes home and his/her name is written down in the *Lamb's Book of Life*.

The first step in making reconciliation with us is through our faith and relationship to Jesus Christ, for we are made new creatures in Christ Jesus (2 Corinthians 5:17). Old things in our rebellious days are over, and we are new in Him. It is this new life that allows us to come back into right relationship with God, and reconciled us back to Him (5:18).

We are not friends of God, but we are enemies because of our rebellion and transgression against Him and His righteous law. No matter how good we are, our righteousness is as filthy rags in the sight of God. We all deserve nothing more than Hell. It must be understood to the church that songs proclaiming "I am a friend of God," speak only of those in Christ. The rest are not a friend of God. We are only friends through Jesus Christ; otherwise we make Christ's death of no effect. Outside of Christ's reconciliation, we are alienated from God, and in our minds, enemies by our wicked works. Yet now, He has *"[reconciled] all things to Himself"* (Colossians 1:20-21).

This complete reconciliation takes place after Armageddon, but before the Marriage of the Lamb. Christ is a friend of God, and when God sees us through the righteousness of Christ, only then are we acceptable; only in Christ can we address God, and be heard; only in Christ is our sin not imputed (not credited to our account, nor counted against) to us.

How blessed we are when God no longer looks at us as sinners, but as the Redeemed. The book of Romans reminds us of this blessing:

"Blessed are those whose lawless deeds are forgiven, and whose sins are covered; Blessed is the man to whom the Lord shall not impute sin" (4:7).

One of the outcomes and results of Tribulation, will be that all sin and rebellion will be put down; in us, in angels, and in Hell, as Satan will be bound, and all transgression and sin will end; it will be finished, and reconciliation will be made for iniquity by bringing in everlasting righteousness in the fullness of Jesus Christ our Lord (Daniel 9:24). He has also committed, or assigned unto us, the *word* of reconciliation (9:20) That is, He has given to us by the anointing of the Holy Spirit, the same anointing that rests upon Jesus who is *The Word* to speak the word of reconciliation into people's lives. Our appointment as Ambassadors of Christ is to speak the word of reconciliation to all people. To be reconciled back to God by the blood of the Lamb is one of the greatest of accomplishments by our Lord and Savior when He presented His blood on the mercy seat in Heaven (Hebrews 9:24-28).

HEAVEN ALSO RECONCILED

When Jesus Christ puts down all the enemies, even Heaven will be restored to its original peace. Ever since the rebellion of Satan and His angels, Heaven has been at war: *"And war broke out in Heaven"* (Revelation 12:7). That war will go on until at the beginning of the Tribulation, when Satan and His angels will be cast out of Heaven and will be sent to Earth. This will wreak havoc with the aid of demons out of the pit (Revelation 9). The first of three woes is *"woe to the inhabitants of the earth and the sea! For the devil has come down to you, having great wrath, because he knows that he has a short time"* (12:12).

Meanwhile, up in Heaven for the first time in ages, they have a breath of fresh air and cry out:

"Now salvation and strength, and the kingdom of God, and the power of His Christ have come, for the accuser of our brethren ... has been cast down" (12:10).

My point is this: after Christ deals with the accuser of the brethren, even Heaven is made at peace. Then at Armageddon, the accuser and trouble maker, that old dragon the serpent—Satan is taken from the earth and "cast into the bottomless pit ... and set a seal on him ... till the thousand years were finished (20:1-3). Now, restitution, restoration, and reconciliation can be made in the whole universe.

6. *Christ will bring a completion*—It is known as the consummation or quick, final conclusion to all things. For instance, where Christ speaks of the Tribulation being shortened in Matthew 24:22, the Greek word is *Koicboo* meaning a quick and final conclusion. Christ has allowed Satan plenty of time to prove Himself and complete His rebellion. Now the mystery of God—those things kept secret in the battle plan, is made plain; the *"mystery of God*

[is] finished" (Revelation 10:7). There is no more time for Satan and rebellion; "It is done!" (10:6, 16:17). Christ brings it to a short and sudden completion. All of the purposes for this final confrontation in the 70th week of Daniel, or the Tribulation is complete (Daniel 9:24). That phase of rebellion is over, the plan for completion is done, and God, through Christ, begins again to complete what He started in the first place.

7. *Christ shall make a consummation*—From the word *Kabah* in Hebrew, comes a word that is clearly a part of the final end. Isaiah prophesies that *"those who forsake the Lord [in the end times] shall be consumed"* (1:28); Kabah, i.e. like our slang kabash, which means to lay one out with a punch. Daniel 9:27 says that at the cutting off of the sacrifice in the midst of the Tribulation, there will be an overspreading of abominations which makes a desolation, *"even until the consummation which is determined [by God in His plan] is poured out on the desolate,"* those who have fallen into abomination.

This verse tells us beyond question that except for the restoration of those things useful to Christ and God in the coming Kingdom, all else will be consumed by fire. Isaiah 10 further comments on this consummation to come in the end-time. When the Lord Jesus Christ comes to complete His work on Mount Zion and on Jerusalem, the Remnant of Israel will return and the glory of the Lord will become like a burning fire to kindle a light upon Israel (Isaiah 10:16). The holy one of Israel will be a flame upon Israel to devour the thorns and briers, not weeds, but tares sown in the field of the Lord's harvest field (10:17). And a remnant of Israel will return, and in that time, the consumption (kabah) decreed shall *"overflow with righteousness. For the Lord God of hosts will make a determined end in the midst of all the land"* (10:22-23).

A decree is an official declaration, or signed order of the will of a King. The will of Christ who is the coming King of the Kingdom has decreed, or ordered this consummation before the setting up of the Kingdom of Christ. It is *determined* by the Lord Jesus Christ, and it will be.

When the great "I AM" says "I will," It is, or will be! Hide and watch, take it to the bank, when Christ says will be, it will be!

HEAVEN OPENED FOR SECOND TIME (v.7)

This is the second time in the Book of Revelation that Heaven has been opened. We have been allowed to see through the veil between Heaven and Earth several times, but not through an open door. The first time the door was opened was in chapter 4. There, it was open to take the Saints out of Earth and into Heaven. The second time it was opened on Earth to let the saints, together with Christ, come back to Earth. We should note that Heaven's door is not open until after the Marriage Supper of the Lamb, an indication that the Marriage Feast will take place in Heaven.

> *"The ransomed of the Lord shall return, and come to Zion with singing, with everlasting joy on their heads; they shall obtain joy and gladness, and sorrow and sighing shall flee away"* (Isaiah 51:11).

And Isaiah 35:10 echoes the same. In a chapter that speaks of the Millennium we read:

> *"And the ransomed of the Lord shall return, and come to Zion with singing, with everlasting joy on their heads. They shall obtain joy and gladness, and sorrow and sighing shall flee away."*

I have been part of that Joyful sound many times as the

saints stood and sang "I have heard the joyful sound, Jesus saves, Jesus saves…" from the great song written by David, recorded Psalm 89:15, *"blessed are the people who know the joyful sound."*

Christ will get rid of all rebellion and corruption in both Heaven and Earth, and the Universe will forever by free from corruption:

> *"But there shall by no means enter [into] it anything that defiles, or causes an abomination or a lie, but only those who are written in the Lamb's Book of Life"* (Revelation 21:27).

When Christ gets finished, and before we move into the New Jerusalem, He will absolutely clean up this universe so that our work area will be OSHA approved, as it were.

Thank God for my new life in Christ Jesus my Lord; for without His change in my life, if I were to go to Heaven in that natural and unredeemed state, I would be part of the pollution and defiling of both life and eternity, maybe even the abomination of the city; thank you Jesus, for changing me and trusting me enough to write my name in the Book of life.

> "Is my name written there, on the page bright and fair, in the book of thy kingdom, is my name written there?" (Mary A. Kilder)

CHRIST DRASTICALLY CHANGED - A MAN OF WAR AGAIN (v.11-21)

Christ rides a war charger—a white horse. We have seen this white horse a number of times in the Scriptures. His name for this event is *Faithful and True,* showing that what He is about to do, is because He is faithful to keep His promises and is true to His Word.

"And in righteousness He judges and makes war"(19:11). I doubt if we can say that any war in the history of man has been entirely a righteous war, but this will be a completely justified war.

This brings us again to a *meanwhile*. We have been watching what has been taking place in Heaven, while on Earth, the vials are being poured out. Near the beginning of Armageddon, the Marriage Feast took place in Heaven. We will not even hear or see those scenes, for we will be totally caught up in Christ, and the celebration and praise time in Heaven. Now immediately after the Marriage Feast, Heaven's door opens, and Christ and His army are shown as engaged in the battle at Megiddo. From verse 11 throughout the rest of this chapter, are scenes which tell in greater detail the events of the Battle of Armageddon, and God and Christ's part in that battle.

THE WORD DIPPED IN BLOOD (v. 13)

He has been a Savior; then He was a Judge; now He is a Conqueror—a man of war:

> *"His eyes were like a flame of fire, and on His head were many crowns ... His was clothed with a robe dipped in blood, and His name is called The Word of God"* (Revelation 19:12).

He has many crowns, and shall be called by a new name that no one knows (Christ's campaign to Zion) (Isaiah 62:2). This is the same man that came from Bozrah with blood on His garments (63:1.) He is the same one who visited Zion and who trampled out the wine press of the wrath of God after His campaign to Zion (Revelation 14:19-20). I believe his second coming will begin with His campaign first to Zion, and then He will meet the Antichrist at Megiddo, *"and the armies in heaven ... followed Him on white horses"* (19:14).

OUTCOME OF CHRIST AND ARMAGEDDON

Now His Bride has become His army as we head for Armageddon. I am not sure that a lot of people attending churches and claiming Christ as Savior are going to be prepared for this phase of Christ's ministry. Our *peace gospel* and *positive confession*, and *God is good all the time* message, will not be germane here. He now is not a gentle Savior and Intercessor, but is Commander-in-Chief of the warriors of Heaven. Of course, for us, nothing is said of our deployment, only our enjoyment. I do not believe we, the Church will be engaged in the Battle of Armageddon; only the Word of Christ and *"the brightness of His coming"* will be needed to defeat the beast and the armies of Hell (2 Thessalonians 2:8).

OUT OF HIS MOUTH, A SHARP SWORD TO SMITE THE NATIONS (v. 15)

We are told in 2 Thessalonians that Christ will smite the Wicked one (Antichrist) with the "breath of His mouth and destroy with the brightness of His coming" (2:8). This is the same event as we read about in Revelation when "He should strike the nations. And He Himself will rule them with a rod of iron" (19:15).

We now see Him, not as Savior or Judge, but as treading *"the great winepress of the wrath of God"* (14:19).

Christ and the Church are joined with many of the mighty ones of Heaven. Isaiah shows us that He will face the *"blast of the terrible ones,"* but by His own blast, the *"terrible ones will be diminished"* (25:4-5). Joel, in reference to the Battle of Jehoshaphat, speaks of meeting the mighty ones—the angels, and again, Isaiah mentions the Tribulation period by saying, *"the Lord will punish on high* (wicked principalities and powers in the heavens) *the host of the exalted ones, and on the earth the kings of the earth"* (24:21).

NOW HE ALLOWS HIMSELF TO BE CALLED BY HIS RIGHTFUL TITLE (v.16)

Only when He defeats the final enemies at Armageddon, will Christ allow Himself to be called by His rightful title. He consistently wanted to be known by a more humble title—*Son of Man*, during His earthly life. Similarly, all the way through the Book of Revelation and the time of judgment, He prefers to be called the *Lamb*, another humble servant title. Now and only now, when He is set to rule the nations and defeat His and our arch-enemy, will He allow Himself to be called the *"King of kings and Lord of lords"* (19:15, 11:15; Psalms 2:2, 6-7; Zechariah 14:9). God the Father, in the presence of the angels and the Church, must have put this name upon Him.

CLEANSING THE EARTH OF THE RAVAGE OF ARMAGEDDON *(vs. 19:17-18, 21)*

These two verses are a bit gruesome unless we contemplate what the battlefield will be like after Armageddon. Along with the ravages of war and the greatest earthquake since the beginning of time, together with violent weather, it will be a disaster. We are told that the blood down in the valleys of the field of battle will run to the horses bridles (Revelation 14:20).

These birds mentioned *"that fly in the midst of heaven,"* will be God's cleaning agents used for disaster relief (19:17). They are called forth from Heaven, showing Heaven's concern over cleansing the earth. I don't know whether God will cause a great surge in the birth of eagles, vultures, and other birds of prey, or just create them from Heaven, but from somewhere, a great numbers of birds will come. It is called the *supper of the great day of God.* Both Isaiah 34:3-6 and Zephaniah 1:7-11 speak of the same slaughter. Ezekiel 39:17-20 speaks of this same event, adding the beasts of the field, along with the birds of the air.

Revelation 19:18 is a very gruesome verse, but it describes what the world has seen many times, only magnified several times over. God will cleanse the battlefield of Armageddon's ravage to prevent disease and sickness as we begin the New Millennium (see Ezekiel 39:17-20).

EPITAPH OF THE ENEMIES OF GOD AND THE CHURCH (Vs. 19-20)

This is another picture of Armageddon. It is the end of all the goat Gentile nations that made themselves enemies of God by rejecting Christ when He preached to them.

First we are shown the fate of all of the earthlings, who have gathered at the call of demons, devils, and evil spirits, and who have given themselves to the beast, and received his mark, name, and number in their foreheads and hands (16:13-14, 19:20). And let us note the fact that they were *"gathered together to make war against Him who sat on the white horse and against His army"* (19:19). That is the Lord Jesus Christ; they were also making war with us—His Army. Satan and his followers have been making war against Christ and His Church for over 2000 years, so it's about time that we win that war.

Next, we are shown the fate of the esoteric side of the battle (19:20). Even though the beast, represented here by the Roman prince, the little horn, the false prophet (Antichrist), the worker of miracles, and all who worshipped the beast and His image, and are a part of Earth's crowd, they are nevertheless incarnated with Satan and his evil spirits. All of them are headed to *"the lake of fire"* which is burning like brimstone— hot cinders on the rim of a volcano (19:19-20). All were slain with the sword of Him that sat on the horse. Are you ready for this phase of Christ's work? Can you handle it when He is no longer a gentle Savior and Shepherd? No, He is a man of war! Paul said *"therefore, consider the goodness and severity of God"* (Romans 11:22).

BINDING AND IMPRISONMENT (chapter 20)

The first three verses of chapter 20 must follow closely with chapter 19. In these verses, we are told of the fate of the dragon, that old serpent, which is the devil and Satan, who is bound for 1000 years.

There will be a great cleansing on Zion—physically, morally, and spiritually. Zion has been cleansed from the abomination that makes desolate, and has been prepared for a great coronation feast in Zion, after the defeat of Satan's host (Daniel 9:27; Isaiah 25:6-9). I suspect that this will be the time of His entrance into the great gate, the East Gate of Jerusalem. He will come as a conqueror.

When the British army had conquered Jerusalem on December 17, 1917, Sir Edmond Allenby and his entourage made preparation to enter Jerusalem. They prepared a car, opened up the Jaffa Gate to allow the car passage, decorated the Jaffa Gate, and made plans to celebrate him as a conqueror of Jerusalem. When the time came and they were ready to enter the city through the Jaffa gate, Sir Allenby refused to get in a car and even on a horse; he declined to be honored as a conqueror. Humbly, he walked through the gate with his hat in hand, weeping as he walked. When asked why he did not want to be honored as a conqueror, he replied:

> "No one has a right to come into Jerusalem as a conqueror except He to whom it rightly belongs."

Of course, He was referring to Jesus Christ, the King of kings and the Lord of lords, when He comes. Such should be the honor and respect paid to the Great I AM, the Alpha and Omega, and He who is called:

"Wonderful, Counselor, Mighty God, Everlasting Father, Prince of Peace" (Isaiah 9:6).

He alone is worthy to receive coronation as "King of kings and Lord of lords" on Mount Zion and the Temple Mount.

The first three verses of chapter 20 will complete the binding of Satan and the Antichrist. After that, chapter 20 will allow us to contemplate the theocratic government of the Millennial Reign of Christ our Lord.

CHAPTER 20

THE MILLENNIUM AND BEYOND

I wrote an adaptation of this little story years ago and thought it might be good to open this chapter with, as it fits so well here:

"The Devil's mad, and I'm glad, and I know how to tease him;

Dig him out, the deceitful lout, and in Jesus' name defeat him!"

> *"And they sang a new song, saying: You are worthy to take the scroll, and to open its seals; for You were slain, and have redeemed us to God by Your blood out of every tribe and tongue and people and nation, and have made us kings and priests to our God; and we shall reign on the earth"* (Revelation 5:9-10).

This text, taken from the 5th Chapter of Revelation, shows us how this whole Book ties together. Everything written there was with exact fore-knowledge, looking forward to the final end. These songs were sung at the Throne when the Lamb first appeared and took the Book of our Inheritance in anticipation of the events written here in Chapter 20.

We could outline this Chapter as follows: 1) The binding of the devil; 2) The Millennial Reign; 3) Satan loosed for a season; and 4) The Great White Throne of Judgment. We will take each of these in turn and the sequence in which they happened.

TIME-FACTOR - 7 YEARS AND 1000 YEARS

It is important to get a good grasp of the time-factor. We must realize that the whole Book of Revelation, from chapter 5 to this point in chapter 20, has happened in less than seven years. A good part of it takes place in only 3½ years. This Chapter will cover a period of 1000+ years. Wow! If we don't catch a good perspective of this time-line difference, we will have a tendency to take a negative view of Revelation. When the ratio between the seven years and 1000 years is factored in, we see again what an absolutely positive book this is.

THE BINDING OF SATAN (V. 1-3)

A dear older woman got up to testify in a church service and everyone could see that she was haggard and frustrated. She said rather excitedly, "The Devil's been after me all day, praise His holy name, and He's about to catch me, glory to God!"

Well, we can laugh a little and sympathize with her and understand her sincerity, but praise God, the day is coming when the Devil will not be after us, nor will He be about to catch us, glory to God! We will enjoy one thousand years plus, an added eternity, without worrying about Him being after us, for He will be chained, bound, and locked up. He will have to serve his entire sentence without the possibility of parole.

The binding of Satan and His casting out from Earth in Revelation 20:1-3 is stated very simply and without much ado. For Jesus the Christ who is the Lord of glory, it probably would be no big deal. Jesus said that He handled Beelzebub with His little finger even if he did not go peacefully (Luke

11:19-20). It is no effort for Christ; after a great war in Heaven, he was cast out of Heaven indicating a battle, and he came to Earth with great wrath, showing that was no peaceful exit (Revelation 12:7-9).

Satan and his angels had only been cast out of Heaven less than three years before Satan's binding, but three years of the Devil loose and a host of demons out of the pit, would be enough (Revelation 9)! They possibly had been loosed on the Earth about five months according to Chapter 9, but it was enough to be one of the worst *woes* to the Earth. Now He is being removed from all inhabited parts of the universe and will no doubt be even more violent. He does not leave peacefully. In fact, He has to be chained with a great chain, and when He reaches the bottomless pit where His fellow cohorts are, He is put in solitary confinement with a great seal put upon His prison house. (See also Isaiah 14:4-6, 24:21-22, 27:1, 51:9). He cannot be released before His time is up. He will then be loosed again for a short time (20:7) and at the end of that time He will become a four-time loser and be sentenced to death (20:10).

This event is referred to a number of times in the Old Testament and is a theme of the final great victory of the *Day of the Lord.* Compare Isaiah 14:9 to Babylon and the great crooked Leviathan (See also Isaiah 27:1).

He is forced to be openly revealed to the earthlings. Until this time, he has been allowed to remain totally esoteric, not exposed to earthly sights, sounds, or knowledge. Except for the insight that we receive through the revelation of God's Word in the Scriptures, we would not know that He even exists. Those who do not accept or study God's Word, remain willingly ignorant of His wiles. To them, He is completely unknown except for fun-poking and the brunt of jokes as an evil clown.

Never is Satan thought to be real by the unregenerate

world. He has hidden himself behind his symbols: the Serpent, the Devil, and the Dragon; and He has acted through his principalities and powers that have ruled the darkness of this world from Satan's place of wickedness in high places. Never has He been forced to reveal himself, but instead, remains behind the scene. It will be at Armageddon where He will be plainly exposed to the world as that Great Red Dragon, deceiver of the nations associated with demons and devils, and the arch-enemy of Christ and God. He is the source of all evil perpetrated upon the human soul, since He himself is also inclined toward evil (Ecclesiastes 9:3).

There will be no more demonic deception during the whole Millennium after this terrible one is put down. He and all of his cohorts will be bound at this time. Even the demons, such as those who filled the demonic of Gadara, know that at some time, they will be bound in the pit, for they cried out to Christ,

"What have we to do with You, Jesus, You son of God? Have you come to torment us before the time" (Matthew 8:29)? Hell knows it has a time of judgment coming.

Today Satan is not bound; He is loosed in the Earth. There is however, a sense in which he has already been bound.

1. He is still free to tempt and torment the saints. He is our adversary who *"walks about like a roaring lion, seeking whom he may devour"* (1 Peter 5:8). We overcome him daily in Jesus' name.
2. He is still *"the accuser of our brethren"* before the throne of God (Revelation 12:10). We overcome His accusations by the word of our testimony.
3. We overcome him today by preaching the Word of God and taking authority over Him in Jesus' name. The seventy evangelists returned to Jesus rejoicing and saying, *"Lord, even the demons were subject to us in Your name"*

THE MILLENNIUM AND BEYOND

(Luke 10:17). Jesus responded with the same joy and said, *"I saw Satan fall like lightening from heaven"* (10:18). That was a vision coming to the Lord as He anticipated the final fall of Satan from Heaven (Revelation 12:9) He has been bound in Jesus' name for 2000 years by the authority taken by preachers, evangelists, and pastors, who are in the gospel outreach.

4. He has not been bound in deception. The first warning Jesus gives to us in Matthew's Gospel was, *"take heed that no one deceives you"* (24:4). He is still free to deceive. Jesus ordered Him, *"Get behind Me, Satan!"*

5. (Matthew 16:23) Jesus again said to Peter: *"Satan has asked for you, that he may sift you as wheat! But I have prayed for you that your faith should not fail"* (Luke 22:31). We must live close to Jesus and trust Him every day, to keep us from deception because He is still loose to *"[transform] himself into an angel of light"* (2 Corinthians 11:14). He is able to work signs and wonders to deceive (2 Thessalonians 2:9).

6. He is still loose to fill our hearts with lies and evil intent, and take advantage of us (Acts 5:3; 2 Corinthians 2:11).

7. He has not been bound in His deception of the nations, even though He has been controlled in part by the preaching of the Gospel. At his final entrance to Hell, he was called, "You who weakened the nations" (Isaiah 14:12)!

No chains on Earth can bind Him in these liberties except the Name of Jesus Christ. He respects no other name as also shown in the story of the demonic of Gadara. (Mark 5) He can only be bound in Jesus' name. No nation or its rulers and kings can handle Him. He is called the *"Prince of the power of the air"* (Ephesians 2:2). Our only defense is to put on the full armor of God (Ephesians 6:11-17). Through the fallen nature of unregenerate man, He destroys, corrupts, and fulfills His rebellion in every way possible against God, Christ, and the Saints.

I have good news from the Book of Revelation of Jesus Christ. Satan will not only fall like lightening from Heaven, but his wrath on Earth will be finished and Christ will chain him up along with all of his fallen angels; the principalities, and powers, rulers of the darkness of this age, and spiritual wickedness in high places, and cast them into the bottomless pit which was designed as the prison-house for them.

What a wonderful and different world it will be when Satan and all of his cohorts are totally and completely bound by the authority of Christ. All rule and authority of Satan will be put down, and a new and true One World Order will be set up under the reign of Christ, David, and the Saints, to fulfill the real purpose of the World Order today (1 Corinthians 15:24-28). Hallelujah! However, the rest of the dead will not live until the 1000 years are over; this will appear at the great White Throne of Judgment. (Revelation 20:5)

With Satan and his cohorts bound, Christ will be free to set up His theocratic government (Revelation 20:2-6). With King David and the twelve apostles ruling over the redeemed remnant of Israel; and the Church, after the purifying of the Great White Throne Judgment; Christ the King of Kings and Lord of Lords will rule the Gentile nations under God (20:5-6). There will be perfect peace and health on Earth under the rod of Christ:

> "*Therefore the strong people will glorify You; the cities of the terrible nations will fear You*" (Isaiah 25:3).

By the time Armageddon is over, the nations will know that Christ is Lord (Ezekiel 38:23, 39:7, 21; Zechariah 14:9).
We have counted 85 times in the Book of Ezekiel where

THE MILLENNIUM AND BEYOND   665

the prophet declares: *"... that they may know that I Am the Lord."* All nations will come to see and seek the Lord and receive His Word and Commandments. The government will be *"upon His shoulder"* and there will be universal peace (Isaiah 9:6-7; Micah 4:1-4).

CORONATION OF THE KING

Christ will rule from Jerusalem after the setting up of the kingdom and the coronation of the King when Christ is inaugurated as the King of the earth (Revelation 11:15; Zechariah 14:9). There will be a victory-march through the Eastern Gate and a fabulous banquet feast on Mt. Zion in Jerusalem (Isaiah 25:6-9). There, He will break bread with us and serve the first communion of the Millennium (Matthew 26:29; & Mark 14:25). "I say unto you, I will not drink henceforth of this fruit of the vine until that day when I drink it new with you, in thy Father's Kingdom."

What a day that will be! All of this takes place before eternity ever begins. This is the same Victory March spoken of in Isaiah 51:11, when the redeemed of the Lord come with Christ to Mount Zion (Zechariah 14:4; Revelation 14:1). It will be the time when the nations are judged, the sheep nations enter into the Millennium, and the goat nations turned into Hell (Matthew 25:31-46; Jude 14, 15).

THE 1000 YEAR MILLENNIUM

The subject of the Millennium has been one of the most controversial of all of Christ's promises to us for the End-time, and yet nothing has been made so clear and simple in the Scriptures. Six times between Revelation 20:2 and 20:7, the terminology, *"a/the thousand years"* is used. Twice we are told that Satan will be bound a thousand years. Then we are told that *they* lived and reigned, and are going to reign a thousand years here on Earth.

Who are *they*? There is no question in my mind who *they* are. *They* are the saints of God, the Church of the Lord Jesus Christ (Matthew 19:28, Luke 19:17, Revelation 3:21, 22:4-5); *they* are the ones made kings and priests (Revelation 1:6); *they* are the armies of Heaven that returned with Christ (19:4); *they* also may include the Tribulation Saints who were martyred for not taking the mark, name, and number.

There are ten terms in Scripture which represents the Millennium. In Revelation, it is called *"a thousand years"* (20:2-6); Ephesians calls it the *"dispensation of the fullness of time,"* and *"the ages to come,"* (an age of this world, not of Heaven) (1:10; 2:7). In Isaiah, it is called the *"day of the Lord."* (*Yom-* Hebrew for *day,* meaning a cycle) (13:6). In Mark, it is called the *"Kingdom of God"* (14:25). Matthew calls it the *"Kingdom of Heaven"* and the *"regeneration"* (3:2, 19:28). In Acts it is the *"the times of restoration"* (3:20-21). In Colossians the *"Kingdom of the Son of His love"* (1:13); And last, in 2 Peter it is called the *"Everlasting Kingdom of our Lord and Savior Jesus Christ"* (1:11). When we take all of these terms and put them together, we get a good cross-section of what the Millennium will be like.

THE MILLENNIUM - A PROMINENT THEME IN SCRIPTURES

The word *millennium* comes from the Greek word *Chilia* and means simply 1,000. It defines the earthly reign of Jesus Christ in His earthly kingdom.

The Millennium is, along with the 7 years of Tribulation, called the *"Day of the Lord."* This term is used in Isaiah, Jeremiah, Ezekiel, Daniel, Joel, Amos, Obadiah, Zephaniah, Zechariah, and Malachi. It is revealed to be a sabbatical rest, being the 7th of a 6,000 year period of man's existence— one thousand years for each day of Creation. God rested on the 7th day and we, with Christ, will rest and worship during this

7th of the Thousand Year period (Hebrews 4:4-6).

Many of the early fathers spoke of the certainty of the Millennium, including Irenaeus, Enoch, the Epistle of Barnabas, the Testament of Adam, The Jewish Talmud, and others; (*"Prophesy in the News,"* by the late J.R. Church - November 2011).

No subject is any more prominent among the Old Testament Messianic prophesies than the Millennium. Every detail of its living conditions is comprehensively, thoroughly, and meticulously itemized. With very careful, precise, and specific research, we gather great insight on the life and times of the Millennium. In the Appendix, we will make a list of many of those texts for the student who desires a deeper study. Be careful to separate the Heavenly Kingdom from the Earthly.

According to Revelation, this Millennium is known as *"the first resurrection"* (20:5-6). Those that take part in this first resurrection, the *"second death"* will have no power over them, because *"they shall be priests of God and of Christ, and shall reign with Him a thousand years."* (20:6) In a few more verses, we will study about the final judgment at the Great White Throne, and in it, we will understand the meaning of the second death. Daniel 12:1 shows us the two Resurrections which, by that verse, seems to happen simultaneously. However, by Revelation 20, we know these events happen one thousand years apart.

CONFUSING CONCEPTS OF THE MILLENNIUM

The millennial concept, an idea put into the minds of fallen man in his earliest infancy, hinted that an earthly king, by divine authority, would at some time rule an all-powerful World Order kingdom. This has been an easy deception for Satan to use to force upon all ruling monarchs through the ages, the possibility that they might be the *coming one*. It was easily adaptable, especially to those kings who came in the series of empires which were part of the continuing rebellion of Nimrod. Nimrod had set up an idolatrous system of self-worship and presented himself as the Son of a Virgin, even though he was actually Semiramis's husband. This supposedly *virgin-born son* was depicted in the star sign, Virgo. Even Nebuchadnezzar caught the idea; from a warped sense of his own godlike quality, and completely misunderstanding God's intent as revealed to Daniel, he built a great image of himself in the Plains of Shinar in Babylon and demanded that the world bow down to him.

He was the first type of an Antichrist, who set himself up as a god in the place of God's beloved Son. Every ruler, king, and Caesar, from then on, through the evil lies of an Idolatrous system of self-worship, believed themselves to be the Great Messiah who would rule the world with a rod of iron. No concept has been so used of Satan to deceive the heart of great rulers, than the concept of a coming Millennial Reign of the Messiah.

In the Middle Ages, the Catholic Church with its self-loving Popes who dared to believe themselves to be the Vicar, (actual earthly representative of Christ) let Satan fill their hearts with a false idea of a thousand-year reign, thinking one of them should be the Messiah and reign as the king of Jerusalem. He would supposedly reign from Jerusalem. This was the impetuousness which inspired the Crusades. It was called the *Chiliastic Doctrine and Interpretation of the Millennium.* A further explanation of this concept and a detailed explanation of this Chiliastic idea can be found in the introduction to our writing.

The Crusaders took Jerusalem from the Muslims, and set up the office of King of Jerusalem. They built forts and castles all around the premise of the Holy Land, and planned a thousand year reign of their self-appointed *Christ's.* Of course, after eight crusades, the effort totally failed, but the concept did not go away. It was this concept that was in the idolatrous hearts of the Wilhelms, and of Hitler. An understanding behind Hitler's Third Reich will show that there were three efforts to revive the Old Holy Roman Empire and to revive the Crusades. This was the cause of two World Wars. And as I mentioned earlier, deep in the recesses of the occult societies of the *Kings of the Blood*—those who believe they are from Mary Magdalene's son by Jesus Christ, there is the plan to again establish a Millennial Kingdom which will supposedly be ruled by one of them someday.

While we speak of the prominence of false ideas about the Millennium and how they play a major part in world politics, we should mention Satan's false interpretation of Revelation and how He imagines himself as the great Messiah, and the head of the coming thousand year period. He plans to set himself up in the person of what the scripture calls the Antichrist, and become the proprietor of the thousand years by ruling it through the nations that he controls, and by a One World Order of His own making.

This is why all of the satanic Secret Societies have developed the philosophy and hope of a One World Order. It is prominent in the Templars, the Rosicrucians, the Masons, and is especially promoted through the New Age and the United Nations. We must be especially discerning during this time to understand that the dream of Humanism and its millennium of peace and security in forming the present day World Order, is a pseudo-Millennium dream of world powers, which is only a mockery of the real thing that will come with Christ's second appearing. It draws its impetuous ideas given to us in Revelation, and will support a false Christ at its head.

We must mention the Jewish concept. Among the sages of Judaism, especially in the Kabala, there is an idea of a thousand years of Jewish bliss when Israel will be the center of the world and Jerusalem the seat of power. It is a legitimate hope, clearly taught in the Messianic prophesies. If these precious Rabbi's and Sages of Judaism would accept their Messiah, Jesus Christ, and include Him in their interpretation of the golden age of Israel concept from the Messianic prophecies, they would be pretty close to the promises as shown in Revelation. It is sometimes confused with greater Israel, and causes concern.

Let us be careful to stay close to exactly what Christ has shown us about the coming Millennium, and not to be persuaded to deviate into a very subtle misconception of it.

CHRISTIAN CONCEPTS OF THE MILLENNIUM

There are three distinct concepts among the Christian Churches. The *Pre-millennial* thought, indicating those that take the millennium literally and believe the Church will be raptured before the Millennium. The A-*millennial* concept teaches that there will be no literal Millennium and it is only allegorical and being fulfilled through time. The third concept is a P*ost-millennial* view which teaches that the Church is bettering itself through time and through human ingenuity, and it is building its own Millennium.

I am sure you have already realized that our view is totally based upon a literal interpretation of the Revelation, and we believe Christ will return and set up his own Millennial Kingdom on Earth.

SATAN LOOSED

One of the most puzzling parts of the Revelation of this book is the following texts found in Revelation 20:7-10. We are plainly told that at the end of the thousand years, *"Satan is released for a little while"* (20:3). No part of the Revelation has been questioned, studied, and misunderstood as much as this short Revelation. It seems in the offing there is another deception of the Nations; another rebellion; another Gog and Magog; another siege against Jerusalem and the Saints; another Armageddon; and another judgment. This time it seems there is an eternal binding of Satan, the Beast and False Prophet in the Lake of Fire, all coming at the end of the Millennium. In our finite thinking, it seems so wrong to allow such a time right after the thousand years of bliss. However, God has said, *"My thoughts are not your thoughts, nor are your ways My ways"* (Isaiah 55:8). Therefore, we will have to try and understand His thoughts and ways.

However, we are warned of its eventuality in verses 2 and 3 of Chapter 20. Twice we are told plainly that Satan would be bound for only a thousand years, and after that, He *"must be released for a little while"* (Revelation 20:3). For reasons we hope to explain at least in part, there is a *must* in Christ's purpose for His release.

It seems to the author that God and Christ must be making a point which involves Christ's continual contention, and that is, even though Satan has played a major part in the fall of man, there is still the fact that the heart of man is *"only evil continually"* (Genesis 6:5). The wise Solomon found out what God told us all along, and that was *"the heart of the sons of men is full set in them to do evil"* (Ecclesiastes 8:11). Psalms 52:3 agrees with what Christ told us in John 3:17,18: *"You love evil more than good."* Jesus said, *"men loved darkness rather than light, because their deeds were evil"* (John 3:19). Then they rejected the light in Christ and turned to their evil deeds. Paul wrestled with his own spirit and said *"I find then a law, that evil is present with me, the one who wills to do good"* (Romans 7:21).

HUMANISM CHALLENGES GOD AND HIS WORD

In our present age of Humanism when Christ's insight

into the evilness, inherent in man's nature, is being especially challenged by the whole world's humanistic philosophy. The humanist believes that man is inherently good, and evil is only caused by environment, poverty, lack of education and refinement.

To the humanist, religion plays a large part in, and is actually most of the root cause of, man's tendencies to do evil. These social reformers and manipulators of man's consciences deny any existence of evil in the form of dark spirits in the realm of Satan's Kingdom. Any inherent evil in man's character has substituted the born- again experience for character modification, sanctification in the Spirit for self-improvement, and righteousness as cultural refinement. This is human perfection without God, Christ, or religion.

Humanism has and is, deeply penetrating into even the most avowed Evangelical churches. For instance, it comes in the doctrine known as *Kingdom Now*, and is supported and taught by many of our foremost leaders. Another is *Replacement Theology*; and yet another is the *Emerging Church*, teaching that the Church replaces the Jews in Prophecy and the Jews have no place in the last days. Some say that all Scripture is to be interpreted, not literally, but allegorically. They teach that if the church could live up to all the Old Testament laws and commandments, we would conquer society and world politics, and restore righteousness. This would make it possible for us to take over all politics and government, form a Christian nation, set up the promised Millennial Kingdom, and make it ready for Christ to come. They completely overlook the fact that our Constitution forbids a state-controlled religion. They also deny the sinfulness of man.

However, we find that God's Word is proven right, and God is justified in judging man as basically evil and sinful. In the Millennium, everything will be changed to give man his

THE MILLENNIUM AND BEYOND

best chance of redemption by himself. Also, many other things will be changed; his culture, his environment, no devil, no demons, and no influence from Hell. Everything is changed except the heart of man. During these thousand years, failure in the race of man cannot be blamed on the devil, Satan, demons, or any other evil in high places. They cannot say the failure of man is caused by environment, for they will have the best of environments. They cannot say it is lack of knowledge, for they will have the best of education. They cannot say it is caused by poverty, for there will be no poverty.

Consider that these people, born during the Millennium, have not been redeemed by the blood of the Lamb. They are simply obedient by the force of a rod of iron. They are made to obey, not from the heart, but by fear and force.

The experiment of the Millennium is to see if unregenerate man, free from all influence of environment, poverty, and Satan, can redeem themselves from their evil nature and the tendency to rebel against the truth of which God and Christ have spoken. Can man regenerate himself by his own will through cultural perfection and self-improvement, or through character modification, gradually overcoming the Adamic nature, and become pure? And further, can unregenerate people through direct association and relationship with Christ in the flesh, willingly submit themselves to the will of God and come into a righteous relationship with Him, as our humanists will have us believe?

Judging by what we read in Revelation 20:9, humanism has not and cannot work. Man, by his own righteousness, cannot and will not overcome his tendency to sin. He cannot perfect himself, and even a perfect environment will not allow human nature to perfect itself. Christ, even with His physical presence without the spiritual regeneration of a new birth, cannot change the nature of man. He may rule with a rod of iron and force human beings to submit, but as soon as they are no longer under his iron fist, they quickly revert to their old sinful nature.

We learn by this experiment that reformation is certainly not regeneration. They should have learned this fact during the dispensation of the grace of God. We learn again that it is;

> *"Not by works of righteousness which we have done, but according to His mercy He saved us, through the washing of regeneration and renewing of the Holy Spirit"* (Titus 3:5).

And we realize again, that we are not what we are in Christ by any righteousness or refinement of our old nature, but instead, "having been born again, not of corruptible seed but incorruptible, through the Word of God which lives and abides forever" (1 peter 1:23).

Even the Jews, the seed of Abraham, have to realize, that with all the law and commandments which were certainly given by their great Jehovah, and with all the manifold wisdom, power, and revelations which God shared with them, none of this has brought any change to their old nature. Even under the old law, they found it absolutely necessary for Christ to regenerate their old nature by,

> *"[giving them] a new heart and [putting] a new spirit within you; I will take the heart of stone out of your flesh and will give you a [compatible] heart of flesh"* (Ezekiel 36:26).

We see that we must be changed from the inside out, not the outside in, and all just to break our old stubborn self-righteous pride which came to us from the rebellious nature of Satan:

> *"For by grace you have been saved through faith, and that not of yourselves; it is the gift of God, not of works, lest anyone should boast"* (Ephesians 2:8-9).

It is not a religious experience or a moral conversion that changes man, but rather a new nature, washed and renewed daily by the Word of God, Jesus Christ our Lord.

These are truths that need not be preached to the born-again crowd. Verse 9 shows the truth of it when we see that after people had been in the presence of Jesus Himself and witnessed his great power and glory, and subject to a perfect environment, they were still more at home with Satan. Therefore, were judged and doomed by the same fire that would consume Satan and his entire crowd.

THE DEVIL AND HIS FOLLOWERS AND THEIR FINAL DESTRUCTION

It comes to me when I contemplate this second chance for Satan himself (along with the Roman Prince and the Antichrist) to realize that their failure was the failure to repent. Even after a millennium of bondage and Christ's rule on Earth, they just continue on in their rebellion and corruption. Nothing is said here of any repentance on their part, nor on the part of the fallen angels. A second time Satan is cast into the lake of fire and brimstone, along with the beastly worshippers and the False Prophet where He and his crowd are tormented day and night forever and ever (19:20).

Satan is destroyed in the physical body as the Antichrist, but we must remember, his full existence began long before He was incarnated into the Antichrist. Daniel 11:45 reminds us from a physical perspective how He will *"come to His end, and no one will help him."* Ezekiel gives us an interesting detail of his physical end. God says, *"I cast you to the ground, I laid you before kings that they might gaze at you"* (28:16-18). We are further told that His physical destruction will come from a *"fire from your midst"* (28:18). Today there are documented cases where human beings out of no evident source, just catch fire from within and burn to a crisp. Evidently, the Antichrist will die in this manner.

LEVIATHAN—THE PIERCING AND CROOKED SNAKE

This final destruction of Satan and His entire ilk is in part the fulfillment of Isaiah 27:1. Isaiah, Chapters 24-26 give us many details about the Tribulation period. He immediately ties in the end of the Tribulation and *that day*, with the destruction of one called *Leviathan*. He is identified with the *piercing serpent* and the *crooked snake*.

In antiquity, this piercing serpent is remembered in the garden as a dangerous killer. In the star signs from the original *Gospel of Adam*, he was known to be a conniving crooked sneak. Always, Leviathan is an alternate name for Satan. He is the dragon of the sea (Psalm 104:25-26); the same dragon that we deal with several times in Revelation, especially the dragon that gives the beast his seat, power, and great authority.

Evidently Satan, after God cursed him, was manifest on Earth as this creature described here. He is spoken of in Psalms as frolicking in the *"great and wide sea"* (Psalm 104:25). Job 41 says that *"out of his mouth go burning lights; sparks of fire shoot out"* and makes the deep a *"boiling pot"* (41:19-20). He has *"terrible teeth all around [and] his rows of scales are His pride"* (41:14-15). One thing we should say here is that all of the myths and legends are based in reality; the basis of the Great Dragon of ancient literature, and the mascot of the Eastern societies described here, are very real. This creature existed in Job's day. He is extinct today and probably one of the dinosaurs whose skeletons we found worldwide. Even though the physical body he lived in is extinct, the seraph himself is still very much alive and frolicking among men as *"accuser of the brethren"* (Revelation 12:10). We would have no clues to his existence if it was not for the Bible.

This is the ancient earthly creature in which Satan was manifest before the days of the flood. He is the very one we deal with all through Revelation, and the one that Christ punishes and puts in the pit for a thousand years, finally destroying Him in the eternal Lake of Fire (Revelation 20:1-4, 10). Satan is not a myth and Hell is not a joke! Hell is very real, *"prepared for the devil and his angels,"* but expanded for all who reject Christ and His forgiveness (Matthew 25:41).

Therefore, this revelation that Satan is loosed again after the thousand years shows us a second time that the human race is tested to see if it can become righteous without Christ and His atoning Blood. This is the significance of *"Gog and Magog."* (Revelation 20:8). Gog is symbolic of leaders, and Magog, of the common people. It is not that the Gog and Magog of Ezekiel 38 are here again at the end of the Millennium. These are two different groups, but driven by the same demonic spirit of Gog and Magog, and the same deceptive spirits that motivated the multitudes against Christ in the Tribulation. The same demonic spirit that led the nations to Armageddon is the same spirit that *"went up on the breadth of the earth and surrounded the camp of the saints and the beloved city. And fire came down from God out of Heaven and devoured them"* (Revelation 20:9 - see also 2 Peter 3:10-14).

Satan is not impressed. Even though He has seen all of the wonders of the New Jerusalem and all of the glory of God and His Son, He still tries to attack the Holy City, 'New Jerusalem.' This presages the hardness that can develop in the heart of a sinner toward God when he hardens his heart and refuses to repent.

The real significance of this tells us that the Judgment will include not only Satan, the Antichrist and the False Prophet, but also those who, after the Millennium, still worship the Dragon and the Beast. These are the ones who are of the same spirit of idolatry as those that received the mark, name, and number, and chose to be part of Satan's World Order. Revelation says that the number of them was a great innumerable host, as many as the sands of the sea (20:8.) Revelation 21:8 shows us the ones who will be in this Judgment:

"But the cowardly, unbelieving, abominable, murderers, sexually immoral, sorcerers, idolaters (self-loving), and all liars shall have their part in the lake which burns with fire and brimstone, which is the second death."

This great number would be those who were born during the Millennium, those who were over 100 years old as the Millennium started, and those over 100 years old, will be accursed (Isaiah 65:20).

"The heart is deceitful above all things, and desperately wicked; who can know it" (Jeremiah 17:9)?

Oh how easy it would be to escape judgment for our sins. No wonder Paul says in the agony of his spirit, *"How shall we escape if we neglect so great a salvation"* (Hebrews 2:3)?

THE FINAL CRIMINAL COURT JUDGMENT, THE GREAT WHITE THRONE

"And I saw the dead, small and great, standing before God, and their books were opened. And another book was opened, which is the Book of Life. And the dead were judged according to their works, by the things which were written in the books" (Revelation 20:12).

Oh, my dear friends, there is something so terrible and final about what we are reading here. This is the final end of the Judgment presaged in the 5th Chapter. Christ postponed this final judgment until He could open the seals and fulfill all that the prophets had said about these last days.

He waited for the fulfillment of Daniel's 70th week, the 7 years of Tribulation, and the final assault upon Him and His authority.

He will set up a Kingdom and rule in righteousness, first to fulfill His Messianic promises to the Jews and the Church, and to provide for them that golden age. However, He will also make it a testing time for the unregenerate that would not let Him save them from themselves. It demonstrated the justice and rightness of having to separate the unrepentant and rebellious forever from the universe, which He had to cleanse of all iniquity.

There are seven separate judgments in Scripture. They include:

1) *The Judgment for Saints.* It was completed at the cross. *"He who believes in the Son has everlasting life; and he who does not believe the Son shall not see life, but the wrath of God abides on him"* (John 3:36).

2) *The Judgment of Servants.* We who are saved, become stewards of the things of God and will be judged by our faithfulness at the Judgment Seat of Christ (2 Corinthians 5:10; The Bema-Romans 14:10).

3) *The Judgment for sinners at the Great White Throne.* *"And I saw the dead, small and great, standing before God, and the books were opened"* (Revelation 20:12).

4) *The Judgment of Nations—the sheep and the goats* (Matthew 25: 31-46).

5) *The Judgment for Israel.* It will be the *"time of Jacob's trouble, but he shall be saved out of it"* (Jeremiah 30:7).

6) *The Judgment of the fallen Angels* (Jude 6, 2 Peter 2:4).

7) *The judgment of Satan and His cohorts*: the Beast, the Antichrist, and the False Prophet.

At this time, all opportunity to be saved is over. Satan has had His last chance, the world of nations is judged, and judgment calls up all unsaved and all citizens of Death and Hell for Judgment from the books of records. None of the Saints are mentioned here; only Death and Hell. This is the second death, and it has no power over those in the first Resurrection (Revelation 20:6). Think about it! ... born once, die twice; born twice, die once. Selah!

"The Lord knows how to deliver the godly out of temptations and to reserve the unjust under punishment for the day of judgment" (2 Peter 2:9).

And again, referring to people who are willingly ignorant about the flood, Peter said:

"The heavens and the earth which now exist are kept in store by the same word, reserved for fire until the Day of Judgment and perdition of ungodly men" (2 Peter 3:7).

There is a record being kept and everything will be accounted for. Only those things confessed and forsaken will be blotted out. What a rejoicing on that day when we realize the full impact of Christ's forgiveness. We will then understand what Paul meant when he said:

"For I know whom I have believed and am persuaded that He is able to keep what I have committed to Him, until that day" (2 Timothy 1:12).

Here is a more understandable way it could read: "I know the one in whom I have put my trust, and I am fully convinced that He is able and will keep unto Himself all that I have placed in His trust, in the day of Christ's coming and judgment."

We feel sorry for those who trust their good works to get them through this Judgment. The trouble with trusting our own goodness was well expressed by Will Rogers when he said, "There is so much bad in the best of us, and so much good in the worst of us, it's hard to know who should judge the rest of us."

When we hang our wash out to dry which may seem clean, it will look awful dingy beside the righteousness of Christ.

However, there is another Book which was opened, and it is called *"The Lamb's Book of Life"* (Revelation 21:27). All of the names in this Book have already passed the bar and been redeemed by the blood of Christ. An old song that I love to sing, asks a question:

> "Is my name written there, on the page bright and fair, in the book of thy Kingdom, is my name written there?" (Mary A. Kidder)

There was a time in my life, when for an entire week, I could not rest or sleep until I answered that question. Ask yourself, "In the Book of thy Kingdom, with its pages bright and fair, tell me Jesus my Savior, is my name written there?"

And then another verse says:

> "Yes, my name's written there, on the page bright and fair, in the Book of thy Kingdom, yes my name's written there." (Mary A. Kidder)

It is only after this final and total judgment when the whole universe has been purified and all rebellion and sin is gone, that we are ready for the New Heaven and the New Earth of Chapter 21:

MARANATHA! THE LORD IS HERE AND SEES!

CHAPTER 21

NEW HEAVEN AND NEW EARTH

There is an old song I love to sing:
"There is Coming a Day"
"There is coming a day, when no heartache shall come, No more clouds in the sky, no more tears to dim the eye, And forever I will be, with the one who died for me.
What a day, glorious day that will be."
"No more sickness no more pain,
No more parting over there...."
Jim Hill, Author

A Preacher who had burned out in the ministry, resigned, giving up as a pastor and took a job as a lifeguard. He was fired after just ten days, and when he went in to get his final check, he questioned why he was being fired. The boss looked at him rather puzzled, and said, "Well, we don't know what to think of you. We hired you to rescue people in trouble who called for your help. Several have drowned during your employment and we noticed that whenever someone was raising their hand and calling for help, you just sat there on your stand and said over and over the strangest thing, and you kept repeating, "I see that hand, yes, I see that hand."

It has its humorous side doesn't it? However the sad thing

is, there are thousands of missionaries, pastors, and evangelists all over the world who are weary with the burden of souls. They have weary nights of pleading prayer, and week after week of services where they have cried and pleaded for people to get right with God. Like our friend in the story, they can't get away from their calling. In their sleep they wrestle with the call on their lives for people to come to God.

What a relief it will be when there is no more need of the burden of preparing an evangelistic sermon; no more pleading nights in prayer; no more wrestling with the burden; no more gut-wrenching burden for souls; no more appealing for people to respond; and no more broken hearts after the service, for those you love who did not respond. Yes, every one of our beloved ministers and soul-winners know the heartbreak, when all we long to do is to point people to Heaven and this New City we are studying about now.

Evangelist Billy Graham is said to have approached a boy on the corner of a city in which he was holding a crusade, and asked if he could tell him how to get to the post office. The little fellow politely pointed the way. Then, it is recorded, that Billy said to the boy, "I'm preaching each night down the street at this church and if you will attend, I'll tell you how to get to Heaven." The little fellow looked up at him rather puzzled and said, "Mister, if you don't even know the way to the post office, how are you going to tell me the way to Heaven?"

THE HEAVENLY SIDE OF REALITY

Sometimes we who are endeavoring to show people how to get to this Heaven that Jesus told us about in Revelation 21, can only hope that we are sure of the way. Fortunately, our great assurance is that the Man who went away to build it, said:

"I am the way, the truth, and the life" (John 14:6).

NEW HEAVEN AND NEW EARTH

Jesus also said:

"I go to prepare a place for you, and if I go and prepare a place for you, I will come again and receive you to Myself; that where I am, there you may be also" (John 14:3).

What we are about to enter in the next two Chapters, is probably the most intriguing and fascinating part of the enigma of Revelation, and may also be the hardest to understand. It brings us insights into a dimension of existence that none of us have ever seen. The Bible is the only text we have to give us any reliable understanding of the heavenly side of reality. It is often very sketchy and written in cryptic symbolism and takes the Holy Spirit's help to understand. However, if we seek to know, we then shall know the fullness of its blessing.

What we are able to see and understand of this other world from which Christ reveals to us in these Chapters of Revelation, certainly excites and challenges us to deeper research and commitment. As we read these lines in the 21st Chapter, we are impressed with wonder, and may think: wow, fantastic, cool, or whatever our expression of *awe* may be. Immediately, we think it is unbelievable and incomprehensible. Yet, I do not believe that Jesus gave us anything that we could not understand. However, to prove our earnestness, He kept it analogous so that we have to study to know its full reality.

1. **It must be revealed to us by the Spirit of God**

    Paul did tell us that these things which are prepared for those that love God and Christ, are things that can only be understood by the Holy Spirit who *"will tell [us] things to come."* (John 16:13) Quoting from Isaiah 64:4, Paul said:

"Eye has not seen, nor ear heard, nor has it entered into the heart of man the things which God has prepared for those who love Him. But God has revealed them to us through His Spirit. For the Spirit searches all things, yes, the deep things of God" (1 Corinthians 2:9-10).

What we can comprehend of these texts, we must find through prayer and the leading of the Holy Spirit that Christ told us would *"guide [us] into all truth....and tell [us] things to come"* (John 16:13).

Isaiah has great insight into the Church Age and the last days. So much so, that his Book is called the New Testament in the Old. He first received the above insight:

"For since the beginning of the world men have not heard nor perceived by the ear, nor has the eye seen any God besides You, Who acts for the one who waits for Him" (Isaiah 64:4).

We are limited to our five senses: see, hear, smell, taste, and touch. Any dimension beyond those earthly experiences, is beyond our ability to understand.

2. **We cannot conceive of the transcendent God living among us.**

    "The Tabernacle of God is with men" (Revelation 21:3). Verses 20:3, 4 continue the mystic of what John is seeing and revealing to us from Jesus Christ. A great voice, a loud and shouting voice, speaks out of Heaven, and tells us to *"behold"* which is a term indicating something almost unbelievable for us to grasp (20:3). How can we comprehend and experience the place where God *tabernacles*, or lives among us? Some of us have experienced the presence of God in what measure He limits Himself to us in the flesh, by allowing us into His presence, and we can hardly keep from being overcome.

How could we ever endure Him living among us?

The great transcendent God who dwells in a light that no man can approach unto, whose home is among the vast starry reaches of a Universe we can barely conceive of, the Creator and Sustainer of all that is made, wants to dwell here on this lowly globe with us. On a chart of just our galaxy, NASA can only point out the location of our sun and solar system. Our Earth is so infinitesimal (incalculably small) that it can hardly be found in our Galaxy alone; and our Galaxy is only a small example of the billions of Galaxies in our Universe. Awesome beauty lies in parts of it, and yet the eternal God wants to dwell among those redeemed out of a very troubled Earth. He desires to dwell among us so much that He sent His only begotten Son to die for us, and called Him *"Immanuel... God with us"* (Matthew 1:23). He became a lowly man in order to dwell among us.

Only as we are able by the Spirit to comprehend and accept the incarnation of Christ, as both earthly flesh and at the same time, eternal divinity, can we grasp the idea of God dwelling with us:

"And the Word became flesh and dwelt among us, and we beheld His glory, the glory as of the only begotten of the Father, full of grace and truth" (John 1:14).

Even in the New Heaven and New Earth, we will still be finite beings and so dependent upon Him. Oh God forgive us, for this is beyond our comprehension or ability to conceive, therefore even the best of us are not humbled or appreciative enough.

3. **Cryptic symbols from ancient Old Testament texts are analogous**

Like the Old Tabernacle was a complete symbol of the Messiah with every color, type of material, furniture, tapestry, measurement, and all cryptically reflective of Christ, so was the New Earth and a New City of Jerusalem in their description in Revelation 21 and 22. They are filled with symbols and types and shadows of the Old Testament and New Testament Messianic texts. From the very first impression which John expresses as he sees the New Jerusalem coming down out of Heaven, we see the beginning of symbolism. He was deeply stirred with the exciting emboss of the Church and the Bride of Christ in its every feature. The Spirit even helped him to see that *She* was adorned for her *Husband,* whom we immediately know to be Christ. In verse 21:9, John is invited to follow one of the angels who delivered the last plagues and said, *"Come, I will show you the Bride, the Lamb's wife."* John had to be *"carried away in the Spirit"* and from this, we learn that we will have to be *in the Spirit* in order to understand these symbols from antiquity. Paul showed this same thing when he spoke of things that the eye could not see, and ear could not hear, when he said:

"But God has revealed them to us through His Spirit. For the Spirit searches all things, yes, the deep things of God" (1 Corinthians 2:10).

To see the many types of the *Bride of Christ* in the description of the New Jerusalem, will take some studying. It will still be a literal city. We will at least touch on some of them in our next Chapter.

Now, as we proceed through the rest of Chapter 21, we will see many reflections of Christ from the Old and New Testament texts, but we shall also see how Christ is reflected and characterized in His Bride. The names of the twelve Tribes of Israel (21:12); the names of the twelve apostles of the Lamb (21:14); the Light, which is Christ (21:23); the measurements (21:15-17); the stones

NEW HEAVEN AND NEW EARTH

of fire (21:20); the gates of pearl (21:21); and the Lamb as the Temple (Old Testament Tabernacle.) (21:23) All of these are types of the Messiah, Christ the Lamb, and are deep things of God, understood only by those who walk in the Spirit.

4. **A dimension beyond our human experience.**

NO MORE *MORES*

Revelation, Chapter 21 carries us further into the *unbelievable*, as this passage says:

> *"And God will wipe away every tear from their eyes; there shall be no more death, nor sorrow, nor crying; and there shall be no more pain, for the former things have passed away"* (21:4).

Besides that, we shall hear later that there will be no more night, no more sea, plus no more devil or demons, for the adversaries are all bound in the pit. Oh, Hallelujah! Verse 8 tells us that there will be no more fear, no more unbelief, no more abomination, no more murder, no more whoremongers, no more sorcerers (drug addicts and drug pushers), and no more liars. If we follow over to verse 27, there will be no more defilers, no more abomination or the making, (filming or writing or producing) a lie. And, according to 22:15 no more dogs, (the human kind) no more sorcerers, no more whoremongers, no more murderers, no more idolaters, and no more loving and making of lies.

Over 20 social ills of our present society will not be there. And I think without deviating from truth, we can say there will be no more bitterness, no more anger, no more wrath, no more clamor, no more evil speaking, and no more malice. All will be kind, tenderhearted, forgiving, merciful, meek, peacemakers, and pure in heart. We could go on enumerating those qualities which are listed as the characteristics of the redeemed throughout the gospel message.

The elimination of these will completely change our lives and existence. Every ill of our godless society will be eliminated and only godly righteousness will exist in that New City. How can we begin to comprehend such a living condition like that? I think I would like to be there and endeavor to get my family and friends there also. It would make our burdens well worthwhile.

These conditions would not be possible unless Satan is bound, the Antichrist and False Prophet removed; anarchy in the spirit of man is broken and given a new spirit; the fallen nature of man is changed and he is given a new heart; the curse is lifted off of the earth; and all authority and power is put down and delivered to Christ, by God. Isaiah gives us an early insight into these things that are shown to us by Christ. In Isaiah 25:8, He places these same promises right after the Tribulation in Isaiah, Chapters 24-26, and also in the middle of the Millennium texts (25:6-12).

Now God repeats what He has said in Revelation 21:1, and presaged in Isaiah 65:17. This time, however, He puts His own signature to it. It is a signed and sealed document, attested by the Man who rose from the dead, and we are sure He knows what He is talking about. It seems that Christ had to pull John back out of a dream. He told John to stop staring in awe and write down what He is going to say: *"for these words are true and faithful"* (21:5).

Then, He puts His signature to it by telling us again who He is, the same one who began this Revelation of Jesus Christ—the Alpha and Omega, the beginning and the end. He then renews some fantastic promises to the ones who *"hunger and thirst for righteousness"* and to the overcomer *"who shall inherit all things."* (Matthew 5:6; 21:7) Only the overcomer's of Revelation, Chapters 2 and 3 who are the Church, will

NEW HEAVEN AND NEW EARTH

be participators in this New Heaven and New Earth. Even the Jews will have their inheritance in the earthly restoration of the Promised Land—the New Jerusalem and the Temple Mount on Mount Zion. *"But you have come to Mount Zion and to the city of the living God, the heavenly Jerusalem, to an innumerable company of angels, to the general assembly and Church of the first born who are registered in heaven, to God the Judge of all, to the spirits of just men made perfect"* (Hebrews 12:22-23).

WHO WILL NOT BE THERE

Verse 8 is a disclaimer. Along with the Revelation 21:27, it tells us who will not be in the New City: the fearful and the unbeliever, the abominable to God, the murderers and whore mongers, sorcerers (drug peddlers and addicts) idolaters, and liars. Also mentioned in this passage is anything else that would defile the city or make it unclean; and those who work abominable acts—any defilement of the Law of God, or any who lie (21:27).

Note that in both of these texts, liars are mentioned. In a day when lying has become so common, it behooves us to take notice. Only those written in the *Lamb's Book of Life* will make up the society of the New Jerusalem. The rest will be in the Lake of Fire with Satan and the Antichrist, and will be called up before the Great White Throne (see also Chapter 20).

I feel that I must take some time to help us understand the difference in the New Jerusalem which comes out of Heaven, and the New Jerusalem that still sets on Mount Moriah in Israel. Please bear with me as we try to understand all that is written here, as it compares and relates to many Old Testament foresights in Messianic prophesies, and which are relevant to these very things.

THE EARTH NOT DESTROYED, JUST RENOVATED

There is much controversy concerning the true meaning of the New Heaven and the New Earth. The question arises about whether or not they are completely destroyed down to nothing, whereas before, they were spoken into existence by God, through Christ, who is the *"Word of God"* (John 1:1). Or, will they be changed or renovated, like three times before; once in an early renovation from the fall of the original Earth under Satan, and again *made* (remolded, as you would a piece of clay) in six days. Then there was the Earth before the flood, which perished (2 Peter 3:6). The word 'perished' in this passage, does not mean to disappear or be demolished and cease to exist. Peter goes on and tells us that the Heavens and Earth which exist now by the same word, are kept in store, reserved unto fire against the Day of Judgment and perdition of ungodly men.

It is always difficult to translate words from one language to another. Translating spiritual writings into English is especially difficult, because English is strictly an earthy language and doesn't have a lot of terms that understands the eternal truths. However, by consulting with the original texts, we can arrive at a better understanding.

Peter uses the term *Pleugo*, meaning *"pass away"*—flee, change, or renovated (2 Peter 3:10). It is used in several other places in the New Testament: twice again in Revelation 6:14 and 16:20, where it means to escape, like a criminal from captivity. It indicates that the Earth has been kept in bondage and will flee away to be re-created into a new Heaven and a new Earth (Romans 8:20-21). All of the texts that mention the New Heaven and New Earth have similar language (Isaiah 65:17, 66:22). And in verse 12, the word *"dissolved"* again means a change of the elements. Nowhere does it ever say that the Earth will be completely destroyed.

In fact, we have ample texts which tell us plainly that the

Earth and the Heavens are forever, therefore eternal. Psalms 78:69 speaks of *"the earth which He has established forever."* Psalms 89:36 says the Throne of David, like *"His seed* (or family) *shall endure forever."* His throne is not a heavenly throne, only an earthly one. Psalms 104:5 tells us that the Lord *"laid the foundations of the earth, so that it should not be moved forever."* And Ecclesiastes reminds us that one generation after another passes away, *"but the earth abides forever"* (1:4). It has been shaken at times by the presence of the Lord (such as at Sinai) and will be shaken again so that the mountains come down and the seas roar, but never to be destroyed completely. Here, as in all other texts where the New Heaven and New Earth are mentioned, it means a complete renewal and renovation.

As we have said, there is a lot of debate as to whether the Earth will be destroyed by fire and cease to exist, or whether it will be completely renewed. Only the texts of the Old and New Testaments can settle this question. To answer scripturally what the truth is, we will have to climb over a heap of carnal, godless, and unbiblical information that floods our media, books, television, and movies, and erroneously uses the Bible text to fascinate the unsuspecting public with sensational *end of the world* lies.

First of all, as we have listed some above, there are many verses that plainly tell us the Earth is eternal. Great and wonderful prophecies are made to Abraham, Israel, and the Jews; promises of an eternal Earth. Those who have fallen for the lie of the doctrine called Replacement Theology which we discussed earlier, leave no place at all for the Jews, Israel, or Jerusalem in Christ's Revelation. They completely dismiss the Messianic prophecies of the Old Testament as an allegory, and they say it only has meaning as it applies to the Church. They are quick to interpret everything in Chapters 21 and 22 of Revelation, as all allegorical and spiritual, leaving no room for the real New Heavens and New Earth here in Revelation or in the Messianic texts for Israel, in the end-times.

The Earth was built by an eternal God, to be inhabited for eternal purposes, and it is going to be renovated and customized for the eternal Kingdom of His dear Son.

CAN GOD KEEP HIS PROMISE TO ABRAHAM, ISAAC AND JACOB?

Now my beloved, I have to propose a consideration. If God cannot or will not keep His promises to Abraham, how can you and I expect Him to keep His promises to us? Either God is truth and every man a liar, or God is not truth, and we can reject all promises, or at least hold them in suspect and not be sure whether He can be trusted or not. To bring a final solution to Jerusalem, and settle the Jews in their old estates inside the promised borders, is a very difficult task for our world, but it may or may not be for God. I submit this: providing us with Eternal Life and an Eternal City built in Heaven and coming down to set on the earth for a thousand years, is a far greater task, but depends on the same God who made promises to Abraham. Therefore, I depend on a God who is big enough to keep His promises to Abraham and Israel in order to trust Him for His great and exceeding promises to us.

THERE WILL BE AN EARTHLY JERUSALEM ON SIGHT IN THE HOLY LAND

By the authority of a faithful God and the claims of His Word, I declare to you that there will be a New Jerusalem in the Holy Land on the hills of Moriah, and it will be the seat of David and his Kingdom. The Jews will inhabit it as their capitol during the Millennium. Jerusalem will be the capitol of the world out of which goes the Law and Truth. Let's see if we can find tests and promises to back this up.

First of all, we read in Hebrews, Chapter 11 about an insight which must have come from knowledge and writings that we do not have, telling us that Abraham looked for a city and a God who would build that city for Him. We know that back as far as promises made to Abraham, there would be a city built for his seed in the last days. He made the same promises to David. (Psalms 89:36)

A LITERAL EARTHLY JERUSALEM AND A LITERAL HEAVENLY JERUSALEM

A long ongoing dilemma fills the writings and preaching about these two cities. We do not take issue with them, for we are left with a lot of space not explained. I will give my personal observations over the past 50+ years and leave the reader room to analyze and study the information available to us and try to decide.

With the concept of an eternal city, the Scriptures as well as other ancient writings, have set a hope in the heart of humanity for such a city from the beginning. Evidently, God had this city in mind from the very beginning and shared His hopes with His prophets even as far back as Enoch, who speaks of it in his writings. The concept of *Plato's Republic* leaned on it, and Aristotle drew from it when he wrote *The Tale of Two Cities*. Rome was thought to be the Eternal City through a misinterpretation of The Revelation. The Antichrist twisted the promise to Israel that Jerusalem would be the place of God's throne. Thinking to make himself the Messiah, he will set up his throne on the temple site, claiming that he is God (2 Thessalonians 2:4). This was also the hope of the Crusades who planned to set up a King of Jerusalem on a throne in the Temple Mount. Even many of the fairy tales and legends subtly allude to that fanciful city, such as the *Pied Piper* and *Alice in Wonderland*. The Muslims have their city—*Mecca*; the Catholics have their city—Rome; and the Jews have their city—Jerusalem. We Christians have *"no continuing city [here on Earth] but we seek the one to come"* (Hebrews 13:14).

A LITERAL, PHYSICAL JERUSALEM IN ISRAEL

This is an absolute and unquestionable promise to the Jews. There can be no doubt to any student of the Old Testament Messianic texts, that the Jews and Israel are encouraged to look for a golden age of the earthly city, Jerusalem, sitting on the hills of Moriah in the Holy Land. I can say with confidence that there are hundreds of texts which speak of that glory of a New Jerusalem yet to come here on the Earth at Moriah in the Holy Land; it will be built and inhabited right on the spot where Jerusalem now stands.

The present Jerusalem, although highly revered by Christians, Catholics, Orthodox, Muslims, and Jews, is really only a shadow of what is promised. But we suffer disappointment and despair, for we are told that this present Jerusalem is full of sin and not redeemed. Even in the days of the two witnesses in Chapter 11, Jerusalem *"spiritually is called Sodom and Egypt, where also our Lord was crucified"* (Revelation 11:8). The city is still in jeopardy and will yet be compromised. Part of the Temple Mount will be given to the Gentiles for 3½ years. Zechariah 12:1, 2 describes that time just before the Lord makes the city a world center, when Jerusalem will be a *"cup of drunkenness to all the surrounding people."* We are told that in the days just before Jesus returns, Jerusalem will be under siege from the armies of the world, that is, the Armies of the Nations, or the World Order troops, like NATO. Half of the city will fall and be sacked (Zechariah 14:2). However, the next verse says at that time, the Lord will enter the war. His feet shall stand on the Mount of Olives, and He will come to Mount Zion with 144,000 Jews to take possession. It will be renovated along with the rest of the earth and become the city promised to the Jews and to David, their resurrected king.

Over 700 years before Christ, Isaiah looked past his day and saw a time coming in the *"latter days"* when a New Jerusalem would be exalted upon the mountains which includes the Lord's house and the Temple Mount (Isaiah 2:1-4). It will be established and the nations of the world will flow into it, and the cultural and social center of the world will reside there. People will come to receive instruction in His ways, and how to live in His paths. The religious center of the world will be there. From Jerusalem, Christ will judge all nations, therefore the Legal and Judicial Center of the world will also be there, and the Department of Peace and Safety will be there also, because from Jerusalem, will go forth policies allowing all to destroy their war equipment and turn their finance into peaceful endeavors. And here is the great news: there will be no more war! This same text is written in Micah 4:1-4, where is added the exciting detail that Christ shall reign over them in Zion. Zechariah, Chapter 13 sees a great city which has a fountain flowing from the house of David and is cleansed from its sin. A city to which there will be a mass Aliyah, and there they will meet a man with nail prints in His hands (13:5-6). The Jews, in mass, will realize that Christ is their great Messiah, and there will be a weeping in the land, and great conversions will take place with the help of 144,000 Jews with Jesus. Chapter 8 speaks of a great restoring of Jerusalem to a glory that never has been before.

Throughout the Psalms, there are songs written to and about, the coming eternal city of Jerusalem: *"The Lord builds up Jerusalem;"* (Psalms 147:2) we will be *"Standing within your gates"* (122:2); the Lord will reign from Zion (146:10). We are to *"pray for the peace of Jerusalem"* and never forget her (122:6,

135:21). Isaiah concurs that the Lord will reign in Zion (Isaiah 24:23); and the Lord has *"performed* (finished) *all His work on Mount Zion and on Jerusalem"* (10:12). *"People shall dwell in Zion at Jerusalem"* (30:5) and God said, *"for Zion's sake I will not hold My peace, and for Jerusalem's sake I will not rest until her righteousness goes forth as brightness"* (Isaiah 62:1).

Ezekiel's book makes it beyond question that there will be a glorified city during the Millennium. He describes it Chapters 40 through 48. There, in elaborate detail, a new temple is shown in this city. Remember there is no temple in the heavenly Jerusalem, because the Lamb is the temple thereof (Revelation 21:22).

These are only samples of the texts which are replete with the promises of a literal Jerusalem setting on the Mountains of Zion in the Millennium.

A HEAVENLY CITY THAT IS ALSO A PHYSICAL REALITY

None of these seem to have any part of the New Jerusalem coming down from God out of Heaven. There seems to be another New Jerusalem, not for the Jews, but for the Church, the body and Bride of Christ, and the Lamb of God. Paul relates to this city in Hebrews 13:14 where he says, that here on this Earth, *"we have no continuing* (eternal) *city, but we seek the one to come."* Earlier in Hebrews 12:22-29, he enlightens us further about our city. He tells us that going beyond the literal earthly city and Mount Zion, we come to a *"Mount Zion and to the city of the living God, the heavenly Jerusalem"* (12:22). We will note the cryptic symbolism as the earthly Jerusalem and earthly Mount Zion are duplicated in Heaven. Paul said in that city will be found the *"general assembly and Church of the first born who are registered in Heaven, to God the Judge of all, to the spirits of just men made perfect; to Jesus the Mediator of the new covenant"* (12:23-24).

In correlation to the earthly city of the Jews in an earthly Jerusalem, Ezekiel tells us plainly that there will be a temple built and he describes it in detail. Revelation 21:2 concurs there is a city that comes down from Heaven. However, there will be no temple in the heavenly Jerusalem, for the Lamb is its Temple. (Revelation 21:22)

It becomes contextually clear that we must accommodate two different cities. 1)There is a Millennial city—a holy city promised to the Seed of Abraham as a place for the throne of David; and 2) there is a holy city not made by man, coming down to rest on the earth, which is the home of the Saints who are redeemed in Christ. We cannot completely explain or even comprehend these two cities side by side, nor one over the top of the other; but never mind, we are dealing with things that have never been seen nor comprehended by mortal man.

I will now share a bit of practical understanding as I try to see these two cities resting upon the Earth. It seems to me the new city that comes down from God (the one Jesus built and prepared for us) will hover over the old but newly renovated city of Jerusalem, where the Temple will be built on Moriah, and the throne of David will exist with twelve thrones, one for each of the twelve apostles (Matthew 19:28; Luke 1:32, 22:30). It may be that the reason why the foundation stones are called by the twelve apostles of the Lamb is that they are all Jewish and are the foundations of the New Testament gospel, and make the connection between the two cities (Ephesians 2:20; Revelation 21:14). These twelve foundations extend down from the heavenly city to rest around the earthly city. It is as if the earthly city is a suburb of the heavenly city, and they interact one with the other with Christ ruling them both, including the dominion over David and the earthly city. Christ is also Lord and King of the New City.

ISRAEL AND THE JEWS DO HAVE A PLACE IN THE MILLENNIUM

There is absolutely no doubt that Israel and the Jews have a leading role in the Millennium and the Eternal World to come, even though information about their place in the events of Revelation is very sketchy. However, a careful study of Old Testament Messianic texts, and especially those that reveal details of the Millennial time are abundant with insight into the Jews and Israel in the last days.

A study of texts such as Isaiah 60 - 66, reveals to us what we actually see in our current world events today. The only two redeeming societies in the last days will be the Church and Israel. Jesus said He would bring us together as *"one flock and one shepherd"* (John 10:16). The original, literal text as given to us in the NIV, says that the bringing together of the Church and the Jews results in making us perfect (Hebrews 11:40). It is clear that the Church and the Jews will celebrate the Feast of Tabernacles together every year in the Millennium:

> *" And it shall come to pass that everyone who is left of all the nations which came against Jerusalem shall go up from year to year to worship the King, the Lord of hosts, and to keep the Feast of Tabernacles"* (Zechariah 14:16).

We will camp out in the earthly Jerusalem together with the pilgrims of the world from every nation left after Armageddon, and together with the Jewish people, we will have an Old Fashioned Camp Meeting.

Because there is an extreme amount of anti-Semitism in our world, and Replacement Theology which is heavily taught even in the evangelical world of Christianity, (denies Israel any promise or place in the Millennium) I feel it is necessary to reinforce the promises made to Israel and the

NEW HEAVEN AND NEW EARTH

Jews for the end-time. However, I can say without question, that the Old Testament Messianic prophecies are replete with promises for Israel and the Jews in the last days. I will reference just a few of them. God said to David that He would establish His kingdom forever (2 Samuel 7:16). That, along with the everlasting kingdom, God would *"appoint a place for my people Israel and will plant them, that they may dwell in a place of their own and move no more"* (7:10).

In Isaiah's prophecy of the Christmas story, God said that when Christ returned, there would be no end to His government (Isaiah 9:7). Then we must not overlook the following clear statement of Israel's rule through David's throne:

> *"... upon the throne of David and over his Kingdom, to order it and establish it with judgment and with judgment and justice from that time forward, even forever. The zeal of the Lord of hosts will perform this"* (Isaiah 9:7).

Most of the end of Isaiah, Chapter 65 is clearly Millennium statements. We note that these references to the Millennium are preceded by reference to the New Heavens and the New Earth, and will leave us with the impression that the following verses were about them. However, verse 18 begins with the word *"but"* (Hebrew, *Kisim*, meaning *never-the-less* or *in-contrast*). Therefore, the rest of the verses describe something in contrast of the New Heaven and New Earth. It is fairly plain that the rest of the chapter describes the Millennium. It is during the Millennium when He creates the earthly Jerusalem:

> *"For, behold, I create new heavens and a new earth; and the former shall not be remembered or come to mind. But be glad and rejoice forever in what I create"* (Isaiah 65:17-18).

We note then, that there is a definite place for Jerusalem and His people, Israel. And they will enjoy peace forevermore.

These few chosen texts will illustrate how the whole Messianic prophesies are full of references to Israel's eternal promise of a Golden Age and a New Jerusalem, and Israel's place in the New Kingdom. Therefore, we must intercalate these Messianic prophecies into what we read in Revelation in order to get the full picture.

The New Testament supports the fact that Christ intends to put the Church together with the Redeemed Jews as the saving agencies in the Millennium. For instance, we read in Galatians:

"So then, those who are people of faith are blessed and made happy and favored by God [as partners in fellowship] with the believing and trusting [the seed of] Abraham" (3:9, Amplified Bible).

In Ephesians 3:6 (Amp.) we read the same thought:

"... That the Gentiles are now to be fellow heirs [with the Jews], members of the same body and joint partakers [sharing] in the same divine promise in Christ through [their acceptance of] the glad tidings" (Amplified Bible).

Those that try to cut Israel out of the final blessings and promises are, in my humble estimation, willingly ignorant. No one can be a serious student of the Bible, and especially the Messianic prophecies, and ignore the obvious promises to the Jews who have accepted the Gospel.

PHYSICAL BODIES AND SPIRITUAL BODIES

A word is in order about the difference in bodily form that will be our existence in the New Heaven and the New Earth. It is obvious that we will have to be changed, and that is exactly what Paul reveals to us in 1 Corinthians 15:51. We are also told in 1 John 3:2:

> *"Beloved, now we are children of God; and it has not been revealed what we shall be, but we know that when He (Jesus) is revealed, we shall be like Him, for we shall see Him as He is."*

It is obvious that we will retain our individuality and identity. Some of the eastern religions (a concept adopted by the New Age Luciferian Cult) try to say we will lose our personal identity and in some mystic, mysterious state of eternal existence, melt away into some kind of cosmic soup, and enter into a mystical, universal body of God. We all supposedly become *spirit* and exist in the mass of spirit that is made up of us all, as well as God. This is the kind of nonsense you can expect to fall into when you follow Satan. He is lost and lives in spiritual darkness; he has been confused about reality ever since his fall.

Some try to tell us that Christ's high priestly prayer in John Chapter 17, hints at what the Buddhists and Hindus believe. Jesus did say that He and the Father are one, and that He is in us and we in Him, just as the Father and He are one, so He wills that we be in one. (paraphrased) None of this however, hints that we are melted into some universal soup of spirit, and lose our identity in Him. Our soul is our eternal identity and there is no hint anywhere in the text that we lose our soul as we enter this eternal city. In fact, *"I shall know just as I also am known"* (1 Corinthians 13:12).

WE WILL NOT LOSE OUR PERSONAL IDENTITY

What we read here and in all prophecy, gives us every reason to know, that although we will be changed, we will be like Him; and certainly Christ has retained His full identity and individuality. His appearance to the disciples shortly after His Resurrection shows us this fact without question. He said to Thomas, "Reach your finger here into my side and see that it is Me, and not a spirit (John 20:27). Then He sat down and dined with them. We are plainly told in Philippians 3:21 that our spiritual bodies will be *"conformed to His glorious body."* We will still be physical and yet free from gravitational pull and all of the weakness connected to the earthly body.

Oh yes, beloved, we will be real in a real city, with real people all around us, secure in our identity. We shall know as we are known, just as Abraham, Isaac, and Jacob will be known in the Kingdom of God.

At the same time, we will in some way, perhaps mysterious to us today, be one *in* Christ and one *with* Christ. Paul told us our change is a mystery, and tried to deal with it when questioned. If the great Paul, whose life is heavy with revelations, can explain it no further than what we read in these verses, I do not expect myself or any other to explain it, short of when we see Him as He is.

Certainly there are many questions we would like to ask, but most of them will have to be answered when we get there, and I think it is not wise to take more space in this writing. What we do know is that we can make plans to be there by the directions given to us in the Gospel of Christ, and that our wonderful Lord and Savior is waiting for us there. We shall see Him; we shall behold Him whom we have loved but have never seen. An old chorus we used to sing says,

> "Oh, won't it be wonderful there, having no burdens to bear; joyously singing, with heart bells all ringing, Oh won't it be wonderful there!" (George Jones)

We will cover the rest of Chapter 21 in the next Chapter, which will include all of the description of the New Jerusalem. Here we will see how it images the Bride, the Lamb's wife. Then, in Chapter 22, we will see the conclusion of this wonderful matter. PTL!

Chapter 22

THE HOME OF THE BRIDE

A TOUR OF THE CITY AND A LOOK AT THE BRIDE: "HERE COMES THE BRIDE"

This chapter accurately describes the Bride of Christ in Messianic cryptic symbols.

As we begin to study what is shown to us about the New Jerusalem and how it reflects the characteristics of the Church, the Bride of Christ, and their mysterious relationship to Christ, we will become increasingly fascinated with our bond and spiritual romance with Christ, a relationship that will last for a thousand years and then for eternity. So let's trail along with John as he follows the angel to *"show [us] the Bride, the Lamb's wife"* (Revelation 21:9).

NEW JERUSALEM, BOTH A PHYSICAL REALITY AND CRYPTIC SYMBOL

The description we are given of the city is both literal and metaphorical. It will have a two-fold meaning as we go along. It is both a real physical city with real physical features, yet at the same time it reflects cryptic images of the Bride of Christ. It has a likeness to the Old Tabernacle which we know reflects the Messiah in all of its structure and furnishings.

The first key to understanding the mystery is to grasp

what we are seeing here. The City is a real physical place that Christ has built for us as His gift to us in marriage. When Jesus said that He was building a place for us, he used the Greek word *topos* which means *a location on a map*. So, just as we can find our way home on a map, we can also find our way to our eternal home and say with assurance "this is my place" or "this is your place." The City came out of Heaven (a place) to Earth (a place.) It is a real place in real time with real people, and built upon a real foundation and promise. Isaiah saw it (60:21); Jesus willed it and built it (John 17:24, 14:2); Abraham looked for it (Hebrews 11:10); the prophets prophesied about it, the philosophers anticipated it, and every emperor tried to build it. (Babylon and Rome) All religions have the hope of either the real thing or a counterfeit; but we are going to see it, receive it, and live in it.

Our eternal home is not in Heaven, but in the New Jerusalem. It will be right here on Earth, an eternal city on the new Earth. This city moved out of Heaven (its construction site) and John saw it *"coming down out of heaven"* (Revelation 21:2).

We are told other things about this earthly eternal abode. God Himself, the Father of our Lord Jesus Christ and the Father of the Bride, is going to move His permanent headquarters here (21:3). It is beyond us to understand why God wants to leave the glories of His Heavenly Abode and dwell here with us, but that's what we are told. It says that *"God Himself will be with them and be their God"* (21:3). When you view the minute place this little planet fills in just our galaxy, let alone the great Universe beyond (see NASA's view of our Galaxy) it is an absolute enigma for God to want to dwell on Earth with us.

A REAL, NOT AN IMAGINED CITY

To know that our eternal home is a real place may make it

a bit more attractive to some of us, including myself.

One day, I was trying to excite a man to prepare for Heaven. I was sharing with him about the Lord while he was very busy in his car repair shop. Suddenly, he stopped his work and looked up and said,

> "Reverend, why would I want to go to Heaven? I don't think I'm really all that excited. First of all, I don't want to spend eternity flitting around on a cloud doing nothing but harping on a harp. I like to be busy and I don't know how, nor do I want to learn how, to play a harp. And besides, I don't care a thing about lying around in my night shirt all day; I like to get dressed in the morning. Is there any place else I can go?"

Oh how glad I was to turn his attention to Revelation, Chapters 21 and 22, and show him the real city that isn't even in Heaven, but is a very busy place right here on Earth. It is not a cloud, but a city, and we will be fully clothed and active. And as for the harp, I suspect there will be a full orchestra and choir there, whether I play an instrument or not.

OLD TABERNACLE AN EXAMPLE

We have learned in an in-depth study of the Tabernacle in the Wilderness, that it is not only a pattern of heavenly things, but is also carefully crafted to represent the Messiah, Jesus Christ. Although it is an actual physical building, every minute detail of the Tabernacle can be found to represent the Lord in every minute detail of His life, His character, His death, burial, resurrection and ministry. It is a metaphoric symbol to us on Earth and in Heaven. Christ is cryptically revealed to us in every part of the materials in the Tabernacle.

So it is with the New Jerusalem. Just as the Tabernacle was a physical structure, yet reflects the Lord in *type and shadow*, the New Jerusalem is built after the same heavenly pattern and reflects every minute detail of the Bride of Christ- her life, nature, character, and ministry to Christ. It reflects every intimate relationship of the Church to Christ, our Husbandman. As we walk with John and the angel (our fellow companion) in a tour through the New City, we will be challenged to see the actual physical structure, expressing and manifesting the characteristics of the Church as the Bride of Christ. It is up to us to search out the cryptic metaphors that reveal the Bride to us.

THE CITY'S PHYSICAL PROPERTIES - THE HOME OF THE BRIDE

First, let's consider the actual physical aspects of the city.

It is 1500 miles square which calculates out to 2,250,000 square miles (Revelation 21:16-17). That is the distance between Seattle, Washington and Mexico City; or between Fresno, California to the Mississippi River. Dividing it up between 8 billion believers, it leaves about 6 acres for each person. Take out 8 million miles of roads and 1/3 for businesses, and you still have 4 acres each. That is a nice little piece of this Heavenly City. And all of this is only on the ground floor. We are also told that the height of it is equal to the width and breadth. Is it a pyramid or a mountain? Like the tower of Babel, it ascends upward to an elevation of 1500 miles high, with the foothills on the bottom and the lower mountains and valley each ascending upward to the top of the Mountains. On top is the throne of God and Jesus Christ. It is also the eternal *"Mount Zion"* (Hebrews 12:22); the *"city of our God ... [and] His holy mountain"* (Psalms 48:1); and *"it is Mount Zion on the sides of the North, the city of the great King"* (Psalms 48:2).

"Great is the Lord, and greatly to be praised, in the city of our God, in the Mountains of His Holiness. Beautiful for situation, the Joy of the whole Earth, is mount Zion on the sides of the North, the city of the great King" (Richard Smallwood, from Psalm 48:1,2. (See Psalms 47 for more of the setting).

John could stand at the top and see the entire city before him on every side; its streets, its rivers, its orchards, and its fields. A fountain flows from out of the Throne and divides into twelve streams which make their way to each of the gates; the Tree of Life lines the banks of each stream.

The City Chambers are at the thrones of the Church where the Church rules and reigns with Christ. Its foundation is the Kingdom of David and the administration of Israel. The terrain of the earth will have to be changed to accommodate it, if it sits on the Earth.

It may however, hover just above the earthly city of Jerusalem as we mentioned in the study of the last Chapter. If it hovers above Earth, it would cover all of the Middle East, and would overshadow the complete millennial borders of the Promised Land which was bequeathed to Abraham. However, it will not matter, for either way the earth is going to be renovated to accommodate all of this. As a matter of physics, if it was placed on the eastern seaboard of the United States, it would extend from Main to Florida and from New York City to the Rockies. Its sheer weight would tip the continent into the sea. Also, it is possible that it will be suspended above Earth. Whatever happens, the last great earthquake and fire is going to completely cleanse and change the earth to accommodate God's plans.

MATERIALS IN ITS CONSTRUCTION

The materials of its construction will be gold, diamonds,

pearls, and precious stones in quantities that the earth cannot supply. Whatever happens, *Science News* reported on 3/14/87 that 'star-dust' is studded with diamonds. Gold is manufactured in the universe as well. Pearls 80 feet high and 30 feet wide, cannot be supplied by the earth, but Heaven can supply it. Remember, it is being built in Heaven and not on the earth, nor of the earth.

Then there will be those precious stones that Isaiah saw (54:11-12). Ezekiel said they were taken from Satan's glory (Ezekiel 28:13-18). It also carries its own foundation stones garnished with the best of the universe.

Out there somewhere, is enough gold to pave 9,000 miles of freeways and multiple thousands of miles of avenues and streets; and enough pearls to garnish 12 gates, 80 feet high, 30 feet wide, and an equal 30 feet thick; each gate made of a single pearl. With Christ as the Chief Corner Stone and a foundation of pure Jasper, a clear and pure form of diamond which the Earth has never produced, we will have a city that is *out of this world*. The ancient City Atlantis may have been its closest earthly likeness.

It took God six days to make all that we have in this inhabitable earth. Jesus said He went away to *"prepare* (build) *a place for [us]"* (John 14:2). Now, He and Heaven's crew have been building it for 2000 years. What kind of home is it going to be after two millennia of construction? He said there *"are many mansions"* prepared just for us (14:2).

Remember, it came down from Heaven, therefore it was constructed somewhere out there In God's vast Universe and brought here to Earth. The materials used in the construction of the city are not polluted or impure as the materials of Earth, but are as pure as Heaven itself. For instance, our gold on Earth is polluted gold, even that which is considered of the purest form. My son-in-law, Mike Filkins, worked for a gold processing company where they not only mined the gold, but processed it as well. I have had the privilege of watching the whole process, from the mining to the laundering of it, and then putting it in its raw form into the furnace where it came out as pure as they were able to make it. But even then, it is said to be only 93% to 96% pure.

In Fort Knox, most of the gold is considered junk gold (i.e. melted down jewelry) as well as other gold- bearing paraphernalia. However, the gold of Heaven is pure 100% gold. What a honeymoon cottage it is; and it is prepared for us by our Bridegroom.

CONCEPT OF AN ETERNAL CITY SET IN THE HEART OF HUMANITY

The concept of an eternal city has been revealed in Scripture and other ancient writings, and has been set in the heart and hope of humanity since the beginning. Evidently, God had it in mind and shared it with his prophets and faithful, even as far back as Enoch, who speaks of it in his writings. The concept of Plato's *Republic,* leaned on it, and Aristotle wrote of it in the *Tale of Two Cities.* Rome drew from its concept when it became known as the *Eternal City*, and the Antichrist's diversion of the promise to Israel that Jerusalem would be an eternal city. However, He decided to claim it as his own. As mentioned earlier, its concept is subtly alluded to in many legions and fairy tales like the *Pied Piper*, *Alice in Wonderland*, and many others.

Also, the Muslims have their city - Mecca; the Catholics have their city - Rome; and the Vatican, and the Jews have their city - Jerusalem. However, *"we have no continuing city, but we seek one to come"* (Hebrews 13:14).

Abraham looked for *"the city which has foundations, whose builder and maker is God."* (Hebrews 11:10) We are plainly told that God has *"prepared a city for them"* (11:16). It is a real city with *metes and bounds*, and will be setting on location over Mount Zion during the Millennium. It is described for us in detailed earthly terms, and as we walk through it and observe its symbols of the Bride, we must not forget its reality.

As we behold the physical city, we are going to be shown hidden and secret symbolisms that reveal the characteristic of the Bride of Christ. As we have said it is analogously written in order, that only those who really love Christ will be interested enough to search, analyze the evidence, and learn what it really means to be a member of the Bride of Christ.

SOME ARE LOSING THEIR APPETITES FOR HEAVEN

We used to talk about Heaven a lot more than we do now. Every part of the description of this city has been the subject of countless Sunday School lessons, sermons, and Bible studies. We've talked about the streets of gold, the gates made of one single pearl, the foundations of precious stones, the Tree of Life, and the river of the water of life. We have always been given full assurance of their reality. We have talked about this city and sang songs like, "When I Get up to Heaven," "In the Sweet Bye and Bye," and "A City Four Square." We've anticipated meeting each other with songs like "I'll meet you in the morning." Oh, how I love to hear people sing about Heaven!

Then came our present affluent times and people have become so content and satisfied with what they have here, that we increasingly center our interest on what Christ provides for us now, and less on what our eternal promises are. It seems that many people have lost their appetites for Heaven thinking Earth will always be as it is now.

I am finding, to the shock of my soul, that some are beginning to question whether there is a Heaven or even Hell, and also being told that if they are interested in Heaven, it will have to be something similar to what we have here on Earth right now. This makes it all the more necessary that we talk about Heaven and the New Heavenly City in this writing. Heaven is certainly real, and this City is real and only those who long for it, will walk its streets.

Even among those who talk and sing a lot about Heaven, I have yet to hear any mention of the similarity between the city and the Lamb's wife. Without taking away from the physical reality of the city, let's look at some exciting similarities that reflect the Bride of Christ.

HERE COMES THE BRIDE

"Come here, and I will show you the bride, the Lamb's wife" (Revelation 21:9).

Someone has told a little story on Adam about the first time he saw his bride, Eve. They said God had put him to sleep in order to perform surgery and take one of his ribs out for the construction of Eve. God worked and worked on Eve to make her just what He thought Adam would like. When He was finished making her, God placed Eve within a few feet of Adam. When Adam awoke and took one look at Eve, his first exclamation was "WHoo—Man" and that's how we got the word "woman!" As we walk through the city we will be looking for symbols of Christ and His Bride. What a beautiful, attractive, and desirable wife she will be; Whoo—man!

I don't know if we can attach any scriptural reality to this story, but it does illustrate our excitement at a first look at the Bride. I hope we can find as much excitement as we take our first look at the Bride of Christ. The Church is first presented by Christ *"as a bride adorned for her husband"* (Revelation 21:2). Never does a bride look more appealing and desirable than when she anticipates her wedding day and gets herself ready. That's what is meant as Christ anticipates the marriage to His Bride, the Church, saying, *"His [bride] has made herself ready"* (Revelation 19:7). The first thing a bridegroom notices about the bride is her "beauty beyond compare" and that she has made herself ready. So it is with the Church who has prepared herself for the marriage reception to her Bridegroom. Some may take offense to such a close comparison of the relationship of Christ to His Church, but Paul said that married love in its purity is a cryptic facsimile of the Love of Christ for His Church (Ephesians 5:25-27, 31-33).

As we walk with John and the angel through the city and see the characteristics of the Bride in every part of its physical features. I hope it is as exciting to you as it has been for me, preparing notes for this study for over 60 years.

We will put Revelation 21:9-22:6 together in-as-much as these verses are all a study of the New Jerusalem, and how it reveals here in cryptic symbolism the characteristics that make up the Church which is called the Bride of Christ, or the Bride of the Lamb.

THE WAY OF A MAN WITH A MAID

Paul's observation about Christ's spiritual love for His Church surely agrees with what we will find in Proverbs. As John views the New Jerusalem coming down from God, he has an impression that at the time, he cannot understand or describe its whole meaning. As he views the actual physical city, the Holy Spirit impresses upon John's heart that this city is *"prepared as a bride adorned for her husband"* (21:2). He does not completely comprehend the connection between the city and the Bride of Christ, but a little later in verse 9, it will be fully explained to him. There is an intriguing mystery about Christ and His Church:

"This is a great mystery, but I speak concerning Christ and the Church" (Ephesians 5:32).

Paul was speaking of the great mystery that should and does accompany every marriage. It is the wonder of two persons becoming one in the Lord. Proverbs, chapter 30 gives us another insight into the mystery of marriage. In verses 18-19, Solomon speaks of 4 things that are too wonderful to be understood. One is the way of an eagle in flight; the second is the way a serpent moves across the ground; the third is the way of a sail-ship on the sea; and fourth, he startles us by touching upon the subject found in Revelation 21 where it speaks of, *"the way of a man with a virgin"* (Proverbs 30:19).

"The way of a man with a virgin" is too wonderful for anyone else to understand or describe. The enigma is far beyond our ability to comprehend or explain. And Solomon surely should know after trying to work out a viable relationship with over a thousand women. He said he could not find the quality of a good woman among the thousand (Ecclesiastes 7:28). There is nothing that upsets things on the earth like an odious woman who is married. But Solomon also declares, *"He who finds a wife finds a good thing, and obtains favor from the Lord"* (Proverbs 18:22). In Chapter 32, Solomon says that, *"a virtuous wife ... [has] worth far above rubies"* (31:10).

LOVE AND RELATIONSHIPS ARE KEPT SECRET AND ARE NOT FOR PUBLIC DISPLAY

The point is, no one really can understand the relationship between a man and his mate, let alone understand the relationship of Christ with His Church. A marriage is a relationship that is beyond comprehension to anyone but the man and wife themselves. I learned in over 50 years of marriage counseling, that I could give some timely and helpful advice, but must never think that I truly understood the couple's relationship. Every marriage is different and each man and woman works out many integral details that only they can understand; most of which they cannot and/or would not express. Sometimes the relationship in marriage is a bit of an intriguing mystery to us, ourselves. Most intimacies are totally private and not a spectator sport for public consumption. It loses its sacredness when put on display.

Certainly Paul, by the Holy Spirit, has picked up this fact as it relates to Christ and His Church. It is a great mystery, and as John is called upon to follow the angel to be shown Christ's Bride, we enter into some very intriguing and wonderful insight to the Church, and her characteristics and relationships to Christ.

The relationship of Christ and the Church was kept secret and only known to the heart of God until it began to be revealed through Paul (Colossians 2:3; Romans 16:25; Ephesians 1:9, 3:4, 9). The mystery of the Bride with Christ will not be made fully manifest until Christ makes her manifest or fully known, at the Marriage of the Lamb, and when she makes her appearance with Him. (Romans 8:19) Until then, *"the whole creation groans and labors"* in earnest expectation waiting for the Bride's manifestation (8:22-23). It was only revealed so that Paul could:

> *"[Betroth] you to one husband, that [he] may present you as a chaste virgin to Christ"* (2 Corinthians 11:2).

We probably will not understand the full relationship between Christ and His beloved Bride for some time, for we are told that it will take ages to come for us to:

> "..comprehend with all the saints what is the breadth, and the length and depth, and height; and to know the love of Christ, which passes knowledge"(Ephesians 3:18, 19).

It seems it will take ages for us to begin to comprehend our relationship with Christ:

> "... *that in the ages to come He might show the exceeding riches of His grace in His kindness toward us in Christ*" (Ephesians 2:7).

Certainly we cannot begin to comprehend the depth of Christ's love for us, nor can we fully understand our love, devotion, and commitment to Him. One of the great mysteries of a man with his virgin, and surely the mystery of Christ and His Bride, is the deep love that is within them. Christ's love for us and our love for Him is a great mystery *"which is Christ in you, the hope of glory"* (Colossians 1:26-27). There is a relationship between the Father and the Son, and between them and us, which only can be understood and revealed by the blessed Holy Spirit of God.

MANIFESTATION OF THE CHURCH

Not only is this the "Revelation of Jesus Christ" but also in a very real sense, it is the Revelation of the Bride. Until now, the Bride is kept in secret from the raw godless world. The world *"waits for the manifestation on the Son's of God."*

(Romans 8:19) We have not yet been revealed to the world. We are still waiting for the *"redemption of our bodies"* (v 23); *we are made "ready"* for our salvation which is *"ready to be revealed in the last time."* (I Peter 1:5) The salvation of our souls was complete when Christ died on Calvary and presented His blood on the Mercy Seat of Heaven, but we speak here of the salvation of the body being delivered from death and corruption.

That deliverance takes place at the Revelation of Jesus Christ. We have received the salvation of our souls (ibid v.9) but there is a part of our salvation which has puzzled the prophets and sages for centuries, (vs.10-12) inasmuch as the Church has been "hidden' and will be hidden until it is manifested and revealed.

Therefore we are to keep on "*hoping to the end for the grace that is to be brought unto you at the revelation of Jesus Christ.*" (ibid v.13) So we learn that the Bride is making herself ready, and will be ready at the revelation of Jesus Christ. Our salvation is to be complete and ready to be revealed at the time of the bridegroom's own "revelation. This is confirmed by Hebrews 9:28 where we read: "*So Christ was once offered to bear the sins of many; and unto them that look for Him shall He appear the second time, not to bear sin, but to bring salvation*" (NIV). Oh what a revelation it will be when this ungodly old world sees Him manifest in all His Glory, and also sees the Bride of Christ revealed in all Her Splendor, as having "*made herself ready*" and is "*coming down from God out of Heaven*" (Revelation 21:2). Our full salvation will be revealed at our full manifestation at the coming of the Lord. No wonder there will be a shout from Heaven and a trump of God.

"Be ready therefore also; for the Son of man comes at an hour you think not."

A VIRTUOUS WIFE AND A VIRTUOUS BRIDE— THE CHURCH

> "*Christ also loved the church and gave Himself for it, that He might sanctify and cleanse it with the washing of the water by the word, that He might present it to Himself a glorious church, not having spot or wrinkle or any such thing, but that it should be holy and without blemish*" (Ephesians 5:25-27).

As Paul said, and my point is that we hope Christ, in the mystery of His marriage, has found us to be "*a glorious church, without spot or wrinkle or any such thing, but that it should be holy and without blemish*" (Ephesians 5:26, 27; 2 Peter 3:14).

We have been, as a body, growing in those virtues pleasing to Him, in the *"perfecting of the saints"* (Ephesians 4:12, *KJV*) as the body (Church):

> *"Till we all come to the unity of the faith and the knowledge of the son of God, to a perfect man, to the measure of the stature of the fullness of Christ"* (Ephesians 4:12-13).

We must be worthy and comparable to Christ, to be a true equal mate.

Those that are separated and called to the Marriage Supper of the Lamb, will be a select number who have made their priority, not to miss Hell or be religious, but to come up to a measure of maturity (perfection) that is worthy of being His Bride.

THE BRIDE GIVES THE INVITATION TO THE MARRIAGE (22:17)

"And the spirit and the bride say 'come'" (Revelation 22:17)!

Now we will go toward the end of Chapter 22 at this time, because I feel it is important to show this characteristic of the Bride. The Bride, under anointing of the Holy Spirit, reaches out to all. It is also certainly the spirit of the Church to make invitation to everyone who will hear, to come and be part of the Marriage to the Lamb—God's wonderful Son, Jesus Christ. Every day we Christians are witnessing to everyone we can and inviting them to share in our joy. All over the world, missionaries of every denomination are inviting every kindred, nation, people, and tongue to join in the wonderful hope of Heaven, both here and for eternity, with Christ our Savior and Husbandman. Therefore:

> *"The Spirit and the bride say, 'Come!" And let him who hears, say, "Come!" And let him who thirsts come. And*

whoever desires, let him take of the water of life freely" (Revelation 22:17).

As we have said above, the description given of the city is both literal and metaphorical. There is a call to everyone within the reach of the Church, to witness by the power of the Holy Spirit (Acts 1:8). Sometimes people get a little agitated with us when we try to witness to them; if they could only understand it is the Holy Spirit urging us to call them to the city and to the Bride.

THE SPIRIT'S VISION OF THE BRIDE - THE LAMB'S WIFE

This city is not only its physical properties, but also the people who live there—the Church, the Body, and the Bride of Christ. What we see in the physical properties will reflect what we are able to know spiritually about the people who are the Bride. The personality of Christ is also reflected in the Bride. As mentioned prior, it is the same Biblical fashion as the Old Testament Tabernacle in the wilderness, where Christ and Israel were represented in all of its building patterns, materials, furniture, and rituals. Both Christ and His Bride are symbolized in the characteristics and colors of the stones, the gates, the walls, the foundations, its light, its rivers, trees, and all other properties. Therefore we do see the Bride is represented in this city.

We are going to go into many of these details and reveal the *"The Bride; the Lamb's wife"* (Revelation 21:9). Through the Spirit of God and the revelation of the Church given to him while in exile, Paul was able to see this wonderful enigma of Christ and His Bride. He said in Romans 7:4;

> *"Therefore, my brethren, you also have become dead to the law through (becoming part of) the body of Christ; that you may be married to another, even to him who*

was raised from the dead."

CHRIST AND HIS BRIDE - THEIR MAIN ATTRACTION AND INTEREST

If it is a God-like marriage, for the man, it is all about his bride; and for the woman, it is all about her bridegroom. The first thing we see that reflects the Church, the Bride of Christ, is that the city is all about the Lamb of God, Christ our Savior. So it is with the Church.

For us the church, it is all about the Lord. Everything else in our lives is auxiliary, and only secondary. Christ is all in all.

When my wife and I were first married over 57 years ago, a comment was made to me about her by some of the women of our church. They said to me, "You know, we can't get Marvelle to be interested in anything else but you; you are all she is interested in talking about." I must admit, she was my main interest also. Her beauty, her character, her mannerism, her all around qualities, and her devotion to me and our future children, outside of Christ, was my major interests. And so it is and has been through the years, and should be for any rightly married and happily united couple; it is *"the way of a man with a virgin"* (Proverbs 30:19).

So it is with Christ and His Bride—the Church. All we want to talk about is our Lord, our Husband in the Spirit. He takes up our total interest. And as we have commented several times, starting with Chapters 2 and 3 of Revelation and continuing through the book, the Church takes up His major interest. All through the Revelation, we always find Him in the midst of, or in the company of, His Church. To care for, nurture, and provide for; to lead and feed, and promote the eternal welfare of His Church is His greatest interest (Revelation 7).

As we view the city as the Bride of Christ, we are soon impressed that it's all about Christ. And as we notice the features that represent Christ, we see how these are also the temperament, disposition, and nature of the Church, the Bride of Christ. In the exact pattern and principle as we are given in the gospel, *"we shall be like Him, for we shall see Him as He is"* (1 John 3:2).

This is the same John that is writing the Book of Revelation. As is evident in all of his writings and mannerisms, He had a special personal relationship with Christ in the Holy Spirit. He loved Jesus the most and was known as the *"disciple whom Jesus loved"* (John 20:2). He also had very special insight and understanding of the divinity of Christ. As he walks through the City with the Angel, he would have a special insight to the cryptic symbolism hidden in the physical attributes of the City itself. However (and I'm sure with the approval of the Lord) He chose to leave those symbols analogous (to be analyzed) so that we the Bride, are hidden from the casual critic and available only to those who, like the Bereans, *"searched the Scriptures daily to find out whether these things were so"* (Acts 17:11).

First, John 3:2 notes that even now, we are the sons of God, but struggle in our everyday lives to be more like Him. We will not display all of the charm, characteristics, mannerisms, and qualities of Him until we are changed and appear in His likeness. We will be like Him when we see Him as He is now, in His glory and power, at the right hand of God almighty, and His majesty on high.

What will be reflected in the attributes of the physical Eternal City will be His qualities and distinct traits *as He is,* and His characteristics will be an indicator of the qualities of the Bride, as she will be like Him.

Now let's walk through the City and see first the attributes of Christ, and then reflect upon them, as will be the spiritual features of the Bride.

First we note He is still *"the way, the truth and the life"* of His new City and the Bride (John 14:6).

Christ is the Life of the City: The whole city radiates with His life. The Life of Christ is the life of the Church, the Bride. It also is true with a biblical and godly human Bride. Her life takes on the life of her husband.

Christ is the Light of the City: Revelation 21:23 says, *"The Lamb is the Light."* The light of the Church is Christ. He is the light of Life. We sing:

"In that city where the Lamb is the light; In that city were there cometh no night."

"And the nations of those who are saved shall walk in its light" (21:24).

The light is perfect and represents Christ. It is the "Glory of God" that rested upon Christ, "a most precious stone, like Jasper stone, clear as crystal" (21:11). The whole foundation was made of jasper stone, and the complete wall of it was also Jasper (21:8-9).

We must be reminded that we the Church are *"also, as living stones being built up a spiritual house, a holy priesthood, to offer up spiritual sacrifices acceptable to God through Jesus Christ. Therefore it is also contained in the Scripture, 'Behold, I lay in Zion* (the New City) *a chief corner stone, elect, precious, and he who believes on Him will by no means put to shame'"* (1 Peter 2:4-6).

And again, *"having been built on the foundation of the apostles and prophets, Jesus Christ Himself being the chief corner stone ..."* (Ephesians 2:20).

We see then that the walls and the foundations are reflective of the light of the Lord Jesus Christ, and as it gloriously shines in the Earth's night, it fulfills in a greater measure what Christ said: *"you are the light of the world"* (Matthew 5:14). So with the above, we see that:

Christ is the walls and the foundation of the City. The names of the twelve apostles are placed on the foundation's stones in agreement with Ephesians 2:20 above.

Christ's glory is reflected in the precious stones of the City. Herein is part of the wonderful mystic of this city as it reflects Christ and all of His glory to the Church. It is voiced and taught in the ancient circles of those who contemplate the Messianic texts that Lucifer's purpose was to strip Christ of all of His glory and power, and assume His place in the plan of God. When He is humbled, His prince-hood taken, and His purpose is to supplant Christ, it is generally accepted that Christ would receive the glory that was taken from him (Ezekiel 28:13-19). If this is true, it is well documented here in Revelation 21:18-20, for we find the same beautiful *"fiery stones"* with which he was decorated when he first appeared in Eden. These stones are listed in Ezekiel 28:13 and are the exact same stones that make up the wall of the New Jerusalem. We have seen that the jasper stone is a representation of Christ in its pure light.

This indicates to us that Christ has received the beauty and glory of what Satan tried to steal, and now it has become part of the heritage of the Church. We, through Christ, will be given the beauty, glory, power, and position of Satan. Christ and His Bride now wear the beautiful stones of fire that once was the beauty of Lucifer. We will discuss this more in detail later in the writings of this Chapter.

Christ is the way in the city: The twelve gates represent the way, and certainly Christ is the way for the Church and the Bride. The ways of the Church are the ways of Christ. We follow Him wherever He leads:

"These are the ones who follow the Lamb wherever He goes" (Revelation 14:4).

We used to sing the chorus:

"Where he leads me I will follow, where He leads me I will follow, where He leads me I will follow. I'll go with Him, with Him, all the way."

And one verse has relevance here:

"I'll go with Him through the judgment, I'll go with Him through the judgment, I'll go with Him through the judgment, I'll go with Him, with Him all the way."

Oh yes, that is the spirit of the Bride.

Christ is the truth in the city: Revelation 21:5 says *"Write, for these words are true and faithful."* It is under signature of Christ Himself, that all these things are absolutely reliable. They are truthful and have been faithfully revealed to us.

Christ ascended down from God: This city came down from God out of Heaven and took up a humble earthly abode (Psalms 113:5-6). So, Christ came down from above. He who dwelt on high yet came to this lowly earth, an earth that is so lowly in the universe that even our solar system cannot be seen by the Hubble telescope in the vastness of our universe. From the great Heavens, he came down because He *"remembered us in our lowly state"* (Psalms 136:23). Christ *"made Himself of no reputation ... [and] humbled Himself"* (Philippians 2:6-7). (The Greek word is Kenosis—to pour out, to drain oneself and to claim no reputation; see Isaiah 53:12) He chose to dwell with whoever is of a "contrite and humble spirit" (Isaiah 57:15). He seeks to revive the spirit of the humble and to renew the hearts that are broken, and to lift us up to His heavenly estate, the New City. *Christ is the Bread of life in the City:* The manna which came down from Heaven. In the City is the Tree of Life—the manna from Heaven to the Church *"for the healing of the nations,"* just as the husband is the breadwinner for his Bride (Revelation 22:2).

Christ is the Water of Life in the City: The "River of the water of Life" flowing from the Throne of God and the Lamb is the *"fountain of water springing up into everlasting life."* (22:1; John 4:14) Christ is the springs of living water for the Church.

Christ is the Temple in the City: "For the Lord God almighty and the Lamb are its temple" (21:22). There is no other place of worship than at the feet of Christ. All of the Old Testament purpose for the temple or tabernacle is fulfilled in Christ.

Christ's Book of Life, the only register in the City (21:27). Just like on our passports, every membership card has the stamp of Christ on it. I would dare not go to this city without going with the Church, for it is the only number there.

Christ is the sacrifice that broke the curse in the City (22:3). The throne of God and the Lamb are there and his servants shall serve Him.

The way to Christ will never be closed (21:25). We may go in and out at our leisure, but Christ will always be available to us when we need Him as He is even today in our earthly service to Him. John was not to seal the sayings of this Book, for the promises in it are always available to the Church.

Christ is the absolute assurance of living in this city. The right to live here is strictly by His signature or spoken will:

"And they shall bring the glory and the honor of the nations into it" (21:26).

For instance, the thief on the cross had no other qualifications going for him only that Christ said, *"Today you will be with me in paradise"* (Luke 23:43).

THE BRIDE AND THE GLORY (v.11)

The first thing we are told about the Bride when we begin

to view her is her light, as she is reflected metaphorically in the features of the city. It is like a stone most precious, like the jasper stone. We have already talked about the jasper stone which makes up the city's total foundation and walls. It is a pure form of gold and represents Jesus Christ. Revelation 21:23 says that the light represents the Lamb, for *"the Lamb is its light."* We already know, as this verse tells us, that the saved of Earth walk in the light of the Lamb who is the light of the city, and is therefore, the light of the Bride in Christ, the light that comes from a reflection of His Glory (21:11). However, this verse says that the Bride has that glory upon her. She has the glory on and in her. For those of us who walk in the light of Christ and have the glory of the Holy Spirit in our lives today, we will carry it right on into our eternal home. Just like the *aura*, or light that lighted the body of Adam and Eve in the garden of God, so having been cleansed from sin, the glory will return to our skin. We will be like Christ, for we shall see Him as He is.

THE WALLS OF THE CITY (v.12)

The walls are our protection and our security. The walls are made of Jasper, and the Jasper is reflective of Christ. Therefore, as we view the Bride in the city, we see that Christ is the walls all around us and He is our *Jehovah Jireh*, our provider and our protector.

The Bride is also the care and protection of her husband, as Solomon shows in Proverbs 31. She protects his honor and his reputation, so we the Bride have been the bearer of Christ's honor and reputation while here on Earth. This is the nature of a true Bride.

THE GATES (vs. 12, 20)

The gates are our way; our way is Christ. They are each made of one pearl (21:21). Christ is our *"pearl of great price"*

(Matthew 13:45). As we have entered through the door, which is Christ Jesus, we are quickly impressed with two things; 1) The tremendous price that Christ paid for us to be there. A pearl is created by the extreme agony of the mother oyster when a small piece of sand gets into its bosom and agitates it for its lifetime. Christ paid the price of giving His all to win us the chance to enter this city; and 2) the tremendous value of the city, which is the Kingdom of Heaven. We the Bride have found that one Pearl, which is of great price. It is worth selling out everything else of value, and purchasing our citizenship into this city in the Kingdom of Christ.

Of course, pearls are a famous adornment of a bride, and no doubt, part of the Bride of Christ's adornment as well (1 Timothy 2:9; Revelation 21:2). Pearls represent gifts of great value, like the pearls of great price that adorn the Church, given out of His great riches, and beyond compare.

Each of the gates was captioned by one of the twelve tribes of Israel. As one enters the gates, he or she is reminded of the awesome heritage of the Bride. The Bride should always honor the family of the groom. And to the amazement of those who have preached that God still holds a grudge against the Jews and Israel and has cut them out of the heritage and power, the first thing they see are the supposedly cursed names of the Tribes captioned on the gates. God wants us to be reminded of the royal heritage upon which we, the New Testament Church is built upon. They were the door and entrance into the Kingdom. Pause at the gate, pay respect, and be reminded of your heritage. Jesus, Himself was of the Tribe of Judah, and that name will be there. Paul was of the Tribe of Benjamin and that name will be there also, along with all the rest of the sons of Israel. The twelve apostles (except possibly one) were all from one of these Tribes.

Those carnal Christians who are saved, but have not

thrown off their old carnal ways and tend to carry the anti-Semitism of hate toward the Jews, will be totally embarrassed to see these names so honored by God, Christ, and the Church. And what of those who have reveled in the deceit of Anglo-Israel doctrine about the ten lost tribes of Israel when they find that there are no lost tribes as far as Christ or the Bride of Christ is concerned? Every time you enter a gate, you'll regret your lowly attitude toward the Jews and Israel. Even Dan, although he was absent, has been reinstated.

METES AND BOUNDS OF THE BRIDE (v. 17)

We are not referring to her size; but the metes and bounds, or the measurement of the city, does have metaphorical reflections of the Bride of Christ. The city is foursquare, the width is the same as the breadth, and the height is equal. The reach of the city is the same—North, South, East, or West. We are commissioned to go into the whole world and teach all nations. Every nation, kindred, tongue, and people are the width and breadth of the Bride. And of course, her height is the far reaches of Heaven. How high have you reached on the scale of your life's reach?

I like to tell stories to illustrate many of my points: A preacher was in the company of one of the great ranchers of northwest Texas. The rancher was seeking to impress the preacher of the size of his domain. He said to the preacher, "Just as far as you can see to the east, that's mine; just as far to the west, I own that; as far as you can look to the North or the South, that's how far my land extends." The preacher stood silently for a moment, and then said, "How far do you own upward?"

Christ said, *"Lay up for yourselves treasures in heaven, where neither moth nor rust destroys"* (Matthew 6:19). If you belong to the Bride of Christ, the Church, the body of Christ, you own it all, *"for all things are yours"* (1 Corinthians 3:21, 22).

We can make a draw on the bank of Heaven at any time that we have need, if we have an account up there. How much are you depositing up there? How much do you own Heavenward?

PRECIOUS STONES (v. 19-20)

"Garnished with all manner of precious stones."

As we said briefly above, here we are presented with another analogous (a matter to be studied and analyzed) part of the Book.

As I note the list of the stones, I am immediately reminded of two major places that same list of stones can be found in the Old Testament. The first is the list of the same stones in Eden (Ezekiel 28:13). By the context, we realize that this is some pre-Adamic Eden, sometime in the ancient past when Satan was *"the anointed cherub who covers;"* a protector and light-giver of the Throne of God. He was full of wisdom, perfect in all His ways, and had his throne on the *"mountain of God"* where he was made the prince over this world by God (28:14).

As pertaining to our subject at hand, Satan *"walked back and forth in the midst of fiery stones."* (Ezekiel 28:14) There is something we don't understand in this dispensation of time. These fiery stones were in Eden and may have accompanied Lucifer or circled God's presence. It seems that there was a close correlation between the fiery stones and the Throne of God. Anciently, they are called *Stones of Judgment;* therefore they must be related somehow to God's Throne of Judgment.

Second, they were placed on the breast plate of the High Priest and reflected all of the colors of the rainbow. As stones upon the High Priest's breastplate, they were also called the *Stones of Fire and of Judgment.* The fiery stones on the breast plate of the great High Priest also contain the names of the twelve tribes of Israel, as do the precious stones in the foundation of the New Jerusalem. Thus, they also remind us in the days of the Tribulation and the final fulfillment, that Israel is still upon the heart of our great High Priest, and are part of the New Jerusalem.

THE SPOILS OF SATAN'S KINGDOM

These *fiery stones* or *precious stones* pick up some cryptic symbol from the ancient past. In receiving the spoil of Satan's Kingdom, Christ also becomes guardian and protector of Mount Zion, the mountain of God where Satan had His headquarters. He is of course, perfect and a pure reflector of the light, just as Satan once was. The Urim and Thummim, light and perfection, which lay on the heart of the High Priest, reminds us that Christ is now the "light and perfection" as our High Priest, and shares that light and perfection with His Bride, the Church. In some cryptic sense, the colors of the rainbow around the Throne are reflective of the character of the Lord, and now of His Bride, and are inscribed and engraved like a signature to show that *"they shall know that I am the Lord"* (Ezekiel 28: 24).

Now they are the foundation of the New Jerusalem. All of the symbolism concerning these stones will probably not be understood until He explains it to us as we walk through the City with Him. But, there is enough told to us in the above references, that we can make some strong and well supported conclusions.

One of the evident conclusions, and the one which pertains to our study here, is that the glory that once belonged to Satan has been transferred to our High Priest, Jesus Christ, and He is sharing it with those of His Bride as part of the dowry of marriage.

The precious stones somehow were the light and glory of Eden, and reflected the light of God in Christ with every color of the rainbow. That glory was transferred to the High

Priest, and became the glory of Christ Jesus, who hands it to us, His Bride. All that Satan sought to have and be in his rebellious quest for equality to God, he lost; it is given back to God's Son who now has received the *"glory and honor and power"* and dominion when Satan was unworthy to take the Book (Revelation 4:11). In the new City, they may be seen in the rainbow around the Throne, and reflected upon the sea of glass as we saw in Revelation 15:2.

WHAT WE WILL RECEIVE AS SPOILS OF SATAN'S KINGDOM

One of the principles of the Kingdom of Heaven is that God will take from those who received, but failed in caring for it, and give it to those who were faithful in their stewardship of the Lord's possessions (Matthew 25:28-29, 21:43; Mark 6:11; Luke 16:2; 19:24; Revelation 2:5). When Satan is judged:

> *"I cast you as a profane thing out of the mountain of God, (Zion) and I destroyed you, O covering cherub, from the midst of the fiery stones"* (Ezekiel 28:16).

The stones evidently were Satan's holiness and when He is thrown out of Heaven; His place will be filled by Christ and His holy Bride (28:15). We will receive:

1. Satan's glory, the covering or clothing of the stones of fire (Revelation 21:19-20).
2. His glorious position (21:16).
3. His glorious name, "Son of the morning."
4. His beauty in the stones of holiness will be our clothing (21:19).
5. His place in Paradise. He was kicked out of the garden of God; we are grafted in.

6. His place among the stars of God. His power, dominion, and authority also has been stripped from Him and given to Christ, who gives it to the Church.

BRING THE GLORY AND HONOR OF NATIONS INTO IT (v. 29)

As we have seen in previous parts of this study, the nations of those who are left, will come up year after year *"to worship the King, the Lord of hosts"* (Zechariah 14:16, Isaiah 60:12, Acts 15:17). The labor, sacrifices and devotion of our missionaries and their supporters, will be realized as the nations which allowed the gospel to reach part of its people, and who are saved from destruction of Armageddon, are opened up to the full acceptance of the gospel of Christ and will be allowed as guests in the New Jerusalem and hosted by the Saints (Zechariah 14:16).

ABSOLUTELY UNDEFILED (v. 27)

Nothing that in any way would defile it will be allowed inside its walls. Anyone who lies, or loves and makes a lie: who lives in falsehood or figment of imagination; who is defiled morally, spiritually, or mentally; or any who are an abomination to the Lord will be allowed. It all exists by and through the Lord, the Lamb of God.

Don't be deceived, not all are going to Heaven or will be in this city. There are those who are *within,* and there are those who are *without.* In order to have the *in's,* you have to have the *out's.* In fact, the Bible clearly tells us that there are going to be more *out's* than *in's.*

There are a total of eight classifications of *outs* listed:
1) Those who are contrary to society: whoremongers, adulterers and fornicators, thieves, murderers, and drug addicts and peddlers.

2) There are those against God. Sorcery—Phar-mak-eia, i.e. drug pushers, idolaters, and materialism; things that take pre-eminence over God.

3) Those who manipulate truth—liars, and that make lies and all pretense, hypocrisy (acting like something you are not) all resistance to absolute truth and honesty (22:15).

4) All anti-Christ actions and attitudes; unbelievers, fearful—those who are afraid to confess Him, abominable, and dogs (the lowest cast of society).

Matthew tells us to *"enter by the narrow gate; for wide is the gate and broad is the way that leads to destruction, and are many who go in by it. Because narrow is the gate and difficult is the way which leads to life, and there are few who find it"* (7:13-14).

Once we have entered into the city, we have a secure and lasting relationship with Christ. Let's look back at Revelation:

> *"He who is unjust, let him be unjust still; he who is filthy, let him be filthy still; he who is righteous, let him be righteous still; and he who is holy, let him be holy still" (22:11).*

There is going to be no change after the Millennium and the final judgment at the Great White Throne of Judgment (Revelation 20:11-15).

THE WATER OF LIFE

As we said previously, the water of life is coming out of the Throne of God, unpolluted, clear as crystal. It is the same water that Ezekiel saw in the New Jerusalem, that watered Eden (Ezekiel 47:1; Genesis 2:10). It is the same water that Christ told us about and was spoken of in Isaiah 33:21 and Joel 3:18. It is both a real river and a broad river that flows out of the throne, dividing into twelve heads flowing out of each gate to water the whole Earth. And, it is the spiritual water that flows through the Gospel of truth to bring life and sustenance to those who are washed in its flow. It is also the water of the Holy Spirit poured out upon the thirsty as the Holy Spirit fills us with *"joy inexpressible and full of Glory"* (1 Peter 1:8). All of these are contained in the cryptic symbol of the water of life.

THE TREE OF LIFE

Here again we are taken back to the beginning and the Garden of Eden, where we first heard of the Tree of Life and how, after the rebellion of Satan, its way was kept at the garden of the gate in Babel. It is known in Eden as the *"tree of the knowledge of good and evil"* and it was forbidden by God that we should partake of its fruit.

The New Age, taking their cue from Satan, says that Adoni is a mean God, for He keeps us from knowledge, and those who are looking for excuses to blame God, take no effort to read their Bible and find out the truth. It is not knowledge that God wanted withheld from us, but only carnal knowledge (evil knowledge.) God knew well that the weakness of our flesh, or self-nature, would destroy us with carnal knowledge, and it has.

Once we are redeemed and delivered from our flesh and self-nature, then it is no longer prohibited, and God can place the Tree of Life at our disposal, for carnal knowledge will no longer be a danger to us. Proverbs 11:30 tells us that wisdom is a *"Tree of Life,"* that will fill us with God's wisdom and understanding.

"Wisdom is the principal thing; therefore get wisdom. And in all your getting, get understanding" (Proverbs 4:7).

THE FINAL ATTESTATION OF TRUTH (22:6, 7)

These things, by the testimony of Christ, and sworn

under oath, are the truth, the whole truth, and nothing but the truth, so help me God. This Book is a legal document, attested to, with under-oath testimonies, and properly signed and sealed by notary. There are three testimonies:

1) The angel - *"these words are true and faithful"* (22:6);

2) Jesus - *"I Jesus, have sent my angel to testify"* (22:16); and

3) John - *"I John, saw and heard these things"* (22:8).

It is signed twice:
1) by John (22:8); and

2) by Jesus Christ Himself (22:16). As a legal document, it must not be changed or misread without penalty (22:18-19).

An altar call is made (22:17). There are three who call us to the altar at Jesus feet:

1) The Spirit who woos us to Christ;

2) The Bride, the Church which is and has been calling sinners to repent for 2000 years (About 5 billion have responded, most of them in our lifetime); and

3) the hearers, all of us who have heard and have turned back to others out of love and concern, calling them to God. My whole purpose in this writing is to call you to Christ.

Our response is crucial. If we miss the final altar call, we will remain judged throughout eternity (22:11). The unjust remains unforgiven; the filthy (morally and spiritually) remains unclean and unforgiven. However, if we will hear the call and respond, the righteous will never be defiled again, and the holy will never be polluted again.

Our final heartfelt appeal to Christ is, *"Even so (no matter what) come, Lord Jesus"* (22:20)! Like a lonely bride waiting for the return of her beloved husband, we wait and long for His return. This is the daily cry and prayer of the Church. We have a longing in our hearts for Jesus; do you long for Him to come?

We have this assurance; three times in these last pages of attestation He says:
* *"I am coming quickly"* (suddenly) (22:7).
* *"Behold, I am coming quickly"* (suddenly) (22:12).
* *"Surely, I am coming quickly"* (suddenly) (22:20).

Like a legal document, these sayings in the Revelation of Jesus Christ, are to be kept. We are to read them, hear them, and keep them (Revelation 1:3). To *keep* is to preserve them, guard them, and act upon them. Like a legal document, it is kept unchanged, guarded so that it may become the legal document to be acted upon and deliberated. It is not to be confusing or unclear (2 Peter 1:19). It must be a more sure word of prophecy; not obscure.

Let us not be as those spoken of in Luke 24:25: *"Oh foolish ones, and slow of heart to believe in all that the prophets have spoken!"*

A final reminder from the author: Remember, it all has to do with "the Bride, the Lamb's wife" (21:9); The Lamb is the Temple (21:22); The Lamb is the light (21:23); *"The Lamb's Book of Life"* (21:27); The Lamb and the Throne (22:1); and again, the Lamb on the Throne (22:3). The whole book opens, follows, closes, and involves Jesus Christ the Lamb. That is what our writing is all about. It is the *"Revelation of Jesus Christ!"*

This final ending was all prophesied with the Christmas text. In Isaiah, the ninth chapter where it was foretold with explicit clarity that God's Son would be born to us. The text then jumps completely over at least the next 2700 plus years, and brings us to this final end of the Revelation of Jesus Christ, and to the very reality that we are reading about in the

19th to the 22 chapter. A hope placed in every son of Adam, and every soul of the seed of Abraham who hoped in their Messiah. That hope is set in the hearts of the Church a new at every Christmas season around the World. We read the final glorious end of the Revelation of Jesus Christ in Isaiah 9 6:

"For unto us a child is born, and unto us a Son is given, and the Government will be on His shoulders. And He will be called Wonderful, Counselor, Mighty God, Everlasting Father, Prince of Peace. Of the Increase of His government and peace, there will be no end. He will reign on David's throne and over His Kingdom, establishing and upholding it with justice and righteousness from that time on and forever. The zeal of the LORD ALMIGHTY will accomplish this."

EVEN SO, COME LORD JESUS! PTL! AMEN! (SO BE IT!)

APPENDIX

CHRIST IN THE REVELATION

SPECIAL BOOKS AND PUBLICATIONS

PUBLICATIONS BY THE AUTHOR:

"Jerusalem-Rushing Toward the Midnight Hour"

21st Century Press, copyright 2004 (www.21stcenturybooks.com) 2131 W. Republic Rd., Springfield, Mo. 65807

"Post Saddam Iraq in Bible Prophecy" Christian Services Network,2004 (CSNbooks.com) 1975 Janich Ranch Ct., El Cajon, Calif. 92019

REVELATION AND DANIEL-THE CLOSED BOOKS

Jesus had a profound understanding of the Book of Daniel, and we see this in His many references to Daniel, both in His time of ministry and in His dictates of the Book of Revelation of Jesus Christ. To the Jews, all through the late Old Testament period, the Book of Daniel was a *closed book* (Daniel 12:6). Jewish commentary on the book is very limited for that time. Actually, the Book of Daniel remained a *closed book* to the Church as well, until the awakening in the early 1900's. For this reason, the Book of Revelation of Jesus Christ was also virtually a closed book until the same awakening, because of its extreme reliance on the Book of Daniel for understanding. When the Spirit chose to *open* the Book of Daniel to the Church, it follows that the Book of Revelation of Jesus Christ should also begin to be opened to our understanding. One is the hand and the other is the glove, as they fit one another so closely. Of course, it certainly was not closed to our Lord. In our day, the Lord Jesus Christ is opening both the books of Daniel and Revelation to the Church, but commentators must intercalate the truths and revelations of each into the other in order to understand them.

The angel told Daniel that he would have a distinguished place in the last day when his Book would be opened to understanding. Ezekiel also spoke of Daniel's influence in the last days when he said, *"Though these three men, Noah, Daniel, and Job, were in it, they would deliver only themselves by their righteousness"* (Ezekiel 14:14).

The Rapture and the Resurrection are prophesied in the Book of Daniel. The fall of Jerusalem and the rise of a New Jerusalem; the times of the Gentiles as depicted in the great image of Nebuchadnezzar's dream and spoken of by Jesus in Luke 21:24; the Abomination of Desolation; and the Tribulation are all clearly understood by our Lord from the Book of Daniel. (Matthew 24:15, 21-23) He and John fully understood from Daniel, the final 70TH week of years which the great messenger from God said were determined upon the Jews and the city of Jerusalem (Daniel 9:24). All of these are interwoven subjects both in the Book of Daniel and in the Revelation of Jesus Christ, where we see our Lord's knowledge of Daniel (see Daniel 9:27, 12:1).

Remember, Daniel himself lived during the time of the Great Empire of Babylon and the first Empire of Nebuchadnezzar's vision, yet he clearly saw the end of these kingdoms in their mature and mutant form - the ten Kings represented by the ten toes of the Image. This brings us right down to the day of the Coming of the Lord who would crush this whole system of world powers. Daniel saw the Lord as a rock cut out of the mountain without hands, cast into the feet of the image, and the whole system of worldly empires coming down. All of this depicts Christ's coming which will bring down the devil's world of kingdoms as shown in the Book of the Revelation of Jesus Christ. Christ will bring a complete end to the reign of the Gentiles. As shown in Daniel, and again in Revelation, this final end will come down at the end of the two long legs of the 4th Empire, Rome, with the two legs representing the Eastern Orthodox and the Western Roman legs of the Empire. In those days, Christ will set up his Kingdom *"which shall never be destroyed."* (Daniel 2:44, 7:18; Revelation 19-20) We could say that Daniel's book shows the history of the Devil's kingdom of the *Times of the Gentiles* from head to toe, and also show the Kingdom of Christ which destroys Satan's Kingdom in the end. All of this in Daniel agrees perfectly with Revelation. Daniel gives information which cannot be found in the Nevi'im—the Prophets, nor in the Law, and neither in the Kethubim—writings of the Jewish unique books among the inspired texts.

It is these many references to Daniel which promotes our suggestion that the Book of Daniel is actually the introduction to the Revelation of Jesus Christ. I believe we can accurately say that the essence of the whole Book of Revelation rests in the concepts of Daniel. Note the following Chapters in Daniel as they are related by our Lord in the Book of Revelation: Chapters 2, 7, 8, 11, and 12, noting in particular 2:44, 45; 7:24, 27, 12:1, 2. Christ our Lord almost seems to disappear in Revelation, but His activities during the Beast's time can be followed, when related to companion Scriptures in Daniel. In a few Chapters, such as Chapter 14, He appears by name and His appearance can be seen more clearly by intercalating texts as seen in Daniel. We will expound on many of these later. Daniel also has much to say about the character of the Antichrist and His activities during His period in Revelation.

3 ½ YEARS, 42 MONTHS, 1260 DAY-SYNDROME

NOTE: All of the texts that relate to this syndrome are found in the Book of Daniel and in the Book of the Revelation of Jesus Christ. This in itself, shows the close correlation between the two books and the reason why I chose to make the Book of Daniel the introduction to the Book of the Revelation of Jesus Christ.

All of the references to the above syndrome are during the last 3 ½ years of the Tribulation and all are during the reign of the Antichrist:

1. Daniel 7:25: Antichrist sets his own calendar for 3 ½ years

2. Daniel 8:14: Years set to cleanse the temple

3. Daniel 9:27: Shows the midst of the last seven years

4. Daniel 12:7: Years from the abomination to the end of Israel's persecution

5. Daniel 12:11: Years to the end of the abomination

6. The above references perfectly correlate with references in Revelation.

7. Revelation 11:2: Court of Gentiles in the Temple, given to the Antichrist

8. Revelation 11:3: Witnesses witness during the Antichrist's reign

9. Revelation 12:6: Israel remnant flees and is persecuted

10. Revelation 12:14: The persecution of Israel

11. Revelation 13:5: Years that the Beast, or Antichrist, to Continue

Each of these references have to do with Jews in the last 3 ½ years of the Tribulation, and all relate to the period of this false Christ, the Antichrist. They either use the year scale, or the month scale, or the day scale, all of which equals 3 ½ years. Daniel 12:11 adds 30 days. This probably represents 30 days to actually complete the upset of the Beast and His kingdom, and cleans the Temple area of the Holy Mount. Then Daniel adds another 45 days to the setting up of Christ's millennial reign. This makes 75 days between the fall of the Beast and the actual setting up of the Kingdom of Christ.

The 2300 days of Daniel 8:14, has to do with the daily sacrifice that was "taken away" or disbanded. This would be 160 days short of the 3½ years. This likely relates to a time at the beginning of the Covenant. It probably took a while to get everything set up and Kosher, in order to begin the sacrifices.

CHRIST – NUMBER OF TIMES BY NAMES OR TITLES IN REVELATION

The Lamb. He is only referred to as the *Lamb of God* four times in the whole New Testament, all of them in the Book of John. In my opinion this fact is because the Jews, including the disciples, had not fully understood the connection between the *Sacrificial Lamb* and the *Messiah,* as a man. John the Baptist spoke by revelation when he, for the first time, called Jesus *"the Lamb of God who takes away the sin of the world."* (John 1:29) Of all the gospel writers, only John understood this and only in his writings is Jesus so named. Yet, He is called *The Lamb* 27 times in the Book of the Revelation of Jesus Christ:

(5:6,8,12,13, 6:1,16, 7:9,10,14,17,12:11, 13:8,11, 14:1,4,10, 15:3, 17:14, 19:7, 9, 21:9,14,22,23,27, 22:1,3).

He is called by His proper name *Jesus* 7 times: (14:12, 17:6, 19:10, 20:4, 22:16). Five of them are in the first chapter where He is introduced. Only twice is He mentioned by name in the actual Revelation texts. Once in chapter 12:17, where we are told that the remnant of Jews in exile in Edom accepted Him as Messiah. The second time is in Chapter 22:21, where He becomes personal signatory and guarantor of the writings in 22:16. He greets us personally in v. 22 (1:1,2,5,9, 12:17, 22:21).

He is called *Lord* 26 times:
(1:8, 4:8,11, 11:8,15,17, 14:13, 15:3,4, 16:5,7, 17:14, 18:8, 19:1,6,16, 21:22, 22:5,6,20,21).

Otherwise, we find him only in metaphorical and cryptic symbolism. It is in these texts, that we must make our closest search for the Christ in the Revelation.

THE MESSIAH AND THE SUFFERING SERVANT

Isaiah's writing of the suffering Savior can be found in the 52nd and 53rd chapters of his book. Isaiah is said to be the writer of the New Testament, and the Church age in the Old Testament. Chapters 50 through 66 are largely about the Church as well as the Jews, in the last days.

Starting in Isaiah 52:14, note how hesitant he is to introduce a suffering Messiah. He admits that many will be astonished at his teachings concerning the Messiah as marred in his body more than any other man. Then in verse 53:1, he continues to note their astonishment and questions whether any of his peers will be able to accept what he writes: *"Who hath believed our report? And to whom is the arm of the Lord revealed?"*

Who can believe this and who can see this revelation, he asks? Then he speaks of the Messiah's lowly estate. He would grow up as a tender root out of dry ground (53:2). Roots that grow up without water are very weak and have little chance of growing strong. The Messiah also would have nothing attractive about Him that the Jews would desire (53:2).

Now Isaiah really shocks them with what is impossible for them to believe: that the Messiah and great King would be *"despised and rejected by men"* (53:3). He would be *"a man of sorrows and acquainted with grief"* and the Jews would hide their faces from Him (53:3).

Now Isaiah begins to get into language that I believe the Holy Spirit intended to introduce the Jews to the idea that this Man, the Messiah and suffering Savior, was indeed related to the Lamb of God which takes away the sin of the World:

"He has borne our griefs and carried our sorrows; yet we esteemed him stricken, smitten by God, and afflicted ..." (53:4).

And throughout the next several verses, there is more language which can be associated with the sheep, and the Suffering Lamb. He was *"led as a lamb to the slaughter"* (53:7).

When you make this lamb of slaughter an,
"offering for sin, [God will] see the travail of His (the Lamb's) *soul, and be satisfied"* (53:10-11).

It is said that the travail of this suffering Savior,
"brought as a lamb to slaughter [will] justify many, for He shall bear their iniquities" (53:7, 11).

He would,
"[pour] out His soul unto death" and make intercession for *"the transgressors"* (53:12).

What a wonderful revelation this was over 700 years before the Messianic Lamb would actually suffer at the hands of sinners to bear the iniquity of many.

WHY CHRIST REFERRED TO HIMSELF AS THE LAMB 27 TIMES

The purpose of Christ referring to Himself as the Lamb 27 times in the Book of the Revelation, is the fact that He is dealing with the Jews in most of the Revelation. Therefore, in order to bring them into full acceptance of Himself as the Messiah, He will need to convince them that He is their sin-bearer, as well as their great Redeemer. He will accomplish this sometime during this Tribulation period. I believe it will be when He reveals Himself to the Remnant in Edom. There, He will come to plead with them, ie. He will present a legal claim before them. When they suddenly grasp the full impact of Him as both their Lamb that takes away their sin, and the great king that is ready now to plead their cause before the whole world, a revival will break out and *"all Israel will be saved"* (Romans 11:26).

We can see Israel's conversion to the Lamb by noticing that this remnant returns with *"the testimony of Jesus"* as the 144,000—the Redeemed, coming up to Mount Zion *"[following] the Lamb wherever He goes ... being first-fruits to God and to the Lamb"* (Revelation 12:17, 14:4).

It is always the Lamb that fights for the Jews and Israel in the Tribulation and during the time when Satan takes his best and last shot at their destruction. It is the Lord who shortens the time for the elect's sake.(Matthew 24:23, Israel is the elect.) He will not have to shorten time for the Church's sake, for they will be gone in the Rapture (Matthew 24:22). It is the remnant of Israel who is fleeing from the onslaught of the devil, the dragon, of whom it is said that they (the Jews) overcame Him by "the Blood of the Lamb and by the word of their testimony, and they did not love their lives to the death" (12:11).

ZION, ENIGMA AND NATURE OF ITS ETYMOLOGY

When we consider the Lord and 144,000 coming to Zion, (Sion in Greek New Testament) we should pause for a brief study of the word and meaning of Zion (Revelation 14:1).

Before the UN General Assembly, Iran's former President Mahmoud Ahmadinejad, joining a long historical line of satanically inspired rebels and terrorists, made a statement that will judge him in eternity. He said, "Soon there would be a world without Zionism." Little does he know or care that there has never been a world without Zionism, and there never will be a world without Zionism. One of these days, Zionism, in its final enigmatic form, will outlast all of the world's anti-Zionist nations including Iran, which will be destroyed along with Russia, Ethiopia, (Sudan) Libya, and Turkey on the Mountains of Israel.

There is a special and extra *mystery*, the real and the metaphoric application of Jerusalem and Zion, in the teleological progress and program of God's redemptive plan.

In all of the texts as we study them, there is continually lingering very near the surface or just beyond our immediate concepts, and hovering just above our realization, the essence of Zion. It very gently touches its wings to the far distant past, and then ever-so-slightly overshadows the near past, the present, and the future. Its final enigma comes again to the surface when we are able to turn the mystical key to its cryptic symbolism and behold it in its full glorious and eternal light as it emerges as the New Jerusalem in the final Chapters of Revelation.

Like a dolphin, Zion may at times swim just beneath the surface so as to show only a shadowy image, slightly discernible. Then suddenly, it may plunge to the surface and come into full view, only to dive far into the hidden depths where, although we know it is still there, we must wait for it to emerge again to be sure of its presence. Even then it may submerge without us catching it, so we wait again for its shadow.

So it is with Zion. As writer Gary Stearman so clearly describes regarding Zion in his article in *Prophecy in the News* entitled *Zion: the Enigma of the Ages:*

> "[Zion's] sheer weight in importance and few terms can match its grandeur."

Within its etymological concepts are the revelation of the fulfillment of God's purposes and promises for all people, including the Church and Israel. Its enigma belongs to Israel first, then the Jews, and finally the Church, and carries through to the New Jerusalem.

According to ancient Jewish folklore Zion's connection with Jerusalem began when God, seeking to illustrate how terrible and devastating it was for Adam & Eve to sin, God took little lambs from Abel's' flock which were pasturing on Mt. Moriah and slew them as sacrifices to make clothing of skins for them. From that time on, God called the mountain Salem which means peace, for it was there that peace was made between God and man, through the Sacrificial Lamb which appeased a righteous God enough to take away the guilt of sin. That sacrifice continued in Moriah as a memorial down through the long ages.

The Mount became a very sacred place to God and He placed a very special Priest to guard the Mount. This priest was serving there down to Abraham's day, and the Sacrifice continued until the Temple was built in that very place. **There, God placed His name and commanded His sacrifice to continue. That is why Abraham was called back to sacrifice His son, Isaac. The enigma of Zion surfaced** there, for *"God will provide Himself a sacrifice---in this Mount, you shall see it."* **Jerusalem, meaning "Jehovah brings Peace," represented the earlier place where God provided peace between God and Man.**

We must try to understand its relationship to not only Jerusalem, but more specifically, the Mountains of Moriah. And in grappling with the subject, we must ask the question:

This is why these particular mountains already were so significant to God at least 1000 years before Abraham was directed there for the sacrifice of Isaac?" Already, God had established Moriah and Salem (Jerusalem) as a very holy place worthy of His special attention, and a place for the dwelling of His name and the presence of His Holy Spirit

Psalm 87 speaks of its unique place as being the very foundation of this strange place called Zion. This psalm the Church together with the 144,000 will sing when Christ comes to Mount Zion: It says: *"His foundation is in the holy Mountains"* (Zion) (87:1). In the Jewish lore, this Psalm is said to speak of God's home, which he loves far more than all the homes of Jacob – Israel (87:2). It is called from ancient times, even pre-flood days, the *City of God*. Already, it is known as the home of *"those who know me"* (87:4). And in some enigmatic way, it is called *Zion* from the very foundation, or from the beginning of the peace treaty between God and man.

In the time of the foundation of redemption, this place was already called Zion. Thus, Zion is connected with the place where peace was made with sinful man. Can it be overlooked that this same word 'foundation', or *yecuwdah*, is the same word used in Isaiah 28:16, where God speaks of this foundation being laid in Zion for a foundation stone? Certainly, this speaks of Christ's blood sacrifice being the settlement, or establishment, of our peace with God.

And where was God's home when he visited Eden in the

cool of the day? Could Psalms 84 give us a hint when it speaks of God's beautiful home, and that place being Zion?

"How lovely is your tabernacle, O Lord of hosts? ... and how "blessed are those who dwell in your house" (84:1,4)?

The writer is well aware that such a thought is beyond our immediate understanding, and yet it fits well within the perimeters of the enigma of this place and situation called Zion, as our eternal home shown us in Revelation.

If we are to put any weight of plausibility on ancient Jewish tradition, we may find answers to the enigma of Jerusalem and Zion.

Why was this place so well-known even before the flood, right after the flood, and long before David "took the stronghold of Zion"(2 Samuel 4:5) and made it his capitol and the place of his throne, long before a Temple was built and the law of sacrifices was performed there.

Why did God move Abraham to return there? And why did God sanctify this place for the throne of David and the ancient Temple to be built there? What else would make it so special to God that He would "put His Name there and send a Pre-incarnation of His blessed Son to safeguard its sacredness? Thus, we see Zion as representative of an earthly throne which will be re-established in the prophetic future to the sacred place of the Kaphor (blood sacrifice) at the Holy of Holies on the Temple Mount.

Today, Zion represents the divine nature of the work of God through the Messianic Hope as well as to the geophysical location on Earth. It is no longer a human essence of his work, but the inner work going on in the hearts of those Jews who return to the land in hopes of the final Kingdom of David. It is also the same work in the hearts of the Church who hope and long for, the Kingdom of Christ.

Zion is the touch of deity, calling the Jews back in the return and calling the Church in rapture to her eternal home:

"..unto mount Sion, and unto the city of the living God, the heavenly Jerusalem and to an innumerable company of angels. To the general assembly of the church of the first born which are written in heaven, and to God the judge of all and to the spirits of just men made perfect" (Hebrews 12:22-23).

The same hope that has been whispered into the heart of believing Jews and Christians alike through the ages from such texts as Isaiah 2:2-4 and Micah 4:1-3 and pulled them here to mount Zion by the same Spirit of the living God who will anoint Christ Jesus when, as a Lamb slain, comes in victory with 144,000 of His Jewish converts to Mount Zion (Revelation 14:1).

It is the work of God, not the work of man, pointing them to the coming kingdom of the Messiah, which will complete the enigma of Zion. It is from that depth, the depth of the eternal soul of God and the eventual fulfillment of our hope (the hope of the final destiny of Zion, planted deep in the hidden recesses of the soul of all believers today as well) each of us finds the root of our dissatisfaction and longing. It is that depth in Christ's own soul that is calling to the depth of God's heart—Zion, which is the source of Christ's own longing and the essence of our longing yet today.

Oh beloved, as I muse on these thoughts, I find the same tearful experience of David even today. I sense it in my soul and in the soul of every true believer with whom I worship, among whom I go up to the house of God, and with them enter into praise. Sitting here typing these thoughts, tears are rushing down my cheeks, and from way down within me is an ache, a longing which started in my soul when I first met Jesus. A longing for that day when all of God's promises will be realized and we stand in His presence, see Him face to face, and are able to contain all of the fullness of Him in the glorious reality of the Zion that David longed for. An old chorus caught it for us so well:

"There's a longing in my heart for Jesus, there's a Longing in my heart to see His face. And I'm weary, oh so weary, as I travel here below, I've a longing in my heart for Him" (author unknown).

From the Book of Psalms:

"But you, O Lord, shall endure forever, and the remembrance of your name to all generations. You will arise and have mercy on Zion; for the time to favor her ... has come " (Psalm 102:12-13, 18).

We believe that time will come as shown in Revelation 14. Then, Psalm 102 says:

"For your servants take pleasure in her stones, and show favor to her dust. So the nations shall fear the name of the Lord, and all the Kings of the earth your glory. Now let the nations and their rulers tremble before the Lord, and before His glory. For the Lord shall build up Zion; He shall appear in His glory ... This will be written for the generation to come that a people yet to be created may praise the Lord. For He looked down from the height of His sanctuary, from Heaven the Lord viewed the earth, to hear the groaning of the prisoner, to lose those appointed to death" (102:14-16, 18-20).

Verses 21 and 22 in the King James Version says:
"The name of the Lord will be declared in Zion and His praise in Jerusalem, when the peoples and the kingdoms

assemble to worship the Lord in Zion when the people are gathered together and the kingdoms, to serve the Lord."

We believe that day spoken of in Psalms 102 is presage to Revelation 14 when the Lord comes to Zion.

NATIONS MENTIONED IN THE LAST DAYS

BIBLICAL NAMES:	PRESENT NAMES/COMMENTS:	TEXTS:
BABYLON	IRAQ	EZEKIEL 32:11, ZECHARIAH 5
PERSIA	IRAN	EZEKIEL 32:24, DANIEL 10
JAVAN	GREECE	EZEKIEL 27:13, 19, DANIEL 10
ROME	EUROPEAN UNION	
KURDS	IRAN/TURKEY/SYRIA	ISAIAH 22:6
ISHMAEL	ARABS	PSALMS 83
PALESTINE	HOLY LAND	JEREMIAH 25:29, PSALMS 83
		EZEKIEL 33:24
AMMAN	EDOM/ MOAB/	
	JORDAN	JEREMIAH 25:4, 21, PSALMS 83
	MOAB	PSALMS 83, ZEPHANIAH 2:9
AMMAN	EDOM	AMOS 1:1, 6, EZEKIEL 25:1
SIER , IDUMEA		EZEKIEL 35:1, 7,15 36:5
	BOZRAH	EZEKIEL 22:18
SYRIA	GOLAN HEIGHTS	EZEKIEL 22:18
	DAMASCUS	ISAIAH 17:1-14
LEBANON	SAME, TYRE	
	AND SIDON	EZEKIEL 31:13, 15, 116, 32:30
MIDIAN	GILEAD &	
	GOLAN HEIGHTS	PSALM 83
EGYPT,	CUSH LIBYA,	
	ETHIOPIA	EZEKIEL 27 & ISAIAH 19
LUD AND PHUT		EZEKIEL 32:2, 15,1
LIBYA	SAME	EZEKIEL 38
ETHIOPIA	SAME 7, & SOMALIA	EZEKIEL 38
SAUDI ARABIA	SAME	EZEKIEL 39
ASSYRIA	IRAN	PSALM 83, EZEKIEL 27:23, 31

THE DAY OF THE LORD AND MESSIANIC TEXTS

It can be stated as a matter of fact that the Book of the Revelation of Jesus Christ is essentially a detailed account that brings to a conclusion all of the last-day Messianic prophecies of the Old Testament. With each of these carefully studied, related to, and intercalated into the Book of Revelation, we get a complete picture of the Messianic Promise. These prophecies are generally categorized under the title, *The Day of the Lord*, *The Lord's Day*, *that Day* and many other terms,. It is also occasionally spoken of as *The Day of Visitation*. Rather than try to work all of these texts into the writings, I chose to expose a rather detailed account of the prophecies of *The Day of the Lord* in the appendix for the convenience of those who wish to make an in-depth study of the subject as it relates to Revelation.

The terms, *Day of the Lord*, *Lord's Day*, or just *That Day*, can be found at least 62 times in the Old Testament texts: in Isaiah 20 times; in Jeremiah 4 times; in Ezekiel 1 time; in Daniel 3 times; in Zephaniah 5 times; Zechariah 18 times; and the last 62 times, in the rest of the minor prophets. They actually represent in general; the whole time between the Rapture and Revelation, the 7 years of Tribulation, and the last four battles of Tribulation, each are said to take place in the Day of the Lord. The final Battle, Armageddon, and Christ's coming to set up His Kingdom is also said to be in Day of the Lord. In other words, the whole circuit of His Revelation back to Earth.

The following is a summarization of these texts which generally state their information as it relates to the Book of Revelation:

Isaiah 2:12: *"The Day of the Lord will come in the last days when God will judge the nations and exalt Israel with the Holy Mount."*

CHRIST IN THE REVELATION

Isaiah 13: 6 and 9: speaks of the Day of the Lord as a day of destruction, cruel with wrath and anger which will destroy the sinners.

Isaiah 24:21: In the midst of Tribulation texts (chapters 24-26) speaks of the day when the Lord will deal with principalities, powers, rulers of the darkness, and spiritual wickedness in heaven (Revelation 12).

Isaiah 25:3-9: Speaks of the Day of the Lord when the terrible nations will be brought low, and the Lord for whom both Israel and the Church has waited for, will appear.

"Behold, this is our God; we have waited for Him, and He will save us; we will be glad and rejoice in His salvation" (Isaiah 25:9).

Isaiah 26: Judah will sing of His salvation and a cry will go out to *"open the gates"* (6:2; Matthew 25:33-34).

Isaiah 27:1: Just after the Rapture, "in that day, the Lord ... will punish Leviathan, the fleeing serpent," and slay the dragon, all very much a part of the Revelation story. Verse 13 says, *"In that day that great trumpet will be blown."*

In Isaiah 28:5: *"The Lord of hosts will be for a crown of glory and a diadem of beauty to the remnant of His people."* He will sit in the gate of judgment, Isaiah 28: Almost all of the rest of Chapter 28 is about the Day of the Lord, and has some most interesting insights into the day that Christ comes to Zion. It deals with the treacherous and scornful men who will be ruling Jerusalem at that time. They are said to be men who will be very much in control of Jerusalem and the Temple Mount, who made a covenant with death and Hell (28:15a). They are people who have hidden themselves behind secrecy and lies and say that when the final end comes and the scourge of the Lord comes, it will not come to them, for they have *"made lies [their] refuge, and under falsehood [they] have hidden [themselves]"* (28:15b). I believe this speaks of the supra-national sovereigns of world finance to come.

Isaiah 29 – 34: In that day, the blind will see, and the deaf hear, the meek and the poor brought to joy and rejoicing, and the terrible one, Satan, will be cut off. In that day, Jerusalem will be defended, preserved, and delivered.

Isaiah 35-60: packed with Messianic prophecies of the golden era of Israel. They also speak clearly of the Gentile Church and all the blessings mutually shared with Israel during the Messianic Day. The New Jerusalem is described in 54:9-12 and the Temple built on Mount Zion which in the days of Revelation will be a *"house of prayer"* for all people (56:7). The ungodly of both Israel and the nations are exposed in Chapters 57 through 59. However, in Chapter 60, we see the promise of the Jews returning to Israel, and also a blessing upon the Gentile Church. The day of the Lord's vengeance is spoken of in 61:2 and is expounded upon and detailed in Chapter 63.

Daniel: in verses 2:44-45, the 'Day of the Lord' includes the days of the ten kings, which play a prominent role in Revelation 13 and 17. In Daniel 7:13, and 14, the Lord comes near before the Ancient of Days (God), and He is given dominion to set up His Kingdom. This all happens in the context of Revelation.

Joel 3:14 and 18: the Day of the Lord plays a prominent role when the Armies of all nations gather in the Valley of Jehoshaphat near Jerusalem. It is these armies (also spoken of in Zechariah 14:1-4) which prompt the Lord to come to Zion.

Obadiah 15: speaks of this same event and says the Day of the Lord will see deliverance come from Zion.

Micah 4:1-4: speaks of the Day of the Lord as being the time when Mount Zion will be exalted as a center of worship for all nations from which the Messiah, Christ Jesus will judge all nations and end all war.

Zephaniah 1:7-18: mentions the Day of the Lord seven times and gives much detail that explicitly matches what we read in Revelation. Chapter 2 continues details about the Day of the Lord, especially mentioning Gaza's destruction during that time. Chapter 3 mentions the Day of the Lord four more times and shows it to be the time when God gathers all nations to pour out indignation and wrath upon them (3:8). In a sense, we could intercalate the whole Book of Zephaniah into the events of Revelation.

Haggai 2:7: speaks of the time in the Day of the Lord when God will shake all nations, and *"the desire of all nations"* shall come, i.e. that long-awaited Messiah, Jesus Christ. The time will see the House of the Lord filled with glory (Revelation 15:8).

Zechariah: is full of *the Day of the Lord*. Eighteen times it is spoken of, starting with His coming (3:10); to build His temple (6:12); and re-establish Israel in Her land (8:11). Zechariah 12 speaks of the "Day of the Lord" five times, when Jerusalem will be surrounded by armies of the nations, and becomes a *"cup of drunkenness"* or trembling (12:2); and the Generals of the IDF will become very strong (12:6). In that day, He will defend Jerusalem (12:8) and the Lord will seek to defeat all nations with a horrible plague that will come against Jerusalem (14:12). Mount Megiddo, the place of Armageddon is mentioned in verse 12:11. Every word of these texts can be intercalated into Revelation's events.

Zechariah 13: the Day of the Lord will see a fountain opened in Jerusalem, and all idols cut off. Verse 4 shows 2/3 of Israel cut off and 1/3 brought through the fire, all a theme of Revelation.

Zachariah 14: is a classic Chapter that rises to a magnificent height among all of *The Day of the Lord* texts. Seven times, the Day of the Lord is mentioned here and the details given of that day, which will enhance the Book of Revelation gloriously. The gathering of the nations against Jerusalem (14:2) and Christ's feet standing on Mount of Olives (14:4). The living waters flowing out of Jerusalem speaks of the river flowing from the throne (14: 8; Revelation 22:1).

The great battle where Judah Joins the Lord in His fight at Jerusalem, will result in the wealth of the nations that are being funneled into Jerusalem (14:13-14). Then, the people of the nations who are left after Armageddon, comes up to Jerusalem to celebrate the Feast of the Tabernacles every year (14:16). The rest of the Chapter describes millennial scenes around Judah and Jerusalem. Brother, if you can't find the Book of Revelation in these texts, how can we help you!

Malachi finishes up the glorious prophecies of the Day of the Lord, where in 4:1, he speaks of the day that will burn like an oven. Here is real global warming and it does not involve the carbon footprint or emissions, or any other man-made cause, but a solar, God-created thing that we have nothing to do with. Then, the coming of Christ with *"healing in His wings,"* closes the great texts of *The Day of the Lord* in the Old Testament (4:3).

WE MUST UNDERSTAND THE OLD TESTAMENT TO UNDERSTAND THE NEW

It is a very dangerous attitude that rejects or at least ignores the Old Testament message, especially when we study the Book of Revelation of Jesus Christ. Jesus, Himself said that He did not come to destroy the Old Testament law, but to fulfill it. And, His Revelation is His final fulfillment of the Messianic prophecies of the Old Testament (Matthew 5:17). There are, by my count, over eight-hundred references to the Old Testament text in Revelation, and over two-hundred, fifty direct quotes. Jesus said again:

"Search the scriptures, for in them you think you have eternal life; and these are they which testify of me" (John 5:39).

Keep in mind at that time, there was no New Testament scripture, only the Old Testament. Therefore, we were admonished to search the Old Testament in order to find Christ. There must be an understanding the Old Testament message if one is to understand even the basics of salvation because according to Jesus, we could miss the message of our salvation by not knowing what the Old Testament has to say.

In Christ's own teaching then, we dare not trust our salvation to the New Testament alone. Just before His ascension, Jesus explains the meaning of His message:

"…beginning at Moses and all the Prophets, He expounded to them in all the Scriptures things concerning Himself" (Luke 24:27).

It is important to understand that everything in the New

Testament is predicated on the Old Testament. As we study the scores of references to the Day of the Lord, it will become evident that the Old Testament is the basis for the Book of Revelation.

The Old Testament shows that the entire motif, or dominant idea forming a distant design of the Book of Revelation, is the exact same motif of the Old Testament message. This very motif is embodied in the subject found in the New Testament, is the foundation of Revelation. We will study namely, The Day of the Lord, The Lord's Day or that day.

Seeing Christ in Revelation will bring many Old Testament Messianic prophecies into focus, revealing the Great Day of the Lord.

The more we see what is the real "hope of His calling [and] the riches of the glory of His inheritance in the saints," the more we will understand Revelation (Ephesians 1:14-18). It is the theme of Revelation of Jesus Christ that tells us of the earnest of our inheritance until the redemption of the purchased possession. Revelation is all about Jesus winning back possession of the earth from Satan. It is to be given back to both Israel and the Church as they serve under His kingship.

The more we delve into the depths of the whole of scriptures, the more we see that every book, both Old and New Testaments, ties together the whole teleological and eschatological view of Revelation as projected in the Old Testament Messianic hope.

The Revelation of Jesus Christ shows the day of the Lord beginning with Christ coming to rapture the Church, and ends with His second coming to put down all rebellion and set up His Kingdom on Earth. We are clearly told in several texts, especially Daniel chapter nine that the Day of the Lord will be seven years long with forty-five days added to the setting up of Christ's Kingdom.

This ends with the setting up of the Kingdom of Christ

right after He destroys the great Gentile imperial system (Daniel 2:44). It refers to The Day of the Lord explained in detail according to Joel chapter two. It is the day Enoch spoke of and Jude records in verses fourteen and fifteen. It is the day Paul sees in 1 Corinthians 15:24 and 2 Thessalonians 1:2-10, 2:8.

THE FOUR BATTLES OF TRIBULATION CONNECTED TO THE DAY OF THE LORD

One of the great insights into the Book of Revelation of Jesus Christ from the Old Testament is the prophesied battles of the Tribulation period which are not covered by name in Revelation, but their devastation is foreseen. We can confidently place these battles in the Tribulation period because of the mention of the "Day of the Lord" connected to each of them. There are four different theaters of war mentioned in connection to the Day of the Lord. They may also basically be one continuing Battle.

THE BATTLE IN THE VALLEY OF JEHOSHAPHAT

Possibly, the opening volley of the Tribulation war's, is known as the Battle of the Valley of Jehoshaphat found in Joel chapter three. The scene for this battle and the Day of the Lord appears in the book of Joel where we read:

"Blow the trumpet in Zion, and sound an alarm in My holy mountain ... for the Day of the Lord is coming, for it is at hand" (Joel 2:1).

This battle is to be at the time when God has returned his people to the Land (Joel 3:1). At a given time, connected with events told to us in the Book of Revelation, God will "gather all nations" into the "Valley of Jehoshaphat"

(Joel 3:2). The valley of Jehoshaphat is the area where King Jehoshaphat met the armies of Moab after they had crossed the Dead Sea into Israel. You may remember that he faced the enemy with his choir, and as they sang, God discomfited them and the enemy slew their own people. Israel only had to pick up the spoil (2 Chronicles 20). Today, it is called the Valley of Berachah from Baruch, which means "the valley of blessing." (20:26).

This area was never called the Valley of Jehoshaphat outside of the prophetic reference. It would appear that the Spirit of God has changed its name for emphasis in light of the Tribulation battles that will take place there. "Jehoshaphat" means, Jehovah will Judge. At some time in the near future, great hoards of Muslims will gather there in defiance of the Jewish State of Israel. The issue over the West Bank will bring them there (Revelation 20:2). When the international community finally forces Israel to give up the West Bank, a time that seems very near, Israel's resistance will bring the world down upon them. The West Bank is better known as Judaea and Samaria.

It is conceivable that this is the time when the Lord will come to Mount Zion (Revelation 14:1). Joel 2:32 says by that time, "*Mount Zion in Jerusalem shall be [delivered].*" And later in Joel,

"*The Lord also will roar from Zion, and utter His voice from Jerusalem ... but the Lord will be a shelter for His people ... so you shall know that I am the Lord your God, dwelling in Zion My holy Mountain*" (Joel 3:16-17).

So it seems that the Lord will already be in possession of Mount Zion. Joel also declares in that day, that

"*... [God] will sit to Judge all the surrounding nations. Put in the sickle, for the harvest is ripe*" (Joel 3:12-13).

This is a direct reference to Revelation fourteen. Now, take notice of the next verse,

"Multitudes, multitudes in the valley of decision! For the day of the Lord is near in the valley of decision" (Joel 3:14).

It is called the valley of decision because this is the place where Jehovah's final judgment upon rebellious nations will be issued, and where He makes His ruling and sentence. However, here again we find indication that God is still pleading with the nations according to verse twelve when He cries out *"Let the nations be wakened and come up to the Valley of Jehoshaphat."* Even when time is up for the world, our merciful, Jesus gives every opportunity for mankind to change plans, repent, and cease fighting against God and Christ.

No doubt, there is a connection between these texts about the Day of the Lord and the Book of Revelation, and their direct relationship to the Tribulation battles. Speculation suggests that the great commotion caused by the battle at the Valley of Jehoshaphat is going to involve Iran and her co-conspirators, attracting the attention of Russia who has long looked for an excuse to invade the Middle East. That brings us to the second, more notorious Tribulation battle.

THE BATTLE OF GOG AND MAGOG (EZEKIEL 38, 39)

The battle of Gog and Magog's invasion into Israel is most likely the best known of the four Tribulation battles. For many centuries, as far back as the invasion of Babylon and Rome, there was speculation about this future assault by Russia and her allies upon Israel in the last days.

According to Scripture, we can know this battle will take place when the Jews have returned to their land, placing it in the same proximity of the Jehoshaphat battle and tying it to our day. Ezekiel makes it perfectly plain:

"In the latter years you will come into the land of those brought back from the sword and gathered from many people on the Mountains of Israel, which had long be desolate; they were

brought out of the nations, and now all of them dwell safely" (Ezekiel 38:8).

Both Ezekiel 38:12 and also 39:25-27 say the same thing. Israel's birth opens up a clear understanding of scores of prophetic events and gives us their time of fulfillment. So it is with the battle of Gog and Magog—Israel's birth gives us the exact time.

Next, we note that this offensive will be an interfering intrusion into the affairs of Israel because of the International troubles over the "Mountains of Israel" (Ezekiel 38:8). This is a significant event mentioned four times in relationship to the onslaught against Israel (Ezekiel 38:8, 39:2, 39:4, and 39:17). Remember, the West Bank is the mountainous regions of the State of Israel. Tightly connected to the West Bank is the Golan Heights which was a part of the heritage of Israel's twelve tribes. In Ezekiel 39, this is called the Valley of Hamon-Gog, meaning the burial of Gog (39:11). It is also part of the West Bank debacle. It becomes evident that this battle, like the battle in the Valley of Jehoshaphat, also involves trouble over the West Bank. Take note that God said He would be the one to conquer them (Ezekiel 38:4). It is a bit disconcerting to some, to think that God would cause this battle against Israel. However, many times over, the texts indicate God's direct involvement in assembling all nations into Israel in the Day of the Lord for the purpose of bringing final judgment upon a wayward world of nations. Also regarding the battle of Jehoshaphat, God said He would gather the nations and "bring them down" (Joel 3:2). And in Zachariah 14:2, God "will gather all the nations to battle against Jerusalem." Zephaniah declares God's "determination to gather the nations" together for the purpose of pouring out His wrath upon them (Zephaniah 2:8).

Russia's allies include Iran, the horn of Africa, Libya,

CHRIST IN THE REVELATION

Germany/France, and Turkey. This very scenario appears to be developing in our day. God will bring Tribulation like judgment upon these armies, and only one in six will return home (Ezekiel 38:19-23, 39:2) Several times in these two chapters, that day is used to reflect its relationship to the Day of the Lord in Revelation. The entire thirty-ninth chapter echoes the Tribulation woes found in the Book of Revelation.

THE BATTLE FOR JERUSALEM

The next Tribulation battle detailed in the Old Testament and connected with the Day of the Lord is found in Zechariah, chapters twelve and fourteen. The first verse of chapter fourteen begins with:

"Behold the day of the Lord is coming ... For I will gather all nations to battle against Jerusalem" (Zechariah 14:1-2). The connection to the Tribulation becomes evident in the rest of the chapter when reading about the coming of the Lord to do battle for Jerusalem against a world that has set itself against the "Lord and His Anointed" (Psalms 2:2). The flight of Israel is connected to the time of trouble and the "abomination of desolation" which takes place in the midst of the Tribulation week (Matthew 24:15). Zechariah continues by saying, *"and the Lord my God will come, and all the saints with You"*(Zechariah 14:5).

No doubt, this sets the scene in Revelation when the Lord comes to Zion in His day with His saints *"and He shall reign forever and ever!"* (Revelation 11:15).

The dividing of Jerusalem mentioned in Zechariah 14:2 is reflective of Revelation 11:13 and 16:19 where 7000 will die in this battle against Jerusalem. The earthquake mentioned in 11:13 is the same earthquake associated with Christ's feet touching the Mount of Olives in Zechariah 14:4.

The tragedy of nuclear exchange, as is alluded to in Revelation is found in verses 12-15 of Zechariah 14. And to add to our understanding of Revelation's Tribulation woes, we are told in Zechariah 14:16-21 that all nations will not be destroyed at Armageddon, but after these battles are over, they will come up to Jerusalem at the Feast of Tabernacles each year to worship the King, Jesus Christ.

All of the forgoing information shows the close relationship between the Old Testament Messianic prophecies of the Day of the Lord and the coming of Christ in the Book of the Revelation.

ARMAGEDDON

Revelation sixteen records the last battle to come at Megiddo in central Israel. It will be the final battle of the *"great day of God Almighty,"* the final skirmish between Satan and Christ.

All four battles named above will be in and around Israel and will concern the controversy over the West Bank and the Temple Mount. They will involve the Terrorist Nations of Ezekiel 32.

Hal Lindsey, over TBN, quoted the Editor and Chief of the Intelligence Digest who said:

"I have come to the conclusion that what is taking place in the Middle East will bring the world to its last battle. I know nothing about the Bible. I draw my conclusion from the data we gather for the Digest."

Insight from this world leader and mover shows us that we are drifting toward the World's last Battle today.

www.ingramcontent.com/pod-product-compliance
Lightning Source LLC
Chambersburg PA
CBHW070712160426
43192CB00009B/1156